JUDY

Books by Gerold Frank

THE DEED
THE BOSTON STRANGLER
AN AMERICAN DEATH
JUDY

In Collaboration

I'LL CRY TOMORROW
TOO MUCH, TOO SOON
BELOVED INFIDEL
ZSA ZSA GABOR

JUDY

Gerold Frank

HARPER & ROW, PUBLISHERS
NEW YORK, EVANSTON
SAN FRANCISCO
LONDON

FIRST EDITION

Designed by Gloria Adelson

Library of Congress Cataloging in Publication Data

Frank, Gerold, date
  Judy
  Includes index.
  1. Garland, Judy.   I. Title.
ML420.G253F7   784'.092'4 [B]   74–20402
ISBN 0–06–011337–5

TO MY GRANDCHILDREN

CONTENTS

A NOTE TO
THE READER

EVERYTHING IN THIS BOOK COMES, so far as possible, from firsthand sources—that is, as I learned it, in person, through interviews extending sometimes over months, with those who participated most intimately in Judy's life. This is therefore a book written from the inside. It is the only biography of Judy Garland written with the complete cooperation of her immediate family: her only surviving sister, Virginia (Jimmy) Thompson, the last of the three Gumm Sisters, who has until now never spoken about Judy to a biographer; Judy's three children, Liza Minnelli, Lorna Luft and Joey Luft, with whom I have sat for weeks and who until now have given only the most fugitive interviews about their remarkable mother; and Judy's husbands, David Rose, Vincente Minnelli, Sid Luft and Mark Herron. (I have not spoken with Mickey Deans.) Of these, Sid Luft was married to Judy for thirteen years; for an additional six, both before and after their marriage, save for a few intervals, he either directed her career or was involved in her life. During these nearly nineteen years he undoubtedly knew her more intimately than any other person, and, like Judy's sister, has until now spoken to no other biographer.

Thus, to these persons closest to Judy, I want to express my deepest gratitude, the more so because, though they opened her life to me with the utmost candor, and allowed me complete access to family data, letters and other private papers, they have exercised no editorial control over what I have written. None of her family—nor any of the nearly two hundred other persons who played roles in her life and have allowed me to be privy to these roles—has read a word of this text. To be entrusted with such a wealth of personal matèrial, to be used as he sees fit, is for the biographer to assume a heavy obligation, the more so if it is his goal to say, *This is the way it was really; this is the true Judy.*

To many others I must also express my thanks. Chief among these is one person—Dr. Marcus Rabwin, who bore a unique relationship to Judy, beginning even before her birth and encompassing the whole of her life, and who was, as well, the lifelong adviser and confidant of her parents, Frank and Ethel Gumm. I must single out, also, Mrs. Marcella Rabwin; Mrs. Norma Patterson, Ethel's sister, who grew up in the Gumm household with Judy; Joanna (Peg) DeVine, Cecilia Sues, Jan Pravitz and Helen Fisher, Ethel's oldest friends; Mrs. C. E. (Muggsy) Miller and Edward White, Judy's closest grammar-schoolmates; Mrs. Betty O'Kelly Dimon, Judy's confidante throughout high school and in later years; Mrs. Minnie Gumm, Judy's aunt; Mrs. Irene Mathias, Judy's cousin; Mrs. Judalein Sherwood Havens, Judy's only niece; Jack Cathcart and Robert Sherwood, once Judy's brothers-in-law, married to her sisters, Suzy and Jimmy; Johnny Thompson, Jimmy's present husband; and Vern Alves and Carleton Alsop, Judy's strong supports in some of her most difficult (as well as happiest) days.

Among her professional associates, I am particularly indebted to Benny Thau, L. B. Mayer's chief lieutenant; the late Arthur Freed, a prime force in directing Judy's career; Dore Schary, production head of MGM in Judy's last years there; Howard Strickling, Mary Mayer Schroeder, Ann Straus, and Lester Peterson of the MGM Special Services Department; Mary MacDonald, her teacher at MGM; and Dottie Ponedel, Judy's foster mother, confidante and makeup genius.

I am also grateful to still another category of persons who have helped me understand and shape the Judy of this book; they include Dr. Karl Menninger, Dr. Augustus S. Rose, Dr. Herbert I. Kupper, Dr. Fred W. Pobirs, Dr. Lee E. Siegel, Dr. Daniel G. Morton, Dr. John L. Frank and Dr. Lester Coleman.

It would be an imposition on the reader to list here the scores of Judy's screen colleagues—the celebrated actors, directors, musicians, choreographers, song and script writers—to whom I am deeply obligated. Since I have interviewed virtually all of them, their contributions will be easily recognized. (They will be found in the list of Acknowledgments following the text.)

For assistance in background research I must thank Dr. Homer Pittard, Rutherford County archivist of Gumm, Tennessee; Paul Myers, Curator of the Theatre Collection, New York Public Library; and Lottie Cogen, John Graham and (in London) Gordon Gush, researchers.

And I would be especially remiss if I did not state my endless gratitude to my editors, Buz Wyeth and, in particular, Ruth Pollack; to that master of copy editors, Dick Passmore; and, finally, to my wife, Lillian, who has passed with me through the anguish and ecstasy of these pages with wisdom, love and encouragement beyond any words of mine to express.

GEROLD FRANK

FOREWORD

ALTHOUGH I FIRST MET JUDY GARLAND in London in 1960, I came to know her in the spring of 1968 in New York, when we were brought together by a publisher who thought I might write her autobiography. She had attempted this several times before, each time with a different writer. In each instance the project ended almost as soon as it began. Because Judy had been in and out of psychoanalysis for many years, it was assumed that she would be accustomed to the process of exploring her life, and would not find it difficult to tell her story. Who here or abroad did not know it in roughest outline: from child vaudeville star through *The Wizard of Oz* and the all-too-many musicals, the exploitation by her mother and Metro-Goldwyn-Mayer, the regime of sleeping pills and wake-up pills, the broken marriages, the concert tours, the suicide attempts, the repeated illnesses and nervous breakdowns and inability to perform invariably followed by triumphant comebacks in which she transformed audiences into manic worshipers screaming, "Judy, we love you!"—yet, through it all, the endless, heartbreaking, unavailing search for personal happiness so achingly captured in her song "Over the Rainbow"?

By any measure, an extraordinary personal history. But the fact was that she did find it difficult to talk about herself. In many instances, it was too painful. In some, she was too ashamed. In others, she sought to maintain a mystery about herself, a reserve, a defense, so that people would not find out her vulnerable qualities and, with this knowledge, hurt her. Since her troubles as well as her triumphs were so well known, it always seemed open season on Judy Garland. People treated her like a common possession. They bandied about her name, her problems. They *knew* her, knew what was wrong or right about her, what she should do, how she should handle her life. She found this amusing and annoying, and at times resented it fiercely as an invasion of privacy, even though she knew this was the price she paid for being taken into people's hearts. "Everybody says they know me—they know the *real* Judy," she once complained to her daughter Liza. "Nobody knows me! Not *me!*" Liza, then in her precocious teens, and always one of the most perceptive of creatures, had to agree. "I don't know you, Mama," she said, and she meant it. "I only know that I don't." Judy flashed back, "Then you know more about me by saying that than anyone else."

Invariably when she talked about herself, the entertainer took over. It was the best way to evade and avoid. The result is that the huge wealth of newspaper stories and magazine articles, even after her death, and the books based upon stories she herself told, or on interviews she gave, must be suspect, especially where they are autobiographical. Judy was not an accurate source with respect to herself. She exaggerated outrageously, invented gleefully and over the years changed her stories—they were performances, too, and she aimed to please, and to entertain. There is no doubt that Judy Garland lived in her own special world of fantasy. Telling stories, making up stories, was a good part of her life. Living itself was to her a marvelous and exciting adventure, but at the same time, and in its own strange way, a journey involving nameless, awful terrors; and with her ingenuity and antic humor, she could fit whatever happened, however harrowing, into that adventure.

She abhorred dullness. I have seen, and propose in these pages to cite instance after instance, how she changed her autobiographical accounts as the years went on; and when, at certain periods, a paranoiac note suffused much that she saw and did, what had at one time been merely tall stories, enormously funny improvisations touched by her mordant and often macabre wit, became accusations, almost unbelievable tales of cruelty and suffering at the hands of others. At least, in the later years. That she once, almost *in extremis,* called Peter Lawford, an old friend, to come to her rescue, exhibiting her face bleeding with what appeared to be tiny razor cuts, and sobbed that her then husband, Mark Herron, with whom she had had a fight, had "come after me with a razor"—only to have it disclosed that she had inflicted the cuts on herself—is but one of many such episodes. It was exciting, it was dramatic, it was masochistic, it was wildly feline, it was *acting*—and it brought sympathy, sympathy, sympathy, which she needed as a drowning man needs oxygen. Make no mistake, we are dealing here with a most complex creature. Thus, where at first there had been stories of charming self-mockery, wry accounts of episodes in which she was the hapless but lovable butt of malevolent forces out to frustrate her, there was now the cry of helpless, impotent rage at those who she thought had destroyed her and against whom she fought valiantly—yet still ready, suddenly, to break up with almost hysterical laughter at the duplicity and fiendish absurdity of everything about her. In consequence, there grew up a tremendous mythology, most of it contributed by Judy herself.

Another instance may be cited which became an integral part of that mythology. Writing in a magazine in January 1964, Judy described how she and Mickey Rooney were worked beyond endurance while making the musical *Babes in Arms*, in 1939. "They'd give us pep-up pills to keep us on our feet long after we were exhausted. Then they'd take us to the studio hospital, and knock us cold with sleeping pills—Mickey sprawled on one bed and me on another. Then, after four hours, they'd wake us up and give us the pep pills again, so we could work another seventy-two hours in a row."

This story is untrue. Yet it, and others similarly cruel—that her mother, to punish her, would silently pack her bags and pretend to forsake her, alone, in a hotel room in a strange city, or prevented her from having a normal warm relationship with her father—have found their way into nearly every biography of her. These were the tales told by Judy Garland, the teller of tales; this was the mythology; and in the years since her death, they have been repeated, refurbished, retold.

I had some inkling of this when, early in 1968, an appointment was made for Judy and me to meet again. It was arranged by Sid Luft, her third husband, and father of her two younger children, Joe and Lorna Luft. Though their marriage had ended years before and Judy had been married and divorced since, they maintained an amicable relationship. Luft and I were to join her at 10 P.M. in her suite at the St. Moritz Hotel.

We two dined earlier at the nearby Plaza Hotel, where Luft was staying. He took the occasion to explain that Judy was a night person, rarely able to be herself until late in the evening. Just before ten o'clock he interrupted dessert to telephone her. She was not ready. Eleven would be better, she said. At eleven she was still not ready; nor at midnight. At 1 A.M. she was nervously asking Luft if I could possibly wait until 2 A.M.; and it was not until then that he returned from the phone to say she could see us now. We had been drinking the hours by in the Plaza's Oak Room bar, and during the brief walk to the St. Moritz, Luft said Judy was extremely nervous about meeting me and needed the time to prepare herself.

I was nervous, too. This woman who was already a legend and part of the very folklore of our time, this terrifyingly explosive, unpredictable superstar, presented a challenge to any writer; and especially to one who would have to work with her in the intimate, almost psychoanalytical relationship of the literary collaborator, who becomes confidant and confessor as well as personal historian—and, in the end, alter ego, taking upon himself if possible the very shape and sense of her identity.

In my days as a foreign correspondent I had interviewed a number of the makers and shakers of the world—popes and presidents and Nobel Laureates—all, I thought, with a certain aplomb, but walking down the twelfth-floor corridor at the St. Moritz on my way to the suite of Judy Garland, the entertainer, I was surprised at my own apprehension. I found myself saying fatuously to Luft, "I almost feel like asking you, 'How shall I act?' " He said, with a brief smile, "Just be yourself," and knocked on her door.

It was opened by a handsome, dark-haired man in his thirties who introduced himself as Tom Green. He was her fiancé and personal manager. I did not make out Judy immediately. Then I saw her. She was seated on a sofa on the far side of the room, wearing a dark dress, surprisingly tiny, thin, a child, a waif, staring at me, her huge black eyes searching my face with an expression at once strained and frightened. The moment was indescribable, but it was not her gaze, anxious as it was, that held me. She had made up her face as a clown, and it was behind this laughing, slightly grotesque, makeup that she had been able to meet me: a scarlet dab on the tip of her nose, black lines drawn starfish-like from each eye, the furrowed, absurd cheeks, the hectic coloring, the black touch on the tip of her chin. . . . I had

been ill at ease, but what must she have gone through in these hours
—putting off the meeting, and putting it off, and finally seizing on
this way out, to hide behind this façade—the wistful, lovable little
clown whom no one would dare to hurt?

My heart went out to her: that she should have been so afraid of
me! I wanted to put my arms around her and comfort her and say,
half-overcome by the tenderness welling up in me—that vulnerabil-
ity that was Judy could destroy one!—half-laughing at the irony, and
altogether embarrassed by my sentimentality, "Judy, you didn't have
to . . . I was terrified to meet you, but you were terrified to meet
me. . . ."

But I said nothing like this. We shook hands, she offered drinks, and
after a few pleasantries we began to discuss the book. At one point
we talked about her mother. "If you want to put my mother into it
—and you probably will—O.K.," she said. She made a grimace. "But
my mother was so terrible, so sadistic to me, I could only laugh at her.
It was the only reaction—laugh, or die. She was good only to create
chaos." She gave a bitter laugh. "She'd slap me across the mouth and
shout, 'Go out there and sing!' She was completely impossible. She
called me a whore—I was two years old!" Judy stared at me. "Can you
imagine anyone calling a two-year-old baby a whore?" I said I could
not. "I guess if I must talk about her, the only thing I can say is that
she taught me how not to be cruel to my children. I should be
grateful for that, I suppose."

Judy's harsh description of her mother was not new to those who
had read interviews with her. I asked, had she ever questioned an
aunt or uncle as to what troubled her mother? Why she should have
acted in that way? No, Judy said, and went to another subject. She
had tried telling her story before, she said, but could never do it. Now
she hoped she would be able to do it with me. "I think it's an interesting life—I know it is. And I'm not the daughter of tragedy, you
know."

It is difficult to convey the quality of Judy's speech. She warned me,
"You'll find I slur my words sometimes. You'll have to get used to it."
She also had the habit of pausing after every few words, giving each
phrase a special nuance of tone or emphasis, with now and then a
brief, reflective "mmm" as though turning over in her mind precisely what words to choose. "I think—" pause—"it's an . . . mmm
. . . interesting . . . life." Pause. "I . . . know it is. And I'm . . . mmm

... *not* ... the daughter of *tragedy*—you know." All this gave her speech an unusual musical lilt, and her words subtle differences in meaning, so that one was not always sure how much was candor and how much satirical play. As she said "daughter of *tragedy*," her face was illuminated by a smile that was half gamin grin, half pure irony, and you knew at once that she recognized the idiocies about herself, and knew exactly how people saw her.

Suddenly, completely serious, she said, without pause or any special inflection, her words hard and direct, and the more effective because they came from this tiny clown, "I have gone through hell, I tell you, a hell no one, no person, no man, no beast, not even a fire hydrant could endure!" Which led her, in the ensuing silence, for no reason at all into a hilarious, grotesquely visual story. As she told a story, one saw at once that she put on a performance. She could not tell it seated. She had to leap to her feet, take a stance in the center of the room, dash away, return and, in a kind of hysterical moment with a fling of one hand and an antic glance, set a scene—strut, mug, grin, use her body as expressively as her voice, and end on a high note next to you, hands on your shoulders as you sat in the chair, bending over you, her head leaning against yours, her cheek pressed to yours, shaking with laughter, laughing with you at her, at the insanity of things, making you part of her experience, enveloping you so warmly, so intimately. . . . This girl, this woman, projected a laser beam of pure emotion. Suddenly there were no barriers between us, I had known her all my life, we were one, I was her slave, her knight-errant. Indeed, that power that could so affect an audience of thousands became overwhelming when directed at an audience of one.

She talked then of her children, how proud she was of them. "I always have to tell them to sit down when I bawl them out," she said, laughing. She had been talking about fifteen-year-old Lorna, tall and slender and coltish, and like her mother vibrating with energy, who had come into the room to say hello, flash an utterly captivating smile and leave. Luft and Tom Green had left long before so we would be alone. Judy was saying, "I'm standing here—" she stood in the center of the room—"just under five feet, one hundred pounds—the fat shows at one hundred five or one hundred ten and I have been one hundred fifty—my head back, looking up and shaking my finger at my baby towering over me!" She enacted the scene, head back, finger wagging warningly.

So the night went, swiftly.

On another occasion when I knocked on her door, I heard her voice. "Come in." It was thick, the words slurred, the voice of a drunken woman. There was a fumbling with the lock, then she managed to pull open the door, staggering back. She looked at me blearily. Cowering on the sofa, in a corner, was a frightened Lorna, and on the floor, an overturned empty vodka bottle, scattered about it a confusion of pills. *No*, I thought, and turned to her. She burst into laughter and threw her arms around me. On the sofa Lorna almost choked in a fit of giggling. Judy's voice was in my ear. "Oh, God, you should have seen your face!" And then: "I just didn't have the heart to disappoint you. . . ."

Yet we really never got under way. Like the others, this book was not to be. She was entering a long, often difficult period, the last year of her life. It was a time of alternate despair and joy, a time of accidents, illnesses, concern over financial debts, a time during which we made less and less contact. Finally she left the United States to live and work in England with the man she was going to marry, Mickey Deans, a pianist and entertainer whom she had met when he was manager of Arthur, a well-known New York discotheque. She left on a high note, convinced, as she told her friends and family, that she had at last taken hold of happiness and this time it would not escape her.

And in London, the city she loved, in the hours before dawn of Sunday, June 22, 1969, twelve days after her forty-seventh birthday, the final chapter came in the story she had yet to tell.

I have tried to tell it in the pages that follow.

BOOK ONE
BEGINNINGS

*"For such a mixed-up life later,
it started out beautifully."*

1

WITH A CERTAIN POETIC JUSTICE that Judy Garland, given her delicious sense of irony, would have found marvelously appropriate, this book about her and her extraordinary life begins with the adventures of a doctor. Not quite a doctor, really; at the moment, still a medical student. His name was Marc Rabwin, and in the summer of 1920 he was nineteen, and one of the brightest freshmen at the University of Minnesota Medical School in Minneapolis. He could not know it then, but he was destined to play a major role in the scenario the fates were about to write for Judy Garland—and this even before she was born.

Marc's father owned the only movie house in Eveleth, a small town in northern Minnesota. From his high school days he had helped his father run the theatre, and had gone as far as Minneapolis to rent films for him. This summer Marc decided he knew enough about the business to earn vacation money by trying his hand as a film salesman himself. The W. W. Hodkinson Company of Minneapolis, which had a stock of some fifty silent Westerns, assigned Minnesota and adjacent territory to him. It would be his job to call on small-town movie operators, like his father, and persuade them to rent Hodkinson pictures rather than those rented by Paramount, Goldwyn and other giants of the industry.

On a bright July day Marc was sitting in a day coach rattling through rural Minnesota, being briefed by a group of older salesmen. Someone asked, would he try to make Grand Rapids? Not Grand

Rapids, Michigan, but Grand Rapids, Minnesota, a remote papermill town of fourteen hundred people not far from the Canadian border. Marc checked. Yes, he had it on his list. "Forget it," one of the older men said. "Don't waste your time."

Why? Marc asked. Grand Rapids was hard to get to, he was told, there was only one movie house in town, the New Grand, run by a Frank Gumm, an impossible man to deal with. Gumm was extremely nervous, he had a hair-trigger temper, he hated salesmen, he simply wasn't civil. . . . "Skip it," he was advised.

This warning only challenged Marc. He would call on Frank Gumm and sell him. Two evenings later, after a slow ride through the iron country of northern Minnesota, he reached Grand Rapids. Suitcase in hand, he walked down the town's one Main Street, looking for the theatre, and found it to be a one-story clapboard structure with a painted wooden sign above it. In the lobby he came upon a blue-eyed, dark-haired man in his thirties, of medium height, who was simultaneously tending the popcorn machine and taking tickets. The show was about to begin. Yes, yes, he said irritably in a surprising Southern accent, he was Frank Gumm, and, as anyone could see, he was busy. If Marc wanted to take his chances and hang around—"Just keep out of my way, though"—until after the picture began, he might find some time for him.

A few minutes later Gumm led the way into a cubbyhole office. The man, Marc saw, clearly lived up to his billing. He was nervous, he fidgeted, he paced back and forth as he talked. Marc also made an on-the-spot diagnosis. Minnesota was in the goiter belt, and though Gumm had no visible goiter, neither the telltale bulge at the throat nor the prominent eyes, he was obviously hyperthyroid. That would explain his nervousness, his irritability. But more astonishing to Marc as their conversation continued was the realization that Frank Gumm took to him; that Gumm liked him and he liked Gumm; that, despite his mannerisms, he was a charming man with a quick, spontaneous laugh and genuine warmth. It was an almost instant rapport; the chemistry was just right; within ten minutes they were friends. That night Gumm not only contracted for several films from him, but invited him to stay at his home and work the neighboring towns from there for the two weeks or so he'd be in the area. "We don't have a decent hotel here," Gumm said, "and anyway, my wife's the best cook in town."

Marc accepted the invitation. Gumm took him into the back of the theatre and the two sat in the darkness watching the film unfold while a vigorous piano accompaniment sounded in the pit. Gumm leaned over. "That's Ethel down there at the piano," he whispered. "She's got the fastest fingers on the keys you ever saw."

When the show was over, Gumm introduced Marc to his wife. Ethel Gumm was a plump, spirited little woman just under five feet, with snapping black eyes that missed nothing and, like her husband, brimming over with nervous energy. She almost ran as she darted about on her high four-inch heels helping close up the New Grand. Marc, the medical student, suspected that both might have goiters. Ought he not advise them to do something about it? The Mayo Clinic in downstate Rochester was famous for its work in the field. He decided he would bring up the subject later.

In the next two weeks Marc found himself taken into the family almost as though he were a grown son. Ethel was as hospitable and outgoing as her husband, and Marc fell in love with them and their two little girls, Mary Jane, five, and Virginia, three. Evenings, after early dinner—Ethel *was* a good cook, if given to rich gravies and puddings topped with whipped cream—she took her place at the upright piano in the living room, the two little girls arranged themselves behind her, and there would be a nightly musicale for Frank and Marc and any neighbor who might drop in. Ethel was coaching the two girls, patterning them after the Duncan Sisters, Vivian and Rosetta, one of the reigning sister acts of the day. At seven o'clock, when the New Grand opened, the entire family adjourned to the theatre. Ethel sold tickets until the picture began, then went to the piano in the pit. While the film was on, Mary Jane and Virginia— Janey and Jimmy—sat in the first row, directly behind her, as enthralled watching it the fifth time as the first. Friday night was entertainment night. Then the two girls had their chance to perform before an audience. At intermission Ethel remained at the piano; Janey and Jimmy slipped backstage, where Frank helped them change into costumes Ethel had made for them. They would wait for an opening chord from their mother, and then bounce on stage, to go through the Duncan Sisters act based on *Uncle Tom's Cabin*— Janey playing Eva, and Jimmy, in blackface, her hair in corkscrew curls, playing Topsy, the two raising their voices in a plaintive duet, "I Never Had a Mammy," while Ethel directed them from the pit.

The Gumm home was a warm, easy household, with everything revolving around music and the New Grand. Frank told him something about himself and Ethel, and Marc listened, fascinated. He and Frank had much in common: Eveleth was hardly larger than Grand Rapids, and he could listen sympathetically as Frank unburdened himself on the headaches of running a small-town movie house, and especially of his campaign against block booking. This was a high-handed practice in which the major film companies forced the movie operator to contract for a "package" of films in advance, giving him no choice but to accept the bad with the good—a subject that made Frank turn purple when he talked about it.

But what intrigued Marc was Frank's picaresque background and Ethel's story, which complemented it. Frank, one of five children, had been born in Murfreesboro, a hamlet in the Tennessee hill country not far from Nashville. The family, of German, Scotch and French ancestry—nonetheless, Judy always called her father a "charming Irishman"—had been among the earliest settlers in the state; the village of Gumm, half a dozen miles away, had been given its name by one of his forebears. Both parents died when he was twelve, leaving an older sister to rear the others. Frank, who had been a soprano soloist in the Episcopal church choir, ran away from home to join a minstrel troupe. He showed Marc a snapshot of himself, aged thirteen; he was in blackface, grinning like a young Al Jolson, complete with bowler, vest, black string tie, long trousers, and clutching a ukulele under one arm. Then he and a younger brother sang on trains between Murfreesboro and Chattanooga, with Frank passing the hat among the passengers for coins. Later his voice, which had changed to a sweet tenor, led a rich suitor of his sister Mary to put him through the Sewanee Military Academy, a private preparatory school, where Frank was an ornament of the choir. At eighteen he entered the University of the South to study business administration; but the lure of vaudeville was too much, and he left to go on the road again.

He met Ethel one January day in 1914 at the Princess Theatre in Superior, Wisconsin, where he was leading the audience in song while the verses appeared on colored slides flashed on the screen, and Ethel was playing the piano in the pit. It was her duty to provide appropriate music for the film and, when an itinerant performer like

6

Frank Gumm appeared between showings, to play his accompaniment.

She had looked up at him with those flashing black eyes, and it had been love at first sight. He was twenty-seven; she was, she said, twenty (after the children came, she took three years off her age, and to the day of her death never admitted to those three years), and as soon as the manager of the Princess introduced them, Gumm realized this was an ambitious, resourceful girl. He was impressed. Like him she came from a remote little backwoods town—Michigamme, Michigan—one of seven children of a railroad engineer who could never make ends meet. She had been forced to quit school in the fifth grade, and was completely self-taught. She had wanted to play piano more than anything; she played by ear as a child, then took lessons, a quarter a lesson, until she was proficient enough to get a job selling sheet music in a five-and-ten, singing and playing her own accompaniment. When Frank met her, she was working there during the day and at the Princess at night. It had to be a whirlwind courtship because his engagement was for only two weeks; but Ethel had a mind of her own and when Frank went on to his next job, Ethel left with him: they were Mr. and Mrs. Frank Gumm. Frank's family always felt he had married a little below his station: more than half a century later Mrs. Minnie Gumm, an aunt, could say, "I always liked his little wife—but, you know, she was a Northern girl."

Now Frank and Ethel put together an act: "Jack and Virginia Lee, Sweet Southern Singers." As a team—Ethel had a modest contralto voice—they toured the tiny Gus Sun circuit, made up of small rural movie houses in the Central and Northern states that could afford only one act of live entertainment between the first and second showing of the film. Their opening number won the audience. The curtain rose to show Ethel seated in great dignity at the piano on the stage, Frank standing beside her. He would introduce himself. "Good evening, ladies and gentlemen. My name is Jack Lee, and this is Virginia Lee, my wife." Ethel would rise from the piano bench and take a little bow, then resume her seat. Then Frank, in his soft Southern drawl: "Virginia Lee will now open our program by playing 'Alexander's Ragtime Band.' I would like you all, please, to observe how small her hands are."

At this Ethel turned sideways on the bench and held up her hands, palms out to the audience, showing them from right to left and then left to right again, smiling sweetly and modestly to the applause; then she would turn and play, her fingers flying over the keyboard.

They were on tour when Ethel found herself pregnant, in Grand Rapids, Minnesota. They could not travel from one tank town to another with a baby. Frank looked about town. The New Grand's lease was available if he wanted to go into partnership with a local citizen named Fred Bentz. They would run the show as a family affair, cutting down expenses. Frank would be manager and ticket taker, Ethel musical director (she would play the piano in the pit for the films), Bentz would be projectionist, and Mrs. Bentz sell tickets. Frank had put all their savings into a diamond ring he wore on the fourth finger of his right hand, where it flashed dazzlingly when he strummed his ukulele. He gave up his ring as his share of the down payment, and the Gumms settled in Grand Rapids. Mary Jane was born September 24, 1915. Virginia came along as an Independence Day baby on July 4, 1917, in the midst of the great war. They had their family now, Frank said. Their vaudeville days were behind them.

When Frank took over the New Grand, one of the first things he did was to introduce a series of weekly amateur nights. The theatre had an excellent stage, unusual in small-town picture houses. This had been one of the reasons Frank leased the New Grand. A few days before, he attended a dance at the village hall. He approached two brothers, Robert and Wayne Gilbert, who had been pointed out to him as members of the Methodist church choir, and said, "I understand you two boys sing." Robert replied, "We try to do our best." "Well," said Frank, "how about singing in our amateur show down at the theatre? We're going to have them every Friday night."

That Friday night between the first and second showings of the film, he appeared on stage with them, all three in white flannels, red vests and straw hats. Frank strummed his ukulele, Ethel presided at the piano, and the trio sang "By the Light of the Silvery Moon" and other songs of the day. The amateur nights caught on—and within a few years among those who entertained between films were the two Gumm Sisters. Nothing fazed Ethel. She sewed costumes for the girls to complement their songs—Irish, Scotch and Spanish costumes —and even tried her hand at songwriting. The girls first practiced with Duncan Sisters records played on their wind-up Victrola. Ethel put the songs in a key they could manage, adding here and there a grace note of her own improvisation. By the time Marc Rabwin came on the scene, the two Gumm Sisters were a permanent feature of Friday night entertainments at the New Grand.

At home, Marc observed, Frank was the most affectionate of fathers. He would get down on the floor to play jacks with the girls, and shamelessly indulged them. Ethel, it was clear, was the disciplinarian of the family. She bustled about under a full head of steam, rising at 6 A.M. to do the day's cooking and baking—one of her specialties was a carrot cake—coaching the girls, making both their everyday clothes and their stage costumes, taking moments off to jot down lyrics of songs she was forever writing and, when evening came, hurrying to her duties at the New Grand; yet she still found time to organize weekly bridge parties, play the organ in the Episcopal church (where Frank was choirmaster) and preside at meetings of the Eastern Star. As everyone said, Ethel was a born manager. Frank was no less busy. In addition to running the theatre (and playing the piano in the pit when Ethel was not there) and directing the choir, he also worked during the day as an advertising salesman and society reporter for the Grand Rapids *Weekly Independent.* As operator of the only place of amusement in town, he knew everyone. He hardly had to leave the lobby of the New Grand to pick up his social notes.

Marc left Grand Rapids with the promise that he would correspond regularly. To Janey and Jimmy he was already "Uncle Marc." Before he said good-bye he asked Frank if either he or Ethel had ever been told they had goiters. No, Frank said, surprised. Ethel had a touch of high blood pressure, and he had a running ear which bothered him now and then, but otherwise their health was fine. Marc suggested tactfully that Frank's jumpiness and Ethel's hyperactivity might be due to hidden goiters. "I'd look into it one of these days," he said.

In Eveleth that autumn, after Marc returned to school in Minneapolis, the elder Rabwin found himself in trouble. The family theatre—the Empress—was really a store that Marc's father had converted into a movie house. He had always dreamed of owning a new modern theatre in which he could show first-run films. He had finally been able to build one across the street from the Empress, which he named the Regent. Having done so, he gave up his lease on the old building, assuming that it would revert to a store, as he had found it. Instead, the owners, angered by his move, decided to operate the Empress in competition with the Regent. There simply were not enough people in Eveleth to support two movie houses— surely not enough to make a success of the Regent, into which a great deal of money had been put. In desperation, Marc's father offered to buy the Empress. The owners refused. Rather than sell to Rabwin, they would gamble on outstaying him and have the field to themselves when he failed. Marc's father, caught in a vendetta he had never anticipated, was beside himself. He called on Marc at school: had he any ideas what to do?

Marc had urged his father to expand. He felt part of the responsibility was his. He decided to take a year off from medicine, return to Eveleth and operate the Regent himself. He could spare the year, for he had skipped a grade in high school. Meanwhile, he suggested that his parents go to California for the winter. That would remove the immediate pressures on his father, and give both parents a relief from the bitter Minnesota cold which sometimes dropped to 40 degrees below.

After his father left, Marc went to the telephone and called Frank Gumm in Grand Rapids. "Frank," he said, "I want you to go to Eveleth and buy a theatre." He explained the situation. It would be a great favor. "When you get there, you're simply a theatre operator from Grand Rapids and you're looking for one to buy around Eveleth. Buy it. I'll send you my check for five thousand dollars now. If that does it, fine. If not, my father will take care of it."

Frank Gumm carried out his mission. Within the month he went to Eveleth, stayed there ten days, became acquainted with the owners of the Empress and offered to buy their theatre. They sold it to Frank. He held it for a week, then resold it to the Rabwins and returned to Grand Rapids. Now the Rabwins could operate both theatres or close down the old one, as they wished. Marc's parents went to California for the winter, and Marc took the year off.

Late one night the following winter—early November 1921—the buzzer sounded in the room Marc Rabwin, now a second-year medical student at the University of Minnesota, occupied in a student boardinghouse on the Minneapolis campus. When he opened the door, there stood Frank Gumm. "I'm sorry to bother you at this hour,

Marc," Frank said. "But I've just come in from Grand Rapids and I've got to talk to you." He was obviously agitated.

A minute later he was telling Marc his problem. He had once done Marc a favor; now he wanted one in return. He had come these nearly two hundred miles for help. Ethel was pregnant. It was entirely unexpected. She—they—weren't prepared for another child. She—they—didn't want another child—five years after Janey and Jimmy. It would be a burden. Ethel was about two months pregnant. Frank indicated that she had tried all the old wives' remedies—the huge doses of castor oil, the rough wagon rides—nothing had helped. Marc was in medical school, so perhaps he would know what to do so they wouldn't have this child.

"Frank, you're talking about abortion," Marc said. "That's terribly dangerous." These were the days before antibiotics. Abortions were not only illegal, they were often followed by fatal infections. No reputable physician would attempt one. Ethel could die at the hands of some back-alley abortionist who might not even be a doctor. Marc explained this to Frank. "If Ethel got through it safely, there could still be aftereffects that might last the rest of her life," he said. For these reasons, even if he knew where to send him, he would refuse to do so.

Marc was always to remember the scene in his small student's room, his football pennants on the wall, his books and microscope under its glass dome on a battered wooden table near the window, his gooseneck lamp throwing its yellow light on the medical text he had been studying, and Frank pacing nervously back and forth as he listened. Marc concluded, "Look, Frank, let her have the baby. After the baby's born, you wouldn't take a million dollars for it."

Frank stopped his pacing. O.K., he said, finally. He'd persuade Ethel to go through with it. They'd abide by Marc's advice. He spent that night on the sofa in Marc's room and the next day took the train back to Grand Rapids.

Ethel had to wait for her baby nearly two weeks beyond her expected time. In the hope that it would be a boy, they had already named the child Frank, Jr., but it was Jan Pravitz, a neighbor, who predicted as they waited, "It's going to be a girl. She's taking her time. She's primping." And it was a girl, born at 5:30 A.M., June 10, 1922.

One of Frank's first calls was to Marc. The baby weighed seven pounds. She looked like Ethel. They had named her Frances Ethel Gumm.

As it turned out, she was never called Frances by anyone in the family. The name seemed not to belong after she had been thought of so long as Frank, Jr. It seemed easier to call her Baby. And so, like it or not, she was known to the family until her twelfth year. In school they lessened her mortification by making it Babe. But Frances never really took.

It was Baby Gumm, formally known as Frances Gumm, who became Judy Garland.

2

YEARS LATER JUDY, talking about her first appearance before an audience that had already become impatient, said, "Late—as usual," and then with a mischievous flash of her dark eyes, "I knew I wasn't wanted. And after two girls, I might at least have had the decency to be a boy. I wasn't primping, God knows; I was fighting not to be born. If I could have talked that morning, I would have said, 'Look, I object to you as much as you object to me!'

"But I had nothing to say, then—or ever."

Yet it really wasn't that way. At the beginning, Judy's memories were happy ones, memories out of a child's story book, recollections of a gay, music-filled household in which everyone sang—mother, father, sisters, uncles and aunts—of a doughty, irrepressible Grandmother Eva, who wore a narrow black velvet choker about her neck, caught with a bright pin at the throat, who loved to hug her grandchildren and cheat at poker, and a fat, jolly Aunt Norma, over 250 pounds (that heritage of weight from her mother's side was always to be Judy's cross), who once toured small-town vaudeville as a member of a "Beef Trust" chorus line, and made such meltingly marvelous doughnuts that Judy and her sisters sold them about town.

As Judy herself put it, "For such a mixed-up life later, it started out beautifully." She remembered Grand Rapids as all charm and gaiety, a lovely town of little white houses surrounded by blue lakes, and tiny ponds, the corner house she lived in with a truck garden in back and corn growing wild between the sidewalk and the curb in front, the snow all about—it started snowing in September—and ice skating, with hot green mint tea to drink afterward.

And always the snow. Years later, when Judy played Esther Smith in the moving and delightful story of a turn-of-the-century American family in *Meet Me in St. Louis,* the lovely snow scenes almost brought her to tears, for they recalled so vividly the winters in Grand Rapids, and particularly the Christmas holidays. Just as the Smith family celebrated Christmas in St. Louis, so the Gumm family celebrated it in Grand Rapids. Judy and her sisters had their own special Christmas Eve observance. For days before, no one was allowed to walk in the front yard, to ensure a clean blanket of snow. Then the day before Christmas Frank would hasten home after the first show, at 9:30—there was really no business after that hour on Christmas Eve—and Judy and her sisters, waiting for him, would lace up their leggings and, all bundled up against the bitter cold, go out into the yard and make angels in the snow.

Judy described how it was done. You stood stiff, arms flat at your sides; then Daddy, holding you by the shoulders, let you fall slowly backward onto the snow, so that you lay there on your back. Then you swept your arms in wide arcs like a bird, and moved your legs in similar fashion; then, keeping yourself stiff as a board again, Daddy pulled you up carefully, so as not to spoil anything. Then you all ran upstairs and looked out the bedroom windows at the angels imprinted clearly in the snow, complete even to wings and gowns! Then, to warm everybody, Ethel gave the girls big glasses of hot milk with Thompson's Chocolate Malt stirred into it. A large round can was always kept in the pantry next to the extra room where Bella, the Swedish housegirl, stayed. Bella's family had a farm twenty miles from town, too far for her to go back and forth to school each day. The Gumms needed a girl only from late afternoon on, because the New Grand (except on Saturdays) did not open until 7 P.M., and Ethel did not leave for the theatre until after dinner. The arrangement worked out nicely all around.

Winter meant snowball fights, too. Judy when she was very little watched enviously as Janey and Jimmy built fortresses of snow and chose sides with other children. If you hit anyone with a snowball, it counted a point for your side. The day came when her sisters allowed her to get into the snow with them. She was so thrilled to be with the older children that she stuck her head up above the fortress, and a boy named Bernard threw a snowball with a rock in it, which nearly stunned her. She burst into tears. Her big sister Janey took after him, pummeled him furiously, and when he broke away, threw tin cans after him; then she took Judy in her arms and put snow on the bump and comforted her. The memory of the warm glow that enveloped her as she nestled in her sister's arms was as fresh and vivid to her through the years as though it had happened yesterday. To be comforted, to be babied, to be *held*—never were there enough of those moments for her.

Judy's memories of summers there—the Gumms were to live in Grand Rapids until she was four—had the same story-book quality. When her older sisters allowed her to play with them, she was ecstatic. They taught her how to use Mason jars, taken from the cellar where Ethel kept the jams and preserves she put up each fall, to catch bees and hornets, then watch the insects buzz about inside. There was high drama, too—the heartbreaking funeral of their pet bird, a crippled blue jay they had found in the back yard. They tended it carefully, putting a splint on its broken wing, but it died. They lined an empty cigarbox with tinfoil to make a coffin, laid out the bird, then had a long funeral procession in the back yard to the garden, where they ceremoniously buried it with a little cross to mark the place. The girls all wore hats—they put Ethel's hat on Baby, almost covering her eyes—and it was all mournful and wonderful. Then they returned to the house to find Aunt Norma had just arrived. They were so disappointed that she had missed the funeral that they dug up the bird and buried it all over again, complete to the procession, hats and all.

Often Baby fought with her sisters, and took advantage of what was clearly becoming her special position in the household. She was indulged, not only because she was Baby, but because everyone in the family knew they had almost lost her.

When she was little more than a year old, she came down with a frightening illness marked by a high, persistent fever and an inability to keep any food on her stomach. As days passed, she seemed to wither before their eyes, becoming so emaciated that her arms and legs looked as thin as pipestems. It was a fearsome thing. The fever

14

raged, it would not be brought down, the doctors were powerless. They spoke vaguely of "acute acidosis"; they admitted that she was becoming more and more dehydrated, and that if this continued, she would die.

The crisis came one nightmarish midnight when Frank and Ethel hurriedly bundled her up in blankets, carried her out to the family Buick, and drove with her all night through a blinding snowstorm over eighty miles to a hospital in Duluth, where a specialist waited, to see if he could save her. She was not expected to live. There were no sulfa drugs then, no penicillin. When, after nearly a month in the hospital, they brought her back to Grand Rapids, everyone knew that Baby had almost died. It was the first of several times that she became desperately ill. Baby was fragile, Baby was vulnerable, and she grew to take advantage of it.

She was self-willed, she wanted what she wanted when she wanted it, and had no hesitation from the first in making her demands known. "She was spoiled rotten," one of her sisters was to say. Janey and Jimmy were always at each other, two sisters fighting over toys and possessions and the like; but there was too much of an age difference for them to pick on Baby.

At the beginning Baby did a lot of crying. She was always hungry. Ethel was old-fashioned and proper and insisted on nursing her, though she did not have enough milk. The baby seemed to do nothing but cry until the middle of the third month, when she was placed on formula. Then she stopped. But in almost nothing else was Baby Gumm frustrated. She was indulged by the entire family, and in her first years particularly by her sisters.

At 7 A.M. the morning she was born, Frank came home from the hospital. Janey and Jimmy were up, unable to sleep because of the excitement. They crept into bed with their father. He told them they had a baby sister. "Oh, that's keen," said seven-year-old Janey. "Now we got something to play with." What should they call her? Frank asked. Janey, who liked glamorous names (she was to change hers from Mary Jane to Suzannah later), could not think of one glamorous enough for their new sister. Jimmy, who was always the most practical, spoke up. "Let's call her Baby." For the two girls, she was a live doll to fondle and fuss over.

They doted on her. She was pert, she was quick, she was adorable with her little turned-up nose and her bright black eyes, which, like

Ethel's, missed nothing. They marveled at her idiosyncrasies. If she took a dislike to anyone, the left side of her face reddened and broke out in perspiration; but since that happened if she was fed certain foods—shrimp, for example—they didn't quite know what to make of it. She came down with sudden earaches. When she was two, she had to be rushed to the hospital and have her ears lanced. It was done without anesthetic, Ethel holding down the screaming child while the doctor worked on her. Fear of pain—pain of an earache, toothache, childbirth, physical pain of any kind—was to haunt her always. Years later, however, Judy could paint a hilarious picture of herself as Ethel ministered to her. An old country treatment for earache was the application of hot salt. Ethel would fill two of Frank's socks with salt, heat them in the oven, then hang them over Judy's head so each foot hugged an ear. "I'd sit on the couch in the living room with those socks full of hot salt hung over my ears—I looked like a cocker spaniel most of the winter," Judy would say.

But there were treats for her, sometimes. Marian Latz, whose father owned the town's general hardware store, Latz's Emporium, was Jimmy's best friend. The Latzes lived directly above their store, about five minutes from the Gumms. They were the only Jewish family in Grand Rapids, and very Orthodox. Often Jimmy was invited for Friday night dinner, and when she was a little older, Baby found herself asked to come along.

Jimmy and Baby, her fingers clutched firmly in Jimmy's hand, would walk down Main Street, past the Pokegama Hotel, and Mrs. Zizer's bakery, and Gunner Smith's blacksmith shop where, if they peeked in, they could sometimes see Mr. Smith, who had a wooden leg and a mustache and chewed tobacco, all but lost in a shower of white-hot sparks as he hammered at his forge, until they came to the Emporium, half a dozen doors beyond. Once upstairs, the two little girls would sit primly at the table with Marian, her two brothers and Mr. Latz, a sober little man who wore a tiny black skullcap perched on the back of his head. The large dining room table sparkled with white linen and two tall brass candlesticks held a place of honor in the center. Mrs. Latz, a buxom woman, had a small apron tied over her dress, which showed glimpses of many petticoats as she moved about. She would be the last to sit down. First she would light each candle carefully with a kitchen match, then remove her apron and, standing before the candlesticks, place both hands, palms down, against her forehead as though shading her eyes, and then, her eyes closed, rock gently back and forth, murmuring strange words in Hebrew, right out of the Bible. "She's saying grace," Jimmy explained to her little sister. Since Daddy said grace every night, this was only partly mysterious. But then, when Mrs. Latz took her place at the foot of the table, Mr. Latz, presiding at the other end, would bow his head with the black skullcap perilously atop it, and murmur grace all over again, at the same time cutting a twisted loaf of bread beside his plate. It was all mysterious and wonderful, and the Gumm girls felt privileged to be part of it.

It *was* a treat for Baby to go with her older sister, and she was always grateful. Her first consciousness of a moment when her sisters treated her meanly—their first memorable really angry fight—occurred one day when the two girls came home from school, each munching on a candy bar. They had forgotten to buy one for her. The moment they walked into the house Baby began yelling, "Gimme a bite of the candy!" Neither girl paid any attention to her. Aunt Norma came in and immediately took Baby's part. "Why, you two selfish girls, you give your poor baby sister a bite." Whereupon Janey and Jimmy threw the candy on the floor rather than give it to her. Aunt Norma promptly locked them in an upstairs bedroom for fifteen minutes—this was punishment in the Gumm household— while Baby fell upon the two candy bars and stuffed herself with them before Aunt Norma had a chance to wash them off.

Suddenly, at the age of two, the world opened up for Baby Gumm. She made her stage debut. It was at her father's theatre on New Year's Day—Thursday, January 1, 1925. Nothing was quite the same after that.

Almost as soon as she could toddle, she had tried to line up with her sisters behind Ethel and mimic them. At the beginning her attempts to sing and dance threw them off, and she was shooed away. She nagged and begged. When Ethel said, "Baby, you're too little," she went into one of her screaming fits until Ethel compromised— she took her along on Friday nights and at intermission let her stand backstage in the wings peeping out at Janey and Jimmy as they sang and danced.

One day Frank taught her and a playmate, no bigger than she, to sing "My country 'tis of thee," accompanying them himself on the piano. The other child faltered halfway through, but Baby sang every word, sustaining the tune to the end, her voice clear and pure, and surprisingly strong for so small a child. "Say," Frank said admiringly to Ethel, later, "Baby Gumm is good, she is." It was Judy's first memory of praise for her voice—her first notice.

Not long after this Grandma Eva, who then lived in Duluth, came visiting during the Christmas holidays. She took Baby with her to the Christmas Day matinee performance by the Gumm Sisters, and held her on her lap. As Janey and Jimmy danced the Charleston and then went into their songs, her grandmother became aware that this child on her lap was not only rocking in rhythm to the music, but was accompanying her sisters under her breath. She knew the words, certainly, even if she couldn't pronounce them all.

Janey and Jimmy swept off to great applause, then waited a proper moment in the wings before returning for their encore. Grandma Eva could not restrain herself. She pushed Baby off her lap. "Baby," she whispered, "go on and get up on the stage." But Baby dared not. She already knew it was not wise to cross her mother, privileged though her own position in the family. While Ethel could be loving and open, she wanted things done her way; not only could her temper be even more frightening than Frank's, but she also possessed a strong, piercing glance; when annoyed, her glare could reduce the older girls to tears, especially if they had done something wrong. Baby made her way to her mother in the pit. "Mama, can I sing, too?" Whether because of Frank's praise or for whatever reason, Ethel's response was gentle. She put her finger to her lips. "Not today, Baby —but next week."

She was as good as her word. She fashioned a white net dress for her, sleeveless, low-cut in front, with the edging of a little white bodice showing, and then taught her "Jingle Bells."

The following Thursday afternoon—New Year's Day—as her sisters performed, Baby, all dressed up (Janey and Jimmy had pinned little sprigs of holly on her dress, as their contribution), waited in the wings. Frank knelt at her side, ready to unleash her at the right moment. Baby's appearance was to seem impromptu and unrehearsed—the littlest Gumm unexpectedly appearing to the surprise of everyone. Mary Jane and Jimmy came off, blowing kisses; there was applause; everyone expected them to appear again for their bows; instead, Frank let go his hold and gave his daughter a gentle push: "You're on, Baby."

As Ethel had rehearsed her, she was to bounce on stage carrying a little dinner bell, make a deep bow, and go into her song, ringing the bell at the appropriate moments: "Jingle bells, jingle bells, jingle [sound of bells] all the way . . ."

Baby carried out her instructions like a professional. She marched out, showing not the least sign of shyness at the audience's gasp of surprise, laughter, then applause, planted herself in the center of the stage and began to sing on the right note, in perfect pitch, and keeping perfect time.

She finished and made her bow to rousing applause. As it died down, Ethel beamed up at her. "Get off, Baby, you're through." Baby shook her head. "I wanna sing some more," she announced, and started the chorus all over again. Ethel began to choke with laughter, but played the accompaniment. From the wings Frank's stage whisper was unmistakable: "Baby, come off—come off!" Behind their father Janey and Jimmy were beckoning frantically to her. But Baby would hear and see nothing. When the applause rose even louder after the second chorus, she bowed and promptly went into her third; and once more Ethel, all but helpless in the pit, had to hurry up on the piano to catch up with her. There was no stopping Baby; now she was in her fourth chorus, singing and ringing her bell; for the first time she had come under the spell of the lights, the music, the applause, and after the fifth chorus Frank Gumm strode out onstage to waves of laughter, picked up his little daughter, threw her over his shoulder and carried her off still energetically ringing the bell at the audience and singing to them over his shoulder until they both vanished into the wings. And then the audience heard the bell backstage.

Now they were three.

The Gumms might well have remained in Grand Rapids and—it is pure speculation, of course—Frances Gumm might never have become Judy Garland had it not been for one thing: Marc Rabwin's parents had become so enamored of California during their visit there that they determined to move permanently to the West Coast. They waited only until Marc, their youngest son, received his medical degree in June 1924. That year the elder Rabwin, having educated his six children, retired. He sold the Regent in Eveleth and moved with his family to Los Angeles. Marc moved, too, to be near them, along with his eldest brother, Harry, who began the practice of law there. By 1926 Marc was chief resident at the Los Angeles County Hospital.

In his correspondence with the Gumms, Marc had written glowingly about California, its climate, its growing opportunities. Frank Gumm decided that the Gumms, too, should go west. He would try his fortune as a theatre operator in California. Marc made the decision easier by promising to help Frank find a theatre. Several other reasons lay behind the Gumms' decision to follow the Rabwins. The West was booming; oil had been discovered in Texas; stories of Southern California's swift expansion were filtering back to the East. There was also an important personal consideration. Ever since Baby's almost fatal illness, she had been increasingly susceptible to colds and fevers. Nor was Frank's ailing ear helped by the hard Minnesota winters. They decided they would take a long summer vacation to the West Coast, working their way through North Dakota, Montana and Washington, and down to California, where they would investigate the possibilities of leasing a movie house in Los Angeles. Though the only people they knew there were the Rabwins, in mid-June 1926, with the three girls in the back seat of their Buick touring car, they set out on their drive.

To help pay their way, Frank and Ethel returned to their old vaudeville act. They became again Jack and Virginia Lee, Sweet Southern Singers, and performed in such towns as Devils Lake, North Dakota, and Kalispell, Montana. When they arrived in a town with a movie house that had a stage—most small-town picture houses had simply a screen dropped from the ceiling against the back wall —Frank introduced himself to the manager, produced the 11-by-14-inch theatrical posters he had had printed advertising their act, and made a deal to play one night—or even two—for a percentage of the house. Then the entire Gumm family busied itself putting up posters in front of the theatre and on fences all over town. Often Frank and Ethel had to make up for their performance in the comfort rooms of the nearest gas station. One thing they were assured of: they had a built-in claque in the three girls who sat in the front row at every performance and applauded loudly when their parents appeared.

Now and then, if it meant additional pay, the three Gumm Sisters followed them on stage, whereupon Frank and Ethel hurried into the audiences and applauded with even more enthusiasm.

By this time all three girls were stage veterans, dancing the Charleston, Janey and Jimmy had played their Topsy-and-Eva routines and sung their duets, and Baby had danced and sung her solos.

This roundabout trip—over two thousand miles—was enlivened by Baby Gumm. She was impish and uninhibited. Every so often Frank noticed that passing cars swerved dangerously close to them, and as they went by, the heads of driver and passengers turned as if on swivels to peer delightedly into the back of the Gumms' car. Frank, glancing into his rear-view mirror, saw why. There was Baby between her two sisters, who faced front, as well-bred children should. But Baby's back was to him, she was on her knees on the seat, pressing her forehead against the back window and making faces at the passing cars: her fingers in the corners of her mouth stretching it as wide as possible, pulling down the skin under her eyes, sticking out her tongue, her thumbs in her ears, wiggling her fingers, mugging outrageously, putting on a full show. "Baby!" Frank would shout angrily, and Baby subsided—for a little while. There was always this difference between the sisters: Janey, taller, slimmer, darker-complexioned, restrained, to whom some things would always be sacred, taking after her father in appearance; Jimmy, warmer, more open, who resembled Ethel; and Baby, the cute one, the cutup, the scene-stealer, who absorbed attention and was instantaneous in her reactions, and who looked like both Ethel and Frank.

So the Gumms worked their way westward, town by town, and one Friday afternoon Marc, on duty at the hospital, was called to the phone. "Marc, we made it!" They'd all arrived, and checked into an inexpensive hotel down the street. When they met later, it was like a family reunion.

The following Sunday Marc had a full day off. He spent it driving Frank from one small town to another on the outskirts of Los Angeles, looking for a theatre to lease. Ethel and the girls meanwhile visited the studios, Ethel to survey the possibilities of bookings for the Gumm Sisters, or even for a piano-playing or teaching job, when and if they decided they would move permanently to California.

The two men had no success that day or the following Sunday, but on the third Marc decided to go into the country to Lancaster, a rural, isolated town on the edge of the desert north of Los Angeles. He happened to know of it only because it was the furthermost community to which he, as chief resident, was permitted to dispatch County ambulances for emergency pickups. He had ridden the ambulance there several times himself, and knew Lancaster to be a busy, self-contained town. Most important, it fulfilled a basic requirement for Frank. There was only one movie house, and therefore no competition, and no likelihood of anything like the Rabwins' unhappy experience in Eveleth.

That noon they parked in front of the Antelope Valley Theatre in Lancaster. Frank liked it immediately, particularly because it, too, like the New Grand, boasted a genuine stage, and he could put on live entertainment as he had in Grand Rapids. A quick lunch at a nearby restaurant elicited the information that the theatre had been built a few years before by Whit Carter, the town's leading citizen, and promptly dubbed "Carter's Folly" because it seated five hundred persons—then the town's entire population. But, as Frank and Marc learned, the theatre had a monopoly. It was the only one for miles around. It actually dared charge half a dollar instead of the customary quarter. Moreover, Lancaster was a supply center for farmers within a fifty-mile radius. On its Main Street were garages, blacksmiths, auto dealers, farm-implement stores, branches of J. C. Penney's and Woolworth's; and with farmers and their families driving in on weekends to shop, the Antelope Valley Theatre had to do well. Because the town was a gathering place—the American Legion, the Eastern Star, the Kiwanis, Elks, Masons and other fraternal orders had chapters there—it offered full scope for the Gumms' talent for sociability. And since the New Grand had seated only two hundred and charged a quarter, and the Antelope Valley seated five hundred and charged twice as much, this would be a step upward for Frank Gumm.

All this seemed to balance the less attractive features of the town: that the heat sometimes reached 120 degrees in the summer, and that Lancaster was on the road to nowhere, so that once you drove to the end of Main Street, there was little beyond save sand, lizards, sagebrush and sun.

That afternoon Frank and Marc called on Whit Carter. A onetime vaudevillian held the lease, which was coming up for renewal the following May 18, but he wanted to start moving on, and was ready

22

to give it up at that time. The rent was within reason. If Gumm wanted to take the theatre over then, Carter would make the deal. The Gumms decided they would go back to Grand Rapids, Frank would sell his share in the New Grand to his partner, Fred Bentz, and then return to Los Angeles, where he and Ethel were sure to find jobs to tide them over until the Antelope Valley Theatre was available.

They drove back to Grand Rapids and carried out their plan.

On October 26, 1926, the proceeds of Frank's share of the New Grand once more invested in a diamond ring, Ethel and the girls left by train for Los Angeles, Frank following in the family Buick.

Their departure was an event in Grand Rapids history. In a front-page story, the *Herald-Review* reported that Frank Gumm had sold out his interest in the New Grand and was going west with his family. It was tribute to the affection in which they were held that no less than half a dozen farewell dinners were given them, climaxed by a banquet under the auspices of the Episcopal Guild of Grand Rapids, at which the Gumm Sisters gave their final performance in town.

Once the Gumm family was back in Los Angeles, Marc Rabwin's brother, Harry, became Frank's lawyer and drove down to Lancaster with him to draw up a formal lease for the Antelope Valley Theatre. Once more Frank Gumm's diamond ring served as a down payment.

Which explains why in May of 1927 Frank and Ethel Gumm and the three girls—Baby turning five, Jimmy ten and Janey twelve—found themselves living in a remote little town on the edge of the hot, inhospitable Mojave Desert of California, sixty miles from Los Angeles—hardly a place from which to launch a career—anybody's career.

3

FOR THE NEXT SIX YEARS—from Judy's fifth through her eleventh birthday—the Gumms were to live in Lancaster, trying to make the best of what, it became clear after a while, was a disappointment. The tranquil years ended in Grand Rapids. Judy began to experience what later was to create a fierce resentment in her (although at first she luxuriated in it, as any child would)—the idea that she was only a voice, a musical toy—she described it as "winding me up to sing, and then putting me back in the closet when they were finished with me."

It began quite unwittingly. During their six months in Los Angeles, the Gumms rented a house in West Hollywood. They immediately became friendly with Lester and Peg DeVine, who lived across the street. Peg DeVine owned real estate, which she managed herself; she was brisk, warmhearted, down-to-earth—the sort of woman who climbed up on the roof of her house with hammer and nails and repaired the shingles by herself. She and Ethel each recognized herself in the other, hit it off at once and became lifelong friends. When Ethel had to leave her house during this period, she would ask Peg to take care of Baby for the day. This happened often. Baby was not old enough for kindergarten, Janey and Jimmy had been put in school, and Frank, to support the family, had gotten a job selling advertisements for the Hollywood *Citizen-News*. Ethel, with her customary enterprise, was able to book herself as a pianist at lunches and tea dances. Peg, who was childless, was only too delighted to be in charge of Baby and would take her along with her to her bridge parties. She invariably introduced her with the words, "This is Frances, she'll sing for you." Frances obediently sang, the ladies were impressed, they fussed over her and then turned to their cards, leaving her to amuse herself as best she could. More and more it was being made clear to her that this was her value, her importance, her role: her voice was everything.

The child stole Peg's heart. She drew affection from one, this bright, bubbling little girl with her astonishing memory—so quick to learn—but Peg thought Frank an overly indulgent father, and she made no secret of her disapproval. Several nights a week she and her husband dropped across the street to play cards. When it grew late, Ethel made the girls jelly sandwiches and sent them up to bed. But until then Frances—if Frances was Baby's name, then Frances it would be to Peg—was in everything. When Ethel was busy with Janey and Jimmy, Baby would not be left out of it. All by herself she would reach up to the kitchen drawer, open it and take out a deck of cards and tease her father into playing with her.

Their game was the simplest one possible. Frank placed the deck face down on the floor between him and Baby; each then turned over a card. The higher card took the other.

The first time Peg watched she could hardly contain herself. Whenever Baby turned over a card that was lower than her father's, she simply pretended that it was higher, and took the trick. Frank turned up an eight, Baby a six. She said, knowing it was not so, "Daddy, mine's a ten," and triumphantly took the hand. Frank said nothing. Peg could not remain silent. "Frances, that's not right," she said sharply. "It's a six and an eight takes a six." Frank tried to shush her. "Peg—"

Peg held her tongue, but after the girls were sent upstairs with their jelly sandwiches, she turned to Frank, outraged. "Ohhh, that's terrible, Frank, what you're doing to that child. Building into her the idea that she has to win all the time!" No, Frank said, with utmost seriousness. "I want her to win, and when you play with her, Peg, let her win. She just hates to lose." *What a terrible thing to accustom a child to,* Peg thought. *How will she ever meet disappointment?* On another occasion, on the same subject with Frank, Peg said, "You and Ethel simply can't say no to that child. It's not good for her. What you need in this house is discipline."

Frank looked at her coldly. "Peg, that is a word that belongs in the dictionary. We don't use it around here."

Whatever the case, there was no question that Baby adored her father. Ethel was not one to get down on the floor with her, but Frank, as he had done with Janey and Jimmy when they were small, always found time to play with her. It was true, of course, that Baby was all affection, an emotional little girl who was easily hurt, whose eyes saw everything and who was sensitive in ways surprising in a child so young. One of Peg's first presents to her was a little white apron she had made from one of her husband's old shirts. She was delighted with it and could hardly be persuaded to take it off, even at bedtime, until Peg one afternoon, proud of her own frugality, said, "You know, Frances, I made that out of one of Uncle Lester's old shirts."

Nothing could make Frances wear it again.

Once, at Sunday lunch after church, Jimmy asked her father, "Dad, what are your forefathers?" Baby spoke up. "I know. The four fathers are the father, the son, the Holy Ghost and the real one."

Everyone laughed, whereupon she burst into tears. She could not bear to be laughed at. The moment she cried, everyone, it seemed, fell apart. "Oh, Baby, what is it?" Janey or Jimmy would say, and Frank would take her on his lap and comfort her. When she wanted something, and put her mind on it, she wanted her way, and screamed at the top of her lungs if she did not get it—and no one punished her. Baby was never spanked, never locked in her room, never sent to bed without her supper, although the older girls were. Instead, the entire family tried only to make her stop crying. "Now, come on, honey, you poor little thing, *please* don't cry. . . ." Frank would cuddle her in his arms, press the tip of her nose with his forefinger and croon, "Now, now, my little monkey-face . . . it isn't that bad . . ." until finally she would relent and suddenly be herself, a winning little minx who could wind anyone around her tiny finger. Peg thought, *This adorable child, without knowing that she is, is a little tyrant.*

Yet she had to admit that, with all Frank's indulgence, he still held to definite rules of propriety. Once eleven-year-old Janey uttered an annoyed "Oh, my Lord!" Frank, a pillar of the Sunday school, said severely, "I trust you're talking about Lord Byron, Janey." Ethel, too, was strict in her way. Frank had taken the girls with him one afternoon to a matinee. Ethel asked which theatre they had gone to. It had been the Rex. Baby said, "It's the Sex, Mama." Ethel recoiled. "Baby!" she exclaimed, shocked, and then realized that the child had no idea what the word meant. Sex was never talked about in the Gumm household. Judy was to learn about babies from Jimmy, who gained her knowledge from the naughty girls in the schoolyard. Judy never dared ask her mother about it: she knew Ethel's face would look as though she'd said something dirty.

The moment the Gumms arrived in Lancaster, they did their best to plunge into the life of the town. They tried to ignore the heat, the scorpions scuttling about the walls of the white stucco house they rented across the street from the Antelope Valley Joint Union School, where Baby would begin kindergarten and the older girls go into the higher grades. Frank became choirmaster at the Episcopal church, Ethel its organist. The girls joined the choir, and twelve-year-old Janey began teaching dancing to a youngsters' class. Ethel also put together a four-man band, with herself at the piano, which played for

Saturday night dances at the Elks Hall. Frank was busy running the theatre, attending his Kiwanis, Mason and Rotarian luncheons, hurrying about town each Friday morning to place his showcards, "Coming Next Week," in shop windows, paying off each merchant with a pair of tickets.

A week after he leased the theatre, Frank and Ethel gave a gala show to introduce themselves to the town, and got their first notice in the Antelope Valley *Ledger-Gazette:* ". . . the little daughters completely won the hearts of the audience with their songs and dances." No one could say it was not an auspicious beginning, especially after Frank shortened the name to the Valley Theatre, put in a cooling system and introduced amateur nights, as he had done in Grand Rapids, to take advantage of the wide, deep stage.

But Baby had hardly begun kindergarten when she came down with the illness that had nearly taken her life in Grand Rapids. This time its terrible progress was even swifter. Again the local doctors were baffled, and though they did all they could, nothing helped. The Gumms, in panic, telephoned Dr. Marc in Los Angeles. Baby was terribly sick, she had barely survived last time, this time she was even worse. . . .

Marc acted instantly. He knew about Baby's earlier ordeal. The description of her condition now was frightening. For some reason, it was clear from this child's history, she was extremely vulnerable to infections of this nature. If she was to be saved this time, only the finest medical care could bring it off. The pediatric service in the Los Angeles County Hospital was known throughout the country. Its chief, and Marc's close colleague, was Dr. Oscar Reiss, a brilliant pediatrician, who later founded the world-famous Reiss-Davis Child Study Center in Los Angeles. If Baby could be admitted to his service, they might pull her through. But under California law she was not eligible to enter the County Hospital: they could accept only charity cases. The rules, understandably, were very rigid.

Marc's appeal to the superintendent was so effective that a County ambulance was sent speeding the sixty miles to Lancaster. Marc then asked Dr. Reiss if he would take personal charge. When Baby was brought in a few hours later, with a distraught Frank and Ethel riding in the ambulance, Dr. Reiss was waiting. She was critically ill, devoured by fever, so dehydrated that she had to be given fluids intravenously to support life. Dr. Reiss worked over her with Marc at his side. Again it must be remembered there were no antibiotics. Such virulent infections were often fatal even to those with strong resistance. It was days before she was out of danger, and nearly a month before she could be released from the hospital—and then so pitiably emaciated, her legs so spindly, that Peg DeVine wept when she saw her.

Judy never forgot the tortured, surrealistic days and nights of that illness, nor the devoted care given her by Marc Rabwin and Oscar Reiss. (Years later, when her daughter Liza was born, she insisted that Dr. Rabwin be present at the delivery and that Dr. Reiss become Liza's pediatrician.) During her illness, Frank and Ethel moved in with Peg, so they could be with Baby every day. After she was out of danger, Ethel brought her to recuperate at the DeVines'. Frank commuted between Lancaster and Los Angeles, and Grandma Eva Milne, who was now living with the Gumms, kept house for him and the two older girls.

By September of that year—1927—Baby was well enough to return to Lancaster and enter kindergarten. Then she had to undergo a new ordeal. Many of her nights were made almost unbearable by hay-fever attacks. She was allergic to a local night-blooming plant. She would awaken usually around 10 P.M., her eyes swollen and running, crying, "Mama, I can't breathe." Ethel would dress herself, wrap a blanket about Baby, bed her down in the back seat, and drive off toward Los Angeles and pollen-free ground. She would drive for hours, circling the low mountains near the city while Baby slept. Then toward dawn, a weary Ethel would turn the car back to Lancaster.

There were difficulties for Ethel, too. Lancaster was a strait-laced community, far more constricting, far more rigid, than Grand Rapids, which was essentially an industrial town. Lancaster was a community of storekeepers and farmers. To this rural, extremely conservative population, the fact that the Gumms, however active in community life, were show people and had traveled about the country as entertainers in vaudeville, so closely allied to burlesque, and were training their three daughters for that kind of life, too, was hardly likely to bring them full social acceptance. Though there had been a story in the *Ledger-Gazette* at the end of the year commending the good work the Gumms had done for the town, Ethel still felt a veiled hostility from the older families.

Her unhappiness was compounded by tensions that were beginning to show in her marriage. Before they left Grand Rapids, a neighbor gave Ethel the name of a cousin, a woman who lived on the West Coast. When Ethel got round to looking her up, she was astonished —it was one of those amazing coincidences—to find that she lived in Lancaster, and only a few houses away.

Her name was Laura Gilmore. Like Ethel, she was in her midthirties. Her husband, Will, was an engineer with a degree from the University of Nebraska. They had three children, too. Will, of Indian-Irish stock, a few years younger than Frank, was tall, broad-shouldered, with aquiline features and jet-black hair—a handsome, vigorous man. Laura Gilmore loved nothing more than bridge, as did Ethel. The Gilmore children, two boys and a girl, were about the same ages as the Gumm girls, and soon they were playing together after school and in each other's houses as much as in their own.

The two couples became a foursome. Laura and Will Gilmore, and Ethel and Frank Gumm, went everywhere together. Then Laura suffered a stroke. More and more, while Frank was busy in town and Laura kept to her home, Ethel and Will were thrown together. Out of this developed a closeness that was to cast a pall upon Judy throughout her life. The knowledge came slowly to her, and although some years after Frank's death, and that of Laura, Ethel married Will and thus legalized a relationship that had broken Judy's heart when she became old enough to understand it, she never quite forgave her mother. It was one of the accounts that could never be settled between mother and daughter and that helped to underwrite the great bitterness that separated them later.

But in these first years in Lancaster Judy knew none of this— nothing of the reason for the disappearance of the tranquillity she had known in Grand Rapids. She knew only that now there were violent arguments between her parents. And, in a strange way, these became associated in her mind with remembered automobile rides, late at night, along winding mountain roads, her mother driving, and she lying bundled up and terror-stricken in the back seat. Hay fever played no part in it in her memory. What she did recall was lying in bed trembling, hearing her mother and father quarrel with each other through the night, then falling asleep, then becoming aware that her mother was in her room, waking her, dressing her, saying, "We're leaving Daddy." Judy would begin to cry. "I don't want to leave Daddy." Her mother would say, sadly, "Oh, Baby, you don't love me," making her cry even more, then take her out to the car, put her in the back seat and, "to release her frustration, drive, hour after hour, sixty miles an hour, hell-bent for election, around mountain curves. . . . I would be just terrified. I don't think I ever went to bed at night without wondering if I'd be wakened and taken out into the night."

Wherever truth may lie in this "Rashomon" story, this is how Judy remembered it. Whether fantasy or not, its effect on her was as if it had happened. Her father, from whom she always feared she would be taken, was dearest to her. Busy as he was, he found time for her. They had a nightly ritual. Before she fell asleep, he came up to her room, she crept into his lap, and he would sing softly to her and then listen to her prayers. She loved his quick, rollicking laugh—her own was to be like it, a full-bellied whoop of laughter when something delighted her—and she loved his dry sense of humor. At one point he hired a girl to sit in the glass booth outside the Valley Theatre to sell tickets, while he took them and tended the popcorn machine inside. "Mr. Gumm," the girl asked, "how do I let you know if I make a mistake and short-change someone?" Gumm grinned. "Just rap on your glass with a sponge, my dear." Judy liked that.

In a family album she and her sisters pored over, they always paused at a photograph of their father with a mustache, wearing a derby—an immaculately dressed man, very dapper, very handsome —his diamond ring gleaming on his fourth finger. It had been taken before any of them had been born, and was all part of his exciting early years in vaudeville. The snapshot Frank had shown Marc Rabwin in Grand Rapids was in the album, too, and from Jimmy Judy learned more about the family. Aunt Mary's suitor—the rich merchant in Murfreesboro who paid for her father's education—somehow could never bring himself to propose to her. Aunt Mary began to waste away with a mysterious crippling disease which put her in a wheelchair, and one day she wheeled herself onto a bridge over the river and as the sun sank, pushed herself, wheelchair and all, to her death in the waters below. She had ended it all, Jimmy said, because she loved him too much to be a burden if he did ask her to be his wife.

Jimmy had accidentally overheard her father tell the story to one of his brothers when she was seven.

They never knew she knew, and Baby must never talk to Daddy about it, because he was religious and taking your own life was a sin. So it was a tragic, delicious family secret, the more so because Aunt Mary had had an exceptionally beautiful voice and might have gone far.

Show business and railroading, an odd combination, ran all through the family. Ethel's brother, known as "Jack Milne the singer," was a charming little man who had fourteen children and worked during the day for the North Star Railroad and presided at night as master of ceremonies at the popular Green Parrot nightclub in Duluth. Though Ethel's mother, fun-loving, irrepressible Grandma Eva, came from a devout Dublin family (*her* mother had been reared in a convent), she shocked everyone when she came to America in the 1870s and married Judy's grandfather John Milne, Sr., the railroad engineer, a self-proclaimed atheist who championed Robert G. Ingersoll, the freethinker and defier of God. If Grandma Eva was a handful, she met her match in Grandfather John, a fierce Scotsman. Baby listened wide-eyed to Janey's stories of Grandfather John chasing Grandma Eva down the street, brandishing his cane, and Grandma Eva in turn crowning him with a tin pitcher. It was easy to see where their mother got her temper. And though Grandma Eva always described her family as "pigs-in-the-parlor Irish," and invariably said "ain't" no matter how often Ethel corrected her, the fact was that Grandma Eva's father—Judy's great-grandfather Hugh Fitzpatrick—was first cousin to Ulysses S. Grant, later President of the United States, and looked so much like him, black beard and all, that you might have thought them twins. And like President Grant, he was a man of strong language and strong drink.

Whatever the situation between Ethel and Frank, Ethel now began spending more time on the girls' careers. Some of this concentration stemmed from her unhappiness, some from her dissatisfaction with Lancaster—save for the Gilmores, all her friends were in Los Angeles: the Rabwins, father and sons, the DeVines, even Jan Pravitz from Grand Rapids had moved there—and some from her need to fulfill herself through her daughters.

But no one could have been more single-minded and more devoted. She enrolled the three girls in Lancaster's only dance school, playing piano for the classes in return for a reduction in their tuition. She made them practice singing an hour a day. She taught them piano—but only Janey persevered long enough to play with any competence. She spent sixty dollars to buy three violins by mail order from Sears, Roebuck & Company, in Chicago—if the Gumm Sisters could do a turn on three violins, it would certainly enhance their act, but none of the girls did well.

And finally, because she felt they were talented—particularly Baby, who captivated every audience—and because she had taught them all she knew, and the training at the Lancaster dance school was hardly professional, in late 1927 she enrolled them in Mrs. Meglin's School of the Dance in Los Angeles—Frances, five; Jimmy, ten; and Janey, twelve. She did this though it meant they could take lessons only on weekends since they had to go to school in Lancaster during the week.

Ethel's decision to make this move marked a great step forward in the girls' careers. Mrs. Ethel Meglin was a dominating figure in the world of professional children. Her school was a place of discovery for many child performers, among them, later, Shirley Temple. Children whom she accepted automatically became "Meglin Kiddies"; she booked them to appear at clubs, benefits and other affairs, and, most important, twice each year she produced a widely publicized *Meglin Kiddies Show* at Loew's State in downtown Los Angeles, where they were seen by talent scouts from the studios and radio stations.

Ethel had met Mrs. Meglin when she was looking for a job during the Gumms' first days in Los Angeles. She had taken to her at once —Ethel had a natural affinity with other managerial women—and the two Ethels became close.

Now began a new, strenuous routine. Each Saturday morning at 7 A.M. Ethel roused the girls, washed Baby's shoulder-length hair and put it, still wet, in tight leather curlers, packed the girls with their costumes in the back of the Buick and drove three hours over dirt roads to Los Angeles. At Meglin's she watched them take soft-shoe and tap dancing in the morning; fed them sandwiches she had prepared beforehand at lunchtime; and watched them again in their afternoon lessons—ballet, buck and wing, and acrobatic dancing.

Saturday night was a treat. Ethel would take them to Loew's State, or the Paramount, or Warner's Hollywood—wherever there were performers from whom to learn. They would stay over Saturday night in a small hotel, the four in one room, so the girls could attend a second day of classes at Meglin's on Sunday; and at 4 P.M. Ethel would drive them back to Lancaster in time for a late dinner. Always there was song; Janey would begin "Old McDonald Had a Farm," and "The Old Gray Mare" and whatever new songs they'd heard shortened the long miles to home.

For Judy, it was a confusing period. She enjoyed it, yet she disliked it. It was the beginning of the dichotomy suffered by every child performer, who forever after regrets a lost childhood, yet would not have forgone the magical world of show business, even if that was the price that had to be paid. But the result is always a sense of being cheated out of what every other child has as its birthright. To be in the limelight at Mrs. Meglin's—to know, as was apparent after the first few sessions, that Mrs. Meglin doted on her as a talented pupil —was gratifying, even though in Judy there seemed to be a bottomless pit into which all praise vanished. But she did not like being pulled out of bed (all the girls liked to sleep late, in contrast to Frank and Ethel, who sprang out of bed early and wide awake the moment their eyes opened)—and missing the fun of playing with other children on weekends.

Judy's inseparable companion in Lancaster was Ina Mary Ming, so close to the Gumms that Frank became her godfather. Because she had a merry tomboy face, it was her fate to be nicknamed "Muggsy" Ming; and Muggsy's picture of Babe—as Judy was called in school— was of a thin, rather intense child, gay, mischievous, loving, but quick to tears and subject to stomach-aches—particularly when she had to go off to Los Angeles each Saturday. Later, when Janey and Jimmy became more interested in going to Saturday night dances in Lancaster than to Meglin's in Los Angeles, Ethel took only Baby; and Baby often refused to go unless Muggsy came along. At seven, eight, nine, Judy was already being torn by her opposing needs. Ethel took her to auditions for children's parts at the movie studios quite often: she tried out for a role in *Daddy Long Legs,* with Slim Summerville, at Universal Pictures, but lost to another child—and she complained to Muggsy, "Mama's always taking me before strange people and I have to sing for them—I sing, and nobody smiles, nobody does anything, nobody says anything. It's awful!" Yet by the accounts of others, Judy enjoyed the trips to Meglin's—she had far more friends there, and more to her liking, than in Lancaster.

Both portraits of Judy are probably true. From her earliest days the reaction of her audience was essential: it was intolerable for her to appear before impersonal, undemonstrative film executives when she was accustomed to rapturous acceptance from others. To win *had* been built into her; to lose was unbearable.

Muggsy disliked Ethel. She found Frank gentle and generous— Judy could always manage to take her friends into the Valley Theatre free; Aunt Norma, who had joined the family, jolly and affectionate; Grandma Eva always waiting, when they came from school, with hot cocoa and cinnamon toast; but she feared Ethel. Though Mrs. Gumm was hospitable, and there were always mouth-watering tidbits on the table, she was brusque, businesslike—a "get-out-of-my-way" woman. You did what she told you, you ate up your food if she told you— everything had to go her way.

Always there would be this conflicting portrait of Ethel, painted by Judy and Judy's friends as an inexorable stage mother, by Ethel's friends as a misunderstood, determined woman who only wanted the best for her children.

But the Meglin connection was important. It led Ethel to build up the first professional appearance of the Gumm Sisters—the first act for which they were actually paid: ten dollars each—for a week.

4

EARLY ONE SATURDAY AFTERNOON in Los Angeles, during Christmas week, 1928, eleven-year-old Ann Rutherford, a child radio star who would become better known as Polly Benedict, Mickey Rooney's sweetheart in the Andy Hardy films, went with her older sister to the first matinee at Loew's State Theatre. The girls watched the film, the name of which they would not remember, and then the opening act of vaudeville, equally easy to forget.

Then the card on the side of the stage was flipped to announce: "The Gumm Sisters." Ann Rutherford there had her first glimpse of

Judy Garland, as Baby Gumm. Neither she nor her sister would ever forget it.

In the pit a plump little brown-haired woman in glasses played with the speed and metronomic beat of a player piano. But on the stage . . .

First the two older girls, tall and gawky, one thirteen, the other eleven, pranced out in their frilly costumes, and bringing up the rear, with an inimitable strut as if to say, "I'm just as big as any of you," was a sturdy little six-year-old, with a funny Dutch bob, a tilted snub nose in a radiant little face with huge black eyes—and when, after all three tap-danced with arms linked, Baby Gumm stepped forward and sang "I'll Get By," the hackles rose on the back of Ann's neck. The audience sat transfixed, and when Baby Gumm finished, there was such a roar of applause and demands for encores that, though Ann was little more than a child herself, Baby Gumm's face was tattooed forever in her memory.

Ann was not alone. It was the beginning of a phenomenon—a child who, once seen and heard, was never forgotten. Word of mouth was then just starting to spread, word of this enchanting youngster billed as "Little Miss Leather Lungs," who poured forth such a torrent of sound, without a microphone, in a voice so round, so rich, filling the theatre, that Louella Parsons wondered in her column if Baby Gumm might not really be a midget. No child could have such a voice—and such power.

The difficulty was that at first Baby Gumm wasn't even named. The reporter for the Los Angeles *Record*, writing about the *Meglin Kiddies Show* at Loew's State on December 22, 1927, was overwhelmed. Out of the scores of children who appeared during the afternoon's performance, one child stood out. He had seen her somewhere before and had to write with annoyance, "Once again we can complain only of their unprogrammed appearance. We have no names with which to lay tribute to. One small miss shook these well-known rafters with her songs à la Sophie Tucker."

It was, of course, Baby Gumm, her name lost in the long list of Kiddies.

Mrs. Meglin, impressed by the sisters, and especially by Baby Gumm, though they had attended only a few classes and had paid hardly enough tuition to entitle them to appear in the semiannual show, had allowed them to perform. Janey and Jimmy sang in the chorus, but Baby Gumm was presented as a single—a solo performance. She appeared as Cupid, a red sash diagonally across her small costume as a quiver for her bows, her hair in curls down to her shoulders, a little bra across her flat chest, singing "Dinah."

There were more than two hundred children in the show. Judy was the only child Mrs. Meglin thought strong enough—at the age of five —to handle the stage alone. It was extraordinary recognition—and none of it would have come about had Ethel not had her wits about her. Under California labor laws, no child under six could appear onstage. Ethel learned that a representative of the Gerry Society, which rigidly enforced these rules, would attend the rehearsal. When it came time for Judy to rehearse, Ethel sent Jimmy onstage. Jimmy was old enough to appear, and Ethel had her birth certificate to prove it. The Gerry Society representative left, none the wiser.

The Gumm Sisters' appearance in the Christmas show of 1928 climaxed the hardest kind of work by Ethel and the girls. By trial and error, Ethel had developed a far more sophisticated act than the Duncan Sisters imitation in Grand Rapids. The two older girls had always sung together: Ethel had never been able to persuade them to sing alone. But Baby loved it. At the beginning their act consisted of Janey and Jimmy harmonizing together, then Baby appearing alone, to do her acrobatic dances and sing her solos—torch songs made popular by Sophie Tucker and Helen Morgan.

Almost by accident, the Gumm Sisters became a trio. One Saturday morning in 1930 Gus Edwards, Hollywood's leading child impresario, conducted auditions at the Paramount Studios in Los Angeles for the next edition of his famed *Gus Edwards Review*. Ethel, overlooking no chances, drove the girls to Los Angeles. The Gumm Sisters had their opportunity; Edwards, impressed, could not use them, but he let them off gently. "You're all very musical," he said, "you've all got good ears. Ever think of doing a trio?" He turned to Ethel. "There are no children's trios."

Ethel pondered his advice as they drove back to Lancaster late that day. So the trip to Los Angeles would not be a total loss, she had taken the girls to the matinee at Loew's State, which featured the Brox Sisters, like the Boswell Sisters a top adult singing trio. In the rear of the car as they drove back, Jimmy said, "Let's try 'What Do I Care?' " —a favorite Brox Sisters number, which they had just heard. Ethel, behind the wheel, said over her shoulder after they finished, "You know, you're pretty good. That's not a bad idea. We'll do it."

Thus their act was improved and broadened. The two girls sang duets, as before; then with Baby, they appeared as a trio; then Baby did her own numbers. She had a larger role.

A Paramount booking for one week was their first engagement as a trio. They were billed, as usual, to follow the opening acrobats—the least desirable spot. After the first show the manager promoted them to next to last on the bill—the most desirable position. At the end of the first week, they were held over two more, and then an additional fortnight.

Ethel, inspired, had choreographed a genuinely successful act. Now the curtain rose to show her seated at the piano, dressed in a low-cut, sleeveless white net dress with double ruffles on shoulders and sides decorated with tiny pink rosebuds. Then the three Gumm Sisters danced out—all wide smiles, and in dresses almost identical with their mother's—dresses which had taken Ethel hours to sew and press.

In their first number the three girls sang together, Janey singing alto, Jimmy melody, and Baby tenor. At the finish they danced off, Baby the last of the three, with a back kick and a flounce of her little rear end—a kind of "brrrupt!"—to sign them off.

Janey and Jimmy reappeared, to take formal positions by the piano and sing their first duet, "I Never Had a Man," with appropriate gestures in which they had been drilled endlessly by Ethel. During the applause they retired and Baby appeared. Now she was in the Egyptian harem outfit which Ethel had made for her acrobatic dances—dances in which she had been coached by Ethel Meglin herself, who had once been an acrobatic dancer. She wore filmy dark-blue pantaloons with little white pants underneath, spangles and bracelets on her arms and ankles, an embroidered white band across her chest, which represented a bra, and a filmy veil. For the next few minutes she did her cartwheels and back bends and splits and flips, finishing to great applause. Meanwhile Janey and Jimmy had changed into Irish costumes (also made by Ethel) to sing "Did You Ever Go into an Irishman's Shanty?" and a ballad or two; then they were off and Baby Gumm appeared in her original costume to sing her solo, "I Wanna Be Loved by You," which brought down the house.

They were on their way now, and sometimes their adventures were hilarious. Taskmaster though Ethel might be, she had a quick sense of humor, she saw the drolleries about her, and often mother and daughters were like four schoolgirls on a lark, giggling over what took place.

One weekend Ethel booked them into a little theatre outside Los Angeles: a matinee Saturday, then a performance between the two film features that night, then the same thing Sunday. For this the Gumm Sisters, including Ethel as accompanist and manager, would receive $25. The theatre had minimal facilities, no locks on the doors, not even makeup lights; the stage was too small even to accommodate a piano. Ethel would have to play in the pit. Nonetheless, they went ahead: the money might enable them to break even for food and hotel.

The Gumm Sisters trooped out as usual. There was no spotlight, only the harsh white footlights. Standing in the order of their height, arms linked together—first Baby, then Jimmy, then Janey—they launched into their first number, a fast tune, "Stay on the Right Side, Sister," which was given double excitement by Baby and Janey snapping their fingers in time as they sang.

A moment later they became aware that the most awful odor of garlic was pouring back at them. In the front row were a dozen teen-agers, squirming with delight. They had squashed cloves of garlic in the tray of the footlights, and as the bulbs grew hot, the garlic came into its own.

Baby, always sensitive, began to gag, but she had to giggle, as did the other girls. The stage was shallow; there was no retreat. Ethel looked up from the pit, furious: she knew nothing because the air currents were from the rear of the house to the front. She continued to play briskly, but her eyes flashed fire, and the girls could read her lips: "You stop that! You don't do that! What's the matter with you?" Jimmy, one arm about each sister, could do nothing. Janey, though she giggled, was also near tears—of the sisters, only Janey really took vaudeville seriously—and it was Baby who tried to snap her fingers in the direction of the footlights to signal their distress. Somehow they managed to finish the number.

Ethel, outraged as she was, had to go into the next song. This was a lovely ballad, "Beside an Open Fireplace." Usually the girls sat demurely on a bench, looking soulfully at the audience, but this theatre had been unable to provide even a bench, so after gulping what fresh air they could backstage, they hurried out and standing arms linked together again, facing front, began their number.

Halfway through, something came hurtling out of the audience and struck Janey in the stomach and bounced to the floor. There it lay, open before them—the debris of a half-eaten salami sandwich. This was too much. Baby gave one of her characteristic whoops of laughter, Jimmy burst into laughter, too, and even Janey, unable to maintain her dignity, broke up. As if at a signal, they sidestepped their way into the safety of the wings, arms still linked.

Ethel came backstage. "Well!" She knew it all now. "Let's go out for a bite," she said. They went in their car to find the nearest restaurant before returning for the evening show. Suddenly Ethel turned the car around. "We're going home," she announced. "We don't need their twenty-five dollars. That's the most awful place I've ever seen. You don't want to go back there, do you?"

No, no, they agreed. And they drove back to Lancaster, mother and daughters feeling closer than ever.

It would not be fair to say that Judy was unhappy in Lancaster, although their stay there, without their knowing it, was drawing to a close. Yet she was always to speak coldly about the town and its people. One of her favorite stories was of a night before Halloween, when a group of classmates came begging to her house to borrow Gumm Sisters costumes for a big party the next night. The party was held—"but we weren't invited," she said. "We were those awful show people and not good enough." The evidence is questionable. The Gumm Sisters were celebrities in Lancaster, their names printed often enough in the *Ledger-Gazette*, and when they found time to appear at local events, they were regarded with something like awe by other children.

Judy had wanted mightily to belong to a select little club, the Jolly Cavern Kids, who met in a deep cave where they sat amid flickering candlelight to sing songs and exchange ghost stories. Finally she was initiated with Muggsy Ming and Ruth Gilmore—Will and Laura's daughter, who was a few grades ahead—and Ed "Junior" Carter, who lived next door and played groom to Judy's bride when the Fifth Grade Mothers staged a musical climaxed by a mock wedding. Judy always complained that her classmates were told not to play with her, but Ruth, and Junior, and Muggsy Ming and such other friends as Lauranna Blankenship and Vera and Ardis Shrimp (Judy would giggle, "Did you ever hear such names?") were only too happy to be with her, famous or notorious. She was warm, instantly sympathetic and already something of a comedienne; as Ruth Gilmore said, Babe could make the most ordinary experience sound hilarious.

In school she was not a good student, but she grasped things swiftly, and with her almost photographic memory, the work came easily. Most of the time she disdained homework. She knew her power to charm adults. Janey, the only honor student among the three sisters, would say, "You can't skip your homework, Babe. What'll you tell your teacher?" "Oh, I'll talk my way out," she would say. Ethel's voice would come from the kitchen: "Now, Baby, you just sit down and do it!" Grumblingly she sat down, but ten minutes later she was into something else, or out romping with Waffles, her wire-haired terrier, and no one pressed her further.

She was surprisingly athletic. She spent hours at the high school pool with her sisters. It was the most sensible place to be when the thermometer soared over 100. In the dusk she played in front of their house—Run Sheep Run and Kick the Can; in the gathering darkness she limbered up on the lawn, turning her cartwheels and somersaults. At night, when the air was pollen-free, she and her sisters sometimes might not be in bed until midnight, lying out on the grass, the cool of the desert sweeping in on them, the stars low and enormous in the sky.

Often there were unexpected guests. Peg and Les DeVine drove down frequently from Los Angeles for a night of cards, and tart, practical advice from Peg, who felt like an older sister to Ethel. (The first time the DeVines stayed over, Peg discovered to her horror that Ethel took Frances' breakfast up to her in bed every morning.) Or Marc Rabwin, his roadster packed to the rumble seat with fellow interns and nurses, and bearing a dozen steaks, showed up for an impromptu cookout at the Gumms', and to plead for Ethel's marvelous "Damn-it-to-hell!" cakes—cupcakes filled with chocolate and whipped cream, so called by Frank because Ethel, frustrated once when the cream refused to whip, exploded, "Damn it to hell!" And here, as it had been in Grand Rapids when Marc was a student, he and Frank sat back in the living room after dinner and Ethel sat at the piano and there were the two girls—and Baby. She was Marc's pride, and he watched her growing up with an interest second only to her parents'. He could not get over her. What a delightful, gifted child she had turned out to be!

Partying or not, Judy lived a full, busy life in Lancaster. She played in Gilbert and Sullivan operettas at school. (Ethel was always on the parents' committee that sponsored these performances.) She sang in the church choir, she went biking and roller-skating, and she began having crushes, sudden and intense, on the older boys. From the first, boys, to Judy—because she had no brothers—were special and she was always able to invest them with qualities far beyond what others might see in them.

Her first real crush, however, was not on anyone in Lancaster; it was a little later that she fell madly in love with Robert Donat, the British actor. *The Count of Monte Cristo* was being shown in a theatre in which the Gumm Sisters appeared, and Judy would stand in the wings, night after night, watching it, and though everyone seen from that angle was grotesquely elongated, including Donat, she lost her heart to him. She cut out every picture of him she could find in the fan magazines and pasted them on the walls of her room. Finally she could not rest until she wrote him her first fan letter. In time she received an autographed photograph—"To Frances Gumm, my admirer, With sincere best wishes—Robert Donat"— with a note from his secretary. She compared the signature on the photograph with that on the note, and burst into tears. It was the same handwriting. He hadn't even autographed it himself. Yet she slept with his picture under her pillow.

The problem of boys was to be not only Judy's, but her sisters', too, because of Ethel's distrust of boys. There was a misunderstood incident when Janey, thirteen, had a crush on a boy named Mark Settle, and Jimmy, eleven, was ecstatic about his best friend, Brandon Castle. One Saturday night, while Ethel and Frank were at the theatre, the two boys came over to the house, unknown to the Gumms. Frank drove home at 9 P.M. to pick up six-year-old Baby, who was to do a solo at the Valley Theatre. The two older girls, in panic, hid the boys in their bedroom.

In the car on the way back to the theatre, Baby asked, "Daddy, do you like boys?" Frank looked at her, wonderingly. "Why, yes, Baby," he said. "Well," she asked, "why did Janey and Jimmy hide Mark and Brandon in the bedroom when you came home?"

The two girls did not hear the end of it. When Janey was to reach seventeen and start dating, Ethel would insist that she take fifteen-year-old Jimmy along, as chaperone. It was to make for tears and tantrums, and a Judy who cried with her sisters in sympathy. But Ethel was firm. "I hate to see young girls boy-crazy," she said.

Ethel's surveillance was hard to accept from the beginning, because of the whispers which did not escape the town's teen-agers in a place as small as Lancaster. Ethel Gumm and Will Gilmore—well, yes, the Gumms and the Gilmores, great friends . . . Yes, Laura is taking to a wheelchair, and Ethel is such a marvelous companion. . . .

Judy, always quick, always aware, did not comprehend it fully. In later years she spoke gingerly about it. Her mother, she told a friend, was "attracted" to Gilmore. "I don't know what kind of a relationship they had," she said, as though she did not want to admit the truth to herself. "I know it was very strange—it went on for twelve years.

"For years there was no marriage," Judy said, speaking of her parents. She recalled a long separation, during this period, when she and her mother lived in the Gates Hotel in Los Angeles, while her father remained in Lancaster with her sisters. "I don't know why my parents decided to stay together—perhaps it was for the sake of the children," Judy said.

The move back to Los Angeles was inevitable—and it came in 1933. It was due partly to the depression, ushered in by the great stock-market crash of 1929, and partly to the fact that Frank Gumm was pouring money he could not afford into the Gumm Sisters' career.

They hadn't quite expected it to turn out that way.

From 1927 to 1932 the Gumm Sisters, shepherded by Ethel, tiny and indomitable, darting about from agent to theatre manager, had appeared everywhere in the summers and on winter weekends: in Los Angeles, in Pasadena, in Long Beach, in towns up and down the Coast, in San Francisco, even as far north as Seattle. One summer, rather than make the tiring trip each weekend to Los Angeles, Ethel rented an apartment there for herself and the three girls. They kept busy. They appeared on radio programs, at Bank Nights, in the annual Meglin productions and in a few film shorts in color. Judy auditioned for the title role in one called *Cinderella*, but was turned down as "too plain." But the sisters appeared in *The Land of Let's Believe*, in which they were maidens on the moon in fantastic bubble costumes; in *The Old Lady in the Shoe;* and, before Judy was signed by MGM, in *La Fiesta de Santa Barbara*, in which they sang as Spanish dancing girls in shawls and black brimmed hats. In the main, a happy time for Judy. Nearly always she was happy onstage. Once or twice a sudden, inexplicable twinge of apprehension had swept through her a moment before she went onstage, but always the applause when she appeared had restored her.

Yet for all their work, the money the Gumm Sisters earned rarely covered their expenses—food, travel, hotel, costumes, music and dance arrangements, and commissions for agents. Frank had to pay the difference each time, and the cost represented a major drain on the profits from the Valley Theatre, just beginning to feel the effects of the crash.

Frank began to fall behind in his rent to Whit Carter. The girls had no idea he was pressed. Neither Frank nor Ethel ever talked about money in front of them; and on the road Ethel, who handled every penny, gave them pocket money on request. "Take what you want from my purse, Baby," she would say. Ethel, who had been forced to be on her own from the age of ten because of lack of money, who had missed an education for the same reason, wanted her girls never to be driven by need of it, as she had been. Neither Judy nor her sisters were ever told, "We can't afford it." Some other reason was given. The result was that the girls rarely gave a second thought to the need to economize, as Peg DeVine repeatedly and warningly pointed out to Ethel. "That's bad training," she would say sternly. "When those girls grow up, they'll let money slip right through their fingers." Ethel pooh-poohed that.

Only once was Judy even vaguely aware of a money problem. Her parents were talking worriedly in front of the theatre. She walked up and asked, "Daddy, can I have a nickel?" Frank looked down at her, the faintest lines of annoyance in his face. Then he pulled half a dollar from his pocket and gave it to her. "Take the whole thing," he said. Judy protested, "I only wanted a nickel," but her father said curtly, "Take the whole thing. Just go." It was as though her asking for money was the last straw—it no longer mattered whether it was five or fifty cents.

In the spring of 1931 Ethel tried to ease the situation. She got a job as teacher of piano and "personality singing" at the Kusell Dramatic Dance Studio in Los Angeles, the largest on the West Coast. Maurice L. Kusell, the owner, who had been dance director on several musical films, also hired Ethel to conduct the orchestra for his mammoth *Stars of Tomorrow* revue at the Wilshire Ebell Theatre that July. The Gumm Sisters appeared, but it was Baby Gumm whom he singled out as the only solo performer—this in a three-hour production involving more than five hundred children. Yet even here Ethel accepted less salary in return for Kusell's promise to help choreograph the girls' act.

By late 1932 Frank Gumm was so far behind in his rent that Whit Carter reluctantly notified him that unless he could speed up his payments, he would have to assign his lease to another operator the next summer. Frank found this impossible. The Gumms resigned themselves to giving up the Valley Theatre.

Frank consulted Marc and Harry Rabwin. In March 1933—a low point not only in the Gumm fortunes but in the country's, for the newly inaugurated President Franklin D. Roosevelt had just declared a four-day bank holiday, to prevent a run by panicky depositors—the three men drove about the outskirts of Los Angeles and finally found a smaller, less expensive movie house in Lomita, a suburb. Frank arranged to take it over when he turned back his lease in Lancaster. Interestingly enough, neither Judy nor her sisters ever knew that their move from Lancaster to Los Angeles was forced by their father's financial troubles.

Ethel could not wait to get to Los Angeles. In June 1933, a few days after Judy's eleventh birthday party, Ethel rented the furnished upstairs of a duplex in Los Angeles and moved there with Judy, Jimmy and Grandma Eva. Aunt Norma was on the road and now lived in northern California. Because Janey was in her last year of high school and begged to graduate with her class, Frank remained in Lancaster with her until the end of the school year. Once a week the family was reunited when Frank and Janey drove up to spend the night.

Judy's introduction to Los Angeles was far happier than to Lancaster. She enrolled in the Lawlor School for Professional Children, known as Mom Lawlor's. For the first time she went to school with her peers, children in vaudeville, radio and films whose lives would cross hers through the years.

She came home glowing the first day. "Well," she said, "I met

Mickey Rooney. He's just the funniest. . . . He clowns around every second!" She had been assigned her desk when suddenly a freckle-faced boy burst late into the room, stuck a note under the teacher's nose, and took the desk next to hers, where he began fidgeting, pulled a comb out of his pocket and began combing his tangled hair. When he got it caught, Judy helped him release it. He reached over and shook her hand. "Thanks," he said. "My name's Mickey." "You're welcome. My name's Frances." They got along famously. A few weeks later he left, telling her he had been signed by Metro. But there were other classmates: Donald O'Connor; Gloria DeHaven; Bonita Granville; Frankie Darro; Marjorie Belcher, who was to become Mrs. Gower Champion; Dawn O'Day, who was to become Anne Shirley; Leonard Sues, trumpet player—actors, singers, dancers, musicians, all were Lawlor students.

Though it was a place for show-business children—it held classes only until noon, so students could rehearse or work professionally in the afternoon, and even obtained the all-important labor permits—the Gumm Sisters there, as in Lancaster, were celebrities, for it was a small school, its graduation class no larger than ten children. When the Gumm Sisters appeared at the Paramount or Loew's State or Warner's Hollywood, Judy's entire class turned out en masse to applaud.

It meant a new excitement for her. Her very first month in Los Angeles had brought a special triumph. One of the Gumms' first dinner guests in their new house was Kusell, who took the occasion to ask a favor. The B'nai B'rith, the largest Jewish fraternal order in the country, was sponsoring an enormous benefit affair at the Ambassador Hotel. Kusell was on the entertainment committee. He had a brilliant idea. He wanted Judy to appear, to sing only one number, and this nothing like anything she'd ever done before. It would be "Eli, Eli," that moving, heartbreaking song of Jewish lamentation, which expressed the very soul of his people. If Ethel agreed, Cantor David Blanko, a revered artist in the field, would teach her how to sing it. He knew, Kusell said, that she could belt out songs, drive like a pile-driver, like a young Sophie Tucker; but she had a way with a ballad, too, and if she sang "Eli, Eli" . . . Ethel took to it at once. "Oh, my," she exclaimed. "A little Irish girl singing that song—it will bring down the house." She was right.

A few days later Cantor Blanko, a heavy-set, impressive figure, appeared at the Gumm house, and with Ethel at the piano, he taught Judy how to sing "Eli, Eli." Her voice, so rich and pure, with such a moving vibrato, already had a tear in it; after his instruction the sob in her voice was no less than his. Judy sang. The audience was shattered. They could hardly endure it; their applause and weeping made for an evening of such emotion as she had never known before.

It was a good omen. How was she to know that, in time, "Eli, Eli" would serve as a bridge of tears to Louis B. Mayer and the incredible world of MGM?

5

SOMEWHERE IN THE DISTANCE, like the Emerald City in the Land of Oz, Metro-Goldwyn-Mayer indeed waited; but Ethel, Judy's hand clutched securely in hers, had to knock on its portals and those of many other studios a considerable time before they opened. On September 27, 1935, Judy signed a seven-year contract with MGM. Before that happened, however, she was to have a number of adventures, among them her transformation from Baby Gumm to Judy Garland.

That came about as a direct result of Ethel's insistence that the Gumm Sisters should drive from Los Angeles to Chicago to appear at the World's Fair—"The Century of Progress"—in the summer of 1934. Frank was violently opposed to the idea.

Judy came home shortly after noon from school one day to find her parents shouting at each other. It was June of 1934, the family were together again in Los Angeles, and now this loud argument. "What?" her father was demanding. "A woman and three girls driving more than halfway across the country by themselves? You're out of your head, Ethel!"

Ethel thought it a marvelous opportunity. It would be only for two months, the girls would be back in time for school in the fall. She had already gotten a top booking at the Fair—$300 a week at the Old Mexico Restaurant—as well as a two-week nightclub date in Denver, halfway there, which would help pay expenses.

"A nightclub?" Frank cried. "The Gumm Sisters singing before a bunch of drunks?" Yes, a nightclub, Ethel said. Since there were no theatres at the Fair, only clubs and cafés, the girls needed the experience. Frank looked at her. What about Baby? The child was only twelve. No one under sixteen could sing in a nightclub. Suppose the Gerry Society came down to check on Baby?

Ethel had an answer for that, too. She was booked simply as Baby Gumm. No first name. If questioned, she would say she was Virginia Gumm, and produce Jimmy's birth certificate, showing that she'd turned sixteen last July 4. Baby had developed physically; no one was likely to know any better. And hadn't almost the same subterfuge worked when they thought they might have to keep Baby off the Meglin show because she was only five?

In the end, Ethel, as always, won. Judy was thrilled. The World's Fair, Chicago, show kids coming from all over the country—that was exciting. "Hot diggety dog, we're going!" Ethel explained they'd have to do it on their own. Since Daddy was so set against it, they'd take no money from him. He insisted on giving her a book of traveler's checks, but she'd saved up a little money, and they'd all live on bread and water before they'd touch a penny of his money. Agreed?

The girls, caught up in the spirit of it, agreed.

With Ethel at the wheel, Judy at her side and Jimmy and Janey in the back with their boxes of costumes, they set off. They had their first shock in Denver. Ethel, without knowing it, had booked them into a gambling club, and Denver police had just clamped down on gambling. There were no customers. But Stevens, the owner, told Ethel he was not closing up his place. The city administration was to change any moment—he was waiting it out. He was keeping his band, and their engagement was still on, if they didn't mind an audience made up of only Stevens and a table of friends.

For the next two weeks the Gumm Sisters sang and danced to a table of ten persons each night—one more adventure for Judy to regale her friends with in later years.

Once they arrived in Chicago, they took a two-bedroom suite at the St. Lawrence, a first-class hotel. They were, after all, earning $300 a week. The Boswell Sisters, whom they idolized, were staying there as well. The fact that the Old Mexico was not on the Fair grounds proper, but on the boardwalk of the adjacent island, that Judy and her sisters had to practice in the hotel basement because guests complained, and that Ethel had to spend hours each afternoon pressing their costumes in the sitting room, did not dampen their spirits.

They were all in a euphoric mood, those first days of July 1934. The Fair was an enormous playground, a child's extravaganza, a toyland come alive. Judy was never happier than when, like the girl next door she always wanted to be yet never could be, she rode the roller coaster, gorged herself on popcorn and pancakes and ice cream, and marched about chewing sticky mouthfuls of cotton candy.

Their performances were the talk of the Old Mexico. Ethel had worked out a dramatic framework for a number which became a stunning climax to their act. When it was time for Judy's solo, the curtain rose on a darkened stage, showing a figure seated on a piano, legs crossed, Helen Morgan fashion. She was as indistinct as a shadow, swathed all in black, a black shawl drawn tightly over her head, and down the sides of her face to her chin. The stage was black, she could just be made out. The pianist was Ethel. When the girl began to sing, her face alone became visible, spotlighted by a single light. A marvelously robust, mature voice soared over the audience, and when she finished singing "My Man," the applause rocked the house. Then the lights went on, and there was not a grown woman, but a child— twelve-year-old Frances Gumm, her hair in long black thick curls to her shoulders, and little pink bows on her dress and her shoes. The house rocked again. Incredible! How could a child sing like that?

The trumpet player in the band at the Old Mexico was a tall young man in his twenties with wavy hair named Jack Cathcart, who played half a dozen instruments with equal skill. After the first show he sought out Judy. He could hardly find words to express his admiration. "That's the most phenomenal thing I've ever heard," he said. "You know, you just put your arms around that audience." She bloomed under his praise.

She introduced him to her mother and sisters. He was warm, likable, with a contagious laugh, and after the show he joined them for a bite. Before the evening was over, he and eighteen-year-old Janey were talking only to each other. The next day he called on Janey to take her swimming in Lake Michigan. That became a daily occurrence thereafter.

Before the end of the first week Ethel drew $35 in advance. They were spending money faster than they had expected, and the Old

Mexico management was tardy with its salary checks. There were preproduction bills to pay, they explained, but everything would be straightened out before the month was over. At the end of the third week the blow fell. The Old Mexico had to close. Someone had absconded with the money.

Ethel hurried in to see the manager the next morning. She found him sitting gloomily at the bar with two equally gloomy friends. "Look here," said Ethel hotly—she suspected all nightclub owners—"we have to have our money! We came out on your promise that we'd have this engagement through the Fair."

The owner looked at her sourly. There was nothing he could do. He knew it would be difficult for them to get a new booking, but he had his own troubles to think about.

That afternoon they moved out of the St. Lawrence into a small furnished apartment and Ethel called on the William Morris Agency, the largest theatrical agency in the country. She came back greatly cheered up, to report that tryouts were held each Friday at the Belmont Theatre in downtown Chicago. The agency screened new acts there. If the Gumm Sisters went on Friday night—no pay, of course—a Morris man would be there to catch their act.

On Friday the girls got their costumes together, Ethel spent the day washing and ironing, everyone had her hair done, and they appeared at the Belmont—and stopped the show. The audience actually came to its feet, screaming and applauding. The applause would not cease, they came out bowing repeatedly because they had no more numbers, the next act could not start—the management finally had to turn out the lights to stop the applause so the show could go on. Ethel could not wait to get to the Morris office the next morning. She returned utterly crushed. Not a soul from the Morris Agency had shown up at the Belmont. They had done the sort of thing one reads about—*actually stopped the show*—and no one with the magic power to book them had seen it!

They felt ridiculous, they felt humiliated. They had started out so confidently, and with such high hopes in spite of Frank's disapproval. Now their job was gone, they had been bilked out of their money, they had done a sensational audition which no one had seen, they were down to their last few dollars—

"Mama, I'm hungry." It was Judy.

"All right, Baby. Go up and see what we have for breakfast," Ethel said. Judy vanished into the tiny kitchenette to look into the refrigerator, and came back to announce wryly, "There's an egg—and half a loaf of moldy bread."

"That does it," said Ethel. She tossed her head. "I said bread and water, but not moldy bread." They drove off to Henrici's, an expensive restaurant-bakery, where they ordered a huge breakfast topped off with bowls of blueberries and thick cream. Ethel cashed the first of Frank's traveler's checks.

For the next five days she made the rounds of clubs. There were no engagements. Everywhere entertainment had been booked weeks before. The traveler's checks dwindled. Ethel had calculated it carefully. They could last three more days if they economized by sleeping in the car on the drive back to Los Angeles. (It would not be the first time.) But if nothing turned up in the next seventy-two hours, they'd be forced to give up and go back, defeated, the summer a total loss.

Just before noon the next day—Saturday—Janey was called to the telephone. Judy, who watched such matters enviously, said, "He's calling earlier today." It was Jack Cathcart, but more excited than Janey had ever heard him. "Kid, go to the Oriental Theatre, all of you, as fast as you can. They canceled an act five minutes ago—they'll need a replacement. You might get fired, but at least you can do one show!"

Mother and daughters were at the Oriental within the hour. The theatre, in downtown Chicago, featured a special stage production with George Jessel, as master of ceremonies, pulling together ten acts of vaudeville. A singing group had been so dreadful the manager fired them after the first show. Bill Paley, the drummer in the Oriental pit, was Jack's friend, and had telephoned Jack immediately after the firing.

The girls arrived just in time to go on. As usual, they were second on the bill. Jessel had only a moment to meet them before he went out on stage to introduce them. "Ladies and gentlemen, it is my pleasure to present a new act—the Gumm Sisters!"

The audience tittered, then laughed. Perhaps it was Jessel's delivery, but they laughed. In the wings the girls reddened. They went out, however, and when Baby, sitting on the piano, sang "My Man," the effect was even more dramatic than it had been at the Belmont.

The manager promoted them on the spot—as so often before—from second to second to last.

Gratifyingly enough, Jessel was one of those most impressed. After their second show, he took Ethel aside. How old was Baby Gumm? Twelve? My God, he said fervently. He had never heard such a mature voice from a child. She sang that torch song like a woman with a broken heart. Then: "Mrs. Gumm, I can't go out and keep introducing your girls as the Gumm Sisters. That's ludicrous. It gets a laugh, and you're not a comedy act. You've got to change your name."

Ethel knew he was right. They had suffered through the Glum Sisters, the Crum Sisters, the Dumb Sisters, the Rum Sisters. More than one theatre manager had suggested changing their name. But no one of Jessel's stature had spoken out so strongly. All right, said Ethel. Change it to what?

Jessel was on his way to introduce the next act. "I'll think of something," he said over his shoulder.

A moment before it came time for them to go on again, he was at their side, smiling. "I've got your new name."

The girls cried, excitedly, "What is it? What is it?"

He said, "You'll see," and walked out on stage. He went into a brief patter, and then said, "Now I'd like to introduce—the Garland Sisters!"

The girls almost did not go out. It took a moment before they realized he meant them. Jessel had to peer into the wings and beckon to them, muttering "Come on" under his breath. When their act was over, they crowded about him. How had Mr. Jessel come up with Garland? It sounded good. He explained he had been on the phone between shows with Robert Garland, the theatre critic of the New York *World-Telegram*, an old friend. He'd hung up just before going on stage and that was the last thing on his mind.

Now they were the Garland Sisters—Janey, Jimmy and Frances Garland. Ethel automatically became Mrs. Ethel Garland. "Who's your agent?" Jessel asked. They had none. "Oh, you must have one," he said, and telephoned his agent—ironically enough, the Morris office—and next morning, a taciturn young man with a cigar, named Sam Bramson, appeared backstage with a contract for them. It made the William Morris Agency the representative of the Garland Sisters in a deal with the Oriental Theatre, paying them $350 a week—five shows a day—the Morris agency to receive its customary 10 percent commission for the duration of their run.

They finished their stay in Chicago in a blaze of glory, the more pleasurable for Judy because of Donald O'Connor, a schoolmate at Lawlor's, who was appearing with his family at the State Lake Theatre in Chicago. The O'Connors—father, mother and five boys— were old-time vaudevillians. Donald, three years younger than Judy, had a secret crush on her. Not only had they both been child performers from the days they could toddle, but Judy was bound to him by a special tie of sympathy. They had met even before Mom Lawlor's. In San Francisco, the summer earlier, the Gumm Sisters had played the Golden Gate, the O'Connors the Fox, several blocks away. Their performances then came at different times. On the day after the Gumm Sisters opened, Donald walked to the Golden Gate to catch Judy's act, and she walked him back to the Fox to see his.

They had both giggled over Judy's review in the San Francisco News, which referred to "the Gumm Sisters, who harmonize, and have a strong-voiced small woman who imitates and sings in a big way." At least, said Judy, sighing, "They've moved me up from a midget." At the Fox a long flight of steps led down to the stage entrance. When they reached the bottom, Donald's mother was waiting, and without a word slapped him furiously across the face—this in the presence of his girl! They both broke into tears—mothers could be so cruel! Only later could Donald explain that his only sister had been killed by an auto when she was six and wheeling him, then a year old, across the street. He was the last of seven children, and had been warned never to cross a street alone. He had disobeyed when he went to the Golden Gate by himself. Judy never forgave Donald's mother.

Yet they had hilarious memories. Now, in Chicago, and each time they met in the years to come, Judy always greeted him with "Have you heard from Haji Ali?"—the signal for them both to roar with laughter. Haji Ali was an amazing Turk, as Judy put it, "the man who threw up for a living." At one time or another both had worked on the same bill with him. Wearing a large purple turban, his wife as his assistant, Haji Ali came on stage and proceeded to swallow seventeen hazel nuts and one walnut. Then he walked into the audience to let anyone tap his stomach smartly and hear the nuts rattle. Then he returned on stage to announce, "Now I will bring up the hazel nuts and when you want me to bring up the walnut, holler." He brought them up, one by one, each a hazel nut; when someone shouted "Now!" he gulped once or twice and brought up the walnut.

But it was his grand finale that convulsed Judy and Donald. He built a fire on stage, drank a glass of water, on top of which he drank a glass of kerosene; then, to quote Judy, "He'd throw up the kerosene on it and make the fire enormous, then the water came up and put it out." And she would add, laughing, "And God help the audience if he ate any lunch that day!"

Donald always added an epilogue: Did she remember the time Haji Ali went to a fancy restaurant, came down with ptomaine poisoning and had to be rushed to the hospital to have his stomach pumped?

It was a triumphant Ethel Garland and three Garland Sisters who returned in September 1934, flush with money and success, to Los Angeles to confront Frank Gumm. Jessel, proud of his role, became an advance man for Judy. He introduced Ethel to Billy Wilkerson, publisher of the Hollywood *Reporter,* who sponsored a Newcomers' Night each Sunday at the Trocadero Café, a popular restaurant on the Strip. Presently everyone was going there to hear Jessel's latest find, Frances Garland, whom he had discovered at the World's Fair.

The high spot of those weeks was the Garland Sisters' official recognition by *Variety,* the all-important trade journal of show business. Bittersweet though it was for Janey and Jimmy, the Garland Sisters' first indisputably professional review appeared in *Variety* for November 4, 1934, covering their appearance at Grauman's Chinese Theatre:

Hardly a new act, this trio of youngsters has been kicking around the coast for two years, but has just found itself. As a trio, it means nothing, but with the youngest, Frances, 13, featured, it hops into class entertainment; for if such a thing is possible, the girl is a combination of Helen Morgan and Fuzzy Knight. Possessing a voice that, without a P.A. system, is audible throughout a house as large as the Chinese, she handles ballads like a veteran, and gets every note and word over with a personality that hits audiences. Caught on several previous shows, she has never failed to stop the show, her current engagement being no exception.

Still, with all this, no movie studio called. In vain Ethel tried to break down the doors. Sometimes the results were not only discouraging but baffling. She managed to obtain an audition for Judy at 20th Century–Fox, for a dramatic and singing bit—that of a young immigrant girl brought to the United States. Judy was to be heard by Sol Wurtzel, head of the studio. A few minutes before the audition, Dore Schary, then a young free-lance screenwriter, dropped in to talk over a script. "I only have a few minutes," Wurtzel said. "I've promised to hear a child singer called Frances Garland." Schary said, "Hey, she's great. I've heard her." He had been at Proctor's Palace not long before and came away with Judy's rendition of "Little Man, You've Had a Busy Day" ringing in his ears.

"O.K.," said Wurtzel. "Come in and listen, too."

Schary followed him into the other room. There sat Judy, in a white dress with puffed sleeves, wearing bobby sox, looking a little frightened, and beside her, her mother, a tiny bespectacled woman in black, smiling hopefully at them.

Judy sang, her mother at the piano. One song, and then a second. At the end, Wurtzel thanked mother and daughter, and they left. "What do you think?" Schary asked. He had been moved by her. But Wurtzel had already dismissed Judy. "She's got a big voice for so little a girl," he said. It was his only comment. They returned to discuss Schary's script. Again it was brought home to Judy, as she drove glumly back with her mother: audiences and friends might love her, but what did it matter?—the important listeners remained indifferent.

One of Judy's problems was her in-between age. She knew it. "I wasn't a child wonder and I wasn't grown up," she said later. Had she been younger, like Shirley Temple, she would have had a better chance. At every audition one saw scores of little girls, all with their Shirley Temple curls. Had she been older, she might have been a candidate for a bit part as an ingénue.

But forces were at work behind the scenes. While Judy and her sisters were completing their triumphant stay in Chicago, in Los Angeles Marc Rabwin, at thirty-three still a bachelor, had met an attractive and unusual girl. She was Marcella Bennett, at twenty-six executive secretary to David Selznick, the producer. Marc was already a well-known surgeon; Marcella was warm, intelligent, highly capable, one of the few persons who could handle the demands made upon his staff by Selznick, a man of volcanic and almost inexhaustible energy.

Marc and Marcella met, took the measure of each other and fell almost instantly in love. Less than six weeks after they met, they were married. In that brief time Marcella learned about Marc—and, inevitably, about the Gumms. They were obviously a part of his life. Marc made this clear. "You've got to meet these people before I can marry you," he had said, implying that if the five Gumms didn't approve of her, he might have second thoughts about their marriage.

Shortly after Ethel and the girls returned from the Fair, Marc took Marcella to the Gumms' for dinner. It was typical country food served to them by Ethel, the atmosphere homey and pleasant, with Grandma Eva helping in the kitchen. And again, after dinner, Ethel at the piano, the three girls, now all taller, arrayed themselves in order of height behind her and a little to one side—and now it was Frank, Marc and Marcella who sat back, listening.

And now it was Marcella who could not get over Judy.

She thought, *I work in the picture business, I know something about entertainment. I just can't believe what I'm hearing and seeing —this kid is so adorable, she has such a voice.* The older girls sang beautifully, their harmonies were perfect, but they seemed so dignified, so staid: there was no excitement in them. But Judy, in contrast, mugged and grimaced, she was bursting out of herself, her eyes all but popped, and how she *loved* to sing for those who enjoyed her.

From that moment on, Judy had still another champion.

Some months later, in the spring of 1935, Marc and Marcella gave a huge party at their home in Beverly Hills. Those present represented a cross-section of two worlds closely allied in Hollywood—the medical profession with its growing profusion of psychiatrists and analysts, who were just beginning to minister to the troubled egos and psyches of celebrated performers, and the world of the film industry. The Gumms were of course included. The Rabwins chose a moment to present Judy to their guests.

She sang, with the expected result. Everyone was overwhelmed. She was a *Wunderkind*. When the girls appeared a little later with the *Fanchon and Marco Revue,* the critic of the Los Angeles evening

Herald-Express was so impressed by Judy that he invoked the name of the great Sarah Bernhardt herself:

Not your smart, adult-aping prodigy is this girl, but a youngster who has the divine instinct to be herself on the stage along with a talent for singing, a trick of rocking the spectator with rhythms and a capacity for putting emotion into her performance that suggest what Bernhardt must have been at her age. It isn't the cloying, heavy sentiment her elders so often strive for on the vaudeville stage, but simple, sincere feeling that reaches the heart.

It was the most perceptive review so far, seizing on Judy's special and unique quality.

And still no movie studio beckoned to her. Even *Variety* remarked on it. Covering the Garland Sisters' appearance at the Paramount a few months later, it said: "The Garland Sisters are the new hits of this program. Little Frances Garland seems to have been mysteriously overlooked by local talent scouts because this remarkable youngster has an amazing amount of talent for both stage & pix shows."

The Rabwins had invited to their party an intimate friend whom they particularly wanted to hear Frances Garland. This was Joseph L. Mankiewicz, a screenwriter and director at MGM. He had come to Hollywood from New York five years before at the suggestion of his older brother, Herman, himself a distinguished screenwriter. Marc and Joe, both bachelors then, had become close, living at each other's houses. Marc not only enjoyed Joe—he was a gifted writer, a brilliant, sardonic conversationalist—but also greatly respected his judgment. Joe had been out of town, and not at the party.

When he returned, both Marc and Marcella descended upon him. He had to hear Frances Garland. She was sensational. "I've lost my mind over that kid," Marcella said, and she wasn't one to be easily swept off her feet. She ought to be in the movies, they both said. She was a natural for Metro and Metro was a natural for her. More than any other studio, MGM, the top studio in Hollywood, was like a family. Everything was done for newcomers there, from fixing their teeth to teaching them correct diction. What couldn't they do with Frances, already so extraordinary—and this with only the coaching of her parents, who, at their best, were third-rate vaudevillians! Metro hired the finest voice coaches, choreographers, directors, writers. Metro had the greatest talent and was always open to new talent.

Joe was doubtful. No kid singer had yet broken into films. Only Shirley Temple, and she was not a singer, and because of Shirley

56

Temple and Jackie Coogan and Jackie Cooper, stage mothers and their youngsters had invaded Hollywood. He saw little hope in that direction.

"Just the same, listen to her," Marc said. The Garland Sisters were to appear next week at the Wilshire Ebell Theatre, before going on to a summer engagement at Lake Tahoe, Nevada. Marc and Marcella were going to hear them and, like it or not, Joe must come along.

When the Garland Sisters opened at the Wilshire Ebell Theatre, Marc and Marcella, with Joe at their side, were in the audience.

Judy sang. And in his seat Joe Mankiewicz, who was to win half a dozen Oscars as a screenwriter and director, underwent a memorable experience. He sat transfixed. Not only the power, but something electric, a quality, a timbre, in her voice touched that audience like a charged wire and sent it out of itself. He could only compare this tingling, explosive sensation to what he had felt when he first heard Al Jolson sing at the Winter Garden in New York. Nobody could capture an audience as Jolson had—and as this girl did now. This child sang "Stormy Weather" and "Be Still, My Heart!"—songs that would be ludicrous coming from any other twelve-year-old. Yet he was overwhelmed. Something emerged from that little figure on the stage that cut right to your heart.

When the Rabwins took him backstage and Joe, then twenty-five, met Judy, not yet thirteen, she could not know, and he could not know, that in later years he would become one of the most important male figures in her life. She only knew that this attractive, quiet-spoken man with his quizzical brown eyes and slow smile was Marc's dear friend, and he only knew that, when he saw her on the stage, his first thought had been: *This child has a strange and rare beauty. She is like something out of a forest.* . . .

Joe determined he would bring her name to the studio's attention.

A few days later he talked about Frances Garland to Ida Koverman. Mrs. Koverman was a strategically important figure at Metro. In the next months the name of Frances Garland was to assail her from all directions. Mrs. Koverman's title was assistant to Louis B. Mayer, the sentimental and ruthlessly businesslike executive who ran Metro as though it were his personal fiefdom, but her duties went far beyond that of an assistant. She was invaluable to him for her intelligence, her intuition, her discrimination, her devotion. To many she was the power behind the throne. A Scotswoman and widowed—she had been born Ida Brockway—she had been Herbert Hoover's confidential secretary for years before he became President. Originally she had hoped to be a concert pianist. She knew music and was a patron of the Los Angeles Opera. Tall, gray-haired, beautifully mannered, wearing a pince-nez, she moved quietly about the empire that was MGM, aware of everything and her hand in everything. She had an eye for talent. She was credited with prevailing upon Mayer to sign Clark Gable, after he had been turned down by Jack Warner because his ears were too big; Robert Taylor, Jean Harlow, Nelson Eddy, and many more of Metro's highly publicized stable of stars—as Mayer boasted, and as the legend read across the front of the administrative building, "MORE STARS THAN THERE ARE IN HEAVEN." Childless, her husband dead many years before, Ida devoted her life to Mayer and MGM; she knew everybody's troubles and was everybody's aunt. If anyone would be sympathetic to the promise of a Frances Garland, it would be Ida. Whereupon Joe spoke to her, eloquently, persuasively, and Ida listened, and took down Frances' name. But nothing happened. It was true: Metro wasn't interested in kid singers.

Meanwhile, Ethel and the girls had driven to their Tahoe engagement. It was at the Cal-Neva Lodge, built on the border between the two states—the state line ran through the middle of the dance floor —and a place particularly appreciated by more than one Hollywood figure who dared not appear in California because of legal embarrassments, but could appear at the Lodge as long as he remained on the Nevada side.

Frances Garland became Judy Garland at the Cal-Neva Lodge. She took her first name from Hoagy Carmichael's new hit, "Judy," and from the line, "If she seems a saint and you find that she ain't, that's Judy!" She liked the name—"It's peppy!" she said—and she liked the sentiment. Judy might not have taken her name had not Mary Jane announced a few days before that she was now to be known as Suzannah. "If you can do it, so can I," said Judy. "I'm finished with Frances. And I don't want ever to hear 'Baby' again!" Both girls made the change in the face of Ethel's disapproval. Judy, of course, had been christened Frances Ethel after both her parents, and there had been a Great-Aunt Mary Jane. To Jimmy, who had to learn their new names overnight, it was a great annoyance, particularly because of

Judy. She was maddeningly stubborn about it, refusing to answer to, even to look up at, the sound of anything but "Judy."

The Cal-Neva engagement assumed importance in Judy's story only after it was over, and Ethel was already driving the girls to their last booking in Kansas City before their return to Los Angeles. Judy as usual sat beside her mother in the front seat, her hair, just washed, in leather curlers, Suzy and Jimmy in the back with the costumes. They had gone about twenty miles when Suzy, the only one of the girls who was clothes-conscious, suddenly cried out, "Mama, I left our hats in the cabin!" She had been in charge of their costumes, but she had had other things on her mind at the moment. Changing her name had been only part of her self-assertion. She had fallen in love with a saxophone player in the band at the Cal-Neva named Lee Cahn. This, on the heels of her starry-eyed summer with Jack Cathcart, the trumpet player in Chicago, the summer before, had been too much for Ethel. She thought band musicians charming but unreliable, philanderers at heart, who made the worst kind of husbands. She had tolerated Cathcart's attentions to Janey—the man *had* done them a good turn—but she had been relieved when they were done with Chicago. When it started all over again in Tahoe, and again with a band musician, Ethel was upset. "When will you get interested in someone who knows what to do with a slide rule instead of a slide trombone?" she demanded. It rubbed the girls the wrong way. Nobody forgot that Will Gilmore was an engineer. So Suzy and her mother had had words about Lee Cahn, and Suzy was unhappy.

Now when she said she'd forgotten their hats, Ethel said, "It's not worth turning back. We'll send for them." After another five minutes, Suzy groaned, "I left the music there, too." The hatboxes were on a closet shelf of their cabin, the sheet music under the boxes.

Ethel turned back. They needed the music for their Kansas City engagement. An hour later they pulled into the Cal-Neva parking lot. Suzy was sitting silent and sullen in the back. Judy, in an old pair of shorts, her hair in curlers, was dispatched to fetch the forgotten baggage, while Ethel kept the motor running. Halfway to the cabin she was stopped by an excited man—Bones Remer, manager-bouncer at the Lodge. He had been drinking with friends in the lower bar and through a window saw the Garland car drive up. He had dashed out to grab Judy by the hand. "C'mon, kid, there's some people here you just got to sing for."

Judy held back. "I can't," she said. "We left some things in our cabin. That's what we came back for. Besides, Mama plays for me and she's in the car."

"Don't you worry about that," Bones said. "Get your stuff and beat it right back here. I'll take care of your mother." Judy came back, struggling with a huge red hatbox, to find her mother out of the car, looking annoyed, and Remer at her side. "Ethel, she's got to do it," he was saying, and Ethel: "But we're late now, Bones." "Just one song then," Bones pleaded. "Ethel, these people are very influential— you'll be surprised when you see who they are." All right, said Ethel, just one song then.

At a table in the downstairs bar were four men. One, a heavy-set man with a square, unsmiling face, who kept his cigar in his mouth as he was introduced, Ethel recognized immediately from his photographs—Harry Cohn, the formidable head of Columbia Pictures. The others were introduced: Lew Brown, a songwriter and executive of Columbia; Harry Akst, another well-known songwriter; and Al Rosen, an agent. They had obviously been discussing Judy because Bones brought her forward with the words, "This is the little girl I was telling you about."

One of Judy's most successful numbers was "Zing! Went the Strings of My Heart." Ethel sat down at the small upright in the bar and Judy sang. Then she sang two or three other numbers, growing unhappier by the moment. It was obvious that Bones and his friends had been sitting around having a last long drink before he closed up the Lodge for the summer. They were not really in the mood for an audition.

Then Akst said, "Judy, is there any other song you'd like to sing?"

She said, "I know 'Dinah.'" It was one of her most popular numbers.

Akst rose, grinning. "Honey, I'd love to hear you sing that." And to Ethel: "Mrs. Garland, would you mind if I accompany her? I wrote it."

Ethel was all blushes. She had forgotten that he was the composer.

Akst played, Judy sang, everyone applauded. Harry Cohn rolled his cigar in his mouth but remained silent. "She's terrific," Akst exclaimed. And then, earnestly: "Why isn't she in pictures?"

Ethel said, in Judy's hearing, "I think it's because she just isn't pretty enough."

Akst shook his head. "What a voice!" he said.

Al Rosen gave Ethel his business card, she gave him her phone number and address, and they returned to the car. As they drove off, Ethel summed up the experience: "We'll never see any of them again."

She was wrong. Two weeks later Frank Gumm answered the phone. It was early afternoon. Ethel was out shopping. The caller was Al Rosen, the agent. Could Judy get down to Metro at once—within the next hour? He had set up an audience with Ida Koverman! But right away!

Judy was in the back yard playing ball with her wire terrier, Waffles, dashing about among the avocado trees. She was in sneakers and dirty pants, a rumpled blouse, her hair cut short in a Buster Brown haircut. Frank called her. "We're going to audition at Metro," he said. "Let's go." Judy looked at him with dismay. "Daddy, I look awful—I'm a mess. I can't go like this." "C'mon," said Frank. "They'll like you as you are." She got into the little Chevrolet Frank used about town and they drove down to Metro.

What had happened was that, like prayers sent heavenward by Tibetan monks endlessly prostrating themselves before their prayer wheels, the efforts on Judy's behalf by her many champions had finally all reached the throne at MGM at the same time. When the Garlands drove away from the Cal-Neva Lodge, Lew Brown, who had written such hits as "Life Is Just a Bowl of Cherries," tried to persuade Harry Cohn to sign Judy. "My God, Harry," Brown had cried. "When you close your eyes, you think you're listening to Nora Bayes." Cohn refused. Al Rosen, equally enthusiastic, telephoned Benny Thau, general manager at Metro and Mayer's right-hand man. Thau, a taciturn, careful businessman, who negotiated all Metro's contracts, listened to Rosen as Ida Koverman had listened to Mankiewicz, but did nothing. Rosen thereupon telephoned Jack Robbins of the music publishing firm of Robbins, Feist & Miller, who published the songs of Arthur Freed, an MGM songwriter and favorite of Mayer, who was beginning to groom him to become a producer. "I can't get my foot in the door at Metro," Rosen told Robbins. "You've got to get Freed to listen to her. This girl has got something!" Robbins telephoned Freed. Freed sighed, "Oh, not another singer!" —but, reluctant to turn him down, agreed.

The upshot was that Al Rosen received word to bring his new

discovery to Metro. Ida Koverman would be glad to listen to the Garland girl. The name had ticked her memory: Garland. That must be the child Joe Mankiewicz had talked and talked about.

Al Rosen met Frank and Judy at the door and took them into Ida's office. Judy sang several numbers, Frank accompanying her. Ida did not like his playing, and rang up Roger Edens, Metro's music arranger and vocal coach, who came down and politely replaced Frank at the piano.

"What popular songs do you know?" he asked Judy.

"I know 'Zing! Went the Strings of My Heart,' " she said. She sang it. Ida said thoughtfully, "Mr. Mayer should hear her." She immediately went in to see him. It was a difficult time in his life—he was engaged in internecine disputes involving Irving Thalberg—and he said, "Oh, Kay, I don't want to be bothered with these child singers. I'm so low." Ida prevailed upon him. "No, no, no, this girl's voice is different. It will stun you."

They all adjourned to Mayer's huge white office—everything was white, the enormous circular desk, the furniture, the walls, the carpeting, even the grand piano in the corner, and the room was fragrant with the aroma of the expensive cigars Mayer smoked. It was Judy's first sight of the remarkable figure who would control her fortunes—and her destiny—for the next fifteen years. He sat behind his desk exuding power and authority, a solid, impeccably dressed man, his gray hair (he had marked his fiftieth birthday) brushed neatly above a high forehead, sharp-nosed, thin-lipped, his black eyes alert and appraising behind shell-rim spectacles. He rose briskly to greet the group—Mayer, like Ethel, was attuned to a faster beat, and moved swiftly and decisively—shook hands gravely with Judy (to her astonishment, he was only an inch or so taller than she), saw that everyone was seated and then sat down to hear her.

Judy sang. Mayer listened impassively. It was not his style, enthusiast though he was, to reveal himself at an audition—certainly not with an agent present. It made for difficulties when the contract was negotiated. After the third number, he demanded, "Do you know any opera?" Judy became nervous. Here was another monarch who was not impressed. Frank's temper took over. He did not like Mayer, he did not like authoritarian types, he had never gotten over his resentment toward the major film companies, who had forced him to accept block booking. He said to Judy, "Come on, that's enough. You don't have to sing any more." With that they left.

Ethel was waiting, upset, when they returned home. That he had taken Judy "looking like that!" for an audition was bad enough; that he had walked out . . . "Oh, they weren't interested anyway," Frank said.

Next morning, however, Al Rosen called again. Mrs. Koverman wanted them to come back. Edens, musician, composer, arranger, vocal coach without whom Ethel Merman hardly sang a note, a superb stylist and a master of phrasing, thought she was excellent. This time Ethel saw that Judy was dressed in her best and drove her to the studio. Mrs. Koverman said to Ethel, "Mr. Mayer is very interested. Would you mind if she sang a few more songs?" They went to Stage 1, one of the great music stages at MGM. Arthur Freed was there, as well as Edens, and Ida, as part of her campaign for Judy, had also asked Jack Cummings, a producer, who in his own right, but also as Mayer's nephew, carried considerable weight.

Mr. Mayer would be there in a few minutes.

As they waited, Ida took Judy aside. She obviously liked her, Judy realized. "Dear, do you know 'Eli, Eli'?" she asked. For the first time something like hope beat at the back of Judy's mind. Yes, she said. She knew it very well. "Oh, wonderful," said Mrs. Koverman. She looked at her. "You sing that toward the end, my dear."

Mayer came down. Judy sang several jazz numbers, then a ballad, and then "Eli, Eli." The huge room was silent as the rich, throbbing voice rose and fell. Mayer listened, again studiously noncommittal, but his eyes glistened as he rose, thanked Judy and hurried out.

In the next hour Cummings spoke to Mayer, Ida spoke to Mayer, and Freed, who perhaps of them all was first to appreciate Judy's potentialities, gave Mayer no peace. "Isn't she terrific?" he asked Mayer. "She's fantastic." Koverman was equally insistent.

Mayer said, all right—sign her.

She was signed. Without a screen test. And, as it developed, without anyone at MGM having any idea of what precisely to do with her.

6

ONE MIGHT PAUSE FOR A MOMENT HERE and consider to what it was that L. B. Mayer signed Judy Garland. It was a magical contract delivered that September day in 1935, a day of triumph for Judy. Bubbling over, she told Jimmy, "Hey, I'm going to work at Metro! I'm going to be a movie star!" She was unable to sleep that night with the excitement. It came at precisely the right moment, a watershed moment in the fortunes of the Gumm family. Less than one week before, on September 24, Suzy's twentieth birthday, the eldest Gumm daughter had gone to Reno and married Lee Cahn—what Ethel feared, a musician as a son-in-law, had come to pass. Ethel did not attend the wedding. They had gone to live in San Francisco, where Lee played with Horace Heidt's Californians. It marked the official breakup of the Garland Sisters.

The MGM contract could not have come at a more propitious time. Frank Gumm's finances, though not precarious, were sufficient to keep things going, but no more than that. The Gumms could hardly become rich from their small movie house in Lomita. So thirteen-year-old Judy, the littlest and the youngest, was on the way to becoming the main support of the family.

Frank, Ethel, Grandma Eva and the two girls gathered around the kitchen table and read the contract Al Rosen had negotiated for her. It was difficult to believe the figures—Judy starting at $100 a week and going up to $1,000 a week by her twentieth birthday! It was an incredible contract to be given in the depression to a young girl without a screen test, whose film experience consisted of a few fugitive moments singing in a handful of Grade B shorts. The contract, between Metro-Goldwyn-Mayer and "Frances Gumm, professionally known as Judy Garland," had to be approved by the California Supreme Court because Judy was a minor. One of its most important clauses was a guarantee that Metro, until Judy became eighteen, would furnish "such educational and welfare facilities as may be legally provided."

This would bring the first real change in Judy's life. She would leave Lawlor's to enter the school on the MGM lot in Culver City, a genuine grammar school under auspices of the Los Angeles Board of Education. She would attend classes from 9 A.M. until noon five days a week with other contract child performers—they were known as Metro's "studio children," with Ida Koverman playing the role of house mother. Judy was ecstatic: "I'll be going to school with Jackie Cooper and Freddie Bartholomew!" She had read all about them. Freddie Bartholomew, nearly two years younger than Judy, had been signed the year before. Jackie Cooper was her age; she had wept over him in *The Champ* with Wallace Beery at the Valley Theatre when she was nine, and bit her fingernails over his adventures in *Treasure Island* a couple of years later. She looked upon them both with a kind of awe.

After school she could look forward to being taken over by one of the most extraordinary finishing schools in the country—Metro's Special Services Department—and the process of grooming her for stardom would begin.

If she was put to work in a film, she would be excused from classes and do her lessons on the set. A temporary schoolroom would be set up for her on a corner of the stage. Black fabric partitions, which were usually used to help carry out a lighting scheme, would be hooked together to form a small ten-by-ten room, in which a desk and two chairs would be placed. When a break occurred in the shooting—often it might be a wait of an hour or more—the time would be utilized for lessons. She would go into the little room with a teacher assigned to stay on the set at all times. Then a call—and she'd be back on the set again. The time was religiously observed: at any moment the teacher could call, "School time," and everything would stop while Judy worked with her teacher. California labor laws were strict. Every child under eighteen had to receive three hours of schooling and one hour of recreation in each eight-hour day—and it was the teacher's responsibility to see that this was carried out. Nor could any minor remain unaccompanied on the set, and if Judy left to go into town for lunch, or interviews and other Metro assignments, she had to be accompanied by either her teacher, otherwise known as a "welfare worker," or a member of the studio publicity staff.

From 9 A.M. until 5 P.M., five days a week, Metro supervised her life. All this until she became eighteen.

But the money! There were options, which meant that at specified intervals Metro could drop Judy (though she could not leave) or "pick up her option," with increases each time. One hundred dollars a week for the first six months, $200 a week for the next six; then (each time the option had to be picked up) $300 a week the second year, $400 a week the third, climbing by ever larger raises until her salary reached the $1,000-a-week mark. And during the seven-year period, the contract could be renegotiated to reach even higher levels.

Ethel said, "Now, we're going to be sensible about this." It was true, as Peg DeVine said, that none of the girls really knew the value of a dollar. Money had come too hard to Ethel for her to allow anyone else to manage it. Now this money was to flow in steadily, in increasing amounts, and something should be done about Judy's future. Ethel had consulted two old Grand Rapids friends, George and Helen Fisher, who had recently moved to Los Angeles. George sold insurance. He had recommended that the Gumms immediately take out two annuities for Judy, one to pay her $100 a month for life at age twenty-five, the second to pay an additional $500 a month for life at age thirty-five. Then, if she wished, Judy need never work again. George had calculated that with $600 a month for life, and the savings Judy would have accumulated in the intervening twenty-odd years, she should be financially independent. "At least," Ethel said, "she'll never starve, no matter what." Ethel had arranged to pay the first premiums from Judy's first paychecks.

Ethel had other plans, which would be carried out in the next months, including the purchase from George Fisher of a $50,000 insurance policy upon her life, which at her death would pay $15,000 to each girl and $5,000 for funeral expenses. Frank already had a nominal policy on his life. Assuming Judy did well, and Metro picked up her options, she was now really embarked on her career. Suzy was married; eighteen-year-old Jimmy was dating with an enthusiasm which suggested she could be married in a year or so. At last a sense of financial order and stability had settled upon the Gumm family.

There were, to be sure, a number of rather harsh, even terrifying, clauses in Judy's contract. They suggested some of the pressures that would come to bear on her later. If Judy's physical appearance changed or her voice became impaired so that she could not perform satisfactorily, she could be suspended without pay. If the damage was deemed permanent, her contract could be terminated. She could be suspended for many reasons, among them her refusal to accept a role assigned to her, or committing "any act or thing that would tend to bring her into public hatred, contempt, scorn or ridicule or tend to shock, insult or offend the community." She had to be ready to appear anywhere, in any city here or abroad, at any time specified, to perform before the camera, or on stage, or on radio, or in order to be fitted for a wardrobe, or to be interviewed, or "for such other purposes" as Metro might decide. She was not allowed to sing in public, be photographed, or her voice recorded or her name used without the studio's written permission, but Metro could lend her services to any other person or studio *without* her permission. To sweeten the arrangement, there was a letter signed by Mayer himself saying that she could take radio or other engagements so long as they didn't conflict with her MGM duties.

There were other clauses—the contract ran nineteen legal-size pages—but the essence of it was unmistakable: The studio owned her. Her voice, her face, her name—all were Metro's.

These conditions, however, were customary. After all, the buyer paid well for what he bought. Ethel signed (Judy was a minor), and on October 1, 1935, Judy Garland officially entered the strange, the overwhelming, the enchanted province of Metro-Goldwyn-Mayer.

She entered a very special world indeed. No other studio was quite like Metro. Time-worn though the phrase was, it *was* a dream factory —a place where dreams were manufactured—and one entered it at the risk of forgetting what reality was. MGM was the largest, the richest and the most efficiently run; there were other studios, of course—Warner Brothers, Columbia, Paramount, 20th Century-Fox, Republic, RKO Radio, Universal, Samuel Goldwyn—and other studios had stars, but none so many as Metro and of such glitter: here, under contract in Judy's time, were Greta Garbo and Spencer Tracy and John and Lionel Barrymore and Joan Crawford and Norma Shearer and Clark Gable and Hedy Lamarr and William Powell and Melvyn Douglas and Myrna Loy and Robert Taylor and Jean Harlow and Lana Turner and Rosalind Russell and Robert Montgomery and Wallace Beery and James Stewart and Mickey Rooney and Jackie Cooper and Buster Keaton—the list was always growing.

But equally as important as this roster of stars was the studio's carefully worked-out technique of training, grooming and building its players. Something of this had been in the minds of Marc and Marcella when they suggested to Joe Mankiewicz that Metro was the place for Judy. The care and protection of these beautiful people was not left to chance. No other studio had so skilled and efficient a Special Services Department.

Under Howard Strickling, chief of Publicity, a staff of thirty-five men and women devoted themselves to making life easy and smoothing the way for contract players, on call for whatever their needs. Every player had an aide assigned to him or her, to check daily with the performer, to arrange appointments for publicity and promotion, to take care of errands of every kind.

Under Mayer, Metro was geared to turn out fifty-two films a year, one a week, an astonishing production. This figure was chosen because theatres which offered stage shows changed them once a week. Mayer wanted to supply these theatres with a new Metro picture every week—no other studio need apply. Loew's, Metro's parent company, owned hundreds of theatres across the country, and it was a beautiful arrangement. Loew's MGM turned out the films, Loew's theatres showed them. To ensure the sale on a mass basis elsewhere, Metro had instituted the system of block booking against which Frank Gumm had fought so bitterly as far back as Grand Rapids— the purchase in advance of a year's supply of films, the bad with the good and no control beforehand over what films one might receive. Later the government outlawed this practice as monopolistic.

Metro was the factory that turned out these films, and the technique that made it possible had been awesomely refined. To produce one picture every seven days, a stable of actors and actresses had to be available at all times under contracts committing them to work in any film to which they were assigned, and in any role chosen for them. To provide the films in which these players were to appear, a stable of screenwriters had to be available at all times committed by contract to create the screenplays, either as original pieces of work or as adaptations from books, stage plays and magazine stories. To transform the screenplay into a motion picture, there had to be a stable of producers, committed under contract to put together players and story. This was a most complex operation, which involved assigning directors (taken from a stable of directors, committed to direct whatever film they were assigned), using musicians under contract to score the films and, in musicals, songwriters under

68

contract to write the appropriate tunes, cameramen to film the action, set designers to create the scenes, dress designers to create the costumes, makeup artists, beauticians, hairdressers and—to back these up, and keep the physical plant in continuous operation (a film a week, a film every seven days the year round)—a huge staff of carpenters, metalworkers, electricians, lighting experts, tailors, cobblers, cooks, physicians, nurses, technicians of every kind, machine shops—more than 140 departments—an army of artisans all to be used with a God-like authority to create the very shape and feel of life itself.

The Metro statistics were staggering. At one point its makeup division would handle more than twelve hundred makeups an hour; its telephone exchange make as many long-distance calls each day as a city of fifty thousand; and in its search for film properties, a thousand plays, novels and short stories would be read each month.

Factory *was* the word for it.

Thus, in Culver City, itself an ugly little town, there rose this magical kingdom which turned out dreams, packaged in roughly one-hour-and-forty-five-minute segments, to entrance the sixty millions who went to the movies each week. Judy came to Metro when motion pictures were everybody's other life. Millions lived vicariously the lives of the stars, intimately sharing their triumphs and failures as recounted by magazine after magazine and in dozens of Hollywood columns, and this mirrored and remirrored, magnified and remagnified without end. Such was Hollywood, and such was MGM, "the Tiffany of the studios," a vast, walled, crenellated, turreted fantasy land, half papier-mâché, half wood and cement and iron and steel, covering two hundred acres where some three thousand highly skilled men and women, paid and pampered on a regal scale, devoted themselves, each in his own way and with his own talent, to the task of making dreams emerge as reality. One could understand why in his time L. B. Mayer was to become the highest-salaried executive in the country.

Before Judy was fed into this extraordinary mechanism, much would be done for her. A fortune in education and grooming would be expended upon her. At first she would simply go to school, and after school spend time with her voice coach, Roger Edens. But in time she would be given dancing lessons, diction lessons, drama lessons, French lessons, lessons on making up for screen and street, lessons in deportment, how to walk, how to carry herself, how to respond to interviewers. Physical therapists would work with her and specialists devote themselves to taking pounds off her as they sought at the same time to put pounds on others. All her rough edges would be smoothed over and honed down, and when she emerged, she would be a finished product, buffed and polished—a product calculated to please.

7

JUDY'S FIRST SIGHT OF HER NEW SCHOOL enchanted her. Ethel drove her there the first day, and once they passed through Metro's great west gate, they came suddenly upon it. There, perched among the huge three-story-high rectangular sheds, some as long as a football field, housing Metro's giant stages, was the MGM school, which looked as though it had dropped out of the pages of a child's fairy-tale book: a little one-story wooden schoolhouse, actually painted red, with a gabled roof and chimney and a diminutive front porch, complete to rocking chair, with three wooden steps leading up to it from a neatly cobblestoned pavement.

Once inside, Judy and her mother found themselves in a large room with a blackboard along one wall, a dozen wooden school desks complete to inkwells in the upper right-hand corner, and a small office. There they found the teacher, Mary MacDonald, a slender, dark-eyed woman with black hair severely done up in a bun, and a gold watch pinned to her shirtwaist. On a table near her desk was a wind-up Victrola, and a pile of records.

There were only four other students. There was Mickey, and much warm greeting, and then Terry Kilburn, Gene Reynolds and Dawn O'Day, all child players under contract. To Judy's disappointment, neither Jackie Cooper nor Freddie Bartholomew was there. Miss MacDonald explained that both boys had private tutors, Jackie because he had a complicated schedule, and Freddie because his Aunt Cissie, his guardian, feared he might lose his British accent and so had imported a tutor from England.

70

When Ethel left, Miss MacDonald looked after her thoughtfully. They had talked together briefly. Ethel had explained that Judy was a sensitive child, but then she had added something no other mother had told Miss MacDonald: "I don't want her frustrated—ever." Miss MacDonald was a disciplinarian and a stickler for rules (when she was on the set, she consulted her watch regularly to make sure that every child received its full three hours of schooling), and Ethel's words ruffled her. It was quite understandable that some mothers wanted everything made easy for their children, but Miss MacDonald was not one to cater to anyone. It was too bad Judy came from Lawlor's —their students tended sometimes not to be well prepared—and if she bore down on her in class, this child might well feel frustrated.

But it turned out differently. Judy surprised her. She was an attentive student. Because both Mayer and Mrs. Koverman loved good music, and Mayer purchased entire European libraries on his frequent trips abroad, the MGM music library was considered second only to that in the Library of Congress. Miss MacDonald spent an hour a day teaching music appreciation to Judy, and later to Deanna Durbin, another teen-age singer, who arrived not long after.

Both girls listened eagerly to records Miss MacDonald had brought over from the music library, which she played on the Victrola. Judy, to her surprise, loved classical music—"Oh, much more than jazz," she said, and then added unexpectedly—the words sounded so matter-of-fact coming from this ardent, sensitive little thirteen-year-old, "but everybody says the money's in jazz." Judy amazed her, too, by her genuine love of poetry. Miss MacDonald had taught no other child who, assigned James Russell Lowell's poem "The Vision of Sir Launfal," so rich, yet so difficult, memorized huge stretches of it because she wanted to, and recited it not only beautifully and movingly but with comprehension. This girl, Miss MacDonald thought, was not only talented (news of the new singing sensation had spread through the studio) but responsive to imagery.

Mickey and Judy were a pair to Miss MacDonald, so much alike— not only in age and size (Mickey was a year and a half older, and then about the same height), but in their extraordinary energy and readiness to perform at the slightest opportunity. Judy was really no trouble—she at least could manage to sit still, while Mickey bounced about in his seat—but when they were together, they struck sparks off each other. The combination taxed even Miss MacDonald's iron control. At Mom Lawlor's they had exchanged mash notes: Mickey's "I love you, Judy, do you love me?" and Judy's heartfelt "Oh, yes, I love you too, Mickey." But when they met again here, Mickey, a compulsive mimic, always performing in class or out, could not help mimicking her. Then he succumbed completely to her, became extremely protective of her, and they established a lifelong friendship.

In the afternoons, before she went to one of the small studios for her sessions with Roger Edens, her voice coach, she had to go through her appointments at the Portrait Gallery. This was a building devoted to still photography over which Ann Straus, a fashion expert who came from New York, presided. Miss Straus occupied a special niche at the studio, not only because she was efficient and genuinely friendly to the younger players, but because she was related by marriage to the Mayer family.

Here in the Gallery began the process of publicizing Metro's newcomers, particularly those who bore promise. Here they posed for the first publicity stills to be sent out to the newspapers and fan magazines announcing Metro's latest acquisition. Here they were appraised almost clinically by a team of photographers, beauticians and fashion designers to determine how best they should be presented to the public, how they should be clothed, what colors suited them, what physical features were to be emphasized or suppressed, how they were to be lit, and at what angle they should be photographed. Dressmaker forms were made of their bodies, on which their costumes would be cut and fitted.

Going through the Gallery, for all its good services, was one of Judy's unhappiest experiences. She was looked over, and the first reaction was unfavorable. It was the time of tall, slender, long-limbed American beauties, and the report that went out on Judy was not flattering. Garland was short, plump; she had no neck. There was a slight curvature of the spine. If you wished to be cruel (or, as some Metro executives thought, witty), you might even say she was a little humpbacked. (Once L. B. Mayer said, "How is my little hunchback this morning?" He meant it affectionately, but it was a heartless joke.) This general disparaging assessment of her physical traits haunted Judy.

But it was true. Scoliosis—a slight curvature of the spine—ran in the family. Grandma Eva handed it to Ethel, who handed it to Judy, who was to hand it in lesser degree to both Liza and Lorna. Judy was one-half inch under five feet. Her legs were long but—as she was to quip, now ruefully, now bitterly—they seemed to be hitched to her shoulders. She was short proportionately from waist to shoulders; her neck was short (wherever possible, she was dressed in low-cut dresses to give her neck a longer look); her shoulders were simply too broad for her body. There were other matters that would have to be dealt with. She had a bad bite. Her teeth were not bad, but out of alignment in front. Judy balked at having them permanently capped. She would have to wear portable caps before the camera. Her nose could be improved upon. The early photographs of Baby Gumm showed such an adorable child with that upturned little nose and huge brown eyes. Her eyes were fine, large and beautiful, with a depth and darkness that arrested you, but her nose was no longer so retroussé —little rubber disks would have to be inserted to bring that about. She would be given the caps and disks to carry with her in a little pillbox in her purse when the time came.

They would have trouble with her as she went into her adolescent years. They would have to bind her breasts to keep her no more than fourteen for the next few years, and later, to give her a shapely waist, squeeze her into a rigid "love corset"—a cruel harness of canvas and metal stays which required a woman on either side to pull the strings tight. The problem of streamlining Judy was to be compounded by still another unwelcome heritage from Grandma Eva and Ethel—the tendency to put on all additional weight above the waist—which only exaggerated the top-heaviness of her figure, the more so because her legs remained remarkably slender.

For Judy this emphasis upon what she lacked was a source of extraordinary humiliation. From it grew, in those teen-age years, what was to amount almost to an obsession—the conviction that she was not physically attractive, not sexually desirable, to men. It was unfair, the comparisons she made between herself and other girls already on the lot or soon to be signed: Lana Turner and Elizabeth Taylor and Hedy Lamarr and Ann Rutherford and Kathryn Grayson and June Preisser and June Allyson. A compulsive masochism would not let her forget it. It did not help for Ethel to point out that she had not been signed as an actress, or to decorate the screen, or because her walk brought whistles from the stage hands. She had been chosen for her voice, her ability to put over a song, the mesmeric effect she had on audiences as a singer. What had been true at five, when Peg DeVine took her about, was now true at thirteen and fourteen and fifteen and sixteen: they wanted her only for the voice, and the voice alone—and there was so much more she longed to be wanted for. It was both her solace and her cross.

The road was painful from the bewitching little Baby Gumm through the stubby, barrel-shaped teen-ager to the Judy whose beauty, if not traditional, was glowing and mysteriously warm and deeply moving and in its way sexually powerful as no classical beauty could be. The Judy whose personal magnetism, whose pure femininity, mixed with what Mankiewicz had seen and felt—*a strange and rare beauty . . . something out of a forest*—an infinite tenderness, a quality of almost naked emotion in her eyes, her voice . . . would bring to her any man she wished to have.

Reassurance came from Roger Edens. Had there been no Roger Edens, there might not have been the Judy Garland the world knew. More than anyone, Edens shaped Judy's voice, her manner of singing, her phrasing, her choice of songs—even how she dressed. This tall, slender, elegant man, perfectly tailored, gentle-spoken but firm, satirical, austere in his choice of friends, a quintessential musician with superb taste and a biting wit—all traits Judy admired—built upon her innate talent to help her establish the style which became second nature to her. She was Ida Koverman's pet, but so far as she could be anyone's creation, she was Roger Edens'.

Edens was a Southerner. His accent was not unlike Frank Gumm's, which further endeared him to Judy. He had done for Ethel Merman what he was now to do for Judy. He had launched Ethel as a singer, becoming first her accompanist, then her arranger and then her voice coach—yet far more than that. He taught her how to hold a word, a phrase; he gave her much of what became her style. She depended upon him. When Merman came to Hollywood a couple of years before to appear in a Goldwyn production, she brought Edens with her to do her numbers, one of which, "Eadie Was a Lady," became a classic. He was to write many more. He had impressed Carmel Myers, the silent screen star, who gave several dramatic recitatives on *The Rudy Vallee Show*. After Ethel Merman returned to New York, Edens had remained in Hollywood as a free-lance music arranger and composer. He had written Miss Myers' music and special material. She spoke to Ida: "He's the best talent around—he can play, perform, coach, do anything." Ida alerted Arthur Freed, who was beginning to surround himself with a group of gifted people to be known as "the Freed Unit" at MGM, and later produce most of the studio's great musicals in the next decade and more. Freed, equally impressed, hired Edens. This had been several months before Judy joined MGM.

Now, with Judy, Edens worked to temper her voice. Ethel had billed her as "Little Miss Leather Lungs." Not always necessary, that volume, that strength. And the songs Judy sang, chosen by Ethel— inappropriate, ludicrous! A seven-year-old singing "If I Had You," a twelve-year-old singing "My Man"—they made Judy more of a curiosity than an artist. In addition, Ethel had taught Judy gestures, in generous number. Edens limited her to one a song.

"Don't use your hands at all except in one final gesture—and let that be the big one," he told her. Judy could not read a note of music (as a matter of fact many singers could not), but Edens had only to play a number—even the most complicated—for her to sing it almost perfectly the first time and flawlessly the second. Part of his task, Edens realized, would be to move Judy away from her mother's musical control. It would make for friction, because Ethel was very much in Judy's life. She drove her to and from the studio every day; she rehearsed her and was her accompanist. Because in the first months the studio had nothing for Judy to do, she was allowed to appear on a *Shell Chateau* radio program (Wallace Beery, a Metro star, was master of ceremonies), and to cut a series of Decca records (good publicity for a new Metro contract player)—and Ethel had accompanied her each time. If one thing was clear, it was that light-years separated Ethel's musicality and that of Judy. Judy possessed an inborn sense of taste so that, ignorant and relatively untrained as she was, she knew the real from the shoddy.

When Edens first heard Judy on Stage 1, he was almost unnerved. The first note she struck was so rich and pure, her control throughout, in both high and low registers, unbelievable. He thought, *This is a phenomenal talent, but it lacks a style.* All the elements were there, however: a voice that was a completely natural and beautiful instrument; an almost photographic memory; and, though Metro's fashion department might groan over the problem of clothing this girl's figure, all shoulders and legs with a tubby barrel in the middle, it was, as Edens put it, "the perfect anatomy for a singer, built around a supermuscle of a diaphragm." Add to this her intelligence, her instinctive musicality, her willingness to throw herself into her work with such ardor, such energy, that concentrated heritage of vitality from both parents, whose lives had been spent trying to slow down . . . He had only to coach, to bring out, to channel, to refine.

They worked together each afternoon. Judy would bounce in on him, a chubby little girl in a white middy blouse, brimming over with eagerness. Edens was completely taken by her. She was so anxious to please, so affectionate, so grateful for her talent and his appreciation of it. *Lord*, he thought, *what a sweet girl!* Sometimes their sessions went two hours, three hours. Often he had to order her to go home; it was the only way to end the session: she could have sung all night. She trusted Edens, she adored him. To be with Roger Edens was a reward that helped assuage a great deal. In his presence she was not found wanting, she was all promise and greatness yet to be.

She needed all the support, all the reassurance, she could have at this juncture in her life. For less than seven weeks after her contract had been signed, Frank Gumm died.

There had been no warnings, really. On a Saturday afternoon he had been well, and on a Sunday morning he was dead. This event, the most traumatic of her childhood, occurred while Judy slept. It was a theft in the night; she had no chance to exchange a word with him, and she knew of it only after it happened.

The suddenness and unfairness of her father's death—the way he was taken from her—remained a wound to her all her life, an experience of such depth and poignancy that she never really emerged from its shadow.

Judy spent Saturday afternoon, November 16, 1935, with a girl who had been at Mom Lawlor's with her. They had gone down to see MGM's newest musical, *Broadway Melody of 1936*, important to Judy for two reasons. Arthur Freed had co-written the songs and music, and Roger Edens had scored it and done the vocal arrangements. The two girls returned to her friend's house humming one of the catchier tunes, "Broadway Rhythm," played records until nearly six o'clock, and then Judy went home. Jimmy had gone out on a dinner date and would not be back until late.

Judy went up to bed around ten o'clock. Her father was resting on the sofa in the living room, not feeling too well. "I think I've got a cold coming on," he said. His ear had bothered him a little; it had begun to run. He'd taken some quinine cold tablets. In the kitchen, Ethel and Grandma Eva were busily putting up canned peppers for the winter. Judy kissed her father good night and went upstairs.

She never saw him alive again.

She was wakened early Sunday by Jimmy bending over her. "They took Daddy to the hospital last night," she whispered. She told Judy what had happened.

Frankie Darro, Jimmy's date, had brought her home just after midnight. They were startled to see all the lights on in the house. Jimmy hurried in just as Ethel, looking upset, was leaving. "They had to take your father to the hospital," she said. "I don't know what it is." And she all but ran out to her car and drove off.

Jimmy was shocked. Her father had been enjoying his newspaper when Frankie picked her up earlier. Grandma Eva, in robe and slippers, was up, too, when she came in. "Gosh, your daddy's awful sick," she said worriedly. "Maybe it's pneumonia." Ethel and Frank had gone to bed not long after Judy, but just before midnight Frank had become so sick that Ethel had to telephone Dr. Marc, who had been asleep. He hurried over, at once called an ambulance and went with Frank to the Cedars of Lebanon Hospital. Ethel, who had been in her nightgown, stayed behind only long enough to dress. It was at that moment that Jimmy had arrived.

Jimmy had gone upstairs. Judy was sound asleep. Jimmy wondered whether she should wake her, and decided against it. There was nothing Judy could do. She undressed quietly in the bathroom and slipped into bed. She reassured herself. Their father had never been seriously ill. He had been in a hospital only once before. That had been when they still lived in Grand Rapids. He and Ethel had gone to Mayo's in Rochester at Dr. Marc's suggestion, discovered that they both indeed had goiters, and both underwent thyroidectomies. No real illness since then—and that had been years ago.

When the two girls hastened downstairs the next morning, there was Ethel in the kitchen preparing breakfast. How was Daddy? He was still in the hospital, Ethel said soberly. "He's not doing very good," she added. She had been there all night. Dr. Marc was still there. She had come home only to bathe and change clothes, to make breakfast for the girls and go right back.

Just before noon there was a telephone call. Grandma Eva called a cab and she and the two girls went to the hospital. When they arrived, Dr. Marc, his face solemn, took Jimmy and Judy into the waiting room and told them gently that their father had died. Everything that could be done for him had been done. He had died of a massive hemorrhage of the mastoid.

Judy and Jimmy were in a state of shock. They could not take in what had happened. Grandma Eva took them home. Ethel remained at the hospital. She had telephoned Suzy in San Francisco, and she and Lee were already on their way to Los Angeles.

The two girls sat in the living room, dazed, while Grandma Eva wept softly. It came home more sharply to them when Ethel returned later, weeping. Neither Judy nor Jimmy had ever seen their mother cry before. Whatever the calamity, she had never wept. More than anything else this broke through their numbness and underlined the enormity of what had happened. Both burst into tears.

Somehow the afternoon went on. Ethel lay on the same sofa where Frank had lain in the living room, being comforted by Fred Walsh, an elderly neighbor, who had lived next door in Lancaster. When Judy and her sisters lay on the grass at night, looking up at the stars, Mr. Walsh would sometimes join them and tell them about the constellations. He was an atheist, like Grandfather John, and he often read the Bible to the two girls, showing them annotations he had made in the margin, pointing out discrepancies and absurdities in the text.

Now, in the late afternoon, Suzy and Lee arrived, and there was another fresh torrent of tears.

Seven o'clock came, and no one had eaten. Grandma Eva dragged herself into the kitchen to fix some pork chops and fried potatoes.

The front doorbell rang.

Judy, tear-stained, went to the door. There stood their dentist, Dr. Bill Halverston, and his sister, Leonore, all smiles. "Surprise! Surprise! Happy birthday, Ethel!" And they piled into the house, carrying gifts wrapped in gaily colored paper and shining ribbons.

Bill and Leonore, seeing Ethel on the couch, staring at them with something like horror, her eyes red with weeping and a handkerchief to her face, stopped short. Ethel moaned, "Oh, my God!" and began crying again as though her heart would break. All three girls burst into tears and rushed into another room. They had all realized at the same time what had happened.

This was Mama's thirty-ninth birthday. Frank had arranged a surprise party for tonight and had told no one in the family.

Then followed a merciless ordeal. For the next hour guests arrived, gay, noisy, in festive spirits, with cries and shouts of "Happy birthday!" the moment the door was opened and before they could realize how woebegone the face of the thirteen-year-old girl who opened it. Later the ordeal was somewhat lessened when Leonore and Bill, who had been neighbors back in Grand Rapids, took up their station on the porch and warned newcomers as they came up the front steps. Those, then, who still wished to come in to what they expected to be a joyous occasion but had turned out to be a wake did so. Presently the house was full of somber, shocked friends.

Late that night the three girls sat numbly in the living room. "I didn't even see Daddy," Judy said, again and again. "I didn't even have a chance to say anything to him." Her sisters were more fortunate. Suzy had had her father for her twenty years. Jimmy had known him for her eighteen. Judy had known him the briefest time, and even in that time so desperately less than she had wanted. The separation she always feared had come with such suddenness, such cruel abruptness. It was such a loss!

She would look for him again and again, and always in vain, in every man she would ever meet, and fall in love with, the rest of her life.

She took the pillow from the sofa upstairs with her when she finally went to bed that night. It showed a tiny stain from the fluid that had escaped from her father's ear as he lay on it. She was to sleep on the pillow for many nights afterward and fought furiously to keep it, as it was, unwashed, uncleaned, against every attempt to take it from her.

Dr. Marc explained to the girls what had happened. Their father had grown up with a running ear—he'd had it from boyhood. Such middle-ear infections were common, and little could be done about them. A child came down with a sore throat, the infection went into the middle ear, and the eardrum had to be lanced, or it ruptured by itself. Judy had suffered such infections, but hers had run their course and vanished. Frank's, however, was a chronic infection. This time

an abscess had developed without his knowledge—an unusual occurrence because generally the pain it produced forced the patient to
summon a doctor. With no warning symptoms, the abscess had suddenly ruptured, the infection had entered his brain and spinal fluid,
and he had collapsed. Only then had Dr. Marc been called. Frank
had died within a few hours of what Dr. Marc described as an "overwhelming meningitis."

Many years later when Judy was asked by Liza how she felt when
her father died, she said, "I thought, 'Now there is no one on my
side.'"

JUDY'S FIRST YEAR AT MGM was a tantalizing mixture of frustration
and fulfillment. What helped take her out of her immediate grief
after her father's death was the speed with which events occurred.
There was, however, one constant. Always, from now on, there was
to be a boy on the scene. She was to go from one crush to another.
She was nearly always to be in love, or else falling out of love and
about to fall in love with somebody else. In the brief intervals when
there was no one, she was bored and unhappy, marking time; when
there was someone, she was alert, alive and enchanting everyone
about her.

Judy was the ultimate romantic. From the time even before she
could walk she had sat wide-eyed in her father's theatre, absorbed
and enthralled by the fantasy love lives unfolding before her on the
screen. A good deal of her childhood had been spent acting out those
fantasies, singing make-believe love songs under artificial palm trees
and crooning ballads of heartbreak in front of fake fireplaces, and
moving amid canvas scenery which pretended to place her on Broadway or in Paris or on a sunny beach in Spain. Now, in adolescence
and girlhood, she was suddenly plunged headlong into that dream
world made even more authentic, more believable. When she

walked into the MGM commissary, there were Clark Gable and Robert Taylor, real as life. (She and Deanna Durbin actually lunched with them—two teen-agers, Frances Gumm from Grand Rapids, Minnesota, and Edna Mae Durbin from Winnipeg, Canada, a foursome at one table, laughing and *flirting* with Clark Gable and Robert Taylor!) If she wandered through the make-believe streets in the world of MGM when the stages broke for lunch, there were kings and courtiers in their scarlet robes and ladies-in-waiting in plumes and brocades sweeping out of this set or that. Everything was make-believe, and it was not difficult, if one was conditioned to it, to walk right through the looking glass and live blissfully on the other side. And the essence of this make-believe was to be caught up in the transports of love. Judy had been singing of love and romance from the age of three, and the lyrics she grew up on, the words forever running through her head as she moved from Baby Gumm to Frances Gumm to Frances Garland to Judy Garland, spoke poetically of love and the bittersweet loss of love—one trembled, one trembled for it to arrive, to find and probe the full meaning of it.

Companionship with the opposite sex was to become an integral and basic need of her life. Psychiatrists would seek to determine whether it was the loss of her father, or the absence of maternal warmth in her earliest years, or simply an exquisite and vulnerable sensibility in search of its complement in another, that made this need so powerful, forever repeated, satiated and then unsatiated. But it was fundamental, and the male leitmotif ran pure and strong through her life. She was never to have very many intimates among women. She appreciated yet secretly resented beautiful women, and rather disdained the plain. She was happiest in her relationships with men, and only completely happy when she was in love. But her relationships with men were always fraught with peril because of her deep-seated doubt of her desirability, and her need, therefore, to test them, to be wanted by them with a hunger, a devotion and a knightliness no man could be capable of. By sheer imagination, by the power of her yearning that it should be so, she invested them with qualities out of her world of make-believe; she made princes of each one, sometimes indeed princes of paupers. . . . And since these were such qualities as they could never live up to, that even her imagination could not sustain for long, in the end it was, it had to be, disillusionment.

And then, incurable and obsessive romantic that she was, she would begin again.

A swift sequence of events led to Judy's first appearance before the camera. The studio had signed Deanna a few weeks after Judy, to play in a film based on the life of Madame Ernestine Schumann-Heink, with the celebrated opera star appearing as herself, and Deanna to play her as a child. But the project was repeatedly postponed by Madame Schumann-Heink's illnesses, and then given up. This left Metro with an embarrassment of riches: two young girl singers with no property in mind for either, and each taking home an increasingly larger paycheck as time went on.

L. B. Mayer called in Jack Chertok, in charge of the studio's Short Subjects division, and explained, "We've got two girls whose options are coming up and we don't know which one to keep. Can you help us decide?"

MGM owned a title, "Every Sunday," slated to become a full-length musical someday. Meanwhile, the title had to be protected, and the best way to do that was to make a short subject entitled *Every Sunday*. "I can kill two birds with one stone," Chertok suggested. He would put Judy and Deanna in the short; the theme would be jazz versus classical music, and the two girls would be friendly competitors, appearing at Sunday band concerts. To maintain suspense, a story would be whipped up: Judy sang jazz, Deanna had an operatic voice. It all made good sense, for it would provide a perfect opportunity to compare them.

"Fine," said Mayer. "Go ahead. See if you can shoot it by Monday." He was going away on one of his summer trips to Europe in a few days and wanted to see the short before he left.

This was Wednesday. Chertok had four days to prepare. By Monday morning, a shooting script had been dashed off and costumes chosen. The shooting took less than a week, but before the film could be processed for screening, Mayer had left with orders that it be put aside to await his decision when he returned.

When he did come back weeks later, he ordered *Every Sunday* screened in the presence of his executive staff, which included Margaret Booth, his chief editor and film cutter, almost legendary in the industry because of her unerring judgment. They all sat in silence as the two-reeler unfolded. Ida Koverman, Benny Thau and several others were in Judy's camp; but Margaret Booth was one of those who preferred Deanna. The girl was taller, prettier in the conventional sense, a slender, beautiful child with faultless teeth and a dazzling smile, and her voice, full, round and powerful, was that of an operatic soprano—astonishing.

For a wavering moment Judy's future hung by a thread. Then Mayer decided, "We'll keep them both." The order went out to put them together as a singing team in a musical.

Then, to Mayer's dismay and fury, it was learned that in his absence no one had picked up Deanna's option and Universal had signed her for the leading role in a Joseph Pasternak picture, *Three Smart Girls*.

Mayer raged. For a time it appeared that Judy was simply forgotten. Fortunately, while Mayer was gone, Edens had been seeking ways to keep her busy. One of his projects had brought her to the notice of a 20th Century–Fox scout. He and his wife were childless; in his own way he had begun to fill part of the vacuum left by Frank Gumm's death. He had become Judy's mentor and guardian at Metro, maintaining a polite relationship with Ethel, yet slowly weaning Judy away from her musical influence. Edens, as musical director of the Chesterfield radio hour, had gotten Judy a weekly guest spot —writing dialogue and music for her. Fox, hearing her, asked for her loan to play a small part in a college football comedy, *Pigskin Parade*. Since Metro would receive Judy's compensation and still had no picture for her, Judy awoke one morning to find herself loaned out to Fox to appear in her first full-length film.

Judy, bubbling over, read her part. It was hardly designed to delight her. She was to play a barefooted hillbilly girl in pigtails. Was this how 20th Century–Fox type-cast her? She never forgot that George Jessel had originally seen her in much the same way. In that first matinee at the Oriental Theatre in Chicago during the World's Fair, Jessel had played her for laughs when he brought her out on the stage alone. There was at the time a pigtailed little girl comedienne named Pinkie Sis Hopkins—homely, freckle-faced and blushing— who always looked as though she'd just come in from milking the cows. Jessel, as he admitted later, had thought of Judy as in the same mold. He introduced her as "Pinkie Frances Gumm," and engaged in a silly patter. "How much money do you want me to pay you for singing, Pinkie?" he asked. Judy: "I'll do it for a lollipop, Mr. Jessel." Jessel, with a chuckle: "Oh, I've got myself a bargain!" Only after Jessel heard her sing had he suggested changing her name. But that was how Jessel, an experienced, professional showman, had seen her at first glance.

Her first assignment at Metro—on the Saturday of the week she had been signed—had not helped her self-esteem. An MGM publicity aide took her to the Los Angeles Coliseum to sing between halves at the University of Southern California football game. At the half, after the rival bands finished marching, Judy was brought out and lifted onto a platform before the cheerleader's microphone. They had dressed her in a knee-length skirt and middy blouse, and someone had stuck a red-and-gold USC rooter's cap on her head. She was introduced as MGM's new contract player, Judy Garland, and launched into the school song, "Fight on for Good Old USC," blasting it out across the field. She was halfway through when the home team raced out on the field and Judy's voice—and Judy—were completely blotted out as eighty thousand fans rose to their feet in a thunder of cheers and applause. There was no use continuing; she was forced to stop in mid-song. No one seemed to care. Someone lifted her down again, and, trying to fight back tears of humiliation, she was escorted back to anonymity on the sidelines.

Now, in *Pigskin Parade*, her part could have been written for Sis Hopkins. It was a silly story about a mountaineer football team from the South which by mistake had been invited to play Yale in New Haven. Its quarterback was a ham-handed country bumpkin, Amos Dodd, played by Stu Erwin. Amos' astounding ability to send watermelons sailing over the fields had made him the team's passing star. Judy was his freckle-faced kid sister, Sairy Dodd—barefooted, in a tattered gingham dress, her hair parted severely in the center and in long braids down her back. To make her even more homespun, the Makeup Department stippled freckles on her face. The coach, Slug Winters, was Jack Haley; the coach's wife, Bessie, was Patsy Kelly. It was a film geared to broad comedy and horseplay. Amos made calf eyes at pretty Laura Watson, a local girl played by Betty Grable, and the leading man, Tommy Barker, smooth, elegant, with dark eyes and a deep romantic voice, was Tony Martin, the singer. In addition to Betty Grable, there were two other pretty girls in the cast, Arline Judge and Dixie Dunbar. Compared to them, Sairy Dodd was little more than comic relief and really had very little to do.

Judy knew no one on the Fox lot. It was Patsy Kelly, warm and outgoing, who saw her distress at her role, and her frustration as she waited to do what she did best—to sing—and tried to make her feel at home by inviting her to use her dressing room. Judy always said to her afterward, "You were the first one to be nice to me."

Not only the role disturbed Judy, but the fact that it was such a bit part. "Why don't they give me more to sing?" she demanded of Patsy. "Why can't I sing?" Fox had asked for her because of the Chesterfield broadcast; Edens had told her they also liked her Decca records. If it was her voice, why didn't they make use of it? She knew at this point that her fate and Deanna's presumably were wrapped up in *Every Sunday*. Now Fox had borrowed her, she had a second chance to show what she could do, and they had given her three brief numbers in an hour and thirty-five minutes of film. She asked the same question of an assistant director. No one paid attention to her.

Patsy comforted her. "That's the way they wrote the script, Judy. Just wait. You'll get your chance."

Judy bided her time, impatiently.

Ann Rutherford, newly signed by Metro, walked into the Wardrobe Department one afternoon and was brought up short by the sight of a young teen-age girl in bobby sox, with a sturdy little bell-shaped body, standing in the center of the room, tears running down her cheeks as two fitters laced her into a tight corset—the kind of heavy canvas foundation garment used by portly ladies. The two women, one on either side, pulled hard on the laces, squeezing the girl tighter and tighter. It was a humiliating sight, and Ann turned away. Later, she said to her own fitter, "That poor kid looked so familiar. Who is she?" Her name was Judy Garland, she was told. She was a singer, there was talk about whether her option or Deanna Durbin's would be picked up. . . . Ann thought, *There's something so haunting about that sad little face.* Then she recalled the girl's marvelous smile when she was let free and allowed to dash out of the room—and it dawned on her. This had to be Baby Gumm, whom she had seen at the Paramount that Saturday matinee so many years before! *That voice, that personality,* thought Ann. *She'll stay.*

Patsy Kelly was right. When Judy got her chance in *Pigskin Parade*, she made up for everything else. She was required to sing a ballad to Tony Martin, "It's Love I'm After," and despite her comic garb she sang it with such intensity that the entire cast, watching, was in tears. They burst into applause, ruining the take. There were actually cries of "Bravo!"—unheard of on a professional set. The scene had to be taken over again. The director and assistant director hugged her. They were sorry they had treated her so cavalierly. Jack Haley came over and hugged her, too. "You're terrific," he said. *"Now* I remember you." He realized he had heard her at the Trocadero. He'd never forget that voice. It had that Caruso note in it.

Nonetheless, Judy did not like herself in *Pigskin Parade*. She watched it at a preview with Ethel. "It was the most awful moment in my life," she said later. "I was frightful. I was fat—a fat little pig in pigtails. My acting was terrible. It was just little Kick-the-Can Baby Gumm—just dreadful." She grabbed her mother's arm. "Mom, let's go, I can't bear to see myself." Ethel prevailed on her to stay through the picture. The reviews were hardly raves. The *New York Times* spoke of her "pleasingly fetching personality," and said she knew "how to sell a pop song." She was described as "cute, not too pretty." That was something she didn't have to be told.

If anything assuaged her discontent at playing Sairy Dodd, it was the fact that she had met—and conquered—Jackie Cooper. They had been introduced at one of her first MGM publicity parties on Halloween 1935. He had heard of her. "Ida Koverman has a new singing sensation"—the word had swept like wildfire through the studio. They had much to talk about. He was tutored privately not only because of his busy schedule but because his mother thought life on a film lot was abnormal for a child, and wanted him to pal around as much as possible with neighborhood kids. He'd been Metro's first child star, and was now in the last year of *his* seven-year contract. His mother, like Judy's, had been a pianist in a vaudeville act, and he'd been in show business since he was three. They were both old-timers at the age of thirteen. He invited Judy to his home for dinner—the first time she had been to a boy's home for dinner by herself—and she came back so impressed by that fact that she had been served pâté de foie gras that she wrote an essay about it for Miss MacDonald's class.

They were on the phone to each other for an hour at a time. She confided in him all her doubts about *Pigskin Parade*. She wanted so badly to sing. "I want to be the best singer in the world," she told him. They lied to each other about their ages. *My God,* Jackie thought, *she's older than I am!* He'd learned that she was born in June 1922, three months before he was. He told her he was six months older, which at once made him more than a year her senior because she solemnly assured him that she really had been born in June 1923. They began going steady. Everybody knew it was Judy Garland and Jackie Cooper.

Meanwhile, Ethel had been busy. When Frank died, the family had been living in a small house on Mariposa Lane in Hollywood. Judy's options had been regularly picked up; she was now earning $300 a week, as well as money from records and radio appearances. They moved to a larger home; Ethel bought a two-story pink stucco house with a porch swing and a large lawn, and a swimming pool in the back—their first swimming pool—at 180 South McCadden Place, not far from Peg DeVine. Ethel had made another good friend—Ida Koverman. The two women, both widows, both eager to advance Judy's career, became confidantes.

Once Ethel furnished her new house with the help of Jackie's mother—Mabel Cooper was a professional interior decorator—Ethel began giving Friday night parties for Judy and her friends. They danced to records; there was no drinking, no smoking; Judy and her girlfriends were not allowed to go out alone on dates. They were introduced to boys in proper fashion at each other's homes. Since none of the boys was old enough to drive—they had to be sixteen—their parents drove and called for them.

One day there was a honk outside the house on McCadden Place. There was Jackie, sitting in state in the back of a touring car. Judy ran out. "I wanted to be able to take you places myself," Jackie explained. To parties, even perhaps to movies. He had made such a fuss that Mrs. Cooper hired a young mechanic from the corner garage as his chauffeur so that from now on Jackie could pick up Judy and take her wherever they wanted to go. "Oh, scrumptious!" cried Judy. This was going steady in style.

Now Jackie drove her often to his home, particularly on Sundays, when everyone knew the Coopers held open house. For his fourteenth birthday, September 15, 1936, he put together a four-man band to play for a dance in his basement rumpus room, with himself at the drums, entertaining Judy and his other guests—all part of the young, young film colony: Mickey and Deanna, both fifteen; Judy, not yet fifteen; Peggy Ryan, fourteen; Freddie Bartholomew, going on thirteen; and Donald O'Connor, going on twelve. They talked about Mr. Mayer and Ida Koverman. Everyone liked Ida, but no one could warm up to Mr. Mayer. He was God Himself.

If this was the beginning of Judy's romantic period, it was also her giggly period. She found a perfect foil in a girl her age, Betty O'Kelly, like her petite and quick, with the same sense of humor, but far more shy. Betty was a student dancer. The two became inseparable, Judy the leader, Betty the willing follower. They attended movies together, they mooned soulfully over Fred Astaire in *Swing Time,* they played records by the hour, they ate and slept at each other's houses. Betty had difficulty keeping up with Judy—she was so full of pep. When Betty was ready to fall into bed from exhaustion, Judy was still bouncing about, saying, let's do this or let's do that.

(More than twenty years later, Judy would greet Betty with a wry "My God, you wanted to go to bed at night!")

During these months Judy went swiftly from crush to crush. She began to see less of Jackie. His schedule was getting in the way. She was in a highly emotional state, involved in a secret and forbidden crush on an older man—Bobby Sherwood, her sister Jimmy's beau.

Young Sherwood was twenty-three, a six-foot, handsome, easygoing blond guitar player in Metro's music department. No one knew how Judy really felt about Bobby—not Bobby, surely not Jimmy, not even Judy's blood sister, Betty O'Kelly. (Judy and Betty had taken a solemn oath never to smoke, and to seal their pledge they had pricked their wrists with a needle and commingled their blood.)

Bobby Sherwood had the added glamour of being married and separated from his wife. He had studied music, become a skilled arranger and then the guitarist in Bob Crosby's band before moving to MGM. Jimmy's interest in him—a band musician *and* a married man—led to tense scenes in the house on McCadden Place. Despite Ethel's hostility, he began calling on Jimmy and often took her to the amusement park at Long Beach. Sometimes he said, "Want to come along, Jude?" and Judy dropped whatever she was doing to join them. Jimmy began to realize that her kid sister preferred their company to that of her own friends. Bobby was amusing, he could be witty, and when he talked to her about music, about which he knew a great deal, she listened with complete absorption. The idea that Judy looked upon him as anything other than her adored "Big Brother" Bobby never occurred to Jimmy—or to Bobby.

Then came an afternoon when Jimmy answered the telephone in her upstairs bedroom. It was Bobby. A few days before, he had told Jimmy what she had been desperately hoping for. He had decided to divorce his wife and to marry her. Now he was saying, "I don't think I can go through the divorce courts here, Jimmy—the laws are just awful. Let's go to Vegas." He told her his plans. She would join him and his sister there, where they'd form a vocal trio—he could get them a booking at the Flamingo Hotel—and work for the six weeks he needed to establish Nevada residence and get his divorce.

"Great!" exclaimed Jimmy. "Oh, that's wonderful. That's grand, Bobby."

Within a minute after she hung up she heard the sound of steps on the stairs and Judy came into the bedroom. She was crying. "I didn't know you were going to get married," she said. Jimmy was so shocked—Judy must have been listening on an extension downstairs —that she hadn't even the presence of mind to be indignant. Instead, she said, "I would have told you except I was afraid to tell anybody because I wasn't sure he was going to marry me. He's still married." Then: "But why are you crying?" Judy blubbered through her tears, "Because I'm so happy for you." It was then Jimmy realized that her sister had a crush on the man she was going to marry. She was taken aback. Then she thought, *Oh, well, she's just a kid, she'll find someone her own age.* Aloud she said, "Promise me you won't tell Mama." Judy, sniffling, sighing heavily, promised.

Not long after, Jimmy revealed her secret to Ethel. Bobby was getting a divorce. She was going to Vegas and they'd be married the moment he got it. Jimmy's announcement brought on a family crisis. First Suzy—now Jimmy. Ethel tried her best to control herself.

"You're so foolish, Jimmy," she finally said. "He's got a wife. What makes you think he'll stay married to you if he doesn't stay married to her?"

"Because he loves me," said Jimmy, Judy at her side for moral support.

Ethel said, "He loved her."

"Oh, Mama," Jimmy said, "they just aren't suited for each other."

Ethel said, "He's just not suited to be married, Jimmy. None of them are!" And she stormed out of the room, slamming the door.

It had been a bad week for Ethel. There had been an unfortunate angry scene with Peg DeVine. Ever since Frank's death, Peg had been counseling Ethel to do something about her future. Frank's insurance could go only so far. Suzy was married, and away, and now here was Jimmy, preparing to go off. It was high time Ethel began thinking about herself.

Peg said, "Ethel, you have got to get a contract that pays you at least ten percent of Judy's salary. You have to have your own contract, either with Judy or a separate one with the studio that pays you, because you have to have some kind of income."

Ethel stared at her. "My daughter wouldn't leave me destitute! For Heaven's sake! She's my child!"

Peg said, "Ethel, you are wrong."

Ethel said, "Get out of my house!"

Peg marched out, highly insulted.

Jimmy left 180 South McCadden Place. She went to Vegas, lived alone in a hotel for six weeks, then became Mrs. Robert Sherwood. Ethel had not attended Suzy's marriage to Lee Cahn in Reno. She did not attend Jimmy's marriage to Robert Sherwood in Las Vegas.

Nor did Judy. Her two sisters had married, and she had not been at either wedding. Because Suzy and Jimmy were truly in love they had married the men of their choice despite warnings and protests, and so many scenes, and so many tears.

For Judy, the romantic, it was only too true: Love's way was fraught with suffering. That was how it was.

9

HAD IT NOT BEEN THAT L. B. MAYER, always emphasizing the family spirit of MGM—one for all and all for one—delighted in celebrating birthdays, his own and those of his stars, Judy might never have gotten her great chance. It came almost by accident.

Mayer saw to it, with the help of Ida Koverman, that birthdays were celebrated with parties on the set, their size and elaborateness determined by the star's importance. At 5 P.M., when shooting ended for the day, a huge birthday cake would be wheeled in and Mayer himself would come down, impeccable in dark suit, dark tie and white-on-white shirt, to help cut the cake and lead everyone in singing "Happy Birthday."

He organized studio picnics, with tugs of war and card games, and dancing and swimming parties; he instituted a series of Sunday brunches at his Malibu Beach house. Attendance was compulsory if one was invited. After an abundance of food which included finnan haddie, Mayer's specialty, everyone arranged themselves comfortably in rows of chairs in the enormous living room, a screen rose up out of the floor, and his guests were treated to the latest MGM movie, yet unreleased.

Mayer's particular pride was the MGM commissary. He turned it into a huge family dining room, with blue and white walls, colorful photo montages of scenes from great MGM movies, waitresses in smart blue and white uniforms with blue and white menus featuring dishes named the "Clark Gable Special" and the "Broadway Melody of 1938 Sandwich." Each craft had its own table: actors at one, directors at another, writers at a third, so that each group would be thoroughly informed as to what was going on in its own field. To prevent these highly paid members of the family from going off the grounds to lunch in Beverly Hills (and so waste precious time) Mayer had done his best to transform the commissary into a gourmet restaurant where excellent food could be had at half the price it cost outside. He had hired a fine chef, who lived at the Mayer home for two months while Mrs. Mayer instructed him in the art of Jewish cooking, with emphasis on a rich, chunky chicken soup that became so celebrated that even foreign visitors had heard of it. Mayer's chicken soup, which took a full day of slow cooking to prepare, and his apple pies, made after his mother's recipe, were the butt of innumerable jokes, but everyone agreed they were delicious. The commissary operated at a loss of $50,000 a year; Mayer believed it worth it. He lunched there daily and brought his most distinguished guests there. Before he entered his private dining room at one end —named the Lion's Den for Leo, the MGM lion—he moved briefly among the various tables, greeting everyone, great and small, the benevolent patron smiling and chatting graciously with his faithful protégés.

Mayer's intimates knew his own Horatio Alger story: his trip as a child in steerage from Russia with his wise, vigorous, remarkable mother, whom he worshiped, and his gentle, ineffectual father; his boyhood in St. John, New Brunswick, Canada, where in knee pants he went about the streets with a little wagon collecting junk for his father's shop, meanwhile haunting the synagogues dreaming of a career as a cantor; his introduction to the early nickelodeon film industry, and his swift rise due to his business acumen and skill in judging the tastes of the American public; his puritanical values, his explosive rages, his unabashed sentimentality, his extraordinary ability to cajole—ready to weep instant tears or fall to his knees in prayer to win his point—his respect for Church, God and Motherhood, and his present unchallenged eminence as monarch of all he surveyed. He *was* MGM, and although other studio heads were powerful, he was the most powerful.

At this time MGM's most important star was Clark Gable. Gable's thirty-sixth birthday fell on February 1, 1937. Mayer decided to give him an elaborate party on the set of *Parnell,* which Gable was shooting with Myrna Loy. Arthur Freed was summoned and told to devise "a musical divertissement" in Gable's honor. Freed, in turn, called in Roger Edens. "Roger," he said, "dream up something."

Roger's first thought was of Judy. Here was her chance. Metro was really doing nothing with her. She was simply being wasted. There had been a quick summer two-week trip to New York in 1936 with her mother, where she cut several more Decca records and sang over WHN, the MGM station. The high point of that trip, she had told Edens, was hearing Artie Shaw and his band at the Hotel Lexington. She was so excited that she marched backstage and introduced herself to Shaw with "I'm Judy Garland, I'm a singer with Metro, I just had to tell you how great your music is."

Shaw looked at her in astonishment. He was then twenty-six, he had organized this band only the year before, and he was experimenting in jazz with string and brass arrangements which were too avant-garde for most of his listeners. "How old are you?" he demanded, and when she told him fourteen, he hugged her in delight. "My God, sweetie, you're really something! Do you realize that nobody but musicians like what we're doing? The public hasn't the foggiest idea." He marveled that a girl so young should have the ear and the perception to appreciate such music. Shaw's praise had buoyed her up, but as the months passed after her return to the Coast, and she had nothing to show for them but *Every Sunday*, a four-day two-reeler that meant nothing, and her loan-out to Fox for *Pigskin Parade*, while Metro, her own studio, still had found no picture for her, she had become almost despondent.

This had only been intensified by Deanna Durbin's success. *Three Smart Girls*, recently released, was a tremendous hit, and Deanna had been hailed as a new singing sensation. Frank Nugent in the *New York Times* could not find enough flattering things to say about her. Her voice "was velvety and bell-like"; she had "an ingratiating impudence which peppers her performance and makes it mischievously natural"—why, that was how Judy's notices used to read back when she was Baby Gumm.

Judy had been taken to a preview by Lester Peterson, an MGM publicity aide assigned mainly to Mickey Rooney, and sitting next to Lester, she actually bounced in her seat with impatience as she watched the picture, exclaiming repeatedly under her breath, "When am I going to get my chance! When am I going to get my chance! I can't wait!"

The day the local reviews appeared Judy could not hide her feelings. She had not won, she had lost, and she could not bear it. She and Deanna had vied with each other as peers, they had been thought of as a singing team—why, Mr. Mayer couldn't decide between them—and now, in a few short months, look where Deanna was and look where she was! Deanna Durbin recognized as a star, the lead in a smash musical success already talked about as one of the ten best films of the year, and Judy Garland trailing far behind as comic relief in something called *Pigskin Parade*.

The next morning Ethel telephoned Ida Koverman. Judy was in a state, she had cried all night. Ethel could do nothing with her, Metro had forgotten she existed. Ida said, "Bring her right over." When Judy came to Ida's office, she ran to her and, throwing herself into her lap, cried like a child. "I've been in show business ten years and Deanna's a star and I'm nothing!" The columns were already reporting that Universal would star Deanna in an even bigger musical film, *100 Men and a Girl*, with Leopold Stokowski, the conductor—"And

I'm still taking Music Appreciation from Miss MacDonald!"

Ida comforted her. One really could not blame Judy. "You just wait," she said. "You're going to get your chance, you'll be starred, and you're going to have your footprints in Grauman's Chinese— you'll see."

Now Roger, fired by his idea of using Judy for Gable's party, consulted Ida, who had been his sponsor at Metro, too. It was a propitious moment: Judy's sobs still rang in her ears. Wonderful! she said. Mr. Mayer and every top executive would be there. What a captive audience for their girl!

That next morning Edens told Judy, and she caught his fire. She knew exactly what she wanted to sing—Roger's own arrangement of "Drums in My Heart," which he'd done for Ethel Merman, a great song.

Roger said no. This led to a brief little scene in his office. Roger said, in effect, "Judy, you're too young—and too unsophisticated to sing a song like that." Judy protested. She knew the kind of song she could do—it was precisely this type of number she belted out to such enormous applause: she tore down the house each time she sang one. Roger was firm. "That's for Merman, not for you," he said. "Drums in My Heart" was as inappropriate for fourteen-year-old Judy as "My Man." He explained. If she was to do justice to herself, she must be herself when she sang, not an imitation, however sensational, of Helen Morgan or Ethel Merman or Sophie Tucker. She must sing something related to her, believably her—something she had never done before. He would have something for her when she returned the next day.

Roger had a specific number in mind. He would write a special piece of material for Judy based on one of the dramatic recitatives he had put together for Carmel Myers.

By the time Roger saw Judy the next day, he had whipped up what he wanted her to do and had had it enthusiastically approved by Arthur Freed. Judy rehearsed it and loved it. Neither Freed nor Edens could know then, nor could Judy, that what Edens had devised would overnight catapult her into her film career and place Arthur Freed firmly on his way to becoming the most successful producer of movie musicals in film history.

What had happened was this.

Carmel Myers had done a special three-minute dramatic monologue, half-speech, half-song, based on her own idea, in her Rudy Vallee series. The lyrics had been hers; Roger had set them to the tune of "You Made Me Love You," and added a musical background of his own. Miss Myers' story dealt with a teen-age girl who worked as a maid at the Biltmore Hotel in Los Angeles, who had quarreled with her boyfriend. To cheer herself up, she had taken the bus to MGM, to see the stars—and, if she was lucky, Clark Gable, who was her idol. She asked the guard at the gate if she might sit on the curb and wait for Mr. Gable to come out. The guard said, all right—but she was an adorable child, and he told her she could sit on his chair just outside the gate. She did so, and a few minutes later Gable himself walked out of the gate. He saw her and said, "Come here, Miss." "Who, me?" she asked. "Yes," he said, and when she approached timidly, he asked her, with his heartbreaking smile, "Would you like a ride?" "Oh, Mr. Gable, I'd love it. You've been my idol for years." "Hop in," Gable said, opening the door of his Rolls-Royce, which had just driven up for him. On the way to town, she poured out her story to him. When they reached the Biltmore, she asked to be let out at the employees' entrance. Gable did so, bidding her good-bye with the advice, "Now, you go back to your boyfriend. Everything's going to be all right." And he smiled at her a second time in a way that broke her heart again.

At this moment someone touched her shoulder. She sat up with a start. It was the guard. "Did you see Mr. Gable? He just drove by in his car." "Oh, my goodness," she said. "I must have fallen asleep, I must have been dreaming. I thought I'd met him and we had the most wonderful talk."

Roger had called Miss Myers. Would she mind if he rewrote what they'd done together on Gable into a new piece of special material for Judy Garland? Oh, no, said Miss Myers. She knew Judy and liked her. Months before, Mr. Mayer had telephoned her—she and the Mayer family had been friends for years—that he and Mrs. Mayer were taking a new young singer they'd just signed named Judy Garland to Sophie Tucker's opening at the Mocambo. They'd reserved a table, but they would be late—would Carmel look after her until they arrived? Carmel found Judy sitting alone, joined her and was immediately enchanted. After Sophie Tucker's first number, she turned to Judy to find tears streaming down her face. "Is anything the matter?" she asked, alarmed. No, no, no, Judy said. And then, with an intensity that astonished Carmel, she exclaimed, "If only I could sing like that!" Carmel had come away thinking, *Nothing's going to stop that girl.* She was delighted that Roger, her protégé, was working with Judy.

Roger ingeniously rewrote Carmel's story. The girl became Judy herself, writing a fan letter to her idol, Clark Gable. She was to pour out her heart in a half-recitative, half-song to a photograph of Gable, leading into "You Made Me Love You." She was to be herself, a star-struck teen-ager, not a precocious mimic of Helen Morgan or Ethel Merman or Sophie Tucker. "Oh, gee, Mr. Gable," Judy's fan letter began, "I don't wanna bother you, but I am writing this to you . . . I just had to tell you about the time I saw you in *It Happened One Night.* That was the first time I ever saw you, and I knew right then that you were the nicest fella in the world. I guess it was because you acted so—well, so natural-like, not like a real actor but like any fella you'd meet in school or at parties." She recited this against a musical background with absolute believability. "And then one time I saw you in a picture with Joan Crawford—" her words ran almost breathlessly yet shyly on—"and I had to cry a little, because you loved her so much and you couldn't have her—well—" and here she was sweetly reasonable—"not until the end of the picture anyway. And then one time I saw you in person." Her voice rose subtly in excitement, bringing the listener up with her. "You were making a personal appearance in the theatre and I was standing there when you got out of your car, and you almost knocked me down. Oh, but it wasn't *your* fault—" quickly, apologetically, self-effacingly—"I was in the way. But you looked at me and—" an embarrassed little laugh —"and you smiled. Yah, you smiled *right at me*—" hearing Judy, you were there yourself, as overwhelmed as she—"as if you meant it, and I cried all the way home just because you smiled at me for being in the way." Silly, wasn't it? she was saying over her tears, every inflection, every nuance, of her voice perfect. "Oh, I'll never forget it, Mr. Gable, honest Injun." Even here, what could be bathetic was true and believable. "You're my favorite actor. . . ." Then she went into the song.

Judy, wearing a little brown straw hat and a black and white dress with puffed sleeves and a scooped neck, was led by Roger and Ida (with whom she had had a reassuring lunch in the commissary) to a piano that had been wheeled to the center of the set. She sat down on a little wooden box and, gazing at a framed photograph of Gable, with Roger accompanying her, she sang, "Dear Mr. Gable," and sang it with all her heart.

It was a sensation. Gable, deeply moved—he actually wept—came to her, hugged and kissed her—at which she broke into tears, too—and as they clung together, the flashbulbs popped. Later he sent her a gold charm bracelet, each charm a miniature musical instrument, the largest charm a tiny golden book which opened to show his photograph and the inscription, "To Judy, from her fan, Clark Gable."

Judy had to repeat her performance a few weeks later before Metro's national exhibitors' meeting. This was a major MGM promotional event. Hundreds of important distributors and exhibitors were brought to Hollywood as guests of the studio for a week of dining, entertainment and previews, climaxed by a gala ball held in their honor. Since there was no nightclub in town large enough to accommodate them, MGM transformed Stage 25—its largest sound stage—into a vast nightclub. Food was catered by Hollywood's most fashionable restaurants, and Mayer used the occasion to show off the studio's prize assets.

Judy, dressed in a little white organdy frock with ruffled shoulders which made her appear even younger, sang her song to Gable—and once more there was an ovation. When Gable himself appeared again to thank her, to hug and kiss her, it was pandemonium—and Judy had to repeat it once more. Many exhibitors, watching Judy that night, felt they were seeing film history made. The reaction was unanimous. They wanted this girl put on the screen, and as soon as possible.

Now Judy's team rode high: Freed, who had been so enthusiastic in wanting her signed and had supervised the musical divertissement; Roger, who had guided Judy through her role; and Ida Koverman, who had supported them all. Judy was called into Mayer's office the next day, and Mayer and Ida beamingly told her they were rushing her into a major film, *Broadway Melody of 1938*. Her chance had come.

The film was already in production. The script had to be rewritten to make room for her to sing "Dear Mr. Gable"—and since she was in the film anyway, they wrote a part for her, with a last-minute billing as "That New Hot Little Singing Sensation." She was to play the talented daughter of Sophie Tucker, who ran a theatrical board-inghouse in New York City. Sophie, a typical stage mother, constantly pushed Judy forward to show what she could do—which would give Judy the opportunity to sing not only "Dear Mr. Gable" but several other songs written by Freed and Nacio Herb Brown and arranged by Roger, as well as appear in a dance number.

Broadway Melody of 1938 was the latest in a highly successful series of musicals. They began with *Broadway Melody*, which won MGM its first Oscar for Best Picture of the Year (1929). *Broadway Melody of 1936*, with songs by Freed and Brown, had starred Robert Taylor and Eleanor Powell. The same formula would be used in the new film; the same director, Roy Del Ruth; songs by Freed and Brown; Taylor and Powell starred again, with a cast that included Sophie Tucker, George Murphy, a song-and-dance man, Buddy Ebsen, a dancer, and Willie Howard, the fabled comedian of the Broadway stage.

Now Judy was really taken in hand. From this moment the frenetic years at MGM began. She was never again to be idle for long. She was swept into a whirlwind of activity. Roger worked with her on her voice; Metro's drama coach helped her with her lines; and since she had a dance number with Buddy Ebsen, Dave Gould, in charge of the dance ensembles, rehearsed her soft-shoe and tap routines; while Hal Loomis, the MGM physical therapist, worked to streamline her figure. Not that Judy at this point was really fat; the real poundage would come later. But she was definitely husky, and unfortunately the camera always made one appear much heavier. (He was trying at the same time to put pounds on a lean young newcomer, James Stewart, whose favorite food was chicken, a diet hardly likely to fatten anyone.) Judy underwent a physical examination—Arthur Freed reported later that she was "strong as a young horse"—and, with a physician's approval, in order to cut down her appetite she began taking tablets made of Benzedrine and phenobarbital.

Surprisingly, they had little effect on her appetite. From childhood Judy had been accustomed to huge breakfasts—ham and eggs, potatoes, French toast, butter, jellies—and at both lunch (she always lived near enough to school to come home for lunch) and dinner to Ethel's generous helpings of food. When they were on the road, there was a fourth meal, the midnight supper after their last show, not to mention Judy's special weakness, Hershey chocolate bars; and although she attempted now, with Ethel's help (who herself had a weight problem), to eliminate fattening foods, she was still developing, she was working strenuously, using up tremendous amounts of energy, and she had a genuine need for food. But if the tablets failed to dampen her hunger, they produced other, more dramatic effects.

One day she was hurrying down a corridor and almost collided with Ann Rutherford. "Oh, Ann, I'm so sorry, I ought to look where I'm going." Judy spoke so rapidly that the words all but ran together. Ann looked at her. "Boy, are you full of pep," she said. Judy laughed. "I don't know what it is," she said almost apologetically, "I can't seem to form the words fast enough to get them out of my mouth—" and hurried on.

Benzedrine had been introduced to the film colony only a year before Judy was signed, but by now this wonder pill was in every medicine cabinet. No one thought of it as an evil drug. Few had sufficient experience with amphetamines to learn their dangers. One knew only that they took away appetite, and so were miraculously helpful if you needed to lose weight; that they enabled you to stay up for hours without sleep, a priceless boon if you had dialogue to write, or lines to learn, or parties to go to; that they not only miraculously wiped away exhaustion but gave you a wonderful sense of well-being. Some users complained that Benzedrine made them tense and irritable. Then it was found that the addition of phenobarbital eliminated many of these troublesome side effects, in a pill called Dexedrine. Still later a new refinement was added, amobarbital, and these became known as Dexamyl. Doctors in Beverly Hills were delighted to be able to dispense euphoria in a little yellow tablet to their patients, particularly to actors and actresses whose egos were forever hostage to their latest reviews.

Ethel had been consulted when Judy first took the tablets. Ethel herself was no stranger to medication. Since her thyroidectomy, she had been required to take thyroid pills daily; she also took pills every day for her high blood pressure, and once in a while a sleeping pill; and no one in the Gumm household had ever counted how many aspirins or quinine tablets Frank or Ethel or the girls swallowed to fight off headaches or earaches or colds. But when it became evident that Judy's medication had no great effect upon her appetite, and only speeded up a girl who was already full of bounce, so that at 3 A.M. Judy was moaning, "Mama, I can't sleep," and Ethel was forced to give her a sleeping pill, only to find that Judy, never able to get up early, but who had to be up at 6:30 A.M. for her day's work, was now as one drugged and so needed a Benzedrine to get herself awake, Ethel said, "This is no good—you've got to stop it." Judy agreed and gave up the yellow tablets—then.

Once shooting began, Judy's rigorous new schedule made her feel sometimes as though she were juggling half a dozen balls at the same time. Before, she had only to be on the set at 9 A.M. for school. Now she had to rise three hours earlier to be ready when the makeup people arrived at the house each morning at 7 A.M. to work on her, and then drive her to the studio for the start of shooting at 9 A.M. (Only minors were given this service. Once Judy became eighteen, she would have to be on the set at 7 A.M. for makeup and hairdressing there.) "With my mug, they ought to start working on me at 5 A.M.," she said to Betty O'Kelly, who had been hired as a dance stand-in. Judy still had to get in her three hours of schooling daily. Since she could no longer attend Miss MacDonald's classes, her lessons had to be given on the set, which meant that, having recited her lines as Betty Clayton, the boardinghouse keeper's daughter, she would have to take advantage of an hour's pause by hurrying into a cubicle with Rose Carter, her set teacher, to recite algebra or history. "It's a wonder I don't spout fractions the minute they holler 'Camera!' " she said, giggling, to Betty.

In addition, Judy was now taken over by MGM's efficient Special Services Department. Each morning Judy was telephoned by Mary Schroeder, a quiet, diplomatic woman of thirty-five, who had been assigned to her by Strickling. Mary felt protective toward Judy. She had seen Judy's humiliation at the Coliseum that Saturday when Judy, just signed, had been forced to stop ignominiously in mid-song.

Mary served as Judy's liaison in publicizing *Broadway Melody of 1938*, and Judy's role in it, and her morning calls were to give Judy her promotion schedule for the day, which had to be fitted in between and after shooting. Today, for example, they would spend most of the lunch hour on a Halloween sitting in the Gallery: Judy, dressed in a tailored suit, smiling prettily against a background of huge grinning pumpkins. Though it was only April, the film was to be released in the autumn, and a Halloween feature (which had to be prepared months in advance) in a magazine such as *Photoplay* or

Good Housekeeping would build up both Judy and *Broadway Melody of 1938.* At five o'clock, when shooting stopped on the film, Judy would have to remain for several affectionate mother-daughter stills taken on the set with Sophie Tucker. Carmel Myers had told Ida about Judy's reaction at Sophie's opening at the Mocambo; the word had gone down through channels to Publicity, who immediately recognized its value; and now a photograph of Sophie and Judy gazing fondly at each other would appear in a magazine over a caption revealing that young Judy Garland wanted nothing more in all the world than to become as great a singer as Sophie Tucker.

As soon as these stills were finished, Judy was due for a fitting in Wardrobe—a dress had to be let out or taken in, depending upon Judy's weight, which vacillated from week to week. The days were long. More than once dinner had to be held for Judy until nearly eight o'clock, and then there were her lines to learn and, what Judy found particularly aggravating, school homework to do—although Rose Carter burdened her with as little of this as possible.

When Mary Schroeder gave Judy her schedule each morning, she also asked for human-interest items to feed the columns—anything to warrant a mention of Judy Garland's name. With paragraphs she had gathered, or manufactured to enhance Judy's image as the all-American teen-ager, Mary turned out a feature article on Judy. Each night, she and her colleagues on the publicity staff assigned to other films in production brought their material to a meeting with Strickling's "planting" crew.

This was made up of aides who placed such stories where they would do the most good. Some dealt with "trade" publications, such as *Variety* and the Hollywood *Reporter;* others with newspapers and news services, here and abroad; still others with magazines. The planters worked closely with specific columnists, knowledgeable in what to send to Louella Parsons rather than Hedda Hopper, or to Walter Winchell rather than Jimmy Fidler. They were familiar with the columnists' professional jealousies, and skilled in keeping them happy. They acted as two-way conduits, passing back requests for exclusive interviews or special features. Everyone on Strickling's staff read everything his colleagues had written, so that each knew at all times what was going out to the world about MGM players and MGM pictures.

Strickling himself was a personable, highly diplomatic man in his mid-thirties with a slight stutter, who had a wide acquaintanceship in Hollywood. He had been a newspaper reporter in Los Angeles. Extremely loyal to Mayer, skilled in his profession and remarkably levelheaded, he kept an alert eye on all that happened in the studio. No secrets were held from him. Each of his aides, familiar with the personalities and problems of the stars to whom they were assigned, reported what was deemed important for Strickling to know. Everything was streamlined, everything was funneled. Strickling had Mayer's ear at all times. For MGM's huge and complex human machinery to move smoothly, talent had to be kept happy, their every need anticipated and friction of any kind eliminated at once.

There was a continuous, up-to-the-minute interchange of information among Mayer; Benny Thau, his vice president; Eddie Mannix, his general manager; Sam Katz, his administrative executive; and Ida Koverman, privy to everything, and particularly close to the Music Department. The internal intelligence at Metro was superb. A falling out between Ethel and Judy in the McCadden Place house in the morning was known to Ida by noon, and measures were already under way to meet the problem.

In this sense Metro was a closed society: love affairs, adulteries, abortions, brawls or seductions on the set, gambling, drug or alcoholic excesses—all were known, but all, where possible, were kept within the MGM family. Only in this way could Metro protect its talent, which, as Mayer warned repeatedly, must be treated as precious jewels. This meant, too, that in cases of major scandal Strickling's apparatus—as good a word for it as any other—worked miracles of suppression or interpretation—whatever was required to maintain MGM's good name as well as the sterling character of its stars.

Judy knew her new estate when in the midst of making *Broadway Melody* she and Ethel were invited to a picnic celebrating Mayer's own birthday that July 4. Mickey Rooney and Ann Rutherford, who were then shooting their first Andy Hardy film, had also been invited. Judy and Ann had exchanged notes about Mr. Mayer, particularly what happened if you dared go in to see him with a request. Judy had done so after her scene with Ida Koverman. She had been told you could always see Mr. Mayer about your problems because he liked children, particularly children like herself and Ann, who were close to their mothers. When you went into his office, as Ann put it so well, your problem dissolved in the first ten minutes, along with his tears, because it didn't matter what you wanted, he looked at you tenderly, and he could cry if you asked him the time. (Strickling had once described him as the best actor on the lot.) The tears would cascade down his cheeks and he would reach over and pat your hand gently —you'd think, *Oh, my goodness, I am disturbing this loving man, so busy with so many important matters*—and he would say, "My dear, I was unaware. Don't you know the plans we have for you?" This in his beautifully melodious voice. He would look out the window and say, "Someday your name will be all over the top of this studio along with Metro-Goldwyn-Mayer because we have more stars than there are in heaven, and we plan to list the names of our stars. . . . Your name will be up there, my dear." Another pat of the hand, the ringing of many telephones on his desk, and you were dismissed. Judy would leave, but he had reassured her. Mrs. Koverman had told him how distressed she was—"We must find parts for her," he had been quoted as saying, and they had, had they not?

Today Mr. Mayer could not have been nicer. He danced with Judy, dashing in his white sporting outfit and rakish white hat, and looked on beaming while Ida and Ethel sat talking in the sun and the three young players swam in the pool, wrestling each other on the diving board and fell shouting and squealing into the water. Then later everyone had roasted hot dogs, Mayer doing the honors himself, and toasted marshmallows and drank soda pop. It was a happy afternoon and an augury of the future for Judy, because when *Broadway Melody of 1938* was released in the early autumn of 1937, Judy needed little comforting. Here, said the critics excitedly, was MGM's answer to Deanna Durbin. They spoke of Judy's "amazing precocity" as singer, dancer and actress, and particularly of her "heart-rending song about her unrequited love for Clark Gable."

Her footprints in the Grauman's Chinese forecourt were still before her. But she had appeared in only her first full-length MGM film, and she already had a song that would forever be identified with her.

In quick succession she found herself in two more films. *Broadway Melody of 1938* was no sooner finished than she was put into her first picture with Mickey Rooney, a lighthearted race-track story called *Thoroughbreds Don't Cry*. Here she was Sophie Tucker's niece, and Mickey a brash young jockey who lived at Sophie's boardinghouse.

Thrown together on the set now, Judy and Mickey, both two years older than when they had been in Miss MacDonald's class, were even more irrepressible. They worked together beautifully, Mickey helping Judy where he could out of his vast experience, so that she had a lark making *Thoroughbreds Don't Cry*. Much of her sense of comedic timing came from him. He was always "Mickey" to her, but she was often "Joots" to him, because he was in too much of a hurry to pronounce "Judy." Both had the same spontaneous antic humor; both were born mimics, caricaturists able to catch an essential quality —the ridiculous, the pompous, the stupid—with the slightest gesture. They struck sparks off each other: a glance, a cryptic aside in a language their own, and they were both off in peals of laughter. And Judy's laugh now was a lusty one, rolling and tumbling out of her like water over rocks and building until she would be doubled over, clutching her stomach—a laugh so infectious that no one could withstand it.

"We were the space people of our day," Mickey said later. "We just had to look at each other and we'd crack up—we knew instantly what we were both thinking."

Most of these antics took place off camera, but the two kept even the stage hands laughing. Waiting for a scene to be set up, Mickey, in as many minutes, became Carmen Miranda, the Brazilian dancer, prancing about with a wicker wastebasket for a hat; or Harry Lauder, the Scottish comedian, stumbling over his cane; or Lionel Barrymore, harrumphing and growling with his thumbs in his suspenders. Judy, when she was able to control herself, became a dying Sarah Bernhardt; a precious, black-gloved Gertrude Lawrence; or a hilarious Maurice Chevalier, her lower lip outthrust and a white fruit bowl for a straw hat.

As inevitable, a crush developed between the two. Judy confessed this to Ida. She already knew her pattern. "I have to have a crush on somebody," she said, almost defiantly, and then added a plaintive "but they never last."

Her career moved swiftly. In the late fall of that year she appeared in *Everybody Sing*, with Fanny Brice, the star of the Broadway stage, and Allan Jones, the Broadway singing star—and Judy now had equal billing.

She was, very definitely, on her way.

10

ON A BRIGHT SUNDAY MORNING IN NOVEMBER 1937, Arthur Freed breakfasted with L. B. Mayer at the latter's Malibu Beach house. Freed had brought along a scrapbook of reviews of *Broadway Melody of 1938*. The picture was a financial success, the front office in New York reported with pleasure. But it was Judy everyone wrote about. The two films she had made so quickly since—*Thoroughbreds Don't Cry*, just released, less than three months after *Broadway Melody of 1938*, and *Everybody Sing*, just completed but yet to be released—were all very well. But this girl, Freed said, needed a role that could tap her unusual potentialities. He wanted to make a film with Judy, and wanted Mayer's permission to find a property and buy it for her.

Over their finnan haddie they talked about it. Mayer listened attentively. Freed, now in his early forties, personable, enthusiastic, was a many-faceted man—pianist, singer, actor, lyricist—who had owned his own theatre before coming to Metro in 1929 and, as a prolific songwriter, with Nacio Herb Brown had turned out such hits as "Singin' in the Rain," "Pagan Love Song," "Wedding of the Painted Doll" and many others. Mayer respected Freed for both his musical knowledge and his astuteness in recognizing ability. In years to come Freed would bring to MGM such gifted people as Vincente Minnelli, Gene Kelly, Kay Thompson, Busby Berkeley—giants of the musical film. What Freed and Edens had accomplished with their musical divertissement and then with Judy in the film only confirmed their value. Mayer now had his opportunity to promote Freed from a songwriter to a producer of musicals. The timing was right, too. The Freed-Brown songwriting team was breaking up because Brown wanted to go off on his own. So Freed's proposal fell in with Mayer's own plans.

All right, Mayer told him. Find a property for Judy. He went on: since we have nothing for her now, we'll use the next few months to build her up—send her out on a twelve-week personal-appearance tour in connection, where possible, with her new film, *Everybody Sing*. The film was to open in Miami Beach in late January. After that it would be shown at Loew's State in New York, then in Ohio, Pennsylvania, Michigan—the heartland of America. Arrangements would be made with Judy's agent to put her in the stage show with the picture in each city. The film would help Judy, Judy would help the film. Assign Edens, who seemed to know how to bring out the best in her, to write special material for her, and put Edens in charge of the tour. Mrs. Garland would have to go along, of course—Judy was still a minor—but Edens, not Ethel, would be her accompanist and musical director. Let Judy enjoy herself—go on a shopping spree when she hit New York. Metro would pay the bill. The girl deserved it. She had done three pictures in less than six months. Meanwhile, it was up to Freed to find the right property for her.

A property, Freed said, that would make better use of Judy the person. That girl had a way with a song that could pull you out of your seat—nobody disputed that. But there was something far more to Judy—something in her character, in the fresh wonder-touched quality of her personality, in what emanated from her not only when she sang but when she spoke—a yearning, a reaching out with a purity and genuineness of feeling that tore at your heart. That quality had to be captured, and this could be accomplished only by a script written with Judy in mind. If you analyzed the remarkable success of "Dear Mr. Gable," it was precisely that that Edens had done—he had suited the story to Judy, the Judy he saw behind the funny plump little girl who could sing scorchy songs and dance and do imitations.

As for Judy's last two films, *Thoroughbreds Don't Cry* was really Mickey Rooney's picture. Judy did little but sing a few numbers and do several imitations; and in *Everybody Sing*, while her role was more important—she sang five numbers—she still had to compete with Fanny Brice and her Baby Snooks routine, and the sexy attractiveness of Lynne Carver. The advertisements for *Everybody Sing* printed Judy's name in letters the same size as those of Fanny Brice and Allan Jones, but promised moviegoers a special treat: "Get an eyeful of lovely Lynne Carver, M-G-M's new glamour girl!"

Judy needed her own film, a musical—built around her.

When Freed left Mayer's Malibu Beach home, he was a man with a mission.

It is necessary to pause here and explain what had gone on behind the scenes before Mayer and Freed's breakfast meeting, for this had much to do with the direction of Judy's career. Mayer had been paid an important visit by Judy's agent—Jesse Martin. It had been Martin who, as chief of WHN's Artists Bureau in New York, had put Judy on the air during her brief visit there in 1936. Hearing her, Martin had become almost hysterically enthusiastic. He and his wife, Lorraine, had lavished every kind of attention on Judy, taking her to Coney Island, letting her have her fill of hot fudge sundaes out of Ethel's sight, driving her and Ethel about town, escorting them to the latest Broadway shows—Martin had been beside himself with affection and admiration for Judy. "Ethel, she's going to be a star, a star!" he had exclaimed. "I tell you, if she ever appears on stage at the Paramount, they'll have to get out the mounted police to handle the crowds!" Ethel had been impressed. As a young man Martin had roomed with Benny Thau, now Mayer's chief lieutenant, and a power as vice president of MGM; Martin's father, a distinguished rabbi, had been an intimate of the late William Morris, founder of the giant theatrical agency which bore his name, and had even officiated at the marriage, many years before, of Abe Lastfogel, the present all-important head of the agency. Ethel had considerable respect for what she considered the interplay of Jewish clannishness in the movie industry. Jesse Martin was obviously well connected, and knew his way about on both coasts. When he confided to Ethel that sometime in the future he would leave New York to become an actors' agent in Los Angeles, Ethel invited him and Lorraine, when that time came, to stay with them in their McCadden Place house until they found an apartment.

When the Martins came west, they accepted Ethel's invitation. They stayed with them three weeks—and Ethel asked Martin if he would take on Judy as a client.

She explained that she had discharged Al Rosen some time before and had been managing things herself. Martin could not help being momentarily taken aback. Everyone knew how strenuously Rosen had worked to sell Judy to the studios, and how he had persisted until he managed to open the door to MGM. Ethel obviously wasn't one to let sentiment stand in her way.

She told him she liked his ideas, his enthusiasm for Judy, and, all-important, Judy liked him, she trusted him, she would listen to him. Even more: Harry Rabwin, Dr. Marc's brother, who was her lawyer, had told her that Lastfogel wanted the Morris Agency to represent Judy. Rabwin quoted Lastfogel: "That girl's absolutely got something. I want to represent her and I don't ask ten percent; seven and a half percent will be O.K." This was unheard of. Nonetheless, Judy liked Jesse, and if Jesse would take her on, they'd have a deal. The upshot was that after much discussion—Lastfogel had even come up with a signed contract, and Ethel had carried it about with her, postponing and postponing signing it—Jesse Martin had become Judy's agent.

Now, when the question arose of Judy's tour, Martin was ready. Back in 1936 he had predicted Judy's stardom. Now, calling on Mayer, and bolstered by a deluge of letters which followed Judy's highly successful guest appearance on *The Chase and Sanborn Hour,* he was doubly eloquent: more, to test his conviction, in the last few days he had offered Judy to the Paramount in New York on a four-a-day schedule, asking them a staggering $5,000 a week—and they told him they were ready to consider $3,500!

Mayer bristled. The Paramount? Judy was under contract to Loew's-MGM. How dare Martin think of booking her into an opposition theatre! If she played New York, it must be Loew's State or Loew's Capitol. But they couldn't justify paying $3,500 a week to a performer already under contract to them for $300 a week. Finally, Martin compromised. If Loew's would allow him to negotiate for as much money as he could get for Judy's appearance in cities where there were no Loew's theatres, he would cut the Paramount price in half—to $1,750—for her personal appearance at Loew's State in New York, and in any other Loew's house during her tour. Naturally he would understand that her $300 a week contractual salary would not be paid to her during that time.

Thus it was arranged.

In the luxurious suite she and Judy occupied in the Palmer House in Chicago, Ethel was dashing off a cozy letter to Peg DeVine. The date was March 15, 1938:

Dearest Peg:

Well, at last I have a little time to write you. I have been answering all the damn fan mail. About 100 letters a day! It was about to get me down. Now I have a girl who comes in three times a week for about four hours, which leaves me a little time to write my own letters.

After Pittsburgh next week we have one more week in Detroit, then back here for three days, and then a couple of days in Grand Rapids—and then back home. And am I glad! So many places wanted Judy, we may be home in three weeks, and if no picture is ready for her, we come back here again for two or three weeks. We have had a wonderful trip, but I'm ready to come home for a while. We have seen more people that knew us when, or knew somebody we knew, or is some long-lost relative. . . .

Next trip, Peggy, you'll have to come along and help me answer mail and take care of Judy's clothes. No fooling! I really need help. Bye-bye, see you soon, should be home April 3 or 4th. Will call you.

> Lots of love from Judy and me,
> Ethel

Ethel's flare-up over Peg's blunt warning to get herself on the MGM payroll had long been forgotten, but it had led Ethel to talk to Mayer; and since she was now working for Metro on Judy's behalf, acting as everything from secretary to chaperone, and, as mother and guardian of the artist, accepting the responsibility to see that Judy carried out her obligations to Metro, an arrangement had been made by which Ethel received a weekly salary stipend out of Judy's salary.

It was, as Ethel wrote, a wonderful trip. For the first time Judy was getting star treatment, the kind she would receive for the rest of her life. At the world premiere of *Everybody Sing* at the Sheraton Theatre in Miami Beach, there were klieg lights sweeping the sky, Judy and Ethel arriving on a train from Hollywood that included a special coach filled with movie critics, and then a triumphant motorcade to the Roney Plaza Hotel, where, as the newspapers respectfully reported, "Miss Garland will rest and prepare for her personal appearances at 8 and 10 P.M."

Her appearance at Loew's State in New York had been the greatest triumph of her life so far: her name in enormous letters on the marquee—Judy Garland headlined the bill. She had begun opening night tense and frightened. (When Jesse Martin first told her the sums of money he had negotiated, she had thrown her arms around him and cried in panic, *"What will they want of me for that money, how can I live up to it? I won't be able to do it, but oh, it's so wonderful, thank you, Jesse, thank you . . ."*) She had clung to Ethel's arm backstage, while in the pit Roger Edens played her introduction.

When she went onstage, she teetered on her high heels, her legs trembling so uncontrollably that she almost collapsed until she discovered that if she locked her knees, making her legs rigid from hip to toe, her feet planted slightly apart, standing flatfooted and solid, she felt secure. It was a characteristic stance she would always take thereafter. Her first notes of Roger's arrangement of "Take Me Back to Manhattan" were tentative, and though Roger whispered encouragement, the audience began to break out in a rash of coughs—always the mark of disaster in the making. What saved her was a baby's cry in the balcony. It came in a sudden moment of embarrassed silence; it seemed as though the baby were trying to mimic Judy's attempt, a moment before, to hit a note. This struck her as so absurd—that infant was trying to help her, that baby could do what she could not—that, as had happened so many times before in the adventures of the Gumm Sisters, Judy began to giggle and, despite herself, burst into laughter. Her infectious laugh won the audience. They laughed and applauded. Suddenly she was at home, enveloped by the delighted affection that flowed over her—and she went into her songs, sure and true. She sang "Dear Mr. Gable," and then the spectacularly popular "Bei Mir Bist Du Schön," and many others; and when she finished, there was a mighty roar of applause. They liked her, they liked her tremendously.

Backstage, she received like a prima donna, flanked by a beaming Ethel and Roger, in a dressing room banked with flowers. Two young songwriters in the audience were among the first to come backstage to visit her; they were Sammy Cahn and Saul Chaplin, who had collaborated on the English version of "Bei Mir Bist Du Schön." It had originally been the work of Sholom Secunda and Jacob Jacobs, Yiddish songwriters. Judy could scarcely believe Chaplin's words. What she had done with that song! "Judy, we've heard every kind of version—yet you made it different. You made it yours!" She had done everything technically that every skilled singer did, but she had put an emotion into it. "It just knocked me out," he told her. He all but bowed to her in deference. Then came Artie Shaw, who kissed her on the cheek, bringing a flush to her face, and took her two hands in his and told her with his almost hypnotic intensity, "Now I understand why you were so smart. What a voice, what an ear you have! You're great, Judy, you're going on to great things!"

There was another distinguished musician in the audience that night. He had no reason to go backstage to greet her. He had been struck by the emotional longing in the girl's voice, the ache for fulfillment—he could not put his finger on it. But he thought as he

110

Judy, age fifteen, attending a preview of *Broadway Melody of 1938*.
(Pictorial Parade)

Frances Ethel Gumm, in
Grand Rapids, age 1½.

The Gumm Sisters, 1929: *(l. to r.)*
Suzy, Jimmy and Baby Gumm.
(Nancy Barr)

1933: *(l. to r.)* Suzy, Jimmy and Judy.
(Pictorial Parade)

Mother Ethel and Judy at the house on Stone Canyon Road, 1939. (Pictorial Parade)

Family portrait: Judy with Ethel, sister Jimmy (Mrs. Bobby Sherwood) and three-year-old Judalein, Jimmy's daughter. (Pictorial Parade)

Lunch at MGM: *(l. to r.)* Freddie Bartholomew, Peggy Ryan, Mickey Rooney, Deanna Durbin, Judy, Jackie Cooper. (Pictorial Parade)

Off-camera antics on the set of *Listen, Darling,* 1938: *(l. to r.)* Freddie Bartholomew, Judy and Scotty Beckett. (Pictorial Parade)

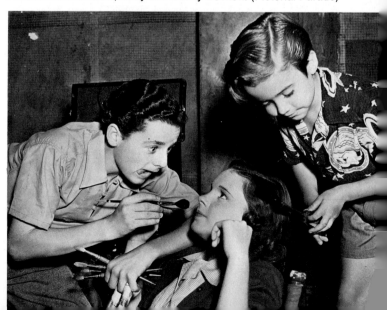

Judy and Ray Bolger dance down the Yellow Brick Road in *The Wizard of Oz,*
1939. (Pictorial Parade)

Judy, with Tom Drake, in *Meet Me in St. Louis,* 1944. (Cinemabilia Inc)

Judy and Mickey Rooney in *Babes in Arms,* 1939.

Studio portrait, *Presenting Lily Mars,* 1943.

Joseph L. Mankiewicz in 1961. (Pictorial Parade)

Artie Shaw with his band, 1938. (Pictorial Parade)

On the set of *The Clock:* Judy, Robert Walker and Vincente Minnelli, 1945.
(Pictorial Parade)

Adolphe Menjou, Ronald Colman, Judy and Mickey Rooney attend a broadcast for the British War Relief Association, 1941. (Pictorial Parade)

Co-stars Judy and Fred Astaire on the set of *Easter Parade,* 1948. (Pictorial Parade)

Judy with Barron Polan, friend and confidant, 1943. (Pictorial Parade)

Hedda Hopper, David Rose and Judy, 1941. (Pictorial Parade)

Peter Lawford with Judy at
the Mocambo, 1944.
(Pictorial Parade)

Judy dancing with director
Charles Walters at Ciro's,
1943. (Pictorial Parade)

Mr. and Mrs. Vincente Minnelli on their wedding day, June 15, 1945. (Jack Albin)

Frank Sinatra joins Judy and Van Johnson at the Mocambo, 1943.
(Pictorial Parade)

Judy with friend and manager Carleton Alsop, 1949. (Pictorial Parade)

Judy's musical mentor, Roger Edens, escorts her to the premiere of *The Song of Bernadette*, 1943. (Pictorial Parade)

Sid Luft and his wife at the premiere of *A Star Is Born* at the Pantages Theatre, Hollywood, 1954. (Pictorial Parade)

left the theater, *That girl is all yearning, all hope for the wonderful world that lies on the other side of the moon.* He was E. Y. ("Yip") Harburg, the lyricist, who could not know that within the next year he would be called to Hollywood to write the unforgettable words of a song called "Over the Rainbow" for the girl he had heard this night. So it might be said that a strange magic was at work even then on all who knew and were touched by Judy.

If Roger Edens had been a man who allowed himself to write in *Variety*'s colorful Broadwayese, he himself might have dictated *Variety*'s review:

Youngster is a resounding wallop in her first vaude appearance (as Judy Garland). Comes to the house with a rep in films and after a single date on the Chase & Sanborn radio show. Apparent from outset that the girl is no mere flash, but has both the personality and the skill to develop into a boxoffice wow in any line of show business. Applause was solid and she encored twice, finally begging off with an ingratiating and shrewd thank you speech.

Roger, after all, had coached her on how to end her act, and what to say if she had no more encores prepared.

The scene was repeated in city after city. When they reached Grand Rapids, they found it was Judy Garland Day. The New Grand still stood, and Judy, deeply touched, appeared on the same stage where more than twelve years before she had sung "Jingle Bells" and first felt that magical enveloping wave of acceptance flow over her from the audience. Ethel drove her by the white corner house in which they had lived, and which in her memory had seemed so much larger. Another high point came in Columbus, Ohio, where she was inducted, the first girl in history, as the Sweetheart of Sigma Chi, after the famous college song, by the Ohio State University chapter of the fraternity. This led, thanks to Howard Strickling's alertness, to a four-page picture spread, "Life Goes to a Party," in *Life* magazine —the first of many stories on Judy to appear in *Life*.

Although Judy was two months short of sixteen, MGM publicity described her as fourteen. So the press wrote about this astonishing little fourteen-year-old miss, and Judy played her role. She chattered away, giving the first of what was to grow into a vast repertoire of interviews mixing fact with fiction, depending upon how much she felt like improvising. No, she didn't wish a film career, she said. She was in pictures by accident. Someone had heard her singing around a campfire when she was on vacation at Lake Tahoe, and that had led to her MGM contract, thanks to Mr. Louis B. Mayer, whom she loved, as she loved the studio. Actually, nursing was to be her life-work. As soon as she graduated from high school she would become a trained nurse. She was going to build a hospital for crippled children on land she owned in California, with gay walls and colorful decorations because she had been hospitalized as a child and had never forgotten how dreary and frightening that experience was.

At the same time she spoke excitedly of her shopping spree with Roger Edens. He had taken her to the finest Fifth Avenue shops in New York, and bought her a complete new wardrobe (the first time —she did not say this—that her clothes had not been chosen by Ethel).

Roger had told Freed he could not take Judy on tour without outfitting her from head to toe. In his opinion, she had been frowzily dressed as far back as he knew her. He could not tell Judy that, despite her intelligence, her instinctive sense of quality, she simply had no taste in clothes. She would always have to be advised how to dress properly. She had never bought her own things. Ethel had shopped for the girls, ordering dresses and coats sent out on approval. The three sisters disliked shopping for clothes. After years of putting on and taking off costumes backstage, it was an ordeal. Even when they were grown, Ethel shopped for them. She simply ordered three of everything—three dresses, three houserobes, three hats. Now, when Judy walked into a shop, she nearly always chose badly. The same was true of Jimmy. Only Suzy had a real clothes sense.

But there was a moment in New York when Roger, after all the shopping was done, took Judy to dinner in the Rainbow Room high atop the RCA Building in Rockefeller Center. They stood at one of the huge picture windows, looking down over the exciting, dream-fraught panorama of Manhattan spread below them, at night a fairy-land of lights and towers and spires floating like a vision between the two rivers. Roger was not one for gestures, or for melodrama. He was always low-keyed. But he indicated the city below her with a sweep of his hand and said, "Judy, all this will be yours one day."

This—from Roger. She was in tears.

Arthur Freed had found his property for Judy. It was *The Wonderful Wizard of Oz*. Freed had read the Oz stories as a boy of nine, and

112

had been enchanted by the story of Dorothy, a lonely, lovable orphan who lived with her Uncle Henry, a Kansas farmer, and his wife, Aunt Em. Both were stern, careworn, kindly but joyless persons, and Dorothy's only playmate was her small dog Toto. One day she is caught up by a cyclone that whirls her through the sky and deposits her, unhurt, with Toto in her arms, in the magical Kingdom of Oz, as rich with color as the plains of Kansas were gray, and as full of happy people singing and going gaily about their work as her own uncle and aunt were dour and silent.

This fairy tale, in which the girl goes off on a journey with a straw man, a tin woodman and a cowardly lion to find the Wizard of Oz and plead with him to give each what he most truly wishes—the straw man a brain, the tin woodman a heart, the lion courage—required a young girl with precisely the kind of innocence Judy projected—that quality of wide-eyed trust, without coyness and artifice. One would almost have thought that L. Frank Baum, the author, had had Judy in mind when he described Dorothy: "She was loving and usually sweet-tempered, and had a round rosy face and earnest eyes. Life was a serious thing to Dorothy, and a wonderful thing, too, for she had encountered more strange adventures in her short life than many other girls her age."

The original book had been written in 1899 by Baum, a New York printer and editor. As the years passed he wrote other Oz stories. Baum had desperately wished for a daughter, whom he would have named Dorothy. When fate ordered otherwise and gave him four sons, he had poured out in his Oz stories all the wonder and fantasy that would have delighted the daughter he never had. They became an obsession with him. He set up his own company to produce a series of films based on them—there had even been a Broadway musical production many years before—but the films failed. Eventually Baum's company went out of business, and Samuel Goldwyn acquired *The Wizard* for $40,000. He had held it now for nearly five years and done nothing with it.

Freed asked Mayer's agent, Frank Orsatti, to buy the book without telling Goldwyn why he wanted it. Orsatti was one of Mayer's closest friends. He had been his bootlegger during prohibition. In early 1938 Goldwyn sold *The Wizard* to Orsatti for a profitable $75,000.

Judy was still on tour and *The Wizard* had not yet been bought when Freed excitedly dashed off a memo to Mayer listing the cast he had envisaged. For Dorothy, Judy, of course; the Scarecrow, Ray Bolger; the Tin Woodman, Buddy Ebsen; the Cowardly Lion, Bert Lahr; Aunt Em, Edna Mae Oliver; Uncle Henry, Charles Grapewin; the Wizard, W. C. Fields. There was to be a great deal of negotiation before anything was done. Nick Schenck, the head of Loew's in New York, wanted Shirley Temple to play Dorothy, if she could be borrowed from Fox. She represented sure box office in a project that would involve a tremendous amount of money.

All this put Mayer in a dilemma. Fond as he was of Freed, this was too ambitious an undertaking for Freed's first musical attempt. Musicals were always expensive; the technical costs would be overwhelming. Fantasy demanded the most extravagant special effects, especially this one—a full-fledged cyclone, houses, trees and people floating through the sky, witches and fairies appearing and vanishing in bursts of flame and floating bubbles, not to speak of an army of flying monkeys, and the Munchkins, which would mean bringing midgets from all parts of the world. To top all this, part of the picture would have to be filmed in Technicolor, still a new process, to emphasize the contrast, as Baum had done in his book, between the drabness of Kansas and the magical, rainbow-hued magnificence of Oz. The budget could go over two million dollars. Mayer knew the sorry history of the earlier film attempts. Even were the picture well done, fantasy was a gamble at the box office. Both children and parents had to like it. *The Wizard of Oz* probably would not be commercial, and most likely MGM would have to write it off as a prestige picture.

Mayer told Freed in as many words: "I can't take a chance on you going down the drain—and the studio as well—with this. You can begin it, but I am going to bring in Mervyn LeRoy as the producer. You will be associate producer." Mayer had just hired LeRoy at a reported $6,000 a week away from Warner Brothers, where he had directed such classics as *Little Caesar,* with Edward G. Robinson, and *I Am a Fugitive from a Chain Gang,* with Paul Muni. LeRoy not only had experience as a producer and director, but happened to be married to Doris Warner, daughter of Harry Warner, head of Warner Brothers. Mayer was not unaware that there might be certain advantages to be derived from what was both a social and business relationship.

Mayer reassured Freed further. Since LeRoy was currently spending much time on his newest film, *Dramatic School,* starring Luise Rainer, Freed would have an almost free hand in the story conferences, in helping cast the picture, and, since music was his field and not Mervyn's, in hiring the songwriters. Freed wanted to have his good friends Harold Arlen and "Yip" Harburg, the songwriting team whose musical *Hooray for What!,* starring Ed Wynn, was a Broadway hit.

Then Mayer, the diplomat, spoke to LeRoy. He knew how busy he was, but would he become producer of *The Wizard of Oz,* and work with Arthur Freed, who wanted to learn the ropes? As a songwriter Arthur would be helpful in developing the story line of Dorothy's songs, making them fit smoothly into the plot, and so knit together the entire production. In too many musicals songs were inserted that simply had nothing to do with what was going on. Arthur would guard against this.

The die was cast. It would take several months before the book was adapted, a screenplay approved, the songs written and fitted in, the appropriate players signed, the challenging special effects and special makeups created—how do you produce a straw man, a tin man, a lion, all of whom speak and all of whom are believable?—but a tentative date, autumn 1938, was set for the inception of what would take nearly a year before it reached the screen.

Judy returned from her tour to celebrate her sixteenth birthday with a party given by Ethel. Everyone was there, from old family friends like the Rabwins and DeVines to some thirty of Judy's friends from the various studios. Ethel had a treat for her: follow a red ribbon from the front door upstairs through her room, downstairs again, out the back door, beyond the swimming pool, around the corner to a side street, and there Judy would find her birthday present—a red roadster, her first car.

There were other surprises, one sad, one happy. Suzy's nearly three-year-old marriage to Lee Cahn had broken up, and she was now back living with them; and Jimmy, who lived not far away in Los Angeles now with her husband, Bobby Sherwood, who had his own band, had become a mother. She had given birth in May to a little girl, first named Judy Gail, and later "Judalein"—little Judy, in German, to differentiate her from big Judy, who now had her first and, as it turned out, only niece.

In these months there was a third surprise, not at all welcome to Judy and her sisters. Laura Gilmore had died the year before, and now Ethel, the widow, and Will Gilmore, the widower, were beginning to see each other. Gilmore now lived not far from Los Angeles, and Ethel would visit him there, or he would visit her. The girls were glad that Ethel had male companionship—she had never been seen with another man after Frank's death—but did it have to be Will Gilmore with his crisp, authoritarian, slide-rule mind?

Yet Judy had little time to concern herself with these family developments. She had hardly returned when she was thrown into two more quick pictures, pending the final decisions on *Wizard* and the date when the project finally got off the ground. While she had been on tour her future had been discussed by others than Arthur Freed. By this time Mickey Rooney had played the role of a boy called Andy Hardy in two Grade B films which had done astonishingly well at the box office. Both were extremely low-budget productions. The first was *A Family Affair*, released in April 1937, in which Mickey first appeared as Andy, the likable adolescent son of Judge Hardy, then played by Lionel Barrymore. The second, released a few months later, was *You're Only Young Once*. This time Judge Hardy was played by Lewis Stone, because Lionel Barrymore was in London. A new girlfriend was introduced for Andy—Ann Rutherford, as Polly Benedict. *You're Only Young Once* did so well that a third picture with the same basic cast was turned out so swiftly that it was on the screen only three months after its predecessor. By now the Hardy name was known, and this film was called *Judge Hardy's Children*. Again, it was successful. Budgeted at $200,000 dollars, it had earned a million and a half. The others had done almost as well.

New York was jubilant. Howard Dietz, in charge of national advertising, sometimes spent $800,000 advertising a high-budget picture, with questionable returns; whereas he spent as little as $75,000 advertising these inexpensive Andy Hardys—and look at the money they brought in!

Clearly, Metro had found a paying formula, and an inexpensive one, in these homespun, small-town family pictures, in which the brash but basically decent Andy was teamed with his outwardly stern but always understanding father, and Polly Benedict as his girl-

friend. The MGM executives thought of everything. Polly was sufficiently taller than Andy to make their young love affair more laugh-
able than dangerous. There was nothing the most prudish audience
could not accept.

Now a fourth Andy Hardy picture was on tap. The MGM unit
turning out these B films was headed by Joseph Cohn and his associate, Carey Wilson, as assistant producer and scriptwriter, who also
genuinely enjoyed working with younger players, even inviting
them to parties at his home and encouraging them to confide their
teen-age love problems—all of which helped give the scripts
verisimilitude. Cohn subscribed to one of Mayer's cardinal star-
making principles: *You build unknowns by pairing them with
knowns. One pulls up the other.*

MGM history exemplified this repeatedly. Norma Shearer worked
with John Gilbert and Lon Chaney and became a star; Clark Gable
was paired with Norma Shearer and became a star; though Robert
Taylor was a star before *Camille,* it was his appearance in that film
with Garbo that ensured his fame; Myrna Loy and Rosalind Russell
were paired with Taylor and Gable, and they became stars. Ann
Rutherford was already becoming known for her work with Mickey
Rooney; and before the Andy Hardy series would be over, eleven
more would be turned out in the next eight years, and they would
have been used to catapult such young players as Lana Turner,
Esther Williams, Donna Reed, Kathryn Grayson and others into
prominence.

Cohn and Wilson called on Benny Thau, who was in charge of the
B units. Cohn said, "My feeling is that this Andy Hardy series could
use some new strength—we need a fresh face that will help the
picture." He had Freddie Bartholomew in mind. Freddie had just
finished *Captains Courageous.* He had been magnificent. He was
ripe for more exposure and it could only help the series.

Thau once more came to Judy's support. A small, dapper man,
cautious, deliberate in action in sharp contrast to Mayer's quick,
decisive movements, Thau carefully fixed a cigarette in his holder
and thought the matter through. "No," he said, finally. "Freddie
Bartholomew doesn't need help. He's established. The one that
needs help is Judy Garland. She's just on the edge of big things—let's
put her into it." He had observed how well Judy and Mickey had
played off each other in *Thoroughbreds Don't Cry.*

The new picture was named *Love Finds Andy Hardy*, and a part was quickly written in for Judy, the new face in the Andy Hardy series. But she was not to play the girl for whom love came to Andy Hardy. Instead, her role was her first as Betsy Booth, who, in the Andy Hardy stories, always was the sober, sensible, not too pretty but true-blue friend of Mickey, but never his girl. In this instance she is an out-of-town visitor who falls deeply in love with Mickey, who hardly gives her a thought because his head is turned not only by Ann Rutherford but even more by a sexy, red-haired newcomer named Lana Turner, a protégée of LeRoy whom he had brought to MGM with him.

Compared to Ann and Lana, both tall, slim and beautiful, Judy is a simple, plump little plain Jane who has to advise Mickey in his unhappiness while she suffers the pangs of her own unrequited love. It was even more painful for her to realize that Mickey, now eighteen, could hardly keep his hands off Lana. In the picture Judy helped him out of his dilemma, but if any message was coming through to Judy in this, her fifth feature film—and the fifth in which she was cast as the girl whom no one whistled at—it was the same message and only confirmed the conviction relentlessly gnawing in her during her most susceptible years—that men looked elsewhere than at her.

Even before *Love Finds Andy Hardy* was released that summer of 1938, Judy was shuttled into the second film, *Listen, Darling*, in which she was paired with Freddie Bartholomew.

The making of this picture had its own ironies for Judy, one particularly painful. For the first time it was not she who had the crush —but the boy, Freddie. And this in real life. Bartholomew had always been a year or so too young for Judy's crowd. Though Freddie already had behind him such fabulous roles as Greta Garbo's son in *Anna Karenina*, and starring in such major productions as *David Copperfield, Little Lord Fauntleroy* and *Captains Courageous*, he was not yet fifteen. He was taller than Judy, but she still looked on him as a delightful and intelligent younger brother.

But Freddie's crush on Judy was genuine. He believed himself madly in love with her. Each time he called on her, the very picture of the well-turned-out British boy, he presented her with a single gardenia. In a private code they alone understood, he wrote her ardent love notes, which he faithfully pinned each morning on her dressing-room door, where MGM publicity aides tried vainly to decipher them before she arrived.

Judy at this point had begun to write poetry—always tragic, as adolescent verse usually is, and the theme nearly always her death because of rejected love. One of her most effective and romantic poems read:

> Would that my pen were tipped with a magic wand
> That I could but tell of my love for you,
> That I could but write with the surge I feel
> When I gaze upon your sweet face;
> Would that my throat were blessed by the nightingale
> That I could but sing of my heart's great love
> In some lovely tree flooded with silver,
> Sing till I burst my breast with such passion,
> Sing, then fall dead to lay at your feet!

After all, had not Juliet at the age of fourteen taken her life for love of Romeo and had he not done the same?

The poems were not written to anyone real but to the *verray parfit gentil knight* Judy waited for, but Freddie glowed with the knowledge that Judy liked him and that when they went to the movies they sat holding hands through the entire picture.

The greatest irony, however, came to Judy in the plot of the picture they were making together.

The theme of *Listen, Darling* was simple. Mary Astor was the widowed mother of Judy and her little brother, Scotty Beckett. Freddie was Judy's best friend and confidant. Judy's mother, a lonely woman, was being courted by Gene Lockhart, a hard-bitten, unsympathetic disciplinarian, a man neither Judy nor Freddie could endure—and whom Judy's mother was prepared to marry. Unable to persuade her mother to give him up, Judy and Freddie, with Scotty's help, actually kept her captive in a trailer while they drove about until they found the right man for her. And in the final scene Judy's mother married the man everyone loved and wanted as a stepfather, gallant, warmhearted, understanding Walter Pidgeon.

One can imagine how Judy felt, playing this role before the camera even as the story was unfolding in real life at home as Ethel saw more and more of Will Gilmore. For when Gilmore came over to visit Ethel, and the two spoke about their children—the widow with three daughters who had no father to confide in or consult, the widower with two sons and a daughter who had no mother to confide in or consult—and when there were disputes between Judy and Ethel, Gilmore invariably gave Ethel moral support, and both bore down on Judy. The real-life ending for Judy was far less happy, because Ethel ultimately secretly eloped with Gilmore to Yuma, Arizona, to Judy's chagrin and utter bewilderment, as well as that of Suzy and Jimmy, on November 17, 1939—the anniversary of Frank Gumm's death.

Suzy and Jimmy, speaking out of their own experience, tried then to explain it to Judy. Perhaps it was Ethel's way of seeking to erase the terrible pain of their father's death by replacing it with a joyous deed—her marriage to a man she loved. And after all, it was Ethel's birthday as well.

But Judy did not, could not, accept it. It was four years to the day since her father died, a day sacred to his memory. And her mother and Will Gilmore: What had been their relationship as far back as those first years in Lancaster, when she lay awake late at night, trembling, while her mother and father had at each other so bitterly? What secrets were there between them that made her mother seem to distrust all men with the exception of Will Gilmore? How long had these two loved each other, how much had her father known, how deeply had he been hurt? And her mother had dared to do this now —and on this day—and with this man.

Judy never forgave her.

It was one more accounting that would never be settled.

For years Judy was to say, "That was the most awful thing that ever happened to me in my life. My mother marrying that awful man the same day that my daddy died."

#

WHILE PREPARING TO BE TRANSFORMED INTO DOROTHY OF *The Wizard of Oz,* Judy fell in love, deeply and over her head, for the first time. The man was Artie Shaw.

It was in 1939, and it began in the spring; it grew through a year which saw important and emotional family changes at home. It was an exciting, now happy, now despairing roller coaster of a year for Judy, and it became a preview of what was to happen so often in the years that followed.

Judy had won her role in *Wizard*, though for a while it had been anything but certain despite the fact that Harold Arlen and "Yip" Harburg had come to Hollywood to write the songs—for Judy, for no one else. Mervyn LeRoy, the producer of *Wizard of Oz*, although always insisting that he envisaged Judy from the first to play Dorothy, was still under pressure from New York to borrow Shirley Temple from Fox. Not only was Shirley certain money in the bank, but she was ten years old—a far more suitable age than Judy, now nearly seventeen, to play a naïve little girl who believed in witches and fairies. Though Shirley Temple was basically not a singer, this astonishing child did everything well. She had sung in films. Indeed, MGM front-office interest in her was so strong that an outraged Freed had to dispatch an even more outraged Roger Edens to audition Shirley for the role. He returned with a negative report. Consummate little actress that Shirley was, in song, in personality, in *soul*, Judy was Dorothy.

In the end the matter became academic when Fox refused to loan Shirley out.

Judy, assured the part, accepted the news with a certain equanimity. No one involved knew they were embarking on what was to become a classic: that for generations to come Judy Garland would be Dorothy, and Dorothy would be Judy Garland; that *The Wizard of Oz* would become an annual feature on television to enchant millions of children and adults all over the world.

All that mattered then was that in the winter and spring of 1939 Judy would be making her seventh picture, *The Wizard of Oz*—and that at the same time a major interest was Artie Shaw, who was now one of the world's most popular bandleaders. And he was now in Los Angeles.

Shaw's appeal was not only musical—bandleader, composer, virtuoso clarinetist—but he had a reputation as a man of serious thought and constant self-appraisal who suffered fools badly, spoke his mind sharply, without regard, apparently, for consequences, and was, beyond all this, a man whom the most glamorous women found all but irresistible. In his late twenties, he was already twice married and twice divorced, and was seen escorting some of the most beautiful girls in town.

He had come to California to appear with his band at Los Angeles' largest dance hall, the Palomar Ball Room, to continue his broadcasts on the *Old Gold* radio program, and to play himself in a film with Lana Turner called *Dancing Co-ed.*

It was, to all intents, Artie Shaw's year in Hollywood.

On the night of February 10, 1939, his opening night at the Palomar, before a huge audience which included Judy and her mother, halfway through his performance Shaw collapsed and had to be rushed unconscious to the hospital, where he was to remain for weeks on the edge of death.

What had happened was this.

Some time before while playing in New York Shaw had come down with a strep-throat infection, plus complications, which briefly hospitalized him. Judy had wired him flowers and a get-well message. Shaw, with the help of a newly discovered miracle drug, sulfanilamide, fought off the ailment and, still highly dosed with sulfa, came to California. What neither he nor his doctors knew was that he was extremely allergic to sulfa compounds. This had finally caught up with him at the Palomar.

Now, in the hospital, it was discovered that he was suffering from a rare, nearly always fatal blood disease known as granulocytosis, brought on, apparently, by his earlier medication. The illness was comparable to leukemia in that one's white corpuscles were destroyed faster than the body could manufacture them. Less than ten persons had been known to have survived it.

Judy, though fully involved in *Wizard,* insisted that Ethel and she visit Artie at the hospital. He lay unconscious for days, with brief moments of lucidity. On the third visit Ethel balked. That she had not done so immediately was something of a wonder. Given her attitude toward musicians, her disapproval of Suzy's and Jimmy's marriages to them, now tragically confirmed by a weepy Suzy at home, and the possibility that her youngest and most vulnerable of daughters might now be going in the same direction, her reaction was understandable. But Judy would not hear of staying away; and when her mother refused to accompany her, Judy drove over every few evenings in her roadster with her friend and MGM publicist,

Betty Asher, newly assigned to her by Howard Strickling.

One of Shaw's first memories when he finally came to was of Judy's face hovering over him: "That absolutely marvelous little face, with freckles, the brown eyes, the reddish hair, looking at me with consummate tenderness"—mythlike, dreamlike, not real. He could hear her whispering, "You're going to be all right, Artie. . . . Don't worry. You'll be all right." She had come there many times, the nurses told him. Whenever he awoke, it seemed she was there, leaning over him, the Constant Nymph, encouraging him, comforting him, willing him to get well.

When he grew strong enough to leave the hospital for a little while each day, Judy appropriated him as her private outpatient, taking him on long drives. She gave him her warmth, her enthusiasm, her delight in him, and he was overwhelmed by tenderness for her—he had never had a sister, and she was close to what he would have wanted if he had had one. He never thought of her as someone to be made love to—the idea had simply not occurred to him. When he wanted that, there were others to whom he turned; with Judy it was pure delight in her as an adorable companion, a joy in being with someone he loved in a very idealistic way.

He could hardly contain himself in teaching her, in conveying to her his own excitement about himself, themselves, the world. He knew he was on the top. He was young, he was handsome, he had money, and in this city in which they found themselves, this dreamland . . . He would joke with her as they drove, saying, "You're little Frances Gumm from Grand Rapids, and I'm little Arthur Arshawsky from the Lower East Side of New York, and look where we are!" He would have her stop the car, and breathe deeply. "Smell the wind, Judy—when it's right, like now, it's all orange blossoms, you can smell the fragrance of the whole San Bernardino Valley." And the people here, gifted, talented, each beautiful in his own way, gathered here, in this one incredible town, from all over the world . . . "We're the chosen few, Judy, we're the chosen people! We've got no place to go but up, and it's never going to end!" Judy would laugh, and cling to him, and he would hug her, and try to convey to her what an absolutely marvelous creature she was—eager, lovely, outgoing, thirsty for knowledge, just beginning to feel the wonder of being young and alive.

He was amazed, as he had been in New York, that she should have understood the music he and his band played at the Hotel Lexington three years before. And her sense of humor! That laugh of hers, that belly laugh that caught everyone and rendered them helpless, it just burst out of her—she could roll on the floor, clutching her stomach, howling with glee. He could make her laugh, and, laughing together, they were two golden people in a golden world.

When he was nearly recuperated, they continued their drives, but he did not return to the Palomar; his band stayed on, to play there, to make its broadcasts, and the papers announced simply that he was still recuperating. He lived quietly in a house he had bought on Summit Ridge Drive.

Meanwhile, with everything going well financially, Judy and Ethel agreed to build a large, four-bedroom house for themselves on exclusive Stone Canyon Road in West Los Angeles, near Sunset Boulevard. Again, Jackie Cooper's mother, Mabel, was the decorator. The new Garland home had every possible game facility, from tennis and badminton courts to a swimming pool, and garden walks and pinball machines, even a solarium, with a complete suite for Judy on the top floor. It contained a bedroom almost as large as a living room, big enough to entertain her friends, her own dressing room and bath. There was a double bed in a little alcove, covered with cushions, and a huge bookcase which, when a hidden button was pressed, turned to reveal a secret Alice-in-Wonderland room for Judy. There was a separate entrance leading to her quarters so she could have privacy.

The building of the house had been, in a way, partly to please her mother. She considered it her mother's house. Judy enjoyed the rewards of her growing fame, but she knew how even more meaningful it was for her mother. Ethel had been writing songs, music and lyrics both, as far back as Judy could remember. Ethel had even brought some of these to Arthur Freed; a politic man, he had kept them a decent interval, then returned them. None had ever been published.

One afternoon months before the house was built, Judy confided in Jesse Martin. Ethel had driven Judy over to visit Jesse and Lorraine, who lived only five minutes away. Usually the two women talked comfortably in the kitchen about everything from recipes to MGM politics, while Jesse and Judy enjoyed their own tête-à-tête in Jesse's den.

Judy seemed dejected; she sat silently in the window seat, looking out at the Martins' garden, but her mind obviously far away. "What's the matter?" Jesse asked.

"Oh, I don't know, Jesse." She sighed. "Everybody's telling me I'm getting too fat. I'm sick of hearing it."

"Don't worry about it," he said. She would grow out of it. Suzy was slender, and so was Jimmy. They'd grown out of it.

"But I take after Mama," Judy said. Did he know she had an aunt who weighed over 250 pounds? Suddenly the words poured out of her. "You want to know something, Jesse? I just *hate* this business. Do you know why I'm in it and why I want to be a big success?"

Jesse, always a patient listener, said, "No, Judy, but I'd like to hear it."

"Because I want to take care of my mother. I want to build her a big, big house. I want to see that she has everything she wants, she's worked so awfully hard all her life—then I don't want to have any more of this business. I hate it."

Martin looked at her—sixteen, looking years younger in slacks and a sailor blouse. This was a child! Why should she have such concerns in her head?

"Honey," he said, "that's wonderful of you to want to do that, but you really don't know what decisions you want to make about this business. When the time comes, you quit, if that's what you want." But only after she had made the big success she hoped for.

"I'm making it now, Jesse," she said. There was nothing boastful in the way she said it.

Right, said Jesse. She went on: "I just want to do these things for my mother. Then I really really don't want any part of it after that."

That was how they left it. He thought, *There's an unhappiness somewhere in this child,* and he could not explain it. Perhaps that had something to do with the heartbreak in her voice when she sang. But what was it?

When the house was built, everyone enjoyed it. Ethel became even more the hostess. Because Judy was beginning to feel the pressure of *The Wizard of Oz,* Ethel thought it wiser not to forbid her to see Artie Shaw. She made the best of the situation. She invited him and some of his band to dinner—at least everything would be aboveboard there. His band included Buddy Rich, a brilliant, explosive drummer, and several of Shaw's friends—among them, of all persons, Jack Cathcart, the trumpet player in Chicago who had gotten the

Gumm Sisters their job at the last minute when the Old Mexico failed at the World's Fair, and then had spent most of that summer with Suzy. He had just moved to Los Angeles from Chicago.

It was a happy coincidence for Judy's eldest sister. Suzy and Jack were delighted to see each other again, and, ultimately, Suzy divorced Lee Cahn and became Mrs. Jack Cathcart. In the strangest way the circle was always rounding itself for the Garlands. Again, Ethel had to accept what seemed to be a sardonic fate. Her girls were constantly involved with band musicians, and even if they divorced one, they simply married another.

Judy's seventeenth birthday party, June 10, 1939, was celebrated with Artie and a few of his players. Artie brought along a close friend, Phil Silvers, the comedian, who was to immortalize the brash, larcenous Sergeant Bilko on TV many years later. Judy found Phil the funniest of men, and the three, Artie, Judy and Phil, went everywhere together. As Judy's present they had cut a special record—a hilarious Phil Silvers–Artie Shaw burlesque routine written especially for her.

Music and books brought Judy and Artie together as much as anything else. He would tell her about a whole world he was just becoming involved with, of knowledge and experience that he could never make his own as long as he remained doing only what he was doing.

Books were a great vicarious way of living a life, he told her. He gave her James Stephens—*The Crock of Gold, The Demi-Gods*— books that he treasured, that he thought were beautiful and from which she would benefit—the kind of books a girl who had not a lot of education would not be likely to have read. She would come to him later and say, "Why did he say this? He could have said that." Her perceptiveness never ceased to astonish him. Like Roger Edens, Shaw was constantly astounded by that inborn sense of knowing the good from the shoddy, that inborn sense of discrimination.

But what also constantly surprised him was her low self-esteem. Perhaps for the first time, and to the first man whose intelligence she respected and who had no obligations to MGM, or to her mother— someone upon whom she could rely implicitly, who was not a sycophant, who had no favors to seek from her—she revealed herself. What emerged was a shocking and constant denigration of herself, of her appearance, of her image to others as a woman.

"I'm not beautiful," she said. "You wouldn't call me pretty. You know that's true." Artie would explode. "What's the matter with you? You're crazy to say that." Judy: "No, I'm not. I'm homely. You know I'm homely."

"Judy, you're not a classic beauty, but you're beautiful—"

"No, look at me. My neck is too short. I should have been a football player." A laugh. "I'm a hunchback. I'm little. My legs are long and my body is all hunched up and I have this funny nose and my face is all squashed down—"

Yes, Artie would say, hugging her. "Yes, that's right, and you're Judy, and Judy is beautiful, and if you'd only get that straight . . ."

She loved to hear this, but he had begun to understand that words of praise fell into a bottomless pit. She could not be reassured. He was not to realize until later that Lana, with whom he was beginning to work in *Dancing Co-ed*, and with whom he found it difficult to talk, was Judy's ideal of what a girl should look like.

It was not only that she felt that beauty had escaped her. To Artie, who knew music, she could confide that her singing, so praised by everyone, the one reason for her existence as far back as she could remember (indeed, if she attended a party and was not asked to sing, even though she might not have wanted to, she would leave puzzled and humiliated), brought her far less satisfaction than anyone thought.

"I've got this vibrato," she said. "I can't control it." Artie could not disguise the fact that Judy spoke the truth. When there was no control, the vibrato could become a disaster. Judy knew it. "I stink," she once said, suddenly, bitterly. "I'm not a good singer." And then, in the depth of self-deprecation: "I can't sing." And she couldn't help adding, "You listen to Billie Holiday or Helen Forrest." They both sang with Shaw's band. "Now, those girls can sing," Judy said. She would look sadly yet challengingly at him. "I couldn't sing with your band, Artie. You know it. You know it damn well."

Again he would have to say, "That's true—but so what?" Judy was a show singer. Judy was a virtuoso, a law unto herself. "A show singer has a different kind of musicality, Judy. You sell your personality through a song whereas most singers sing the notes, they sing the tune, they-just-sing-it." Judy could never be simply one more instrument in a band. What she did with a song, no one else could do: she made it hers, she put the stamp of her warmth, her tenderness, her intelligence, her belief upon it, so that it became something glowing and incomparable—how dare she say, "I stink!"?

The extraordinary thing was that Shaw had no idea that Judy was in love with him—physically, emotionally, intellectually. Sometimes when he took her home, and now and then when he hugged her, or was about to kiss her on the cheek, he found her lips on his, and she was kissing him, not as a sister but as a woman. It would surprise him. He would hold her by her shoulders and say, "What are you doing? What are you up to, you idiot?" And she would say, "Nothing, nothing," and laugh. He thought she was having fun with him, playing sex games as young girls do. He could only explain it to himself later by thinking, *I was young and busy with my own life.*

But if it was not evident to Shaw, it was evident to Ethel. The day came when there was a loud, furious confrontation. Ethel said, "I forbid you to see Artie again. You're with him all the time. He's not the man for you. If you don't know any better, he should. He's been married and divorced and married and divorced and he knows his way around." Ethel knew something Judy did not. Ann Rutherford had been fascinated by Artie Shaw, too—those brooding dark eyes in a dark-complexioned face that had something Mephisthophelean about it—something deliciously menacing about this man, created by this combination of arrogant intellect, intensity and obvious virility. When Shaw was working with that sexiest of girls, Lana Turner, in *Dancing Co-ed,* Ann was in the cast, too, and Artie had telephoned her for a date. Ann's mother had said no. Definitely no. Why, that man's had every girl in town! And Ann had to forgo going out with fascinating, dangerous Artie Shaw.

What might have developed then is unknown, for Artie, having completed *Dancing Co-ed,* and with his band committed to engagements elsewhere, left California; and Judy fortunately found herself busier than ever working on *Wizard,* and completing her last year of schooling as well as carrying out a number of personal and radio appearances. Artie bade her good-bye with a kiss on her tear-stained cheek, and she hugged him and then let him go.

She was now on an intricate schedule. It took two hours each morning for her to get her makeup on. There had been difficulties on every level. The picture had taken six months of preparation. LeRoy had first brought in George Cukor as director. He became dissatisfied after a few tests, and was followed by Richard Whorf, who in a few weeks was replaced by Victor Fleming, a middle-aged, onetime cameraman and highly skilled in the use of color, who remained until the last few days, when he left to direct what was to become another classic, *Gone With the Wind*.

Metro had problems with Judy. She was obviously too well developed for Dorothy. She still had to be fourteen, her magic age. Miracles of adjustment were worked on her. Not only was she once more squeezed painfully into the "love corset"—it cost wardrobe $100 to make it—but her breasts had to be bound as well. Early in this period there was the temptation to take Benzedrine again, but Judy was so excited making the film that she seemed to need less sleep than ever before, and awoke each morning brimming with energy—unusual for her. But it was *her* film. She was working with three of the biggest names from the musical stage—Bert Lahr, Ray Bolger and Jack Haley, whom she'd liked from her days in *Pigskin Parade*—and *she* was the star. The film was built around her. A film which, so went the reports, would not only exceed the two-million-dollar budget but might even reach three million before they were finished.

Arlen and Harburg were working daily on *her* songs, Harold on the music, "Yip" on the lyrics. They had taken houses a block apart in Beverly Hills, not too far from her, and since Harold had a piano at his place, each morning "Yip" went there to work. The songs they were writing were written for *her*, not for whoever might later be cast in the film. Harburg still remembered the quality of yearning he had heard in her voice so many months before in New York.

A new world was opening to Judy. She was now meeting not only these very special persons from New York but their friends: Ira Gershwin, the lyricist, who told her he had first heard her sing at the Trocadero—"And I liked you then, Judy!"—and Ira's wife, Leonore, a celebrated hostess. The Gershwins' home on North Roxbury Drive, with its huge living room, its two pianos, its tennis courts and spacious garden with flowered trellises, was a gathering place for some of Hollywood's most exciting people, among them Oscar Levant and his wife, June. Ira's brother, the supremely gifted George, had died only two years earlier. Oscar, one of his dearest friends, was very close to the family—wry, witty, a superb pianist, a man of erudition—and before long Judy and Oscar were writing poems to each other. In much the same way as she had enchanted Artie Shaw, she enchanted Oscar Levant, and both loved her in the same way.

Behind the scenes in the making of the film LeRoy was facing numerous problems. Mayer wanted W. C. Fields to play the Wizard: who better to play a humbug? He offered him $150,000. Fields turned this down as not enough. LeRoy asked Ed Wynn, fresh from his triumph in *Hooray for What!* Wynn thought the part was too small. He refused it. Frank Morgan was finally settled upon, and went into movie history with it.

Then Buddy Ebsen, whom Judy had danced with in *Broadway Melody of 1938,* the first choice for the Tin Woodman, came down with a respiratory disease growing out of a makeup problem. He was to be completely encased in a tin suit, save for his face, neck and hands; aluminum dust was blown over him, so that his skin would match the suit. Ebsen inhaled so much of the dust that he had to be hospitalized, and was forced to drop out of the picture. Jack Haley then replaced him. This time the makeup artists used aluminum paint, and Haley found he could manage, although he was miserable perspiring under the paint, and wretched because he had to remain upright: it was impossible for him to sit in his tin suit. So that he could rest between scenes, the studio carpenters contrived a special resting place—an ironing board with foot and shoulder cuffs, leaned against a wall—and each time there came a rest period—especially when Judy's teacher called, "Judy—school!"—Haley made his slow, robot-like way to his board, was fitted into it and promptly fell asleep—this to the profane comments of Bert Lahr: "That son of a bitch could sleep hung on a meat hook!" Lahr was an insomniac and could never nap, though he was able to lie flat in his lion's costume.

Special effects also achieved miracles of illusion with Lahr. His extraordinarily expressive face lent itself marvelously to that of a lion, but there remained the problem of how he was to express the Cowardly Lion's emotions with his tail—wagging it with joy, lashing it about in fury, or curling it between his legs in shame. This was solved by rigging a long traveling boom above him, out of camera range, on which a man with a rod, like a puppeteer, manipulated Lahr's tail by invisible wires.

Then a new problem presented itself. It dealt with the Tin Man, who is discovered standing in a field, stiff with rust, unable to move. When he finally speaks, what kind of a voice should he have? The Straw Man could have a hoarse, low voice; Lahr's own inimitable speech, by some magic of its own, seemed perfectly suited to the Cowardly Lion. The Tin Man's voice posed a problem. Fleming and

Haley discussed it. Haley's son, Jack, Jr., was then four years old. Haley said, "You know, I tell him bedtime stories I make up each night, and I make up the voice, too. I begin with—" his voice took on a thin, falsetto quality—" 'Once upon a time, a long time ago . . .' " Fleming grabbed at this. "Try it just that way," he said. Haley did. When Judy and the Straw Man, after oiling the Tin Man's joints so that he can bring his arms down, ask what happened to him, Haley speaks in the voice he used to Jack, Jr.: "Well, a long time ago I was standing here . . ."

Perfect, said Fleming.

Judy was given star treatment. She had her own dressing room, a yellow trailer on wheels, with its own bathroom, her name on the door, and decorated as she wished with Degas reproductions, a gaily colored cretonne-covered daybed, a record player and family photographs on her dresser. In the making of *The Wizard of Oz* she began to display a habit of privacy that was to mark her behavior on the set in all her pictures thereafter: she tended to stay by herself in her dressing room, with either her makeup girl or a few of the other players. Seldom was she to mix with others on the set. Now she spent much of her time with her teacher, Rose Carter, taking her lessons in her dressing room instead of in the small cubicle that in the past had been set up on one corner of the stage. She still had to receive her three hours of lessons a day.

Although Judy always told funny stories of her struggle, while dancing up the little yellow road, with Lahr, Bolger and Haley, because they presumably tried to squeeze her out of the picture (on a Jack Paar program twenty years later she had her audience doubled up with laughter as she quoted Fleming roaring from a high boom: "Hoooold   it!   You-three-dirty-hams-let-that-little-girl-in-there!")— none of this was true. The Straw Man, the Tin Man and the Cowardly Lion skipping up the road through Oz with the little girl who was to lead them hidden behind them simply made no sense, but, as she told it, it became one of her marvelous, funny stories.

Her social life widened. She went out with Billy Halop, who was one of the Dead End Kids, Mickey Rooney, Peter Lind Hayes and Leonard Sues; the Levants took her to concerts; Bobby Sherwood, her brother-in-law, took her to several musicales at the home of his friend Groucho Marx.

Judy's closest friend on the set was Margaret Hamilton, who played the fearsome Miss Gulch back in Kansas, and then the Wicked Witch of the West. They became Maggie and Judy almost at once. Margaret Hamilton had come to Hollywood from the Broadway stage. Before that she had taught kindergarten for several years. She represented an altogether new type of person to Judy, who found herself talking to her as if she were a favorite aunt.

One afternoon she said excitedly, "You know, I'm going to do what everybody does," and when Maggie asked, "What is that?" Judy said, "I'm going to graduate with the University High School class. I'm going to go up with everybody else and get my diploma. And I have my dress!" And like a fourteen-year-old, indeed, she brought the dress next day for Maggie to see, holding it up against herself to display it. "Do you like it?"

Miss Hamilton thought, with people reading about how wild movie stars were, they ought to see this girl—a star if ever there was one —so thrilled over graduating. Judy unburdened herself, but not without exaggeration. "You know, I've been in this business since I was four years old—I've been supporting my family since then, so I never got to do the things other kids do. I used to sing and dance—I sort of kept the family together, I guess. I never knew what I earned, but that's what I was told."

When Margaret expressed sympathy, Judy went on, "I guess I really never had a chance to do the things most children do. That's why I'm so excited about graduating with a real high school class, like everybody else—carrying my corsage, walking up the aisle with the rest of the class and getting my diploma from the principal. . . . I remember," she went on, suddenly, "stopping at some little station in some little town—we were always on trains, you know—and there were two or three little girls out in the back yard. One was pushing a buggy around, another was swinging on a swing, and one was playing with a doll. I remember pushing my nose against the window and thinking, I just never had dolls like other girls—"

"Didn't you want them?"

"Yes," said Judy. "I suppose I must have had them—either I couldn't hold on to them or my mother wouldn't bother taking them with us—but I never had a doll that I could feel close to, that was a kind of friend the way little girls seem to have dollies—you know."

Margaret was touched. She would have been astonished to know that at this time Judy was telling Betty O'Kelly—and years later would tell her daughter Liza—that she never liked dolls, never wanted them because they were inanimate and reminded her of dead people, and so enjoyed other toys and living pets much more.

Margaret could only say, "Oh, that's too bad, because they're so much fun. It's a shame you didn't have them." She herself was the mother of a three-year-old boy.

"Oh, I got along all right, but I remember always wishing I could have one," said Judy, ". . . and have the time to play. But I never did."

She had to go then, and she left Margaret Hamilton feeling very sorry for her.

Director Fleming, a man who had married late in life and had no children of his own, treated Judy with great tenderness, and made her days on the film some of the happiest so far. The escapades of the Munchkin people, who were all midgets, many of whom had to be brought over from Europe—there were not enough Singer Midgets in the United States—kept everyone in a state of shock and hilarity backstage. LeRoy had housed them in a hotel in Culver City, and some of the wilder episodes occurred there.

Though everyone—from the players to the grips—was inclined to treat them as they would retarded children, they were adult men and women in their twenties, thirties and forties, with all the energies, appetites and habits of adults. When Judy learned that a woman was employed in the ladies' room at the Munchkins' hotel and that a male attendant was similarly employed in the men's room, assigned to lift each Munchkin to the seat of the toilet, hold him there and then lift him down again, she almost fell to the floor laughing at the picture this evoked. The men, she was to say later, pinched her when she passed by. (There was a folklore which held that midgets possessed unusual sexual prowess, and they took advantage of this, she said, propositioning her on the slightest pretext; and if some unsuspecting executive condescendingly greeted one with "How are you, my little man?" or a watchman unthinkingly said, "Hey, son, what are you doing smoking a cigarette?" the reply might be a venomous "Go fuck yourself, you silly bastard!"—or worse.)

The difficult, intricate makeup required every principal to have an attendant of his own follow him about, because some of the makeup was so delicate that one dared not even touch one's face. Miss Hamilton had a nose and chin attached, as well as a single long hair that had to be fastened to a huge wart, not to speak of a repulsive moist green makeup applied to every visible part of her face, neck and hands. This was always dripping off. She had to be fed and attended almost like an infant. The sets—Munchkinland and the rest of the Kingdom of Oz—were highly uncomfortable. As a new process, Technicolor necessitated lighting that was almost unbearably hot, and hours were spent experimenting with dyes trying to achieve true colors.

Mervyn LeRoy was everywhere, and Arthur Freed, though his name was not to be on the production, virtually lived behind the scenes. He worked with the writers, Florence Ryerson, Edgar Allan Woolf and Noel Langley, who adapted the original book into a screenplay, and spent hours with Arlen and Harburg. Since Judy could not read music, Arlen would play each number through once or twice after she had memorized Harburg's lyrics. Then she would sing it—and, as usual, turn out to be letter perfect the second or third time. Freed would shake his head unbelievingly. "That girl can learn a number while they're setting up the camera!" Everything she did confirmed his conviction that he had to find more films for her, that there was no limit to her potentialities.

Then a new dilemma faced them. Twelve songs had been written when it became evident that still another was needed: a transition song before the cyclone struck that transported Judy from the farm in Kansas to Munchkinland, and set her on her travels toward the Emerald City of Oz. It would have to bridge reality and fantasy. "We have to have it," said Harold.

Since he wrote the music first and Harburg then fitted the words, this was essentially Harold's problem. He knew what he wanted, but he didn't have it: a ballad, a song with a broad theme, something with a sweep to it, a sustained, rich, sonorous melody that would seem to move Dorothy from one world into a different one. The middle section of the tune might hop, skip and jump, be as catchy and fast-moving as the others in the picture, but over all this song had to be music that fitted the wide plains of Kansas, that suggested great spaces, and then a soaring into even wider spaces.

Arlen, a conscientious man, brooded over it. Freed said, "Harold, you're daft, taking it so to heart. You're too anxious. Take it easy— it'll come to you."

Harold and Harburg agreed they needed something with an almost symphonic quality, a feeling of the open sky and the vaulting blue of heaven, and with it a yearning to get off the earth and be somewhere else—and thinking again of the power in Judy's voice, something in the soul of that child that cried out to one, a yearning for everything good and right on the other side of the moon as Judy had first sounded to him in New York, Harburg all but shivered. The words would have to come to him, he knew, and Harold must produce the music that would *make* those words take shape in his mind.

Arlen moped about his house. Nothing came to him. He talked to his wife, Anya, and one night, trying to follow Freed's advice—put it out of your mind, it will come to you—he and Anya got into their car to drive the twenty minutes or so to see a movie at Grauman's Chinese Theatre. So that he would have nothing at all to concern himself with, not even traffic lights, Anya drove and Harold sat beside her in the front seat, his mind blank.

And suddenly, out of nowhere, and without his being conscious of what was happening, the theme presented itself to him, as they were driving down the dark, wide, quiet, tree-lined length of Sunset Boulevard in Beverly Hills just before it suddenly breaks into the brilliant, bustling, street-lighted effulgence of Hollywood's Sunset Strip. Arlen exclaimed—years later he could chuckle at the banality of the scene, for it could have come from the worst B movie—"Annie, I got it! Stop the car! Stop the car! Pull over to the curb. Quick!" He was yanking a notebook from his pocket and jotting something down.

He was writing as fast as he could by the light from the large show window—he realized it only later—of Schwab's Drugstore. Schwab's, where for years would-be starlets would sit at the drug counter dreaming of being discovered as Lana Turner (so the fanciful legend went) had been discovered; Schwab's, where many another pretty girl would wander amid the magazine racks and candy counters hoping to attract the attention of the directors and producers and screenwriters always dropping in for a quick sandwich and coffee.

Anya had stopped the car at the curb in front of Schwab's.

And there the melody of "Over the Rainbow" was written.

Within minutes Mrs. Arlen had turned the car around and they had driven back home. Arlen telephoned Harburg. "Yipper, come on over—now." Arlen, excited and triumphant, played it for him.

Harburg's face fell. What he said in essence was: "Harold, you're crazy. This is for Nelson Eddy and Jeanette MacDonald, not for a little girl from Kansas! It's too big, too broad, too operatic."

Arlen was crushed. "It's all I've got, Yipper," he said. "I just can't come up with anything else."

Harburg was crushed, too. It had hurt him to say this to Arlen, and how did he know he was right? After a disconsolate moment, he said, "Why don't we ask Ira to hear it? Let's see what he says."

Arlen was even more depressed. He thought, *Now I'm completely dead.* They both respected Ira Gershwin's musical taste, but Harold knew that Ira hated ballads unless they had a twinkle to them.

Presently Gershwin was there. Arlen played it again, this time with a sinking heart, without any of the triumph he had felt before. "Yipper, that's a very good melody," Gershwin said. Harburg said, with an excited note in his voice, "Harold, you didn't play it that way for me—you had all sorts of embellishments, you played it like Beethoven beginning a symphony." It occurred to Arlen that Harburg was right: in the first flush of triumph, he had played it so majestically, with so symphonic a quality, that the listener would ask, as Harburg had asked, "What's this got to do with a little girl in Kansas?"

When Freed heard the simpler version, he, too, liked it; and in the end, everyone agreed that the number would do as the transition song.

Now Harburg began to think about the words to fit the music. He thought, *Suppose I were a child in Kansas, and had never seen anything colorful in my life, living on those gray, gray plains, and I wanted something else . . .*

He played with his fantasy. He put himself in Dorothy's shoes, standing in the gray colorlessness of the Kansas dust, in a dry place, without grass, without flowers, gray not only with dust but with the gray, careworn faces of Aunt Em and Uncle Henry, and the gray of the mud in the gray pigs' pen and the gray of the weatherbeaten house and porch and fence, and the gray trapdoors leading to the storm cellar. He thought, *A child would say, "Gee, that's the place I want to go, to the rainbow, over the rainbow to the other side, where there's always color and good and beautiful things—oh, if only I could go there, but I'd have to fly there, but I can't fly, only birds can fly . . ."*

Perhaps, he thought, he was influenced by the thought of Judy, too: Judy, this child who, as he knew, had lived from her earliest days in the world of fantasy. Fantasy had been for her the only reality she knew, and she was trying always to chase these fantasies and seize them—and what was fantasy at its most pure but yearning for what lay on the other side of the rainbow in the sky?

Every writer is, of course, himself as well as the character he writes about. Harburg could identify in his own way with Dorothy-Judy. He had been brought up in the New York slums—to him, far worse than the plains of Kansas—and so beating behind the words was his own yearning, his dreams as a boy of escaping his own drab, depressing surroundings.

He thought, too, of Judy as a product of show-business people, who in his mind had not the same umbilical relationship to their children as other parents had. They could not, because once their child became part of the act, the relationship had to turn into a business one. Such children lost their identities as children, and so lost their childhood, and when this took place, they entered the world of dreams to find a substitute, a fulfillment.

Thus Judy or Dorothy, Dorothy or Judy: the constant reaching out for the never-never land that doesn't exist, for the rainbow that is, always and forever, an illusion.

All of this worked its own magic on Harburg as he labored over the words; and when he had them down to his satisfaction, he notified Arlen. "Beautiful!" said Harold. Then Judy, Freed and Edens were called in, and Arlen played his music on the piano while Harburg recited his lyrics. His small audience was excited. Judy tried it; and there, in Arlen's living room on Rodeo Drive, they all heard Judy for the first time sing the song that would be her trademark, none of them knowing it at the time, but all aware how perfectly words and singer became one.

Yet, for a brief period, when the first screenings disclosed that the film was far too long, "Over the Rainbow" was almost cut out. Jack Robbins, the music publisher, was among those present who said, "Nobody's going to sing that song anyway—the whole score is over the heads of teen-agers. What's the point of even having that fantasy song in the first place?"

LeRoy and Freed both wanted it in. A furious Freed went to see Mayer, prepared to say, "We're going to a third preview at Grauman's Chinese. If 'Over the Rainbow' is out, you can take my songs and everything else—I'm handing in my resignation." At the same time, he tempered his threat, particularly to a man like Mayer, who, he knew, liked him, and had great expectations for him.

He had a quid pro quo in reserve. Everyone agreed that, with or without "Rainbow," Judy had done a magnificent job. Freed, even before *Wizard* was completed, had been talking to his agent in New York, Leland Hayward, asking urgently for another inexpensive musical property which he, Freed, could produce by himself, with Judy in it. Hayward said, "How would you like *Babes in Arms?* I think I can get it for you for twenty thousand dollars."

Freed jumped at the chance. *Babes in Arms* was a Broadway hit, with a score by Richard Rodgers and Lorenz Hart. And what he could do with it! Freed said, enthusiastically. He had a brilliant idea. This would be not only for Judy but for Mickey, too. They should be teamed more often—they were terrific together. Mickey would play a young vaudevillian, Judy his girlfriend and singer; Mickey would sing for the first time, and there would be the two of them, unparalleled each, pals and lovers. Everything was there for box office.

Whenever Freed had a plan he wished to press on Mayer, he made use of his knowledge that Mayer was at his most expansive and relaxed on Sunday mornings, at his Malibu Beach house, and there, once more over finnan haddie, and with the Pacific surf sounding its own reassuring obbligato to Freed's persuasive voice, he said:

"Just think, a Rodgers and Hart score—I'll write a few more numbers—we'll buy 'God's Country,' which Harold and Yip wrote for *Hooray for What!*—it's great—and Roger will write additional material, we'll get Berkeley to direct—it'll be my first musical and I'll bet everything I've got on it. I got to do it!"

Mayer said, go ahead.

And in the end, of course, so far as *Wizard* was concerned, LeRoy, Freed, Edens, Arlen and Harburg won out: "Over the Rainbow" stayed in.

Who could have known that the words Harburg had found would become the leitmotif of Judy Garland's life?

12

IN THE NEXT FEW MONTHS, which saw Judy shuttling between final work on *Wizard* and beginning shooting on her next film, *Babes in Arms*, with Mickey, which was completed in little more than a month, Judy's life became increasingly complicated.

On August 17, 1939, *Wizard* opened at Loew's Capitol in New York, with Judy and Mickey in person, with Ethel along, as well as a retinue of MGM press aides. There were the two of them, the greatest pair in show-business history—Mickey was becoming the No. 1 box-office film draw at a time when nearly a hundred million persons went to the movies each week, and Judy's star was moving up with astonishing speed. Only the year before, she had opened at Loew's State to a reception which filled Times Square; now Broadway was simply overrun with their fans.

Judy and Mickey appeared in person four times a day. Judy had a little habit which endeared her even more. In shoes she was now taller than Mickey; and she would appear surreptitiously to push one shoe off with the toe of her foot, do the same with the other foot, and then, in her stocking feet the same height as Mickey, go into her act with him. On one occasion she collapsed backstage just as she was about to go on: she simply slumped and fainted. Whether it was exhaustion or a sudden drop in blood sugar (she virtually lived on Coca-Colas when she could), she was unable to go on. Mickey covered for her, ad-libbing and clowning cleverly, and in a little while Judy, who had been given immediate medical attention backstage, had revived. Before reaching New York she and Mickey had undergone the grueling ordeal of "breaking in" their act by being rushed through personal appearances in three cities—Washington, New Haven and Hartford—and from the moment they had arrived in New York, they had to cope with welcoming committees of teen-age winners of MGM contests in some seventy Loew's theatres, as well as luncheons and constant interviews. Judy's collapse was her first from overwork—and the forerunner of many later.

At home pressures were growing. On November 17, Ethel's birthday, came her elopement with Will Gilmore, and a series of unhappy domestic scenes in the Stone Canyon house. Now Judy deliberately used only one entrance to reach her room so that she might not accidentally come face to face with her stepfather.

In the midst of this, there were startling newspaper headlines: Artie Shaw, playing at the Hotel Pennsylvania in New York, called his band together one night and said he was leaving. He had had it. He was quitting. He was taking a long vacation. And he vanished. No one knew where he was. He had walked out of hundreds of thousands of dollars' worth of contracts. Since only a few days before in an interview he had said something to the effect that jitterbugs were morons, this added to the belief that Artie had temporarily taken leave of his senses and that when he became himself, all would be well again. His agent had pleaded, "Just stick it out for two more years and you'll never have to worry about money again for the rest of your life." Artie had exploded, "Yes, but I'll have to worry about my sanity." And he had left.

Judy read the news in Hollywood. She tried to reach him, but she didn't know how. A few days later, in the midst of the upheaval brought about by her mother's marriage, there was a telephone call. It was Artie.

"My God, Artie, where are you? My God, what did you do, walking out like that?"

He was calling from a motel in Little Rock, Arkansas. He had left New York at dawn, driven day and night through a snowstorm, grabbed a few hours' sleep in a motel somewhere in Virginia, and was trying to think: what to do, where to go, what now with his life?

She heard him say, "I called you because I just didn't know who to talk to, Judy, and since I've got my house in L.A. I thought if it wouldn't be too much of a hassle, I'd come out there now and stay at my place. What do you think?"

Not now, Judy said. There was too much excitement over him. "Artie, I'd love to see you, but I don't think you should come out. You just don't know what's going on here. Where's Artie Shaw? That's all people talk about. You're the mystery man. You fell off the earth!"

At her suggestion, then, he decided to stay out of sight for a while. He drove to Mexico, to Acapulco, where he remained until Christmas, then drove back to California.

Meanwhile, Judy had pressed her hand and shoe prints into the concrete in the forecourt of Grauman's Chinese, and now she was there with all the stars, and particularly Deanna Durbin, who had, nonetheless, been given that honor earlier, after her second hit, *100 Men and a Girl*. Deanna had literally saved Universal studios from bankruptcy, and, like it or not, Judy always felt a rivalry with her. Mayer assuaged much of this by presenting Judy with a check for $10,600—a "voluntary bonus" for her personal-appearance tour with *The Wizard of Oz*.

Her reviews were all her heart could desire. She was perfectly cast; she had "wonder-lit eyes"; the picture was "a delightful piece of wonderworking." Two months after *Wizard, Babes in Arms* opened, increasing both Judy's and Mickey's popularity. *Babes in Arms*, Freed's first musical production, turned out to be the biggest money-maker of the year for its cost.

Now, with Artie back in town, Judy had gone out with him. There had been another terrible confrontation between Judy and her mother. She was not to see him again.

On the face of it, Judy bowed to the dictum. But, actually, she did not. One day Judy telephoned Jackie Cooper. He was surprised by her call. It had been quite some time since they had seen each other. She'd been very busy—she wondered, would he like to take her out?

"I'd love to," Jackie said. She gave him the address of her Stone Canyon Road house. They had not seen each other so long, he'd never been in it.

Ethel greeted him in friendly fashion when he came to pick up Judy. "Now, behave yourself and get back at a decent hour," she told Judy—it was her invariable send-off. The two went to dine at Brittingham's, a popular restaurant known for music as well as food.

Jackie brought her up to date on himself. He no longer had a tutor but went to Hollywood High School, like any normal kid. He'd taken Lana Turner to his school prom, he'd dated other girls, he'd finally gotten out of that dreadful child-star syndrome at Metro, having completed his seven-year contract, and was now free-lancing, working at Universal and other studios.

At the end of the evening, when he drove her home, they sat talking in the car for a few minutes. She looked at him and said, "Jackie, I'm going to trust you with something very important to me." As she put it, she had "a terrible crush" on Artie Shaw. Her mother absolutely disapproved of him. Just the same, she'd been seeing him on the sly, at his place. It was getting more and more difficult for her to get out of the house at night.

Jackie was an old buddy—they'd been each other's first steady dates in Hollywood. Would he do her a great favor—play "beard"—or front—for Artie? Start to date her again, pretend that he was going steady with her again, call for her two or three evenings a week to take her to dinner and a movie or dance, but really drop her off at Artie's? Jackie could go off on his own then, so long as he returned to pick her up at Artie's around midnight and get her home "at a decent hour."

And Jackie—how could one deny Judy anything?—agreed.

Later, he thought how well she had handled it so he would not be too hurt, waiting until the evening was over to let him know why she really had wanted to see him. She could be the most solicitous, the most delicately understanding of persons when she wished to be. He could not help admiring her. He knew what it was to have been a child in a world of grownups, always controlled by them, always carrying on your shoulders responsibilities and duties that other kids did not, and how glorious it was to move beyond that control, beyond those responsibilities, and do what *you* wanted to do, to carry out your own desires—not what was wise, or sensible, or advisable, or profitable. . . . To Jackie Cooper, just seventeen, Artie Shaw, nearly thirty, was all but venerable; as a consequence, Judy, dating this middle-aged man, seemed so much older, so much more mature, in his eyes.

But the game lasted briefly. It had to come to an end, and Jackie ended it. He had become growingly interested in a girl named Pat Stewart. Now with his duties to Judy, days passed when he did not call Pat, and finally he told Judy he could not continue playing beard. Judy would have to find someone else to take on the job.

Judy did—this time her sister Jimmy.

Now, so far as Ethel knew, Judy began dropping over two or three evenings a week at Jimmy's. Their baby, Judalein, was a year and a half; Judy doted on her tiny namesake and so there was no valid reason for Ethel to question these visits.

Judy would drive off to see the Sherwoods, ostensibly; instead, she drove directly to Artie's. If Ethel called Judy at Jimmy's, either

Jimmy or Bobby covered for her by saying she had gone out to pick up cigarettes or ice cream and would call back the minute she returned. Then they'd alert Judy at Artie's.

Jimmy played this role with great reluctance. But Judy was dancing about starry-eyed. "I'm in love with Artie Shaw," she confided to Jimmy. "If only he'd ask me to marry him!" Judy and her mother were not getting along. The marriage to Gilmore had made their relationship very tense, and when Gilmore assumed the role of stepfather, siding with Ethel in any dispute between her and Judy, Judy became furious. Jimmy had decided that anything was better than to risk alienating her sister completely from her family; and if doing this for Judy would help, she would go along with it.

Besides, Artie had once told her something that always remained with her. He had said he divided women into two essential categories: those he talked with and those he went to bed with.

She sensed—she could not be sure, but she was almost sure—that Artie was with Judy because he could talk with her. There was an honesty and a directness about the man that made Jimmy as certain as she could be under the circumstances that he would never attempt to take advantage of her kid sister. Besides, he had been taking out Betty Grable, whose marriage to Jackie Coogan had just broken up—there were even reports that Betty and Artie were secretly engaged, although Artie denied this—and he was seen with other beautiful women all the time.

As for Judy, more and more she unburdened herself to him. He would understand. One of the first things her mother had done was to buy a car for Gilmore's oldest son. She had bought a big Packard touring car for herself—to Jesse and Lorraine Martin she explained, "We need this for show."

Before, as Judy explained it, there had been only her mother; now there was her mother and her stepfather. And the studio. Sometimes they had to hold supper for her at home until eight o'clock, she was kept so busy at Metro. And working Saturdays, too. Suddenly, bitterly, it came from her: "I want to quit. I'm going to tell them all to go to hell! I don't care. I don't like what I'm doing. I don't want to go up to Metro and do that goddamn stuff and compete with those beautiful girls—why should I have to compete with them? I'm Frances Gumm and I'm not going to compete with them. And why is my mother . . ." And so it went on.

Clearly she felt both love and hate for her mother, a great ambivalence. Yet Judy understood that her mother wanted a good life for her, for her sisters, for all of them; that she wanted Judy to be successful and happy and wanted to discharge what she saw as her duties to this gifted child of hers. Judy and her sisters had agreed, when they thought about it more calmly, that Ethel and Will had probably married because it seemed the practical thing to do—each to help the other with their children. But there had already been disputes on money matters between Ethel and Will, both strong-minded, determined people. Almost as soon as they were husband and wife Will had turned to Ethel and said, "From here on, I intend to take over all the handling of business in this family." To which Ethel had retorted, "Like hell you will! Handle Judy's money? Never!" And so it had really gotten off to a bad start.

Judy complained. She couldn't understand her own place in things: was it the system, was it people, was it the world itself? All she knew was that she had to fight, that it was all so unfair! Here she was, the youngest in the family, working her head off, not getting enough sleep, trying to learn about life and about herself, yet being treated like an infant even though she was the family's major source of income. "I'm a slave!" she cried. "I want to quit!"

And still Artie knew—and she knew—that she did not mean it.

It was the dilemma of all who are caught in a golden vise, struggling to escape even as they fight to remain.

He had escaped. Or had he?

On another occasion she poured out her heart about her films. In *Babes in Arms,* while she found it wonderful to work with Mickey, she was again the girl on the outside: in the story she is Patsy, about to be given her chance, the biggest of her life so far—to sing with Mickey's band—only to be supplanted at the last moment by pretty June Preisser. She actually had a line to say to Mickey (and it must be believable, because Mr. Mayer wouldn't let her say anything the audience wouldn't believe): "I know I'm no glamour girl," like June Preisser. And now, after *Babes in Arms,* they were putting her back into another Andy Hardy film, this one called *Andy Hardy Meets Debutante,* where she again played plain little Betsy Booth, while Andy naturally again fell in love with much prettier debutante Daphne Fowler.... Always the girl on the outside, and never allowed to grow up. The pleasure of attending the premiere of her own film,

144

Babes in Arms, was almost spoiled by Mr. Mayer, who told her when she wanted to wear a gown designed by Adrian, Metro's famous designer, "You're too young for anything like that." Judy wept before he relented and allowed her to wear it.

Bobby Sherwood, while living at the Stone Canyon house, had observed how hard Judy was working. Often she would want to go to a party, or invite Jane Withers and other friends over, but could not, saying regretfully that she had to get to bed early because she had to be on the set early.

Artie tried to comfort her. The pressures upon her and the financial pyramid she supported on her shoulders were unfair. And in that winter and early spring of 1940, he knew she was not getting enough sleep. She was beginning to take sleeping pills to help. Whether overstimulated at night or because she had to go to bed early so she could be at Metro early the next day, she would say, "Oh, Christ, now I'm going to have to take one of those goddamn things or I'll be up all night." Everyone was taking sleeping pills. If you were up late— and Judy loved to stay up late—and had to rise early the next morning, you took the pill to get as much sleep as possible—and if, in order to wake up and function, you had to take a wake-up pill, you took a Benzedrine, or later the newer, improved pill called Dexedrine. Everyone did—the writers, the directors, the actors. It was part of the course—of everyone's course.

So the early weeks of 1940 passed, until a terrible morning in February. Ethel, as was usual now, woke Judy by knocking on her door, bringing in her breakfast tray, on it the morning paper. Ethel was halfway down the stairs when a piercing scream from Judy brought her rushing back: Judy was sitting up in bed, sobs catching at her, the newspaper unfolded to an enormous black headline:

ARTIE SHAW ELOPES WITH LANA TURNER

Ethel stared at her. "Well, so what?"

Judy burst out, "But I love him!" And then it all came out: she had been seeing him, she had seen him only three nights ago. She wailed, "He didn't say a word, he didn't tell me anything"—and that this night, when she had no date with him, he had eloped with Lana Turner! To lose Artie, to lose him so unexpectedly, and to lose him to someone whose beauty and sex appeal she envied so much . . .

No one could understand the marriage. Artie and Lana disliked each other on the set of *Dancing Co-ed*. Lana complained to reporters that he was arrogant and egotistical, and Shaw had never hidden his disdain for Lana and the world he assumed she represented.

Ethel had no sooner stamped down the stairs, for once almost speechless, than Judy got on the phone to Phil Silvers and sobbed hysterically, "How could Artie do this to me! How could he!" Phil tried to comfort her. Phone in hand, he looked across the table at a friend who had joined him for coffee that morning—Saul Chaplin, the songwriter, who had gone backstage in New York two years ago to tell Judy how beautifully she had sung "Bei Mir Bist Du Schön." Phil, after a few moments, gave the phone to Chaplin, who added what words of comfort he could find. Judy would not stop crying. She was still sobbing when she hung up.

The two men looked at each other. Only a few minutes before Judy's call, Betty Grable had called Phil from New York for the same reason, but there had been no tears in her voice. She shouted over the phone, "That son of a bitch, who does he think he is! Doing this to me!" And she had hung up, furious. Judy had hung up, destroyed. Phil said, "I'm going over to see Judy—I just have to try to make her feel better." He himself was not altogether innocent in what had happened for he had played a role, wittingly or unwittingly.

Surprised as everyone had been by the elopement, perhaps no one had been more surprised than Shaw himself. He had not seen Lana since finishing *Dancing Co-ed* the summer before. Now that he was back in Hollywood, Phil had taken him one night to Metro, where Lana, striking in a skin-tight gown and looking her loveliest, was working on a second picture, *Two Girls on Broadway*. Phil introduced them: Shaw was never sure whether Phil did this because he had forgotten they'd worked together in a film or did it slyly, roguishly, knowing they had all but insulted each other on *Dancing Co-ed*, and wanted to see what would happen now.

Whatever the case, on the night of February 8, 1940—Lana's twentieth birthday—Shaw took Lana out. According to one report, she was to have gone to dinner that evening with Gregson Bautzer, a handsome young Hollywood lawyer and highly eligible bachelor about town whom she expected to marry, and Bautzer had telephoned at the last moment to say he was ill. According to another story, Shaw telephoned her that night and Lana promptly canceled her date with Bautzer to go with Artie. That evening Shaw found Lana not only enormously sexy, but sweet, unpretentious and, above all, a girl who wanted a home and children more than a career. Since this was how he, too, felt, disenchanted as he was with show business, he was completely taken by her. As he later admitted privately, "The reasons for what we did were totally insane, but they seemed valid to her and to me at that point"—and in the next few hours they flew in a friend's plane to Las Vegas and were married by a justice of the peace.

When the headlines hit next morning, Shaw was astonished by the barrage of publicity, as he had been astonished by the explosive reaction to his walkout in New York. For the next few days he and Lana hid in a friend's guest house. When the excitement died down, they went to Shaw's own house on the hill. There, a day or so later, Shaw received a telephone call from an angry, stuttering, almost incoherent woman. "You monster! Do you know what you've done to my daughter?" It took him nearly a minute before he realized that this must be Mrs. Ethel Gilmore, Judy's mother.

He was shocked. Judy's mother hardly existed for him, save in Judy's complaints to him, or Judy's words, "Mom won't let me out," or, "I've got to arrange something so I can see you, Artie." Vaguely he remembered meeting her, a short, dumpy woman whose features he could not even recall. He remembered months before when he went to Judy's house for dinner, a huge St. Bernard dog almost knocked him down when the door opened, and there was Judy in the doorway, and somewhere behind in that house was Judy's mother. She was a vague presence, that was all.

Now when this woman raged at him, "Do you know what you've done to my daughter, you terrible, irresponsible . . . ?" Shaw, completely puzzled, could only say, "I don't know what you're talking about. What do you mean?"

"My daughter's practically had a nervous breakdown on account of you, you contemptible—"

"You're talking about Judy?"

"Yes, who the hell do you think I'm talking about?" Ethel almost screamed.

Shaw said, still incredulous, "You're talking about Judy and me?"

Ethel was even more furious. "How dare you run off and marry that woman without—"

He began to understand. His voice was like ice. "Judy and I are friends, Mrs. Gilmore. We were never anything but friends." Judy's mother obviously believed he and Judy had had an affair. "You know, I never touched Judy sexually—I never had anything to do with her as a boyfriend." And though Ethel was sputtering at the other end, he went on, "I'm her friend, and she's my friend, and we love each other, and she'll always be part of my life, but it's got nothing to do with what—"

This was his first inkling of Judy's reaction to his marriage. It stunned him. He had had no idea. When Ethel banged down the receiver, and the conversation ended, he tried to reach Judy at Metro. He did not get her until the next day. Then it was a tearful, subdued girl who said, "I hate her for calling you. I'll never forgive her. She shouldn't have done that."

They met later that day. He told her they must work out an understanding. She listened as he explained that he loved her in a way he would never love anyone else. He loved her now and he would always love her. And then, unaware that he was putting into words what was her own bar sinister, that he was confirming her deepest fears, her most despairing image of herself, he said in words whose unmistakable sincerity only tore her apart the more, "Lana is a whole different thing, Judy. Lana is a woman I'll have sex with." She was looking away, silent. "You know, you and I—" He stumbled for a moment. "I never thought of you in that way and I didn't think you thought of me in that way."

No, Judy said, with a small laugh. She didn't think of Artie that way. And of course he didn't think of her that way. Never had she been a better actress than here, before a man whose perceptions were as acute as her own.

He never knew.

Nor could he know that, no matter how her intellect appraised it, in the depths of her being she felt he had forsaken her. The first man who had forsaken her was her father. Now it was he. And this would be the pattern she would follow, whether she was actually forsaken or because she would make it come about. How much of this was her need to see herself as a victim, one cannot know. But a victim is forgiven everything; a victim is one for whom everyone is sorry; a victim is an object drawing from everyone sympathy, compassion, affection, love. If by no other way, then by this way.

148

The night of the morning Judy woke to be served breakfast and the news of Artie's elopement with Lana Turner, she was to be a guest on Bob Hope's radio program. She had gone through tantrums of tears all through the day. She had said she would not, she could not, sing that night; it took all of Ethel's and Jimmy's encouragement and sympathy for her to allow herself to be driven to the studio to rehearse the show before it went on the air. Then she learned she would have to sing a love ballad. She forced herself to sing it at rehearsal, tears streaming down her face. The orchestra leader on a show across the hall was David Rose, a twenty-nine-year-old composer and arranger, to whom Judy had been introduced some time before by Jackie Cooper. It was impossible now not to notice her emotional state. The reason why was no secret, for Shaw had brought her to the program once or twice before.

There were two hours to show time after the rehearsal. Judy retreated to her dressing room, and remained there. A knock on her door—she opened it, her face tear-stained. Rose stood there, one hand held behind his back. He grinned at her. "Here," he said, and with a flourish brought forth from behind him a huge slice of chocolate cake, topped with whipped cream. "My mother made it," he said. "I had some left. It's for you."

Judy stared at him and his consolation offering, and then burst into laughter. "Oh, David," she cried, and pulled him into the room. "I've got another fork somewhere here, and you can share it with me. How did you know this was just what I needed!"

That night she went out with David Rose—the first of many dates with the man who would become her first husband.

13

IN THE WAKE OF THE ARTIE SHAW DEBACLE, Judy began to grow up.

In the months that followed, her life took on a new direction. Much was to happen before her marriage to David Rose more than a year later. If there is to be found a first watershed period in her life, a time which saw not only the maturing process but an intensification of her struggle for independence—the struggle of Galatea to free herself from Pygmalion—it would be here. David Rose was part of that struggle, as was a new confidante, Betty Asher, her publicity aide. Betty was a slim, sad, rather unattractive girl, daughter of Ephraim Asher, a producer for Carl Laemmle. Her parents had been divorced when she and her brother Bill were small, and their father had been given custody. Betty was five years older than Judy: bright, sophisticated, extremely resourceful in a pinch—the sort of person who always brought you the very thing you wanted for your birthday. Judy responded to her instantly, not a little intrigued because she was also reportedly the girlfriend of Eddie Mannix, an important MGM executive, which gave her a certain cachet. She became not only Judy's aide, secretary and buffer to the world, but one of her closest advisers. She had earlier been assigned to play much the same role with Lana Turner, and belonged to the bigger, wider, more exciting world which attracted Judy.

Of all the men one might think Judy would marry, David Rose seemed hardly a leading candidate. His age—thirty-one when they married—was right; Judy's interest was always in older men, whom she could admire. But he was remarkably quiet; at parties he might let half an hour pass before making an observation, apparently having no need to enter the conversation, neither challenged nor excited by it; mainly he listened, utterly relaxed, smiled pleasantly and remained silent. In contrast to most of the men to whom Judy gravitated, he was not a wit, though he had a dry sense of humor which could keep Judy laughing, which she loved; and he was a serious man with an unusual musical facility. He had the respect of people Judy respected: Harold and Anya Arlen, and Bobby Sherwood. They spoke admiringly of his ability to listen to a Sibelius recording in D major while writing a new arrangement in E flat for an Irving Berlin song. One understood how he could be musical director and arranger for four radio programs simultaneously.

Born in London and brought to America as a child, he had come from Chicago only three years before. He had formed an orchestra with a preponderance of strings—a new idea then—and so had gathered a certain fame as an innovator as well as a talented musician.

He was going now through a separation from his wife, Martha Raye, the comedienne. When Judy became Mrs. David Rose in July

150

of the following year, she would be the third of Ethel's three daughters who, by whatever fate was Ethel's lot, had chosen husbands from the ranks of musicians.

In the late spring of 1940 Judy received a special "juvenile" Oscar from the hands of Mickey Rooney, for the best juvenile performance of the year in *The Wizard of Oz*. There was talk. Why should she not have been eligible for the regulation Oscar? But, as Judy had lamented to Shaw, "they" simply didn't want her to grow up.

In June 1940, on her eighteenth birthday, Mayer himself opened his house for her and her guests, a tribute to her growing importance. Two months later he tore up her original contract, which still had two years to go—she was now reaching the $750-a-week level—and replaced it with a new seven-year contract which raised her immediately to $2,000 a week for three years, then $2,500 for the next two, and $3,000 for the remaining two. It gave her a new fame, for since she was still a minor until age twenty-one on contractual matters, though an adult at eighteen as far as marriage was concerned, the contract had to be approved by the Superior Court of California, and so received considerable publicity.

The figures had been hotly discussed at home by Ethel, Will, Peg DeVine and Harry Rabwin, Ethel's lawyer. Will, as the businessman of the family, said, "They shouldn't start her at one hundred thousand a year—it should be three hundred thousand." Peg said, shocked, "Will, that's an awful lot of money." Wiser counsel prevailed, and on August 28, 1940, Judy signed the contract and Ethel signed a rider in which "as mother of the artist" she guaranteed that the artist would carry out "each and all of her obligations," and agreed that the compensation being paid Judy would take care of them both. Then mother and daughter privately settled on the sum of $125 to be taken out of Judy's check and paid each week as salary to Ethel.

Since Judy had actually built the Stone Canyon house for Ethel, this was taken into account. Ethel thought her stipend should be larger. Peg said, "My God, Ethel, who needs $500 a month to live on? You should live on $375 a month and save the other $125." Ethel said, well, at least Judy should pay the tax on it, but then subsided, and made her peace with the arrangement.

The renegotiation of Judy's contract had been inevitable. Despite her traumatic experience with Shaw, by autumn of the year Judy had done two more films, *Strike Up the Band,* a campus musical with Mickey as a drummer and Judy as his girlfriend and singer—like *Babes in Arms,* it was directed by Berkeley, with a comparable show-business formula—and *Little Nellie Kelly* with George Murphy, in which she danced, sang and played a dual role, first as mother, then as daughter, born as the mother died bearing her; and, as Murphy later reported, did so well in the death scene that even the watching grips had to leave the set because their sobs were picked up on the sound track. The two films were released that autumn within two months of each other, the first in September 1940, the second in November. (It must be remembered that the Andy Hardy pictures had been done in twenty to twenty-five days, while the musicals rarely took more than forty days.)

Both of these were produced by Freed, whom Mayer now gave virtually a free hand. Everything Freed had done so far, from that first "musical divertissement" in which Judy introduced her "Dear Mr. Gable" song, had been touched with gold. Now he had been building up his producing unit, recruiting more and more gifted people from New York to help him carry out his objective of producing first-rate musical films. It was the right time, a comforting way for the public to turn away from the depressing war news from Europe. Hitler had marched into Poland the preceding September, and the newspapers made somber reading; music, gaiety, color, beautiful girls and romantic love affairs were a welcome antidote.

One day, after Judy finished a dance routine with Mickey, Freed arrived on the set of *Strike Up the Band* with a tall, slim man with enormous black eyes and a slight nervous stammer, and courtly manner. This, said Freed, was his new production assistant, Vincente Minnelli, the New York director and stage designer. Minnelli had directed *Hooray for What!,* the Broadway hit for which Harold Arlen and "Yip" Harburg had written music and lyrics which had led to Freed's hiring them to do the same for *Wizard of Oz.* It was a casual meeting. Vincente suggested to Freed a way to handle a troublesome piece of stage business. It was so simple and yet so ingenious that both Judy and Mickey were impressed.

Freed had seen *Little Nellie Kelly* as a George M. Cohan production on Broadway, and immediately told Cohan he wanted to buy the film rights for Judy Garland. Cohan might have thought twice, but Judy's name was already magical. The picture, in turn, gave her a welcome change of pace for it allowed her to play, however briefly, her first adult role as Nellie, the mother.

By the spring of 1941 she was completing a film that at the beginning elated her—her first glamorous part—*Ziegfeld Girl*, with a cast which included Jimmy Stewart, Tony Martin and Jackie Cooper, and in which she was dressed by Adrian and given the same glamorous treatment as her co-stars, Hedy Lamarr and Lana Turner. She was actually billed ahead of Hedy, already world-famous because of her notorious nude swimming scene in the European film *Ecstasy*.

On the face of it, Judy was rising as fast as her star could take her. She was finishing her twelfth film; she was earning $2,000 a week, less Ethel's salary, but increased by moneys from radio and recordings, which her new contract allowed so long as they did not conflict with her Metro duties; and she was growing more and more in love.

David Rose's divorce from Martha Raye would not become final until May 15, 1941. Judy had been seeing David since the preceding spring. She had also gone out with Peter Lind Hayes, with Robert Stack (this, a public-relations suggestion by Ida Koverman, who thought they looked well together, but neither felt strongly about the other), with Dan Dailey, Jr. and with Jackie Cooper, both of whom had been with her in *Ziegfeld Girl*. But she dated Jackie as surreptitiously as possible, because he was then going steady with Bonita Granville. Jackie and Bonita were always together at parties.

At one of these Jackie was surprised when Judy came up and said, how come that they hardly ever saw each other any more? There was no resisting Judy. The next night Jackie found himself beginning quietly to see Judy again. But he soon felt miserable at what he was doing. He and Judy were involved in something clandestine, and he knew nothing would come of it. What surprised him, in the middle of his own guilt, was that Judy seemed to enjoy it: the secrecy, the intrigue, even—it seemed—Bonita's suspicions and obvious distress when the three unexpectedly came upon each other at a party. She, Judy, had taken Jackie away from Bonita, and although this really wasn't true, Bonita *thought* it was. Even though it was only a game, Judy was getting the best of both possible worlds. *I don't like that,* he thought, *I don't like it in me and I don't like it in her.* For the first time he thought, *Why is this so important to her? Why should she enjoy it? What is she trying to prove to herself?* It made him feel uncomfortable—stimulating and emotionally exciting and marvelous a girl though she was—and he simply stopped it.

To his surprise, Judy seemed not too perturbed. In the midst of this busy period she had met Johnny Mercer, the songwriter, at a Bob Hope party, and she had been at once taken by him. Some of his songs, particularly "Jamboree Jones" and "Bob White," were her favorites. At the party she was to sing a duet with Bob called "Friendship." Hope suggested that Mercer and she sing it instead, and they had. She was wearing a red dress, she was exuberant, and Mercer told her that he had first seen her when she was a little Gumm Sister. It had been at the Hollywood Bowl, or some such place, she was about seven years old, and she had struck that stage "like a little electrical unit." He admired her tremendously, and she was fascinated by him.

This had all the earmarks of a delicate situation in the making, and Ethel, who missed as little as possible, watched Judy's activities with considerable perturbation. Even if Mercer was a married man, and had been for a considerable time, he was the right age—just turned thirty-one—he was a poet at heart, an enormously sweet and charming man, and obviously enchanted by her. (He wrote the lyrics of two of her later best-known songs, "That Old Black Magic" and one with the sweetly melancholy title "This Time the Dream's on Me.")

Behind Judy's dating, even with David Rose as the man with whom marriage seemed ultimately the most likely, there was a kind of desperation. To have been thrown side by side into the same film with Hedy Lamarr and Lana Turner, even to pose between them for publicity pictures captioned "The Three B's of Beauty, i.e., Brunette, Bronzette and Blonde," was all very well, but who was kidding whom? No matter how high her heels, she was half a head shorter than they, which Makeup tried to remedy by perching a grotesque stovepipe headdress atop her already high hairdo when they posed together: all this only made it worse. And it was clear that Tony Martin, for whom she had always yearned, had eyes only for Lana—in the picture and out of it. Lana was already separated from Shaw. That marriage had lasted less than half a year (their divorce became final in September 1941). Tony might walk over with Judy to watch the shooting on other sets—Myrna Loy in one of her *Thin Man* mystery comedies, or Robert Taylor doing *Johnny Eager*—but it was Lana Turner he dated, and Lana Turner he courted at night.

Little of Judy's true feelings showed themselves on the set, but they were clear enough in more private moments. Judy now took an hour of dramatic instruction daily from Lillian Burns, an MGM dramatic coach. She had worked hard with Lana, who spoke highly of her. Lillian found Judy an instinctive actress. One afternoon she told her, "Let's try a few things to loosen you up dramatically." Lillian greatly admired Thornton Wilder's play *Our Town,* and asked Judy to read the lines of Emily, the girl, while she herself read the parts of the mother, father and others required to give continuity to the scene. She wanted to place Judy in this moving family situation of love, death and faith.

There, in Lillian's office, Judy became Emily. She read the eloquent moving lines spoken by the dead Emily, who, allowed to relive one day of her life, chooses her twelfth birthday and, home again but invisible, poignantly relives the warmth and family love of that day.

When Judy finished, Lillian Burns was unable to continue reading her part. She simply had to go out of character. "Oh, Judy, my dear," she said almost brokenly, "you have a priceless gift. You can be anything you wish in the theater! Judy, there isn't really anything you can't do if you want to do it!"

"Except one thing," said Judy. "Except that when I sit down at a table opposite a man, all he can see is my head. I haven't any neck."

Lillian remembered that she went home, crying, to tell her husband.

The same mood was on Judy after the first reviews of *Ziegfeld Girl,* in which Judy played what might have been a Gumm Sister working her way as a singer and dancer to triumph in big-time vaudeville. But Lana turned out the star, and the one acclaimed. Lillian said to Judy, who had dropped over with a gift, "Judy, I'm so glad the picture's so good—" Before she could go on to praise her performance, Judy had interrupted her. "What does it mean to me? So I had a scene where I cried again." Lana was the beauty, Lana had died in the picture, Lana had the dramatic part. Hedy Lamarr had been loved and wanted in the picture. Judy again was, for all the importance of her billing, in her own mind only a sword-bearer. Lana had the tiniest of dressing rooms, nothing to compare to those given Judy and Hedy, but in the picture a man yearned desperately for Lana, and it was about that that the world turned. Lillian thought, *The trouble is that Judy knows that she's never really the love interest; she has never really played with a handsome leading man to whom she is everything.* She had played with Mickey Rooney, she had played with

Jackie Cooper, she had sung a song, not to Clark Gable, *but to his picture*—could anything be more ironic!—she had yet to play a passionate love scene with a great leading man. On the set of *Ziegfeld Girl,* when Lana bounced by, the electricians whistled; when Hedy swept by, the grips stared lasciviously; when Judy went by, it was "Hi, Judy!" . . .

If she wasn't to find it even in fantasy, she had to look for it, hope for it, in real life.

She threw herself, then, into real life, and Ethel watched one incident after another upsetting her. One episode with David particularly distressed Ethel. More and more they were seen together. David would come to the house, writing arrangements for Judy's Decca records, and helping with both lyrics and music for new songs of her own. (She had by now written nine poems, mainly free verse, which she had bound in different-colored suede bindings, with the title *"Thoughts and Poems,* by Judy Garland," to give as gifts, the first one to Ethel on Ethel's birthday the year before, one to David, one to Roger Edens and others to various intimates, including Barron Polan, who had been Mervyn Leroy's assistant and was an old friend of hers and David's, having dated her even before she knew David. She made each recipient feel that the gift was his alone.)

Musically, she and David were fine together. No one had a derogatory thing to say about David. The man hadn't a mean bone in his body. His mother was a warm, maternal, efficient type; he lived for his work and his hobbies, his latest an elaborate miniature train, but big enough for a person to ride in, which wended its way around the grounds of his house, where he now lived alone, cared for by a housekeeping couple.

Jimmy and Bobby Sherwood now lived in the valley with three-year-old Judalein. On occasional mornings Ethel drove over to take the child off Jimmy's hands for a few hours, as a grandmother's prerogative. She had to pass David's house on the way, and one morning, as she drove by quite early, she saw to her horror Judy's red roadster parked in front. Judy had told her she was going to spend the night with Betty O'Kelly.

One night months before when Judy had first begun seeing David, and it became midnight and Judy, who had said that she was going to the movies with several girlfriends, was still not home, Ethel decided to take a little drive past David's house—and, as she suspected, there was Judy's car. Midnight—and Judy seeing this thirty-year-old man who was still legally married. Ethel drove back home and got David immediately on the telephone.

"Judy is there at your house and you better damn sure have her here in fifteen minutes or I'll have the law on you!" she told him, and hung up. Judy was home in ten minutes, so outraged she could scarcely speak. Then the storm burst. How dared her mother humiliate her, as though she were some wayward child, in front of David Rose! And humiliate him, too!

But this was far more serious. When Ethel arrived at Jimmy's house, she was a study in fury. Jimmy, though flustered, tried to pass it off. "Oh, well, Ma, don't worry about things like that—they're always going on."

Ethel snapped, "Not to my daughter!"

Judalein was all bundled up and ready to be taken. Ethel picked up her grandchild and stormed out. The moment Jimmy heard her mother's car drive away, she telephoned David. When she demanded to talk to Judy, he was indignant: what made her think Judy was there?

Jimmy said sharply, "Davie, this . . . is . . . Jimmy. If Judy's there, I've *got* to talk to her." Then Judy was on the phone, furious. "What do you want?"

Jimmy said, "Honey, listen, you're in trouble. Mama came over this morning to get Judalein and she drove by Dave's and saw your car out front—"

"Oh, Gahd!" came from Judy. Then a wail: "What'll I do?"

"Call her on the phone," Jimmy said. "Get it done over the phone. For God's sake, don't go home and walk right into it. Or else have Dave go over with you so you both can talk to her."

Five minutes later Judy called back. She had telephoned Mama. It had been impossible. They'd just screamed at each other, first Mama hanging up on her, then she calling back, and then more screaming, and she hanging up on Mama. . . . Would Jimmy meet her and David at once at the Beachcomber's? They had to talk to her.

Jimmy found them in a back booth, holding hands, both fortified with a drink. Judy said with surprising calm, "I don't know why Mama's so upset. You know, we're going to get married."

"No, I didn't know," Jimmy said. "Did you tell her that?"

Judy's voice broke. "I couldn't tell her anything. She didn't want to hear anything. She thinks I'm just awful." They had been talking about getting married, she and Dave, but hadn't said anything to anyone, because Dave's divorce wouldn't be final for a while.

Later David spoke to Ethel, and apparently peace was made. At least, the promise of marriage made the romance seem less illicit.

Ethel would have been even more enraged had she known that such episodes, with Betty O'Kelly playing beard for David, as Jackie Cooper had once played beard for Artie Shaw, were not isolated. Judy and Betty went for a weekend to a new hotel at Lake Arrowhead, not far from Hollywood. As Judy put it to Betty, David and Buddy Pepper, a brilliant young pianist, who was later to accompany Judy in her concerts, were going up that weekend to swim, play tennis, have jam sessions with the band. They'd all have a wonderful time. David and Buddy would share one room at the hotel, and she and Betty another. Of course it did not work out that way, but so it would have been explained to Ethel had explanations ever had to be made.

In late spring of 1941 Ethel tried one more strategic approach. She invited Jesse and Lorraine Martin to afternoon tea. Ethel appealed to Jesse. "Judy wants to marry David Rose. It'll be no good for her. He's too old, he's not for her. I don't want her to marry him." She would be home from the studio in a little while. Would he talk to her? She always respected his opinion.

Jesse, his voice noncommittal, said, yes, he would talk to her.

When Judy arrived, he followed the plan that had been laid out by Ethel. He turned to Ethel and his wife and said, after a few minutes, "Why don't you two go into the other room and gab? I haven't seen Judy for a long time and I want to talk to her."

When the women left, Judy looked at Jesse. She said, "You may not think I know, Jesse, but I think I *know* why you're here today." She added, "You are here because Mother said for you to tell me that I shouldn't marry David Rose."

"You're sure of that?" Martin asked.

Judy's eyes flashed. "Positive."

"Well," went on Martin, with apparent indifference, "let me ask you a question. Do you love David Rose?"

"I sure do!" Judy said with spirit.

"Then marry him, damnit!" Martin almost shouted, thinking, *If*

Ethel heard me, all the better. He had promised her nothing. And he could not forget how this child had sat in his den a couple of years before, confessing her unhappiness, her wish to wait until she could buy a big, big house for her mother, and then she would quit the business. Well, the big, big house was here, but she had not quit: of course she would never quit. But she was entitled to have something go her way, if it would only assuage that strange ache of sadness he always sensed in her.

Judy leaped up and threw her arms around him. "I just knew you would say that," she cried. "I knew you couldn't do anything different, that you wanted me to be happy! Oh, thank you, Jesse!"

Ethel had to give up. She confided in her good friend, Ceci Sues, Leonard's mother, "I could still interfere with this marriage, Ceci. If I went to Mr. Mayer and really insisted, I think he'd just forbid it—Judy's career is going so well, and what will people think, a young girl like her marrying a thirty-one-year-old divorced man?—but if Judy has only a year's happiness, it would be worth it to me. Because if I don't let her marry Dave, she'll always say, 'Well, if you had let me marry him, I might have had some happiness.'"

One could hardly blame Judy. While all this was going on, Deanna Durbin, Judy's constant rival, on April 18, had married Vaughn Paul, an assistant director at Universal. It was an enormous church wedding, with all Hollywood present—and now Deanna seemed to seize happiness as well as fame.

Judy at first had played along publicly with her mother's wishes. She might marry in three or four years, she said, and then told *Photoplay* magazine: "I want Mr. Mayer to be at my wedding if I get married, and I want my wedding to be in a church with flowers and music. And I want my mother to be happy about it."

This last observation seemed, then, to dispose of David Rose. Indeed, Judy tried hard to paint a picture of harmony at home. Months before, to Irving Wallace, then a magazine writer, she had said:

"I want everybody to know this. I have the most marvelous mother that's ever lived. She's so different from other mothers. When I act, she's never on the set to tell me what to do and what not to do. When I ask her advice, she gives it. And sometimes, about certain matters, she even asks my opinion! Isn't that swell? My mother never dragged me to casting offices. Other children go every day, but I didn't see a casting office until I reached Hollywood."

But there continued to be dissension over David. The studio was not happy about it; nobody wanted her to grow up and be married. Judy and Ethel at one point had a bitter argument, growing out of half a dozen fractious matters. In the course of it Ethel said, "Well, this is your house. I'll move out and you stay here."

Judy retorted, "No, it's your house. I'll move to David's and you live here."

Ultimately, Ethel yielded to Judy's determination to marry Rose, but she did so with her fingers crossed. She summed up her attitude to the marriage with a statement that shocked David: "Well, what if it doesn't work out? So what?"

It was in something of this spirit that a formal invitation was mailed to their friends, reading in Old English script:

> *June 2, 1941.   1231 Stone Canyon Road.*
>
> *Miss Judy Garland*
> *requests the pleasure of your company*
> *at a tea and cocktail party*
>
> *Sunday, 15th of June, 1 till 5 o'clock.*

Within this folded invitation was the printed announcement of Judy Garland's engagement to David Rose. Ethel had revealed it to the press in an interview three days earlier.

For grandeur, entertainment and importance of guests, Judy's engagement-birthday party—her nineteenth birthday fell on the preceding Tuesday—eclipsed Deanna's wedding. It didn't matter that Judy, after *Ziegfeld Girl,* was once more back playing capable, sisterly Betsy Booth in still another Andy Hardy film, *Life Begins for Andy Hardy.* Here, in the beautiful home that her songs and talent had built, she was coming into her own as a woman with the promise of independence, at last, just down the road.

There were more than six hundred guests, and on the large green grounds Ethel had set up enormous yellow beach umbrellas. Bobby Sherwood's new La Maze Café orchestra entertained (Jimmy was his singer, once more back in show business, and Jack Cathcart's brother, Jim, played in the band, too, so it was all a family affair). Acting Corporal Jimmy Stewart, in uniform, home on weekend leave, was there with his sister, Dorothy, congratulating Judy on her engagement ring. Joan Crawford was on hand, and Ann Sothern, and George Murphy. Judy, swathed in a floor-length billowy gossamer pink gown with a diamond brooch matching her ring, stood in the doorway with David, handsome in a gray suit and white shirt with its long Barrymore collar and his ever-present pipe, greeting the guests, which included Jackie Cooper and Bonita Granville, solidly together again, Johnny Mercer and his wife, Ginger, John Payne and Ann Shirley, Tony Martin and Lana Turner, Lana bouncing little Judalein on her lap, Freddie Bartholomew escorting Jane Withers, now that Judy had long since gone into a higher, older league, Suzy and Jack Cathcart, the Rabwins—Marc, Marcella and Harry—the DeVines and other family friends. There was a giant engagement cake, two hearts entwined and decorated with gardenias; Hershey chocolate kisses and hard candies were distributed, record players filled every room with music, the younger people danced or played the pinball machines, and there was an army of photographers and reporters to make the event a part of Hollywood history. It was "Hollywood's gayest engagement party"; Judy was "Hollywood's youngest prospective bride." The marriage, it was expected, would take place in September.

But Judy was never one to wait.

Unexpectedly, during the shooting of her next film, a musical called *Babes on Broadway*, a natural outgrowth of the earlier *Babes in Arms*, she and David decided to get married. All that the movie colony knew was that Judy and David and Ethel and Will Gilmore were photographed dining in a Hollywood restaurant, all gay and animated, one night in the last weekend of July 1941; and that late Sunday night—actually 1 A.M., Monday, July 28—Judy became Mrs. David Rose at a ceremony before a justice of the peace in Las Vegas. It couldn't properly be called an elopement, since the bride's mother was along. If Ethel, as well as Judy, was deprived of a church wedding (here Deanna was one up on Judy), at least Ethel had at last attended the marriage of one of her daughters. Judy sent similar telegrams from Vegas to Mayer and to Freed. That to Arthur read, in effect: "David and I just married here. Please be happy for us and give us a week for our honeymoon. When I come back it's going to be one take from here on in."

The wedding, so sudden, so far in advance of the time it was to have taken place, made headlines.

Less than twenty-four hours later there was a call from Metro to Mrs. David Rose in Vegas. She was needed back on the set. *Babes on Broadway* simply could not be held up. Judy announced as she came off the train, "Even if we don't get any sort of a honeymoon right now, we're the happiest couple in the world." They were obviously very much in love.

The interesting thing is that David Rose literally drifted into his marriage with Judy. David did not press for the marriage, it was Judy who wanted it. She not only loved him, but wished desperately to get out from under her mother's control. David preferred to hold off, because of Ethel's hostility. But as they continued seeing each other, the result seemed inevitable. He thought, *Well, it all points that way, it all points like it might work out fine.* They enjoyed, both before and after marriage, going to the usual restaurants—Ciro's, the Mocambo, La Rue's—the nightclubs, the house parties. They had friends in common, though he found himself falling in with her crowd, rather than the other way around. His skilled help on her songs and poems, set to music he wrote or arranged, gave her a bracing sense of achievement in a field she greatly respected. Less than a month after their marriage Judy had the marvelous, ego-supporting experience of singing in her own musical sketch, "Love's New Sweet Song," for which she had written the lyrics and David a striking score, on CBS's *Silver Theatre.* She adored this.

Rose was careful to keep his and Judy's incomes separate. Few of the mothers of young girl stars were happy about their daughters' marriages, particularly when the girl earned several times as much as the man. A problem discussed endlessly at the monthly meetings of the Organization of Motion Picture Mothers was: *How do we keep our kids from dissipating their money, especially through a husband?*

David determined religiously, too, to keep out of Judy's MGM affairs—whatever financial dealings she might have there, whatever her professional problems with Mayer, Thau, Ida Koverman, Freed or her other bosses. Judy had her agents to advise her—he knew she had gone through a tearful, painful period months before, when

Ethel told Jesse Martin that he could no longer be Judy's agent. The conversation had taken place in the Garland home. As Ethel explained it, Ida Koverman had told her that no one could really go far at MGM unless Frank Orsatti handled her.

"Haven't I done a good job, Ethel?" Jesse asked, shocked, and not quite sure what to say. Yes, he had, Ethel said. But Judy's future would be more assured with the Orsattis; they handled everyone of importance at MGM, and neither she, Ethel, nor he, Jesse, should stand in Judy's way. She was sorry that it had to be this way.

Jesse had left, shaken, but not before catching a glimpse of Judy, who had been standing at the head of the stairs and so overheard it all, bursting into tears and running to her room. What further confused Jesse was that when he met with Benny Thau at MGM, in order to make the change, Thau said to him, "You don't have to give up Judy's contract." Jesse said, "I'm told that's what I have to do." Thau repeated, "And I'm telling you right now that's not what you have to do. We're satisfied with the way you represent Judy, and have been, and we're telling you we don't think you should sell the contract."

But Jesse, at this point heartsick, said, "No, I'm going to bow out. I don't want any more of it. I don't feel I can do justice to it now and I wouldn't want to do anything to hurt Judy, so I'll just pull out." And he had done so, selling the contract to the Orsattis, as he said later, at a "ridiculous" price. The change was unfortunate for Ethel. The Orsattis soon claimed they could not get along with her, and protested to Mayer; in consequence, Ethel woke one day to find herself banned from the MGM lot.

Later, because they were no longer able to handle her, the Orsattis in turn sold Judy's contract to Leland Hayward, who represented her for some time thereafter.

The separation of David's money and Judy's money was not precisely what Ethel had envisaged. She discussed all her financial problems with Peg DeVine, who was forever berating her for what she considered Ethel's carelessness with money. On one occasion when Jesse Martin was still Judy's agent, Ethel had sent him upstairs for a fresh deck of cards. In the drawer he came upon three of Judy's MGM salary checks, uncashed. He bawled Ethel out. "Good Lord, Ethel, how do you think I'll ever be able to get another raise for Judy? They'll come back with 'Jesse, Judy doesn't need any more money.

Our accountants tell us she doesn't even cash the checks we send her now.' "

When it was clear that the marriage was to go through, Ethel told Peg that she would handle "Davie's money" as well as Judy's. This suggestion, brought to the newlyweds, hardly helped sweeten their relationship.

The marriage itself was doomed from the start. It was actually over in eight months. Both Judy and David were busy with their own careers, and they had completely contrary work habits. David was dedicated to his music; he had, in addition to everything else, a half-hour daily radio program. He found it easiest to write at night, and when they finally bought a house, he had music copyists working almost around the clock to turn out scores for the various instruments. Judy did her best to keep his hours, to remain up with him, but she had to work days. When he was ready to go to sleep, she was just going off to work. The problem of lack of sleep, which had haunted her for years, was still further intensified.

Added to this was a discovery that Dr. Marc had made long before about Judy. She simply was a night person. She did not begin to function well until late in the day. That was how her metabolism worked. Just as there were Japanese clams which, even in the hundredth generation after being transplanted here, still opened and closed according to the rise and fall of the tides in Japan, so Judy's internal clock mechanism had been set from birth to be at its most sluggish in the morning and grow in efficiency as the sun crossed the heavens.

Freed had recognized this problem in Judy, and did his best to see that in *Babes on Broadway*, and in her next film, *For Me and My Gal*, for which Judy had the triple job of singing, acting and dancing with Gene Kelly, as much shooting as possible be done around her, so that she could arrive later. But she was in nearly every scene. This meant that if she was late, and scores of principals, chorus girls, dancers and extras, not to speak of directors, technicians, cameramen and the like, had to be paid to do nothing but wait, the cost became nightmarish.

Although during the early part of their marriage David saw no evidence that Judy was on pills any more than anyone else—by now everyone not only carried wake-up and sleeping pills in their purses and pockets, but passed them about like chewing gum—toward the end of the marriage it was observed that Judy would arrive on the set with dark circles under her eyes—almost as though someone had rubbed on blue eye shadow. Friends who noticed would worry. She wasn't happy, that was clear. She began to forget her lines—something unheard of for Judy, with her photographic memory. It was tiredness, lack of sleep and, over all, the struggle to be a glamour girl.

Dr. Rabwin added his appeal that Judy be allowed to arrive later than others, and wherever this was possible—this must be said for Mayer and Freed—it was arranged.

Once she and Betty O'Kelly were talking about marijuana. They had never tried it. Many musicians smoked it because it speeded up one's mind by slowing down the perception of time, so that ten seconds seemed like a full minute. This meant a player could improvise like mad. Judy wanted to smoke one. Would Dave get her a marijuana cigarette?

He said, I don't use them, but I'll get you one and you can smoke it on one condition: that you do it here where I can watch you so nothing can happen. Judy was all for it. One night David brought home a cigarette. He and Betty watched as Judy, in the living room, smoked it for a few minutes, inhaling industriously, and then stood up. "Why," she said, disappointed, "it's not doing a thing for me. I thought I'd be going over the rainbow! Watch." She walked steadily across the living room rug and when she came to the end of the rug, tried to step down hard and fell flat on her face. Dave rushed to pick her up. She could hardly stop laughing, though her chin was bruised. She had tried to step off the rug, under the impression that it was two feet above the floor.

At the beginning Judy thoroughly enjoyed her new home. Now at last she had a house of her own. She doted on it as though she were a child with a doll house. David had had over a thousand feet of train track surrounding his house in the valley. This was now brought to surround the new house, and as a wedding gift Judy bought him a depot to go with the train, and at one of their first parties all the guests rode on the train about the grounds and the swimming pool, and through a tunnel, pretending to ignore the fine soot that drifted upon their lovely gowns. But it was fun. From below, the sparkling lights of David's trains circling the Rose-Garland house on the hill had the appearance of a child's fairyland high above the city.

Judy turned out to be an admirable hostess. Among the first to come over were Marc and Marcella Rabwin, to find an exuberant Judy: "See, now I'm married and I have my own house and servants." She was very proud. At one party, they invited many people, there were great amounts of food, but nothing very fancy—no champagne, no caviar, and everyone sitting about on the floor. Then Judy said, "We've got to have a show."

With that she stood up and began to entertain, singing, dancing, doing funny bits of dialogue, clowning—she could be enormously funny among friends. Then she said, "I want to introduce you to somebody I love very much." She presented a tall, redheaded youth named Danny Kaye. He was still comparatively unknown in Hollywood, although he had been a hit on Broadway in *Lady in the Dark*, and, with his wife Sylvia at the piano, he had Judy's audience nearly choking with laughter. He became one of her most admiring, and admired, friends.

David tried to compromise on his working habits to make it easier on Judy. He brought an organ down to the pool and worked there in his bathing suit, while Judy and her friends—Betty O'Kelly, particularly, or Jimmy with little Judalein—went swimming. If he worked upstairs, they'd skinny-dip in the pool, between drinks of champagne, hoping David would stop writing and join them, but he did not. He and his copyists wrote till dawn, but at night, when he was not writing, and Judy really should have gone to bed, she'd stay up with him to do whatever he did—go out, visit friends, give parties or ride his trains with him—she simply refused to miss out on anything. But the next morning it was almost impossible for her to get started without an "upper."

On the set she was having other difficulties. She did not get along with Busby Berkeley, the director. She had had her first experience with him two years before when he directed *Babes in Arms,* but she had managed, supported by Freed and Edens. Now it was increasingly difficult for her to work with him. He spent hours concentrating on lights and on his sets, using long stretches of time to place his numerous cameras precisely where he wanted them, and guiding huge choruses through his elaborate, sometimes surrealistically spectacular choreography, and all this at the cost of virtual nervous exhaustion for others. Sometimes he was not ready to shoot until 6 P.M., which meant grabbing a fast supper and returning for hours of night work, sometimes until 11 P.M., which the unions then permitted.

There was no limit to the number of hours one worked, so long as the studio paid overtime for these so-called "golden hours." But it meant that Judy, who not only acted but danced and sang, had to be as alert, as vital in the last take at 11 P.M. as she had been during the first, at 9 A.M. It was to—it had to—take its toll, sooner or later. After all, Berkeley insisted on shooting his ballet scenes, his intricate, kaleidoscopic routines, from every angle, from above, from below, from every side—and later, when he got into his Esther Williams swimming extravaganzas, from underwater.

Some directors speak softly. Fleming, for example, was a paragon of gentleness with Judy on *The Wizard of Oz* set. (It was his calling Judy "Judalein" that led Jimmy later to call her daughter Judalein.) Berkeley was a shouter. To Judy he was always screaming, "Eyes! Eyes! Open them wide! I want to see your eyes!"—to him, her greatest asset. He wanted them to show up on the screen wide and sparkling. His mind worked with lightning-like rapidity, and often he'd bark, "O.K., do it!" Judy and Mickey would stare at him. "Do what?"

It would be hard to find two performers who could grasp directions more quickly, but they did not know what the man was talking about. Berkeley thought he had explained what he had in mind, and he had not. He was authoritarian—something that always put Judy's back up —and she worked with him only under stress. Yet he was the director, and she *had* to get along with him.

Slowly it became known that the Rose-Garland marriage was in trouble. It was no secret to their friends. To Betty O'Kelly one day, Judy said, "I'm miserable. I'm just plain unhappy. Dave is at his music all night and, you know, I really can't blame him for that. I wish I could say that he was a son of a bitch, but he isn't. I wish he'd do something, so I'd be able to put the blame on him, but I can't—he's so nice. And yet I'm miserable."

On another occasion Ceci Sues dropped over to visit one evening. Ceci was a widow; her son Leonard, one year older than Judy, had been a child prodigy with the trumpet, and he and Judy had been featured on programs together from her eleventh year. Ceci had often baby-sat for Ethel when she had to be away of an evening. As it came toward eleven o'clock, Mrs. Sues rose to leave. Judy pleaded with her, "Oh, Aunt Ceci, couldn't you stay a little longer? You know David writes music practically all night and I try to stay awake." Ceci understood then that Judy was "taking things" so she could remain awake. "Stay with me. I'll be alone. I just hate that," Judy said. But Mrs. Sues had to leave, and Judy reluctantly sent her home in David's car, an expensive right-hand-drive British limousine with a chauffeur.

Some thought the trouble between Judy and David was that David was too much on one plane for her; the very calmness and relaxation that had brought her peace at the beginning now bored her. Others thought there was another reason. They said that David had divorced Martha Raye for Judy; and for Judy, the conquest having been made, everything began to run downhill.

But if it wasn't the night work, it was the trains. One night Judy called Tony Martin. Would he and Lana please take her for a bite somewhere? David was busy, she was going out of her mind.

They went to the Brown Derby and had no sooner been seated in one of the booths than Judy burst into tears. She was utterly wretched. David wasn't paying enough attention to her—the man was mad for his music and his goddamn trains. "I'm going to kill myself!" she cried. At this point, before either Lana or Tony knew quite what to say, the waiter arrived. Judy looked up at him. "I want a cornbeef on rye," and added, blubbering through her tears, "and a cream soda, please."

To Jimmy, who visited her so often, she said, a few months later, "I just can't stand it any more." Jimmy asked, "Honey, what's wrong?" Judy said, "He's—oh, all he wants to do is stay and work—and besides, his mother's around all the time." This wasn't quite true. Mrs. Rose did lend a capable hand, as did Ethel, in helping run the house. Judy was so busy that she had to do everything by phone, from furnishing to buying groceries, and it was Ethel who interviewed and finally hired a couple to look after them. It didn't take the help long to discover Judy's shortcomings as a housekeeper. Though, years after, when she became a mother, Judy tried to organize her household by setting up a blackboard in the kitchen on which she wrote in chalk each morning the duties of the day—errands to be done, supplies to be bought—at this point the new Mrs. Rose was still one of Ethel Gumm's daughters. Judy, like Jimmy and Suzy, grew up rebelling against their mother's whirlwind efficiency. The result was that Judy felt almost a stranger in her own home, almost a victim of her own servants.

There was one other factor that might have contributed to the collapse of her marriage. There had been newspaper reports toward the end of 1941 that Judy would soon become a mother, but in the spring of 1942, after a bond tour, she developed what was described as a "strep throat," for which she was treated at the Cedars of Lebanon Hospital. Although some friends said this was cover for an abortion done elsewhere, Ceci Sues understood it to be a miscarriage, and Dr. Marc, then chief of admissions at Cedars, never remembered Judy brought there for post-abortion treatment—a fact he would not be likely to forget. Whatever the case, when Judy left Cedars and appeared in public again, she was thin and drawn: there was no more mention of approaching motherhood; rather one began reading reports of "incompatibility" in the Rose-Garland marriage.

But something quite beyond her or David's control had already taken a hand in their history. Japan bombed Pearl Harbor on December 7, 1941, and the United States was in World War II. This fact would ultimately help hasten the end of their marriage.

On the set at Metro, where in the summer of 1942 she was now shooting *For Me and My Gal,* she enjoyed working with Gene Kelly, whom she had insisted to Freed she wanted in the part though his first screen tests had not impressed the MGM executives.

Judy had met Gene originally as she had met Artie Shaw and almost every other personality she took a liking to. In the spring of 1939, when her mother took her to New York for a three-week holiday after completing *Wizard,* she had seen Kelly in the revue *One for the Money.* She simply went backstage, accompanied by Ethel, introduced herself to him and said, "I just want to tell you I think you're a wonderful dancer." Kelly, in turn, told her how much he admired her work.

A year or so later he was starring in *Pal Joey* on Broadway. Judy again was in New York. Again she dropped backstage, accompanied by Ethel and a retinue of MGM press aides. Again she and Gene traded compliments. This time an MGM aide said, "Mr. Kelly, why don't you and Miss Garland go out?" It would be good publicity for them both. Judy echoed it: yes, why don't we?

Kelly said, "I'd be delighted." They were taken to the Copacabana, where they were seated conspicuously about a huge round table adjoining the stage.

Kelly, then twenty-eight, and a man of independent mind—he was one of the few actors later to tell Mayer off in a letter and get away with it—took Judy out on the dance floor. They danced silently for a few minutes. Suddenly Kelly said, "This is a hell of a date. It's just ridiculous. I'd like to take you out, but I'd never take you out again like this—a ringside table and twenty people surrounding you." Judy drew back, stared at him and giggled. Kelly went on, growing more indignant with each word. "Don't you trust people, or is it your press agents that don't trust people? Do they think I'm going to rape you, or what? I feel like I'm in a goldfish bowl—even worse, like a silly gigolo, your hired dancing partner with these twenty flacks of yours watching me!"

Judy stopped dancing. "You're right," she said. "I want to have fun. I'm going to leave them right here. Will you come with me? Just us?"

"I'd be delighted," Gene said again. "You tell your mother and don't bother about anybody else. We're going out alone. We're going to have a date."

Which was exactly what happened. Judy whispered in her mother's ear, and before Ethel quite grasped what had happened, Judy and Gene were gone, leaving everyone else at the table to watch the floor show, which was just going on. Gene took her to Leon & Eddie's, on East Fifty-second Street, then several other small gathering places, returned her to her hotel at 3 A.M., the regular going-to-sleep time for people in show business, gave her a good-night peck on the cheek and delivered her to her mother. "If we can ever get together again for an evening . . ." Judy said. "You won't believe it, but this is the first time I've been away from Hollywood that I've had an evening alone."

So Judy had been one of the first to recognize Gene Kelly's ability, and she liked and admired him. So had one of Freed's production assistants he had brought from New York, Stella Adler, the actress. Freed had originally given Stella the script of *For Me and My Gal* to read, and Stella had made two suggestions.

For the dancer she recommended Gene Kelly, whom she had also seen dance in New York. But the script called for Judy only to sing, and for another girl to dance. Stella, who later became a distinguished dramatic coach, said to Freed, "Why have two roles? Why not have them rewritten into one and let Judy play that? She's not only a singer—she's a remarkable little actress."

Freed had introduced Stella, a tall, slim girl of striking beauty, to

Judy on the set of *Babes in Arms* a few years before. He brought her over to what she remembered as a little girl sucking on an ice cream cone. "Judy," he said, "this is Stella Adler. She's joining us as an assistant producer." Judy took one glance up at this breathtakingly beautiful woman standing before her, and, like a six-year-old, extended the cone in her right fist—her face down, her eyes looking on the floor, shyly—and said, "Do you want a lick?"

Stella was taken aback at first, then interpreted it as embarrassment and, with a laugh, took her lick. But she had only to watch Judy a few minutes to recognize that she was made for the stage; she was instinctive in what she did. Stella had been one of Judy's staunchest supporters from then on. Not to use her in this double role she thought would be unforgivable.

Freed's value to MGM was both his skill in choosing talent and his readiness to take good advice. Stella's recommendations turned out splendidly, though it meant more work for Judy. Kelly, however, found Berkeley even more difficult than had Judy. He, like Judy, was confused by the director's quick, sudden instructions, and his equally sudden way of handling the camera. Judy not only argued strongly for Gene to remain in the picture, which marked his film debut, but helped him cope with Berkeley.

Another of Judy's strong supporters on the set of *For Me and My Gal* was Freddie Finklehoffe, who had co-authored the script. Finklehoffe, who had also co-written *Strike Up the Band,* was an amusing little man who frequented the race tracks, and could keep Judy in stitches with his gags. In Judy's hearing one day someone had said to him, "You know, Judy has beautiful legs." Yeh, man, Freddie had said, almost with awe, "better than Man O' War." Judy loved that.

Finklehoffe wrote dialogue for her that he would not have dared write for any other performer. He had heard her sing "I Cried for You" in *Babes in Arms,* one of the most sentimental numbers ever written. Yet you believed Judy in it. As intelligent, as sophisticated a performer as she was, Judy herself *believed* it at the time. In those lyrics she was telling a story, playing a role, and, consummate actress that she was, she lived the part. It had therefore the innocence and impact and genuineness of a child who *believed.*

Finklehoffe often had disputes with the front office about his dialogue for her and Gene. Once Sam Katz, Mayer's administrative executive in charge of musicals, snorted, "This love scene will never work." "It will if Judy does it," Finklehoffe maintained. The story dealt with Kelly, a dancer, a wartime slacker who maims his hand so he can play the Palace. He virtually betrays Judy, the sweet, decent girl who trusts him. The plot was an MGM staple situation save that now Judy was teamed with Gene, far more the traditional male leading man than Mickey Rooney (they might have been Ethel and Frank Gumm), dreaming of the day when they would play the greatest of them all, the Palace. Not the Palace, Newark, where Judy and Gene find themselves, to their dismay, but the Palace, New York. There were such lines as "You'll never make the big time because you're small time in your heart"—this from Judy to Gene. But there were also love songs that broke one up—particularly one by Judy called "After You've Gone."

Judy herself argued with Finklehoffe about the dialogue. "Freddie, you can't think this scene will play. It sounds so silly."

Freddie: "Judy, if you do it, it will play."

Judy: "Well, how shall I do it?"

Freddie, nervous and full of energy, almost dancing about her and going into his race-track dialect: "Hell, baby, there ain't nobody gonna tell you how to do it, man. You just do it. Let it come out of your belly the way you do it. It won't work for Joan Crawford, she doesn't have the chemistry, but it'll work for you."

Judy, still doubtful: "But it's so—well, it's so God-awful corny!"

Freddie: "Maybe it is, doll, but when you do it, it won't be."

And so it would be proved.

In one of the frequent ironies in Judy's life, the picture paralleled reality; in it she was on a bond drive, and in truth she was on a bond drive in the summer of 1942, too. Not only did *For Me and My Gal* make Kelly a new film name when it was released that autumn, but with Judy for the first time billed above the title, she was even more the star.

A few weeks later David Rose found himself in the army—and this was the real beginning of the end of their marriage. In 1942 he had been inducted, then transferred to the Culver City Motion Picture Air Force Base. Judy was alone, save for his two weekend visits a month. When he came home, Judy, he discovered, was by no means living the life of a recluse. He would walk into his house in his fatigues and heavy army boots to find a party in progress, with people he hardly knew or had never met.

By mid-1943 some of these were persons Freed had brought in from New York as he built up his producing unit—directors, choreographers, writers—for his growing program of MGM musicals. There was Kay Thompson, one of the wittiest of women, and her husband, Bill Spier, a radio producer. Kay and Roger Edens hit it off at once. There was Conrad Salinger, a music assistant; Lella Waxman, a German-born music specialist and arranger, who became a highly valued assistant to Freed and Edens; Charles (Chuck) Walters, a dancer and choreographer and ultimately director; others were actors—such as June Allyson, Van Johnson, June Havoc, all brought from the East to Hollywood by MGM—all new people, exciting people.

To David, who was getting a far more drab view of the world at the Air Force Base, this seemed a faster, more sophisticated group. They played intricate word games and charades, everyone dealt in wit, satire and put-downs, and he felt out of it. He knew Judy was impressed. She loved intelligence, the outrageously daring, the supersophisticated; always she seemed unable to realize how extraordinary were her own talents, and almost genuflected in awe at those of other persons.

There was no question, too, that David Rose, in his baggy, unpressed fatigues, cut a far less glamorous figure than he had in his white flannels and white shoes, Brooks Brothers slip-over sweaters and Barrymore collars. It seemed to him on these visits home that Judy was learning new things, that she was finding herself in a novel, more challenging milieu, of friends enormously and even wickedly talented, as well as of lesser hangers-on, who flattered her shamelessly, of guests each wittier and more insouciant than the other, and it appeared to David Rose that their own paths—his and Judy's— were moving farther and farther apart. Judy was growing up—fast.

He thought, finally, *Really, if I just get lost, nobody will actually miss me—not even Judy.*

Not only was all this happening, but an extraordinary man had re-entered Judy's life. He had been at the far periphery of it, hardly visible, for several years.

She had met again—and this time with an impact which would all but shatter her—Joe Mankiewicz.

14

IN THE SPRING OF 1943, after a marriage of a year and a half, Judy and David Rose officially separated, although they had not really been living together for some time. It was amicable, it led to an equally amicable divorce more than a year later handled by Harry Rabwin.

There were no fireworks at the separation or divorce. But it was a difficult, confusing time for Judy, and before she became involved with Joe Mankiewicz, there was a brief, romantic interlude with Tyrone Power. She lunched often with him at Fox; once he gave her a copy of the novel *Forever*, by Mildred Cram, in which two lovers who plight eternal love are killed in a motor accident and only then realize their love is now truly eternal. "We'll make this picture together, you and I, Judy," Tyrone told her. Judy was transported. She had taken an apartment on Sunset Boulevard, where her next-door neighbor was Betty Asher, her MGM aide and companion. Judy was in love with the idea of making the film—and with Tyrone.

When she entertained him in her apartment, she kept the champagne goblets he drank from, and the corks from the bottles. Then Tyrone, that spring—he had just turned twenty-nine—having enlisted in the Marines the year before, was sent to the Marine Officer Candidate School at Quantico. Judy exchanged long, ardent letters with him. Once he sent her one of fifteen pages. She could not help telling Freed about it, and to Lillian Burns, her drama coach, she brought the precious copy of *Forever* Power had given her.

"Oh, Judy," said Lillian, despairingly. "Ty is such a nice person, darling, but have you any idea how many copies of this book Tyrone has handed about to girls? Please don't take it seriously, Judy, please don't. You'll never make *Forever* with him." Judy would not be disillusioned. "I'm sure he meant it, Lillian," she said. And when Ty came home on leave, they saw each other. Then, when he was back at the barracks, she learned from Betty Asher that he had been showing her love letters to his bunkmates, which utterly devastated her and finished him for her.

She was now approaching her twenty-first birthday, and working on a new picture, a Joseph Pasternak film, *Presenting Lily Mars,* once more playing a small-town Gumm Sister hoping to make the big time, and falling in love with a Broadway producer, Van Heflin. She was also working with Chuck Walters, a witty, exuberant dancer and choreographer, who had been called in by Freed to help her redo her dance finale in *Presenting Lily Mars*—a number she loved because it was sophisticated. Irene, the couturière, dressed her; her hair up, with a feather in it—she was no longer little Betsy Booth, the sturdy Campfire Girl with little Mickey Rooney, skylarking around.

It was an intricate number, and Walters realized she was not getting it. He said, "Hon-ey! We don't have much time to do this, you're kidding around with it." Judy whispered, "I'm just so damned scared —I can't move like this. I can't do it."

Walters sat down with her. He was always to be on the same beam with Judy. "Who's your favorite dancer?" he asked. Judy said, "Tony DeMarco." "All right," Walters said. "From now on you're not Judy Garland learning a routine, you're impersonating Tony DeMarco." Judy looked at him, wide-eyed. "Hey, that's a hell of an idea!" She went into the dance without any trouble. Somehow, his approach removed the pressure.

She liked Walters, and began going out with him; then she met Joe Mankiewicz again; for a little while she shuttled between the two, and then, all of a sudden, it was Joe and only Joe.

In the years since he had first heard Judy sing at the Wilshire Ebell Theatre, Mankiewicz had moved swiftly upward into the top echelons of Hollywood's writer-director-producers. In 1934 he had written *Manhattan Melodrama,* in which Clark Gable, Myrna Loy and William Powell starred, which led to the successful Powell-Loy *Thin Man* series; he had produced or written films for Joan Crawford, for Spencer Tracy, for Margaret Sullavan; he had done *Philadelphia Story* with Katharine Hepburn and Jimmy Stewart, and *Woman of the Year* with Hepburn and Tracy, the first in which the two were paired and for which Miss Hepburn received an Oscar nomination. Before him was a career which would bring him a reputation as a

Hollywood Renaissance man who did everything with equal skill—wrote, directed, produced.

Now in his early thirties, he was a handsome, arrogant man with a brilliant ability to puncture the pompous (a quality Judy loved), with a marvelously leonine head and deep brown eyes and a smile at once knowing, irreverent, mischievous and even boyish. You couldn't help liking Joe, even if you realized that behind that boyish smile he could be holding the most devastating opinion of you. He smoked a pipe; he was always with it. David Rose smoked a pipe, too, but with Joe the act took on a new glamour. He would chug away at it reflectively, eying it every little while, tamping the tobacco down, silent, thinking; he wore a slouch hat, a tweedy jacket with leather patches at the elbows, and not only Judy, but Ann Rutherford and Joan Crawford and Loretta Young and Frances Dee and many another actress, young or older, envisioned herself walking in the rain with him, confiding her dreams and aspirations to this wise man, this bright, tough idol-breaker and truth-seeker, who saw their potentialities, who could turn to a girl and say, "It's not your beauty or your talent I'm interested in, it's your brain."

Judy was so overwhelmed by him that when she dropped over to see Jimmy, she was now even more starry-eyed than with Artie Shaw. Like Artie, Joe was virile, dynamic, and had no time for bores. He had a fascinating background: he was a Columbia University graduate, he had lived in Europe, he had been a foreign correspondent in Berlin, he had worked at the famous UFA film studios in Germany, he was learned, he knew languages, philosophy, psychology, his father had been a university professor—indeed, the male members of that family—"Mankiewicz men," so the phrase went—were numerous and all a full cut above the rank and file of even the unusual men populating Hollywood. There was no question he could not answer, no platitude he did not expose in all its fatuity, no aspect of the Hollywood dream that he did not analyze so as to reduce it to its true vacuous dimensions. He stimulated her as no other man had done.

And he was such a sharp contrast to the many neuter or bisexual or homosexual men to be found in various capacities on the set, who were giving Judy obsequious flattery, gasps of praise for everything she did: Darling, darling, how wonderful, my God, how great you are! This sort of thing was to grow more and more prevalent in time, but even at this early stage Joe could say, "That's so much shit, Judy, and you know it. You weren't even trying!" Only Roger Edens and later Carleton Alsop, who became her friend and manager, could speak in this way to Judy and get away with it, as the legend built about her.

Joe brought Judy into his fascinating world. He took her to parties with his friends and organized one in a fashion still remembered. It was at Danny Kaye's house, where the audience was treated to an incredibly funny performance of *The Yiddish Mikado.* It was Gilbert and Sullivan in Yiddish. Joe sang Princess Yum Yum; Judy sang Princess Pitti-Sing, and Danny, Princess Peep-Bo. It had originally been written by Max Liebman (who later produced the celebrated TV program, *Your Show of Shows,* starring Sid Caesar and Imogene Coca) for Danny to use at Camp Tamiment on the Borscht Circuit. Only Judy had to be coached in Yiddish to do a proper job. The guests included James Cagney, John Garfield, June Havoc, Sammy Levine, Dore Schary, Laird Cregar, Keenan Wynn, Jimmy, Suzy, Betty Asher and a host of Judy's other friends.

Then there was her unforgettable twenty-first birthday party on June 10, 1943—a Joe Mankiewicz–Dore Schary project, which featured the playing of a record entitled "The Life of Judy Garland," in which Danny Kaye, Keenan and Evie Wynn, Van Johnson and other friends played various roles. It was the *March of Time* format, with irreverent comments from listeners. It opened with Frank Gumm and the two older sisters waiting for the birth of Judy, then Danny playing Baby Gumm at her debut in Grand Rapids, relentlessly singing "Jingle Bells," while the narrator, Mankiewicz, throughout reported portentously on the highlights of Judy's life to date.

These were the people with whom Judy was happiest—performers, musicians, actors, writers, directors—the societal environment she knew best and in which she felt most comfortable. Metro might want to keep her the little soubrette, but she was growing swiftly, and though Mayer had yet to recognize what a comedienne Judy could be, among her friends she was at her funniest, her gayest, and her most enchanting, not scathing, not putting anyone down, but making herself the butt of all her delicious jokes.

But the Garland family life had begun to break up. Jimmy's marriage with Bobby had ended. He had made the mistake of calling regularly on a young girl—she was to become his next wife—who lived around the corner from Peg DeVine, and Ethel, visiting Peg one day, saw Bobby emerge from the girl's house. When this happened again, Ethel, after wrestling with her conscience, finally told Jimmy.

Jimmy had known about it but hoped it would pass. She left Sherwood and later divorced him. Suzy and Jack Cathcart lived in Vegas. Ethel and Will Gilmore, surprisingly enough, had had enough of each other and they, too, had been divorced—an odd ending to so long a relationship capped by so brief a marriage, less than four years.

The huge Stone Canyon house, no longer needed, Ethel sold (at a low price, according to Peg), but made up for it by buying a house Peg recommended as a bargain on Ogden Drive in Westwood. Here Ethel lived with Jimmy, Jimmy's Judalein and Grandma Eva, still going strong. (She was not to die until she was nearly eighty-five.)

Judy had now seen the breakup of each of the three Gumm Sisters' marriages, as well as her mother's; but she still believed fiercely in true love, she would still find the man, and Joe Mankiewicz was that man. The exquisitely torturing fact was that Joe was unattainable. It was not simply that he was married; married men had been known to divorce their wives. But it was out of the question here. Joe's wife —his second, whom he had married in 1939 and by whom he had two sons—was Rosa Stradner, a former German actress, who was a psychiatric patient at the Menninger Clinic in Topeka, Kansas. Joe's suffering broke Judy's heart, but it was clear that under such circumstances he could never leave his wife even if he wished to.

Jimmy now was at MGM, too, because with her divorce she had gotten a job as a script girl at the studio. Now twenty-five, with an engaging personality, as outgoing and affectionate as Judy but far more in command of herself, she had never done anything but sing and be a housewife. Ethel called Ida Koverman and Jimmy, after a three-month training course, got the job, which she held for the next four years. It demanded a clear mind, an excellent memory, an ability to follow the script minutely so that when shooting resumed after a break, even if the next day, everything on the set would be precisely as before.

Now Judy and Jimmy, on the same lot, lunched together several days a week. Judy had one subject: Joe Mankiewicz. She was in love with him. She had given up her Sunset Boulevard apartment and taken the former Mary Martin house down the hill from where Jimmy lived on Ogden Drive. Now and then Judy had Joe to dinner, with Jimmy as the only other guest. When Joe was not around, Judy still could do nothing but talk about him. As always when she was in love, the man she loved was a paragon; nothing he could do was wrong, nothing he could say was wrong. "Oh, he's so brilliant," she said repeatedly to Jimmy. "God, he knows everything! He's the most wonderful man that ever lived!"

And Joe had been talking to her about psychoanalysis. He had read widely in it; he had once wanted to be a psychoanalyst; he was now in analysis himself. He had told her, Judy said, that she ought to go into analysis. "He says I'm a chronic liar," she said. As well as for other reasons, too.

Pooh! said Jimmy. Of course Judy had been spoiled rotten, and she had gotten away with so much from the day she was born, and she was now a big star, and she'd already loused up one marriage but so had Jimmy herself, and Suzy, and even Mama, and Judy was falling in and out of love every other day, but there was nothing mentally wrong with her sister. Of course she exaggerated, but that was part of her performance. She made herself the center of everything. You couldn't call that "lying"—or could you?

Exaggerate—good Lord! Jimmy could fill a book with examples. Judy could never bear the sight of an animal being hurt because when she was a little girl in Lancaster, she would accompany neighbors as they drove out at night shooting rabbits, which had become almost a plague in the area. Their auto headlights would paralyze the animals in the middle of the road, and the men would shoot them dead. Judy had cuddled in her lap a baby rabbit they had saved; the tiny creature lay trembling under her comforting hands. Suddenly the man next to her fired his gun; the baby rabbit in her lap quivered suddenly, and died—of shock. Now just the thought of hurting small animals sent Judy into panic.

A moving story—*but it had never happened to Judy.* It had happened to Suzy, who told her terrible experience to Judy, and from then on it became Judy's terrible experience.

And Judy's hysteria during a thunderstorm, dating back to a night when a torrential near-cyclone struck Grand Rapids and Ethel herself had been so terrified she hurried the children down into the cellar and cowered there with them for nearly an hour until the storm passed. That had happened, too—*but before Judy had been born!* The experience had been so memorable for three-year-old

Jimmy and five-year-old Suzy because it was the most violent storm they had ever seen. Judy had heard it from them, and it, too, had become her experience.

As Jimmy saw it, since Judy saw the world revolving about herself and her imagination was so powerful, she absorbed other people's adventures and made them her own. *And believed them.* Of course it was possible that that was the other side of the coin of Judy's quality: that she put this ability to believe into her songs, and *because she made herself believe them,* she *made* everyone else believe them with a reality that tore her audience apart. . . .

But Joe Mankiewicz saw more than a girl who merely exaggerated. Judy was beginning to have problems at work. She would show up late, despite all her promises to Arthur Freed, who could not be more kind to her, or to Pasternak, who in his sentimental Hungarian fashion forgave her anything. Not only had she trouble arriving on time; she suffered from headaches, and sudden, inexplicable fears. A few years later her complaints would be more specific: a sense of impending doom, an inability to work, a fear that her voice would leave her, or that in some fashion she herself might vanish, even a feeling that she wanted to die. Now, however, her need for help showed itself in an inordinate sensitivity, and a tendency to inflate the tiniest slight —obviously, she was a girl bound for trouble.

When Judy and Joe saw each other more frequently, Ethel's reaction can be imagined. Judy had told him stories about her mother's cruelty to her. How true they were was not really the question: this was how Judy *thought* her mother had treated her, and may have replaced something that *had* happened to her, which had to be brought out and dealt with.

Here, actually, was a tortured little girl who lived in constant terror of unknown things. She was pursued by invisible demons. What were they? The slightest thing could throw her into a panic. Why? He sensed in her an utter lack of inner resources.

Where was *Judy? Who* was Judy? Other than an extension of Ethel —conceived in her, grown in her, born from her, suckled by her, shaped, dressed, taught, directed, applauded or punished, *created* by her? One saw Judy in frenetic activity—work, men, play—existing only when she sang because that alone was what she knew she was. Only when she sang did she have reality; only then was she applauded. A man in love with her meant applause, too—and so she needed that just as desperately.

And she lied. If she wanted something to happen and she couldn't make it happen, she pretended that it had happened. Anything Judy wanted, she felt she had to steal. Everything had to be done furtively. One obvious explanation might be that since Ethel disapproved of much that Judy wanted to do—not the Judy that was Ethel's projection, but the Judy trying to be herself—Judy had to do it surreptitiously. Usually the mother bird fed and cared for the baby bird until it could fly on its own wings. But then it flew. In its own direction. Ethel would really never allow Judy out of Ethel's nest. Ethel and her friends, who always sympathized with her growing ordeal with Judy, saw it as a mother's natural desire to protect a child, a particularly valuable, impressionable child; but what was taking place was sheer substitution. So long as the baby remained Baby, Ethel, the actress, was fulfilled. Once the baby grew up, it disappeared—and so would Ethel.

The need to do things furtively explained a great deal of Judy's "I have to make arrangements"—seeing Artie Shaw by employing various beards, spending nights with David Rose before the marriage by means of ingenious plots cooked up with Betty O'Kelly and Buddy Pepper, and now Jimmy, once more playing beard, saying Judy was here or there when she knew very well she was with Joe.

One might think that Judy's entire life until now had been a kind of penance which she paid for with her talent, an apology for having been born unwanted, and the sex she was born, equally unwanted, and the shape and figure with which she had been born, which caused only trouble and embarrassment. Jesse Martin had sensed this behind her confiding in him that *all she wanted to do was "to build my mother a big, big house."*

One week Dr. Karl Menninger, who with his younger brother, William, ran the famous Menninger Clinic in Topeka, visited Los Angeles. Joe knew Dr. Karl, who had treated his wife Rosa, and now he talked to the psychiatrist about Judy and his own belief that she needed help.

Earlier Mankiewicz had given Judy several books on Freud. She had read them with interest. She seemed open to the idea of psychoanalysis. Mankiewicz arranged for her to call on Dr. Karl, who was staying at the Beverly Hills Hotel.

As Judy reported to Joe, Dr. Menninger had said, yes, she had problems; they could become serious; she needed help; and if she really wanted to be helped, she should begin seeking that aid now.

That Judy was taking pills was no secret to Mankiewicz. Everyone was. But in Judy's case it was not that uppers acted simply as wake-up pills; Judy was using them as much for the euphoria they gave her, which simply compounded her problem by disguising whatever it was that really troubled her. If others were taking pills in order to feel better than normal, Judy was taking them to feel normal.

Joe knew a great deal about pills. In addition to his other distinctions, he had been the first person in Hollywood to try Benzedrine. This had come about by a curious series of coincidences.

One day in early 1934 when Dr. Rabwin, still a bachelor, was staying with Joe, he came home from the hospital and took a white pill from his pocket. "Joe," he said, "you're the perfect guinea pig for this—the healthiest bastard I know. I want you to do me a favor. Take this white pill tomorrow morning early, and tomorrow night tell me how you felt all day."

Joe swallowed the pill with his morning coffee and rolls. He reported to Marc that night. He felt like God, he said. It was unbelievable! He was working on a melodrama—"I wrote fifty pages of dialogue, I went into a story conference, I was absolutely brilliant." No bad effects? Marc asked. None, said Joe, save for a little dryness in his mouth and throat. He looked at Marc. "Now, will you do me a favor? Get me a ton of this."

Marc laughed. No, he had given Joe the only one he had. He explained that the pill was Benzedrine—a new discovery by Dr. Gordon Alles, a brilliant biochemist who had been searching for an adrenaline-like drug to treat asthma without adrenaline's side effects. One compound Alles tested on himself was this drug. He found it useless in asthma, but it had peculiar effects: he lost his appetite completely, he was unable to sleep; he remained astonishingly wide awake and energetic for a period of seventy-two hours. Now, said Marc, just the day before he had unexpectedly seen Dr. Morris Nathanson, who had been his colleague at medical school. Mrs. L. B. Mayer was seriously ill, and Dr. Nathanson had been called to Hollywood for consultation on the case. While here he had dropped in to talk over old times with Marc. Dr. Nathanson was a man of original and inquiring mind, constantly experimenting with new approaches in medicine, and was always carrying his latest find—a new pill or device, or whatever intrigued him—in the pockets of his jacket. Remembering this habit, Marc had asked, almost jokingly, "What are you carrying around with you these days?"

With a grin Dr. Nathanson stuck his hand into the pocket of his jacket and produced the tablet Marc had given Joe. "Very unusual stuff, this," he told Marc. Dr. Alles had given him several tablets, telling him about their unusual effects. He had experimented on himself, he said, and the results had been the same; not only that, student nuns at the University of Minnesota had been using them to stay up long periods of time to study for exams.

Not long after this Mankiewicz began hearing about Benzedrine at the writers' table at MGM. Within six months after he had taken the first tablet, everyone was taking it. The discovery had swept the country.

What Judy had first been given at MGM when they sought to streamline her had been Benzedrine mixed with phenobarbital, because that helped you lose weight. Later, chemists added Amytal Sodium to create the well-known little yellow capsules—the capsules Judy now used, which—proof indeed of one reason she used them— she called "happy pills."

Judy came to a decision. She would go into analysis. Joe had recommended Dr. Menninger, but this posed a problem because he saw his patients in Topeka. Dr. Karl recommended Dr. Ernst Simmel, a German psychoanalyst of high repute who had been Sigmund Freud's colleague, Freud seeing patients in Vienna, Simmel seeing patients in his native Berlin. With the advent of Hitler, Simmel had come to Los Angeles, where he became honorary chairman of the Menninger Foundation.

Dr. Simmel had a special distinction. When George Gershwin had been taken ill in Hollywood in the summer of 1937, suffering from violent headaches, melancholia and a general lassitude, some of the world's best medical specialists had been called to treat him. They could find nothing physically wrong. It must be emotional or psychosomatic—the sort of thing that often happened to persons as gifted as Gershwin. Many of his friends tried to get him over his apathy with jokes and wit and even the suggestion that it was all imagination. Dr.

Simmel had been the man who ruled out their suppositions, and finally an exploratory examination revealed Gershwin's ailment—nothing emotional, nothing mental, nothing psychosomatic, but something genuine and awful: a brain tumor. By now it was too late: it was inoperable. Dr. Simmel's diagnosis won him even greater prestige.

Artie Shaw had been astounded at Judy's lack of ego. This struck Mankiewicz even more sharply because in the intervening years Judy had proved and reproved her talent. Yet her inordinately low self-esteem suggested a plastic creation living a plastic life.

Mankiewicz realized there was no bottom to Judy's sense of inferiority. She did not think that she was sexually alluring. She knew her voice was. Reports had got back to her from producers and actors—how her voice excited them sexually—but she herself, no. But she *was* sexually alluring, and practically every man who met Judy, or was in a film with her, wanted to go to bed with her. She recognized this, yet doubted it—and so constantly tested it. And her sensitivity —that exquisite invisible antenna she possessed which made her almost able to recognize the still unarticulated thought behind a man's eyes—that sensitivity made her play at being whatever it was that he sought. As Mankiewicz saw it, she simply faded into whatever situation the man proposed. If he played the image of a father, who knew what was best for her, virile, commanding, she, in turn, became yielding, helpless, possessable.

If he played the romantic prince, she was the little princess; if the sensitive, female-frightened homosexual, she was the tender, asexual unthreatening comrade. It was all a game and a challenge, and with it came the reassuring miracle of being loved and applauded, and part of the game was that sooner or later she ended up in bed with the man. The going to bed had nothing to do with morality or lack of it; it was, in so many instances, her way of assuring herself that she existed, that she was desirable not for her voice but for herself. If only she could be certain they were going to bed not with Judy Garland, the voice, the star, the name, but with *her*—whoever, whatever, she was!

But sooner or later the man got tired of playing the game and walked out on her; or she feared that this would happen and she suddenly—Judy was later to use a Kay Thompson phrase—"cut him off at the ankles," and the man would unexpectedly find himself out

184

in the cold. Betty Asher and Betty O'Kelly and Judy's few other intimate girlfriends knew it. Judy would say of someone, "He's dead." That was it. The man no longer existed. It was as though she had never known him.

Judy began seeing Dr. Simmel five mornings a week.

Ethel, when she first discovered this, was violently against it. But she knew Judy was having trouble at the studio. In the rider Ethel signed to Judy's contract of August 28, 1940, she had guaranteed that Judy would carry out her obligations to MGM. And more than once Mayer, aware of his rights, had summoned Ethel to say, "Judy's late —she walks off the set unexpectedly—she's beginning to forget her lines. You've got to do something to straighten her out." And Ethel, against her wishes, though frightened of analysis—suppose it siphoned away Judy's talent?—decided it might be of help. She rationalized it in another way. Judy wouldn't go for very long anyway. Having your own analyst was a fad in Hollywood now. Soon enough, Ethel thought, Judy would get bored. She had a short attention span anyway.

Actually, Judy was serious about her sessions at the beginning. But even in analysis Judy found herself performing. She worked on Dr. Simmel as she had been conditioned from her earliest years to work on an audience. And Dr. Simmel remained unimpressed: no applause, no reaction, no protestations of love flowing forward to engulf her.

Judy began to improvise. The teller of tales took over. She made up stories—wild stories of her treatment as a child. Not to get a reaction from an audience frightened her. It always had. It always would. Dr. Simmel listened, but, as it turned out, was not deceived. Judy was still sufficiently in awe of him to fear to call him up to cancel an appointment when it was impossible for her to see him, and she would ask Betty O'Kelly to make the call.

After two or three such calls, taken by Simmel's secretary, Dr. Simmel himself came on the phone one day. He said slowly in his heavy German accent, "Will you tell Judy that I cannot help her if she does not keep appointments"—and added unexpectedly, and by the softness of his voice making the words even more pointed: "And I cannot help her if she continues to lie to me when she does keep appointments. Give her that message."

Still, Judy continued to go, to Ethel's growing discomfiture. One result was that Judy now confided less and less in her. While this was an inevitable development in psychoanalysis—a separation husbands and parents always felt, because the analysand has someone else in whom to confide, and, in digging into herself, often begins to see either husband or parent in a different light—Ethel was hurt. She had always suspected sinister forces at work at the studio. Who knew who had whose hand in this? She had once warned Judy never to be alone in a room with Mr. Mayer, if she could avoid it. In this Ethel's friends were convinced that Ethel was allowing ancient prejudices and gossip to take over. Mr. Mayer was known to have his own ladies, all tall, long-limbed beauties, whom he courted in his own fashion, and Jimmy and Suzy were certain that Mayer looked upon Judy as a daughter and would have been horrified to think anyone would suspect him of having designs upon her, of trying to assault her—or, as the story always went, chase her around his desk.

Sometimes Jimmy drove Judy to her 7 A.M. appointment at Simmel's house, waited for her, and then drove on to the studio, where Jimmy, as script girl, was due at 8:30. If work for Judy began too early to permit a morning appointment with Simmel, she saw him when she left the studio. Sometimes Betty O'Kelly drove her; sometimes it would be Peter Lawford, a new and good friend.

Then, one evening, Jimmy returned home to find Ethel obviously bursting with news.

"Mama, what's the matter with you?" Jimmy asked.

Ethel came out with it. "I went to see Mr. Mayer this morning."

"What in the world for?" Jimmy demanded, immediately on the defensive for Judy. Most of the time she felt as though Judy were her daughter, not her kid sister.

Ethel now became defensive. "Mr. Mayer and I agreed that Judy shouldn't be going to the analyst." She had held off doing anything all this time because she had consulted with Dr. Marc, and he had said it might not be good to cut it off too sharply, that she should let her go for a while. Well, she had waited, and Judy was still going to the analyst, and was still seeing that man Joe Mankiewicz. Ethel was convinced that Mankiewicz had told Judy her mother shouldn't handle her money, that she was too big a star now, that it was time for her to grow up and have her own business manager; he had been

186

telling her all sorts of things—in short, undermining her authority. And so she'd gone to Mayer.

"Why didn't you tell Judy herself?" Jimmy wanted to know.

"Well, I told Judy I didn't want her to go to Simmel any more," her mother said with asperity. "She won't listen to me. I have to get somebody she'll listen to."

"The last person she'll listen to is Mr. Mayer," Jimmy protested. "She doesn't like him."

Well, said Ethel, Eddie Mannix was there, too, and he agreed, and Judy liked Eddie, so maybe it would help. Mannix, general manager of the studio, was a big, bluff Irishman who had once been a bouncer at the Riviera nightclub on the Palisades, in New Jersey, whose general irreverence made him one of the few MGM executives Judy enjoyed.

Then Ethel went on to tell it all: earlier she had ordered Judy point-blank not to see Joe Mankiewicz any more and Judy had retorted, "I'll live my own life. I will do what I want to do. I'm not a child. I've been married. You have to stop treating me like a little kid."

So there was one more confrontation between mother and daughter, and Jimmy was once more in the middle; and as she had done before, because whatever happened she felt she had to prevent a complete break between Judy and the family, Jimmy found ways to help Judy see Mankiewicz without Ethel's knowledge.

Mankiewicz himself had had one experience with Ethel; it was an accident, but it suggested the pressure Judy felt she was under at work—and this had been before Joe was seeing Judy.

Mankiewicz received a telephone call, and when he picked up the receiver, he heard an angry "Hello!" It was a woman. He replied, "Hello." The woman's voice said, "What do you mean, referring to my daughter as 'that goddamn girl'!"

Mankiewicz, nonplused, said, "Who is this?" The voice said, "Who's this? Isn't this Arthur Freed?" Joe said, "No, it's Joe Mankiewicz." The voice said, "Oh, I'm very sorry," and hung up.

Mankiewicz got hold of Freed at lunchtime at the commissary. "Jesus Christ, what the hell did you do to old Mrs. Garland?" he asked. He explained what had happened. Arthur said, "Yes, she called me. I said 'that goddamned girdle, Ethel, not that goddamned girl,'" whereupon Ethel had said, "Oh, I thought you said 'girl,'" added that she was sorry and hung up. They had been having trouble with the special girdle Judy had to wear.

But it gave Mankiewicz a picture of an oversensitive girl, outraged because she thought Arthur Freed, whom she should have been able to forgive anything, had dared speak angrily about her, and she had gone home so upset that Ethel felt it necessary to bawl out Freed himself.

Whatever the results of Ethel's complaint to Mayer, apparently nothing happened until one afternoon in 1943 when Mankiewicz was on the Super Chief, returning from a visit to his wife at the Menninger Clinic in Topeka. Mayer and Howard Strickling happened to be on the train, too, and learned that he was aboard.

Now a porter brought a message to him. Mr. Mayer was in Stateroom X, and would like to have breakfast with him the following morning. In the course of their breakfast Joe brought up Judy's name. The studio, he thought, wasn't doing right by her. She should have more grown-up parts. He'd been thinking—

This gave Mayer an opening he had been waiting for. With the abrupt, for-the-jugular attack he was noted for, Mayer opened up on Mankiewicz. He assailed him verbally as only he could. (Years later, Dore Schary, finding himself in Mayer's office while Mayer was dressing down Harry Rapf, a producer, had to leave the room, he was so humiliated and sickened even to witness Mayer's attack.) This time Mayer said, in effect, if his words can be summed up without leaping from the page, "You _____, you have a hell of a nerve bringing that up!" Here was Mankiewicz, who of all people knew his way around, having an affair with this girl thirteen years younger than himself, filling her mind full of crazy, dangerous ideas, which could only do her irreparable harm. Joe had to stop his association with Judy Garland.

Mankiewicz retorted, in so many words, "It's none of your business!"

Mayer roared, "I'm the head of the studio!"

Mankiewicz said, "Not at all, you're not talking like the head of the studio, you're talking like a very jealous old man!"

If one man's rage could have stopped the train, Mayer's would have. The two shouted at each other, the powerful head of the richest and most influential studio in Hollywood and one of the brightest of his director-producers.

Mankiewicz finally walked out.

In late 1943 he received a summons to Mayer's office. When he walked in, there was Mayer behind his desk, Eddie Mannix on one side, and Ethel herself in a chair. Ethel spoke. She was livid. There was nothing wrong with her daughter she could not handle, she knew what to do, she knew Judy's problems, her not being able to control this or that, her being late, her lying, men, everything . . . behind all this was that—that Joe Mankiewicz. She was saying so here and now, and she knew how to control her daughter, she knew it better than any psychologist or psychiatrist or psychoanalyst or nut doctor. . . .

She no sooner finished than Mayer picked up the litany. What could analysis do for Judy except mix her up? Making her hate her mother, hate her studio, hate Mayer, hate her work? Mayer began inveighing against Mankiewicz from behind his desk, but as he got worked up, he left his chair and began pacing up and down the room, dramatizing every word. It was a Mayer performance at its best, and had not Mankiewicz himself been furious, he would have applauded the old master. But to Mankiewicz it seemed clear that both Mayer and Ethel were themselves badly in need of psychiatric help, that both were terrified as they took turns screaming at him.

He stood his ground. "Look," he said, "this girl needs help." He had originally recommended Menninger because he was the best there was. "You've got a sick girl and she's going to get sicker without help."

The bitter, insulting exchanges became worse.

During all this time Mannix had not opened his mouth. He had simply listened. As Judy liked him, so Joe liked this refreshing Irishman who was honest and direct. The session ended suddenly. There was a moment of silence, more exhaustion than anything else, and then Mankiewicz, who was, after all, basically a dramatist, could not help uttering a classic line. He turned to Mayer and said: "Well, Mr. Mayer, it's obvious that this studio isn't big enough for both of us; one of us has to go."

Mannix all but fell out of his chair with laughter. He was to tell the story, with embellishments, for the rest of his life. Mayer, so outraged that he was silent for once, simply glared at Mankiewicz. These two were finished. Ethel was beyond her depth: she sat simmering with hatred and distrust.

Mankiewicz rose and left the office.

There was, of course, no possibility of his continuing at MGM, although his contract still had two years to go. He took a few months to complete what assignments he had, and went on to write, direct and produce at 20th Century–Fox. He had given up a great deal for Judy and what he thought best for her—he had given up his future at MGM, where he knew Mayer liked and admired him, and where there were no limits to where he might go.

Whatever Oscars he was to win thereafter—and there were many —were at Fox.

The end, when it came between Judy and Mankiewicz, was a fading away, but not before scenes of considerable poignancy. The inevitable had to happen.

Judy telephoned Jimmy to come over and spend the night with her. She didn't even know if she could go to work the next morning. When Jimmy arrived, Judy was curled up on a sofa, in tears. Joe had said, "I think it might be better if we're not together so much." She should try to begin going out with other men, and so slowly find someone else. The two sisters managed to eat some kind of supper, and then Judy began suffering pains—so excruciating that she rolled on the floor in agony. Jimmy called Dr. Marc, who gave her a painkilling shot, and she was able to sleep that night.

Judy tried to carry out Joe's suggestion. She dated Don Loper, then a dancer; Chuck Walters, the dancer and choreographer; Freddie de Cordova, later to produce Johnny Carson's *Tonight Show;* and she became close to Vincente Minnelli. In the summer she and Minnelli went together to New York on a visit; she seemed very much in love with him. But presently she found herself seeing Joe again.

Once more she would have Jimmy over to her house, to cry on her shoulder. Joe was mean, Joe couldn't come over, or Rosa was home from Menninger's on a visit and he was busy with her, or their two sons needed his time and he could not see her. Judy would find herself waiting hours at her telephone for him to call. It was a double burden on Jimmy, because at home her mother literally paced the floor nights in her concern over Judy.

Then one afternoon Judy called Jimmy frantically.

"You've got to come over right away—now," she cried. Jimmy protested. Judy had called her on the set at Metro, she had her script book in hand, she had to keep a dozen different details in mind. She could not come over now, but this was the last day of shooting, she'd steal two hours at dinnertime, from six to eight, and hurry over.

"Please, please," Judy implored her. Jimmy called Ethel, said she wouldn't be home for dinner, and at six o'clock dashed over to Judy's.

She found her in tears. "I'm pregnant."

Jimmy exclaimed, "Oh, God, you're not!"

Judy, in a torrent of tears: "I am, I am!"

Whose child was it? Joe's? Yes. Had Judy told him? No. Well, said Jimmy, you better get on the phone and tell him.

"I'm afraid," said Judy.

"If you don't do it, I will," said Jimmy. "Somebody's got to tell him and let him figure out what to do about this."

Thus supported, Judy telephoned him.

Within half an hour he was there. Jimmy excused herself and went into the bedroom. After about ten minutes she heard the front door close, and Judy came into the bedroom, dabbing at her eyes. "Are you working tomorrow?" she asked Jimmy. When Jimmy said no, Judy said, "Joe's made reservations for us on the train and we're going to New York."

Jimmy stared at her. "Who's going to New York?"

"You and me," said Judy. They were going because Joe knew a doctor in New York "who will take care of me."

Jimmy took a deep breath. "Oh, honey, are you sure you're really—"

Judy said dully, "I'm sure."

But why all the way to New York? Weren't there doctors here? But nobody here must know. Judy wasn't working on a picture at the time; she could go. And Jimmy could not let Judy go alone. To let Ethel know was unthinkable. . . .

Jimmy telephoned her mother. "Guess what! Judy's been invited to New York to audition for a big radio program, and wants me to go with her!"

Ethel was delighted. "I'm so happy she wants you to go, too," she said. At least, there'd be someone there to watch over Judy.

Three days later Judy and Jimmy arrived in New York, getting off the 20th Century Limited at the East 125th Street–Harlem station to draw less attention. Mankiewicz and a friend, a theatrical agent, were waiting. Joe had flown in two days before and was staying at his friend's apartment.

Next morning Mankiewicz and Judy visited the doctor's office. A rabbit test was made. Jimmy waited for them to return, and when they arrived, they said they would simply have to wait for the doctor's report: they expected him to call the next day.

The next morning the phone rang. Joe answered it. "Yes—yes—yes." He turned to Judy. "You're not pregnant," he said.

They celebrated with champagne, and then the two sisters were back on the train bound for Los Angeles. Joe had bid them good-bye, as Jimmy remembered it, a bit stiffly, yet courteously.

But it was the end. It appeared to Jimmy that Joe could not forgive Judy. For the next few weeks Judy telephoned him without reply, left her number at his house and his office, without return.

What was the truth? Had Judy pretended to be pregnant? For what reason? Sooner or later the fact would be determined. She had told Jimmy she was two weeks late in her period, and Jimmy had assured her that that could happen, and it didn't mean one was pregnant. But Judy would not be comforted. And she had been afraid to go to a Los Angeles doctor for a rabbit test—it might get out.

What is curious here is that Judy's memory of the episode is far different. As she recalled it to Liza, years later, the entire event had about it something of the gentle, romantic quality of *Meet Me in St. Louis.* When, panic-stricken, she told Joe that she thought she was pregnant, he soothed and comforted her. He said, "Don't worry. Whatever you want to do, we'll do. If you don't want to have a child right now—" "But I do, I want to have your child," Judy said she had told him. He comforted her again and explained patiently, understandingly, that he was married, that society was not sufficiently advanced to accept that sort of thing—and then he added, "But if you do want to have it, we'll work something out." Whatever the case, she should go at once to New York and he would fly on ahead so that he could meet her, and they would think it through there, away from the prying eyes of Hollywood. When she arrived, Joe was waiting, and took her to a lovely suite he had rented for them at the stately Plaza Hotel. From their window they could see the entire panorama of Central Park during the day, and at night the ice skaters on the beautifully lit skating pond were like a miniature fairy-tale set.

The next afternoon he took her carriage riding in Central Park, the two of them in the back of a fringed and curtained horse-drawn hansom cab, and as they rode through the winding roads, he told her that he had arranged for a private nursing home, where every care would be taken of her. In the course of the following day, with Joe tender and comforting and understanding, she went to the nursing home, where tests were made and she discovered that she was not pregnant.

Indeed, it was her mother's description of the beauty of New York, of Central Park, of those idyllic days she spent with Joe Mankiewicz, that made Liza then and there fall in love with the city and decide that one day New York would become her permanent home.

Judy told Liza, "I really wanted to marry Joe. I wanted him to leave his wife. I didn't like sharing him." And it was then, Judy told Liza, that Joe said to her: You ought to go out more, Judy. It's not right, you sitting at the phone, waiting for me to call. "I got angry then," Judy said. She started going out, and one of the men she saw more and more was Vincente Minnelli; and the day came when she could say with a certain pride to Joe, "Well, I took your advice and I went out, and Vincente and I are in love and are going to be married."

To which, as Judy remembered it, Mankiewicz's reaction was one of shock—and a certain relief.

15

SINCE *Meet Me in St. Louis* WAS THE BRIDGE, really, between Judy and the man she was now to marry, Vincente Minnelli, with whom she would have her first child and who would play an important role in helping make a woman of Judy, the film and its inception are worth contemplation. For of all the pictures Judy did at MGM, this was the one she was most adamant against doing—and it was the one which, like *The Wizard of Oz* and, years later, *A Star Is Born*, is considered a classic and one of her greatest films: all but flawless, not only in the quality of her performance, but in the perfection of the entire cast, and, beyond that, in the beauty of scene, the magically evocative mood of turn-of-the-century America established by Minnelli, the director.

It was to Arthur Freed that the seed of the film was first brought, and this unexpectedly and in a circuitous way.

Judy was preparing for her next picture, *Girl Crazy*—once more back with Mickey Rooney—based on the Broadway hit of the same name. It dealt—one grows weary, but it was one more variation on the same theme—with the girl who finally triumphs, now no longer a little Gumm Sister but a dancing star. The music and lyrics were by George and Ira Gershwin, and since it would boast a cast of fun-loving actors—Rags Ragland, Nancy Walker and Guy Kibbee— the music scored by Roger Edens, the script written by Freddie Finklehoffe, Judy looked forward to it, even as she was trying to make sense of her own life.

One afternoon Finklehoffe was in the New York office of Leland Hayward, the agent. Paul Streger, one of Hayward's assistants, was saying, "Freddie, I've just read some stories and they're great. They'd make a hell of a picture."

Where's the book? Finklehoffe asked. There was no book, Paul said. He'd read the stories in *The New Yorker* magazine. He had a whole batch of the issues that contained them on his desk. They were reminiscences of childhood in St. Louis written by a writer named Sally Benson. "They're darling stories about her growing up at the turn of the century."

At this moment there was a telephone call for Finklehoffe. It was from Freed, in California. "Freddie, you've got to come out right away," Freed said. "I have *Girl Crazy* all set for Mickey and Judy, Norman Taurog is going to direct, but the script needs more work."

O.K., said Finklehoffe. He'd be out in a week or so. "No, right away," said Freed. He had a shooting date to meet. Finklehoffe turned to Paul. "Give me the stories you're talking about." Paul tore them out of the magazines on his desk, Finklehoffe stuck the pages into a topcoat pocket and flew to California the next day. On the plane he read the Benson stories.

Freed had hardly greeted him when Freddie said, "Arthur, I know you've been kicking yourself because you missed out on *Life With Father*." Also based on a series of *New Yorker* stories, this was a

Broadway hit. Freed had loved it, wanted to buy it, but Jack Warner had beat him to it.

"O.K.," said Finklehoffe. He pulled a fistful of the crumpled magazine pages from his topcoat pocket and laid them on Freed's desk. "You listen to me, Arthur," he said, tapping the desk for emphasis. "Here's *your Life With Father.*" Freed began to read. He liked what he read; he saw not only a wonderful, homey part for Judy, but also a part for a pretty dancer he had discovered named Lucille Bremer, as well as for a remarkable little seven-year-old girl named Margaret O'Brien.

Within twenty-four hours the property had been bought for $40,000, and Finklehoffe and his writing partner, Irving Brecher, began working on the adaptation with Sally Benson, who came to Hollywood.

Meanwhile, Judy had started shooting *Girl Crazy* on location in Palm Springs. A tremendous sandstorm came up; everyone left, with orders to return the next day. But when they returned, Judy was not there. She had, so the story went, gone back to Los Angeles with Joe Mankiewicz.

Everyone had to wait three or four days until she returned.

While *Girl Crazy* was being made, Freed gave Judy the script for *Meet Me in St. Louis.* She read it with Joe. He advised her not to do it. Judy would be cast as seventeen-year-old Esther Smith, one of the four daughters of a St. Louis lawyer at the turn of the century, but she, Judy, would not be the star, Joe warned her. The phenomenal Margaret O'Brien, who would play little Tootie—the fourth and youngest sister—would simply run away with the picture. But the role Judy played—a typical Betsy Booth all over again—this time with a secret crush on the handsome boy next door, Tom Drake, who didn't even know it, was the same tripe as before. She definitely needed to be put into more sophisticated roles, Mankiewicz said, like Katie Hepburn, a couple of whose films he had produced. Judy was versatile, too. She deserved something with far more depth and promise to it. Others told her, too, that playing Esther Smith would set her back who knew how many years!

Judy went in to see Mayer—she was by now one of the few who could walk in without an appointment. She simply didn't want to do *Meet Me in St. Louis.* She was very upset about it. Mayer calmed her down. He would read the script himself. He had talked about Judy often with Freddie Finklehoffe, whom he liked. She never realized how much Mayer actually admired her; often she was to say that he saw her only as a commodity to be treated and merchandised as such. Once Mayer had said to Freddie, almost wistfully, looking out the window of his office and reverting to Yiddish phrases, because Freddie understood them, "You know, boychik," (an affectionate Yiddishism for "little boy") "it's too bad that she has to grow up. That Judy! What a talent she is! It hasn't started with her yet—wait—" and, in his dramatic manner, he spread his hands theatrically—"wait until it really starts. *Ich weiss!* [I know!] A real talent!"

Now he read the script and telephoned Freed. "Judy's been up here raising hell about this, Arthur. I've read it and I must say she's right. Because nothing happens in it." He went so far as to call in several other MGM executives. They agreed. What was the story? Nothing happened. A man lived in St. Louis with his family, he wanted to move to New York because he was offered a higher-paying job there, they didn't want to leave, and in the end he yielded to their wishes and they all remained in St. Louis. What was the story?

Only Freed and the director Freed had assigned to it, Vincente Minnelli, stood firm for it. That Freed had chosen Minnelli was one of those mysterious throws of the dice so significant in Judy's life. Freed originally wanted George Cukor to direct, but Cukor had gone off to war. Minnelli had volunteered for the army, too, but was rejected because he was anemic. So he was on the picture. He thought it a wonderful story, he had been working on the script with Finklehoffe and Brecher, repeatedly going back to Miss Benson's stories themselves, for she had caught the flavor of her childhood days beautifully. Minnelli the director, the artist, the scene painter, the creator of moods, saw possibilities in color, emotion and drama that others apparently did not.

Judy, informed that both Freed and Minnelli insisted on doing the picture, decided, *I will go in and talk to this Mr. Minnelli.* Their relationship was a courteous-nod-and-hello one. In addition, Minnelli seemed to move in his own remote, preoccupied aura; he could be a strangely distant man.

She walked into his office. "This script—" she held it in her hand —"it isn't very good, is it?" Minnelli was the kind of courtly man who, if a guest entered, would leap from behind his desk, get a chair, seat his guest and offer her coffee from an ever-present silver pot on his desk, cigarettes, candies, whatever. Although he was a nervous man, one forgot his fidgety quality, even his stammer, because of his charming, thoughtful manners, and it was difficult for Judy to march in, confront him and say bluntly, "I hate this, I don't want to do it." So she had said, "It isn't very good, is it?"

Minnelli surprised her with an absolutely inflexible and assured response: "No, it's marvelous. I think it's very good." He did not understand why she was there. No one had told him how Judy felt about it: that she had actually gone to Mayer himself, that Mayer had telephoned Freed, that there had been conferences up and down the line, and that it appeared that only Freed and he liked it. Freed, skilled at keeping everybody around him happy, had kept this dissension from him. Judy left after a few minutes, having gotten nowhere with this soft-spoken but stubborn man, and quite bewildered. What could he see in this script?

Before a final decision, Mayer did one more thing. Chief among his script readers was a woman named Lillie Messenger. Lillie had a most remarkable ability as a storyteller. If she liked a script or a treatment, she could retell it to Mayer in a fashion that pointed up its potentialities so eloquently that Mayer was won over.

Minnelli and Judy were lucky that Mayer gave the script to Lillie. "O.K.," he said. "Tell me what you think." Lillie was enthusiastic. The flavor of the script was the finest kind of Americana. It was *family*.

That was all that was needed. Mayer would go ahead. In addition, Freed's record was good, and Minnelli's, too. Judy, with all her doubts, yielded.

Judy had had troubles with Berkeley. Now she had them with Minnelli. They began on the very first day of shooting. This man didn't shout, but he could be just as stubborn, just as insistent that a shot be taken and retaken until it was exactly as he wanted it.

The two older Smith sisters were played by Lucille Bremer and Judy. For Judy, what was ironic in the making of the film was that though Lucille was actually a year younger than she—only twenty— Lucille played the eldest Smith daughter, nineteen-year-old Rose, to Judy's seventeen-year-old Esther. Even worse, though Lucille was an amateur as an actress, in the very first scene in which Minnelli directed both of them, Lucille did better than Judy.

The two sisters, preparing to go to a party, look at themselves in their dressing-room mirror and talk about the color of their hair. Judy thought her lines were nonsense and threw them away. She should have said them with absolute conviction. On the other hand Lucille was almost perfect: she spoke her lines as though Judy's were the height of perception. Lucille said her lines believingly because she really believed them.

Time and again Minnelli shot the scene that first morning. Each time Judy failed him. They halted for lunch. Minnelli said calmly, "We'll try the scene again after lunch."

Judy walked into her dressing room and telephoned Freed. Would he please come down? "I just don't know what this man wants. The whole morning's gone by and we still haven't got a shot." She added, "He makes me feel I can't act."

Arthur comforted her. "Well, Vince is from New York and sometimes he's a little hard to understand, but you'll get on fine with him. You'll see."

It took some time for Judy to see, because Minnelli compounded her distress by insisting not only upon working endlessly on scenes but on calling her back to do retakes after she thought she was finished for the day. By this time Judy was being given MGM's top-star treatment. A car brought her to the studio each morning—she was usually the last to arrive—and on the set the word would pass like wildfire, "Her car's coming through the gate—she'll be here any minute." When she appeared, everyone would be on their toes so that nothing might go wrong to further exacerbate the polite coolness between director and star. Judy was accustomed now to remain in her dressing room, being made up, until her call came; then she went before the camera, did her work quickly and expertly, got to her car and left.

There was one difficult scene upon which Minnelli lavished hours of attention. This was one in which the entire Smith family sat about the dinner table, eating and talking: father, mother, grandfather and daughters, each with lines to say. Minnelli saw it as a musical fugue —different instruments repeating the same melody, each in its characteristic way, different voices contributing to the same subject. He felt this simply could not be overrehearsed; everyone had to come into the conversation at the right moment, with the right inflection, the whole possessing a perfect, mounting unity. He had set up the dinner table on a separate set, and each time he finished another scene with a few minutes to spare, he had everyone sit down at the table and rehearse the dinner scene.

This afternoon Judy had finished her sequences for the day, had gotten into her car and was already driving out the gate when the doorman stopped her with a message: "Mr. Minnelli wants you back on the stage to rehearse." This was unheard of; it was like being kept after school; but Judy swallowed her indignation, returned, and Minnelli quietly and imperturbably had her take her place at the table. They rehearsed the scene three times. When they finished, Judy overheard him say, "Well, I know that when we come to shoot it, we'll still have to work on it." She was fuming as she rose from the table. "This is ridiculous," she muttered to Mary Astor, who played Mrs. Smith.

Miss Astor surprised her. "Judy, I've been watching that man. He knows what he's doing. He's absolutely right." It was hard to fault Mary Astor, who had done more than ninety films. Against such experience, Judy had to calm down.

What Minnelli was teaching her—and it was invaluable—was how to be part of a whole. She had always been on her own. She had always been the principal, even back in the Gumm Sister days. Hers had been the solo part. Vincente wanted her to be one of many tones, a voice in an orchestra of many fine voices. This was difficult for her. She had realized it when she told Artie Shaw long before that she could never be a singer in his band, simply one more instrument. But here it was required of her; and once she realized what it was that Vincente sought, they got along much better, and her admiration for him increased proportionately.

Vincente had another supporter on the set. This was Dottie Ponedel, Judy's new and skillful makeup woman. Judy had gotten Dottie as she usually got what she wanted: by making a direct approach. One day Joan Blondell, an old friend, dropped by, her makeup still intact from a picture she was shooting.

Judy stopped her. "Hey, how you look! Who did that?"

Joan told her—a makeup woman named Dottie Ponedel who worked at the various studios. Everyone wanted her: Marlene Dietrich, Paulette Goddard, Joan herself—they all fought over her. Dottie had given Carole Lombard her distinctive look, with that marvelously high forehead, removing the bangs she used to wear, adding a touch here and there, and lightening the forehead, so that it loomed out, a thing of beauty. It was Dottie to whom Director Josef von Sternberg had turned when he wanted plump Marlene Dietrich made mysterious-looking for the film *Morocco*. "Do something crazy and different with her," he had said. And Dottie had given Dietrich the famous sunken-cheeks appearance, and those fabulous eyebrows. Dottie had "magic hands," Joan said.

"I want her," said Judy. She spoke to Mayer, and Dottie became the first and only makeup girl ever to be put under contract by Metro, and the highest-paid in her field. Judy took to her the moment they met. She had walked into her dressing room, carrying in the little box she always had with her the portable caps for her teeth and the little rubber disks used to turn up her nose.

Dottie took one disgusted glance at these and said, "Oh, Christ, throw those things down the toilet. I don't need them. Just let me fix you up a little." She went to work on Judy, raising her hairline, reshaping her eyebrows, her mouth, highlighting and shadowing where she found it necessary. She had become more than Judy's makeup artist; old enough to be Judy's mother, she became her inseparable companion, confidante and adviser, virtually living in Judy's dressing room, as ready for the wildest escapade as Judy, and with the same raffish sense of humor, and just as ready to place Judy's head on her shoulder and comfort her—not to mention the fact that Judy could count on her to do more with a sponge and half a glass of stale Coca-Cola than another makeup girl could do with a painter's palette. Dottie, to whom nothing was sacred, and who Judy felt told her things as they were, thought highly of Vincente. This did him no harm in Judy's eyes.

Presently she grew to know Minnelli on more personal terms. Don Loper, later a well-known fashion designer, was one of the men Judy was going out with at the time. One evening Don called Vincente: Don was taking Judy to dinner, but there was another of Don's friends, a player named Ruth Brady, whom it would be nice to take along. Would Vincente escort Ruth, and make it a double date?

Vincente, a bachelor, accepted. The four went out: Don and Judy, Vincente and Ruth. They got along handsomely. Judy was full of zany stories, and a delightful companion, whatever her private dilemmas; Don and Ruth and Vincente made an excellent audience; and Vincente himself revealed a deliciously dry humor, a quiet, wry sense of the absurd and the ridiculous that Judy found enormously likable. He could do impersonations that were brilliant and devastating—something you would not expect of this remote man.

A few nights later the four went out again. A week later Don set it up once more, only to phone Vincente to say, "I'm sorry, I can't make it tonight, Vince. Will you call Judy and tell her we've got to call it off?" Vincente dutifully called Judy. "I'm sorry, this thing is off tonight because Don can't make it."

Judy, in her own inimitable way, inimitable because her inflection made it seem ridiculously funny yet completely logical, said, "Well, fella, why don't we go out together? We don't have to have Don and Ruth along. We can go out by ourselves."

Judy had never met anyone quite like Minnelli. He had style. The man had had his own Japanese valet when he was twenty-three—and this after a difficult financial beginning. His father had been a musical director, his mother an actress, and he had been part of the family touring troupe, known as the Minnelli Brothers Dramatic Tent Show, which barnstormed the country, and in which he played children's parts. She could sympathize with that.

Then he had gone off on his own. He wanted to be a painter. She loved the stories of his experiences in New York, where he lived on practically nothing in a Greenwich Village flat. Then he found himself a scenic designer at Radio City Music Hall, where he had to create a new show every week; it was invaluable training and he rose swiftly. He was an artist such as she had never known before; she was all admiration. He collected porcelain; he gave her books on art, on music. Not only did he know everyone in the theatre and literary world, from Cole Porter to George Balanchine to Josephine Baker to S. J. Perelman to William Saroyan; he had also known Harold and Anya Arlen before they were married, and the Gershwins when they all lived in New York, as well as Oscar Levant and Dorothy Parker and Moss Hart and Kitty Carlisle. When Judy began going with Vincente, breaking away from Mankiewicz, it was almost like being adopted into another branch of the same fabulous family. She was quite impressed.

It became a courtship, and a beautiful one. He gave her drawings by Max Beerbohm; he had a large library; he explained his enthusiasms. She accompanied him to auctions, picked up lovely bric-a-brac; she fell in love, through him, with antiques.

And throughout it all, Vincente treated Judy always with unfailing Old World courtesy. He placed her on a pedestal—a woman to be adored. Years later his daughter Liza said to him, after an episode with one of his later wives—he was always in love—"Daddy, you let women walk all over you. You just spoil them terribly!"

He had replied, "I thought that was what they were for."

Until Judy met Vincente, she had been treated by every man, with the exception perhaps of Mankiewicz, as a talented child, not a growing woman. She had once said to an interviewer, "I'll tell you who is a good friend of mine, though it's so funny, because she's so glamorous and I'm so unglamorous. That's Lana Turner. We make a funny couple when we walk together." But she knew that if she entered a room with Lana, everyone looked first at Lana, but within five minutes Judy was the one who was holding court, and everyone's eyes and attentions were upon her. So, despite her lamentations and the wry, self-deprecating humor about what she thought was apparent to everyone, she was aware on some subterranean level that there was a beauty, a loveliness, within her. But it was Vincente who made her really feel it. He made her feel a woman: he convinced her that she was extremely attractive. He treated her as an exquisite female, not a talented property.

But he admired her, too, as an actress. Some of her accomplishments amazed him. After a complicated scene had been rehearsed until every move was perfect, and she was about to go before the camera, at the last moment he might find it necessary to give her half a dozen new changes: enter from stage left, not right; turn on this word, not that; the same gesture with a cigarette, not a flower; and the like. She would say, "Yes, yes, yes," and he would wonder almost despairingly, *Am I getting through to her and if I am, how can she possibly keep all these changes straight?*

The unbelievable fact was that she could. She would go before the camera and every last-minute revision would be included as if she had rehearsed them all morning. Fantastic! he would cry. *But she was an actress.* She knew there were a dozen different ways to play a scene and she was prepared to play that scene in any one of those ways.

He knew something of her troubles. He knew her divorce to David Rose was on its way. He knew she was—or had been—involved with

Joe Mankiewicz. It was impossible to keep secrets in Hollywood. Perhaps the closest confidants of the stars were their hairdressers, their wardrobe ladies, their makeup men and women, whom they saw constantly, with whom they spent time alone in their dressing rooms, their maids, their stand-ins.

And these men and women lived vicariously the lives of the glittering stars they served, who confided in them to a remarkable degree, and often took their advice as coming from sound, common-sensical and unneurotic counselors. The grapevine was all-encompassing, on the makeup-room level, on the Gallery level, on the commissary level, on the players' level, on the directors' and producers' level, and finally on the exalted level of the Mayers, Selznicks, Warners, Cohns, Goldwyns and the rest. If that was not enough, there were the newspapers and magazines, the gossip columns, legitimate or run by scoundrels, the blackmail columnists with their "blind" items, not to speak of the headwaiters at the top restaurants, the nightclub managers, the talebearers and jokesters and tipsters: Hollywood was a vast expanse of mirrors mirroring images on and on, like the cover of the old-fashioned Post Toasties breakfast-food box, in which a girl looked into a mirror and saw herself repeated, ever smaller, until the image dwindled into invisibility.

Hollywood was as important a news center as New York, Washington, London, Berlin; newspapers sent some of their best reporters to Hollywood, and Hitler's triumphs in Europe or Churchill's speeches often got the lesser headlines in the Los Angeles newspapers if they had to compete with a major Hollywood story.

Judy's own problems led to difficult moments on the *Meet Me in St. Louis* set. Perhaps the worst dealt with the important Christmas party scene. Some 150 extras were to dance in the ballroom. It was a spectacle of swirling color and beautiful moving couples, all melded together in the tasteful Minnelli style.

Shooting was to begin at 8 A.M. Eight o'clock—no Judy. Nine o'clock—still not there. Ten—eleven—costs were mounting astronomically. Everyone knew Judy was falling in love with Vincente; perhaps she'd quarreled with him the night before. He had vanished into his office, waiting. Whatever the case, she was not there. Freed finally came down. It was now noon. Judy was not to be found. Not at home, not in her dressing room, reachable by no telephone call.

Then she appeared. It was well after one o'clock.

The first to see her was Mary Astor, who was boiling-mad. She had tremendous respect for Judy, and felt an almost proprietary interest in her career. Like so many others she had seen the young Judy as a twelve-year-old Gumm Sister. Then Miss Astor had played Judy's widowed mother in *Listen, Darling,* back in 1938, when Judy was a teen-ager; now in *Meet Me in St. Louis* she was playing her mother again. How could Judy, so professional, so talented, do a thing like this? She said to her sharply, "Well, what is this big-actress act you're putting on! Holding one hundred fifty people up so long." Judy clutched her arm tightly. "Mom, I can't sleep," she whispered. Miss Astor—she was to regret it years later, thinking, *How tired Judy looked, how unobservant I must have been*—said to her angrily, "Well, you get the hell out there or I'm going home."

When Judy took her place, everyone expected an explosion from Freed. If Freed, even good-natured Freed, exploded, he could not be blamed. He alone was responsible for the production costs. But when Freed saw her, he went to her, put his arm about her shoulders and said gently, "What's the matter with my little girl?"

No recrimination, no anger. She made her explanation, fuller than the one she had given Mary Astor. Troubled by insomnia, she'd been unable to fall asleep until almost dawn, had just awakened, and had come right to the set. And he accepted it. Some estimated her tardiness to have cost $30,000 at least: 150 extras paid at an hourly rate, in addition to overhead, cameramen, grips, electricians, sound men, dozens of other employees, not to mention the other players.

Clearly Judy bore a charmed existence on the lot. How Minnelli reacted is not recorded. But on another occasion, when the subject of Judy's tardiness arose, Freed said, naming a dependable performer, "She comes in on the minute and does her work. You can count on it. But what she does doesn't make millions stand on their chairs and cheer. Judy does."

Her friends were beginning to notice a change in Judy. She had not only the dark-blue circles under her eyes, which Dottie could, in a few minutes, make disappear; but she had become thin. Visitors remarked on it. One was Margaret Hamilton. Since Margaret was a free-lance actress, this was the first time they had bumped into each other in years. Maggie, who was then on another Metro film, met Judy in the makeup room. They rushed at each other and hugged and kissed. Then Maggie drew back and looked at her. She was shocked to see how much weight she had lost. "You're getting awfully thin, honey," she said. Judy replied, "I know, but I have to." Maggie had heard that Judy was on a "crash diet." After Judy left, a makeup woman, working on Maggie, asked, "How does it feel to see her after all these years?"

Maggie said, "It's just wonderful, but she's so thin. I thought maybe it's her hair—she's got a very severe hairdo that makes her face seem even thinner."

The makeup woman said, "She has lost a lot of weight."

"Why do they insist on this so much?" Maggie asked. "It doesn't seem to me that it's good for her."

"No, it's not good for her at all," the other said. "But lots of things aren't good for her these days." When Maggie pushed the question, the anonymous makeup woman said, "Well, do you think she seems the same Dorothy you knew?" This led into some minutes of worried conversation. It appeared that Judy had become "difficult." Miss Hamilton bristled. "I just can't imagine that. Why?"

"Well, she's nervous and tense." And of course, there was the divorce she was going through. "The main thing is, she simply can't get her rest," the woman said. And, as she had heard it, "they" were giving Judy something to help her sleep and then something to wake her up again, because she slept so heavily.

The legend was already building up.

Judy herself told Vincente one night they had gone out to dinner that she was taking pills. She brought the subject up delicately: "I use these pills—they carry me through." In later years she would not call them pills. They were "medicine" or "medication." He knew she had been using them to sleep and to get herself started in the morning long before they met.

When she said she used pills "so I can be at my best before the camera," he said, quietly, well, so long as she didn't overdo it . . . He had once tried pills himself, and told her about his experiences. When he was directing *Hooray for What!*, he had been going continuously for some forty-eight hours without sleep, and finally Russel Crouse, one of the play's authors, took him aside. "Look, Vince, you've got to get away and rest for a few hours. We're worried about you. Take this pill right now—" he handed him one—"and set your alarm clock and when you wake, take this one." And he gave him a second.

Vincente followed directions. He went to his hotel, took the pill, fell asleep, slept well, and when the alarm woke him, swallowed the other, and was himself, full of energy again, going through things click! click! click! for another forty-eight hours. It was remarkable. Then, of course, the letdown, the awful collapse—and the enormous temptation, knowing what energy lay in those little pills, to take more. They were dangerous indeed, but for him it had been only a one-time thing.

But Vincente had not the combination of emotional and professional problems that were tearing at Judy. She had to be gay and sparkling in front of the camera at all times, no matter how bone-weary she was from her work, into which she threw herself with all her heart, or how drained she was by her personal problems, which she similarly treated with such life-or-death intensity; she had to, in Vincente's words, "dredge it up"—the gaiety, the sparkle, the personality, the very magic that was Judy. They were paying her enormous sums of money, she could not let them down, above all she could not let herself down, she simply *had* to be Judy.

Vincente himself never precisely remembered how, when the day came, he proposed. But he said something about "I wish we'd be married"—and he found he had proposed, although it had never occurred to him that it would happen. But apparently by his manner he revealed more than he was actually aware of, and Judy was too perceptive to miss it. For one afternoon, when she was leaving her dressing room, she turned to Dottie. "Dottie, I'm going to dinner tonight with Vincente and I think he's going to ask me to marry him."

Dottie said, "Grab him, if you love him. Grab the guy!" And she hugged her.

However it took place, he had proposed. He had taken out many girls, but he had been a confirmed bachelor for nearly thirty-six years. Judy could not know that, though Vincente was not an unattractive man, he seemed to think otherwise; that he had once jokingly told a friend that he would never marry for fear that if he had a child, the child might look like him. In the spring of 1944, when *Meet Me in St. Louis* was being cut, they became inseparable. Freed later gave the entire group a bonus—an all-expense trip to New York. Judy's companion was Betty O'Kelly, who once more found herself not only playing beard but being fixed up by Judy with various male friends, while Vincente became Judy's roommate in place of Betty.

Judy was a born matchmaker. First she had tried it with Betty and Buddy Pepper, three years before; now she did her best to put Betty together first with Bob Alton, the dancer and choreographer, and then Hugh Martin, one of the writers of the superb songs in *Meet Me in St. Louis.*

But when the group returned to the Coast, Judy continued her love affair with Vincente. This became no secret. One day Vincente received a disturbing letter from Ethel. She wrote how amazed and disappointed she was, and how mistaken she had been in him; she had always thought him an honorable man. She could not help feeling outraged that he, a man of his age, would take this advantage of Judy.

Vincente replied immediately. He wrote that he loved Judy and wanted to make her his wife; that he could not marry her now because her divorce from David Rose was not yet final; that Judy had wanted them to go to Mexico so she could obtain a quick Mexican divorce, but he had refused. Mexican divorces were not always recognized in the States, and though they could not marry now, they loved each other and did intend to marry.

Apparently this appeased Ethel for a while. As a matter of fact, after the many difficulties between mother and daughter, a peaceful truce had been established. Judy had given up the Mary Martin house and had moved into Ethel's Ogden Drive house. Ethel outdid herself to welcome her daughter back into her home. She had the top floor redecorated into a suite for Judy, in colors Judy liked, with the white rope rugs Judy delighted in and a completely mirrored private dressing room.

Now Ethel had her three daughters living with her once more; Jimmy, and Jimmy's daughter, Judalein; Judy; and Suzy and Jack Cathcart—and Grandma Eva. Ethel had bought a car for Grandma Eva and hired a woman to drive her to Long Beach, where she could always find a Bingo game.

Meanwhile, Vincente was making Judy even more a part of his world, and in a fashion that merged career and life style both. Kay Thompson and her husband, Bill Spier, had arrived in Hollywood in the summer of 1943. Kay was to remain there for four years before going off on tour with her own show, the Kay Thompson Singers, which also featured the young Williams Brothers, of whom Andy, the youngest, was to become one of TV's best-known singing stars with his own weekly show years later.

Kay and Roger Edens, who had the same birthday—November 9 (which they always celebrated by putting together enormously funny shows)—had collaborated on a brilliant, satiric dance sketch called "Madame Crémeton." This was not for one of their Kay-Roger parties, but was to be featured (as the Great Lady "Interview") in *Ziegfeld Follies,* a new superproduction Freed was putting together, to be directed by Vincente. It was a tremendous project, this musical, combining the talents of Fred Astaire, Gene Kelly, James Melton, Red Skelton, Victor Moore, William Powell, Edward Arnold, Hume Cronyn, Keenan Wynn, William Frawley and Robert Lewis; Judy, Lucille Ball, Fanny Brice, Kathryn Grayson, Lena Horne, Esther Williams and Cyd Charisse. The first idea had been for Greer Garson to satirize her impossibly saccharine Mrs. Miniver role of a few years before. Vincente would start directing immediately after *Meet Me in St. Louis,* which was not to be released until Thanksgiving of that year, 1944. Kay, a singer and exceptional song stylist, did the "Madame Crémeton" skit as only she could do it: superlatively, in high style. However skilled Greer Garson might be, this demanded a professional singer who could act and, equally important, handle satiric lines. Judy was a marvelous storyteller; who better than Judy?

Judy was doubtful. "Can I do that? That high style?" she asked. Kay said, "Just watch me," and she went through it. And doing that number, under Chuck Walters' expert direction, Judy found herself doing things she had never done before and that would become incorporated in her later work. Although by the time Kay came into Judy's life, Judy was already Judy, Kay's influence proved enormous. From her Judy learned a certain way of moving—quick, fast, a manner almost Germanic in its sharp, angular choreography. For example, the trick of resting her head against the inside of her outstretched arm as a song ended came from Kay.

Judy in the late summer of 1944 had begun a new film for Freed, *The Clock,* with Robert Walker. It was a poignant little story by Paul Gallico: a soldier in uniform, alone in New York on a forty-eight-hour pass, knowing no one, meets a girl, they fall in love, are married, and he goes off to war—all in one weekend. All the action took place in

New York City. Judy had been wanting to try a straight dramatic role for some time. Freed read the story in galley proof, he bought it immediately, assigned one of his writers, Robert Nathan, the novelist, to do the script, and a promising young director, Fred Zinnemann, to direct it. But Zinnemann's role in this picture was doomed. Judy had fallen in love, deeply in love, all over again, with Vincente, and this time in earnest. He was completing *Ziegfeld Follies*, and had three weeks of work still to go. Judy wanted Vincente to direct her, and nobody else. But she kept this to herself.

If Minnelli thought he had had difficulties with Judy in *Meet Me in St. Louis*, it was nothing compared to what young Zinnemann now found as he attempted to direct his star. Judy had tooth trouble and didn't show up. Judy didn't like the weather—it was a bad day for shooting, it depressed her. She had nothing against Zinnemann— they simply were not on the same beam.

The three weeks passed. Zinnemann suffered through them; he desperately wanted to make the picture. He felt it was his kind of film. (Later he was to make a distinguished name for himself and win Oscars for other films.) Then early one afternoon Zinnemann walked into Lillian Burns's office; he was on the edge of tears. He had been on *The Clock* that morning, as usual: at noon he'd been told he was off it.

Minnelli himself said he learned about it unexpectedly. He had just finished the *Follies* when Judy telephoned him. Would he have lunch with her? As he recalled it, Judy told him *The Clock* had been "shelved," but she had told Arthur she still had faith in it, she thought it a beautiful story, although there were complaints that in the script every scene was like every other one, two people talking banalities and wandering about New York. Would he take over the picture and direct her in it?

Freed's recollection was that Judy walked in on him one day and said, "Arthur, I know Fred Zinnemann is a talented man, but we just can't seem to hit it off together. I can't work with him any more." To which Freed replied, "I'm sure you want Vincente, right?"

Whatever the facts, Minnelli told Judy he would look at what Zinnemann had shot so far, see what he could do, but he could not take over without Zinnemann's approval. When he viewed what had been done, he made up his mind. "Yes," he told Judy. "I think I can

do it. But you must trust me. You must put yourself in my hands."
He dared say this because he felt she had learned her lesson in *Meet Me in St. Louis.*

He would start from scratch in *The Clock,* he said, revising the script so that New York itself would become "the third character" in the picture. He would use everything he remembered about New York: the little corner restaurants, the teeming, moving, humanity-filled panorama of this extraordinary city he loved and in which as a young man he had had his own share of adventures. He would improvise and invent on the spot, and with Judy and Robert Walker as two enormously likable decent young people, caught in the same wartime emotional crisis many another young couple found themselves in, the picture could not help winning everyone. He had written Zinnemann, he said, and, though Zinnemann was angry with Judy, he gave his approval.

They began shooting *The Clock* in late August 1944. Judy was wonderful. She was growing more and more in love with Vincente. But there were problems with Walker. He was going through a slow, painful breakup of his marriage to Jennifer Jones. He was bitter, vengeful, drinking uncontrollably and, when under this influence, exhibited a frightening change of personality. (Some time later Dore Schary, when he became an MGM executive, took Walker under his wing and persuaded him to go to Menninger's, but in the end could not save him.) In any case, Judy, with her all too poignant awareness of how one could devastate oneself, was like a White Lady to Walker, and of enormous tenderness; she, Dottie Ponedel and Betty Asher more than one night searched out Walker at whatever bar they could find him, brought him home and dried him out so he could work the next day.

At this point another of the apparently inevitable arguments arose between Ethel and Judy—again over Vincente—and Ethel, who was as compelled to take action when angry as was Judy, telephoned Vincente and again gave him a piece of her mind. Judy, beside herself, flew upstairs, packed her bags and, after a tirade which included four-letter words Ethel was astonished that Judy even knew, dashed out of her mother's house and moved into Vincente's.

Ethel was in tears. She was deeply hurt; she had done over the place for Judy, and Judy had stayed there less than a month. There was a small consolation: her old friend, Jan Pravitz, and a girlfriend of Jan's were looking for a place to live. It was difficult to find space in the war years. Ethel invited them to move in, and they did.

In November 1944, *Meet Me in St. Louis* was finally released, to a wave of commercial and critical acclaim. It became one of *Variety*'s All-Time Box-Office Champions, grossing more money than any other film till then save *Gone With the Wind*. Judy wrote Freed a long note, the essence of which, after thanking him, was: "Remind me never again to tell you what kind of picture to make." It was a "ginger peachy show," Bosley Crowther said in the *New York Times*. Among Judy's numbers, one—"The Trolley Song"—became another great Garland hit.

When Judy finished *Meet Me in St. Louis,* it was her nineteenth film in nine years. It brought her, at age twenty-two, to the cover of *Life* magazine. Inside, in the issue of December 11, 1944, was a picture story on the film. The cover portrait shows Judy wearing a white blouse tied in a bow at the neck, a black skirt; she is sitting, hands clasped about her knees, her hair cut short with her bangs turned under, her lips heavily lipsticked to make them fuller than they were, her eyebrows sharply penciled in two sweeping winglike curves (Dottie's work) somehow reminiscent of an Aubrey Beardsley illustration, her mouth slightly parted—an expression on her heart-shaped face at once wistful, thoughtful, slightly troubled.

Judy was growing up, aspect by aspect of her personality, and with concerns everyone thought they knew about, but few really knew. She still struggled with the pills; her weight vacillated; there had been stories that Mayer left orders that no matter what she ordered for lunch at the commissary, she was to be given chicken soup or cottage cheese. There is some truth to these: Van Johnson once took her to lunch there; he ordered everything in sight, but Judy had a plate of cottage cheese put in front of her, with a glass of skim milk. "Cottage cheese?" Van asked. "What kind of lunch is that?" She said, "They have orders here not to give me anything that's fattening." Now she simply bypassed them with the help of Dottie. She now always had lunch in her dressing room. More than once Greer Garson, shooting on an adjacent stage, came by to look in for a moment, and found Judy and Dottie dining, cocktails and all, as well as though they were at a fancy Beverly Hills restaurant.

"How do you do it?" Greer demanded.

Judy giggled and pointed to Dottie. "Ask Svengali here," she said.

"She does it." Dottie dismissed it. She simply ordered the food on the telephone and tipped the delivery boys handsomely.

So now there was a crash diet, with pills.

What saved Judy at this point was that she was so much in love. Her picture on *Life* was a powerful boost to her ego. And Vincente, however difficult as a director, was a thoughtful and sensitive companion.

During this period Judy and Vincente and Kay and Bill saw each other several times a week. They dined regularly together. There was a panache, a swash—sophistication is too limited, too worn a word—in the Roger Edens–Kay Thompson group. At their parties, Judy delighted herself. Their games, many of them intricate word games, were talked about everywhere. Fractured French was to stem from these later. Bill Spier invented idiomatic French witticisms: *Honoré de Balzac: no hitting below the belt. La même chose: your fly's open.* Judy was happy, even on weekends when they all went to Laguna Beach, but self-conscious about her figure—it was all but impossible to get her into a bathing suit. She had an explanation: she burned and broke out, the sun acted as a poison to her, she dared not expose herself.

When the two couples dined, they poked fun at foreign films dubbed in English. Because other languages were usually more wordy than English, the actors' lips were still moving when the English lines were finished—which led to hilarious imitations.

Often Johnny Green, the composer and conductor, another whom Freed had brought from New York, Ira and his wife Lee, and Oscar and June would be on hand. So would Sylvia Sidney and her husband, Carleton Alsop, one of Judy's special people, whom she called "Pa," an urbane Somerset Maugham character—Miss Sidney was his fifth wife—who always had the front table at Romanoff's, knew everyone in town, and had a sulfurous eloquence of invective and, as he admitted, a gift for "character assassination" that kept Judy in raptures.

This was the world in which Judy enjoyed herself through her growing pains, finding her happiness when she was in love and when she was among witty, intelligent, warm friends. And after Artie Shaw and those between, and David Rose and those between, and Joe Mankiewicz and those between, she had Vincente, discriminating and knowledgeable, an artist of taste and a gentle man.

The Clock was finished in early 1945, and it was as Minnelli had anticipated: it achieved immediate success when it was released in May of that year. It had already done more than that: it had sealed Judy's fate to Vincente's.

Vincente had given Judy as an engagement ring a perfect pink pearl set in an exquisitely fashioned ebony shadow box he had himself designed; he also designed the wedding ring—made of gold, encrusted with pink pearls in an ebony setting to match the other ring.

Judy had announced that she and Vincente would have the old-fashioned traditional wedding she had always dreamed of, which neither she nor her sisters had had, for all had been married by justices of the peace. She would wed Vincente in New York, at the charming Little Church Around the Corner, and walk up the aisle of a flower-filled nave to organ music and the moist eyes of hundreds of friends. But this was not to be. Mr. Mayer wanted to be at the ceremony, but could not take the time off to go to New York, and so Judy accepted the next best solution. The wedding would take place in her mother's house. This would please her mother and Mr. Mayer, and once more she and Ethel would try to start a better relationship, and most appropriately, with her marriage.

So the ceremony was held in Ethel's house. The romance which began in *Meet Me in St. Louis*, then faltered, only to resume in *The Clock*, was now complete.

Mr. Mayer himself gave the bride away. The studio smiled at this marriage, for both bride and groom were among MGM's proudest possessions. Indeed, Metro's finest dress designers created Judy's wedding gown and hat, and both hung on display in the Makeup Department, admired by passers-by.

Judy's option was to be picked up again in a couple of months. she would now be earning $3,000 a week, not to mention her fees for radio appearances and the voluntary bonuses Metro paid her. When *The Clock* was completed and, working with Vincente, she had caused no trouble, and her performance had been so heartwarming and so luminous, Metro had given her a bonus of $15,000 "in appreciation of your cooperation and of the excellent services rendered by you." It was as though there had never been any difficulties at all.

Everyone at the studio, from Mayer and Ida Koverman down, hoped Vincente would help give Judy a certain stability. Vincente's long-time friend, Ira Gershwin, was best man; Judy's publicity aide and confidante, Betty Asher, was maid of honor. Arthur Freed was there beaming—he had brought them together; and Ida Koverman and Howard Strickling, as well as Jimmy and Suzy and seven-year-old Judalein and Grandma Eva and the Rabwins, Peg DeVine, and Jan Pravitz and Ceci Sues and a few other dear, close friends.

Everyone congratulated everyone else; and then the newlyweds drove directly to the train station and went, for their honeymoon, to the city of magic which had placed its own spell upon them—to New York, to a duplex penthouse Vincente had subleased on Sutton Place, high above the East River, from whose windows one saw the glittering necklaces of lights that marked the soaring Triborough Bridge—a place of love and romance and infinite dreams of what the marvelous future could bring two such star-touched, fortune-touched lovers.

16

PERHAPS IT WAS FORTUNATE FOR JUDY that her new husband, for all his sophistication, believed in astrological influences upon human behavior. Judy was a Gemini, having been born June 10, and Geminis could be forgiven for acting like Geminis (if you accepted astrology): that is, happy and high-spirited one moment, depressed and moody the next. Judy was also left-handed, and since, as Vincente had heard, left-handed persons were known to have explosive tempers, he could expect—and forgive—that, too, in Judy.

But little of this was in evidence in that summer honeymoon in New York. Judy was very happy. She had just finished *The Harvey Girls,* a musical which dealt with the opening of the first Fred Harvey restaurant along the Santa Fe Railroad in the late 1880s. Judy co-starred with John Hodiak. And although Judy had to play a waitress—a "Little Miss Goodie-Pie"—surrounded by a voluptuous and lavishly mounted chorus of beauties, she was nonetheless happy, because she was in love with Vincente, and the magical armor of the perfect and the superlative in which she encased every man she loved was worn by Vincente, too, in her eyes. In addition, the film had songs by Johnny Mercer and Harry Warren—one of them, "On the Atchison, Topeka and the Santa Fe," like "The Trolley Song" in *Meet Me in St. Louis,* was to become another perennial Garland hit, and win an Oscar as the best song of the year. And in the end, little Miss Goodie-Pie did win and marry handsome John Hodiak, taking him away from Angela Lansbury. The shooting was fun, and MGM threw a surprise party on the set for Judy's twenty-third birthday on June 10, held in a huge Arabian tent with Vincente and Judy taking turns opening her presents. *The Harvey Girls* was not to be released until January 1946, and it, too, became one of *Variety's* All-Time Box-Office Champions.

Now, in New York, she drank in everything like a sponge, the sights, the sounds, the atmosphere, with Vincente as her proud, knowing and loving guide. He sought out little Italian restaurants and Old World tiny Italian bakeries he had frequented in his Green-wich Village days; they were like the lovers in *The Clock,* save that they had months, not hours, to savor themselves and this city; and Judy enjoyed everything. No question of it: whatever her capacity to suffer, it was met by her capacity to enjoy.

Months before, when Freed had given them all their bonus trip to New York, Vincente had taken her to see *Oklahoma!*—then the reigning hit on Broadway. She had told him, ecstatically, that it was the first Broadway show she had ever seen.

Actually, it must have been at least her tenth, or more. As far back as 1939, six years earlier, when she went to New York on her *Wizard of Oz* promotion tour, Ethel had taken Judy to see Katharine Cornell in *No Time for Comedy;* that year, too, Judy had seen Gene Kelly in *One for the Money,* and, on another trip, in *Pal Joey.* But if she could please Vincente, if it would give him pleasure to believe he was opening up treasures she had never before known, she would lend herself happily to that. This was the man she loved and she faded into what he thought of her, what he wanted of her—this growing woman he was helping fashion, with such wide gaps that had to be filled in, in so many fields, and for whom it was such a delight to open doors and reveal new vistas. She was an *appreciator,* and like so many others in the first rank of entertainers, the best, the most enthusiastic, of audiences.

For Judy all the news was good. The Gallup Poll for the first six months of the year listed her as one of the five most popular screen actresses in the country: Ingrid Bergman, Bette Davis, Greer Garson and Betty Grable were the others. This was the third year in a row that she had been on this select list.

Vincente and Judy found their honeymoon coinciding with New York at its most exciting. History was being made: the first atomic bomb was dropped on Hiroshima on August 6, and the second on August 9, on Nagasaki, and five days later they awoke in their penthouse suite to see flags waving everywhere—Japan had surrendered. Judy followed the war news with interest; she had once suggested that wars could be eliminated if armies were all dressed in identical uniforms—or if they were all undressed. Such a simple solution! It tickled her fancy. Judy and Vincente had celebrated V-E Day, the end of the war in Europe, on the West Coast in May; now they celebrated the end of the war with Japan on the East Coast. It seemed the beginning of new times for the United States and the world, as well as for the newly married Vincente Minnellis.

As they got to know each other better, the question of pills, always delicate and painful to Judy, could not be avoided. Vincente told her he could always tell when his actresses were on uppers: they were thin and nervous. Dexedrine did that to them. Judy did not tell him that in the Gumm family every woman as soon as she dropped below a comfortable weight—and this was true of Ethel, and Jimmy, and Aunt Norma and even Grandma Eva (not of Suzy, because she had no weight problem)—became nervous, irritable and difficult to live with. *And this even though no pills were involved.* It had something to do with low blood sugar, or high blood sugar, or metabolism—whatever. Someone once said—and Judy knew it to be so, for it was her fate to come to fruition when the slender was the beautiful—that if she had not forced herself to follow the prevailing sylphlike mode, but allowed herself to become "a little Kate Smith" in those formative years, her history then and later might have been altogether different.

But one night, early in their honeymoon, as they walked along the East River near their apartment, Judy drew a bottle of pills from her purse and in a gesture of hope and freedom threw it into the dark waters of the river. "I'll never take them again," she said. Vincente was deeply moved.

He knew it would be very difficult for her. And he could only guess how long this struggle had gone on. Nor could he know what terrors assailed her, for reasons which psychiatrist after psychiatrist would seek to find. He only knew that when she was herself—when she was not on medication—she seemed to him the most marvelous person in the world. That was the drive she had: she wanted desperately to be such a person; she wanted to do everything that was right.

And the pills were everywhere: in New York, in Hollywood, everywhere. At Metro the dispensary could not provide them without a doctor's prescription, but there was a studio doctor who gave many an actor Vitamin B shots, and, if he thought it advisable, he could prescribe pills. One doctor was known to be quite generous with them; when it was alleged that he was himself addicted, he was later to leave. In cases where players were known to depend upon uppers and downers to a degree that might adversely affect their work, the studio physician was doubly careful; but there were scores of outside doctors to whom Judy could turn for "just something that'll give me a night's sleep," or "just a couple of Dexedrines"; and if not from doctors, then from friends who obtained them from their own doctors ostensibly for themselves and turned them over to her—either because it was impossible to deny Judy anything or because they wanted to remain within her circle.

So there was really never any way to prevent Judy from getting pills; no satanic despot ordered them given to this player or that. Mayer himself was frightened of them, as he was (at the beginning) of psychiatrists, and for the same basic reason: he wanted nobody and nothing, mysterious, powerful, occult or known, to tamper with the God-given talent he so worshiped and wanted to protect in those who possessed it. In short, for Judy there was no restraint save whatever will power she could summon. And she tried.

So there were long periods in which she was medication-free, when she was so happy that there was no need for her to take "happy" pills, or to turn elsewhere than to her own extraordinary resources of energy and vitality.

Toward the end of their New York honeymoon Judy found she was pregnant. She and Vincente went together to the doctor for the test, and knew, in time, that they would be parents. They informed no one at the studio for the moment; Judy's next assignment at Metro was to play a brief Marilyn Miller role in the Jerome Kern story which Freed was to produce. She would have a few songs to sing, and a scene or two, but Vincente would have to get her in front of the camera before she began to show. This was a more troubling problem than anyone outside the family realized, for, in addition to a tendency to put on weight, the Gumm women became enormous when pregnant. Ethel, years ago in Grand Rapids, and Jimmy, years later in Los Angeles, had to go about in long, wraparound coats with huge flares to help disguise their size.

But Judy telephoned her mother to let her know. Ethel never forgot her words: "I'm going to have a baby, Mama. Do you mind?" If there was a sting in the question, Ethel appeared to dismiss it. She seemed delighted: a second grandchild! She told Peg DeVine, with a kind of rueful chuckle, how Judy had phrased the news. And she added, "I'm sure having the baby was Vincente's idea." Ethel discussed the matter, too, with Ceci Sues. Vincente might turn out to be very good for Judy, because, Lord knew, the girl had a father complex: she had really never looked at anyone under thirty. And maybe if she had a baby now, it would help straighten her out. It might be the best thing for her, Ethel thought. At a later date, talking to Peg, she said, "What do you think they're going to call the baby, if it's a girl?" Peg said she had no idea. Ethel said, "Liza." Peg said, "Oh, no—Liza crossing the ice? . . . Why not Lisa. Lisa Minnelli would be like music." No, said Ethel, Vincente had an aunt whose name was Lisa, pronounced "Leesa," and he couldn't stand the name.

What had happened was that one night during a weekend in Boston, where Judy had sung for the opening of one of Vincente's pictures, and they were staying at the Ritz Carlton Hotel, in Suite 904 (which would play a role later in her life), Judy had suddenly awakened Vincente. "I have a name for the baby, if it's a girl." They had already agreed that if a boy, it would be Vincente, Jr. Judy went on: "How about Liza?" She meant Liza, the title of one of George Gershwin's popular songs, whose words went, "Liza, Liza, skies are gray—" the name pronounced with the hard "i." Vincente liked the idea; Ira was his dear friend, the best man at their wedding; it would please him to know their daughter had been named for one of the brothers' songs. And so the parents-to-be agreed, and went back to asleep.

Judy, telling the story to Liza herself, years later, said, "And I added, 'Liza. Liza Minnelli. It will look so good on a marquee.' "

She was playing with the idea, perhaps fantasizing it so far in advance, because at Metro at this time everyone knew how opposed

Judy was to any child's being in show business. Often little Judalein was brought on the set by Jimmy to visit her Aunt Judy, who adored her, and Judy would proudly show her off to everyone. "You just have to see my niece, she's darling!" To get on the wrong side of Judy, a reporter had only to ask, "Would you like to have Judalein in pictures? See her in show business?" Judy would bristle, and retort with surprising sharpness, "I'd wring her neck before I'd let her get into pictures." "Why not?" the surprised reporter would ask. "Because this isn't any life for a child. I want her to be just a plain little girl." She would grow so upset that whichever MGM publicity aide was present—she was rarely interviewed without one of Strickling's aides on hand—would do her best to smooth matters, even going so far as to kick Judy under the table. Then Judy would make amends with a quick joke or witticism.

Vincente and Judy returned to California and began at once on her brief Marilyn Miller role in the Jerome Kern story, in which Robert Walker played Kern, and which was entitled *Till the Clouds Roll By*. It was, as the publicists put it, a "star-studded cavalcade," showcasing the talents of Frank Sinatra, June Allyson, Kathryn Grayson, Lena Horne, Tony Martin, Dinah Shore and many more. Although Freed speeded up the shooting of Judy's part, when, in the autumn of 1945, they began filming her songs, she was just beginning to show.

Vincente called on his usual ingenuity. When she sang "Look for the Silver Lining," she was photographed behind a sink washing dishes, her face smudged and perspiring, only the upper part of her body visible, wearing a checked-gingham housedress; a second number, in which, as she put it, she went from one man to another, "showing out to here," singing, "Who?" she thought riotous; and in other appearances she was kept either partly concealed or, as in a colorful circus number, dressed in a big tutu, while in a horseback scene a double was used.

Like Ethel and Jimmy, she soon became enormous. In January 1946, she arranged for a leave of absence: MGM agreed to continue to pay her new weekly $3,000 salary, even though she would not be working—they would extend her contract by a period equal to the length of her leave—and she could also appear on radio, no more than once a week, at whatever compensation her agents could arrange, provided MGM was mentioned as well as any MGM film "we may designate." It was only good sense that MGM as well as Judy benefit from the publicity connected with any radio engagements she cared to accept.

When her time came, Dr. Marc was on hand to suggest Dr. William G. Thompson, one of the city's finest obstetricians; the decision was made that the child should be born by Caesarean section, but whether this was, as explained at the time, because of her narrow pelvis or because Judy, who feared pain to an almost obsessive degree (even to get her to a dentist was almost impossible), had insisted upon a Caesarean to avoid the pain of childbirth is still a question. But Judy did ask to be anesthetized in her own hospital room, before being taken to the delivery room. The obstetrician who attended Judy when later Lorna and then Joey were born—each also by Caesarean section—said he observed no anatomical condition that would have required a Caesarean birth the first time. But once this procedure has been used, conservative medical practice suggests that it be done in all subsequent deliveries, because the scarred uterus may rupture if labor goes to full term, as in ordinary birth.

Whatever the case, Liza, born without a struggle on March 12, 1946, had the appearance of a little doll when her parents first saw her: no wizened little old man's face, no indentations caused by forceps, no mottled complexion, no signs of the battle most infants have to go through to emerge into the world.

Vincente had worried about how a child of his would look. He need not have: she was a dream! They had shown her to him through the glass, and he looked at all the other babies, with their wrinkled red faces. There was his Liza, lying on a table, waving her hands, absolutely beautiful, pink-faced and crying lustily, but not a wrinkle, nothing!

And Judy? Judy lying upstairs, when she was able to greet her friends, absolutely suffused with wonder that she had a child. *Good heavens, me? Ridiculous. But isn't it wonderful, miraculous, just out of this world!*

They returned to the Minnelli house on Evanview Drive, on a high hill overlooking both Beverly Hills and Hollywood. It was a magnificent structure of pink stucco, almost Mediterranean in feeling, and Judy and Vincente had had it redecorated while waiting for the baby, at a cost of nearly $70,000.

220

They lived in a rented house in Malibu while working together on the job of turning Vincente's bachelor residence into a home for a family. They converted his first floor study into a nursery, because it was a room which had the sun all day long, so that whenever the baby awoke, there was brightness and cheer. A nanny had been hired, proper and competent, named Mrs. MacFarlane, but Judy saw to it that she herself tucked Liza in every night.

Judy and Vincente's living quarters were upstairs: he had designed an enormous dressing room walled in antique glass for her and a chaise longue worthy of Madame Pompadour for her to rest upon.

Ziegfeld Follies was released just after Liza's birth. Judy's Great Lady "Interview" was highly praised. *Time* magazine summed up the production: "A super-spectacular, hyper-Hollywood, triple-Technicolored variety show . . . calculated to send cinemaddicts reeling home in a state of dizzy satisfaction."

The house ran on a strict schedule: Vincente had to report at Metro each morning, and while Judy was on the phone to him a dozen times during the day, she was having a bad time of it for the next weeks. She had been in considerable pain during her pregnancy. On the set of *Till the Clouds Roll By,* Lella Waxman, Freed's music editor and a respected concert pianist in her own right, found herself massaging Judy's legs, because of excruciating cramps in the calves, a not unusual development in pregnancy, and Judy herself was fearful that she might stumble or trip and lose the baby. Now there were complications from the Caesarean operation. These Dr. Marc himself repaired. He had taken care of this girl when she was a child of five, and now he was taking care of her when she had a child of her own. Judy also suffered from a post-partum depression.

She had abstained from "medication" during her pregnancy, lest it harm the baby and because she desperately wanted to carry out her promise to Vincente and herself, and quite possibly withdrawal symptoms were involved. But she tried her best as she fought these various problems to follow the rules laid down by Dr. Spock and other baby specialists.

Like any mother, whether in Grand Rapids or Beverly Hills, she immediately ordered a pink and white beribboned "Our New Arrival" book, and entered all the important facts. Name: Liza May Minnelli (May, after Vincente's mother, Minna—Liza Minna Minnelli was just too much). Date of Birth: 7:58 A.M., Tuesday, March 12,

1946, Cedars of Lebanon Hospital. Weight at Birth: six pounds, ten and one-half ounces (an official memo to this effect was promptly sent by Strickling to Mayer). First Visitors: Me, Daddy, Betty O'Kelly, my mother. Baby's Complexion: rosy tan. Color Hair: dark auburn. Days to Remember: first noticed sound, first smiled, first turned over unaided, first recognized mother . . . father, first tooth, first crawled, first stood. First Party: at home, March 12, 1947, given by parents; guest list: three Rabwin children, Mike & Geraldine Chaplin. What is fascinating is that everything up to the first-year party was obviously written in at the same time—same color ink, same pressure of pen—all in Judy's back-slanting, left-handed script, so that one must speculate that one afternoon, months later, after her depression, Judy had sat down and faithfully filled it all out.

She tried to be an ideal mother. She kept a chart, and if Liza ate when and what she should, she got a gold star; if not, a "booby" star. Although Judy herself was not one for changing diapers and the like, she was to give her children an enormous amount of love and affection: throughout their youth Liza, and later Lorna and Joe, knew that no matter what terrible personal or professional crises their mother suffered—and some were bizarre and infinitely heartbreaking—these were balanced by an endless flow of love. There would always be time, no matter what—one thing that could take Judy out of her troubles was to be needed by someone else in trouble—for Liza to sit with her mother and talk things out, talk anything out, and this mother who seemed sometimes unable to cope with the simplest things would dispense sage and insightful advice that quite overwhelmed one.

17

In the next year and a half the problems that were to plague Judy, off and on, the rest of her life began to manifest themselves more vividly, more frighteningly. She now had not the simple menage to manage that she had had earlier, but the full complement of married life: herself and her career; a husband who went off to his job each morning and had his own important obligations (even worse, to the same employer); the usual household of servants; *and* a child.

Now three facets of her growing up, like rivers moving relentlessly to one churning confluence, were coming together, and they would put her in a state of crisis.

In her first thirteen years of life, she had been programmed not so much to her own needs as to Ethel's needs, to what pleased everyone else rather than to what pleased her. Not that Baby Gumm did not enjoy the praise and acclamation that came to her. Who would not? But how could she know that this would become an opiate to her, and that its absence, or fear of its absence, would bring the most overwhelming terror upon her?

Then there had been her growing up at Metro, from thirteen on, which in the end would scar all her contemporaries, who, like her, had been reared in that same controlled, hothouse world. The very competence MGM prided itself upon—the efficient care and special services it showered upon its players (hadn't Katie Hepburn said—Howard Strickling had made note of it—"I'd work for Metro for less than anywhere else, because of their Special Services Department"?)—this very magic could wreck as well as make lives. For it was not only that Judy, in those formative years, had grown up in a kind of convent, with all that this suggested: constant supervision; constant protection; subservience to authority; rules to be followed, with rewards for obedience (or remaining infantile) and punishment for disobedience; and a rigid, old-fashioned morality, as expressed by the romantic movie scripts she read and lived in which life, as laundered by the Hays censorship office, painted love as ethereal, sexless and forever, and romance outside of marriage as sinful, guilt-building and ultimately and inescapably punished.

It was also—and this most important—that at Metro the usual, normal difficulties of growing up, and the learning experiences which flowed from these, were smoothed over and disguised. Judy Garland could not suffer so much as a pimple without an MGM magician on hand to make it vanish. In fact, MGM had a magical answer for everything, and none of it realistic. Adolescence is a preparation for life, a learning to cope; this preparation and this training to cope were denied Judy.

The studio could handle everything. It made Judy, in those formative years, depend always upon something outside herself, either upon people to take care of it or upon inanimate things or transient events: pills, liquor, parties, games, love affairs, this pastime or that —even roller coasters—to get away from whatever was plaguing you. There was always somebody or something to take care of your problems instead of your facing them and taking care of them yourself. Yet her intelligence made her a person in search of herself (analysis was one path she took) at the same time that she was a person in flight from herself.

Thus, for example, what others might look upon as manna from heaven only made things worse. On November 21, 1946, Metro, for the second time, tore up her contract and gave her a better one. When she was about to earn $750 a week, they had, in August 1940, given her a new contract raising her to $2,000, and going on from there. Now that she had reached the $3,000-a-week level, this November they tore up that contract, which still had a year to go, and raised her immediately to $5,619.23 a week for the next five years, with a promise that she need make no more than two pictures in any one year, that she would star in each picture, and, if co-starred, her name would be billed first. But, as always, there were fearsome penalties if she became physically or mentally unable to carry through: an illness of more than three weeks allowed Metro to cancel the contract, and failure on her part to give them written notification within twenty-four hours of the beginning of such an illness also allowed them to cancel. True, they had so far never taken advantage of the really rigorous clauses of these contracts, but the Damoclean sword always hung over her.

The contract, negotiated through new agents, Berg-Allenberg, Inc., was to take effect with her first day's work on her next film, *The Pirate*, which Vincente would direct, beginning November 21, 1946. It meant she would have eight months' rest after Liza's birth—and if she found herself still not ready to go to the studio, she could have until December 2.

To be paid on the basis of a six-day week nearly $1,000 a day for your time—to be expected to be good enough to earn that fabulous amount—was an extraordinary pressure. You had to be the best—all the time. That meant you had to sleep well—and *deliver*—if not a home run each time at bat, then at least as good as or better than anyone else. You were Judy Garland—you *had* to be good, no matter what. If you took pills to get you out of your depression, then you couldn't fall asleep at night. Or if you went out at night—and you were invited everywhere, because you were Judy and you would sing your heart out until 2 A.M. or later—then you couldn't wake up the next morning. And if you were a night person, and had to be on the set, full of snap and charm and vitality, at 6 A.M., just what did you do? Plus a lovely, adorable baby to teach and help to grow up, when you knew you'd done a pretty dismal job on yourself. And a husband who, however much he loved you, had a certain remote, lost-in-the-clouds quality, with responsibilities for doing his own best work, which only made you even more guilty if you troubled him with your own nervousness, or a sudden numbness of an arm, or an excruciating stomach-ache, or migraine headaches that sent you up against the wall. And an inability to eat—you became thinner and thinner. If you took pills to give you energy and make you feel halfway normal, you felt guilty; but if you stopped them, depending on how many you had been taking and for how long, the withdrawal could bring a grinding, intolerable agony.

And there were other things, too, like colitis, embarrassing to talk about, sending you always to the bathroom—your humiliation about such physical matters went back to your earliest days at MGM. In vaudeville people were dressing and undressing backstage, you were very young, nobody was shy or skittish; but it was agony to be called into a new producer's office at fifteen and stand there to answer such questions as "When is your next menstrual period and how far apart are they?" And "Are they painful?" He had to know how to adjust his shooting schedule to shoot around you if you weren't going to be your best two or three days each month. Or at sixteen to hear two assistant directors discuss the fact that one of your breasts pointed in a different direction from the other, and what was the best way to tape them both down so they didn't protrude too much? Or try to explain there was always a tremor in your hands—no, no, it wasn't palsy, and it wasn't liquor, please—but all the Gumm family had weak hands, if strong bodies, and only Ethel and Suzy had strengthened their hands a little by playing piano, and when your hand trembled as you applied lipstick or mascara, that was what it was, please understand! And you did manage to apply that line firm and straight, just the same.

So one could understand why you cherished privacy, and why you remained in your own dressing room, or your own bathroom, where no questions could be asked and no strangers make notes, for whatever reason. No one really knew how private a person you were, despite that emotional nakedness before the camera. . . .

Now, however she felt, Judy managed to begin, on her last day of grace, December 2, 1946, to work on *The Pirate*. She and Vincente had discussed it as a musical when they were still in New York. It had been written by S. N. Behrman, Vincente's friend; the Lunts had played in the Broadway production four years before. Now MGM would make it, because Vincente and Judy wanted to do it, and she would play opposite Gene Kelly, whom she loved and admired, the whole done against a West Indies background with music, color and scenery handled as only Vincente could. It seemed particularly right when Lemuel Ayres, a designer in the Freed unit, suggested Cole Porter as the perfect man to write the score.

Judy had lost a tremendous amount of weight by the time she finally appeared at Metro. Wardrobe put her in frilly dresses to make her look heavier. She seemed almost a wraith. She began having trouble from the first. She would come regularly for several days, and then not show up for two or three. She was seeing Dr. Simmel—now either Vincente drove her to the analyst after shooting each day, or Dottie Ponedel. Although Judy invariably told Dottie, her partner in crime, each time she emerged, "I lied again. Oh, God, Dottie, I lied so much today I don't know any longer what is true or untrue." She told the same story to Jimmy and others—what fun was it for an actress to play before an audience of one who sat there impassively? You had to lie and invent horrifying things done to you as a child to get some kind of reaction from him. Yet she must have had faith in Dr. Simmel, since she later sent Betty O'Kelly to him. That he was important to Judy was underwritten not long after: a frail man of sixty-five, he was to die in the autumn of 1947 and bring still another traumatic shock to Judy. Beginning with her father, every man in whom she placed faith had, in one way or another, left her.

She began having such difficulties on the set of *The Pirate* that Mayer arranged for Dr. Frederick Hacker, a Vienna-born psychoanalyst who years later became consultant to the Randolph Hearst family after their daughter Patty was kidnaped, to come each day to the set to help Judy get through her work. Mayer paid for it. Although he had been adamantly against psychiatry a few years before, now not only had it become more respectable, but the best medical advice recommended it. So far as anyone in the industry knew, this was the first time a psychiatrist had been in daily attendance upon an actress as she worked in a film. Dr. Hacker made suggestions, not only to Judy but to her colleagues, to help her manage; and when they went into the projection room to look at the "dailies"—the rushes of the scenes done that day—he would sit at her side with Freed, Vincente, Lella, the film cutter and others who watched each day's product.

To add to Judy's problems, she was surrounded by sycophants. She believed very few people. She needed, yet found it difficult to endure, such excessive flattery. Nobody spoke to Judy about herself in anything but superlatives, particularly about her performances on the screen, and this was almost unbearable to her if it was not the truth.

Few performers see themselves on the screen with almost absolute objectivity, as though they were watching strangers. Garbo was one, Fred Astaire was another, Judy was a third. She saw herself so impersonally she could say of her photograph, "I don't like her hair that way," or of herself on the screen, "She could have done that better." Judy had gone through an important scene one day, feeling terrible while doing it, and from the film cutter, sitting in the row behind her, came the words, "Judy—marvelous, marvelous!"

Judy had not been in a bad mood when they had entered the screening room some time before. A moment after she heard these words, she suddenly got up—the dailies were still running, everyone sat in semidarkness—went to the water cooler, pulled down a Dixie cup from the wall container, and out of her pocket came a handful of yellow Benzedrines, which she popped into her mouth, washed them down with the water, said, "I'm leaving," and went out.

She knew what she had done on the screen was not good. She couldn't bear to see herself perform badly, and she knew when it was bad. *They* expected the best from Judy Garland? *They* would never know how good that best had to be to satisfy Judy Garland.

Vincente suffered. On one occasion on the set, when Judy was high on amphetamines and trying to do a scene, Vincente pretended to stumble and fall on her to hold her down, to hide what was happening as Arthur Freed went by, because at that moment Judy was going out of control. When she had returned originally that first day,

December 2, it was to start prerecordings of songs. The vocals in musicals are, of course, recorded beforehand, and when the time came for photography, Judy would go before the silent camera and lip-sync the words to her prerecorded voice. It was these recordings that she now made, though she was not able to begin actual shooting of *The Pirate* until nearly a month later.

At home the situation was a mirror of what was happening on the set. Judy and Vincente were like love birds—or they fought. When she was under the influence of Dexedrine or Benzedrine or whatever she could obtain, her personality changed. Vincente simply tried to live through it. He did not know or recognize this Judy; and the remote, withdrawn quality that was part of his character—intensified by his wish not to exert pressure on her, nor to make her think she was doing badly—only made him seem to her more remote, and even indifferent to her suffering. One result of the pills, which she was taking in a desperate attempt to feel better, was a kind of paranoia. The slightest word or glance, the most minute act, was amplified into a conspiracy against her. It made for even more trouble. And Vincente had quite a temper of his own.

When things grew intolerable at home, either Judy or Vincente would call up the Gershwins. Lee and Ira had what they called a grandmother's couch in a spare room. One night Vincente called; he was trembling with emotion, and almost incoherent when he spoke to Lee. He could not stay that night in his house with Judy. It was impossible. "Can I use your grandmother's couch tonight?"

Lee said, sympathetically, of course.

Fifteen minutes later their bell rang. But it was not Vincente, it was Judy. There had been still another argument, and it had been Judy who stalked out of the Evanview house and came over to the Gershwins. Lee took her to the spare room and Judy lay down on the grandmother's couch, and simply screamed—screamed without halt.

Lee sat next to her, gently stroking her arm, watching her, saying nothing. Judy's eyes were closed, and she was screaming. She did not stop. Whatever anguish, anger, guilt, horror, fear, whatever she wanted to pour out of her, she seemed to be doing at that moment, pausing only to catch her breath, and then go on again.

Lee said, gently, "What can I do for you, Judy? Is there anything I can do?"

And Judy stopped screaming. She opened her eyes and looked at

Lee. "Do you believe me?" she asked. Lee said, simply, "Yes."

Judy resumed her screaming, and Lee sat there, slowly stroking her arm, exorcising the dark horror, until finally there was no more strength in the frail, trembling body, and, with Lee's hand gentle upon her arm, Judy fell asleep.

Lee sat on, silent. Those who knew Judy knew that she could be calmed if one ran one's hand very gently, scarcely touching the skin, up and down her arm. It soothed her. This is what Lee had done and now this child-woman, this mother, slept.

Lee had first met Judy when Oscar Levant had brought Judy over direct from *The Wizard of Oz* set years before. Lee, who had not felt well that afternoon, was in bed. Oscar brought Judy in, introduced her, and Judy removed the little cloth coat she was wearing, placed it neatly on the foot of the bed and stood revealed in her *Wizard of Oz* dress. She was wearing full makeup, she was sixteen and looked twelve, and Lee then and there treasured her.

Lee had watched Judy grow up, but she had not really come to know her well until Vincente became part of Judy's life. Since the Minnellis were always visiting the Gershwins, Liza was almost as much at home in their house as in her own—indeed, one of her first parties and many thereafter (it was always peaceful at the Gershwins', and the same could not always be said of the Minnellis) were held at the Gershwins'. At one party a few weeks before Liza was born, Judy, so pregnant, that belly of hers protruding, sat at the piano with Harold Arlen playing for her while she sang. Lee never saw her more beautiful than she was that evening. And she never sang so well. And so gay and so funny, however she might have been an hour or two, or a day or two, before.

Lee and Judy had become close companions, and Lee, at least fifteen years older, had become (as so many older women did with Judy) a kind of mother confessor. Lee would drive Judy about Los Angeles and Judy would be saying, "Oh, I want some units" (units of property, real estate). She always dreamt of being a woman of property. A free, independent woman, so she could drive about town and point to this building and that and say, "They're mine—they're mine! I finally own something! I've made it! They're mine!"

Once, that summer of Judy's honeymoon, Lee had been in New York with her and suggested, "Let's go shopping for clothes." Lee wanted to go to Hattie Carnegie's. Judy said, "Lee, I can't walk down

Fifth Avenue unless I have protection." Lee, in her ignorance, said, "Oh, c'mon, Judy." Judy had been visiting her at the Plaza, where Lee was staying. They went downstairs but Judy couldn't get into her car, waiting at the curb. Someone had to be there to hold back the hordes of people who pressed forward to touch her. She really couldn't walk those few feet, people would rush forward, clutch her arm, seize her, hug her. Lee and Judy finally got into the car, and went to Hattie Carnegie's, and then returned to the Plaza and entered the Palm Court, off the lobby, to have tea, sitting in a far, quiet corner of the huge, high-ceilinged room, which was almost deserted. Within five minutes the place was jammed: everyone wanted autographs. "Judy, darling, dear—" everybody touching her, saying, "Judy, I love you," pulling her apart almost. *And the laughter,* Lee thought, sitting there now, by the side of the grandmother's couch, watching Judy, trying to will her rest to be calm, restorative. *The laughter. Wherever she went, there was laughter.*

Luckily, little of what went on upstairs at the Minnellis' in their private quarters reached little Liza, in her own suite downstairs, well out of the way. What Liza did remember was crawling upstairs by herself, to be held and cuddled and kissed by her parents, as they sat at their candlelit dinner; and then, after a while, taken downstairs by Mrs. MacFarlane, and then a final hugging and a loving, infinitely tender tucking in by her mother. She had clear memories of her father standing over her, adoring her, and following her about with a camera wherever she went, photographing her; and that her first steps were not taken in her own house but in the Gershwins' when everyone was happy and the Minnellis with their little daughter were Sunday afternoon guests on one of those perfect Southern California days.

But in early July 1947, after Judy had managed to complete her part in *The Pirate,* and had managed as well several public appearances, among them singing on Philco's *Bing Crosby Show,* she reached a point where under psychiatrist's orders she was taken to the Las Campanas Sanatorium in Compton, several miles from Los Angeles, to live under special care and treatment in a bungalow of her own. She had made an attempt—a pretense of one, rather—to take her life. Ethel had been visiting, and was downstairs in the

230

nursery with Liza. Suddenly there was a scream upstairs: Judy had dashed out of her room, after an argument with Vincente, screaming, "Ahhhhhh, I'm going to kill myself!" dashed into her bathroom and slammed and locked the door.

Ethel ran up the stairs screaming, "What have you done!" and she and Vincente tried to break down the bathroom door. They heard Judy sobbing inside, and then the sound of a glass breaking.

Ethel shouted, "Goddamn it, you open this door!" Perhaps because she swore, or because of the fury in her voice, or for whatever reason, Judy opened the door. She had broken a water glass and scratched her wrist: it scarcely bled. Ethel fixed it with a Band-Aid.

Nothing got into the press. But Judy needed help, and the sanatorium was recommended. Judy was completely and desperately exhausted, unable to sleep, afraid of the night, afraid to drive a car, afraid she might harm herself or her child, in the grip of a pill syndrome which led to even more terrors, to an amplification of her fears and apprehensions. She knew that she must be helped through this bad period away from home, from the studio, from the man she loved who was husband at home but director at work, and away from all the responsibilities weighing on her.

Her stay at the first of what she was to call her "nuthouses" led to an entire new collection of funny stories, of which she was always the butt. In one of her favorites, she told how she stumbled repeatedly as attendants escorted her across the lawn from her car to her bunga- low, so that they thought she was drunk, despite her denials; then she discovered next morning when she looked out her window that she had been tripping over croquet wickets in the lawn.

Las Campanas was an expensive place, with many well-known actors and actresses as patients. Because Vincente had been unable to discover where Judy was getting her pills (in this she was to prove cunning beyond belief: friends ordering dresses for her that arrived with Dexedrines sewed in the seams), at the sanatorium the nurses were under orders to make constant searches of her bungalow to see if she had any hidden there. She would suffer this as an indignity, but later these experiences would become part of her repertoire of black- humor stories. She would say to the nurses, "You're wasting your time, girls. There's nothing here. Just knock it off." One of the doctors walked in. She began, "Will you tell the nurses to stop with the looking—there are no pills." Just then a gnat began buzzing about her mouth. She went "Phew!" trying to blow it away.

The doctor said, "Yes, yes, Miss Garland."

"Doctor, there's a fucking gnat buzzing the hell out of me," Judy complained. She began grabbing at the air. "You can't see it from where you're standing, come over here." She would describe the entire routine she had done about the gnat, and the doctor, who had seen nothing—she had spit or blown the insect out of sight—thought he had caught her high on pills again. And everyone searched the more.

She loved to tell such stories. Each evening the "inmates" would gather for a dance. As she told it, "I'm dancing with a handsome guy, who's wearing a beautifully tooled leather belt. I said, 'Oh, that's a marvelous belt.' He said, 'I made it in the therapy thing.' She said, 'Oh, it's really marvelous.' He said, 'Yes, it only cost me $182,000.' "

Both the high and the low point of her stay was a visit from Liza. Judy had insisted on this: she must see her daughter. Liza was less than a year and a half; their meeting can be imagined, tears and laughter and endless hugging. The low point came after the child had left and Judy threw herself on her bed and began to weep—as she was to say later, "I almost died of anguish."

Few knew where she was; that she was ill had been revealed by Louella Parsons in her column that July: Judy was suffering from "nervous exhaustion"; and then again a month later, in August 1947: Judy might have to be replaced in a picture "in case her illness is long drawn out."

After her stay at Las Campanas, she came home for a while, but then a new psychiatrist, Dr. Herbert Kupper, suggested a second sanatorium, the Riggs Foundation in Stockbridge, Massachusetts, and took her there himself. Dr. Simmel, who had recommended Las Campanas, was not only ill but had always refused to make house calls, so he had recommended Dr. Kupper, a younger, American-born psychoanalyst, who would come to Judy—even on a summer afternoon at the Gershwins' tennis courts—if a sudden terror overtook her.

Dr. Kupper had chosen Riggs, in the East, far from California and anyone Judy knew, in the hope that in this completely different New England atmosphere she might come upon realities of life she missed in Hollywood. She would find herself among patients not like those she had known at Las Campanas, many of whom, film celebrities like

232

herself, had psychiatric problems growing out of—who knew what such emotional problems grew out of, but certainly they were not helped by the Alice-in-Wonderland life one led in Hollywood, off-stage as well as on. She would have a better chance to meet everyday people reacting to situations that were real rather than imagined, or inflated from minuteness to catastrophic proportions. A real Esther Smith, distraught and no longer in control of her life because of the death of a child, or an Esther Smith shattered and pill-ridden because of objectively real tragedies . . . In addition, how practical was it to attempt to treat Judy in Hollywood one hour a day while in the remaining twenty-three hours she had to cope with this superheated, superchallenging, superrewarded atmosphere over which she could have no control?

Vincente visited her there twice. After a few weeks he brought her home—a new Judy, still troubled, but able to spring back with that special resilience that was hers, and particularly because a new film, a musical, *Easter Parade*, was waiting for her to begin on December 19. It was a good picture to resume work in, because she would be among people she admired and with whom she was comfortable. Irving Berlin himself had written new songs for her, and had come to California to do them, a great tribute; Vincente would direct, Gene Kelly would be her co-star, and Bob Alton would direct her dances. The cast would include old friends like Peter Lawford and Ann Miller; Johnny Green and Georgie Stoll would conduct the music; the script would be by the Hacketts, Frances and Albert—she knew them all, they were all top-rate, she would be in the bosom of the family. The idea of doing *Easter Parade* also helped assuage the traumatic blow of Dr. Simmel's death on November 11.

Liza was growing fast, as bright and captivating as a child could be, and obviously precocious. Ethel could be an indulgent grandmother, if a disciplining one; she had taken Judy's illness hard, and when Judy was home again, she was overjoyed. Despite the tension between them—one or two words, and either Judy's or Ethel's back would be up—she tried literally to walk on her toes about Judy. Grandma Eva had suffered a stroke; Ethel had put her in a nursing home where now, nearly eighty, she still found Bingo and card games to play (and presumably cheat at). To Liza, Ethel was "Nanna," and Saturday was Liza's day with Nanna. So each Saturday morning Mrs. MacFarlane took the child over to her grandmother's house—Liza always remembered a neat, brightly painted kitchen and a canary chirping in its cage—and one of Ethel's greatest pleasures was to drive Liza when the time came for her first dancing lessons at the studios of Nico Charisse, Cyd's ex-husband. Judy allowed this, but with a kind of guarded reservation: was Liza to be put through the same thing she had been? Yet a child should know how to dance, and even before she walked, Liza bounced about whenever she heard music. (So, too, had Baby Gumm, so many years before.)

Then, unexpectedly, with *Easter Parade* already in rehearsal, Arthur Freed received a telephone call from Dr. Kupper. It would not be good for Judy, he said, for Vincente to direct her in *Easter Parade*. Husband and wife should not be working together under circumstances where Vincente, in Judy's mind, became less her husband and more the alter ego of MGM.

There was nothing for Freed to do but tell Vincente. Vincente was crushed. In a kind of desperation, to help him cope with what was going on both at the studio and at home, he sought out an analyst himself, and after a few weeks Vincente, who had been under intense pressure, was able to accept this new state of affairs and began to busy himself with other work. He and Judy did not even talk about his removal.

Freed called in Chuck Walters. "Chuck," he said, "you did a very good job on your first picture." Walters was essentially a dance director, but Freed had given him the opportunity to direct *Good News*, a collegiate musical with June Allyson and Peter Lawford. Freed's next words almost floored Walters. "I'm giving you *Easter Parade*." *Easter Parade*, a tremendous production, as his second picture! And a new contract. Walters was almost speechless. Freed did not tell him the real reason Minnelli was out and he was in. Walters read the script with great excitement, but found it heavy. The Hacketts were one of the finest writing teams in Hollywood, yet . . . Walters talked with Judy and Gene. They all agreed, and Freed thereupon brought in Sidney Sheldon, a fast, deft writer, to work with Walters until they achieved what they thought was a light, lovely script.

Judy, much as she liked Walters, was on her mettle. "Look, Buster," she said to him one day. "You're in the big time now. You're not doing a little college musical here." She looked at him; she knew why he was there; she knew how well he'd directed her in the exciting dance finale in *Presenting Lily Mars*—and she also knew

234

that he had completed *Good News*. "This is a big picture, an A picture, and I ain't June Allyson, so don't give me any cutes, no batting of the eyes—O.K.?" It was both a warning and a criticism.

Walters loved dirty talk, and he knew Judy liked it, too. He said, "Oh, shit, Judy, you got nothing to worry about."

Sheldon brought in the finished script to Freed, who said glumly, "I've got some news for you. Our leading man has broken his leg." Sheldon thought it was a joke. The picture was due to start Monday —this was Saturday afternoon. Freed said, "No, I'm serious. Gene Kelly broke his leg."

Kelly was a great softball enthusiast, and each Saturday morning he and a group of friends played softball for hours, sometimes two consecutive nine-inning games. This morning he had played and he had broken his ankle. Like that.

"What do we do? Postpone the picture?" Sheldon asked.

"I've got a call in for someone else to take Gene's place," said Freed. Who? Fred Astaire.

"Now you must really be joking," Sheldon said. Fred Astaire had announced his semiretirement the previous year; he was nearing fifty, and he was a grandfather. How could you put twenty-five-year-old Judy Garland . . . "Arthur," said Sheldon, "no audience in the world is going to root for a young girl like Judy to wind up in bed with a guy who is a grandfather. You can't put those two together as lovers. It's a terrible idea. It won't work."

Freed said, "It'll work, kid."

Although Astaire was reluctant to come out of retirement and suggested Freed wait until Kelly's leg healed, when Freed told him they could not wait, Astaire read the script and said he would do it.

On Monday they started shooting. That first morning Sheldon was on the set. He said "Hi" to Judy—he was bright, he was quick, and he could make her laugh, always a basic requirement in her friends. As they were chatting, the assistant director came over. "Miss Garland, we're ready for you." This would be the first shot in the picture.

Sheldon was in the middle of a funny little anecdote. He started to walk toward the set, but Judy grabbed his arm. "Finish your story," she said. Sheldon felt awkward: they were waiting for Judy, and he was telling her some completely unimportant anecdote that could be told later. But she was holding his arm, so he stopped and began to speed up the telling. Then he realized it would take some time to complete it. "Let's go over," he said. Everyone on the set was looking at them. "Let's go through the scene first, Judy, and then I'll tell you." She held his arm firmly and stood planted on the spot. "Finish it," she said.

Something was wrong, he knew. There was almost a note of panic in her voice. He said, gently, "What's the matter, Judy? Don't you want to go over there and start shooting?"

She said no. He asked why. "Well, in this first scene I kiss Fred Astaire. I've never met him."

Sheldon thought, *She idolizes this man.* Everyone assumed they knew each other, and Judy was simply too shy to go over and introduce herself. Sheldon took Judy by the hand, led her to Astaire, introduced them, they went into the scene and all was fine. He thought, as he left later, *On the face of it, she comes out bitchy—the big star who has so much power she can keep a whole set waiting while she listens to an anecdote. Actually, this is a frightened little girl.*

The only difficulty with this account is that she knew Fred Astaire. For twenty-one days they had been on the same train during the famous 1942–1943 Hollywood Bond Cavalcade of Stars, a U.S. war-bond tour made by motion-picture stars with stops in twenty cities. The two had even posed together, his arm around her waist, in a dance-routine publicity photograph in Washington, D.C.

Perhaps it was Judy's great admiration for Astaire that made her play this shy-little-girl role, or perhaps it was genuine panic: once more she was all but in love with her leading man, and because she respected him so, he could do no wrong—and she was at her best. He never recalled seeing her anything but happy on that set. Between scenes they played little skits. He'd say, "This is how I'd play Clark Gable," and mimic him as Rhett Butler; she'd do Scarlett O'Hara. Astaire, too, had been on the stage since the age of four, but his experiences had been happy ones. Once she began telling him about being called a hunchback; when that mood came upon her, he kidded her out of it, or changed the subject; but mainly she showed her best side to him.

Sometimes she came late, but it did not matter. He never saw anyone pick up a complicated dance routine as quickly as Judy. She rehearsed it seriously. She would not stand about waiting to be told what to do; she did what she thought they ought to do, and if it turned

236

out right, Fred said, fine, and they used it. He admired her; one of the reasons he finally went into *Easter Parade* was because he wanted to work with her. Once he had seen a composer begin telling her how to sing his song. Judy walked over to the man and shook her finger under his nose. "Listen, Buster, who's singing this song, you or me?" Astaire felt that if he started directing her, she'd turn to him —"this honest-to-God little performer"—and say, "Listen, Buster, who's dancing this, you or me?"

The plot dealt with Don Hewes (Astaire), who loses Nadine (Ann Miller), his dancing partner, when she accepts Florenz Ziegfeld's offer to appear without him. Astaire, hurt and bitter, bets a friend he can pick out any chorus girl and train her to take Nadine's place. He chooses chorus girl Hannah Brown—it was Judy's luck to be saddled with names that might have been taken from a Girl Scout manual— trains her, they become skilled partners, and fall in love. Nothing really went wrong: the film was shot in forty days.

And Freed had been right about the Garland-Astaire combination. Grandfather or not, everyone rooted for Astaire to get the girl. When *Easter Parade* opened at Loew's State in New York, it broke every record. One of its features was a dance skit, "A Couple of Swells," with Judy and Fred in tramp costume, under Walters' direction. Judy made the little tramp—actually, more an adorable little clown—her own, and it became one of her most admired characterizations.

Obviously, Metro now had a new, unique dance team—Astaire and Garland—and Freed already had the next project lined up for them. It was another musical, *The Barkleys of Broadway,* tailored for them: lyrics by Ira Gershwin, arranged by Roger Edens, again directed by Chuck Walters, story by Betty Comden and Adolph Green. Once more Astaire would lose his dancing partner—this time Judy, his wife, because she wanted to try her hand as an actress—but it would all end happily, and in the cast such dear old friends as Oscar Levant and Billie Burke, who had been the Good Witch in *The Wizard of Oz.* Just more of the same, and the same golden flow of money pouring in. What could be better?

But now events were moving in a direction of their own, and Judy found herself swept along faster and faster, like a frail canoe riding swirling, frightening rapids, trying again and again to seize a rock, a root, a branch, to halt the nightmare descent to a disaster dimly perceived but somehow surely there at the end. When she reached that destination, Judy would no longer be at MGM—and her marriage to Vincente Minnelli would be all but over.

18

THE MONTH THAT *Easter Parade* WAS RELEASED to such acclaim a letter was dispatched by registered mail from Metro to Judy, care of her agents. It was dated July 19, 1948. It read in part:

DEAR MISS GARLAND:

As you know, you have been unable since sometime prior to July 12, 1948, to render the services required of you under our employment contract with you; and it has become increasingly apparent over the past few weeks that your condition is such as to make it unlikely that you will be able in the immediate future to render such services. This conclusion is confirmed by your doctor who advised us that in his opinion you could not without a considerable period of rest and medical care undergo the exertion and strain which would be involved in the rendition of your services in the next photoplay we had planned for you.

You will understand that in these circumstances we would not be legally or morally justified in assuming the risks inherent in the situation.

Accordingly we have no alternative but to elect and we do hereby elect to suspend our contract of employment with you commencing July 12, 1948, and continuing for and during the period of your illness, as illness is defined in such a contract.

We hope you will take advantage of the opportunity thus afforded to restore your condition to the point which will enable you safely and with reasonable assurances of continuity to render your required services. In that connection we would appreciate being kept advised of your progress in order that we may make appropriate plans for you when you are restored to health. . . .

This letter reflected the traumas of the past year and her growing difficulties with MGM—and, at the same time, with her husband. It was one of a series of letters Judy was to receive, now suspending her, now reinstating her, now taking her off salary, now putting her back on, but each time scrupulously extending her contract by the exact number of weeks and days she had been suspended.

238

She had thought, in the spring of 1948, that she was ready to go into *The Barkleys of Broadway.* But she had gained weight and had to reduce. She found herself once more on pills, and then things were bad. She could not stop losing weight. She managed to attend the preproduction meetings in Freed's office: after all, to co-star again with Astaire was a tremendous lift. She sat there with him, listening to Betty Comden and Adolph Green read all the parts in the script so effectively that, when they left, Judy said to Fred, "If we can only do as well as they did reading those parts, we're O.K."

But it was not to be. During 1947, the dreadful year of *The Pirate* and her stays at both Las Campanas and Stockbridge, she had been under suspension for an aggregate of fourteen weeks and four days, according to the letters sent her by MGM (since her salary was roughly $936 a working day on the basis of a six-day week, her suspensions were calculated to the day), and then to top it off came Dr. Simmel's death.

What helped bolster her was the fact that she was seeing a great deal of Carleton Alsop and Sylvia Sidney. She had many reasons for liking, indeed loving, Carleton. She called him Pa, because he used to seize her by the shoulders and shake her, and swear at her; for this little waif was stronger than anyone, able with her jungle cunning to outwit any of them. Only Roger Edens had been able to control her when she was difficult. Roger did it in a more brittle, cutting, English way. "Will Mrs. Gumm's little girl Frances come over here, cut the shit and do what she's paid to do?" If she moved nowhere musically without Roger, similarly in the everyday handling of her difficulties with Vincente and the studio it was Carleton without whom she seemed helpless.

She was trying to make a life together with her husband, but it was an ordeal. At one point Dr. Marc had called in his own family physician, Dr. Fred Pobirs, and it was decided that Judy should live apart from Vincente for a while—or at least there should be another house where they could remain alone or together, as they wished, and so she rented a huge house at 10000 Sunset Boulevard, again high on a hill and invisible from the road, so that one saw only the address sign and an entrance roadway: the house was taken for one year at $1,000 a month. Now Judy was up, now she was down; now she was impossible, now she was utterly charming, delightful, funny, overwhelmingly, incredibly herself. When she was down, she was very down. Then Vincente, too, found himself turning to Carleton for help. He would call Alsop at two or three in the morning, beside himself: they were together, Judy and he, in the new big house, Judy could not sleep, she was sitting on the stairs, she was in an impossible state—Carleton had to come over at once.

Carleton would dress hurriedly and drive over. Some of these sessions were incredible. There sat Judy in her robe, trembling, tear-stained, hunched up on the stairs leading to their palatial quarters, Vincente pacing nervously back and forth. Carleton would arrive, hug Judy, hold her for a moment. What *is* it now, what is it *now?*

"Pa, I can't face a camera this morning."

Carleton would be alternately gentle and stern. She knew what he had told the studio, that they treated her with less consideration than Mayer showed his race horses—that this was a fragile talented girl, and they were torturing her, reminding her of the millions of dollars that depended upon her—how could she possibly come into the studio with that weight on her shoulders? "All right now," Carleton said. "You believed all that shit I told the studio. But remember, they're paying you $150,000 for this picture and you're supposed to go to work to earn it. That means getting up in the morning, that means wardrobe, makeup, hairdressing." He would go on: "I'm not here to discuss the charm of Mr. Mannix, or Benny Thau, or anything about Mr. Mayer. You have a job, you have a contract, they're paying you a lot of money."

By this time Judy would have controlled her trembling, but she might explode at any moment.

"Now, you've got to carry out your job. That you must do. The lies I tell them—because I don't know how much of what you're putting on is fake and how much is real. If it's real, you should have a doctor here, not me. Now, I don't think you need a doctor. I think you need someone to spank your bottom, you little bitch, and send you back to bed. Now, goddamn it, Judy, you go back to bed and go to sleep, or get your ass up and go to work. Go in late and say, 'I feel better,' but go in there!"

Judy would curse him, she would swear like a truck driver, but she would go upstairs and dress and go to the studio—that day.

A few days before her twenty-sixth birthday, in June, 1948, Carleton wanted to buy her something as a gift—something that would cheer her up. He decided to put it to her. "What can I get you for your birthday, you silly little bitch?" She said, "Now, Pa, if you really wanted to do something nice for me, you'd get me Ronald Colman. We've been on the same lot dozens of times since I was a little girl and I never met him."

Carleton spoke to Ronald's wife, Benita Hume, the actress. "Would Ronnie mind being a gift for Judy?"

Ronnie would be delighted. The rest was up to Carleton.

On the evening of June 10, the front doorbell rang. There stood a uniformed delivery boy supporting what appeared to be a manikin. It was Ronald Colman, neatly wrapped from head to toe in cellophane, gaily beribboned, and with a "Happy Birthday" tag from Saks Fifth Avenue dangling from one shoulder. Judy threw her arms around him, carefully unwrapped him, kissed him and then sat down and cried. Getting Ronnie Colman for a birthday present!

But it was Carleton's audacity, as well, that she loved. One evening Ira and Lee Gershwin gave a party in honor of Dr. Gregory Zilboorg, the distinguished New York psychoanalyst, who was visiting Los Angeles. The Gershwins' home was set with eight tables of people playing cards, after dinner, with a psychiatrist at each table. The guests this evening included their friends, Judy and Vincente, Oscar Levant and June, and many more, nearly all of whom had been or were in analysis. Carleton had assured Judy that Dr. Zilboorg was the "mother superior" of all the analysts in the country. He was an imposing man, with an enormous mustache.

At one point Lee Gershwin asked Carleton if he would say a few words on behalf of the assemblage with respect to their guest of honor.

Carleton rose and, in his best Somerset Maugham manner, observed, "So many people have asked me about Dr. Zilboorg—not only about his work but also about his mustache." He and Oscar Levant, he went on, had had a considerable discussion, and Oscar wanted to know "if I thought there was any significance to Dr. Zilboorg's mustache. I said—all I could think of—it's simply the lunatic fringe." And he sat down.

He kept Judy in laughter. She would almost choke over some of his circumlocutions: when he spoke about anyone's sexual equipment, male or female, he would say, "so-and-so's arrangement." Judy would be on the set, ready to rehearse a song, and a director would run up to say excitedly, "We've got a new arrangement for you—" and she'd cry out, "Oh, my God, you've been talking to Pa," and break up completely.

Yet she was not making it. Her weight dropped to eighty-five pounds; she was forced to withdraw from *The Barkleys of Broadway* in early July, too weak, sometimes, to get out of bed. She was replaced by Ginger Rogers, so that the famous team of Rogers and Astaire were reunited for the last time, and Judy's suspension began. This one, in 1948, would last nearly three months.

Carleton and Sylvia decided they would take her to their home on Beverly Drive, where Sylvia would prepare tasteful foods to fatten her up while Carleton, with his humor, as black, as zestful, as outrageous as Judy's, would help sustain her spirits. Above all, they had to get her off pills. Carleton was sure she was getting them from friends; he knew, too, that if Judy visited anyone's home, her hostess would discover when she left that Judy had raided the medicine cabinet of whatever uppers and downers there might be there. Only once was Judy stumped: when she discovered that one old friend had actually put small padlocks on the medicine cabinet. Judy pretended not to notice.

Her monetary problems were endless. She had never handled money, she never signed her own checks, she had no idea what anything cost. She had had a series of agents, and a series of business managers. One of them, Ethel was always to insist, had sold the two annuities she had taken out for Judy when she first signed at Metro, and invested the money in one thing or another. Whatever the fact, Judy was broke, her tremendous income had stopped, as it had stopped the year before during her suspensions, and household expenses—two households now—medical and other expenses, confusion over taxes and a general ignorance of finances had put her in a difficult and precarious situation.

At this point Judy concluded that MGM had deducted something like $100,000 from moneys due her. Carleton checked with her agents. He learned about the so-called "retroactive penalties"— moneys Judy cost the studio by arriving late, or not at all, or by being too ill to function. Judy said, "Pa, they can't do this to me, can they?"

She was sick and in bed in the Alsop house at the time, actually being fed glucose intravenously. Alsop, who knew everyone, went in to see Mayer. Mayer, as Carleton recalled it, said he knew of course that Judy was ill and under suspension, but that "if she could get a little better and come out and do one song in *Words and Music*, I'd pay her fifty thousand dollars."

Words and Music was another MGM "cavalcade of stars," a musical based on the lives of the songwriting team of Richard Rodgers and Lorenz Hart, with Mickey Rooney playing Hart and Tom Drake, who had been the romantic lead in *Meet Me in St. Louis*, as Rodgers. There were nearly a score of cameo roles, by June Allyson, Gene Kelly, Lena Horne, Cyd Charisse, Mel Tormé and others.

Alsop went back and talked to Judy, in bed. She lay there, frightfully thin, a glucose needle in her arm. When he told her what Mayer said, she said, "Pa, get that fucking needle out of my arm. I'm going out there. I can sing, or I'll find out if I can still sing."

Alsop all but carried Judy to his car, drove her to Metro, and Judy sang "Johnny One Note"—belting it out with that amazing power of hers. Her resilience was incredible—to think she came from a sickbed!

Her success encouraged her; she began to eat and drink again, putting on weight almost as fast as she had been losing it. Soon she was well enough to visit the set of *Words and Music* with Liza.

Again Carleton received a telephone call from Mayer. He said, "Carleton, you know it looks pretty silly, with a star of Judy's magnitude to do a number as only she can and to go off to such applause —and refuse to do an encore. We have got to have her do an encore. We'll pay her another fifty thousand if she'll do an encore."

So Judy, now some twenty pounds heavier thanks to Sylvia's cooking, was again driven by Carleton to Metro and sang "I Wish I Were in Love Again" with Mickey Rooney. And she received her second $50,000.

Judy was so delighted with Carleton that on August 4—still under suspension—she sent a letter to MGM stating that Alsop was now her representative.

Metro allowed her several radio appearances in the autumn—a Philco *Bing Crosby Show* on September 11, a salute to WMGM on September 22, and an Al Jolson *Kraft Music Hall* show on September 30. It meant additional money for her.

By this time her health had improved so that she was going out; on October 11, 1948, her suspension ended. And she went into *In the Good Old Summertime* with Van Johnson. She was not happy doing it—in *The Barkleys of Broadway* she would have been in a glamorous role, here she was a clerk in a music shop—but anyone seeing the film would have no idea of this. She looked wonderful, she seemed in excellent spirits, in full command of her part—provocative, pixie, charming, ironic—and the picture has its place in movie history because in it Liza, aged two and a half, made her film debut as Judy's and Van's little girl. The story dealt with two clerks in the shop who cannot endure each other but are each carrying on a secret pen-pal correspondence—of course, with each other, neither knowing it. Judy played the harp, sang such songs as "Meet Me Tonight in Dreamland" and "Put Your Arms Around Me, Honey," dressed in an appealing shopgirl outfit—white shirtwaist with black bow at neck, long blue skirt with leather belt about her waist—and no one could know that she was going through the breakup of a marriage, increased difficulties with her mother, and moving through a period of great change in her life.

That year Jimmy had married again, a quiet, soft-spoken man named John Thompson, Jr., who was—once more, Ethel's luck—a music arranger, for Harry James's orchestra. It had been an elopement to Mexico, followed by a wedding party given by Judy. Jimmy and Johnny later left for New York, where Johnny took a job as an arranger for Tommy Dorsey, but in 1953 he gave up music to take a job with the post office in Dallas, Texas, his home town, and, with Judalein, the Thompsons moved to Dallas to live in an old-fashioned house only two doors from John's parents. As Jimmy wrote Judy, she and her husband were now "out of the Hollywood rat-race once and for all."

Meanwhile, Judy's marriage had fallen apart. There had been two private separations; there was no hiding that, however happy their reconciliations. Then a public separation, with a terse announcement by Vincente: "We are happier apart."

One night, at nearly ten o'clock, during one of these separations, Joan Blondell received a telephone call from Judy. Not only had Joan brought Dottie Ponedel to Judy; Judy and Joan had both been child performers in vaudeville, and later exchanged wild experiences—they both laughed over the discovery that when each was four she'd undergone the embarrassment of filling her pants on stage, and still managed to go through whatever she had to do before escaping into the wings. They had so many other stories to tell, and Joan was warm, forthright and sensible.

244

"Come over and have dinner with me," Judy said now. "I'm so terribly hungry—come on over, Joany."

"Oh, Judy, I had dinner at a quarter of eight," Joan said. "I've given up."

"Oh, please come," said Judy. "Let's have some drinks and talk. Please come." Her voice took on its heartbreaking timbre. "I'm alone in this big place I've taken—"

Joan capitulated. Judy always won anyway. When she finally found the house, there was Judy, looking pretty as the devil. As they greeted each other, Joan could see over Judy's shoulder into the dining room, where the table was set beautifully with silver for two, which seemed odd because she'd told Judy she'd eaten. After two or three drinks, Judy said suddenly, "I'll have to be honest with you." Frank Sinatra, she told Joan, was to have come over for dinner. He'd stood her up. She simply had to talk to somebody, and she'd called Joan.

Oh, of course, said Joan, sympathetically, and they walked into the dining room. But they had no sooner sat down than Judy jumped up. "I've got a headache—I'll be right back. I'm going to take some aspirin."

But when she came back, a moment later, she only toyed with her food. Her hunger had vanished. She wanted only to talk, and as she did, her words growing more rapid, Joan realized that she had taken something more than aspirin.

Judy talked; they went back into the living room, and Judy continued to talk, on a kaleidoscope of subjects. She was humiliated because Frank had stood her up. She was in love with him. Joan realized now that Judy's pupils had become quite dilated—so how much was one to believe? Frank was in love with her, Judy said, and she knew he was going to be her next husband.

Then she talked about the studio. She was outraged at Metro, at how insensitively they treated her; she was outraged at Vincente; she spoke bitterly of her childhood and of her mother, and of Busby Berkeley and how he had worked her, and of L. B. Mayer, and how they had all given her pills. . . .

Joan had heard this before, and, knowing Judy's condition, she allowed all Judy's words to pass by her.

Then for a little while Judy's mood changed. She began regaling Joan with "nuthouse" stories. Once, in one of those sanatoria she'd been in, "they made us march two by two every morning around the grounds for exercise." One morning she managed little by little to get out of place in the procession, slipping back farther and farther in the line as they marched, pushing one girl after another out of place ahead of her, until finally she was at the end of the line and saw two nuns coming behind her. She dashed back and got under the habit of one of the nuns, and so escaped unnoticed when the two nuns emerged from the grounds.

Joan couldn't contain herself. "Judy! Do you think I'm going to believe that, that out of a nuthouse line you slid under a nun's skirt and got away? And that she just kept on walking and didn't even know you were under there?"

But Judy was already on other subjects, again stories grotesquely exaggerated, again bitter reminiscences. The night wore on, Judy talking, talking, talking; and every little while Joan said, "Look, I've got to go, really—I don't relish driving home at this hour." Judy would seem to be on the verge of panic, and Joan had no heart to leave. But finally she rose. Judy looked up at her, the shadows dark under her enormous eyes. "You haven't seen Liza in a long time, have you?"

No, she hadn't, Joan said. She would come over again sometime and see the baby.

"Let's see her now," Judy said.

Joan shook her head. "I don't want to see her now, Judy. My God, it's almost four o'clock in the morning.

Judy said, "Come on, come on."

Joan said, "Judy, don't—" But Judy took her arm and Joan went with her. The house was on a hill, and they went downstairs to the bedrooms. Joan thought Judy would just push the door open quietly, and they'd peek in on Liza, but Judy opened the door, went over to the crib and took the child into her arms. Joan looked at the little face so filled with sleep, and so flushed, as babies are. "What are you going to do with her, Judy? Put her back in bed."

But Judy, the child in her arms, sat down in a nearby rocking chair and held her close, rocking with her.

Joan said, "You love her very much, don't you?" And Judy, rocking with her baby in her arms, said, yes, and Joan, thinking to herself, *How corny can I get?* said, "To get her back to sleep, sing her 'Over the Rainbow.' "

Joan Blondell was never to forget that experience: At nearly four in the morning, in that bedroom, Judy, by this time worn-out and pale, beginning to collapse as the pills she had taken were wearing off, as she looked at that little child in her arms, for the first time in her life had trouble singing "Over the Rainbow."

But she sang it, Joan remembered. *Her voice would crack, tears would run down her face—she crooned the song, so gently, so softly, embracing the baby with her eyes, her voice, her arms, seeing perhaps her own youth,* Joan thought. . . . And all through this, little Liza slept. Joan thought, *Whether she goes off key or not, whether her voice breaks or not, never has this song been sung as it is to this little girl tonight.*

Then Judy rose and carefully put her child back into her crib.

Joan managed then to get Judy up into the living room, found a fur rug on the floor, and simply pushed Judy down on it, covered her with part of it and said, "I'm leaving—you get some rest."

Years later Joan thought: Judy, then at the height of her fame, yet broken in so many ways, singing . . . *God, Judy!* she thought.

Metro had bought a new musical for Judy, *Annie Get Your Gun,* in which she would play the part Ethel Merman had made so great a hit on the Broadway stage—that of Annie Oakley. It meant new, heavy costumes, it meant learning a Western accent, and it meant losing weight again. Once more she was on pills, and in the lowest of moods. She was reminded that Metro had paid more for *Annie* than for any property in history: this would be a $3-million production, all this now rested on her shoulders. To add to the pressure, Busby Berkeley was to direct. While she admired his talent, it was always a strain for her to work with him, and represented still further pressure. Neither she nor he, she was to say later, was in a good mental state at the time.

"I did say, I don't think we're a very good combination right now," she went on. "We started the picture, we did a couple of scenes, and I knew I wasn't good. We made all the prerecordings. But I was in a daze. My head wouldn't stop aching."

The pressure increased on her, and with the pressure, the need for more pills. She lay awake through the night, making telephone calls to friends. She would ring Al Jennings, the assistant director, at two in the morning. "What kind of a day do you think it'll be?" And before he could answer, she would add, "I think it's going to be a gray, dreary day." If only the sun would shine—somehow that became the talisman for her.

Jennings, whom she liked and trusted, tried to encourage her. "No, Judy, it's going to be just fine. It's going to be a lovely day. Now, please get some sleep."

Two hours later, she called him again. "Al, I don't think it's going to be a nice day. It's just going to be foggy and awful." No, Judy, he said. "Now, come on, Baby, get some sleep. You'll have to be on the set soon."

Five A.M. "Oh—" Judy on the telephone again—"I know it's going to be terrible. I don't think I'll be any good." No, no, he said, you're going to be fine.

It was obvious she had been up all night worrying about how she would do, and what kind of a fearful, depressing influence the day would have. She fell asleep around 6 A.M., but did manage to get on the set a few hours later, and sing beautifully.

Then she discovered that her hair was falling out. She tried to make a joke of it: "My God, I can hear it dropping on the floor." Each day it seemed Dottie was using black to restore her hairline. Her skin began to break out. She took more pills. Judy had not shown up for several days. Freed had himself gone to see her, found her in bed and simply unable to be talked to. He did not want to take her out of *Annie:* he had persuaded Mayer to buy it for Judy, and Judy alone. Something had to be done.

Dr. Pobirs went out to see Judy and found her taking Nembutals —she always took Seconal, because it acted faster, but she had obtained these, too, in some way—and various tranquilizers, yet so agitated he could do nothing with her. She took the medication to wipe out her anxieties, and then when she attempted to do without pills, fighting with all her might to avoid them, the result was a physical pain and a sense of suffocation that became so intense that she had to take the pills again. She had built up a tolerance for enormous amounts of barbiturates, amphetamines; in her desire to blot out the agony, she went back into the very thing that had caused it in the first place. Her cure became her illness which became her cure which became her illness. Pobirs called in a specialist in shock treatment and in the spring of 1949, Judy Garland, not yet twenty-seven, underwent for the first time a series of six shock treatments.

248

Pobirs wanted simply to quiet her down enough so that a minimal amount of medication would keep her calm enough to function.

She was able, finally, to return to the set in late March. Again she was late, and increasingly late. There were negotiations for Chuck Walters to come in to replace Berkeley. That seemed a saving grace, but she continued to be late.

On the morning of May 10, 1949, Carleton Alsop walked in on the *Annie* set to find, as he put it, "all hell had broken out."

Judy was screaming epithets, aides were running in all directions, and when Judy saw Carleton, she fled to him, waving a letter that had just come to her from the front office. She all but screamed, "Pa, make those sons of bitches treat me like they do Greer Garson, for God's sake, instead of the little hunchback girl they got from Bones Remer." She burst into tears. "I never lost anybody any money in my life!" she shouted, waving the letter again.

Dated that morning, it was signed by Louis K. Sidney, vice president of MGM, and it read in part:

DEAR MISS GARLAND:
You must be aware of the fact that your contract with us requires you to be prompt in complying with our instructions and to perform your services conscientiously and to the full extent of your ability and as instructed by us.

We desire to call your attention to the fact that on a great many occasions since the commencement of your services in "ANNIE GET YOUR GUN," you were either late in arriving on the set in the morning, late in arriving on the set after lunch, or were otherwise responsible for substantial delays or curtailed production, all without our consent. The damage to us due to these infractions of your obligations under your contract with us is very substantial. . . .

It concluded that if without proper cause she was absent from this point on, or tardy in reporting as instructed, they would do whatever they were entitled to, "including, but not limited to, the right to remove you from 'ANNIE GET YOUR GUN,' to cast someone else in the role of 'ANNIE' and to refuse to pay you compensation until the completion of such role by such other person."

Carleton tried to console her. He would get in touch at once with L. B. Mayer. But Judy went back to her dressing room.

There are three stories of what happened—one by Lella Waxman, one by Dottie Ponedel and one by Chuck Walters. They disagree in details, but they agree in their conclusion: Judy did not return to the set after lunch on Tuesday, May 10—and was fired that day from *Annie Get Your Gun.*

Lella's story is that the Saturday before, Judy came, as usual, late on the set. She was in agony. She simply walked off the picture. Lella was alone with her in her dressing room, and Judy began banging her head against the wall, in pain and anguish, unable to act, to appear before the camera, unable to do anything but suffer, and Lella called Al Jennings, who took her home.

Judy was not at the studio Monday, May 9, but did arrive late Tuesday morning, the tenth. That was when she received the warning letter, and Carleton walked onto the set to find her in a rage—she, who had earned millions for them, now being warned not to be late or she would be fired.

Dottie's story is that she was with Judy that Tuesday morning when she received the warning letter. Judy turned to her: "Dottie, they can't do that to me, can they? If I can't go to work?"

Dottie said, "Yes, they can if you say you won't go to work."

Judy replied, "I'm not going to do it. I can't."

Dottie said, "Come on, do it, Judy, go out and work or they'll fire you."

But Judy persisted: "I won't. I won't. They can't do anything to me. I've got a contract."

Dottie warned her, "But your contract has a clause that says if you won't go to work, they'll fire you."

"Not me," said Judy.

Dottie gave up. "O.K. Don't go. If you don't want to go, don't go."

Walters' story is that his office was a few steps from Judy's dressing room, and that Tuesday he had come on the set to replace Berkeley. Judy came into his office crying. "Chuck, I'm happy you're on the picture, but I'm afraid it's too late. I don't think I can make it. Buzz has just sliced me to ribbons. I cannot do it."

Walters said, "Do you want to have some lunch?"

Judy said, "No, I think I'll go to my dressing room and have a drink."

Walters suggested, "Well, if you want to have it here—"

But she went to her dressing room, and a few moments later called out half-hysterically, "Get the ice out! I'll be right over. I'm going to have that fucking drink! You won't believe—"

Back she came into his office, laughing hysterically, not crying but laughing, yet beside herself. "I'm fired from *Annie!*"

He let her get drunk. "Have another, honey. It's the only answer." She was crying and laughing. "I don't believe it! After the money I made for these sons of bitches! These bastards! These lousy bastards! Goddamn them!"

Walters said, "Let it rip, let it all come out. Let it go!"

The manner of her firing—many of the details Judy herself was not aware of—as much as anything all but destroyed her. Alsop was to say later to Mayer, "If one of your race horses broke his leg, you'd treat him better than you treated Judy. Why didn't you or Benny Thau or someone call her in and talk to her instead of firing her from the picture as you did?"

But it was not quite that way. What happened was that on July 1, 1948, Dore Schary had come to Metro as Mayer's assistant, in charge of production. At one time or another he talked to Judy. He noticed a new hardness in her language: she used four-letter words: "I don't give a shit what they give me." She was angry, she was upset. She felt she was doing too much work, her shooting schedules were too cramped, she didn't want to do so many films—yet at this time she was by contract making no more than two films a year.

Then, as difficulties arose on *Annie Get Your Gun,* Schary spoke to her again. Mayer had talked to her. Freed had gone up to her house to see her, with little result. Schary now told her that she was late, she was not showing up. . . . Her attitude was that she was doing the best she could, and that she felt unwell. Schary decided he had to issue an ultimatum. "Judy, we can't continue with this kind of cost going up and up, and a product we can't use. You're just not right." She was clearly not herself. She said she would try. But finally the moment came when Schary called Nick Schenck in New York. "This is a tough one," he said. He explained the situation. Nearly a million dollars had been spent so far on the film. Judy had already prerecorded eleven songs. But she was now obviously incapable of functioning; she could not, did not, want to go on with it. "This is a tough one," Schary repeated. Everything that had been done so far would simply have to be junked if Judy was removed, and it would be a blow to Judy herself. "But our feeling is to take her out because otherwise you're going to be in a hole—and you won't have a movie."

At the end of the conversation Schenck, who was familiar with the situation from other sources as well, said only, "Do what you have to do."

Schary gave the order.

Lester Peterson, the MGM aide who had been assigned for years to Mickey Rooney (he had been best man at Mickey's wedding to Ava Gardner), and then accompanied Mickey and Judy on their personal-appearance tours, went to Judy's dressing room. He carried a letter to give her and a single one-sentence message: "You are no longer in *Annie Get Your Gun.*"

He would never forget how Judy reacted: with a howl of pain, she literally threw herself on the floor and rolled about in anguish, screaming, "No, no, no!" He was dismayed. He thought she had known before he arrived that she was out. He had no idea that he was breaking the news to her. She knew she was late, she knew she did not know her lines, that she was not functioning. Then she was surrounded by her friends, and he left.

The letter he delivered to her, like the one earlier that morning, was dated the same day—May 10, 1949—and signed by Vice President Sidney again, and it read:

DEAR MISS GARLAND:

You have refused to comply with our instructions to report on the set of "ANNIE GET YOUR GUN" after lunch today and you have also advised us that you do not intend to render your services in said photoplay.

This is to notify you that for good and sufficient cause and in accordance with the rights granted to us under the provisions of Paragraph 12 of your contract of employment with us dated November 21, 1946 . . . we shall refuse to pay you any compensation commencing as of May 10, 1949, and continuing until the expiration of the time which would have been reasonably required to complete the role of "ANNIE" in the photoplay "ANNIE GET YOUR GUN" or (should another person be engaged to portray such role) until the completion of such role by such other person. . . .

That was the fact.

Judy Garland, the greatest singing star in films, had been fired from Metro's most expensive property, *Annie Get Your Gun,* a $3-million musical with songs by Irving Berlin, bought for her and tailored for her and expected to be the most triumphant of her career.

Her salary of nearly $6,000 a week stopped that day.

252

She was taken home.

A few days later she read that Betty Hutton had been borrowed from Paramount to replace her and play the title role of Annie.

19

ON MAY 29, 1949, A THIN, wan Judy Garland entered the Peter Bent Brigham Hospital, associated with Harvard Medical School, in Boston. She had come, it was explained, for a medical checkup: she was overwrought and exhausted; in a fit of temperament, because she had been "insulted" by a minor MGM executive, she had walked off the set of *Annie Get Your Gun,* and had been suspended by MGM.

She was accompanied by a tall, urbane man in his thirties, Carleton Alsop, identified as her "personal manager." She would be a patient of Dr. George W. Thorn, a distinguished internist and physician-in-chief. As Judy pointed out in an interview, her problem was "physical, not mental," it had nothing to do with psychiatry. Yes, there had been something of a sleeping-pill problem—but that was common in Hollywood. "What can you do?" she rhetorically asked Elliot Norton, the well-known dramatic critic of the Boston *Post,* at her first press conference a week after her arrival. "You get so exhausted on a picture that you can't sleep and you know you must sleep because you've got to face that camera early in the morning and it's going to show up every little line on your face." So one took sleeping pills.

Otherwise, she was fine. She was separated from her husband, Vincente Minnelli, the director, but he and their daughter, Liza, who was staying in Los Angeles with him, would both be visiting her soon.

Alsop, her personal manager, meanwhile was staying at the Ritz Carlton Hotel, and would be on hand for whatever assistance he could render.

Actually, the physician directly in charge of her was not Dr. Thorn but Dr. Augustus Rose, an eminent neurologist who was listed simply as one of the consulting doctors in Judy's case.

Behind the decision to go to Boston there had been discussions with Dr. Marc and with Judy's current psychiatrist, and then with Dr. Jessie Marmorston, Mayer's physician and friend. Judy said, "I'll go mad if I just stay around town. I've got to go somewhere to get out of this. I must get my health back, not in a mental institution but in a good hospital." Dr. Marmorston suggested Peter Bent Brigham. Mayer was all for it, when Judy called on him. He himself had been an unpublicized patient there for a minor ailment some months before. Now Judy asked about borrowing money from Metro. She would pay it back when she was able to work again. Mayer said, "By all means, that's the least we can do—pay for your hospital bills."

To clear this he had to call Nick Schenck at the home office in New York. He got Schenck on the phone. The scene, as Judy remembered it some years later: "He put the phone down and said, 'Mr. Schenck suggests that you go to a charity hospital. We're not in the money-lending business.' He just looked at me. I'll never forget what he said. 'You know, if they'll do this to you, they'll do it to me.' He said that he was so ashamed that he, personally, would pay for whatever expenses I would have." Mayer wanted Carleton to go with her to Boston, so she would not be alone. Carleton would receive no salary, but Mayer would pay Carleton's expenses, too, out of his own pocket.

The truth of Mayer's reporting of his conversation with Schenck, whom he did not like, or the truth of Judy's reporting of what she said Mayer told her Schenck had said, poses a question: MGM did pay Judy's hospital bills—some $40,000 for her Boston stay. The records show that MGM loaned her $9,000 on June 28, while she was in Boston, with two provisos: that she would pay it back when she returned to work, but they would not put her before the camera until she came with a letter from Dr. Thorn saying he "reasonably believed" she was able, ready and willing to work. Not only does this cast doubt on what appears to be Schenck's insultingly callous response to Mayer, but it makes clear that the studio did not attempt to force her back to work before she was ready. The accusation that they did, however, would become part of the Judy legend, too.

Judy's first meeting with Dr. Rose impressed her. He was a commanding figure, nearly six foot four, with a comforting manner of speech, a quick smile and a dry, New England sense of humor. She tried to explain what troubled her, after she had spent some days at the hospital going through a complete physical examination which showed everything was fine—liver, blood, heart. But she was tense, nervous, suffering from malnutrition—weighing by then about ninety pounds—and from immense fatigue. She had never been able to put into words precisely what troubled her. When she began talking about it, she became so keyed up she could not go on; it became torture.

Now, under Dr. Rose's calm regard, she was able to separate out some of her troubles. She was in a low mood. She could not sleep; she could not work; she felt she wanted to die; she could not control her temper, and would fly into tantrums at what she realized was the slightest provocation, so that the most minute episode, word, concern, development, was inflated to catastrophic proportions. She was taking pills to sleep and pills to wake up. She was in physical pain; she had migraine headaches; her hair was falling out; there was a rash on her skin. She was abysmally discouraged; her years of analysis had not helped her, she said; she had no respect for psychiatrists, she had seen more than a dozen of them, and they had all failed her. (Dr. Rose had been introduced to her as a consulting neurologist.)

Dr. Rose was encouraged, however, because she had a will to lick her problem. She *wanted* to get well. She was put into a large room, given three big meals a day, with lights out at 9 P.M., whether she slept or not. The first thing she would have to learn was how to eat and how to sleep. "Sooner or later you'll get into the habit of eating and sleeping," Dr. Rose assured her. And she did.

During those first weeks Carleton did a remarkably good job of supportive psychotherapy, carrying out Dr. Rose's instructions. He was with her every moment he was permitted, during visiting hours. She was helped, too, by her friends. Frank Sinatra not only telephoned daily, but sent daily gifts—flowers, bed jackets, a record player, records, perfume—he joked with her on the phone, and promised he would fly up to Boston with mutual friends as soon as the doctors permitted it. And one night he arrived and, with the hospital's permission, took her out for the evening. Mayer himself came up to see her.

On June 10, her twenty-seventh birthday, Liza visited her. By this time Judy was well enough so that Carleton could take her out on trial walks. They would walk slowly, followed behind by Carleton's car, in case of a relapse. On Judy's birthday, she was strong enough for them to pick up Liza and her governess at Boston's South Station, and mother and three-year-old daughter posed for the press, and they spent that day at the Ritz—interestingly enough, in Suite 904, where, less than four years before, Judy had awakened Vincente to say, "I have a name for the baby, if it's a girl—"

After three or four weeks, Judy was completely off medication—completely pill-free, for the first time in years. Dr. Rose had performed miracles. She was sleeping and waking normally. Carleton used great ingenuity in filling her time. He suggested night baseball games and Judy became an ardent Red Sox fan, and, in turn, their mascot; they'd stop practice when they saw her and crowd around as she autographed baseballs.

He entertained her from his vast fund of stories—how he was once drunk with John Barrymore for ten days in a Japanese whorehouse, and of Barrymore's memorable denunciation when, at a chic party in London, Barrymore's hostess told him that a distinguished actor, known to be a homosexual, was to play Hamlet—a role Barrymore himself had made famous in New York.

"What!" roared Barrymore, in his most magnificent manner, "So-and-so play Hamlet? That blazing faggot, that flaming fairy, daring to play Hamlet? Madam, I want you to know that when Hamlet walks on the stage, you should hear his balls clank!"

Now that, said Carleton appreciatively, while Judy doubled up with laughter, "that is the greatest expression of masculinity I've ever heard." Oh, Pa! said Judy, oh, Pa! when she could catch her breath.

After the fourth week Dr. Rose concluded that what Judy needed now in her treatment was self-confidence. Since she was sleeping and waking normally, eating well, there was no reason to keep her in a hospital. He told her she would become an outpatient. She could move to the Ritz, but she was to come and see him at his office at 2 P.M., five afternoons a week. Alsop, who had a room at the Ritz, could drop her off.

The first day Alsop drove her to Dr. Rose's office, several passers-by recognized her as she walked into the building. It was "Hi, Judy," and Judy smiled and waved. Next day there was a bigger crowd when she arrived at 2 P.M.; the third day, still bigger. Soon everybody knew that at two o'clock on weekdays Judy Garland arrived at that building. It became almost festive then. People lined up, now, half an hour before, waiting for Alsop's car to arrive with Judy in it; and when she got out, it was "Judy! Judy!" Shouts, cries, applause. "We love you, Judy!" The papers had been full of her struggle to regain her health

256

after her "nervous exhaustion." Judy would beam, and wave at them, and literally float into Dr. Rose's office, and sit down light and triumphant in the chair in front of his desk.

Dr. Rose would say, with a smile, "Judy, calm down. Just because you had a few people clapping outside—"

Judy: "Oh, you're a mean man!"

And now a strange and curious struggle began to take place: between the physician, seeking to return Judy Garland to reality—that she was Frances Gumm, a real person, not Judy Garland, a plastic creation; that reality was not that fantasy world of hers with people applauding and make-believe love and the dream forever coming true—and Judy, struggling just as mightily to bring this man, this reality-maker, into that very world, her world. She knew she had her audience outside; they adored her; they would wait now for hours for the chance to see her arrive, the chance to see her leave, just to glory in her presence, in the knowledge that they had laid eyes on her, touched her, heard her voice, had her smile at them. *And this doctor seated before her was telling her that all this was fantasy.*

Once, in the midst of this struggle, the noise outside down below grew louder. The crowd obviously was growing. Judy got out of her chair. There were three windows in Dr. Rose's office. She went to each window and flung it open wide, and standing there, while Dr. Rose sat behind his desk, she began to sing at the top of her voice. Her voice filled the room, and outside there was an instant roar of applause, and then cries and shouts: "Judy! Judy!"

Judy looked down, waved at the mass of people below, and sang them an encore.

When she finished, the applause came up to them in waves. The office echoed. Judy looked at Dr. Rose triumphantly.

The physician, imperturbable, unwound to his six feet four inches, looked down on his patient—scarcely five feet high—strode to each window, closed it and sat her down again. "Look," he said. "We can't do this, Judy. If you're going to come to see me, we cannot do this. You're trying to make me into one of your fans. I can't help you in that way. We shall have to meet somewhere else."

He was trying to make her see, but she did not want to see. She had to have someone there to adore her: this was what she had grown up on, from the age of three. Applause and audience approval had become her oxygen. Without it she could not live. She was not gaining any real insight into her problem. She could not be counted upon to sit still, to look into a mirror and say, *This is the way it is. This is life.* She could not say, *All right, I'm restless tonight, but I can do without medicine.*

As a talented child she had been able to get audience acceptance over the rest of the family; she stood out; everything was for her; she was indulged; she took at face value the value others placed upon her.

She became the breadwinner, but she developed no self-discipline. In the routine of the stage performance, she could manage herself, she could perform. Then she was keyed up, she was alive, she had an identity. But after that came the letdown, the return, the transformation from Judy Garland to Frances Gumm—dreadful, frightening, appalling to her. Then she was lost.

She saw what was good in life only when she was performing. If that was taken away, she was unable to deal with everyday matters —brush her teeth, buy a dress, go out in the world. Reality was Frances Gumm, Frances Gumm was reality, and she fled from it through the door her voice had opened for her.

However grotesque, the comparison to Pavlov's dogs was apt. She was put before the public at the age of three, and she began to demand admiration and adulation; and no matter with what largess that came to her, it was not enough. Because it did not register; it could not. It was not going to Frances Gumm, to herself; it was going to the stranger, that created entity, Judy Garland. Yet it had to continue, because it made Judy Garland possible; when the audience was not there, she was Frances Gumm, faced with real life, and she simply had never learned to be Frances Gumm, she had no idea what really fulfilled Frances Gumm: she could only know what seemed to fulfill Judy Garland. The audience gave Judy Garland candy; Frances Gumm accepted it, but couldn't taste it. So no matter what came to Judy Garland, Frances Gumm was forever cheated. And yet she seemed doomed to the terrible, wonderful pretense forever.

One could look at it from another approach.

She had gotten a number of views of herself in her many hours of analysis, from her many analysts. Some of these views she accepted, some she did not.

One was that of the spoiled child: intellectually a woman, emotion-

258

ally a child, infantile in her reactions, who all her life had gotten what she wanted and, like an infant, demanded immediate satisfaction, as a hungry infant demands the breast and is not content until she gets it. If she did not get it, as an infant she cried; as grown Judy Garland she threw a tantrum.

And what had happened? As a result of her talent, her magic?

As it was when she was Baby Gumm: The family (which later became the world) crowded about her, saying, *We love you, don't cry, what is it, hon-ey! Please don't cry.* The world was Frank Gumm, cuddling her, saying, *My little monkey-face, don't cry.* She was not punished as a baby; she was not punished as an adult. Judy could do no wrong. Her friends knew that.

When she came hours late on the set of *Meet Me in St. Louis,* hadn't Arthur Freed put his arm around her and asked, "What's wrong with my little girl?" He did not punish her. For Arthur Freed one could read Frank Gumm.

At three she got away with what she wanted, whether it was her sisters' candy or never being sent to bed without her supper, as her sisters were. At nineteen Jackie Cooper could not blame her when she took him away from Bonita, and in her early twenties when she couldn't get Joe Mankiewicz to leave his ill wife, she had gone so far as to convince herself that she was pregnant.

The other view was that of herself as the one sinned against, the commodity, the thing made use of. This she accepted: that however much Metro might talk about how they loved her, they were really concerned only about her voice, and how she appeared before the camera. Hadn't it always been, *We've got to get her this way for* The Wizard of Oz, *or that way for* Meet Me in St. Louis, *or such a way for* Ziegfeld Girl? It meant she really was just a commodity, a thing to be taken care of for its value, not for its human qualities.

A third view was one she would not tolerate, for it meant looking into herself, and how could you look into yourself if what you feared to find was a confirmation of your deepest fears: that there really wasn't any reason for you to have such a voice, this voice which was your genie in the bottle, this voice bestowed upon you? You really hadn't done anything to deserve it. You hadn't worked to train it. You'd never taken lessons. At a very early age you'd opened your mouth—and, as if by magic, the world had engulfed you with overwhelming love and approval—and it had continued to do so ever since. Where did you get that power? And why could it not be taken away as quickly and mysteriously as it had been given?

As an enormously rich man wonders, *Do my friends like me for myself or for my money?* so Judy never knew whether she was loved for her voice or for the girl she really was. Did her mother love her as she was, or as she expected her to be: not Frances Gumm, but Judy Garland? *But she was Frances Gumm.* That was the shattering part of it.

But there were setbacks in Boston.

Dr. Rose had no control of her once she was outside his office. She could obtain pills—from anyone.

One night, about 3 A.M., Dr. Rose was called by the nurse attending her at the hotel. She reported that Judy was in a hysterical tantrum. Dr. Rose hurried over. When he entered her bedroom, Judy was under the bed, kicking her feet and screaming—being a brat. "Get the hell out of here!" she screamed. Dr. Rose sent the nurse out of the room and sat on the side of the bed while Judy remained under it, screaming and cursing.

He said, "Look, Judy, we are alone—just the two of us. Can't you come out and talk to me?"

She responded again. "Get out, goddamnit. Let me alone."

He got down on the floor, slid his long body under the bed, kept his distance, but talked to her. She pretended not to listen, but after a little while she said, pointing upward, "Let's talk up there."

So both crept out from under the bed—the distinguished physician and the distinguished patient—and sat on the bed and talked.

One can only assume that she thought, *If a doctor is ready to get down on the floor, to crawl under a bed to talk to me, there must be something good in him.*

On July Fourth Carleton, she and Liza went on a holiday. Sylvia Sidney and her little boy—she was doing summer stock through New England—joined them. That Independence Day they were all in Gloucester, and Judy and Liza rode the merry-go-round, and wandered about the town followed by admiring crowds.

One weekend Carleton took her to a summer theatre on Cape Cod. She sat, hunched up in her chair, in the little auditorium; the word spread quickly that she was there. Before the performance began, an actor came out from the wings, stood before the curtain and said, "Myself and members of the cast, and I'm sure the audience, will be as excited as we are to know that Judy Garland is out front." Carleton was to tell her later, "My God, I thought you'd go to pieces. I expected the worst," when the actor continued, "And something that would make this evening so memorable for all of us . . . would be if Miss Garland would come up on stage and sing a song."

Carleton held on to Judy's arm tightly. Anything could happen now.

She turned to him. "Pa," she said, "do you think I have any voice left?" It was both a question and a plea, because he knew that she feared her voice was gone.

He said, "Judy, you'd have a voice left unless they buried you face down and then you'd scratch yourself out and belt the shit out of—"

Her face shone. "Pa, you son of a bitch, thank you!" She rose and walked firmly to the stage, they brought out a camp chair for her, and, sitting there, in the worst possible light, she sang—and suddenly it was not Cape Cod, July 1949, and she a psychiatric outpatient at Peter Bent Brigham Hospital, but it was years before, and a glowing, wondrous Judy shedding magic from the screen to millions. . . . When it was all over, Judy's singing and the play and the applause, Carleton took her back to the hotel, and he wept. Where did she get that power, how could one find words to describe what was inside that girl? Whence came that inner force that could drive this girl—no matter what agonies were tormenting her—to do what she did to people?

He thought, *For good or evil, that strange little hunchbacked girl* (he allowed himself Mayer's offensive hyperbole, the very counterpoint of its grotesquerie burned the thought in his mind), *for good or evil, once you had contact with her, you became in many ways her slave; because in an audience you were a slave; if you became a friend, you were used because you constantly wanted to help her. She drew it from you. And if you had any contact, either as audience or friend, she would never go out of your life. And any time you heard "Over the Rainbow," you would be marked again by her. And she had this extraordinary, strange, explosive ability,* he thought, *to give happiness to the widest variety of people—and out of her own tor-*

ment, really; for she never had any happiness of her own save when she was out there singing, or dancing—performing. Performing . . .

After Judy's stay on Cape Cod—it was lengthened to two weeks, and Vincente and Liza visited her there—she returned to Boston and was told it was all right for her to leave.

Dr. Rose had given this considerable thought. Should Judy go back to work? The question was, how strong was she? How well adjusted? She said she was sleeping. Her skin had cleared up. She had gained weight. She looked well. Or should she remain in Boston for further treatment? He had to help her live a normal life, and a normal life for Judy was not Boston. Her existence was becoming abnormal here. So he decided she should be allowed to return to Los Angeles, and test herself, simply living there; they would remain in touch with a tacit understanding that she would return for another six or eight weeks later, depending on how well she did.

Before she left Boston she had to make a visit, and it turned out to be one of her most moving—and reassuring—experiences.

At one point during her barrage of tests she had been given an electroencephalogram, to determine if there was any tumor or growth in the brain. She had thought, *Oh my God, I've passed all the tests, now they're going to record my brain, they'll get down on paper my thoughts, and I'm a dead pigeon once they know all that. . . . They'll never let me out of here.*

For this test, she had to go to the nearby Children's Hospital, where she found herself taken to the fourth floor and led down corridors past obviously retarded children, some playing vacantly, to a room where she was put in bed. *Naturally*, she thought, *this is a test they give retarded children. Makes sense.* The wallpaper was decorated with little bunnies and pink elephants, and, floating near the ceiling, red and yellow balloons. Then a series of wires were attached to her head, and she lay there while a mysterious machine buzzed and hummed. *Oh, Christ*, she thought, *this is the end of me.* But the test turned out fine; the machine did not record her thoughts, she was assured, and she was greatly relieved.

As she left the room, she learned from the nurse with her that the retarded children were only on this floor; the first three floors were devoted to youngsters suffering from rheumatic fever. At this point Carleton joined her. The children on the lower floors had heard she

262

was there and wanted to see her. They all knew of—and the older ones had seen—*The Wizard of Oz,* and they begged for her to visit them, a hospital official had told him. After consulting with Dr. Thorn, who thought it might be a good idea, Carleton had said yes.

Judy became furious. "Pa, goddamnit, you have no right to commit me to something like that without telling me first," she exclaimed. "It'll just depress me—and it won't do the children any good."

"No," said Carleton firmly. "It will do them good and do you good. Trust me."

In the end, Judy agreed, "Oh, all right, Pa—anything to get out of this joint!"

Judy entered the first ward. She would never forget the sight—seeing those children, some of whom had never walked and would never walk, some of whom she knew would never live to reach their teens. The older children applauded and shouted, "Hi, Judy!" and the little ones, those who could not applaud, were lifted up by their nurses so they could see her. Judy's first reaction was to pull back, startled—"Ohhh!"—an exclamation of shock, pity, then compassion. She turned, stricken, to Alsop. "What'll I do, Pa?" she whispered.

At the foot of each bed was a sign with the large printed initials "TLC," and Alsop said, "Give them what that sign says, 'tender, loving care.' Sit down next to their beds and hold their hands. Sing a couple of notes here and there, something they might remember, and try not to miss any bed."

By this time Carleton need not have told her anything. This was an audience, a loving audience, and, after her first shock, Judy was in charge. She went from bed to bed giving each child all her attention for a few minutes. She was to say later how beautiful they were: "Their eyes marvelously lustrous, with such long eyelashes, and a kind of luminous quality to their skin." One ward had young teen-age children; then, with each ward, the children were younger, and finally Judy found herself with the four- and five-year-olds, all in cribs. And everywhere it was smiles, and clapping, and "Hi, Judy."

Carleton had been right. The visit helped her enormously—as it did the children. Instead of being depressed, she was exhilarated. Judy found herself returning each day. She was finally doing something for an entirely different kind of audience, and with no pay—and she had seen the reward. *She was needed.* And this quality of hers—so many had observed it—this "laying on of hands" which she possessed, this ability to make others feel better, was there.

Now, as she was to leave Boston, she went for a final visit to say good-bye, on the way to the train station with Carleton. The children had been told to expect her, and again—as the first time she set foot in the first ward—she was taken aback. But for a different reason. All of the children had been prepared for her visit: their hair had been shampooed and carefully combed, the older ones wore lipstick, and each child had a tiny bouquet of flowers for her.

Again, it was a laying on of hands. Judy went from bed to bed, with a rustle of sighs and murmurs and tears and laughter following her, and finally she came to one child she had made certain never to miss. This was a five-year-old little girl who the first time had pulled back fearfully into a corner of her crib and huddled there, her eyes panic-stricken. A nurse had whispered to Judy that she was one of eight, her brothers and sisters all healthy, and the family, quite ignorant, hated this child for her illness. They had rejected and even beaten her because she was weak, and she had simply stopped talking. The nurses had tried everything, but she had not uttered a word for nearly two years.

Judy had said, on that first visit, "Well, I'll just sit by her a bit." She sat next to her crib quietly. She did not even say "Hello" or "How are you?" or "What's your name?" She told her only that she, too, was in a hospital, the Peter Bent Brigham Hospital, and told her about her little girl, Liza; and after a few minutes, she left and went on to the next child.

Now, on this, her final visit, Judy sat by the little girl's bed—a trim figure in a hat and blue-gray traveling suit, obviously going away. As Judy had made her rounds, all the other children had said, "Good-bye, Judy," and she had hugged each one, grateful because they had helped make her well during these weeks. Now she said, bending over to kiss and hug this last, silent child, "Good-bye, I hope you feel well," and as Judy described it later: "She suddenly just jumped up on her knees and at the top of her lungs she said, 'Judy!' and she started to cry with her arms around my neck, and she started to talk. . . ." Sometimes the words made sense, sometimes they did not, a pouring out of "Don't leave . . . my mother . . . please . . ." As Judy put it, "Everybody was crying, the nurses were crying, I was crying, and this child was talking at the top of her lungs and I was holding on to her and rocking her. . . ."

Carleton, as moved as she, waited until there was no more time to wait. "Judy," he said gently, "we've got to go or we'll miss the train."

"We'll just have to miss the train," came Judy's muffled voice, her face against the child's cheek. "I'm not going to leave this child while she's talking." She remained for nearly half an hour more, until the child calmed down. Then Judy left.

As she and Carleton got into the car downstairs, they looked up; the children were hanging out the windows, shouting and waving at her.

Talking about it years later, Judy said, "I guess it was one of the great moments in my life when that child spoke like that. I felt I had . . ." She paused, searching for words. "I just didn't give a damn how many pictures I'd been fired from, or how much humiliation . . . I had done a human being some good! I felt right on top of the world."

Then she went back to Los Angeles, and Hollywood, and the strange reality of her fantasy world.

Her return was a calculated risk. Dr. Rose knew she had not gained any real insight into her problem. She still could not be counted upon to look into the mirror and see what was there; she had not the self-control she needed.

In the first days she lost control only once, when, despite herself, and knowing it could only torture her, she insisted upon paying a visit to the set of *Annie Get Your Gun,* which was still shooting. As she stood there, Betty Hutton hurried by, wearing one of the costumes that had been designed for Judy. Betty gave her a cheerful "Hi, Judy!"—and Judy responded with a bitter "You goddamn son of a bitch!" Betty stopped short, and then went on, white-faced. To be replaced, and by someone so happy about it, so full of zest, so bubbling . . . Judy did not lose easily.

Save for this lapse, for a time she did very well at home.

She was back with Vincente. There had been a reunion, and when Judy arrived back on the Coast, the Minnellis were a family again, and now a three-year-old Liza would come up to watch them at their candlelit dinner, dressed in a long dressing gown, looking so adorable it was all they could do not to laugh at her. They had both discovered very quickly that Liza did not like to be laughed at. (That, for whatever it means, was something Baby Gumm could not endure either.)

They knew they must be very careful and take her very seriously.

Vincente would play a game. He knew how easy it was to break Judy up with a funny line, and he would say such things with a perfectly straight face, making her want to laugh—and she dared not, because Liza would think she was laughing at her. Liza was very sensitive about this, and would watch them both like a hawk. Judy would say later, to Vincente, "It's very cruel of you to do that," but he couldn't help it, because it was so easy to make Judy laugh and then watch her struggle not to. As for Liza, she saw far more than they realized. One evening Vincente was lying on the couch, reading. He looked up and there was Liza looking at him. He had no idea what got into him but he said to her, seriously, "You know, I'm not at all happy about France. I don't think De Gaulle is good for France because, you know, they're right on the verge of inflation. I don't see how he's going to manage." Liza was astounded. She cried out, "Mama, come quick, Daddy is talking to me!"—so thrilled that he was talking to her like an adult, not talking baby talk to her. As Judy and Vincente agreed, they had an unusual child.

Indeed, Judy was doing so well that Metro put her into a new production, *Summer Stock*, without informing Dr. Rose. Joe Pasternak wanted Judy for the picture. He had once told her, "If you're half-dead, you're still better than anyone else. Any time Arthur will let you go, I'll use you in anything, if you'll just work for me." And since no one else was asking for her, she agreed and, in the late summer of 1949, began *Summer Stock*.

But by this time she had put on weight again, and once more needed to reduce. She began having trouble on the set. She began calling Dr. Rose several times a day, and sometimes at 2 A.M. He could catch glimpses, in their conversation, that she was slipping.

Then L. B. Mayer telephoned him. Judy was on pills again. She was coming in late; not only late, but unable to function. Would Dr. Rose come to Los Angeles, and take over his patient again, and help her get through the picture? Judy was only happy when she was kept busy, and if she could be helped through this film and prove to herself she could do it, it would be great therapy for her. Metro would take care of all medical fees and living expenses. Dr. Rose accepted the assignment.

He went at once to see Judy in the house at 10000 Sunset Boulevard. He spoke with Mayer, and Thau, and Freed, with Gene Kelly, who was to be her co-star, and Chuck Walters, her director. Judy had feelings of incompetence, failure, inability to withstand pressure. She could not endure people, she could not manage herself. He went on the set with her every day and became her protector and supporter there. Two and a half years before it had been Dr. Hacker on the set; now it was Dr. Rose.

Kelly disliked the script, which dealt with a group of actors who put on a stage show in a barn. He thought it was *Babes on Broadway* all over again. "I really can't do this awful stuff," Kelly began.

"If you don't do this picture," Dr. Rose told him, "Judy will be in great trouble. She has serious problems now and she needs someone whom she trusts implicitly." Otherwise, she would be unable to get through it. "You're the man." Gene said, all right, he would do it. Judy had been his champion in *For Me and My Gal;* he would do anything for her. Dr. Rose really did not approve of Judy's going into a film so soon, but since that was the fact, they would all have to work together to help her. Chuck Walters, too, learned that he was to be part of Judy's therapy if she was to get through the picture.

But it was very difficult. Judy would go before the camera, animated, vital—then suddenly a cold sweat would come over her, she'd hurry offstage, to weep and cry. Dr. Rose would hold her hand, listen to her, give her fifteen minutes of supportive therapy, and she would snap back. Benny Thau said Rose told him he was being forced to compete with people who gave Judy pills at five in the morning. His task was almost impossible.

Judy's tenseness and unhappiness were reflected at home. At one point she and Ethel had a fierce, unforgivably bitter argument, an appalling argument, and Judy exploded: Ethel was to get out of her house; not only that, Mrs. MacFarlane was never to take Liza again to her grandmother's house, her grandmother was not to take her for dance lessons or anywhere else. Worst of all, she didn't want Ethel to see Liza again.

Ethel left in tears. Very well. Grandma Eva was being excellently cared for in the nursing home. Suzy and Jack Cathcart lived in Nevada. Since Judy wanted to have nothing to do with her, and forbade her to see Liza, Ethel simply left Los Angeles. She sold her house and moved to Dallas, to be near Jimmy, Judalein and her new son-in-law, and begin to make a new life for herself there.

Within a few weeks she had obtained a job managing a small movie house, become a popular mistress of ceremonies in little-theatre groups, organized bridge parties, talked about opening a tearoom, and was definitely making her presence felt in town.

Gene Kelly found himself playing a double role—working in the film and giving Judy support. She would not come in for days, or she would show up late. She was fat, and frightened. She had lost *Barkleys of Broadway;* she had lost *Annie Get Your Gun;* now there was a chance she'd be taken out of this film, too, because she was still too heavy. There had been confrontations in the front office and she had pleaded, "Just give me one more chance," she'd not be late, she'd get rid of the weight. . . . It was an agonizing struggle. Sometimes she came on the set at 5 P.M.—the shooting really over for the day—to talk to Gene, to let him know she was there. She would go over to him, and he would hold her in his arms and she would cry because she wanted to work, but something was making her frightened beyond the fright one would expect in someone even in her predicament. This upset Gene; he was supposed to be doing the picture so she would not be afraid. And he knew she was telephoning Chuck Walters at two and three in the morning—and who knew who else she telephoned or saw?—and having a miserable time of it.

Walters, for his part, was invaluable. Judy of course did not know that Gene and Chuck were working almost like surrogate psychiatrists to help her, that all the principals in the cast had been chosen because she loved and trusted them, and all were being briefed by Dr. Rose.

Walters managed miracles of adjustment. When Judy came in so befogged one day, and all she had to do was go up a flight of stairs and still couldn't manage it, Walters placed scenery around her so that she would have something to lean upon every few steps and could reach the top. She was in high heels; to help her, Walters put her in low heels. This required altering all the camera angles; grips, photographers, lighting men, all cooperated willingly, and finally she managed it.

After this scene he helped her to her dressing room. She sat there, exhausted, resting her head on Walters' shoulder. "You're the kindest, you're the most understanding . . ."

Yet there were the characteristic, inexplicable changes of mood. One morning she came in, stepping hard and sure. She was mad at the world. Her eyes fell on Walters, sitting with a cup of coffee, and she pulled up short in front of him. "Listen, Buster," she snapped. "If you think I'm going to act today, you're out of your fucking mind. I'm heading for the hills!"

Walters played his own gambit. "O.K.," he said wearily. His return stare was one of matching disgust; he was as disenchanted as she, and suffering an even greater lassitude. "If you'll wait until I finish my coffee, I'll go with you. Because I feel just as much like making you act as you feel like acting."

It was precisely the right thing to say to her. She reacted instantly, all concern. As always, someone else's needs brought out the Florence Nightingale in her, and made her forget her own. "Oh, honey," she said in alarm. "We got to do it. We got to. Can't we get the crew . . ." and she was full of suggestions how to make his work easier.

"Well, we can try," Walters said dully. He turned to a grip. "George, bring Judy some coffee." And he sat down heavily, his head in his hands. Meanwhile, Judy was muttering to herself. "What in hell am I supposed to be doing today? . . ." He knew he would have to wait it out, but he began psyching her.

"Did you get to bed early?" he asked. "Did you eat something that disagreed with you?" He knew her mood stemmed from pills, whatever pills she had taken.

"No . . ." said Judy. "I just had a rotten night . . ." Her voice trailed off. "I don't even know what I'm supposed to wear in this scene. . . . I had a dreadful time last night. I don't know what it is." Meanwhile, yawning, mumbling, muttering under her breath.

Then, to her dresser: "Greg, what am I supposed to wear today?"

He replied quickly, brightly. "Oh, you know, honey—the blue blouse and pants outfit."

"Well-l-l-l." Judy was coming around. "O.K., Buster. Oh . . . kaay!" She would do it, she would work that day.

She played a plump, serious-minded lady farmer engaged to a hapless, allergy-ridden mollycoddle played by Eddie Bracken. Kelly and his troupe of actors show up in her town, and, to her outrage, she finds that her stage-struck sister, Gloria DeHaven, has given them the family barn in which to stage their show—especially because Gloria has a crush on Gene. Judy, against her will, takes over for Gloria—falls in love with Gene—and proves her talents as a singer and dancer. Bracken was a natural comic; every time she looked at him, Judy broke up. Walters couldn't get a scene because Judy either giggled at the wrong time or was doubled up with laughter. It finally reached the point of near-hysteria: she couldn't even look at Bracken. She fought to control herself. "I'm all right—I'm all right now," she'd gasp. "O.K." from Walters. "Roll it!" The cameras ground, Judy looked at Eddie and it was "Ahaaoohahahahaha!" and she all but fell to the floor laughing, clutching her stomach in her characteristic way.

So it went: *What a bitch of a day,* Walters thought. And, philosophically: *One day in the life of Judy Garland*—and this only on the set!

But he knew how to handle her. Support, support, support! Encouragement, encouragement, encouragement! When she went before the camera to lip-sync a prerecorded song, Walters would keep up a steady barrage of praise and adjurations like a coach, a cheerleader: "Yah, honey! Oh, God in heaven! Marvelous! Marvelous! Keep going, honey! Keep your chin up!" She loved it, she blossomed under such treatment.

Sometimes, however, if he tried to make her feel better about her troubles by expressing a more objective view, she became impatient. He attempted this one afternoon as they waited for a set to be prepared. Outside the women's dressing room there was a little patch of grass. Judy and he lay there on the grass, as one might at the beach, awaiting their call. Judy was complaining about her treatment by Metro. Walters said, as kindly as he could, "Look, honey, you must realize that I'm a lucky, poor little son of a bitch from Anaheim, and you're a lucky, poor little son of a bitch from Lancaster, and why can't we count a blessing once in a while? You never had a singing lesson, I never had a dancing lesson, we're getting away with murder, honey." But Judy would have none of it. "Oh, Chuck, you don't understand anything, you don't know what I'm talking about."

So there were high moments and many, many low ones. The highs and the lows were repeated at home for Liza. Recurrent, real yet dreamlike, through her early years was the memory of the first time she saw her mother in a tantrum, her first "bad" memory. Yet as with so many others in later years, her mother had been able to iron such crises out, so that something good came from them.

Liza was little, wearing a cowboy outfit complete with leather pants and boots, and she was practicing a trick. Lying flat on the sofa, you arched your back and catapulted forward like a spring, landing on your feet. Both Judy and Vincente had been working that day;

270

Judy was talking, pacing back and forth in front of the sofa, Vincente was seated in an easy chair not far away, and Liza lay waiting. She wanted to do her trick a moment after her mother passed by. But her timing was off: when she arched her back and sprang forward, the hard leather heel of her cowboy boot caught her mother sharply in the head.

Judy turned on her in such blazing fury, with such an explosion of anger, that Liza burst into tears, and was ordered downstairs to her room. Moments later Vincente came down. He explained to her that her mother had had a terrible day at the studio, that she had been trying to explain to Daddy what had happened, when suddenly, unexpectedly, the first thing her little girl did was to kick her in the head with her boot. Vincente stuttered as he tried to explain, and Liza said, "Oh, Daddy, I'm sorry—" and burst into more tears.

Then, in a little while, her mother came down. Liza ran to her weeping; Judy hugged her, then sat her down opposite her in a chair and spoke to her as if she were an adult.

It's hard for you to understand, her mother said, but making movies is not always as much fun as you think it is when you come and visit me on the set. She had a job to do there, she said; it was to make people happy. "Do you understand what I mean?" she asked Liza, and when Liza looked puzzled, Judy tried to explain it again. After all, Liza had been on many of Judy's sets, she remembered riding the boom with her father, she had played Judy and Van Johnson's child —she knew a great deal.

"Well, my job . . ." said Judy, and paused. She ran her hand through her hair. "Well, it's like if you go out and play, and, instead of playing, you have to run a race. It's not quite the same—it's playing, but it's hard."

Liza, trying to understand, said, "Un-huh."

"So, when I come home, I'm still a little nervous from the studio, what I've got to do there, and I've got to do it whether I want to or not—and being hit so suddenly like that, I was taking out on you everything everybody did to me all day. And that was unfair to you, Liza. You understand that."

Liza nodded.

Thus the relationship between mother and daughter—and Judy was to remind her of it constantly: *You can always take things out on me, too, if you explain.* And times came when Judy would sit down in front of Liza and say, "O.K. Here it goes," and Liza would say, "O.K., Mama . . ." and whammie! Judy would let go in front of her little daughter. "I can't stand it, I've got the pressure, they want me to do this, I don't feel I can do it, I don't want to do it, they say I'm late and I'm not late, and when I am late, they say of course, as though there's never any real reason for it. . . ." Liza would sit nodding and sympathizing while her mother ranted and raved and got it all out—and then Judy would look at her serious little daughter, as though this three-going-on-four little psychoanalyst were treating her, and burst into laughter, and they'd be in each other's arms, hugging each other.

Liza was precocious, and Liza was perceptive. Her usual place of observation was hiding curled up under the piano, while fabulous and celebrated people moved in and out, and the conversation turned on everything, and Liza would sometimes burst out giggling, and be pulled forth, to be made much of, and hugged and kissed by her proud, her difficult, her wonderful mother.

So there were all kinds of times, good and bad; when good, good beyond belief; when bad, terrible; but never boring, in those first years. Liza remembered her parents living together, then apart. She had a strange, beautiful image of the house in which they lived: all vaporous, pastel colors, a place of antiques, of beautiful pictures, a time of gray velvet couches and stained glass. One night her mother did not come down to tuck her in. She asked, "Where's Mama?" Her father came down later, waking her up, saying, "Mama wants to see us." He had on his yellow pajamas and a robe. He put a robe on her and he drove her to a house Mama had rented high on a hill, and they all moved in there for a little while. And then it seemed they were together for a long time, her father and mother, before they finally separated.

Somehow, then, *Summer Stock* was finished, in late spring 1950, save for an important dance finale which she had been scheduled to do with an ensemble of tuxedoed male dancers. For some reason Walters had not been given the number, and the film was considered complete without it.

The traditional "end of the picture" party was held on the set. Now Judy was in excellent spirits: she was nearly twenty-five pounds overweight, but no work hung over her. At the party the crew gave

Walters a beautiful traveling clock. Everyone kissed everybody, and then Judy went off to Carmel, California, for a vacation with a mystic who promised that he would melt the weight off her.

Walters, after consulting Freed and Pasternak, decided *Summer Stock* simply had to close with the dance number by Judy. Precisely what it was to be, he did not know. But he telephoned Judy in Carmel about three weeks later. She was in high spirits. "Darling, I've lost pounds and pounds. This man's a genius. You should see me!"

Wonderful, said Walters. But there was a little problem about the film. He told her what he wanted.

Judy was butter itself, but with spice in it. She'd been at a party the other night with Harold Arlen. He'd played a song he'd written years before called "Get Happy." Just wonderful! "Chuck, you get 'Get Happy' for me, we build the dance around that, and I'll do it. I'll give you a week—otherwise, forget it."

Walters obtained the song. He talked to Judy again. Yes, she would do it. He explained he'd make it as easy as possible for her. He'd rehearse the male dancers, start the number without her; she could learn it in one day, he'd shoot it in two. If everyone else in such a sketch was busy, even though she might not be doing much, she would appear busy, too.

O.K., said Judy.

She came back from Carmel, sensationally thin.

They started shooting her part. She stood at the proscenium arch, made her entrance, and halfway through, Walters said, "Cut." Judy turned to him. "What did you cut for?" Walters knew this was a ticklish moment; handling Judy required knowledge of her sense of humor, her sense of the ironic, her sense of her own dignity.

He replied, as smoothly as he could, "Hon, we had a little trouble here."

Judy swore. "There wasn't any trouble. What's the matter?"

Walters tried to hedge, but Judy would have none of it. *"What's the matter,* Chuck?"

He said, "Honey, it wasn't very good."

Judy wheeled and stalked off the stage.

Walters thought, *Oh, Christ, me with my big mouth!* He might have softened it a bit, but that could have made her even angrier. He walked into Judy's dressing room. She was sitting there, her arms folded. He said, "Honey, I hated to say it that way, but ... it *was* your first crack at it and you were a little . . . wobbly."

"Shut up!" snapped Judy.

He returned to the set and waited. Presently, Judy marched back. She stood facing him, her hands on her hips. "If you had any class," she said, "you'd use that traveling clock the crew gave you," and turned and marched off again. It was funny, a complete non sequitur; it was clever, it was Judy, but Walters didn't have the heart to laugh. A moment later, and Judy was back, all business. "All right! Let's do it!"

She did—and her memorable singing and dancing bit in "Get Happy," slim-legged, in black tights and a tux jacket and a man's soft hat—the costume had been one of Minnelli's inspirations—still stands as one of her imperishable appearances, in a film that was otherwise completely dismissed. She had lost so much weight that many thought this famous "Get Happy" number had been taken from a film clip shot years before.

It was not to be the first nor the last time that Judy could appear, almost within an eyelid's blink, herself ten years, twenty years older, or herself when young. One day ailing, exhausted, almost comatose —the next, as though she'd just come back from a month in the country. It was during this period that she accepted an offer by Freed to go into a second film with Fred Astaire, *Royal Wedding*, which Walters was to direct, too. June Allyson was to have played opposite Fred, but found herself unexpectedly pregnant. And Judy, riding high, optimistic, and with a chance to work again with Fred and her darling Chuck, replaced her.

The news—how could anyone know where this project would lead Judy?—came as a shock to Walters. He telephoned Freed, almost hysterically, "You can't do this to me, Arthur." He loved Judy, but going through the same thing again . . . "You just can't, I've got an ulcer, I'm a wreck! Not two in a row with Judy—I can't."

Freed reluctantly agreed to find another director. "I'll get you off, Chuck," he said. "Just go home and take care of yourself. I'll make some sort of excuse to Judy—tell her your ulcer kicked up and you've got to stop work for a while."

Gratefully Walters drove to his beach house in Malibu, and set himself for a week or two of rest, books and sun.

The next morning a telephone call from Judy. "My God, Chuck—

I'm so sorry! Arthur just told me about it. I'll be right over." And she hung up.

Walters put down the telephone with a groan. An hour later Judy was there, bustling about. She spent the rest of the day mothering him. "What do you think it is, darling? *Have* you been under pressure?"

Walters gazed at her, marveling: it had been someone else, obviously, who had put him through the grueling days of the past months. He told her, his face innocent, of a pressure in his chest, of a throbbing here. . . . "Oh, I know that symptom," Judy said. "I have it all the time." And it was true, because Walters deliberately chose symptoms he knew she had complained about to make his illness more authentic, and make her more sympathetic, and perhaps leave him alone.

She heated milk for him that day, and prepared dishes of yogurt and Jello, and left at six o'clock with a promise. "I'll be back tonight." That night she returned, brimming over with advice. "You've got to rest, honey, you just cool it and stay off the picture and don't try to do anything." She would bring her doctor down the next morning, she said.

She did. The doctor turned out to be the genius mystic who had taken off her weight in Carmel. Walters played still another role, allowing himself to be ministered to by the man.

On the third morning Judy's secretary arrived with an armload of Judy's clothes and a suitcase. "What's this?" Walters asked in alarm.

"Miss Garland is going to move in for a while so she can take care of you" was the answer.

"Oh, no," said Walters firmly. "You take this right back. I wasn't here when you came in. Take this stuff back and tell Miss Garland you couldn't find me." Then he telephoned Freed. "What do I do now? She's trying to move in, for Christ's sakes, and I'm trying to nurse this ulcer."

Freed sighed. "Leave town for a while," he said.

Leave for where? The situation was becoming ridiculous. Walters telephoned Roger Edens, who came up with a plan. Bob Alton lived on the Pacific Palisades, overlooking the ocean, a few minutes from Roger's. Chuck should pack an overnight bag, drive over to Bob's, park his car there, then walk to Roger's place and stay with Roger for a few days. As far as anyone would know, Walters would have disappeared. "Judy'll be calling me in the middle of the night anyway," Roger said, knowing his Judy.

Walters followed instructions. As Roger predicted, Judy was on the phone at 2 A.M. "Have you heard anything from Chuck?" she asked worriedly. The man had simply vanished. She was very concerned. After all, he was sick. Roger commiserated with her. No, he had heard nothing.

The matter might have rested there had not Alton, all unknowing, called Judy, who had left a call with him—she had been telephoning all of Chuck's friends. Alton said, "I don't know what's happened, darling, but I've just discovered it's Chuck's car that's been parked in front of my house for the last two days, and you know I'm only a block from the cliff—"

Judy came flying to Roger's, hysterical. "My God—maybe Chuck jumped over the cliff—oh, God!" Roger could only blame himself for not letting Alton into the secret.

Walters had to reappear, making some excuse.

But, as events developed, none of this elaborate subterfuge had been necessary. Judy was not to make *Royal Wedding*. All the difficulties of the past seemed to rise like an evil miasma in the next weeks to set up the next to last act for Judy Garland at MGM—and the next to last act of her life with Vincente Minnelli.

IT WAS LIKE THE RERUN OF A NIGHTMARE.

Not a letter, this time, but a telegram, sent to Judy in quadruplicate, so she could not fail to receive it: one copy to her at 10000 Sunset Boulevard, where she was now living during another separation from Vincente, one care of Carleton Alsop at his office, one care of Carleton at his home, and one care of Charles Goldring, Judy's business agent.

It was dated June 17, 1950, and it read:

THIS IS TO NOTIFY YOU THAT FOR GOOD AND SUFFICIENT CAUSE AND IN
ACCORDANCE WITH THE RIGHTS GRANTED TO US UNDER PROVISIONS OF
PARAGRAPH 12 OF YOUR CONTRACT OF EMPLOYMENT WITH US DATED
NOVEMBER 21, 1946 AND WITHOUT LIMITING OR RESTRICTING ANY OTHER
RIGHTS OR REMEDIES WHICH WE MAY HAVE, WE SHALL REFUSE TO PAY YOU
ANY COMPENSATION COMMENCING AS OF JUNE 17, 1950 AND CONTINUING
UNTIL THE EXPIRATION OF THE TIME WHICH WOULD HAVE BEEN REASON-
ABLY REQUIRED TO COMPLETE THE PORTRAYAL OF THE ROLE OF "ELLEN"
IN THE PHOTOPLAY NOW ENTITLED "ROYAL WEDDING" OR (SHOULD AN-
OTHER PERSON BE ENGAGED TO PORTRAY SUCH ROLE) UNTIL THE COMPLE-
TION OF SUCH ROLE BY SUCH OTHER PERSON. ANY AND ALL OTHER RIGHTS
AND REMEDIES WHICH WE MAY HAVE IN THE PREMISES ARE EXPRESSLY
RESERVED BY US.

This came from Loew's, Incorporated, the parent company, and
was signed by Marvin H. Schenck, Vice President. It bore the power
of the home office in New York, it came from on high, and whatever
appeals were to be made to Judy's friends on the scene in Hollywood
would carry far less weight.

June 17 was a Saturday. Judy had simply not shown up at all on the
set of *Royal Wedding*. More than that: she had called up and canceled yesterday's rehearsal. She had stated she would not come.
Letters and telephone calls had been made to her; she had not responded. Dore Schary had been in conferences with Mayer, and with
Schenck in New York, with whom he spoke several times a week.
Schenck and his associates in New York were well acquainted with
her troubles. They had watched Judy grow up, as had Mayer and
Thau and Freed and Mannix and Ida Koverman, all who had known
her when she first arrived at Metro, bubbling and adorable and
brimming over with talent. They knew her troubles only too well.
Now, one doctor after another had been sent to Judy's home to take
care of her. The reports reached New York. Three doctors in a month
—Judy had simply twisted them around her finger. They were men,
and they succumbed. She had made fans and courtiers of them, and
Judy's seductive power over fans and courtiers was almost mesmeric.

When she needed pills, the Devil himself would have been unable to withstand her plea, the catch in her voice, a voice hoarse and almost unrecognizable, the voice of a soul in agony. . . .

Ann Straus, who ran the Gallery, was never able to put one scene out of her mind. Judy was picking up a costume for *Summer Stock;* a moment before, Ann, in idle conversation, had said her mother felt low and she'd just gotten some Dexamyl for her. Judy suddenly excused herself, went into the nearby dressing room, and Ann heard the lock click. A moment later Judy came out. Ann later went into the room, where both their purses were. She opened her purse: her Dexamyl was missing. She opened Judy's: there it was. She took it out of Judy's and replaced it in hers, and took her purse with her.

Late that night, after midnight—far after—Judy called her. She would never forget her voice: it was a voice from the depths, and it said, "This is Judy. Do you have some Dexamyl? I've got a meeting, I've got to have it. Please, oh, please—give me some." Ann said, "Well, I have one—I have one which the doctor gave my mother." Judy said, "Oh, please, I have to have it." Ann said, "But how will I get it to you?" Judy said, "Put it in an envelope and leave it in your mailbox and somebody will pick it up." Ann did so, and within half an hour she heard the scurry of feet in front of her house, then click! click! at her mailbox, and the scurry of departing feet. She never knew who picked it up. But it happened more than once. You could not say no to Judy in her extremity.

Now Schary and Schenck, on the telephone, discussed what to do —Schary, who had first heard her when she was twelve, who had helped write the delightful "Life of Judy Garland" for her twenty-first birthday party, who had joined in the rollicking, inimitable *Yiddish Mikado* of Danny Kaye's. He had himself suffered through *Summer Stock,* through the repeated delays, the frustration and tears and blow-ups on the set, the patient, skilled labors of Dr. Rose, the Herculean efforts of Gene Kelly and Chuck Walters. All this *after* Boston; and in *Summer Stock* he had gotten reports that Judy was taking a new medicine—it made her literally reek of something chemical, like formaldehyde. Schary had telephoned a physician who was an authority on drugs. Yes, there was such a drug—very powerful. It was called paraldehyde, prescribed for people who had taken so much liquor or amphetamines that they needed an especially powerful sedative.

Schary had spoken at once to Mayer. "L.B.," he said, "we've got a very sick girl here, because she can't take this kind of abuse. Her body won't take it. We're in big trouble, and I'd like to do what we did with Bob Walker." Walker had gone on drinking even more; he had been arrested for drunken driving, there had been a page-one scandal with sorry photographs, and Schary, who looked on him as his protégé, arranged for Bob in the summer of 1949 to be sent to Menninger's. "I think you have to talk to Judy, L.B., tell her how much you love her, tell her we'll keep her on salary, or pay her for six months or a year. I'll arrange to get her into Menninger's if she's willing."

Mayer spoke to Judy. So did Schary. Judy refused indignantly. "I'm not crazy," she said.

Schary could not know how upsetting a subject the Menninger Clinic was to Judy. A few years before, Ethel, accompanied by Helen Fisher (whose husband, George, had sold Ethel Judy's original annuities), had traveled all the way to Topeka, Kansas, where Ethel tried to sign Judy into the Clinic. She had also told Peg DeVine about it. "I'm going to have her committed," she said, furiously. "Someone's giving her dope." (Whatever the "dope" was, allegedly heroin, the fact was that Judy did not take to hard drugs.) But Ethel couldn't sign Judy in without Judy's own permission. Ethel, who had so violently opposed psychiatry, had changed now. After all, the attitude toward what psychiatrists could do had altered since the early forties, and Ethel's attitude with it. She was unable to control Judy, she told Dr. Menninger; he was later to remember her visit, her description of her daughter "behaving in ways" beyond her comprehension. She said to him, as he recalled her words, "I know you can help her, but how can we get her here?" Judy, she said, was "back there with all those important friends of hers in Hollywood. I don't think we can get her here."

Ethel was very troubled. When Judy had gone to Peter Bent Brigham Hospital, Ethel had quietly visited one of the psychiatrists treating her. He had asked Ethel, "Have you ever been analyzed?" "Of course not," Ethel had replied, bristling. Now she was more subdued talking to Dr. Karl. Where had she failed Judy? She had tried to do her duty as a Christian woman, with this talented, remarkable child of hers—and now she had been cast aside. Judy used to telephone her to come over, they would get involved in the most terrible arguments, accusatory, bitter, vindictive, and Judy would tell her, suddenly, "Get out! Get out! And don't come back until I call you!" Ethel knew some of this was Judy's pills and liquor talking. Dr. Menninger, before she left, gave her one of his books with a reassuring inscription.

Later Judy was prepared to go to Menninger's, but only if she could take an entire floor and be accompanied by a retinue of friends. Dr. Karl would not permit this. Each patient had his room, and that was that. Once more Judy wanted to transform reality into her world, a stage on which she performed before an applauding audience.

So nothing had come of this. But that her mother should seek to commit her . . . !

What, Schary wanted to know in his conversation with Schenck, were they to do now? After Las Campanas, and the Riggs Foundation, and Peter Bent Brigham Hospital, and psychiatrists on the set, and psychiatrists visiting her home, and the thousands upon thousands of dollars all this had cost Metro, not to mention the costs of the delays due to her not showing up, the turning of two-month productions into six-month productions, the anguish everyone had gone through—Judy had deliberately canceled herself out. She would not come to work. Here was *Royal Wedding*, everyone waiting, everyone on salary, expenses mounting, doctors doing no good, Judy refusing even to rehearse with Fred Astaire, for all her idolization of him.

They would have to take her out of the picture. They would replace her with Jane Powell. It meant Judy's suspension again. How long could they continue what was now becoming a series of catastrophes for everyone concerned? For Judy, for those seeking to help her, for MGM? The girl wanted, but the girl couldn't. Or the girl refused. If MGM could bring into being a healthy, functioning Judy, if that superb talent could be permitted to express itself, MGM would consider itself the most blessed of studios. No cost would be too prohibitive, for she would repay it a hundredfold, this twenty-eight-year-old girl, if she could be well and happy and functioning for ten more years, fifteen more years. . . . But it appeared that everything done succeeded for a while, the evil exorcised, only to reappear, the girl damaging herself the more, and going through greater torment. They all—they and Judy and the doctors—climbed out of the well two feet, only to slip back three. . . .

Schenck spoke. He said, "I think the decision to suspend must come from us here at Loew's." Behind Schenck's words, Schary knew, was the possibility that they were at the end of the road with Judy. They might have to tear up her contract. Therefore this suspension had to come from the home office.

Thus the telegram, Saturday, June 17, 1950.

Forty-eight hours later the newspapers were full of it: "JUDY CUTS THROAT!"

Around six o'clock Monday night, Judy had repeated what she had done before. Talking with Vincente and her secretary, Myrtle Tully, widow of Jim Tully, the writer, she had suddenly rushed into the bathroom, slammed the door and locked it shut. She was screaming, and they could make out the words, "Leave me alone, I want to die!"

As Judy remembered the incident, she just wanted to blot everything out—the past as well as the future. The telegram had been sent Saturday; all day Sunday there had been visits and calls back and forth, as the three recipients talked to each other; Monday Judy had gone over to Vincente's house on Evanview with Myrtle, and she had simply wanted oblivion—for a little while. She rushed into the bathroom, locked the door, broke a glass bottle and ran the sharp edge, not pressing too hard (because that hurt), across her throat, and then stood there, in a kind of limbo, while Vincente and Myrtle shouted and pounded on the door. Then, because she had a child to live for, and there was no point to it all, she unlocked the door.

As Vincente remembered it, after pounding on the locked door he finally seized a chair and broke it down. The bathroom had a cabinet with a collection of antique glass bottles; Judy had seized one of these, broken it and scratched her throat with it. Blood flowed from the wound. While Myrtle tended Judy, Vincente frantically telephoned Carleton, "My God, come over. Judy's cut her throat!"

Carleton drove swiftly to the Evanview house, took the stairs three at a time, to find Vincente running about, hysterical, shouting, "They finally killed my beautiful wife!" Judy lay on the floor, Myrtle pressing a towel to her neck. Carleton kneeled beside Judy and looked at the wound; it was a pretty good cut, but not deep and not long, and then he heard Judy's voice whispering in his ear: "Take care of Vincente, Pa."

Carleton rose and spoke commandingly: "Vincente!" Vincente

turned to him, and Carleton punched him as hard as he could on the jaw. Vincente fell back; Carleton caught him and put him, dazed, on the bed. Then he carried Judy to his car—Myrtle meanwhile had summoned a doctor to be at the 10000 Sunset Boulevard house—and drove Judy there. So far as the press was concerned, what with all the rumors spreading over this weekend about trouble with *Royal Wedding,* the Evanview house would most likely be under surveillance as more newsworthy, because that was where the Minnellis were supposed to be together. But the press found out where Judy was, even though Carleton hired florists to deliver carfuls of flowers to the Evanview house. The press followed the cars, found they had been deceived and descended on Alsop, at the Sunset house.

Alsop, when he wished, could be difficult. (Bringing Judy back from Boston to Hollywood, he had stopped in Chicago and taken her to a department store to buy her several dresses. In a fitting room, she was standing in her slip, when an older woman remarked on her figure. Judy began to go to pieces. Alsop ripped off the woman's dress and said icily, "Sue me. You look very unattractive in your slip.") He said nothing to the press, who by now were ten deep at the door. But according to his account, an MGM representative, having visited Judy, was making his way out through the gaggle of reporters and photographers when someone asked, "What happened?" He drew his finger across his throat in a quick gesture—and Carleton exploded. As he put it later, in his own style, "I was on top of him so fast, like a suppository with no tinfoil on, and I said, 'Goddamnit, how could you do such a fucking, stupid thing, and do it to Judy? You people hiding that nympho with her affairs in Harlem, and that phony stud with the little boys he picks up—you cover them up, yet you do this—' "

Carleton reported that the studio representative replied, "Oh, fuck you, you're so goddamn important, so goddamn arrogant, we will withdraw all MGM support."

Carleton retorted, "She's gotten very little so far," which was far less true than the indignant Carleton knew, but from then on he—not MGM's Publicity Department—handled the press. He became Judy's spokesman. Judy was broke, he said; she took the news of her suspension "very badly." Her wound was slight, no stitches were needed.

Now Judy had other visitors. Dr. Marc was there, and Marcella;

they had known for a long time that, for whatever reasons, the studio had become for Judy a place of torture. She had grown to hate it more and more. She had confided to Dottie Ponedel in recent months that every time she drove through the east gate she became nauseated, nauseated with fear of she knew not what, and threw up her breakfast. Katharine Hepburn marched in. She told Judy of her own troubles making it in films, how she had felt when she was labeled "Box Office Poison" and rated as one of the most difficult of actresses, and she spoke of her difficulties with Spencer Tracy. Spencer, too, had his bad moments; he was not always an easy man. "I've had my own troubles and my troubles with Spence, darling. But you're one of the two greatest living talents we have. Now you get your ass up. The world needs you." And after a few more words of love and common sense, she kissed Judy, ran out the back way, jumped over a rear fence and outwitted the press by taking a short cut home.

Judy needed all the encouragement she could get. Black banner headlines ran, stories beginning: "Actress Judy Garland, her fortune gone and her screen career shattered after years of illness, slashed her throat with a broken drinking glass last night in a hysterical suicide attempt. . . ."

Across the top of the front page of the Los Angeles *Herald-Express* for June 21 ran the words "HOLLYWOOD HEARTBREAKS—STORY OF FAME, FORTUNE AND DESPAIR," with a huge photograph of Judy under the headline "Judy's Future Puzzle After Death Try," and then the smaller photographs of the company with whom now she would be forever associated: Frances Farmer ("Alcohol And Benzedrine Drove Her Into Asylum"); Lupe Velez ("About To Be Unmarried Mother, Took Own Life"); Carole Landis ("She Ended The Heartbreak By Taking Sleeping Pills"); and others—with a caption under Judy's photograph: "ACTRESS JUDY GARLAND (Her Suicide Try Recalls Long List Of Movie Beauties Who Fell Victim To Hollywood Heartbreak)."

One can only imagine how Judy felt reading these—she felt compelled to see everything written about herself, however laudatory or critical or shocking. Alsop did his best to keep them from her, but she got hold of them. She refused to see the press. Alsop spoke vaguely of Judy, Minnelli and Liza taking a trip to Europe in the fall: Minnelli was to start shooting *An American in Paris* with Gene Kelly (this was shot later in the United States). There was talk about Judy playing the Helen Morgan role in a new film version of the Broadway hit *Show Boat.*

Ethel, reading the news in Dallas, immediately flew to Los Angeles. Judy would not see her. She went back to Dallas, quit her job as a theatre manager and said she was returning to live in Los Angeles.

She said to Jimmy, "I can't leave Judy out there. Something calls me back. I wish I had the guts to stay here, but I have to be there, even if she won't let me see her. I have to be near her."

She sold everything in Dallas and moved back to Los Angeles.

Judy came to a decision. She would leave MGM, though her contract had nearly two years to go. In the weeks after her suicide try ("Oh, Mama," Suzy once complained, "Judy's always on. She's on when she's onstage and she's on when she's off—how do you know what's what?") her press had become tremendous. *Summer Stock* would open in New York in September 1950. MGM announced Judy's fan mail had jumped 50 percent since her "despondent act." She was now receiving fifteen hundred letters a week, 90 percent of them wishing her well. MGM announced, too, that it would give *Summer Stock* a gigantic promotion campaign, Judy would go to New York in the fall with Liza and her secretary to promote the picture, and then she'd join Vincente in Europe.

But, actually, behind the scenes Judy had talked to Dr. Marc and Marcella. There must be something more than films for her. She wanted to get out of her MGM contract. There was radio, there were concerts, there was the Broadway stage, the possibility that she might take over Mary Martin's role in the new hit *South Pacific,* when Mary went to London to do the British version. . . . And she had drawn further and further apart from Vincente.

Dr. Marc went to see Mayer, who respected him. Dr. Marc said that Judy wanted to get out of her contract, and that, with all her other problems, the best thing they could do for her would be to release her. Mayer said, finally, "If you think this is best for her, I'd be willing." Marc told Marcella that night that Mayer's attitude was so understanding that he suspected they might be glad to be rid of her. Marc knew nothing, of course, of the long telephone discussions between Schary and Schenck, the meetings between Schary and

Mayer. MGM could have refused to release Judy. After all, they were giving up an important property. In her best time Judy was worth millions of dollars to the studio. Who was to know whether—with her remarkable recuperative powers, her ability to snap back—she might not have those times again? The legend would always have it that MGM fired her. The fact was that she wanted out, and she got her wish.

At the close of business September 28, 1950, Judy's contract with MGM was abrogated. She still owed them nearly half of the $9,000 they had loaned her in Boston. MGM wrote her they would cancel the balance. They would part with no ill feelings.

From October 1, 1935, through September 28, 1950—fifteen years less two days—she had been owned by MGM.

Now she was free. She was still Mrs. Vincente Minnelli, but she would not be for long.

A new future faced her. Judy did not know, no one knew, but it would take its direction from an unexpected source, an unlikely source and, to some, an astonishing source.

And it began—as it would have to begin—with a new man.

She met Michael Sidney Luft.

BOOK TWO

THE MAKING
OF THE
LEGEND

*"Sid, you great big wonderful
lovable son of a bitch, you!"*

21

IT MIGHT BE SAID, ironically enough, that Freddie Finklehoffe, the scriptwriter, was proposing to Judy Garland when she met Sid Luft.

Judy was living in state in a tremendous, three-bedroom suite at the Hotel Carlyle in New York's Upper East Side with her two companions, Myrtle Tully, her secretary, a woman of about forty-five, and Dottie Ponedel. Carleton Alsop had accompanied her to New York; his marriage to Sylvia Sidney was ending (there had been rumors of an affair between him and Judy during his constant attendance upon her, Carleton denying this even while admitting she was all-absorbing, there could be no one else in your life). Carleton, who had once worked for the Central Intelligence Agency, was in New York only en route to another job there in Washington.

The reviews of *Summer Stock,* particularly of her "Get Happy" number, were all she could wish for. Now in New York Judy wanted some fun. Who better with than Freddie, who was always good for a laugh, back to the days when he knocked out silly dialogue for her *Babes in Arms* and the other early musicals? Finklehoffe was going through the last stages of a legal divorce from Ella Logan, the singer, and lived alone in New York.

"Freddie," said Judy, her voice gay over the telephone, "let's go out on the town." She had a limousine at her disposal. She'd pick him up and they'd take potluck.

Their first stop was Billy Reed's popular Little Club on East Fifty-fifth street. At the table Freddie, as usual, kept Judy in giggles. Now that the Minnelli run seemed all but over, and his own with Ella was *kaput*, how about them making for the post together? He was thinking seriously about marrying her, he said. She knew he loved her. She should respect the fact that he was an expert on lady singers—he'd slept with lady singers, remember—and, having been married to one, God help him, he knew what was involved. But it wasn't only the male in him that lusted for her—"You've got to hold me back from jumping on your bones, Baby"—but the gambler, the hundred-to-one-shot man. She excited, she intrigued him. "I'm strictly a long-shot player," he was saying, while Judy, resting her chin on her hand, her head cocked to one side, trying to restrain her mirth, listened. "And, honey, you're sure a long shot in marriage, right? But one day maybe you'll win the Kentucky Derby, and I want to be there."

He was going on in this vein when out of the corner of his eye he saw an old friend approach. It was Sid Luft, known formally as Michael Sidney Luft, ex-test pilot, producer of B pictures, estranged husband of actress Lynn Bari (like Carleton and Freddie, he was going through *his* divorce), fractious man-about-town and sometimes barroom brawler, and, like Finklehoffe, an incorrigible horse-player. They were close friends. They had undergone similar marital disasters. Sid had been a house guest at the Finklehoffes' when all was well with Freddie and Ella; when they separated, Freddie became a house guest at the Lufts' when all was well with Sid and Lynn. When the Lufts separated, both Freddie and Sid found themselves out of the house and were now trying to pick up the loose ends of their lives. Luft was working to produce the life story of Man O' War, the great champion race horse, and if he succeeded, Freddie would have a hand in it.

Now Luft was approaching their table. He was just over six feet, a dark-haired, broad-shouldered, powerfully built man in his early thirties, with a strong, square-jawed face and something of a swagger in his walk, the swagger of a man who knows when he stands drinking at a bar that he can take on any son of a bitch who looks crosseyed at him, but who, unless he was in his cups, would be long-suffering in the face of insults. This night Luft was a study in beige: well-tailored beige suit, beige shirt and tie, and a beige suntan, which made his dark eyes even more glowing; the whole was a handsome picture of male attractiveness.

"Hi, Freddie," he said, cordially. He stood at their table, looking down at them. Finklehoffe sighed resignedly, as a man who knows exactly what to expect and can do nothing about it. He indicated Judy. "You know Miss Garland. . . . This is Sid Luft." And under his breath he muttered an imprecation.

"May I sit down?" Luft asked, smiling at Judy. His voice was smooth as honey. Finklehoffe said coldly, "I don't want any traffic with you at all, Sid. Get lost." He turned his back on Luft, and began talking to Judy again, but she giggled. "Of course—let him sit down, Freddie. Really!"

As Luft pulled up a chair and joined them, Finklehoffe shook his head. "You've heard of this character, haven't you?" Judy said, "Oh, yes, I have." And mischievously: "A great deal."

Luft sat at the table only a few minutes, and then left.

But that began it.

The next night Freddie called him. Luft was staying at the Ritz Tower. Freddie said, glumly, "Judy likes you." The two of them were going to Ben Marden's Riviera, in Jersey, to hear Billy Daniels, the singer, and if Sid had nothing better to do, they'd pick him up at his hotel. Judy had suggested it.

Judy was at her most charming when they called for him, and it was clear as they drove out that the two were getting along beautifully. It was quite late; they had arrived for the last show and they were seated at a table for ten—Billy Daniels' friends and others. Judy, when they sat down, was placed in a chair diagonally away from him, too far for him to talk to her—she was, after all, Freddie's date—but Luft was able to see her more clearly than he had in the comparative gloom of the Little Club. He would always remember her as he saw her then: her black pillbox hat, her black dress, her burnished-gold-colored coat, the way her jet-black hair was cut very short, almost mannishly, across her forehead, her eyebrows similarly straight across, almost as though she were affecting an Oriental look, because the pillbox hat reminded him of something Chinese. She was plump, but not fat. She was quite heavily made up around her eyes, which were large, dark, and sparkling. His impressions were mixed: she appeared mysterious; she laughed too loud; he had never seen a woman who could give one such quick, darting glances. He felt she really didn't see him; something was going on within her, and she was busy with that. Yet he was sharply, intensely aware of her; whatever magnetism emanated from her reached out and touched you, she was magnetic whether you were across the table from her or fifty feet away. It was a kind of energy that came toward him like something almost physical.

The evening ended late; they spent time kidding about with Billy after the show, and then the three began their return to New York as dawn was breaking over the Hudson.

Sitting in the back of the limousine between Freddie and Sid, Judy was obviously enjoying herself. If they had not been able to talk much at the Riviera, they did now, Sid joking, Judy laughing and entertaining him, Sid charming her, Judy responding to his charm, and Freddie sitting gloomily on his side, staring out the window. As they were crossing the George Washington Bridge from Jersey into Manhattan, Freddie broke into their banter, speaking over the steady flip-flop of the tires on the grilled-iron surface of the bridge.

"I've been sitting here like a piece of dead ham," he began. "Judy, I want to tell you something." His voice was grave. "You and I are having a romance—nothing spectacular—" Judy burst into laughter. "And we don't know what's going to happen with it, but I love you and you love me, and we know it's really finished between you and Vince. And you love me, don't you, Judy?" Judy said—it was a voice that could destroy you, Luft thought—"Yes, I do, of course I do, Freddie." The lilt of her voice was like music.

Freddie looked at her for a beat, and went on, "Now, let me tell you about this fellow you just met last night, and out of the goodness of your heart took along tonight. He is the dirtiest, low-down S.O.B. you'll ever meet. He's bad news, and I'm warning you—" Judy, rebuking: "Freddie, how can you—" But Finklehoffe continued: "Remember that Freddie Finklehoffe told you this. I'll go on record. He's doing something right now and will continue to do it and he'll call you, I can tell." He shook his head mournfully. "I get the vibrations—he's on the move. You're a cooked pigeon, Baby."

Judy was hysterical with laughter. She put her arms around Freddie and kissed him. Luft maintained the silence of a man who had been maligned so often that he would not even deign to defend himself. When Judy finally caught her breath, she said, "Why do you say such mean things about him, Freddie?" She linked her arm in each of theirs. "He seems to be such a nice fellow—a darling fellow."

"You better watch yourself, because he's going to nail you." Freddie's voice was sepulchral. He knew it was of no use. The more he denigrated Luft, the more intrigued Judy became. When they dropped Luft at the Ritz Tower, he stood for a moment holding Judy's hand, chatting with her, before the chauffeur closed the door of the car. He said, "I'll call you." Freddie said, "I wouldn't take his calls." Judy said, laughing, "Call me."

Luft telephoned her at the Carlyle the next night. She was not in. He left a message. There was no call back. Two days later he called her again. Perhaps the message had not been sent up. Again she was out. Again he left a message. Again there was no call back. *Well, what the hell*, he thought. *Who needs it?* Women had never been a problem for him.

A few days later, he took a girl to a party at the Stork Club. There friends invited him and his date to a private party at Jackie Gleason's apartment. Gleason was then just beginning to make his way, but had yet to come into his own as one of the most popular TV entertainers in the country. As Luft moved about Gleason's apartment, he saw Judy. She was in animated conversation across the room with Martha Raye, the comedienne. Of course—his mind clicked—they had both been married to the same man, David Rose, the composer. Martha was currently married to Nick Condos, a former dancer, now her manager, who was holding her arm possessively.

Luft did not approach Judy. He was standing near a window, nursing a drink, and Judy walked over to him. He thought she might say something about not being able to get back to him. Instead, it was a simple, cordial "How are you, Sid?" He was slightly reserved, but proper. "I don't know about your switchboard at the Carlyle, but I called you several times. Possibly you didn't get the message." When she said nothing, simply to make conversation, he added, "I told you I'd call, and I did." She said, dismissing his implied rebuke, "What are you doing later?"

"I have a date," said Luft. He pointed out the girl.

Judy said, "Why don't you take me out for a drink?"

Luft said, "I do have a date, Judy."

She looked at him. "What difference does that make?"

Luft pondered that. Carleton Alsop had brought Judy, but he'd done that really as a duty, no more—if Luft were free, he might well take Judy out later. He told her the truth. "I'd love to, but it will be pretty late. The thing is, the young lady I'm with has to get up early.

She's doing some kind of a TV show tomorrow. If she wants to go home early, maybe we can have a drink later."

Time went on. Luft walked about. Judy seemed never very far from him. Carleton was busy with other friends. *Was she following him?* Luft wondered. Then, as he expected, his girl asked if he would take her home. She had to leave. He drove her back to her hotel and returned to Gleason's. Judy was waiting.

"You're alone?" Luft nodded. "Let's go," she said. "I know a place."

It was now nearly 1 A.M. Judy's limousine was outside; she had them driven to the Golden Key, a bottle club. Johnny Mercer was at the piano, singing some of his songs. Judy and he hugged each other like old friends, and presently Johnny was playing, and Judy was singing, and it was not until nearly 5 A.M. that they left, had breakfast in an all-night drugstore, and Judy dropped Luft off at the Ritz Tower. She said, "What are you doing tomorrow?"

He had to go to Philadelphia on business for the day, but "I'll probably be back around seven o'clock or so."

Judy said, "Why don't you call me? I'd like to take you to one of my favorite places for dinner—a late dinner." So it was agreed.

They had told each other a little about their domestic affairs. She was having problems with her husband, Minnelli, whom Luft did not know; she had signed with the William Morris office, now that she'd left MGM, and might go to London to do a concert at the Palladium. He told her his divorce from Lynn was to be final in a few months. They had a two-year-old boy. Judy said, "Well, I have a four-year-old daughter." But all this had been casual, rather than serious—a *We're a fine pair, both in the same boat, neither of us very happy, isn't it ridiculous?* sort of thing. "Yes," said Luft, "we're kindred souls in that department." He thought, *Well, not the most scintillating conversation, not the kind she's probably used to, but what the hell— she's heard about me, and Freddie's warned her about me, and a man would have to think twice about getting involved with her and her problems.*

When he got back from Philadelphia, it was nearly 8 P.M. He telephoned Judy. "Miss Garland is not in," said the operator. He called half an hour later. Same answer. So he telephoned the young TV actress he'd taken to the Gleason party and went out to dinner with her, and dropped her around midnight at her hotel, the Algon-

294

quin. It was a pleasant fall evening. He decided to walk up Lexington Avenue from the Algonquin, at Forty-fourth street, to the Ritz Tower, at Park Avenue and Fifty-seventh Street. He felt let down by Judy—and surprisingly bad about it. He looked up: he was opposite a bar.

He sat at the bar and drank four martinis in a row. It was now nearly 2 A.M. He reached into his pocket to pay the bill and found he had only six one-hundred-dollar bills. When he gave one to the bartender, he was told, "I haven't got any change." "Well, you'll have to get it," said Luft. The bartender called the manager and gave him the bill. Luft owed about six dollars—and wanted to pay with nothing less than a hundred-dollar bill. At this hour of night.

"Come back tomorrow and you'll get your change," said the manager. "How about my coming back tomorrow and paying you?" No, said the manager. He had Luft's hundred-dollar bill.

By this time the liquor had taken its effect and Luft's annoyance was building. "Why don't you and I go outside?" he said. "We'll walk down the street, and get this thing changed somehow."

They started walking down the street. Luft said, "If you don't mind, I'll hold the bill." The manager said, "No, I'll hold the hundred." Luft said, "It's my hundred. I only owe you for four drinks."

When the manager said no, Luft grabbed the bill and pushed the manager to the ground. He had not achieved his reputation as a difficult man in a brawl by backing down. The manager scrambled to his feet and took a punch at him; Luft ducked and swung once, the other went down violently, knocking over a metal trash can. He lay sprawled in the gutter, garbage all over him.

A police car came up. "This man attacked me!" the manager yelled. Luft said, "He took my hundred dollars." Luft had no identification, he lived in Los Angeles, but they could call the Ritz Tower, where he was staying; the upshot was that everybody went back to the bar, the police called, and it was arranged for a bellboy to bring the money to the bar the next morning.

"You better call it a night," said the policeman. "Go on home."

Luft was about to leave; his hotel was only a few blocks away, but he began growing furious with himself, angry at the world. Whose fault was all this? Why, Judy Garland's! If she hadn't stood him up . . .

He went to a booth in the bar and telephoned her. It was 2:50 A.M.

The call got through immediately. He heard Judy's voice. It was not the voice of someone who had been awakened from sleep.

"Judy?" he asked, not quite believing.

"Where have you been?" she demanded.

"Why don't you check with your operator?" he began angrily.

"I did," she said.

"Well," Luft said, "apparently—"

"Where are you?" she demanded in the same voice. "We'll talk about that later."

He gave her the name of the bar.

"I'm coming right over," she said. And a few minutes later he saw her emerge from a cab and walk into the bar, wearing a pert red velvet coat, hatless. Her first words were, with a rueful little laugh: "I was waiting for your call all dressed up, with white gloves and a white hat with daisies on it, waiting at that goddamn telephone for hours. . . ." Now, in the brightness of the bar, he saw her, really, for the first time. He thought, *She is beautiful*—the most beautiful skin, pale, almost alabaster, like a baby's, huge dark eyes and almost jet-black hair, in her red velvet coat, the collar up casually, a diamond pin caught in a scarf about her throat—very attractive, very fresh, as though she'd just come out of a shower.

Then he began to ask questions. How could she be waiting at the telephone for his call at 2:50 A.M.? He'd been calling and calling—

She giggled. Freddie had telephoned her after they dropped him at his hotel the night of their trip to Jersey. "Judy, don't mess with him," he had said, quite seriously. "He's trouble." So she had given orders that she was not in when and if a Mr. Luft called. The hold had remained with the operators after that first order, and when she told him after they'd met again at Gleason's to call her upon his return from Philadelphia, it was not until ten o'clock that she had removed the hold, when, because he hadn't called or shown up, she telephoned downstairs and learned that he'd called and called and had been told that she was out. And so, since 10 P.M. she had been sitting, all dressed up, waiting, at the telephone. For five hours, less ten minutes.

It was 3 A.M. He looked at her, took her in his arms and kissed her. He told her what had happened—she was entranced. "God, I wish I'd been here to see it." He said, "I must have lost my watch knocking that clown into the ashcan. Would you mind helping me look for it?

It's a Vacheron-Constantin and I treasure it."

So at three in the morning, the two of them walked up and down Lexington Avenue, peering into the gutter, pushing the rubbish aside with their feet, looking for his watch. They found it, finally. Luft said, "You know the young lady who was my date at the Gleason party—when I couldn't reach you, I took her to dinner. But that was hours ago. I'm hungry. Can we have our dinner now?"

Tully, on Judy's instructions, had reserved a table for two at a French restaurant, but it was time now for breakfast. They walked to the nearest Childs, which was open all night. It was, as Judy had promised, a late dinner. At 4 A.M.

Now and then Judy giggled. Luft just looked at her.

She had found someone different.

The fact was, as she admitted to him later, she fell in love with him the moment she saw him, as he stood, a study in beige, looking down at her while Freddie deliberately turned his back on him at their table at the Little Club. Freddie had been right. Judy was a gone goose (or pigeon) from the first.

"That Luft," as Judy was to call him, was a new quantity. Vincente could talk brilliantly about Chinese porcelain or the subtle Montmartre ambience of smoke and violence he wanted in a ballet scene; David Rose could talk of the uses of glissando or timpani effects in an intricate song arrangement, but "that Luft" could talk about the Arabian bloodlines of race horses, and what it was like to fly in the Canadian Ferry Command across the Atlantic in the war, or be a nineteen-year-old hod carrier in Coral Gables, Florida, or a high diver in Billy Rose's Aquacade in Cleveland, or work as an agent with Zeppo Marx, or nearly burn to death before escaping from a plane that burst into flames in the air as he was testing it.

Judy was never one to inquire deeply into other people's backgrounds. The world revolved around her, though she could exhibit genuine interest if she liked someone; and Sid Luft fascinated her. In their brief time in New York Luft's imperturbability, no matter what happened, intrigued her.

One Thursday he telephoned her. "How would you like to go to Jamaica Saturday?" he asked. "What a wonderful idea," she said. "I'll be busy tomorrow," he said, "I'll pick you up at noon Saturday. Be ready." She immediately sent Tully to Hattie Carnegie for a complete summer wardrobe. After all, it was cool in New York, but it would be June in Jamaica, which had perfect weather. When Luft drove up at noon, the bellboys were carrying out her bags. "What's all that for?" he asked, in astonishment. "All you need is a light wrap." He looked at his watch. "Come on, the first race starts at one-thirty." She stared at him, then sat down on one of her bags, laughing like a madwoman. "Oh, my God," she was saying. "You meant the race track. And I got myself a whole new wardrobe!"

In November she and Sid returned separately to Los Angeles. Judy was living in the Evanview house with Vincente and Liza, but the marriage, so far as she and Vincente were concerned, was over in all but name: they wanted to ease themselves out of it with the least pain to Liza, who was still too young to understand the full import of a divorce. Now she and Sid saw each other quietly, meeting at a favorite rendezvous, the Villa Nova, an intimate little restaurant on the Sunset Strip, with dimly lit booths and a discreet owner, so they knew their names would not appear next morning in Louella's or Hedda's or Sheilah's column. (The fact that it was at the Villa Nova that Vincente found he had proposed to Judy, years before, is one of those coincidences in Judy's life that pop up repeatedly.) Judy confessed to Sid that she was, as she put it, "sneaking out of the sanatorium" each night. It was now a question of who would make the first move—she or Vincente; and she thought that sooner or later the only honorable thing would be for her to move out of the Evanview house. Finally one night she drank enough martinis "to give me courage" and told Vincente she was leaving, for good. This was it. It was painful for both of them.

She moved out officially the first week in December and took Marlene Dietrich's former apartment on Sweetzer Avenue, off Sunset Strip. She moved in there with Dottie and Tully. Liza remained with Vincente.

Now Sid and Judy could appear publicly. They discovered they had many friends in common. Not only Freddie, but Carleton, too. Earlier, in Los Angeles, Carleton had taken Judy out after she recuperated from her "suicide" attempt. He had been the first to encourage her to appear in public as though nothing had happened, to dine with him at his usual front table at Romanoff's, the most public of places, where Mike Romanoff always greeted her with special attention. Carleton had taken Judy to theatre and nightclub openings as the season got under way, driving her about in a sleek black Cadillac he had bought a year before. Each time she appeared in public on either coast had been a triumph.

When she had gone to the opening in New York of Ethel Merman's *Call Me Madam*, she was all but mobbed by the crowd. When she finally got up enough courage to go to the Capitol Theatre, which was showing *Summer Stock*, she received an ovation. It was "We love you, Judy," and "Good luck, Judy." She seemed never to have been more popular. All her publicized troubles, all her bad press, the fatherly but rebuking editorials in fan publications like *Motion Picture* magazine, which predicted that Judy Garland would "never make another picture," that she had been under "constant guard" while making *Summer Stock*, and that her "shocking attempt on her life . . . proves that we knew what we were talking about," and the "exposés" in such scandal publications as *Hollywood Night Life*, which called her a "pill-head" and worse—all these seemed only to boomerang against the writers. Everyone loved Judy, everyone rooted for her.

Now, with Sid in Los Angeles, nothing surprised her. Not even when she found him calling for her at her Sweetzer apartment, driving Carleton's black Cadillac. Before going to New York and his Washington job with the CIA—it had something to do with Korea— Carleton had been low in funds. Though he had acted as Judy's representative and received 2 percent of her earnings, that had lasted only briefly. In any event he had no need for an expensive car now. Sid had been flush at the moment, and bought Carleton's Cadillac from him for $1,900.

How had this come about? Judy wondered. Sid said, with money he'd won on the horses. Judy listened—she was no lover of horse races, but what a science—or art—he made of it! How could you get angry at a man who told you he bought the car because he'd run $200 up to $3,600 in one race at Santa Anita—and not by chance, but by sound deductive reasoning? He'd gone to the track late one afternoon to bet $200 on a horse he'd chosen after carefully considering his bloodline and record, when he noticed sitting in the stands Slim Jones, an aged, almost legendary stable owner. Jones rarely attended the races, and certainly not so late in the day. Why was Slim Jones there today, waiting for the last race? Sid checked his racing form: one of Jones's stable, No. 8, was in the last race—at eighteen-to-one odds. Now, thought Sid, old Slim wouldn't have taken the trouble to come out there to see his horse lose, not at this hour. If Slim Jones was there, he knew something about his horse no one else did, and No. 8 was going to win, regardless of the bookmakers. Sid changed his bet and put his $200 on No. 8. The horse won, and Sid went downstairs to the window and picked up $3,600 where a few minutes before he had put down $200. Judy could only shake her head. "I never heard of anything like that," she said in grudging admiration.

That night, one of their first public dates, made it quickly evident that going about town with this man would mean not only learning about a world she'd never known, but one exciting moment after another. As they were driving down Santa Monica Boulevard toward the restaurant, Judy became aware that a car was keeping pace with them on their right side.

"Watch out for him," she warned Luft. There was no doubt that the driver, a stranger, was deliberately sticking to them. Luft slowed down to let the other pass; instead, he slowed down, too. Luft speeded up; so did the other. At one point the stranger's car brushed the Cadillac, leaving a long jagged gash in the fender, and only then began to pull away. Luft raced after him.

A red light stopped the stranger. Sid, unable to control himself, leaped out, strode to the other car and, without a word, punched the driver in the mouth. Then he returned to his own car. He was about to get in when the other driver emerged from his car. Judy and Luft saw what appeared to be a giant: the man literally unwound himself as he got out, and they were staring at a huge man, nearly six feet six, built in proportion, his face contorted with rage, and at the moment hurling himself upon Luft, his enormous arms outstretched, like a football tackle charging full speed. As he reached Luft, the latter ducked; the man's body struck the tip of Luft's shoulder and Sid instinctively straightened up sharply; the effect was to catapult the other over Luft's head, to land with a loud crunch several yards away on the pavement.

He lay there, dazed.

Judy, who had watched all this, her fist in her mouth, ready to scream, faint or leap to Sid's defense, was now in a paroxysm of laughter. It could have been a Mack Sennett comedy. A crowd gathered; Luft, imperturbable, walked over and solicitously helped the other man up. On his feet, he brushed off his clothes, looked blankly down at Luft, then staggered to his car and slipped painfully behind the wheel.

Sid helped Judy into the Cadillac, got in himself, backed up sharply and drove swiftly around the car in front of them—the driver immobile behind his wheel, obviously still gathering his wits. Though Judy was beside herself with laughter, Sid was not amused. "Jesus Christ, what a stupid thing to do!" he said. "That's all we need in the press now. Sid Luft and Judy." Judy managed to say, "What do you care?" but Luft responded, "I do care. I care for you. You don't need any of this nonsense—I'm sorry I got mad."

"I loved it," said Judy, and she meant it. All her life she'd been seeking someone to take on the world for her. No one played games with this man. First, the manager of the bar, who found himself tossed in the gutter on Lexington Avenue in New York; now this frightening King Kong character who found himself tossed flat on his back in the middle of Santa Monica Boulevard in Beverly Hills—and Luft was apologizing to her for it! They went on to dinner at the Little Mexico, drinking, dining, dancing—"We swung from the chandeliers," Judy told an appreciative Dottie later—and it seemed to Judy that she and Sid laughed most of the evening.

Judy was bubbling. She had a champion. Luft was the *verray parfit gentil knight.*

He soon discovered, however, that if she saw him in that role, he had to keep to it. She was not one to be played with either. After several dates with her in New York, he had been lunching at 21, where he was introduced to a Mr. Amanda. Luft's first girlfriend in high school had been a Bettina Amanda. They'd gone together for four years, until her mother broke up their romance, and Bettina had married somebody else. It had depressed him deeply; he had even quit school because of it. Amanda was an odd last name. Luft asked, "You wouldn't be related to a Bettina Amanda from Scarsdale, would you?"

Amanda smiled. "She's my niece," he said. Bettina was divorced now, and lived in Denver. Luft could hardly wait until a phone was brought to his table, then and there, and he telephoned her. Obviously, he was still vulnerable. And she recognized his voice—after all these years. "Sid!" she said. "Oh, Sid!" They talked. She said, "Come out to Denver. I'd love to see you." "I will," he said.

Judy was to return to California for various broadcasts—not only with Bing Crosby and Bob Hope but in Tallulah Bankhead's *The Big Show*. She looked forward to these because in radio nobody cared how plump she was, and it was such freedom not to worry about cameras. She wanted Sid to begin meeting her California friends, particularly Roger Edens. Roger was throwing a party for her in two days; she wanted Sid to be there.

Sid promised. He'd have to leave tomorrow for Tulsa, before she left for the Coast, because he had to meet with his associate, Ted Law, with whom he owned a racing stable. Ted was in the oil business, and Sid had to see him in connection with one of Ted's oil-drilling deals, but he promised he'd get back to Los Angeles in time to make the party.

Judy drove him to LaGuardia Airport in her limousine. There was a heavy rain. On the Triborough Bridge, the car stalled. Judy's chauffeur fussed over the engine, but couldn't fix it. Sid, who had once been in the business of buying old cars, repairing them and then selling them, finally got out, looked under the hood, found a loose wire, the car started, and, soaking wet, he made the plane and took off for Tulsa. There he bought a ticket for Denver.

Bettina met him at the Denver airport, they dined and spent the evening together. At 5 A.M. he walked into his hotel, the Brown Palace, and found a telephone call from Los Angeles awaiting him. It was, incredibly enough, Judy. She said, "Sid, you're due tonight at a party at Roger Edens' house. I expect you. Just don't be late. When are you leaving Denver—what plane will you be on?" No recriminations, no bawling out. He said, feeling ridiculous, he would leave that afternoon. He had promised he'd be at the Edens party, and he would not disappoint her. He told her the plane. "I'll pick you up at the airport," said Judy cheerfully, and hung up.

Sid sat down in one of the lobby easy chairs. He was shaken. How did she know he was in Denver? He'd taken the plane to Tulsa. She'd been with him when he bought his ticket. How did she know he was at the Brown Palace? Had she known all along that he lied to her? Had she had her car deliberately stall on the Triborough Bridge in an attempt to make him miss the plane? Paul Riley, her chauffeur, had fussed about twenty minutes trying to fix it, and Luft had found the trouble in as many seconds.

At the Edens party that night he finally said, in some embarrassment, "How in hell did you find me?" Judy answered, with a flash of her dark eyes, "Don't ask me. I have my ways. You know my mother's a black Irish witch, and so am I," and nothing more was said of it.

Not until twenty years later did he learn how she had done it. Judy —by whatever intuition she had—had known he was giving her a story from the very first. In 1970, when Luft was talking with an FBI agent about other matters, the man said, suddenly, "I know you. The name just struck. Once I had to find you and I found you in the Brown Palace Hotel in Denver at 5 A.M. in the morning."

Judy had telephoned J. Edgar Hoover that night—she had only to pick up a telephone, call anybody in the world and begin with "This is Judy Garland" to get through to the person. Though she had never met Hoover, she had called him; Hoover had sent out the order; the FBI had located Sid, notified Judy, and she had put in the call to him.

It was a lesson to Sid. He hadn't realized how determined Judy could be, how ingenious, how resourceful, that she'd stop at nothing to have her way. He was immensely flattered. *He was wanted.* His self-esteem had been struck a shattering blow when Lynn, whom he had loved, said after two trial separations, "I want a divorce," and had obtained an interlocutory decree. They had gone through considerable tragedy together: they had lost their first baby, then separated, then reconciled, their son Johnny had been born, and now she was divorcing him. Lynn was a star, not a big one but a star, and he was desperately trying to make his way in Hollywood as someone other than Lynn Bari's husband. He had produced a film or two: the first had been *Kilroy Was Here,* with Jackie Cooper and Jackie Coogan —a B picture, at Monogram, but a beginning; he wanted to produce more. Lynn thought he had neither the background nor the experience, and he knew she was right.

At this low point he had met Judy. Her interest in him restored his confidence tremendously. As for Bettina Amanda, he *had* to see her again. He wanted to see what being with her would do to him; perhaps the old magic would reassert itself and deflect him from the direction he saw himself going—getting involved with Judy Garland. He had more than an inkling of what that would mean.

Sid remembered meeting Judy even earlier. Their first meeting, come to think of it. Peter Lawford called him one night and asked if he and Lynn wanted to go bowling. Lynn couldn't make it, and he went himself. When he met Peter at the bowling alleys, just above the Cadillac agency on Wilshire Boulevard, Peter's companion was Judy, and Robert Walker was with them, too. Peter had been in *Girl Crazy* with Judy and had dated her, off and on, was one of her oldest, most trusted friends. Sid still remembered what Judy wore that night: a maroon sweater, tan slacks and white sneakers—so little a girl, with hardly any makeup on, just under five feet in her flat sneakers, who bowled with all her might, and not badly. He remembered her as a lot of laughs. He thought she had undoubtedly forgotten all about it, but she hadn't. "Of course not," she said. "I remember you. I thought you were attractive but terribly conceited."

Now, suddenly, unexpectedly, he was dating Judy Garland. More —she began depending upon him.

22

IT BEGAN TO GET SERIOUS IN MARCH OF 1951, just before Judy's trip to England to play the Palladium, which, in size, prestige and tradition, was in London what the Palace Theatre was in New York.

Sid had been drawn into it despite himself.

After he had been introduced to her friends at the Edens party, Judy had been busy with her radio commitments, set up by the Morris office. There were four Bing Crosby shows, a Perry Como show, and then, in mid-February, her first dramatic exposure before a live audience since her aborted suicide attempt. This was *Miss Cinderella*, by Jerome Lawrence and Robert E. Lee, given at the CBS Playhouse in Hollywood. It was a test, and she came through beautifully; there was a great difference between appearing before a small radio audience and in a play. During a rehearsal she sat in the green room with Lawrence. Radio was such a comfort to her, she told him. "I know by heart *all* the plots of *all* the daytime soap operas" —and sitting there, to everyone's delight, she played out several well-known roles.

Judy never had Sid escort her to these events; At her request, Myrtle Tully took him to many of them, but Judy's delicacy was such that she didn't want Sid to find himself in the undignified position of waiting around for her afterward.

But he took her out often the first months of 1951. They went to nightclubs and restaurants; he accompanied her to fittings by Irene, the couturière, to parties given by her and his friends, to the race track, to the theatre; she made him intimate dinners at her Sweetzer Avenue apartment. Tully approved of him; Dottie, who saw Judy happy with a man of action, beamed on him. In public Sid realized he was with a superstar, although the word was yet to be invented. Judy's entrances were always regal. No matter what the nightclub, the moment they appeared the orchestra stopped whatever it was playing and, as a salute to Judy, broke into "Over the Rainbow." Judy would blow the conductor a kiss, nod and smile all around, and they would be led, like royalty, to the best table or banquette.

When he took her to the Stork Club in New York one night, the treatment had been the same. They were given the most important table in the Cub Room, always filled with celebrities. And the celebrities themselves tiptoed over to her, apologetically, with a menu: "Would you please autograph this for my niece?" Judy would say, with a mischievously wicked twinkle in her eyes, "How about one for you?" knowing that's what they wanted but were too embarrassed to ask. Sherman Billingsley, the autocratic owner of the Stork, would see that champagne was sent over for the two of them, as well as expensive perfume for Judy and a gold cigarette lighter for Sid.

In Hollywood, when they were in public, all eyes were on her— and on him. It was a heady thing—being with Judy. And it was, as he soon learned, and as Carleton could have told him, an all-encompassing assignment. Judy wanted him near her all the time.

One night after one of her broadcasts, Judy was to dine with Abe Lastfogel, head of the Morris office, and Fanny Brice. Fanny had been in *Everybody Sing* with Judy, whose respect for her as a comedienne was unlimited. Abe wanted Fanny to help persuade Judy to take the Palladium engagement, which had been confirmed, if she wanted it, for April 8. It was good money: $20,000 a week, from which she would have to pay the customary expenses. But Judy was frightened. She had really concertized only once, and that was in July of 1943 at Robin Hood Dell, in Philadelphia, with the Philadelphia Orchestra, and she had been so nervous "I could almost have died."

Then she had sung on USO tours during the war, but she had not worked since in front of huge live audiences. And none of these compared with what faced her at the Palladium: a sophisticated London audience. She had never really enjoyed her personal-appearance tours while at MGM. At her very first, in New York, she had had a moment of near-panic when, after she had sung, the audiences surged toward her. She cried out, "What are they going to do to me!" It was the fear of the victim as the faceless mob boils toward him. Now, to appear at the Palladium meant not only facing a huge and discriminating audience—all strangers—but it meant thirty-five minutes of songs, twice a night, for four weeks.

Fanny said, "You've got to do it, Judy. For your own good." Judy listened, not completely convinced. She liked and admired Lastfogel, but she was dubious of agents—agents who, like movie executives, were all part of the world she felt had misused her, who had peddled her talent, and whose concern was what was in it for them not for her—a suspicion that always stayed with her. She had deliberately not wanted to discuss the Palladium offer in an office, but over drinks and food, and so they had met at the Brown Derby, with Sid there, at her invitation, as a quiet observer.

Afterward, she talked it over with him. What was his advice? He was an entrepreneur—somebody she'd always needed. At last she had found a man who presumably knew more about a slide rule than a slide trombone. When she met him in New York, he had just come up from Kentucky, where he'd gone to consult Sam Riddle, the aged, multimillionaire owner of Man O' War, about a script Sid had commissioned W. R. Burnett, the novelist, to write. Judy had been impressed. And Sid *had* gone to the Wharton School of Finance and Commerce, at the University of Pennsylvania. That he had gotten there by winning a football scholarship to Penn made little difference to Judy; he had taken courses in business, and he would have her own good interests at heart.

Judy had been secretive about herself and her past. Sid did not pry. He was interested only in the person he saw before him. She knew how to handle him. She allowed him his private life. Only once had she showed what she could do if she wished: when she plucked him from the lobby of the Brown Palace Hotel in Denver, where no one in the world should have known he was. Even then there had been no questions as to why he had lied to her, or who it was he had gone to see in Denver. Nor did he now question her.

But he had learned that she wanted to work not only to be working but to pay off bills. When she and Vincente had married, they had pooled their two incomes, and it came to a considerable sum; but along with Judy's suspensions without salary, Liza's birth and her own doctors (though Metro had paid enormous sums in hospital, sanatoria and doctors' bills, when Judy called a physician on her own, he might charge as much as $500 a visit), there had been the costs of medication, governesses, maids, chauffeurs, gardeners, cooks, cars, limousines rented by the hour (with Judy sometimes forgetting them days at a time), clothes, hairdressers, travel, luxury suites in expensive hotels, Tully and Dottie, the rebuilding and refurbishing of the Evanview house, the Sunset Boulevard house with a second staff there, business managers, agents, publicity firms. . . . By the time Judy and Vincente separated, both were broke, and Judy, in addition, owed nearly $60,000 in back taxes for 1948 and 1949 and was making monthly payments on that debt. All she could be sure of was $171.20 a month from her MGM employee pension plan (this would continue to the end of her life, as certain for her as for a wardrobe girl or night watchman or any other Metro employee). She owed Hattie Carnegie a bill for $11,000—she had shown it to Sid with a laugh: $7,500 was for a fur coat she'd bought on impulse in New York.

It was clear that Judy knew absolutely nothing about handling money. All her life she had simply put her hand out, and the money was there. She didn't even like to discuss it. She never signed checks; she had always given power of attorney to lawyers, to business managers. She had bought some property; nothing had come of that. She had been in one business venture, years before. After Jesse Martin had been dropped as her agent, Ethel, in an attempt to make up for that blow, suggested a Judy Garland Florist Shop, with Jesse and Lorraine managing it and Judy putting up the money. Surely the stars would give it their business, MGM and the other studios would order their innumerable corsages and vast flower decorations from it—but it turned out to be a bad investment.

Now, Judy confided in Sid, except in radio—thanks to Bing Crosby's friendship—nobody, she said, "really wants to touch me here because of all my terrible publicity. They're afraid they can't count on me." But the people in London apparently still loved her. Carleton told her the British press had been repeatedly on the telephone when she was at Peter Bent Brigham: they wanted pictures of her room, how it was furnished—the British public couldn't get enough about Judy. A London appearance should be a natural.

Sid agreed. "I think it's a hell of an idea," he said. "You need a change of scene anyway. If that's the way the business is here, get out of town, get out of the country."

Judy decided to go. She would sail at the end of March on the *Île de France* with Tully and Dottie as her companions. Liza would stay with Vincente (that month Judy announced she had begun divorce proceedings). She began getting together her music, choosing her best songs, discussing the show with Roger Edens, who would write it and add new, topical material suitable for a British audience; visiting (with Sid) Oscar and June Levant and getting ideas from Oscar; and growing more enthusiastic about the project all the time.

After all, making motion pictures had led to sleeping pills, to wake-up pills, to the ordeal of losing weight. Whether she was plump or thin meant little on the concert stage. Some of the most popular divas were enormous women. And there were no 5 or 6 A.M. calls. When she concertized, she could sleep all morning, and not think about preparing for her appearance until six in the evening. It was made to order for her.

Suddenly, a week before she was to sail, she asked Sid: Would he come to England with her?

Sid, after much thought, said no. He was busy with his picture project, he had other obligations, and he was going through court difficulties with Lynn.

Judy accepted his decision unhappily, and left for London. She had begun to count upon him in ways he was not even aware of. Until now she had been surrounded mainly by sympathizers, a retinue of friends and admirers who reacted to her troubles with "C'mon, Baby, it'll be all right, honey. . . ." The echoes went all the way back to her infancy, the placating and the comforting. But Luft, who had troubles of his own, reacted to hers in an altogether different manner. *Straighten up!* he said in so many words. *Who's giving you problems? Tell me and I'll beat him up!*

In the five months they had known each other, although Luft was reticent about himself—he liked to maintain an aura of mystery—what he had told her only brought him closer. They were two of a kind, both with a deep grievance against the way they had been treated—but for widely different reasons.

It had been Sid's lot to be born and grow up in Bronxville, a wealthy suburb of New York City known for its residential restrictions against Jews. Few Jewish families lived in the town; the Lufts were one. Sid's father, Norbert, a watchmaker, owned a jewelry shop; his mother, Leonora, a clothes designer, operated a dress shop. Sid had found himself ostracized as far back as he could remember. He told Judy, "By the time I was five, I knew I was a Jew—a little Jew." There were also few poor in Bronxville, only the rich. And he was a well-to-do Jewish boy, and fair game. From the age of five he had been fighting a hostile environment, taunted and humiliated as "the Jewboy." When he was eleven, his father came upon him beating up a boy in front of his jewelry shop. He pulled his son off the other, dragged him into the shop and gave him a furious beating. How dare he be such a ruffian! He did not know that Sid had come upon the other boy erasing the last letters of the sign on the window, "NORBERT LUFT, JEWELER," to make it read "NORBERT LUFT, JEW" —and Sid was crying too much and was too humiliated for his father to explain that he had been defending him.

It was one of many episodes. He grew up angry. A year later he had been picked up by the police: the headline read, "Boy, 12, Walking Arsenal." He was carrying a .22 revolver, which he had bought for $1.50. He had wild fantasies of getting even with those who mocked and jeered him. He was brought into court and paroled, to his family's shame: a twelve-year-old boy out on probation! When he was fourteen, he tried to join a group of boys playing hockey on a neighborhood ice rink. The captain, a husky boy of fifteen, pushed him sprawling: "No Jews on our ice!" Sid took a punch at him, he was ganged up on, knocked down, the captain beat him so brutally— kicking him with his skates—that he had to be hospitalized, with stitches taken in his face and arms.

It was then, he told Judy, that he vowed to get even. He sent away by mail order to Charles Atlas, a well-known physical culturist, for a set of body-building equipment: bar bells, dumbbells, weights, chest pulls to build his chest muscles and biceps, weights to lift, an exercise bench to lie on while going through his maneuvers with weights. He joined a gym; he became a first-rate boxer, a championship wrestler and swimmer, a star football player, a skilled diver: he built up his body until it was all muscle. At sixteen—that was the year his parents divorced—he could walk on his hands from the cellar to the attic of his house.

Sid had a plan in mind. He never forgot the hockey captain; he waited for his revenge, and finally he got it.

Three years after the episode on the ice, Sid waited one night for the other to emerge from a movie with a girlfriend. When they came out he approached them. He was now an inch taller than his old foe, who had become a high-school football hero.

"You remember me?" he began. "I'm Sid Luft. I've got a little matter to settle with you." And before the other's girl, he slapped him contemptuously, twice, backhand and forehand, across the face, and then shoved him viciously. When the other started to remove his jacket, and his arms were caught in his sleeves, Luft punched him in the mouth with all his might; he fell back, bleeding, spitting out a broken tooth. Someone helped him off with his coat, and, bloody and insane with fury, he rushed at Luft, who ducked, and then gave the other a merciless beating, until the boy was on his knees, his head bobbing, all but unconscious. Luft was now a powerful seventeen-year-old, each punch like a pile-driver. (Years later June Havoc would tell Judy how Sid had lifted the front of her Austin out of the way after a minor collision on Hollywood Boulevard.)

"I was fighting him, I was fighting my folks," Sid told Judy, bitterly, lubricated at the time with several shots of whiskey. "What the fuck were they living in Bronxville for when they were Jews? Why did my folks do this to my sister and me?"

His parents had come from the old country, they had been successful at making money in this hostile town, they had a fine house, a car, a driver—but look what they had done to him and his sister! "Judy," he said, "my folks were gentle people—what sort of a man becomes a watchmaker? But I grew up violent and angry. My sister proved herself. She graduated from high school at fifteen, from Swarthmore at nineteen. But I remember talking to her about being rejected, because of what had been done to us, because we were Jewish and Jewish-looking, by the hatred and cruelty in that town." She was fine now, successful in business, but what she had gone through!

Sid and Judy had been dining in her apartment that night, and Sid, made voluble by the liquor, revealed more of himself to her than he

310

was to reveal for a long time. "My sister went through hell." He looked at Judy. "Baby, I grew up with a knowledge of suffering femininity. But I could always take care of myself; I used to walk around that town with my dukes up, always expecting the insult."

Sid could fight the world with his fists, with his ingenuity and guile. For Judy, he could understand—although he had yet to see her under their terrible spell—pills were the answer to everything, to what she thought she had missed in a childhood she felt had been stolen from her, to the cruelty and thoughtlessness she felt had victimized her. Pills made this frightened little girl ten feet tall. With Benzedrine, she could say, "Fuck you, I don't give a shit!" And with Seconal she could blot them all out, and all the memories of her own guilt, her own responsibility for what had happened to her.

They had met, two hurt, angry people, each feeling humiliated and victimized by a hostile society; each with chips on his shoulders, daring that multitude of invisible enemies to brush them off. Judy and her champion—was it any wonder they fell into each other's arms?

It moved more swiftly than either realized.

Judy sailed March 30. Two days later Sid received a call in his apartment on Sunset Boulevard. It was from Dottie, from the ship. "Could you come over to London, Sid?" She added, "Judy's been thinking about you and I took it on myself to telephone you." Sid hung up, thinking, Dottie wouldn't have made a transatlantic call on her own: Judy had undoubtedly asked her to.

A few days later, after they had arrived in London, another call from Dottie: "Why don't you fly over and surprise Judy? It would set her up so." He was thinking this over when, the next day, a third call came. Dottie was most persuasive. Judy had said, "If only Sid were here to see my opening." Dottie said, "Sid, it would be so great, it would help her spiritually." Judy would open April 8. He could withstand this no longer. He would go for a week—but it must be a surprise. Dottie was not to tell Judy. Dottie was only to get him a reservation at the Dorchester, where they were all staying, and give him the name of the stage doorman at the Palladium.

Luft flew to London, arriving the day before the opening. The moment he had checked into the Dorchester, he went to the Palladium. It was midafternoon. Judy was rehearsing. The doorman let him in and he stood quietly in the wings, watching her at the mike.

She said something to Woolf Phillips, the conductor, then walked offstage to get a glass of water—straight into the waiting arms of Sid Luft.

Judy gasped. This was drama she could appreciate. "I knew you'd be here, darling!" were her first words. And then: "I'm scared."

Sid was at her side from then on. Chuck Walters and Roger had both worked with her on her act. Before she left the States, she had gone over to show Vincente her entire Palladium routine. Though their lives would be separated from now on, save where they were brought together by their little daughter, they would remain friends. He was flattered that she had come to ask his judgment on her act, and he thought it excellent.

Now, in London, the day before her opening, Sid was there to run interference for her. She needed this. Her arrival in London—the first time she had been overseas—was a throwback to every ecstatic reception she'd had in the past. She was told that when the *Île de France* stopped at Plymouth, ships in the harbor welcomed her by sounding their sirens in Morse code spelling "J-U-D-Y." If true, she still couldn't believe it. She took the boat train from Plymouth to London; and at Paddington Station it was as it had been when she and Mickey arrived in New York, so many years before. Police spent nearly half an hour helping her get through the crowd—she finally had to be hidden in a luggage van and driven to the waiting limousine, while Tully and Dottie struggled to keep her many bags together. It was a plump, smiling Judy—Dottie had suggested an auburn color to her hair, as it had been in *Meet Me in St. Louis*—a Judy reborn, who nodded and smiled her way, joking about her weight—"I'm gradually winning my own battle of the bulge," and: "Of course I don't have a double chin." There was no one from Metro now to kick her leg under the table, and she could say, as though it had never bothered her, "I may be awfully fat, but I feel awfully good." And later in one interview after another, she had handled them well, smoothly dismissing all the sensational publicity about her past troubles: "I have come out of the psychiatrist's pantry now and am perfectly fit."

The night before her opening was the closing night for the star who preceded her—Hoagy Carmichael. It was a tradition at the Palladium for the closing artist to introduce—and if possible invite on stage—the artist to follow him. Judy and Sid were escorted to a box that literally hung over the stage, where they remained in the dark until Hoagy finished his performance. Then, after the applause, he looked up at their box. "Ladies and gentlemen," he said, "as you all know, a great little star from America who entertained you with her marvelous pictures is opening tomorrow, and she hasn't been feeling too well, so be good to her." Then he said, "Miss Judy Garland," and the spotlight hit her, and she rose.

Sid thought, *This is the night before, and it's already pandemonium.* Because the entire audience jumped to its feet, shouting, screaming, in a rhythmic chant, "We-want-Judy, We-want-Judy." It was like a fever sweeping the hall. Hoagy said, "O.K., folks—" The house lights darkened, he went back to his piano and began to play "Judy"—the very song from which she had taken her name.

"I can't go down there and sing now," Judy said to Sid. "This is Hoagy's night. It's not fair." His entire act had been dimmed by her unexpected introduction. "Then don't," said Sid. "Anyway, you're not due until 6 P.M. tomorrow—and that's when it's going to be."

And after a while, the audience accepted it. Hoagy saluted her again, she waved and left, and that night's public appearance was over. There was no dispute: Judy was queen—and she had not even begun to perform.

Her appearance, when it came, was all that—and more than—had been expected. She came on after the intermission. She was preceded by aerialists, and balancing acts, and a group of dapper male dancers, and Max Bygraves, a popular British comedian. Judy appeared in the midst of her introduction, almost shyly, unexpectedly—the more effective because it was not the blare of trumpets, a pause and then the appearance of the star, but a realization, that swept over you like an electric shock, that the magical one was there, now, suddenly materialized before your eyes: a surprise that piled drama upon drama. The recitative style, which had been so effective in "Dear Mr. Gable," and for which she had Roger Edens and Carmel Myers to thank so many years before, served her beautifully: she entered almost wonderingly, hesitantly—as if uncertain of her reception—from the wings, and the roar of applause drowned out the announcement of her name. Wearing a lemon, gold-flecked organdie dress, almost like a birthday-party dress, she opened, half-song, half-recital, with "At Long Last I'm Here," before an audience that included standees five deep. Now there was no studio behind her; no one to pick up, fix, repair, disguise: she was simply Judy, she was on her own.

Her opening number had been prepared for this moment, with one verse beginning, "England was so far away, the trip seemed silly," ending with "It's a long, long way to Piccadilly, but at long last here I am."

Nervous as she began, she had only to look up, and there, near enough to throw the boutonniere from his tux lapel at her, was Sid, willing her encouragement. Sitting in another box with a small megaphone was Dottie, shouting encouragement—and directions—to her.

Little by little she went into her songs, some familiar from her films: "Limehouse Blues," "Embraceable You," "Just One of Those Things," "Easter Parade," "Rock-a-bye Your Baby," her accompanist Buddy Pepper. So she was not altogether among strangers, though that sea of faces was one she had never seen before. The extraordinary thing about her singing was that, as always, she grew in power and command as the evening went on; even more extraordinary, before this live audience—the first in so many years—she sang *to them:* rarely had there been such a direct, uninterrupted line of pure emotion from performer to listener. She enveloped each one of them in her tenderness, her gaiety, her loneliness, her longing; she was singing to each, and the words were words of absolute belief: when she sang a love song, each couple in love in that audience felt she was singing to them, singing their song. The audience reacted to her magical ability to overwhelm, to mesmerize, to control and to devastate, to reduce them, individually and en masse, to pure emotional response. More than fifteen years before, Ida Koverman, persuading Mayer to hear "another child singer," had summed up the power of Judy's voice in four words: "It will stun you." When she sang "The Trolley Song," the huge building actually shook, and her other favorites brought ovations such as the Palladium had never seen. In its own strange way it was like an act of love—thrust and response; now audience, now Judy—and if Judy's triumphant close of a song and the audience's ecstatic roar at that very instant were orgasmic—well, why not?

Finally, the time came for "Over the Rainbow." Judy sang it. The program was closing. The lights went on; the audience went berserk; Judy curtsied, as she had been told to, putting one foot behind her

—and, to her utter shame, found herself losing her balance and sinking down until she was sitting on the floor, on one leg.

She looked up and her eyes met Sid's with the unspoken "Oh, God, Sid, help me!" He put his hands to his mouth and shouted at her, "Just get up, Baby, you're O.K. Get up, Baby! You're wonderful!" She gave herself a little push, and then Buddy Pepper was there to help her to her feet. Then she grinned infectiously and spread her hands helplessly, as if to say, "What can I do?" The audience became hysterical. She said she had to apologize "for one of the most ungraceful exits ever made," adding, as she put both hands up to her face, half-acting, half-crying, "What a way to leave a British audience—to fall on your behind." And then she was off the stage.

By this time Sid had raced down and was backstage, so that when she walked off, there he was again, to take her in his arms, hold her tightly for a moment, and then let her go back for her repeated bows. Flowers came up on the stage, so many you could hardly see Judy behind them.

Then it was over, and Judy and Sid, after she had a shower and a brief rest, hurried over to the Café de Paris, where her friend Kay Thompson was also opening that night. The audience gave Judy an ovation when she arrived, and then they went dancing at Ciro's.

The reviews the next day—"Well, what do you think, Judy?" was all Sid could say, as he and Dottie and Tully and Judy sat about in the Dorchester, surrounded by flowers, receiving congratulatory telegrams and reading the newspapers. "Judy Garland a Sensation," ran one streamer; and such reviews: "the most resounding reception ever known in the West End" and "no ovation in the history of the Palladium has been greater."

The British had been prepared for something akin to a wreck of a girl after the headlines of a few months before giving in gruesome detail the story of her "suicide" attempt. And when Judy herself, not a shaking psychopath, appeared and, as the evening wore on, grew more confident, drawing her own Dexedrine from the audience, they were as overwhelmed as she. She had made good, and they had so feared she might not. When Sid held her in his arms, she was so wet, so exhausted, she had given so much of herself, that, after her final bow, he almost had to carry her to her dressing room. But in minutes she had completely recuperated.

A strange thing had happened to Judy on this opening night. For fifteen years her appearances had been before handfuls of artisans on studio sets; she had got some idea of her emotional power over live audiences when she sang at Robin Hood Dell. She had got it again when, unexpectedly, sitting in the little theatre on Cape Cod on her vacation from Peter Bent Brigham Hospital, she had accepted the invitation of the small acting troupe to come up on stage and sing. At twelve she had sung "My Man," and sent chills up one's back; now, at twenty-eight, tempered by what had happened to her, she had drawn from those same notes that same quality of pure emotion, that indefinable yearning which transcended definition.

When it was all over, she had said to her audience, very simply, when they allowed her to be heard: "This is the greatest night of my life. You have made it so."

Fifteen years had vanished, in this one incredible night.

How desperately she had needed that assurance. And it had been given to her.

23

THERE HAD TO BE A MOMENT OF TRUTH between Sid and Judy—and it occurred in, of all places, her hotel suite in Edinburgh, the third week after London. Her month in London had been unparalleled. Every night had been sold out. Opening night they had queued up for four hours in the rain—what other star had fans standing holding up placards, as though it were a political rally, with huge photographs of their idol surrounded by words reading, "WELCOME TO LONDON, JUDY!" and "ALL GOOD LUCK ON YOUR LONDON DEBUT, JUDY!"? Or such accolades as that in one newspaper: "Yes, Judy was a success, the greatest the Palladium has had since Val Parnell [the manager] started to bring Hollywood stars to Britain's No. 1 variety theatre"? And this, one must remember, included the biggest names in American entertainment.

Everyone of importance came to see her, from Laurence Olivier to Maurice Chevalier, who flew in from Paris for her show. The British press treated her as though nothing had happened between the Dorothy of *The Wizard of Oz* and the sensational Judy Garland who now dazzled London. There were cables from the States—the first from Danny Kaye, who was to succeed her at the Palladium—and the reviewers grew more and more ecstatic: hearing Judy was an experience comparable only to the thrill of meeting Winston Churchill or Viscount Montgomery: you knew you were in the presence of the historic, the unique, the irreplaceable.

And Sid remained. He'd promised a week; the week became a month. Judy handled his presence smoothly by introducing Sid as her personal manager. But each night she and her manager dined and danced together after her show, and by the fourth night the captions under their photographs referred to her escort as "Mr. Sidney Luft, the American film producer, who is reputed to become Miss Garland's next husband."

Judy undoubtedly had that in her mind, Sid thought. He was not so sure. She had opened the door to it when Harry Foster, of Foster's Agency Ltd., which represented the Morris Agency, suggested that after the Palladium, and a brief shopping trip to Paris—Judy had never seen Paris—why not a tour of the provinces? Say, six or seven cities in Scotland, Ireland and England—such as Manchester, Dublin, Glasgow and Birmingham—interrupted by a gala performance at the Palladium, graced by the presence of royalty, for the benefit of the late great British comedian Sid Field, who had left a family and many debts, with Danny Kaye as master of ceremonies, and some of America's and Europe's stars to entertain and greet Judy as one of their peers. . . . There had even been a film script sent from the States by Bing Crosby, entitled *Famous*. It had a part for Judy in it, and Bing wanted to know if she'd consider doing it as soon as she returned home.

Judy discussed all this with Sid. He had to advise her, "I'm against doing the film." She'd been in London almost a month, and if one added another seven or eight weeks for the tour—assuming she took it—that meant a total of nearly three months. She was still overweight, and to go back to the States to make a film would mean starting a crash diet once more—the same awful formula as before. He had seen no pills, no medication; as far as he was concerned, that had all been some kind of evil fantasy dreamed up by the press. No, the film was out. Perhaps sometime in the future—but not now. The tour, however, he thought an excellent idea.

"Let's face it, Judy," he said. "With your track record back home, four weeks here, even if you work a miracle twice a day, doesn't prove anything. Nobody's going to think you're for real yet. You've got to go on this tour. It will be good for you spiritually, mentally, physically."

She looked at him dubiously. "Do you think I can do it? At the least, six more weeks, six different cities, six different theatres, two shows a day, day after day . . . ?"

"Of course you can," he said. "See what you're doing here. This is London, a big-city audience. They've had the best, they're accustomed to the best. Can you imagine how you'll be treated in Dublin, for example—you black Irish witch? They loved you in *Little Nellie Kelly*. And the other towns? It'll be something they'll never forget for the rest of their lives."

Very well, said Judy. She would do it. "On one condition—that you come with me."

No, said Sid. He couldn't do that. He was ready to take off now, back to the States. He had commitments.

She said, "I couldn't be away from you, Sid." Then: "I'd really like to do the tour. There's no reason why you can't come along and help me get back on my feet. Your horse picture can wait, can't it?"

In the end he said he would think it over for twenty-four hours. Meanwhile, he discussed the tour with Foster, who had already chosen the cities if she said yes. Sid said, "What about Edinburgh?" It was not on the list. He had been there with his parents when he was seventeen, and he thought the Scottish city a beautiful place. Judy'd enjoy Edinburgh.

Foster dismissed it. "Nobody goes to Edinburgh," he said. It was a bad show town.

So a dispute had already begun. "All right," said Judy. "I'll go one better. You manage the tour, Sid. You select the cities, you do the bookings—the whole thing. Whatever you say, goes. You're my manager—be one." He had told her that at nineteen he had once managed a male singer, and that at twenty-two, because his family knew Eleanor Powell, who had lived in Bronxville, he had spent several months as her secretary, traveling with her; he was not exactly a novice. And, because it was Judy, he succumbed.

So, after London, they went to Paris for a quick shopping trip, and then to Glasgow, where they were joined by their entourage. Minutes after their arrival, a near-hysterical Judy took Sid into her bath-room and opened the window: they were in a railway station. Their hotel was part of the station. "I'm in the john," Judy was saying, "and I can hear every train announcement: 'Track 4'—it's wild!" Glasgow had been a sellout each night, and after each show Max would order up Chinese food, they'd play poker, at which Judy considered herself a shark, and she began telling Sid stories of her vaudeville days. This was the first time since she'd been a Gumm Sister that she was once more on the road—not Pasadena and Des Moines and Detroit, but the fabled old cities of Europe.

Then Edinburgh, his choice. Hotel, fine. But the day was gloomy, until about 5 P.M., when the sun came out. Sid went to the theatre a few minutes before six to check the house, and, to his dismay, in the three thousand seats there appeared to be less than five hundred persons. He stood in shock. *Oh, God Almighty, Foster was right. He said, "Nobody goes to Edinburgh." And this is my management!* He promptly went to a bar and had three drinks in a row.

But Judy did her six-o'clock show as though all three thousand seats were taken, and when he joined her in the dressing room, he said, "Judy, you amaze me more and more. Why didn't you say something when you saw that empty house?" "There's nothing to say," she said. "I did the show. And I loved the audience."

She was trying to prove something to him, but he did not know what—until the evening show. Then the place was jammed—stand-ing room only. Why five hundred people at six o'clock, and more than three thousand at 8:40?

Judy explained. She'd learned about it. The sun was so rare in Scotland that when it shone, nobody wanted to miss it, nobody went inside. But at 8:40, in the darkness, they had come to see her.

In Edinburgh Sid had a set of golf clubs made for her, built to size, with her name engraved on each club. She'd never played golf. Now she went out on the greens and enjoyed herself. Sun, air, walking—he taught her how to play. She taught him how to say "Darling." You had to say it, not as you said any other words; it was a word of magic, not to be wasted. Darling . . . darling . . . *darling.*

And in Edinburgh, on the third day, a typical bleak day, in her suite, where one window looked out on an ancient church wall, something happened. Judy told him she loved him. He found himself responding, I love you, too. There was no talk of marriage between them; what they now had was an affair. Neither knew where it would go. But all was wonderful, so far.

She asked but one thing. He must become her manager in truth. She wanted him to sign a contract. After all, it only made sense. He was booking her, he kept the records. She had said, when he finally agreed to accompany her, that since it meant he could not return immediately to Los Angeles, it was only fair that he receive a salary, and they had agreed on $500 a week. Nothing would change, except that she wanted this managerial contract between them. Now he would publicly carry on where Carleton Alsop had left off: travel always with her, handle her business—she already had a business manager, she wanted to discuss that with him—pay her bills, protect her, do what he could to get her out of debt—in short, help her start anew. She said, "Darling, I need you."

It was true. For Judy a wondrous chapter had opened. Less than one year before it had been the anguished, slow separation from her picture career, from Metro. She had confessed, one night, weeks later, to Dottie, throwing her arms around the older woman and resting her head on her shoulder, as she had once done as a little girl with Ethel, but could do no longer, "Oh, Dottie, you're the only one who knows when I'm not pretending. I used to get sick every time I went through that east gate at Metro. Dottie, I'd give anything if I could go through it again now. . . ." So the break with MGM was always to mean loss to her, no matter how she, and those around her, rationalized it. Sid was aware of this. After discussions with Dr. Marc and Dr. Fred Pobirs, Sid concluded that Metro had let Judy go only after they had convinced themselves that she would never, could never, make another picture; that, indeed, her course was irrevocably downward, and that she might not even live out the year. When Arthur Freed had gone to Judy's house to talk to her about *Annie Get Your Gun* and realized she was not even aware that he was there, when Dr. Pobirs had to call in a specialist to give her shock treatments, when Dore Schary said, "L.B., we've got a very sick girl here" —they had all, in the backs of their minds, begun to write her off. Sooner or later, it had to happen. If her body did not give out, from abuse through medication, or because she drew so much from it in her compulsion to throw every ounce of her energy into her work, if she did not become prey to some fatal illness, she might in a moment of despair cut her throat or take a fatal dose of Seconal.

What bookmaker would take odds on a self-destructive, out-of-control, sick, tortured and unpredictable Judy Garland?

Now it was different. Now there were no pills, no doctors, no psychiatrists, nothing but tremendous nights when she was a phenomenon onstage, and offstage all laughs and games and play and rides and swimming and golf, with a redoubtable devil-may-care lover, a new lover with whom the physical and emotional chemistry was marvelous, and from her audiences, the very breath of life to her —love and acceptance. . . .

It was understandable why she should turn to Luft and say, "Be my manager, my official manager, and let us sign a legal contract between us. I want some order in my life."

Sid thought carefully before he replied. "No. It would be better if there were no contract." He did not want to make it that official— not yet. But—as he saw her face flush, and she began to turn away —"Judy," he said, "don't worry. I'll never let you down."

She walked away from him and stood at the window of her suite in this Scottish city, looking out at a bleak day, at the ancient stones of the church opposite, in a characteristic pose, hugging herself, cupping her elbows in her hands.

He knew she was crying. He knew, too, that he had to make a decision now, beyond simple words of assurance. These were the first days of June 1951. They had been together much of the time for more than eight months, first in New York, then in California, then living together in England, in France, in Scotland. She was dependent upon him now. She was functioning well—a healthy, vigorous woman. Somehow with him she had come out in front of her problems, certainly of many of them. Whether this was because he actually helped her or because, through the strength of her wish for it to be so, she endowed him with powers that exorcised her fears—he would never know.

But he realized that if this was only an affair, it had to end now, in Edinburgh. If it was not ended now, it must lead inevitably to marriage. Judy was a woman who, when deeply in love, wanted to be married. There was that proper, even old-fashioned morality in her, despite whatever rules she broke, however willfully and disdainfully. Judy, who could swear like a fishwife; who, when she wished to be bitchy, *was* bitchy, never missing the mark, knowing exactly how to strike the jugular; Judy, the unpredictable and the outrageous, was at heart a square who sought respectability as much as any choir-singing member of her parents' Episcopal church back in Grand Rapids or Lancaster.

But marriage—Luft was reluctant to think of that. He had been married at eighteen, and divorced a year later. Now he was going through another divorce, a potentially bitter one because a child was involved. Two marriages ending unhappily. After making that difficult journey twice before, he was not ready, emotionally, to start a third.

Judy turned away from the window to face him. Tears were rolling down her cheeks. That she should so expose herself to him—and she was proud, he knew the pride in her . . . He took her into his arms. At that moment—as he was to tell her later, much later—he committed himself to her. He knew that he would have to devote himself to her completely. That would become his lifework. Judy required no less. Her needs, on every level, for love, for affection, for attention, could never really be satisfied. There would always have to be more, more, more. In his egoism, he thought, *I can do it. I am the only man who can.* He had already seen how, as though possessing ESP, she knew when his attention wandered, when his thoughts were not centered on her. (The Denver episode—and they had known each other only a little while then—showed that she saw more than she appeared to see.) It was uncanny. No matter how far removed he was from her, at such moments she would bring him up short with a telephone call, a wire, a cable, a love note, a reminder of her existence, forcing herself sharply back into his consciousness. He had already had letters from her saying, "Write me, Darling, and tell me how much you miss me"—not "Write me, Darling, I miss you so much." She devoured people, and he would be devoured—but he could take that.

Yes, he would lose his freedom, and he liked his freedom. At most, he would be the prince consort. David Rose would always be David Rose, the composer. He had emerged unscathed as Judy Garland's ex-husband. Vincente Minnelli would always be Vincente Minnelli, the director. He would emerge unscathed, too, even praised for whatever qualities of taste and discernment had rubbed off on her. But Sid Luft—Sid Luft would be the man-about-town, the gambler and race-track habitué, that brawling Vegas type who had somehow charmed poor Judy Garland, even gotten her to marry him, so he could use her. . . . He would have to live with that.

Now he said aloud, repeating himself, "Don't worry, darling. I'll never let you down, Judy. Just let me work it out in my own mind." But he knew the commitment had been made.

Judy, for her part, had avoided anything resembling a genuine heart-to-heart talk with him during these months. She had appeared content to permit their relationship to proceed as it had begun—on a fun level. At no time had Luft suggested that he was serious. He had told her he was already a two-time loser. Whatever vibrations came from him were hardly those of the dependable-husband type. And she had been warned against him, not only by Freddie Finklehoffe but by others who took a far less indulgent view of him. She was not naïve. But she had had, as husbands, two gentle men. Luft represented something else again, something unreined, untamed, stubborn and headstrong, dangerous when roiled, one not easily stepped upon, a physical, potentially violent man, but always a fighter in her corner. It was all very well to hear grace notes in one's sleep, and to know the fine points of British porcelain, but perhaps what was needed now was a man of simpler, more basic grain. At MGM she had been surrounded by subtle minds of both sexes, by men whose perceptions quickened her own, infinitely creative, infinitely complex, but whose first duty was to their own artistic souls— who were, in a way, comparable to beautifully arranged feasts of marvelously exotic gourmet foods. Perhaps what was needed now was something as basic as meat and potatoes.

The tour was, as Sid had predicted, a success. In Dublin, she discovered that her dressing room opened on a parking lot—and, to her astonishment, hundreds of people who couldn't afford to pay the rates at the Theatre Royal congregated in the lot, and each night, before and after her show, when she returned to the dressing room, she threw open the windows and sang for them, and they serenaded her in turn.

At the Palladium benefit, Judy was among her own as never before: star after star, name after name, with Danny Kaye an enchanting MC, British royalty in their boxes as much fans as the autograph seekers crowding outside—and before that blasé audience Judy was a towering talent. She *belonged.* The other entertainers sat in curved rows behind her on the stage. Such names: Laurence Olivier, Orson Welles, Marlene Dietrich, Vivien Leigh, John Gielgud, Elizabeth

Taylor, Gloria Swanson, Peter Ustinov, Douglas Fairbanks, Jr., and in the audience the Duke and Duchess of Windsor and who knew what other fabled names—*and she more than belonged.* She sang only two songs, and for the first time Luft realized her power, her command, her importance as an artist, although he had been telling her she had these qualities all along. She sang "Rock-a-bye Your Baby with a Dixie Melody," that Caruso note richer than ever, and Sid looked about him: women were standing on their seats—they had not only risen, they had climbed up on their seats—cheering. The applause was like a tidal wave as it flowed from the audience; it seemed to drive Judy back on the stage until she found herself sitting on somebody's lap in the charmed circle of that illustrious company, her peers.

Then came a trip to the South of France, via the Blue Train to Cannes, and the Carleton Hotel, and swimming in the blue waters of the Mediterranean washing that pure, crystalline beach in front of the hotel, dotted with its gaily colored umbrellas . . . and parties at the Hôtel du Cap, with Judy dancing one night with Sugar Ray Robinson, the sweetest of all boxers, at an open-air nightclub near Juan-les-Pins, and every spectator there on his feet applauding them, two beautiful people, one white, one black, and each a champion . . . and then a joyous party, where Luft drank too much—was it Pernod someone gave him?—and two groups formed, and Judy vanished with one, escorted by Noël Coward, while Luft vanished with the other, finding on his arm a beautiful French blonde who somehow did not become detached from him until he awoke to find himself lying on his back, fully clothed, on the beach in front of the Carleton, in bright sunlight, choking as if he were about to die with sand filling his mouth and throat . . .

He opened his eyes and blinked. There was a face between him and the sky. It was Judy's. She was standing directly above him, both hands outstretched, letting a fistful of white sand fall directly into his open mouth. He had been sleeping off his drunk, snoring, his mouth open, and this was how she had come upon him and how she wakened him.

He sat up with a jerk, sputtering, choking, spitting out sand.

Judy asked no questions.

"I think you better go to your room and get cleaned up," she said.

324

"We've got a lunch date at one o'clock on the terrace." And she walked away.

The European adventure ended early in August. From the beginning, Judy had missed Liza badly. A telephone call to Vincente, and presently Liza, with her governess, Cozy, was there. This had taken place in Birmingham, in July, the last week of the tour. Sid had no idea that Judy could be so maternal; her meeting with her daughter, the way she greeted her, took her into her arms, gloated over her, seemed to expire with every glance at her—it was the revelation of a new Judy to him. Much as he loved Judy, he thought of her as self-centered, the focus around which the world whirled; but with her child, Judy melted, they never had enough of touching each other, she was so delighted, so proud, so overwhelmed, that she was the mother of this little girl. So Liza and her governess had finished the tour with them, and had shared their time together in the sun.

In Liza's presence, Sid had been circumspect. This child had eyes very wide open, like her mother's; she looked hard at what she saw, and Sid was careful not to press himself upon her. She accepted him simply as Sid, her mother's very dear friend.

Judy arrived back in New York, with Liza, Cozy and Tully (Dottie had returned to the United States after the Palladium; it was an extravagance to carry your own makeup girl with you through the provinces), on Sunday, August 12, aboard the *Queen Elizabeth*. Sid had flown on ahead; he could never endure travel by ship or by train, and if he flew, he could be on hand to greet Judy when she arrived. There was no press to meet Judy; that was something neither of them talked about. But a man from *Variety* came up to Judy's suite at the St. Regis (Sid had taken a room on the same floor) to learn her plans. She expected to spend the next two weeks or so in New York, talking with the William Morris people—perhaps a concert tour, to open later at Carnegie Hall, or a return to the West Coast. It was all up in the air. She was reading film scripts—"But look at me," she said, laughing. "I'm overdoing this 'pleasingly plump' business. But I don't care. I never felt better in my life."

And she looked it when she came off the ship. Sid, Liza, Cozy and Tully traveled together, on a desperately hot day, in a hot taxi, to the hotel. That night they put Liza and Cozy on the train to California, and to Vincente.

Next morning the air conditioning at the St. Regis broke down. In the early afternoon of that Monday, August 13, 1951, Sid excused himself and said to Judy, with a kiss, "It's hotter inside than out," and he wanted to walk over to the Morris Agency, in the MONY Building, at Fifty-sixth and Broadway, a few blocks away, and check things out.

Judy, sitting in slacks and a man's white shirt, a fan playing on her, watched him leave. "Good luck, Sid," she said.

Was it the end of the adventure? Garland back, and nobody gives a damn? Sid swore as he went out into the baking heat of Fifty-fifth Street and Fifth Avenue.

24

JUDY SAT IN A DEEP FUNK. Her suite was like a hotbox. Her hair was stringy. She perspired, as usual, on one side. She was plump—no, fat was how the British press put it, and they were right. A concert tour seemed the only sensible thing. Sid had been right. This was no time to think about making another film. In that direction lay unfathomable terrors.

But as usual in Judy's life, the script never turned out as planned (part of this was her own fault, of course; she hated molds and patterns, for they limited her freedom). In this instance Sid Luft's stroll on that dreadfully hot mid-August day was to bring unexpected results.

First he met with Judy's agents. What had they been able to line up for her, after her triumphs in Europe? One thing certain, it appeared: six radio shows, at $1,500 a show.

Luft felt crushed. This, after more than ten weeks of fantastic success in Europe?

Yes, but this was not Europe, where Judy had been acclaimed like a Lazarus risen from the dead; this was the United States. And Judy's history here . . . Luft thought, Why hadn't the entire world been in London those four weeks to see how Judy had come back, how she was in command of her life again?

He was thinking this as, walking down Seventh Avenue, he paused for a red traffic light at the corner of Forty-ninth Street. He stood there absently for a moment. To his right was the rear of the Winter Garden Theatre. Someone said, loudly, "Hey, Sid!" He looked around. A group of girl dancers, in shorts, were lounging outside the stage door, obviously taking a short break between rehearsals. The greeting came from a pretty girl who was married to an actor Sid knew.

Hi! said Sid. What was she doing? It turned out that she was playing the lead in the show. "Wonderful!" said Sid. "Best of luck with it." He exchanged a few more words, then went on, feeling even more bitter than before. This was a nice little girl—but . . . the lead at the Winter Garden? The Winter Garden! A great showplace of Broadway, like the Palace—the Winter Garden, where Al Jolson had made history, and conferred the magic aura of show business on that theatre. And all his Judy had before her was a handful of radio appearances. What a letdown, he thought.

He visualized Judy in the miserable August heat, sweating, hot and uncomfortable and—yes—frightened, no place to go, and very little, indeed, to look forward to. This was dangerous for her, he knew.

Luft had a habit of walking with his head down, deep in thought, and he was doing it now, when he stopped again for a traffic light. This time he looked up to see before him the marquee of the Palace. Drawn by he knew not what, he walked into the lobby. What the Palace had come to! This had been the temple of show business itself in America. Here Sarah Bernhardt, Ethel Barrymore, Lillian Russell, Nazimova, Elsie Janis, Nora Bayes, all the greats had appeared in person, twice a day—but the last of that had been more than eighteen years ago, in 1933. Films had taken over, then radio. Now it was a filthy place—filthy lobby, popcorn containers, boxes of loose paper —the program outside advertising five acts of nondescript vaudeville and a lousy movie for a dollar and a quarter! He bought a ticket and entered the theatre. It took time to become accustomed to the gloom after the bright August sun. It was now about 3 P.M. The place was nearly empty—a few stragglers in a few seats, three drunks in the back row, sleeping it off.

But as he sat there something was turning in the back of his mind, and it was the sort of permutation of acquaintances, circumstances and opportunity which marked the way Luft's mind worked, and which always fascinated Judy. He had parlayed the sight of an elderly owner of race horses, the loneliness of Santa Anita on a dull, late afternoon, into a Cadillac; it was that sort of mental legerdemain that always impressed her. It was taking place again, here in the deserted Palace Theatre.

The Palace was a disgrace. The Palace was owned by RKO. If the girl he had just seen could open at the Winter Garden, God knows, Judy should open at the Palace. He must talk to somebody of importance at RKO. As though a computing machine were clicking away, out dropped the name, from his memory, of Sol Schwartz, vice president of RKO. Some years ago Luft had made a picture at Monogram with a partner named Steve Brodie. Steve had a good friend named Jack Dietz, whose son had celebrated his bar mitzvah three years before. Steve had taken Sid to the party that followed at Dietz's home. There Sid had met a shrewd-eyed theatre operator—Sol Schwartz. They had chatted together, and taken to each other at once.

Luft walked out of the Palace to a cigar store with a telephone booth about a block away. He looked up the number of RKO, got them on the phone and asked for Sol Schwartz.

"Sol," he said, "this is Sid Luft."

As Judy said later, there must have been some kind of telepathic communication going on. For, as Sid reported it to her, Schwartz asked only, "Where are you?"

"I'm in a telephone booth about a block from the Palace," Sid said.

Schwartz said, "Sid, I'll meet you in the Palace lobby in five minutes. O.K.?"

They met. Schwartz grabbed Luft by the arm. "Sid, are you thinking what I'm thinking?"

Luft said, with a grin, "Of course, Sol." There was no question that Schwartz had read of Judy's triumph in Europe, but for the moment Schwartz said nothing of this. "I'll tell you what I'll do," he said. "First of all, let me show you the theatre."

Still holding Sid by the arm, he propelled him into the depths of the lobby. A wide passageway ran from the front doors to the entrance to the auditorium, stairs, with a kind of marble balustrade, leading down. The two men walked down, to a carpeted area below, where, in the old days of glory, amid the gilt and velvet and elaborate furnishings, men during intermission had met at the bar, and one might have thought he was in a little Versailles. It was now hollow

328

and empty. As they walked, an enormous rat suddenly scurried in front of them and scuttled into the darknesses beyond. Luft said, "Sol, grab him. He's the first paying customer."

If Schwartz was embarrassed, he said nothing. Instead, after they had made a tour of the place and he had led the way out, he launched into what he had in mind. Of course he wanted Judy. He wanted Judy Garland to sing at the Palace. "Judy Garland at the Palace Theatre!"

Sid said, "I think we're on the same beam, Sol, but let me put it to you: I want to rent the four walls and put on the show. Two a day. Judy, with five acts of vaudeville. We've just done it for ten weeks in the provinces of England, Scotland, Ireland." And Schwartz knew what she had done at the Palladium. Why not the same thing, the same show, here? If she could set London on its heels, why not New York?

And the Palace was part of Judy's history. In the Andy Hardy pictures, in *Babes in Arms*, in *For Me and My Gal*, it was always the dream—Judy's dream, or Mickey's, or Gene Kelly's—to "play the big time," play the Palace, New York. Well, now Judy *would* get to the Palace. Luft knew that in Judy's mind, if she made the Palace, that would be proof that what had happened in Europe had really happened.

One can only question which man was set afire first by the idea: Schwartz, a slight, wiry man with a full head of black hair, laughing brown eyes, quick-talking, energetic, or the more phlegmatic Luft; in any case, they played off each other as the idea took hold.

"Tell you what I'll do," Schwartz said, excitedly. "You know those beautiful chandeliers we have at the Alhambra at 125th Street, up in Harlem? I'll take them down and put them up here. I'll put in new carpets, new seats, refurbish the entire theatre for Judy's appearance. We'll work out a deal. Opening night, klieg lights, red carpet —everything!"

Sid said, "I'll discuss it with Judy and get back to you."

He found her as he had left her: sitting on a sofa sweating in that fearfully hot room—the air conditioner still not working—on this August day in a city where August can be pure torture.

He said, "Darling, I just took a walk down the street. I think I got an idea you might be interested in." She looked up at him. "What would you think of playing the Palace?"

She jumped up. "Go get it, Sid!" and threw her arms around him.

"That's a *great* idea!" Suddenly she was all vitality. "I've got to call Roger right away."

"Wait a minute, Baby," he said. He disentangled himself. "I haven't even made a deal yet."

She said, "Make a deal," and bounced into the bedroom to call the Coast.

Monday, August 13, 1951. Four in the afternoon of a stinking-hot day. And this time an even more curious Luft parlay: a walk down Seventh Avenue, a girl resting at the stage door of the Winter Garden, a bar mitzvah, an assist by a scurrying rat in the Palace . . .

Judy returned from the phone. She had talked with Roger, with Chuck Walters. They were high on it! Luft called Abe Lastfogel on the Coast: they'd have a two-month engagement, five acts of vaudeville for the first part of the show, maybe Judy doing not thirty-five minutes, as in England, but forty-five or even fifty-five minutes, because they had to put on at least a two-hour show. Inside and outside the St. Regis that day the mercury read 92, but Judy was energy itself: "Let's get out of here, get back to California and put the show together!"

They wrought the miracle on the West Coast. Roger Edens and Chuck Walters (who took time off from Metro for this special duty) mulled over what it must be. Whatever it was, it must outdo the Palladium. It had to be the biggest thing to strike New York since Jolson, the only artist comparable to Judy in what he did to an audience. Roger would write the act, select the songs and create a topical introduction for Judy to sing under the general title "I'm Glad to Play the Palace"; Chuck would choose and choreograph the dances. Then Walters said, and with it he struck the theme that was to lead to the Judy Garland legend: "Roger, Judy shouldn't just make a star appearance at the Palace. Think of the material we have!" There was "Get Happy," with her dancing boys; they'd transport that directly from *Summer Stock*—it had been a sensation. They had "Madame Crématon." He started naming skits, sketches, songs, numbers. "Let's wrap everything together and give the audience a real production, more than they expect—not Judy Garland simply concertizing, but a full-scale production."

"That's a marvelous idea!" Roger exclaimed. So Judy thought, too.

Roger jumped up. "I've got a terrific opening." The song was forming in his mind. "Call the press: It's lovely seeing you, but the first thing I must do is give an interview. . . . Call the *Mirror,* call the *News* . . . call the *Tribune* and the *Times*. . . . Call everybody, for I'm back in town!" And he painted the scene. At her entrance, you wouldn't see Judy at all. Instead, the "Get Happy" dancing boys appear; they move, in their dance, to the left; the audience doesn't know it, but Judy is behind them, unseen, crouching low, moving with them; they start moving to the other side, she behind them, and then they stop, unexpectedly, and Judy, as if unaware, is suddenly seen, crouching, sneaking across the stage—and turns to realize she's visible, the entire audience has seen her—and they go wild. "Judy caught with her pants down!" cried Chuck. "They'll love it."

They worked on pace, Sid, Judy, Roger and Chuck. Chuck had directed the memorable tramp number with Judy and Fred Astaire in *Easter Parade.* Chuck's idea was that they would go from the very upbeat, expanded "Get Happy" number—Judy with her dancing boys the very essence of sophisticated choreography—to the plaintiveness and tenderness of the tramp number—pure vaudeville. What a production it would be!

And so the show was worked out, fifty minutes of highlights from Judy's motion pictures. Roger came up with a medley of songs from her films, such as "Clang, clang, clang, went the trolley" and others she had made classics. And "Over the Rainbow"—the idea of how to sing that bordered on genius: Judy, still in her tramp outfit, with all the lovability of the little tramp, and all the yearning of one who seeks but never finds—Judy, exhausted as she would be, would sit down on the edge of the stage, her legs dangling over, and sing the song that was her song. How powerful, how moving, that would be against the backdrop of what the audience now knew about her, how she had sought, and what she had fought through to reach this moment and sing this song.

They began their rehearsals in California, chorus boys and all, at the Nico Charisse Studio on La Cienega Boulevard, where Ethel used to take little Liza for her first dance lessons. For Judy it was all work, and she threw herself into it, bolstered by still another idea of Sid's—that they plan, sometime in the future, to make a musical film of a picture, *A Star Is Born,* done nearly fifteen years ago, starring Janet Gaynor and Fredric March, the story of a once-famous male actor who becomes a pathetic drunk even as he makes a great star of his wife. Sid had read an item: the Whitney-Selznick people had auctioned off several properties, and a producer whom Sid knew, Eddie Alperson, had bought the rights to *Star.* "Judy, that could be a great property," Sid said to her. Judy laughed. "What's so funny?" Sid demanded. "I wanted to do that picture at Metro after *Summer Stock,*" Judy explained. She had gone to Mayer. "He wouldn't buy it for me. He talked to New York and they said the theme was too depressing and my fans—" Judy mimicked Mayer's mellifluous voice —"wouldn't want to see me as the wife of an alcoholic." She herself thought it great. Would Sid look into it?

At the moment, Sid was under great pressure. The newspapers were merciless. Maybe Judy Garland and Vincente Minnelli might not be going through a divorce if Luft hadn't broken up their marriage. Lynn Bari alleged Sid was behind in support payments for their son, Johnny, though he had enough money to squire Judy about town in a sleek Cadillac and appear with her at the most expensive restaurants and nightclubs. The gossip magazines took over: "THE GREAT DEBATE: SID LUFT IS DEAD WRONG FOR JUDY." . . . "Sid Luft, at 34, is not the mate any friend would select for a girl as sensitively balanced as Judy . . . a man whose business connections resist definition." Judy dismissed it all. There she was, everybody's property again! "Sid's a wonderful guy," she announced. "I feel so happy when he's around. I know we're going to hit it off." And she went blithely forward with her rehearsals.

Luft himself felt chopped up. Everyone was jealous; Judy, who should have been dead or in an institution, was opening at the Palace; he was fighting lawyers and newspapers, was getting little sleep, was constantly on the telephone to New York fighting for box-office prices at which ticket agents balked; and, to top everything, he was suffering from an agonizing cyst on his temple, dangerously near his left eye. Judy sent him to Dr. Marc, who cut out the cyst, gave him medication and told him to go home and get some rest. Sid managed an hour's nap, then rose, impatient, telephoned Judy at rehearsal, and said he'd meet her when she was finished, at a bar not far from the hall.

He arrived there first. He had one Bloody Mary, then a second, then a third. This on top of his medication. Not quite aware of what he was doing, he decided to drive over and pick up Judy, rather than wait at the bar. He drove blithely through red lights, being shouted at by pedestrians at crossings, and found himself suddenly pushing

hard on his brake. Then a crash. He'd struck a car. He said to someone, after he got out, "I'm awfully sorry." The other retorted, "You're
drunk." Sid said politely, almost bowing, "No, I'm not, really—but
I'm sorry this happened."

Suddenly, pushing through the crowd surrounding him, Judy appeared. She had been running. She had heard the crash in the rehearsal hall, less than fifty feet away, and cried out to Chuck Walters,
"It's Sid—I know it!"

She grabbed Sid's arm. "Let's get out of here, honey—quick."
Someone else, weird to Luft because he was a little man in a tuxedo
with a red tie, confronted him, shouting, "Like hell he's going anywhere. He went through a red light! He's a killer! Don't let him get
away!" Sid jerked his arm loose from Judy's, took two uncertain steps
toward the new arrival and swung at him. He broke the man's glasses
—he hadn't even noticed them. The man's nose began to bleed. Judy
grabbed hold of Sid's arm a second time. Another man faced her
belligerently: "If you think he's going anywhere, you're obviously
drunker than he is." Judy promptly turned on him and hit him across
the face with all her might.

Now it was a genuine brawl. Luft heard a police siren. "Judy," he
pleaded, "for Christ's sake, get out of here! Beat it!" He turned to an
elderly spectator. "Get her out of here, please." The other man took
Judy, who, now frightened, allowed herself to be pulled into his car
and immediately hid on the floor in the rear. As the police car pulled
up, she was already on her way to safety.

But of course she had been seen, and there was the story: Judy
Garland and Sid Luft in a free-for-all street fight in the middle of La
Cienega Boulevard, and Judy Garland punching a man in the face.
In Dallas Jimmy read about it and sighed, and Ethel read about it in
the small apartment she had taken and commiserated with Peg De-
Vine, and Suzy read about it in Vegas, and they all agreed: well, at
least, they knew where Judy was, and with whom.

The police asked Sid to walk a straight line; he refused. They
searched his car. They found a .38 in the trunk. It had been issued
to him when he was flying in the Canadian Ferry Command. Somehow it had remained in his possession. He said he hadn't even known
he had it, buried among bags and parcels he was about to move from
Los Angeles to New York. The date was September 30, and Judy was
opening at the Palace on October 16. Everything could be explained,

and he had simply not been himself because of the combination of medication and liquor.

On that note, a few days later, the entire entourage boarded the Super Chief for New York. There they completed their rehearsals in an old hall on Broadway, while RKO finished its refurbishing of the Palace. The elaborate chandeliers had been hung, the new carpeting put down, the place painted and gilded, and the stage, they were told, was sufficiently finished that they could move their rehearsals there.

On a cold evening at the beginning of the second week of October, Judy and Chuck Walters walked together down Broadway to catch their first glimpse of the new Palace. They were just about to cross the street, and a cry came from Judy: "Oh, Chuck, look at that!" And there, above the Palace, in letters of light, each as tall as a man, was the enormous word "JUDY"—with a cutout of Judy singing. This, after the years of heartbreak, the broken marriages, the suicide attempts, the shame and humiliation . . . Judy and Walters stood there and cried.

Walters said, "Honey, you're such a fucking star! . . . Just look!" And Judy, in a hoarse whisper: "Isn't that beautiful? Isn't that beautiful?"

Then came opening night. Sid was at the theatre early, overseeing last-minute details. Walters and Judy took a cab from the St. Regis, where they were all staying. Both had had a drink; both were trying to be lighthearted, trying to play down this opening at the Palace, because if they took it seriously, they might find themselves all but paralyzed. With Chuck, who as always talked dirty, Judy talked dirty, too. She was saying, "Oh, shit, it's just another opening. Fuck it! Fuck it all!"

Their cab got to the little traffic island called Duffy Square where Broadway meets Seventh Avenue—and the street was blocked off. Chuck said, "What the hell's going on here, driver? We've got to get to the theatre." The driver said, "Everybody's here for Judy Garland's opening." He hadn't recognized his passengers. Then it hit them both, and they looked at each other and gulped. This was big, this was really big. Chuck paid off the driver, they got out of the cab, skirted it and walked around to the stage door.

What is one to say about Judy's opening at the Palace Theatre that night of October 16, 1951? Great as the Palladium appearance had been, that was only a rehearsal for what went on inside this theatre that Tuesday night when Judy Garland and the Palace and all its memories of imperishable moments became one.

The box office had foretold the story days earlier. The entire first week was sold out almost at once; opening night was the biggest night Times Square had known since D-Day. There was good reason why Judy and Chuck had to get out of their cab and walk.

Every celebrity from London and New York and Los Angeles appeared to be in that opening-night audience, having walked the regal scarlet carpet laid from curb to entrance, under revolving klieg lights that turned Forty-seventh Street and Broadway into a noonday glare; while two hundred mounted and foot policemen, and wooden barricades, held back the thousands clamoring to get a glimpse of such fabled first-nighters as Lauritz Melchior, Jimmy Durante, Jack Benny, Irving Berlin, Marlene Dietrich, Gloria Swanson, Dorothy Lamour, Lee Shubert, Billy Rose, Jane Froman, Moss Hart, Blossom Seeley, Sophie Tucker (and, later, such nontheatrical personalities as General MacArthur and Walter K. Gutman, then a noted financial analyst for Goodbody & Company, stockbrokers, who was to devote his weekly market letter to Judy: Judy was bullish, a symbol of triumphant America).

The Palladium *had* been only a rehearsal. Here was Judy, plump in black and white, singing her songs; here she was, kicking off her pumps, saying (and winning every woman in the theatre), "My feet hurt"; this one little person filled that entire stage. She sang in the style of Sophie Tucker (who wept in the audience as, years before, little Judy Garland, sitting with Carmel Myers, had wept listening to Sophie Tucker), in the styles of Al Jolson and Nora Bayes and Eva Tanguay, yet she made them all unmistakably her own; and when she went into her trademark songs, it was, as one reviewer said, "the most fantastic one-hour solo performance in theatre history."

Max Bygraves, who had appeared with Judy at the Palladium, was to have done the tramp number with her. When he found it difficult, Chuck Walters took his place in the Fred Astaire part. The choreography Walters had worked out with Edens—Judy sneaking behind her eight boy dancers—was as effective as they had hoped it would be. Judy's face, appearing in the distance like a face dreamed of, as that voice rose without benefit of microphone to fill the hall, mesmerized the audience; and no matter what she did—danced, sang, told stories, paused for a delightful interchange or confession ("I've got ninety pounds to lose!") or traded quips with friends in the audience, mopped her forehead with a yellow handkerchief, stopped to take a glass of water, offering it first to an entire audience—whatever she did was of a miraculous rightness.

No one who was there would ever forget it.

At its height, when she had finished, it was pandemonium: men and women running down the aisles toward the stage, to touch, to see the presence up close, to worship. People standing on their seats, applauding in a paroxysm of emotion, tears streaming down their faces, while on the stage, her tiny, heart-shaped face pinpointed by a single spot of illumination, Judy Garland sang . . . and her soaring voice, capturing emotions beyond expression in words, transported every person in that audience into a world he had never before known.

It was the beginning of the legend.

And the legend grew every night thereafter, and was to continue after her death; whatever happened to Judy herself only intensified the impact of what had gone before.

There then began what might be described as the Garland phenomenon: she inspired an almost godlike adulation among what were later to be known as "Garland freaks," a legion of persons who apparently led their lives vicariously through her; who wrote to each other about her; who put out mimeographed publications—one of the best was "The Garland Gazette"—dealing with her and her troubles; who arranged their vacations so they coincided with her public appearances; who neurotically fed off her and her problems. As with the Jesus freaks a generation later, Judy became part of a religion; more than hysteria, their rituals were a kind of cannibalism: they devoured the image of her, though 99 percent of them never spoke with or touched her. Apparently feeling their own lives empty and wanting, they lived them through hers. This becomes even more bizarre when one realizes that Judy was living, not her own life as Frances Gumm, but a created fantasy life as Judy Garland—who really (and was this not what every analyst tried to make her see?) did not exist.

The Garland freaks were there that night, and perhaps everyone in the audience had a little of their quality. But for the vast majority of those who saw, heard and felt her, perhaps Clifton Fadiman, writing in *Holiday* magazine, captured the mood better than anyone else: "Where lay the magic?" he asked. "Why did we grow silent, self-forgetting, our faces lit as with so many candles, our eyes glittering with unregarded tears? Why did we call her back again and again and again, not as if she had been giving a good performance but as if she had been offering salvation . . . ?" He spoke of the unforgettable sight of her, in her tramp costume, seated cross-legged on the apron of the stage, her small, exquisite, smudged child's face spotlighted so close to the audience, singing in a voice with such yearning, with an ache that tore at everyone's heart, her song, leitmotif of her life so far, "Over the Rainbow," closing with the words no one could answer —certainly not she—against the backdrop of everything she had gone through: the "universal, unanswerable query, 'Why can't I?' . . . It was as though the bewildered hearts of all the people in the world had moved quietly together and become one, shaking in Judy's throat, and there breaking."

If for the audience it was a once-in-a-lifetime experience, we can only guess what it meant to Judy: an elemental force flowed from her —now thankfully outwardly—of such a purity that she dominated the huge hall and its rows of standees, forcing the spectators to become participants in every mood that it conveyed.

Charm, gaiety, childlike innocence, wistfulness—all were there. Now impish, now mischievous; now mimic, now illusionist, now clown, now comedienne—all were there. She *entertained.* Years later Liza, trying to capture what it was in Judy's voice that made listeners feel heartbreak within themselves without knowing why, put it into words: "There was in her a very deep wound, somewhere far down, which she could never close up because she had to use it when she sang, and when she acted. She needed that pain there because it was her work."

When the hurt was beyond her control, then came the terrible times, the private agonies that found their way inevitably into the headlines; but when she could make use of it—as now, when she was in love, and performing where she should perform, in the Palace, and before the people who could see and hear her—the wound was used. *She needed someone to cry over her.* In later years, when with Sid Luft she had two more children—Lorna, born in 1952, and Joey, born in 1955—all three learned that sometimes, in her most difficult crises, the only way she could communicate with them was to make them cry; and then, in moments of unparalleled tenderness, they became mother and children united.

Whatever the mystery of Judy, its spell reigned that night. After each number she would dash backstage, and Sid would be there to give her a sip of tea to moisten her throat, to hug her, others to help her with makeup and costumes, Roger and Chuck to hold her tight and reassuringly for a moment, and then Judy was on again.

And then the show was over.

The curtain calls lasted ten minutes—a lifetime in the theatre.

Judy's dressing room was piled high with flowers, the walls pinned with good-luck telegrams from all over the world, and she, in a Chinese silk gown, after a quick shower, ready to receive, when she suddenly remembered the people who had jammed Duffy Square. She sent a messenger out to see if they were still there. They were. She said, "I'm going to go out the front way—I'm not going out the stage door." She dressed quickly for the opening-night party at 21, and left the theatre by the front entrance. The crowd opened like the Red Sea. Judy walked through, smiling, nodding. Nobody said a word. Nobody tried to touch her. It was the tribute one gives royalty: Don't touch—just look.

Yet in the taxicab to 21 with Walters (Sid was still busy at the theatre), she turned to Chuck. "You know," she said unhappily, "nobody said a fucking word! What was the matter with them?" Walters had to reassure her. "Good God, Judy, nobody's ever *had* such a tribute! Don't you understand—they're absolutely awed!"

So opening night was over, but the extravagant praise continued. *Life* magazine summed it up a few days later, referring to her closing "Over the Rainbow":

... By then almost everyone in the theatre was crying and for days afterward people around Broadway talked about it as if they had beheld a miracle. What they had beheld was Judy Garland making her debut at the old Palace, which was having a comeback of straight two-a-day vaudeville.

But the real comeback was Judy's. The girl with the voice meant equally for lullabies, love songs and plain whooping and hollering deserved the most overworked word in her profession—great. And the long, unhappy years of illness, divorce and declining stardom were over.

Not quite.

Sunday night, November 11, three weeks into her engagement,

while singing "Rock-a-bye Your Baby," she stumbled off the stage and collapsed. She was taken to the LeRoy Sanitarium suffering from "nervous exhaustion," according to Dr. Udall J. Salmon. She had been dieting strenuously and said she also missed Liza, who was in school in Hollywood, and wanted to go back to the Coast to spend Christmas with her. But, said Dr. Salmon, she would be out of the show only a few days and "after a complete rest" be as good as new again.

Judy's collapse came when Sid was not in New York; that afternoon, he'd had to fly to the Coast to answer his drunken-driving charge and deal with an alimony hearing: Lynn was asking for more money for their son's support.

Sid flew back as soon as he could, and was there when she returned to the show five nights later. It was opening night all over again: cheers, flowers thrown on stage, a Judy who closed her performance with a halting little speech still in the tramp costume in which she sang "Over the Rainbow."

Actually, in the months Luft had known Judy, there had been relatively few difficult moments. One had been during the Parisian trip, when Judy was getting fitted at Balmain's, Queen Elizabeth's own couturier, for the gowns she'd wear at the Palladium benefit. Sid had said she looked too heavy in them and refused to let her wear them. It had led to words, a brief chill between them, but Judy's subsequent triumph had wiped that all away.

Then, after they were a week into the Palace engagement, a cruel newspaper review appeared. The critic wrote of Judy's genius, but added, "Our little girl had the face of Judy Garland but the body of a middle-aged housewife." Judy had said nothing, but she had seen it, since she missed nothing written about her. Later that day Sid came home to find Judy devouring a big bowl of spaghetti, smothered in a rich, thick, peppery meat sauce. It was one of her favorites. Sid threw himself into a lounge chair across the room. It was a hot day, and when Judy ate peppery, spicy food, she perspired. It was not a pretty sight. Sid, annoyed, said casually, "Why didn't you order up a steak?"

Judy gave him a glance of anger, but it was more than anger. If Ethel had a piercing, frightening glare, Judy had inherited from her mother a comparable look, a glance that could be so accusing, carrying with it such rebuke for one's insensitivity, that it made one feel guilty and idiotic at the same time. Luft would have given anything to take back his words. It was a recognition that he was right, but why did he have to say it? It was none of his business. Hadn't she suffered enough, didn't he realize how much she had thought about it before ordering it, and fought with herself over it . . . *and don't you think I know how I struggled to get into my costumes here, and don't you think I remember what you said about how I looked in the gowns Balmain made for me . . . ?*

Here was Sid, criticizing again: *What do you want of me, Sid? I can't help it. I know what I'm doing to myself, I'm sick at heart about it, you don't have to remind me of it.*

The next morning a celebrated performer, who was known for her health fads and her solicitude about any friend who was ill, called. She had read the newspaper piece. She said, "Judy, darling, why don't you see my doctor? He knows just what to do." And she gave his name. It was Dr. Salmon.

That afternoon Judy announced, "I'm going to see Dr. Salmon." Her friend had said he was a miracle worker when it came to melting off weight. When she returned, she said, "I like this man. He's promised to get the fat off." And, with a happy smile: "I'm going on a diet, and he's prescribed something for my thyroid."

And, as the days passed, Judy lost weight. She'd been a 14 when she arrived: now she was comfortable in a 10. But a subtle change was taking place in her. Marvelous as she looked in her "Get Happy" number, those long, lithe legs in black, that felt hat set rakishly atop her hair, she was not the same bright-eyed girl-child.

When Sid returned to New York after her collapse, he found her sitting up in bed. "I was dizzy, I wasn't eating, I felt nauseated, I told them not to let me go on, somebody pushed me on stage, the lights hit me, I felt weak, I blacked out. . . ."

Thinking back over the last few days, Sid realized that she had changed since she had begun seeing Dr. Salmon. What were those "thyroid" pills? Was this the beginning of what he had been fearing all the time? He did not know it then, but it was the first installment of his experiences with Judy and her "medication"—some of which were utterly surrealistic, as he was later to view them.

Now he remembered that before he'd left, when she went to bed, instead of talking for a long time, or holding each other in embraces of love, she'd fallen asleep almost instantly.

340

He had watched Judy closely from the beginning of her Palace appearances. At the end of the second week, in late October, her voice began to sound hoarse. Schwartz and he had discussed it. "Maybe two shows a day is too much of a strain on her," Sid said. He was beginning to realize that her very existence as a person was tied up with her voice. That was her most vulnerable spot. At the Palladium she had done two shows a day, but only thirty-five minutes each; here at the Palace, each performance ran almost an hour, and sometimes, on weekends, an hour and ten minutes. Judy gave, always.

Sid reduced the number of shows from twelve to eight a week— from two shows to one on Tuesday through Friday, and two on Saturday and Sunday.

Then one morning he heard her telephone Dr. Salmon. Could he come over to the hotel and treat her? She was too tired to come to his office. For the first time Luft heard Judy slur her words. It triggered something in him. He didn't want to hear that. He wanted Judy always to be in control.

He became incensed despite himself. He walked into her room and said, "Do you mind if once, instead of locking me out, I might be in the room when Dr. Salmon sees you?"

Judy said, "That's between my doctor and me."

"If it were my doctor," Luft said, "you could be in the room. I want to be here when he sees you."

She said, "You're not allowed. Now please get the hell out—now."

Luft turned on his heels and left. Dr. Salmon arrived: a tall, thin man wearing a black cape over his shoulders. Luft had never seen anyone so theatrical outside an illustration for a British mystery play of the early 1900s. Dr. Salmon nodded, went into Judy's room, and closed the door. He emerged after half an hour. Luft escorted him to the door of the suite. Luft had been doing some checking; his uncle, Dr. Israel Rappaport, had told him, "This man has a barnful of New York socialites on pills. They can handle them. She can't. He's not the man for Judy." At the door Sid said to him quietly, "Dr. Salmon, don't ever come back."

"I have a patient."

Luft said, "If you come back in this room, I'll kill you. Stay away from us."

Salmon said, coldly, "I want to hear that from my patient."

Luft said, "You're hearing it from me. *Don't come back.*" Salmon looked at Luft, then walked out. Luft accompanied him halfway down the hall to the elevator. "I'm warning you," he said. "Don't come back." And he returned to the suite.

He had noticed in this period that when Judy woke, she seemed blurred, both in speech and action. But as soon as breakfast had been brought up, and she ate it in bed, her coordination returned; the food seemed to bring her back to herself.

Now, when she came out of her room after breakfast, he said, "Judy, I told Salmon not to come back here." He said it conversationally. To his surprise, she replied, "I think you're right. I'll get in trouble with him."

The Salmon episode ended. Another doctor was called in, and Luft said no more about her pills, or her doctors, for some time after that.

There was, then, only this one incident. Otherwise, Judy's stay at the Palace was a total triumph. Judy was queen of New York. Theatres showed revivals of her films—Loew's State opened a twin bill of *Meet Me in St. Louis* and *Babes in Arms*. MGM brought out a new album, *Judy Garland Sings*—this really was being the toast of the town. Luft watched her in admiration, onstage and off. She was the most feminine of creatures. She had a velvet housecoat; he came upon her one afternoon sewing old English lace on it, to give it an antique look. Her hose had to be seamless or else with a seam that ran perfectly straight down the back of her leg. She always wore high heels in public; she knew it gave a beautiful line to her legs, her proudest physical asset. She had a passion for scarves; wherever they traveled, there was a drawer full of scarves. She hated to fly; when she was forced to, she first fortified herself with a drink, then sat huddled up, knees pulled into a fetal position in her seat, hugging to her stomach a photograph of Liza—Luft with his arm around her, Judy, her eyes closed, a picture of pure suffering. But she loved trains; above all, going into the dining car to eat, looking out the window as the warmly lit houses flashed by (it took her back to her Gumm barnstorming days), or simply to sit at the window and gaze out at the stars. She tolerated champagne, hated caviar, disliked coffee; she loved mashed potatoes, all spicy foods, huge hamburgers, candy bars, hot fudge sundaes. She loved to read. The radio was always on. She hated silent rooms; she despised putting on a hat and going to lunch with a clutch of women.

Max Meth, who conducted for her on opening night, and for the first eight weeks that followed, had to leave for another engagement, and Sid, at Judy's suggestion, replaced him with her brother-in-law, Jack Cathcart, who wrote a wonderful, new overture for her.

One night unexpectedly, Artie Shaw suddenly appeared backstage. He had been with Doris Dowling, an actress he was soon to marry, and a group of friends, when someone said, "Let's go to the Palace and catch Judy." His first reaction was *No. I don't want to.* He preferred to remember the Judy he'd known more than a decade before, the Constant Nymph, the lovely little girl—not the Judy he'd read about. They had gone their separate ways after his marriage to Lana Turner. They had met at parties; they would always be good friends. Since then Artie had married several times, he had become a gentleman farmer, he'd quit the music business and put aside his clarinet—never to touch it again, a most extraordinary thing. He had been psychoanalyzed, and his analysis had taken away from him that sick, hungry need for fame. Hollywood and all it stood for seemed far away.

But, despite himself, he went to the Palace—and, like everyone else, he was completely captivated. Someone said, "Let's go backstage." Again, he didn't want to. He knew what success did to people. He didn't want to find out—he didn't know quite what. Yet, against his better judgment, he went.

When Judy saw him enter her dressing room, though there were other visitors, she leaped at him, throwing her legs around his waist like a child and hugging him. She literally climbed up him. It was like a dance act. "You crazy—" he began. "Artie!" she cried. The others in the room remained, but for the two of them only Artie and Judy were there, off in their own corner, and excited questions and responses: "Jesus, where you been—" "I've heard about you—" "Oh, God, you don't know what happened—" "Wow!" It was like two excited home-town youngsters meeting in the big city. Judy said, "We've all got to go out together." They did—Judy and Sid, Artie, Doris and his friends—but it was still just Judy and Artie. Sid did not seem to resent it; he was at the moment deep in his negotiations on *A Star Is Born*, he was setting up Judy's professional life for months to come, and he seemed to understand that Shaw was like a breath of fresh air to Judy.

Now, from time to time, Judy would call up. "Artie, take me to dinner. Sid's going to be away, and I can't go out alone."

One night he was in her suite, and she was on the telephone to Luft, who had flown to the Coast. The call had something to do with a debt they owed there. Judy said, "Well, darling, take what you need and pay it." When she hung up, she turned to Artie with a rather wistful glance. "Do you think Sid is using me?" And before he could react to this sudden, hard question, she added, "All the men I've known have used me."

Artie reverted to the teacher he had been when they first met. "Judy, it's all a question of perspective. Let me ask you: if they used you, did you use them? Aren't you using Sid?"

She sat down and looked at him, wide-eyed. "You know, I never thought of that." And then she said, honestly, "Yes, I suppose I am." Artie said, in so many words, You're using each other. It's fifty-fifty. We all do. She had to agree. She had seen herself all her life as a victim; it was a novel idea—and one she would never genuinely accept—that she made use of people for her own ends, too.

Artie was to take her to dinner another night when Sid was busy. She arranged a box for him at the Palace, and he'd come backstage and pick her up after the show.

At one point she appeared onstage in a heavy dress. "Pretty classy, huh?" she asked the audience. Then, a moment later: "I don't know, I can't move around with all this heavy stuff on," and she kicked off her shoes and walked around barefoot, with a sigh of relief. The audience loved it: it was so informal, so down-to-earth—getting rid of elaborate trappings.

Artie had been enchanted the first time he saw her do this. But he saw now that she did it again, precisely the same way, with the same sigh—a spontaneity rehearsed and rerehearsed. She had calculated to produce an effect and she had produced it—he felt taken in. The faintest sense of disappointment crept over him. On the other hand, how admirably she had done it, so that even he, a seasoned per-former, *had* been taken in. When she did her little tramp number, she cried exactly on cue, and exactly as she had the first time. And again, the faint sense of disappointment. He tried to analyze it. *He had always associated her with purity:* the absolute, unquestionable, effervescent innocence she had when he first met her. Suddenly he realized that she was as calculating as all the rest. And he wondered: Was that little catch in her voice when they were together also calculated? How much of this adorable Judy was *real*? But when you were with a consummate actress, maybe nothing was real? Maybe he was dealing with her image of herself. Without knowing it, he was trying to cope with the very issues her analysts had wrestled with.

A melange of such thoughts crowded his mind when he went back to pick her up. Judy said, "Hi," and a big hug. "Where we going?" He suggested a restaurant. Fine, she said. "How'd you like the show?" O.K., he liked it fine, he said. She said, "You didn't like it as much though, did you?" Shaw played slow to understand. "Why should you say that?" "Well," she said, "you know, I know why."

Shaw said, "All right, tell me."

"Because all that stuff you thought was just happening, was all worked up, right?" "Yes," said Shaw. "Especially the dress. And the shoes kicked off." She nodded. "Yeah, I knew that would get you."

And they spoke no more of this.

Shaw respected this radar of hers. She was aware at all times of precisely what effect she had on people; it was the essence of the true performer that she should know, and so could both react to and act upon it, and thus make herself one with her audience.

But Shaw noticed something else. Judy had changed. Something subtle had happened in those nearly twelve years. The two of them left the Palace by the front way; her fans were waiting; she signed autographs, and as she did, she bowed her head slightly. She was the little girl who said, softly, gratefully, "Thank you," in a little-girl voice. He wondered how many times she had had to do this, make herself little so she would be liked. Then they got into the waiting limousine. Judy, sitting to his right, waved to her fans—the little-girl wave with her hand held cupped close to her head—"'Bye . . ." The car pulled away. Judy was still sitting as she had been a moment before, her hand still up, the little girl waving the little wave. . . .

Shaw said, "Judy, come off it."

She looked at him blankly.

He said, "They're gone."

She threw an angry, lightning-swift glance at him, and he understood. She didn't like him in that heartbeat of a moment when he brought her back. But then she was back, saying, "Yeah, goddamn it—boy, that's a switch."

In the old days if he had said, "O.K., you can come out of it now," she would have looked at him and giggled. Now it took her longer to come out of the role. She had fallen more deeply into the Judy—Little Judy—role; it was becoming more difficult for her to doff that identity and come back to reality—even the questionable reality of the grown Judy.

Then Sid was back from the Coast, and Artie and Judy saw less and less of each other, Artie finishing a book he was writing about himself called *The Trouble with Cinderella.*

Which, as an epilogue to this episode, was what it was all about anyway.

25

BY THE TIME JUDY CLOSED AT THE PALACE—a sensational, a record-breaking run, originally booked for eight, kept over for nineteen, weeks (with a Christmas vacation on the West Coast)—it was the most successful engagement the Palace had ever had, at the highest prices it had ever charged.

The final night, February 24, 1952, was even more spectacular than the opening. Almost everyone who had come to the first night was there for the last. It was hail and farewell: farewell to New York, and hail to a new Judy in a new career. Judy invited Lauritz Melchior, the great operatic tenor, scheduled to follow her at the Palace, to come up on stage to banter with her. Melchior had his little joke. Rudolf Bing was director of the Met, a difficult man. Melchior told the audience he had closed "down the street" not so long ago "with a Bing," but he hoped he would open here at the Palace "with a bang," and do as well as Judy Garland. And since she had been singing so much to them, why shouldn't they sing back to her? And so the entire audience rose and the great Melchior himself led them in a community sing in "Auld Lang Syne," his powerful voice sounding over the enthusiastic audience's. Judy had sung and sung and sung that night, and taken her curtain calls—it was like good-bye to the town hero—and finally introduced Sid, who was sitting in the front row. He rose and took a bow. The program now contained a line which said, "Production under the supervision of Sidney Luft." Judy

346

proclaimed to everyone that he was, as she was to put it so many times, "my fella."

Never had there been such a night of sentiment, affection and tears. Backstage there had been a particular poignant moment.

Judy was to leave the theatre the back way that closing night. Sol Schwartz was waiting for her. She said to him, "I'm going to miss the Palace, it's like my home." Schwartz said, "Judy, darling, any time you want to play the Palace, it's yours."

It was then that he led the way to the dressing room. At the door, he said, "Judy, this will always be your room, your theatre." Then he swung open the door, and she saw, for the first time, a gold plaque fixed to the wall reading:

> *This was the dressing room of*
> *Judy Garland*
> *who set the all-time long-run record*
> *October 16, 1951, to February 24, 1952,*
> *at the RKO-Palace Theatre.*

Sid had been waiting around the corner. He had just seen Sam Claire, an electrician, who had been doing the Palace marquees for twenty-three years, weeping as he took down Judy Garland's name. Now Sid came into the room.

Judy looked at the two men, her eyes brimming, and ran to the plaque and put her hands on it, caressing it, running her fingers over the engraved words. She was laughing and crying. She turned to Sid. "Oh, Sid, do you think I'll ever have a theatre named for me?"

Why not? asked Sid. Even this could be possible. Weren't the two of them a hell of a team, Baby!

The schedule for the rest of the year, and even later, was already set up. She and Sid were forming a corporation to produce *A Star Is Born*, which Sid was sure would be financed by Warner Brothers. Sid and Judy had already cast two of the parts: Judy, of course, to play Esther Blodgett, who becomes Vicki Lester, the Star, and no less than Cary Grant to play Norman Maine. Cary hadn't been asked yet, but it seemed clearly in the cards. What a part for Judy to return to the films with! What a part for Cary!

Personal matters were being straightened out, too, as the money poured in. Judy still owed tremendous amounts, but little by little the debts grew smaller. Both Judy's and Sid's divorces would become final in March. In that month they took a two-week vacation in Palm Beach, a suggestion coming from no less than the Duke and Duchess of Windsor. They had met the Windsors through Ethel Merman, who visited backstage one night with Charles Cushing, the Duke's friend and business manager, and then Cushing brought the Duke and Duchess to the Palace to see her show. They came backstage, too, and Judy was almost speechless to learn that the Duke knew all her songs, and that when she sang, he would be singing them *sotto voce*, the Duchess beating time in her seat at his side. In Palm Beach, the Windsors and Cushing and Judy and Sid dined together, were photographed together. The Duke, Cushing and Sid golfed together, and Judy held court daily at the Palm Beach Hotel.

On April 21, Judy was to open with her Palace show at the Los Angeles Philharmonic Auditorium—it would launch the Los Angeles Civic Opera season—at last, a triumphant return to the town that had written her off so cruelly so brief a while before, and the one town, other than New York, in which she still wanted to prove herself. A four-week engagement there would be followed by a month in San Francisco at the Curran Theatre, beginning May 26.

For Judy's opening night at the Philharmonic in Los Angeles (she was "Hollywood's Sweetheart"), all MGM turned out. There was a tremendous party afterward at Romanoff's, where she and Sid received an ovation. Judy, in red velvet and an ermine wrap, moving from table to table, hugging everyone—the Mayers, the Warners, the Goldwyns, the Cohns, Ethel Barrymore, Joan Crawford, the Jack Bennys, the Henry Fords, producers, directors, actors, columnists—and everyone beside himself with Judy's "Over the Rainbow" and her closing speech: "It's the happiest night of my life. I've missed you. . . ."

As demanding a script as any Judy could have imagined was playing itself out that spring and early summer of 1952.

Sid watched Judy closely. She was quick-tempered; she could fly off the handle and, just as quickly, be in his arms; she had few bad moments, but she had them, yet nothing so far to compare with the "nervous exhaustion" that had sent her to the hospital in New York —and Sid was becoming growingly expert in judging (and anticipating) the moods of this unique dragonfly personality that was his Judy.

One bad moment came when he was approached in the lobby of the Curran Theatre by a little bespectacled woman with gray hair. "You're Sid Luft?" He looked down at her, smiling, and nodded. "I'm Judy's mother," said the woman. Sid shook hands with her cordially. "I'm happy to meet you, Ethel," he said. She was small, surprisingly small; like Judy, wearing very high heels; like Judy, dark, snapping eyes; like Judy, a projection of vitality—subdued now, he thought. "I don't want to be any bother," said Ethel, "but I wondered if I might see Judy. . . ."

Sid said, "She's rehearsing now." He would go back and see her. Backstage, he waited for a break, then said, "Your mother's in the lobby. She'd like to see you—"

No, said Judy.

There was no mistaking the way she said it. Returning to the lobby, Sid said to Judy's mother, "It's a bad time for her right now, Ethel—"

Ethel said, "Oh, then just forget it. I don't want to interrupt her. I'll see her some other time." Sid, trying to smooth matters over, said that if Ethel wanted to see the show, there'd be no trouble at all in sending her tickets. No, said Ethel, she'd catch the show when she had a chance.

Later that day, Sid ventured to say, "Your mother seems a nice little lady." Judy looked at him. "Don't let her fool you," she said. Sid said, "Why don't you see her, Judy?" Judy said, "Maybe." Sid let the matter rest.

Otherwise all was moving in high gear. Whether one read reviews of Judy in New York, or Los Angeles, or San Francisco, where she had opened on a perfect day, the tone was the same. Judy had come back. A columnist who had written that Sid Luft "was the biggest mistake Judy ever made" was busy eating his words.

But there was more than euphoria in the air.

Late one afternoon in early June, Judy turned to Sid in their suite at the Clift Hotel. Sid remembered the day: it was Tuesday, June 3, 1952. She said, "Darling, I must tell you this. A week ago I went to the doctor. I had some tests made. I called him today. The test is positive. I'm pregnant."

Then followed a strange dialogue. Thinking about it later, Judy would give it a funnier construction.

Sid pulled the ever-present cigarette from his mouth. He said, "Are you serious?"

Judy: "Yes. I'm positive."

Luft: "How long do you think you've been pregnant?"

Judy: "I guess about two months or so."

Luft stared at her.

Judy: "What do we do, Sid?"

Sid: "There's only one thing to do. We'll have to get married."

Judy: *"Have* to?" Pause. "You're not that thrilled about it, are you?"

Sid: "Frankly, I am thrilled, but the timing is crazy. It's way off." And when Judy asked why, Sid said, "We'll have to face it sooner or later. Lynn's lawyer, who's so good with the mouth, is going to be all over me." (The lawyer was later to announce that Luft, having married Judy, was "now half a millionaire.") "They're going to cause us no end of grief." He inhaled deeply. "But we may as well face the music and do it, period."

That was the conversation. Judy was excited. Sid was worried. Judy said, "Let's do it Sunday."

O.K., said Sid.

Where? said Judy. Sid's mind began its permutations. How to do it and keep it secret? Ted Law, his racing partner, his millionaire oil-drilling friend, and, as Sid was working it out, a stockholder in the corporation that would make *A Star Is Born,* had a brother, Bob. Bob owned a huge ranch in Hollister, ninety miles south of San Francisco. He'd telephone Bob and see if they couldn't be married there quietly on Sunday. This was no sooner told Judy than it was done; Bob would be delighted to play host.

Sid went on, thinking aloud. He would use his formal name, Michael S. Luft. She would use her name, Frances Gumm Minnelli. Who in the tiny hamlet of Hollister, California, would know them? They'd not even go to City Hall. Bob had told him he knew a local justice of the peace who'd be happy to officiate at the ceremony at the ranch. Judy and Sid would have to show up briefly at the tiny, backwoods registry office, she would disguise herself in black glasses, her hair in a bun and bandanna, wearing slacks, and that would be all there was to it.

Judy and Sid looked at each other. She said again, "You're not too thrilled about it." He said, "Yes, I am, but—" She looked at him wistfully, but she handled herself well. She knew Sid was apprehensive—apprehensive because of two marriages that had ended unhappily; apprehensive because he had often been written about in uncomplimentary terms; apprehensive because Judy would be pulled into his troubles just as she was getting back on her feet so splendidly; apprehensive because, though he was not a shy man, he was by nature more conservative, less bold, more realistic than she.

So Sunday morning, June 8, 1952, two days before Judy's thirtieth birthday, they drove down in a station wagon to Bob Law's ranch. Bob Heasley, production manager of her show, was at the wheel, Sid beside him. In the seat behind sat Judy and Tully. Judy wore a pair of slacks, sneakers and a man's shirt, her favorite casual wear; it was a hot day, she was perspiring. Sid was not an easy man to frighten, Judy knew, but he was frightened. He was marrying Judy Garland, taking on her responsibilities, taking on a family—and that was something, indeed.

As for Judy, she was like a young bride getting her gowns together. She and Tully had packed quickly; she was elated. She was sympathetic to Sid's concerns. She knew he knew she would have to share with him whatever would happen—that she would find herself involved in his publicity, as she had been involved in his half-drunk, half-medicated brawl on La Cienega Boulevard months before. But she was a doer—she wanted to get married—and it was time. Sid accepted that. They had known each other, after all, for more than a year and a half.

As they drove, now and then he would glance back at her, giving her a sickly look. Judy would smile faintly at him. He could not help admiring her. He could not know that this was—and history must report it—the third time in three marriages that Judy was the loving eager bride and the man she married the loving not-so-eager groom. David Rose himself admitted that he rather floated into the marriage; somehow it seemed right. Vincente could not even remember how he had proposed. What had been his words? "I wish we'd be married," or something like that, and she had jumped at it. And Sid: the best he could manage was his sickly smile. But he admired her. Nothing stopped her. Only a month before, Paul Coates, one of the most widely read columnists on the Coast, had written in the *Mirror* that Judy Garland's mother was working in a clerical job at Douglas Aircraft, in Santa Monica, for $61 a week. Judy Garland's mother forced to work in a factory! Judy's net for one week at the Philharmonic Auditorium in Los Angeles was $25,000; Judy Garland's mother's take-home pay from Douglas Aircraft, little more than a dollar and a half an hour! Yet Judy, despite this painful publicity, could still be Judy, delighted at becoming a bride again, going on with her life in her own way.

They arrived at the ranch, where the Bob Laws awaited them. In the next hour or two, the Ted Laws would arrive from Tulsa. The judge who was to perform the ceremony was there, beaming.

At six o'clock that day the wedding took place. Sid had wanted it to be "short and sweet," and it was—perhaps three minutes. Judy had vanished immediately upon arrival, and when she appeared for the ceremony, she wore a simple black dress, her hair was beautifully done, to her groom she looked exquisite.

Sid passed through it all in something like a daze. He had no memories of the questions of the judge, or his replies. He knew there was Katie Law and Jane Law and Bob and Ted, who was his best man, and Bob Heasley, and Tully, who was matron of honor, and Judy, and that they had champagne after the ceremony, and that he felt relieved when it was over. He put his arms around his wife and kissed her. He whispered in her ear, "Everything's going to be fine, Baby. Don't pay any attention to me, I can't explain, it's hard for me to explain everything that's happening to me—"

She said, "Don't worry. I understand."

She did, indeed—more, even, than might be expected. For after clinking the champagne glasses—because Judy didn't like the drink, she hardly touched hers—they were to have a dinner party at eight o'clock. Since the ceremony had been so swift, it was at most fifteen minutes after six, and Sid turned to Bob Law, while Judy was chatting with the women. "Bob, this is such a terrific ranch—I'd love to see it all." "Sure," said Bob. "I'll show it to you. I'll take you to the top of the hill, where you'll get a good view of it."

When Judy looked around a moment later for her new husband, he was gone. He and Bob were in the latter's jeep, with Ted and Bob Heasley, Sid still in the blue business suit he'd worn for the ceremony and would wear for the dinner. The men had simply vanished.

An hour later Sid and his companions were back. Judy was sitting in a chair, tapping her foot. She said, "Did you enjoy yourself?" Sid, unaware then—Judy never let him forget it later—said, "You know, this is a beautiful ranch. This is how we should live one day. On a farm. I saw cows, and hawks, and even a deer. . . ." Judy said primly, "I'm glad you enjoyed your tour." "I tell you," Sid was saying, enthusiastically, "it's a goddamn menagerie he's got here." Judy said, "That's interesting."

My God, he thought later. *She was mad as hell—and had the class not to let it show.*

They had their wedding dinner, and that night, before they fell asleep, they talked about the baby. What would it look like? With Vincente she had had Liza, with those huge black eyes; what kind of a baby would she have with him?

Sid said, "Well, I come from a hardy people. They've survived all sorts of things, and as far as I'm concerned, this kid is going to be a tough little son of a bitch, whether boy or girl." He laughed. "I only hope it won't be a shrimp like you. I don't want any midgets."

Judy punched him in the ribs, and presently they fell asleep.

Next day they drove back to San Francisco. Everyone agreed, at the Curran that night, when Judy went back to work, that she had never been in better voice.

Thirty-six hours later Louella had the story, the headlines hit— "JUDY'S SECRET MARRIAGE REVEALED"—and Luft was not only taken over the coals in earnest (Lynn had won a judgment that he must double his child support, from $200 to $400 a month), but bookmakers began to make odds on how long the Luft-Garland marriage would last: six months, most likely; perhaps, at most, five years.

Judy dismissed all this. As soon as she finished her engagement, they were back in Los Angeles, living in a house they had sublet on North Maple Drive, in Beverly Hills, which belonged to Joseph and Dorothy Fields, the songwriter. Louella Parsons lived at one end of the street, Hedda Hopper at the other. What could be more symbolic? But what excited Judy was the baby she awaited, and the picture Sid painted of how their life would move from now on.

He had already formed the corporation. He named it Transcona Enterprises. Transcona was the name of a Canadian town he had once driven through: it stuck in his mind; it had just the right ring to it. Judy would own 45 percent of the stock, Sid would own 45 percent; the other 10 percent would be divided between his partner,

Ted Law, who was, in a manner of speaking, his financial adviser as well as dear friend, and Eddie Alperson, the experienced movie man who had originally bought the rights to *Star* at auction. Judy, of course, had always wanted to be a woman of property. Well, now she was. She was an officer and stockholder in a bona fide corporation, with a desk and a secretary, and papers to sign, and memos to send out.

Sid had taken an office on Canon Drive, not far from the house, and hired a production assistant—Vernon Alves—who had worked with him on his Monogram films. Vern, tall, slender, diplomatic—he had been General Mark Clark's adjutant in the war—a gentle and perceptive man, was to become not only Sid's alter ego and closest aide but Judy's companion and confidant. Vern, unmarried, in his thirties, was to play a calming, older-brother role to Judy. Sid had hired him on the closing night at the Palace, in New York, and he had worked behind the scenes, efficiently eliminating technical problems, in Judy's Los Angeles and San Francisco appearances, as well as being constantly at her beck and call. He would play the same role over the next decade.

But however matters moved, everything to do with the film would have to wait, first, on the birth of her child.

And now, for the first time, came the darker moments—so long expected and, save for a lapse now and then, so long not in evidence.

26

THE LAPSES HAD BEEN FEW, but they had already made themselves felt toward the end of the San Francisco engagement. By then Judy was over three months pregnant, there were nights she could have felt better, and she was beginning to feel sorry for herself: in this condition, and working like a machine again. Both Sid and Vern got an inkling of the sort of thing Chuck Walters had experienced—but in a far less virulent form.

A night would come when she simply didn't feel like going out on stage and entertaining. Sid would be out front, taking care of various details; Judy, sitting at her makeup table, would say to everyone in her dressing room, "Out—everyone out but you, Vern. You stay." And as soon as the door closed, she would let go. "I'm not going to work tonight. Fuck the show, fuck them, fuck everything!" But—all the time—she would be putting on her makeup.

And then: "What's that Luft doing? Counting the house? Can't he be here when I need him?" And so on . . . with Vern able by now to make himself almost invisible yet helpfully there, never questioning her but following her lead, all quiet, solicitous attention.

Vern had been the first to know about her marriage to Sid. In her dressing room, she had said, suddenly, "I have a secret to tell you. Sid and I are getting married."

"That's marvelous," Vern had said. "I know it's what you want."

She had said, with surprising candor, "Well, it's what I want, but it isn't what he wants. He wanted to wait for a while. But I have another secret for you. I'm going to have a baby."

This Vern knew; Sid had told him. Sid had said he had mixed emotions about it, but he had said nothing about marriage. Judy had added then, to Vern, "The happiest times of my life are when I'm pregnant."

Judy had been thinking for some time about having a child with Sid. A few weeks before, when six-year-old Liza was watching her make up, always admiring her mother's deftness, Judy had asked suddenly: "What would you think if I married Sid?"

Liza said, "No, I don't want you to marry Sid. What about Daddy?"

"Well," said Judy, "we're not married any more." There was silence for a moment. Then Judy said, "How'd you like a brother or sister?"

Liza: "Oh, Mama, I'd love it."

"Well," said Judy, "if I married Sid, maybe, you know, you could have one."

Oh, said Liza, that would be wonderful. But Liza still was a little doubtful about it, because if Mama married someone else, it meant Daddy wouldn't be around as much.

Then, one night in June, around her mother's birthday, when Liza was visiting her father, they were watching the six o'clock news on TV. Liza was excited. She'd been with her father all day, he'd taken her to the Farmer's Market and bought her a parakeet and she was to stay overnight in his house. Then, there on the TV was a picture of her mother and Sid, and the announcer's voice: Judy Garland and Sid Luft had been secretly married three days ago, and the news had just come out.

Liza's first reaction was hurt: Mama had gotten married without telling her, although, to be sure, she had mentioned the possibility; then she felt upset because she'd missed the wedding and all the excitement; then she realized that the reason she was with her father in Los Angeles, rather than with her mother at her hotel in San Francisco, was because her mother didn't want her around because she *was* getting married. . . . Finally Liza concluded that it really wasn't any of her business, and went into the kitchen and took an Eskimo Pie out of the freezer and comforted herself with that.

Later, when her mother returned from San Francisco and they moved into the Maple Drive house, Liza had moved in, too, with her governess, Cozy, to make up a full menage: Judy, awaiting her new baby; Margaret Gundy, a psychiatric trained nurse who was to help Judy through her pregnancy; Sid; Tully; and Vern Alves there much of the time, to keep Judy company.

The first day in the Maple house, Judy took Liza aside and whispered to her, "Would you call Sid 'Papa Sid' when he comes home tonight?" Liza liked the idea, and her mother seemed as excited as a little girl.

They heard Sid's big black Cadillac drive up. "He's coming," Judy whispered. "Remember." Sid walked in and Liza said, "Hello, Papa Sid." Sid went all red in the face, and Judy laughed, and they all hugged each other—Judy and Papa Sid and Liza. They were a family.

As Judy's pregnancy advanced, it seemed to put odd stresses on her. At four months she was already carrying big. She swore. "Oh, God, five more months of this!"

One day she came home and said to Sid, "I can't raise my right arm." Sid said, "Darling, stop that." She said, "You don't believe me." She walked across the room; the arm swung as though it had no life of its own. Sid said, "Shake hands." Judy said, "I can't. It's gone."

Dr. Pobirs came over and examined her. "It's a spasm, Judy," he said. "These things happen—it's nervous tension. Put the arm in a sling, and it'll go away just as it came."

Sid said, "Let's take a walk. Maybe the air'll do you good." And so Judy, her arm supported in one of her bandannas tied like a sling, walked with him. She gave him a sidewise look. "I don't think you believe me," she said. "You once said something about me always looking for sympathy." Sid protested, "I used the word once." "All right," said Judy. "I'll show you." With her other hand she removed the bandanna. A two-inch safety pin held it. She unhooked the pin, and deliberately jabbed it into the muscle of her arm. "I don't feel a thing," she said. Appalled, he pulled it out. "I'm certainly convinced," he said. "If I had any doubt, I apologize."

As Dr. Pobirs predicted, the paralysis vanished as inexplicably as it came. A week later her arm was fine. The pregnancy advanced without trouble, and the time was now approaching for the birth of her second child. Since the obstetrician who had delivered Liza had died, Dr. Marc recommended Dr. Daniel G. Morton, who had delivered Bing Crosby's boys. He in turn suggested St. John's Hospital, where the rigidly disciplined Sisters would be less susceptible to Judy's manipulation than nurses at a large institution such as the Cedars of Lebanon, where Liza had been born.

Dr. Morton, so he could keep an eye on Judy, had her put into St. John's three weeks before the delivery day, November 21. There followed the slow process of getting Judy off all unnecessary medication. Vern and Sid visited her every day, Vern in the morning, because he lived in Malibu, and passed St. John's on the way to the Transcona office.

One morning, four days before the birth, Vern asked Judy if there was anything she wanted, anything she needed. He thought she seemed strangely subdued. "Do you feel all right?" he asked, solicitously.

Yes, she said. "But there's something bothering me." What was it? Judy said, "I don't know any prayers."

Vern said gently, "But you must know how to talk to whoever it is you want to talk to, don't you?"

No, she told him. She did not know prayers like other people knew. "I'd like to know a prayer that everybody knows."

Vern had no idea that Frank Gumm had been a religious man, a choirmaster, a teacher of catechism in Lancaster; that Judy had grown up in a household where grace was said at every evening meal, and that no Sunday passed that her parents did not take her and her sisters to church. Judy was playing a role, and even Vern was completely taken in.

"Would you like something like 'Our Father'?" he asked.

Oh, yes, said Judy fervently. Well, Vern went on, he was a Catholic, and the Catholic version of the Lord's Prayer was slightly different, but he would teach it to her. He explained that there was also a very short prayer Catholics used called the Hail Mary. "We repeat 'Hail Mary' over and over when we do the Rosary."

Judy's face lit up. "Teach me both of them," she said, eagerly. Vern did, and when she had memorized them, she said humbly, "Now I know these, would it be all right for me to cross myself?"

Vern glanced at her, but she was all seriousness. "Well, it wouldn't be wrong for you to," he said judiciously. "There's no law against it. But you don't have to. Because you now have two pieces of dialogue that you know, and if they give you comfort—fine. That's what they're for."

Judy's eyes sparkled. "Oh, wonderful, Vern. But there's one other thing. I don't have a will." Could he have drawn up a simple will leaving one half of everything to Sid, and the other half to Liza and the new baby? He might ask Bill Hinkle, the very bright young lawyer who had set up Judy and Sid's corporation, to draw one up specifically tailored to her needs.

The next morning when he dropped in, Vern could report that he had seen Hinkle, and Bill would be happy to draw up an informal but binding last will and testament. "It won't be couched in frightening terms, Judy—I mean, it won't terrify you to read it or sign it."

Judy sighed in relief. "It's very important that I do that and get some order in my life."

Not only in the morning, but each night now, on his way home, Vern made it his practice to visit her just before "lights out" in the hospital, and together they recited the prayers he had taught her. Judy was not formal about it; there would always be a conversation about beauty, poetry, ideals, ethical values, the Bible, and then they would find themselves both reciting, "Our Father which art in heaven . . ."

On November 21, the baby was born by Caesarean section. She was small—six pounds, four ounces—blond, blue-eyed and perfect. Judy was delighted that it was a girl, and Liza overjoyed that she had a baby half-sister. Judy and Sid named the child Lorna, for different reasons. Judy, because she had been so moved when she saw Clifford Odets' *Golden Boy*, and Lorna was the name of the female lead. And Sid, because his mother's name was Leonora—and Lorna could be

358

taken as a diminutive of that. And there was a pleasant alliteration about it: Lorna Luft.

Meanwhile, Hinkle had telephoned Vern to say, "I've been working on a hell of a will for her. It's ready." So when Vern visited Judy a day later, he said, "Judy, Bill has the will ready for you to sign—"

Judy looked at him. "Fuck the will," she said. "I don't need it now."

Nor, in all the visits he made to her for the next week that she remained at the hospital, were the prayers ever said again.

Sid was a happy father; he had always wanted a little girl, and here was his own little Judy, his and hers. Judy was to leave the hospital on the sixth or seventh day, and Sid, who had been a faithful visitor twice a day, was in a dilemma. On November 28, the seventh day, he had a horse running at the Bay Meadows race track in San Francisco—a horse called Florence House. When he and Judy had been in Dublin on their European tour, they had visited a famous stud farm. Judy had fallen in love with the beautiful yearling colt, and Sid had bought it as a gift for her for five hundred pounds, and had it shipped to the United States when Judy was appearing at the Palace in late 1951 and early 1952.

Now, having entered the horse in the races in San Francisco, how could he not watch it run? Yet that was the day he was to take Judy and Lorna home from St. John's Hospital. He told Vern to use all his persuasion to keep Judy at the hospital a day longer.

Sid flew to San Francisco; he bet on Florence House; it paid twenty-six to one; he flew back triumphant, walked into St. John's— Judy and the baby were gone. Luft went home. Judy, ensconced in her bed, resting, simply looked at him. He was all apologies. "I don't know. . . ." Judy began to muse, as though this were absolutely beyond belief. "I had to bring my baby home myself." But Sid cajoled her. He had arrived, not only with the money but with flowers, and toys for Lorna, and, after all, the money their lovely little colt had won would pay for Lorna's birth. How could she be angry with him? Now she was the mother of two adorable girls.

But then, subtly, in the next few days Judy's mood changed: a post-partum depression suddenly set in. Not since Judy's collapse at the Palace had there been anything really calamitous. Dr. Pobirs was taking care of her, but it was obvious to Sid that she must be obtaining other medication. Sid instituted a house search, everyone was questioned—clearly Judy was getting pills somewhere. That was the only explanation for her strange shifting moods. Sometimes she changed personality even as you watched. Sid talked not only to Dr. Pobirs but to Dr. Marc; they said, "Watch her." Sid said, "She's so depressed, I can't get her out of it, Vern can't—she's unable even to summon a smile. . . . Crying all the time. Sitting on her bed and crying, or reading and crying, or staring at me. What can I do?"

Vern felt especially guilty. A few days before, Judy had turned to him. "Darling—" she had said, and the way she said it made you weak in the knees—"darling, could you get me two Seconals? I can't reach my doctor, and I really need them." Vern had been warned by Sid: Don't give her any kind of pills. But who could withstand Judy? Vern got her two Seconals, and that started a chain, because she got more somewhere else, and then Dexedrine to knock her out of that, and the combination was torturing her. When she tried to withdraw from them, the need became almost unbearable, the shortness of breath almost intolerable, and in addition she suffered from hallucinations, inflated guilt, terrible hatred of self and others—the result, a compulsion to stop everything, to blot out everything. It was dangerous, Sid was worried, Vern was worried—and finally he told Sid what he had done. "I shouldn't have done it," he said. She had not only prevailed upon him, in a way she had intimidated him. "I'll never do it again," he promised.

When Sid went home—he could not help it—he asked Judy: why had she asked Vern to get her more pills? She had a doctor for that. Look how wretched she was making herself feel. She denied everything. He realized she was drugged even as he tried to reason with her. By an act of will he walked away. But there had been words between them.

Sid returned to his office, leaving an order with Taylor Hardin, the butler. Judy was in her suite, which consisted of an enormous bedroom, a dressing room and a huge bathroom. Taylor was to knock every fifteen or twenty minutes on Judy's door. "Is there anything you need, Mrs. Luft?" And if at any point there was no reply, Taylor was to telephone Luft immediately at his office, three minutes by car from the house.

An hour later Taylor called, upset. The first time he'd knocked, Judy had answered. The second time, she had said, "Will you please stop bothering me?" The third time, there was no answer. He had banged on the door. Still nothing but silence.

Sid was out the door in a flash, shouting over his shoulder to Vern, "Call Pobirs," jumped into his car, drove through red lights and was at the house in no time. He rapped on the door of her suite. "Judy!" —no answer.

He backed up and, with one shoulder down, hurled himself at the door, and was through it as if it were so much plywood. Judy was not on the bed. He knocked on the bathroom door—a heavy door. No answer. He hit that door with all his might, and simply bounced off it. He hit it a second time—it jammed. He hit it a third time—and broke the lock.

He nearly fainted at what he saw. There was blood all over the floor. Using a razor, Judy had cut her throat. He picked her up, grabbed a towel and put it around her neck, placed her on the bed, thinking, *Oh, my God, my darling's dead!* He sat there, pressing the towel to her neck, when Dr. Pobirs, then Pobirs' assistant, burst in almost at the same time. Dr. Pobirs stitched her up. Someone—it may have been Pobirs or his assistant—said, "Judy, you keep this up and you're going to hurt yourself."

So far as anyone could determine, Judy did not know what she had done. Her first question to Sid was "What happened?" She felt the bandages on her neck, but said nothing. Was she acting? Or was it true that the combination of drugs made reality vanish for some unmeasurable time?

But she recuperated, as always, with unbelievable rapidity. While she slept that night with Margaret Gundy keeping watch, Sid and Vern slept on the living room sofas.

Next morning, assured that Judy was still asleep and out of danger, both men went to their offices. About noon Sid walked into Vern's small office, off his own. He said, "Judy just called. We have a command performance." Vern said, "What do you mean?" Sid said, "She wants to see us both—right now." "Oh, shit!" said Vern, and got up.

They walked into Judy's bedroom ten minutes later. Gundy sat in a nearby chair. Judy was sitting up in bed, wearing a favorite silk dressing gown, her hair beautifully done, and a lovely scarf around her neck to hide the bandages. In front of her was a huge tray of what can only be described as a truck driver's breakfast: cornbeef hash, three poached eggs, a stack of toast, a pot of tea, orange juice, marmalade. . . . And this was the girl who the night before had wanted to kill herself.

The two men, feeling like two little boys brought to the principal's office, sat down on a sofa facing her.

She stared at them. Then she spoke. "Sid, I just have to tell you this. You must make a decision. It is either him or me."

Vern, as she saw it, had betrayed her by telling Sid he had given her the Seconals.

Sid's response was simple and immediate. He started to laugh. The more he laughed, the more furious she got, and she called him every name she could think of, interspersed with the usual four-letter words, which had even Gundy turning red, and then—Judy couldn't help it—she began laughing, too.

A day later she was on the telephone to Vern. "Hello, darling, how are you? Why don't you come by and have lunch or something?" How could you get angry at her?

A few days later Sid suggested they give a dinner party, inviting a houseful of people, including Abe Lastfogel, head of the Morris Agency. There were rumors that wild things had been happening at the Luft-Garland home, and Sid wanted to scotch them. It was a highly successful party: the Gary Coopers, the Humphrey Bogarts, the top echelon of the film colony—*and Judy sang.*

Her dress had a high collar, so no one noticed anything. But Sid Luft, standing in the back of the room, listening to her, was like a man in an ague, fearful that the stitches might burst. Nothing happened. The girl was indestructible.

Three nights after the suicide attempt, she had noticed a huge, black-and-blue bruise on his right shoulder. "What's that?" she asked. It was where Sid had nearly dislocated his shoulder breaking down the bathroom door. "I was wrestling with some guys at a bar the other night," he said.

Now things began to happen so quickly one could hardly keep count. She bought herself a rope of pearls, which she could loop around her neck to hide the telltale signs of what she had done to herself. The scar, Dr. Pobirs assured her, would eventually disappear.

Sid and Judy found themselves discussing their new film by the hour. They had both wanted Moss Hart to write the script for *A Star Is Born*, Harold Arlen and Ira Gershwin to write the score and songs, George Cukor to direct, and although shooting would not start for months—Moss, Harold and Ira needed at least four months for their work—the deal for the picture was finally signed between Transcona

Enterprises and Warner Brothers. All this, in December.

In the middle of the month Jack Warner made a telephone call to Sid. "This isn't about *Star*," he said. He had a personal favor to ask. He and his wife, Ann, were giving their daughter, Barbara, a sensational coming-out party in New York the first week of January, at the St. Regis Roof. Elsa Maxwell would handle it. Would Sid—could Sid —prevail upon Judy to sing at Barbara's coming-out party? Before Sid could protest, Jack took the words out of his mouth. Of course Judy wasn't one anyone would dream of hiring to sing at a private party, but since they were in a business relationship, and since Barbara would be terribly thrilled, Jack would be indebted to Judy "if she'd do it for the kid"—he meant Barbara—and in return he would be honored to give Judy any gift her heart desired. And they would all—Judy, Sid, Lorna—be Jack's guests in New York.

Judy liked the idea. It had been a long, troublesome pregnancy, God knew; and this was a chance for a vacation in New York and, since she'd had her baby, a chance to look pretty again. Warner's would handle matters in a first-class fashion, she knew.

So it was arranged.

On Christmas Day, Sid, Judy, one-month-old Lorna and her nurse went aboard the Manhattan Limited for New York. Judy had decorated a little Christmas tree, about two and a half feet high, and wrapped it with bright tissue paper; Sid carried a bucket of champagne and a turkey prepared by Chasen's; and they celebrated that Christmas Day on the train. That night in their Pullman car Sid found a love note from Judy. She was in the habit of writing little missives to him, on impulse, on her cream-colored stationery with "JGL" monogrammed in red. This one said, "Dearest: I wish you a merry Xmas with all my heart and love. May we always be as happy and as lucky and as everything as we are today. God bless you, Judy." At home, she would write on anything she might find. One message, on blue-lined school-pad paper—undoubtedly taken from one of Liza's notebooks—read: "Darling, thank you for the lovely flowers and sweet cards. Sorry I was too petty to say that when you came home in the evening from the races. But I loved receiving them, and I love you so very deeply—forever. Let me help you in whatever way I can, please. Just tell me what to do, and when. Goodnight, my dear, dear husband.—Judy."

What did it matter to Sid what he had gone through—or what

might yet lie ahead? He had entered this marriage with his eyes open, concerned, but overwhelmed by this girl. She was like an elemental force. He had never met anyone like her. He was her slave —even as he believed he was her master. He loved her more and more as time went by.

In New York they were met by a limousine from Warner's, and put up at the Waldorf. They celebrated New Year's Eve at a private party given by friends of Charlie Cushing—the Duke and Duchess were there, and Judy and the Duke harmonized at the piano—at the Sherry-Netherland; and the night of Barbara Warner's party at the St. Regis Roof, Judy was in magnificent voice.

In Los Angeles, early the next afternoon, Harry Rabwin made two long-distance telephone calls. The first—because he knew directly where to call—was to Jimmy, in Dallas. Johnny, her husband, was home, and fourteen-year-old Judalein was having her lunch. Jimmy picked up the phone. Harry said, "Jimmy, this is Harry Rabwin."

Jimmy said instantly, in a voice of horror, "My mother is dead!" burst into tears and dropped the phone. John picked it up. At the other end Rabwin was completely astonished. It was true. And Jimmy had sensed it with the first words out of his mouth. Ethel Gilmore had been found dead at 11:30 A.M. that morning, lying between two cars, in the parking lot of the Douglas Aircraft Company in Santa Monica. She had died of a heart attack a moment after getting out of her car about four hours earlier. It was January 5, 1953. How Jimmy knew it she was never able to explain. Her mother had left Dallas just a few days before after spending the Christmas holidays with them.

Then Harry made another call—to Judy. He had already called Suzy, who with her husband, Jack Cathcart, now lived in Brentwood, a Los Angeles suburb. Harry wasn't sure where Judy was to be found. He knew only the Lufts had gone to New York. He found them at the Waldorf, and spoke to Sid, who was paged in the lobby. After Sid hung up, he was walking, almost dazed, through the lobby. He saw Elsa Maxwell and told her the news. She said, "Oh, don't tell Judy now—not until after she sings tonight. Otherwise, she won't be able to." Judy was to sing at a benefit that night at the Waldorf, another affair of Elsa's.

Luft walked away swearing. He would tell Judy at once—how could he not? He dreaded telling her. He knew it would devastate her. Judy had not seen her mother for a long time. Ethel had wanted to go to St. John's to see her new grandchild, and Judy had left orders that Mrs. Gilmore was not to be permitted to see her. Ethel's eyes were swollen for three days with weeping. She had telephoned Jimmy, who had been outraged. "Oh, Mama, just go into the maternity ward. One of the nurses will point Lorna out to you." No, Ethel had said. Judy had given orders to the doctors, nurses and interns, that her mother was not to see Lorna, and she would not sneak in if that was what she had to do to see her own grandchild. And Ethel had never seen Lorna.

When Sid told Judy, she put her hands over her face and broke down, sobbing hysterically. Then she stopped. "I must get to California," she said. "I must call Jimmy and Suzy." She telephoned them both and, having spoken with them, felt a little better. "We'll all meet at the house," she told them. Though she was utterly terrified of flying, they went by plane that night. She was in an agony of a dozen different emotions; Sid found her biting into a pillow to control herself, even under sedation.

At the Maple Drive house, the three sisters met for the first time in a long while. Harry Rabwin, with Jimmy and Suzy, went to Forest Lawn and made arrangements for a private funeral; and presently Dr. Marc, Judy and her sisters, their three husbands, Jack Cathcart and Johnny Thompson and Sid, Tully and Dottie, all went to the funeral parlor to see Ethel in her coffin.

Vern helped, but it was Judy and her sisters who arranged the services at the Little Church of the Flowers at Forest Lawn Memorial Park. When the funeral director asked Judy if she wanted music, Judy said, "Yes—but unfamiliar music." The playing of any music associated with her mother would have tortured her the more.

The newspapers were cruel: Judy a star—her mother a clerk in a factory. The services were held at noon the next day, all three sisters sitting together in a row, in order of age, as once, so many years before, they had arrayed themselves behind Ethel, as she sat at the piano and coached them. They were all in black, Judy in a long black dress, her eyes hidden by enormous black sunglasses, and all weeping.

Fourteen-year-old Judalein sat thinking of her Nanna, now in her coffin, before the altar and the flowers. Ethel had been a good grandmother to her. What kind of a mother she had been to Judy—what

Judy had against her—Judalein would never know.

Was there something there, about Nanna as a mother? wondered Judalein, listening to the slow, mournful organ music.

In another row, among Ethel's oldest friends, sat Peg DeVine. *Poor Ethel!* she thought, trying to stop her tears. It had been only a few weeks ago that Ethel had driven over to pick her up for a game of poker with several women friends. As they were driving, Ethel unexpectedly stopped the car and began to cry. Peg had never heard a woman cry like that. It was about Judy. She was saying, "What have I done wrong? What did I do that she hates me so?" Peg thought, *Oh, dear, this is terrible.* "Let's keep on going—you'll feel better once we start playing—it'll just be the five or six of us." "No," Ethel managed to say. "I just can't go on." Peg said, "All right, just drop me off back at my house," and Ethel turned the car around, and did so, and they played no cards that night.

She was not a well woman, Peg thought. And the most unhappy woman she had ever seen. She had lately developed diabetes; she had always had high blood pressure. Once she came over to Peg's, and started up a flight of stairs, and Peg, several years older, had to hurry down to the landing and help her up the rest of the steps, she was so out of breath. To get that life insurance policy so that each of her girls would receive $15,000, plus $5,000 set aside for funeral expenses, Ethel had had to take pills to bring her blood pressure down. She never took care of herself. She'd laugh if you talked about it. She'd take a pill, and then a drink. Peg would say, "Oh, Ethel, you shouldn't do that." Peg wept again, and when she dried her eyes, she thought: *Ethel wished that heart attack on herself.*

Jimmy sat there, drained. Only a few days ago she and her husband Johnny had said good-bye to her mother after her Christmas visit to Dallas. One night they had sat all together before the fire—Jimmy, and Johnny, and Ethel, and Johnny's parents, Mr. and Mrs. John Thompson, Sr., and they were talking. Ethel said, "Remember the other night when we went to the midnight service?" This was in the Episcopal church nearby in Dallas. "Do you remember what the minister said? He said, 'We had better keep our wicks trimmed, because we don't know when we will need them.' " Then she had added, "I have an idea I'm going to need mine, soon." The elder Mrs. Thompson had said, "I'll tell you one thing, Ethel, if anybody gets up yonder in heaven, you'll get there." Ethel had said, "Oh, I hope so."

366

Then the services in the Little Church of the Flowers were over, and they all returned to the house, and the word went out that Judy Garland was in seclusion and would see no one.

27

ONE CAN ONLY SPECULATE on what went through Judy's mind during the funeral and in the days after, when, as the newspapers reported, she canceled all engagements. For years after Ethel's death Judy would wake suddenly, a scream in her throat; it was always the same nightmare. She heard her mother's voice crying out, "Help me! Help me!" but no matter how frantically she searched, no matter with what headlong speed she hurled herself down long, dark, frightening corridors crying, "Mama! Mama! Where are you?" she could not find her. Only the despairing voice in her ear.

Before the funeral, when they had all gone to the funeral parlor to look upon Ethel in her coffin, Judy had begun to wail, throwing her arms around Jimmy's husband, crying brokenly, "I didn't want her to die." Johnny could not be sure. Was she saying, *I hated her, I blamed her for my unhappiness, I wanted to hurt her, but I didn't want her to die?* Johnny had said, and the moment he spoke the words he wanted to withdraw them, "Judy, you better straighten up. You have a lot to live with. I wouldn't want that on my conscience," and she had wept, clinging tightly to him.

She knew, as she looked on her mother's face in the coffin, that there had been a night, after one of their terrible confrontations, when Ethel, the strongest of women, had tried to commit suicide. They had had a bitter argument at the Minnelli house, and Ethel had left in a fury. Ethel had gone to one of Judy's doctors and created a scene: he must stop prescribing sleeping and wake-up pills for her. Then there had been the time Ethel and Helen Fisher had gone to Topeka and Ethel had tried to commit Judy to the Menninger Clinic; and in later years Judy would say—and this was unquestionably hallucination on Judy's part, stemming from medication—that Ethel would telephone her late at night at this period and say, in a voice of utmost seriousness, "Judy, you have something wrong with your brain, don't you know? You must be operated upon." With the other pressures on her she simply had not the strength to deal with Ethel, who, in her insistence on ministering to her, succeeding only in agitating and distressing her more. So the day Ethel rushed out of Judy's house and arrived home (as Jimmy told Judy later), she was more enraged than Jimmy had seen her in many months. It was after five in the afternoon. Ethel excused herself and went upstairs. Jimmy began preparing dinner; Judalein was playing in another room.

By the time the food was ready, it was nearly seven o'clock. There had been no sound from Ethel, who was always on time, and they always ate at 6:30. Jimmy sat down to wait for her. She knew her mother had sleeping tablets. Had she taken them, and how many? As though it had been told her as a fact, the conviction rose in Jimmy that her mother had indeed swallowed an overdose, and that if she went upstairs into Ethel's room, she would find her unconscious on the bed. Jimmy was always to remember how she had sat alone at the dinner table, pondering. Her mother was the unhappiest person she knew; she had been unhappy for so long! *What do you do when someone wants to kill themselves? Do you let them? Don't they have the right to end their own suffering? . . . No, I can't, I can't!*—and that thought propelled her out of her chair and up the stairs and into her mother's room, to find her lying, eyes closed, on the bed. She was breathing, but she could not be wakened.

The evidence was on the dresser: a bottle that had contained two hundred Seconal tablets, half-empty. She had spilled some on the floor, she had been so upset; and nearby stood an open half-pint of whiskey. She had not only swallowed the pills, she had chased them down with whiskey.

All this had taken but a few seconds to see and understand, and then Jimmy was on the phone to Dr. Marc. He was there in minutes, he could not rouse Ethel, the ambulance came, he followed it to the hospital, she telephoned Judy and Vincente, and met them moments later at the hospital, and they waited until Dr. Marc emerged to say, "Yes, it was an overdose, but I think we got most of it. She'll be all right." But he would allow none of them to see her until nine o'clock the next morning.

The next day, when Judy and Vincente arrived, a few minutes after nine, Judy white-faced, Vincente holding rein on her and himself,

Jimmy was already there. She had seen her mother, and had been appalled at how terrible she looked—she was barely able to talk, but was slowly recuperating. To Judy, who sat trembling on the bench in the hospital corridor, Jimmy said, "You better go in and see her."

Judy, undergoing a torture of guilt and fear, managed to get the words out: "I don't know, Jimmy . . . Maybe I should talk to my analyst first."

Though Jimmy realized that Judy feared her own breakdown at this moment, she said angrily, roughly, hoping it would shock Judy into positive action, "For God's sake, Judy, at least go in and tell her you're glad she's alive! You can see your analyst some other time!"

Judy had gone in, and had her moment with her mother, and come out shaken.

Now Ethel was dead—at sixty. But her death certificate, filled out by Suzy, still gave her birth year as 1896, not 1893. The cruel newspaper stories continued, and when a statement was finally issued, it said only that, though Judy and her mother had been estranged at the time of Mrs. Garland's death, they had been developing a closer relationship, and Judy had been arranging for the purchase of income property for her mother, now that Judy was getting back on her feet.

What saved Judy now was the intense activity that began to swirl about her. There was Lorna; the purchase of a new enormous house; and the all-encompassing furor of beginning the first of what was planned to be a series of major films with Warner's under the aegis of Transcona. Within a fortnight of the funeral, Harold Arlen, Ira Gershwin and Moss Hart were on the scene, beginning work on *A Star Is Born,* and in constant consultation with Judy and Sid. George Cukor had accepted the job of directing the film. Sid and Judy were both courting Cary Grant, who was doubtful about playing the Norman Maine role.

The Lufts' new house was palatial: a huge nineteen-room stone Tudor mansion formerly owned by Hunt Stromberg, the producer, in Holmby Hills, with a living room more than forty feet long. Sid, the athlete, had built a trampoline in the back yard, on which Liza, Johnny, Judy and he could bounce up and down. He set up pulleys and weights on the second-floor veranda, also, for the children to exercise with. The house had huge bay windows with window seats, and complete quarters for Princess Liza, complete quarters for Princess Lorna, a suite for Judy, an adjoining suite for Sid (if either wished privacy), servants' quarters, a first-floor porch, and a huge lawn, front and back. That Liza was to continue to be a permanent part of the family was tremendously important to Judy. The original divorce agreement stipulated that Vincente was to have custody six months of the year, Judy the remainder, during which Vincente would pay Judy $500 a month for her support. But Vincente had returned to his bachelor way of life, and Liza had been with Sid and Judy since they had moved into the Maple Drive house. Sid's son, Johnny, would move in for a while, too. So there would be Judy, Sid, the three children, and a full retinue of nurses, governesses and the regular staff, which included a butler, cook, chauffeur, maids and gardener. In time expenses at the Mapleton Drive house would exceed $8,000 a month.

Their social life was exciting: a party by Dr. Marc and Marcella for Dr. Alexander Fleming, the discoverer of penicillin, and Lady Fleming; one by Jack Warner for the Duke and Duchess of Windsor, with the Duchess and Judy embracing and Sid and the Duke gripping hands warmly as only old golfing companions can; cocktails with Aly Khan in the Polo Lounge of the Beverly Hills Hotel, with Sid and Aly expertly discussing horseflesh; parties at Cole Porter's, dinners at the Jack Bennys'—choose a name, and Judy and Sid were there. Judy bought Sid a pair of diamond cufflinks she designed herself; he bought her a diamond engagement ring, a little late, but something she had always wanted.

Not that they didn't have lovers' quarrels; now and then Judy would throw a tantrum, but Sid was learning how to handle it: he would put on his hat and walk out. Disappear. He knew Judy could not stand to be alone. She would talk about it later to friends, giving it her own inimitable twist, making light of it. "Oh, Christ!" she would say. "How can you play a scene alone? That's no fun. Now I got to pull myself together and start calling around—'Is Mr. Luft there? Is he in New York? I'm trying to find the son of a bitch.' I can't find him. Three days later my phone rings. I hear that voice: 'Are we through menstruating, honey?' I scream at him, 'Where are you? Where are you? Come home, come home! Yes, I'm through, come home!' " And she would laugh at herself. "He is a son of a bitch, but I love him."

On Mapleton Drive, two houses to their right, on the same side of the street, lived Humphrey Bogart and Lauren Bacall; the Bogarts, too, had a five-month-old little girl, Leslie, as well as a four-year-old boy, Stephen, so Judy and Betty were at each other's places constantly. Across the street lived Art Linkletter; next to him, Sammy Cahn; not far away, Bing Crosby and his four sons; Gloria Grahame —it was quite an exciting street.

Sid and Judy were moving in new, stimulating circles. When they signed Moss Hart, the fabulous "Swifty" Lazar, the demon agent (he represented Moss, as well as Ira Gershwin, Harold Arlen and Frank Sinatra), had celebrated with a party. Sinatra was then separated from Ava Gardner, unhappy, somehow halted in his career, and at this time living with Lazar in the latter's apartment. More than once he came over to the Lufts' and slept overnight on a sofa in the huge living room.

It was at the Lazar party that Sid Luft for the first time met Humphrey Bogart. Bogey, though a menacing figure on the screen, was a small elegant man. He had been drinking that night, and began taking off on Luft. He'd heard all about Luft. What was this character doing on Mapleton Drive, moving in on his, Bogey's, territory? Luft had better behave or else . . .

Sid unexpectedly picked Bogey up by pinning both arms to his sides and holding him at arm's length a foot off the floor, squirming and struggling, yelling, "Put me down, goddamnit!" Sid kissed him on one cheek and said, "You and I are going to be good friends. We won't needle each other, because I'll split your head open, Bogey," and then he set him carefully down.

Bogey, after a moment of near-apoplexy, burst into laughter. Everyone joined in, and the ice was broken. Bogey and Sid began to talk. "How about me doing the Norman Maine part?" Bogey asked. Warner had suggested Bogart, too. But Bogey, already in his fifties, was too old to play opposite Judy, even with a hairpiece. Though Judy was nearly thirty-one, she'd have no difficulty, with a little loss of weight, appearing to be in her early twenties at the beginning of the picture.

Sinatra, too, wondered whether he might not play Norman Maine. Jack Warner vetoed this immediately. Both Judy and Sid had their hearts set on Cary Grant—Judy, particularly, because she had a private crush on him. He would be superb. The descent from the dignity of a charming, elegant and handsome man, a true matinee idol, into a broken, pathetic alcoholic would wring your heart.

It was Sid's job to convince Cary. He discovered that Grant liked the horses, too; and so, though Judy raised an eyebrow over their choice of a place for business discussions, Sid and Cary spent considerable time together at the Hollywood Park Race Track.

Meanwhile, Moss and Kitty Hart had gone to Palm Springs, where Moss was working on the script. Judy and Sid decided to go there, too, for a brief vacation. Presently, they discovered that Harold Arlen was also there.

One Sunday while Sid, Judy and Harold, all in golf clothes, were on the links, Harold absent-mindedly began to whistle a tune. It was something Judy had never heard before, with the catchiest melody. "What's that you're whistling, Harold?" she asked. He blushed. He was caught. He and Ira had finished two songs for *Star* in as many weeks, and they had agreed to keep this a secret. Ira had said, "My God, don't let them know that we did these two so quickly, or they'll expect us to finish the score in no time." And Harold had been whistling one of them.

He fumbled for an answer. "Oh, it's nothing."

Judy grabbed his arm. She knew well enough it must be for their picture. "C'mon, Harold," she said, and she literally dragged him to a little bar on the grounds. "It's Sunday, there's a piano in there, nobody'll be around now—"

She all but ran, pulling Harold with her, Sid lumbering after. She was right: the place was empty. Harold sat down at the old upright; Judy, in her spike shoes, bandanna, little knee-length golf skirt and thick golf socks, curled up on one wooden chair; Sid sat in another; and Arlen played and sang "The Man That Got Away"—Judy's greatest song in *Star*, an Oscar nominee as best song of the year, and thereafter one of Judy's trademarks. When Harold finished, she threw her arms around him. "I love it, play it again!" He did, and then the three hurried over to find Moss and Kitty in their bungalow, and Harold played and sang it for them, too.

By June the Lufts were well settled in their new house. Judy celebrated her thirty-first birthday at the Gershwins', and here Liza for the first time sang some of her mother's songs, before one of the most select audiences in Hollywood. One of the guests was Otto Preminger, who years later was to direct Liza in *Tell Me That You Love Me, Junie Moon* early in her own film career.

Then came the night a delivery boy brought the first draft of Moss

Hart's script of *Star* to the Mapleton Drive house. It was well after midnight, and the entire house was asleep, save for Judy and Sid.

They settled themselves in the downstairs den, curled up in a love seat, reading it together. They would look up at each other—she was crying, he was crying—and then read again.

When they finished, they looked at each other and simply lost control. They were both singing and dancing, hugging each other, crying, laughing. *Their picture.* And what Moss had done! A marvelous job, for Judy a tour de force, in which she could play all her many roles: imp, child, child-woman, lover, dancer, singer, comedienne, mimic, tragedienne, superstar and healer—tender only as she could be, who, even in her own illness, had been able to walk through a hospital room of sick children and bring peace to them by her very presence—*this was a part!* When Sid first thought of *Star*, it had passed fleetingly through his mind, *What a twist: the rise and fall of a great male star, yet with such overtones of Judy's own story . . .*

"We're going to have a great picture, Judy," Sid said.

Judy asked, "Is it too late to call Moss?" He had just come into town, had dispatched a messenger with the script directly to the Lufts and was grabbing a few hours' sleep before a meeting next morning with Samuel Goldwyn. Neither Judy nor Sid went to bed that night. At 10 A.M. Judy telephoned Moss, and told him how grateful she was.

Despite all Sid's persuasive power, his courting of Cary Grant had failed. Cary agonized over the part. Playing a believable drunk was one of the most difficult acting assignments. The natural tendency of an audience is to find a drunk comic. The elegance was there, Cary knew, but he was also a drawing-room comedian of a high order; suppose, despite himself, the broken, drunken Cary Grant brought not pity, but laughter? So he finally said no, though it was his wife, Betsy Drake, who put a firm period to the discussion.

Late one night in the Mapleton house the doorbell rang. It was Betsy. It was a quarter to midnight; she was in tennis sneakers and shorts, she had just come off their tennis court, they had agreed they could take no more, and she shouted, "Lay off Cary!" He couldn't eat, he couldn't sleep, he was going out of his mind because of this choice thrust upon him—just forget him! Sid and Judy were as diplomatic as possible and accepted the decision as final.

Judy and Sid had always had someone else in mind—just in case. This was the British actor James Mason. After Betsy left, Judy said to

Sid, "Get Mason tomorrow. He'll be a better drunk than Cary anyway." They had both seen Mason in a film or two. To see a man of Mason's reserve, Mason's quiet self-assurance, Mason's intimation of what inner torture or public humiliation would do to him, to see Mason slowly degenerate . . . Judy was right.

Next morning Sid was in touch with Mason's agent: the deal was made over the next few days.

The rest of the casting went swiftly. Charles Bickford, an old friend of Judy's, was cast as studio head, Jack Carson as the fast-talking publicity man, forever covering up Maine's drinking escapades, and Sid was to produce. The deal with Warner's was a big one, actually a multimillion-dollar deal: it contemplated their making nine pictures over six years, three of which were to star Judy, two years to a picture, each a three-million-dollar project, with her having approval of story, director, cast, everything; the other six (one would include Sid's own *Man O' War*) to be made without Judy. Warner's was advancing big money, everyone involved was top-rank.

Shooting began officially on *Star* in the fall of 1953, with Judy rather heavy as she went to the prerecording sessions in the weeks preceding. Jack Warner gave her Bette Davis' dressing room, and once more she was in the movie business—on her own terms, and with her husband as her partner. She began slowly slimming down. She was happy. There were not many major roles in the film: Judy, Mason, Bickford, Carson. Judy and Mason liked each other, and Mason had a sly wit that convulsed her. They had met at parties— Mason's wife, Pamela, was as much an outgoing, often outrageously witty woman as her husband was surprisingly shy and reserved. Now, in *Star*, Judy and Mason were to play man and wife in a turbulent love story.

It was Vern's job, among many—he was also associate producer— to drive Judy to the prerecording sessions. Judy liked Vern's driving; he was slow, careful and one of the least abrasive persons she had ever known.

The subject of James Mason came up.

"You know, of course," said Judy, unexpectedly, "I'm going to fall in love with him." "Really?" said Vern. "Oh, yes, I always fall in love with my leading man." True or not (and it was one of the oldest clichés in show business), and however realistic her love-making with Mason on the set later, everything was going well at home. Sid would walk into his dressing room to find pasted on the mirror one of Judy's little notes: "My darling producer—My pride and love for you are endless—Judy"; or even a note on Father's Day from Lorna, which, in Judy's handwriting, read, "To my darling Daddy—Happy Father's Day, and this one our first, only the beginning! Every year I shall love you more. Your devoted (though small) daughter, Lorna."

The picture moved on, but shooting was delayed, and delayed. There were complex technical hold-ups. Warner wanted to do *Star* in both Technicolor and CinemaScope, a process owned by Fox, which not only demanded a payment for use of the lens, but required the film to be shown in certain theatres where Fox had already installed its CinemaScope projection equipment. Warner told Sid and Judy he had a German scientist working on a new anamorphic lens to be called WarnerScope, which he expected to be better than CinemaScope, and so days passed waiting for this to be perfected.

But there was a Pandora's box of other troubles. Five cameramen were to be used, and in the end, Judy was able to obtain from MGM her favorite, Sam Leavitt, who became director of photography for the film. Simply getting him took weeks of negotiation. There were personality clashes. At one point Judy and Hugh Martin, her pianist at the Palace, the man who with Ralph Blane had written such tremendous Garland hits as "The Trolley Song," argued over how Judy should sing a number; the dispute became so violent that Martin walked off the set and left, permanently. The most expensive craftsmen were hired; this was Judy's picture, and it had to be superlative: everyone outdid himself. Warner's had to borrow Jean Louis, Marlene Dietrich's clothes designer, from Columbia; Irene Sharaff came from MGM to costume the "Born in a Trunk" number.

In the end, CinemaScope had to be used, with a cameraman who had never shot in CinemaScope: in Judy's big number, "The Man That Got Away," the rushes were impossible, had to be thrown away, and Judy had to do it all over again. Costs mounted, the rumors increased so that, whatever the delay, it was laid at Judy's feet: she was, of course, holding up everything. She did, but not to that degree. The result was inevitable. Judy sometimes was almost unable to function.

By this time Luft had developed a special sensitivity to Judy where pills were concerned. He had only to hear a word from her on the phone to know; sometimes, as he drove down Mapleton toward the house, he sensed it even before he got out of the car. It was something subliminal; he himself could not explain it. Perhaps it was her breathing the night before; a glance, an impression. It was not necessary for Judy to do anything to trigger this knowledge. If the pills, whatever they were, were in her, anything might touch her off: the sound of the wind, the color of Luft's tie, a falling leaf—and suddenly Luft would find himself saying, placatingly, "Darling, what did I do? What did I say? What wrong fucking move did I make?" For it would be Judy snapping orders: "Get out! Out!" Or: "You're dismissed! Get lost! You're dead—out, out, out, goddamnit!" Or a gentle knock on her door and a tormented, anguished "Come in, quick, help me."

Once Sid had been told that the doctors at Peter Bent Brigham had said that for Judy to function as she wanted to function, because of her body's acclimatization to drugs for so many years, she might always need a minimal amount of medication. There were days she drew a kind of mescaline from the beat of the music itself when she sang, as from the applause; but other times when nothing stimulated and all depressed her, when, no matter how hard she fought, she had to turn to pills, to liquor, to chemical help. Her dilemma was intensified by lack of food; she would go through periods like an alcoholic, but with medication rather than whiskey; she would become toxic; she would be unable to eat—not even a hamburger with peanut butter, which she loved, or mashed potatoes—food that would at least help absorb and dilute the drugs. Sometimes in the Mapleton house Sid would wake at 10 A.M. and find that Judy had been up all night, trying somehow to get through the hours, playing her own records, ringing people up at three, four in the morning. Once she woke up Roger Edens at 3 A.M., put the mouthpiece of her phone next to the record player playing one of her own records. "Isn't that a voice, Roger!" she was saying, in pure hysterical delight. "What a hell of a voice! Christ, it's good!"

Luft had had long discussions, too, with Dr. Pobirs. His interpretation was that Judy had never grown up emotionally. This had nothing to do with her mentality, or sharpness, or cunning—intellectually and physically she was a grown woman; emotionally she was still Baby Gumm.

"When a baby gets up in the morning," Fred said, "and all is well, he coos, he's having a happy time, he has a good day. But if he wakes up on the wrong side, or something starts him off the wrong way, and he begins to cry, you've got a cranky baby all day."

This was Judy. Any stress could precipitate the problem. She couldn't describe what it was because she couldn't describe it to herself. It wasn't actually a pain; it was crankiness, irritability, depression. When she took pills to knock out the depression—she wanted to be gay, entertaining, that was what she had been brought up to be, that brought her all her rewards, her very identity—then the pills, and lack of food, did lead to acute physical pain—to migraine, to drilling lights in her eyes, to a hypersensitivity—which in turn led her to take more pills to knock out the pain. Then, when the pain vanished, there was a great lassitude, a feeling of intense malaise and an overwhelming fear that she'd get out there and be unable to sing, unable to act.

Yet when she was functioning, she was terrific. When she redid "The Man That Got Away," she was thinner, costumed differently and superb. Gundy, her psychiatric nurse, was on the set in street clothes, introduced simply as her secretary, carrying out her doctor's orders. Judy was at the floor of her medication: six grains of Seconal for sleep, and during the course of the day a certain amount of Dexamyl.

How she worked on *Star!* One day the actress Ina Claire, a friend of Cukor's, came on the set and watched Judy; later, she said to him, "That girl should work two hours, and then be taken home in an ambulance! How she gives herself!" Critics were to say later she played scenes with raw nerves, so real that they were almost embarrassed to watch.

Shooting on the main sequences of the picture ended in March 1954. Then there was a period of shutdown and re-examination of what had been done. There came a day, during the shutdown, when Judy said, "Sid, you know I'm in a bind. I know you know, but I've been taking too much medication, even more than you know about. I want to get off it, now."

They went down that morning to Ojai, one of the most beautiful towns in Southern California, to rest, to recoup their strength and to play golf, taking a cabin on the golf course of the Ojai Inn. Sid knew better than to make any suggestions that might upset her. He said, "I came here to play golf. You do whatever you want to do, Baby."

Then: "Would you like to come out on the course with me?"

She said, "No. No golf. I want to get off my medication. I need time to do it. I want you to help me."

He put away his clubs. "O.K.," he said. "You tell me what to do."

She said, "We are going to stay right in this room. I don't want you to go out, or to play golf, or to do anything, but stay in this room and play gin with me, and I'm going to get off what I'm taking by myself."

They unpacked the bags. He ordered breakfast. She ate nothing. He had lunch. She did not eat. By nightfall she was beginning to perspire. Sid thought, *My God, she's going to do it cold turkey.*

She began to tremble. "Just hold me," she said. He put his arms around her. She was trembling and perspiring. "Don't worry about it," she said. "Just hold me." She shook, and it took all his strength to hold her. It was now nearly 11 P.M. No, midnight. They had been spending the hours playing gin rummy, watching television, walking in circles about the room, Judy seized by fits of shaking, Sid holding her.

The sweat started pouring from her. Her trembling increased. "Judy, I better call a doctor," Sid said, as gently as he could. No, she said, no doctor. She grew worse. "Judy, I'm going to call a doctor!" She screamed at him. "No! Don't! Don't call a doctor! No needles, no needles, no doctor, nothing, for God's sake, don't!"

For the next twelve hours, from midnight until nearly noon, they went through mutual agony, he holding her, she screaming into a pillow, into his chest, gritting her teeth, holding on to the wall as he supported her, he taking her back to the bed, holding her down, she suddenly unconscious, then coming back again, fighting, fighting, fighting, until, around noon, whatever it was broke, and she lay limp, her eyes open, no longer struggling, in a kind of peace. She said, weakly, "Darling, order me a steak—a great big steak, with mashed potatoes and butter, and just lie close to me until it comes."

Then there were four wonderful days, of golf, and sun, and swimming, and disbelief that what had happened, had happened. They had actually taken a dangerous risk. It was not the first time Judy would attempt to rid herself of her devils in this manner; she succeeded now because she was still young, "but you took a hell of a responsibility," Dr. Pobirs told Sid later. He should have called a doctor. Judy could have suffered convulsions, she might have injured herself in many ways. But she had won out.

378

Then, after everyone returned to Warner's, and they saw what had been shot so far, it was clear that an important segment was missing from *A Star Is Born*. The audience had to be shown why Judy was such a star. The story said a star was born, but there was no proof. A discussion with Roger Edens and his assistant, Leonard Gershe, led to the conclusion that what was needed was a major musical number which would prove to the audience how great a star Esther Blodgett, now Vicki Lester (as Frances Gumm had become Judy Garland), had become. Thus, the genesis of "Born in a Trunk," written by Roger and Leonard. This was an eighteen-minute musical sequence showing a girl becoming a star, incorporating such songs as "Swanee," "I'll Get By," "My Melancholy Baby," with "Swanee" as the stirring finale with full chorus.

So, ultimately, the picture was made.

At times Cukor had allowed Judy to shoot at night, when she was her best, shooting around her during the day where possible, for she was in nearly every scene. It cost more money, more time; but he worked closely with her, and he was able with his skill to introduce, where necessary, a lightness that balanced the tragedy of the story.

Cukor had directed some of the greatest actresses in contemporary film history—Garbo, Ethel Barrymore, Katharine Hepburn, so many others. Judy aroused his admiration, not only as an actress but because of her quick intelligence, her originality, her captivating humor. And he was excited, too, watching her discover things about herself as an actress. Despite all the films she had made, she had never before been in one which demanded such skill, one which really tried her. Cukor found her a brilliant and creative actress; and he concluded that when she did not come on the set, it was not willfulness, or self-indulgence, or bitchiness; mainly it was that she was not in condition, and knew it. She simply could not bear to see herself appear when she was not at her best.

Cukor, expert as he was at handling women, knew how to deal with Judy. On one occasion, everyone had been kept waiting more than three hours for her to get to the lot, and then she had refused to come out of her dressing room. The assistant director was beside himself; and Cukor, who did not like to fetch anyone, and knew that Judy certainly did not want to be fetched, nonetheless said, "I'll go in and ask her to come out."

He walked into her dressing room. It was large, luxurious, with a huge sofa, and all four walls mirrored. As he opened the door, he saw her sitting at the dressing room table, her head down, resting on her crossed arms, the picture of dejection. He saw her from the back, but because of the mirrors he also saw her from every angle and saw himself as he entered, splintered into a dozen different images. He did not know quite what to say, and he heard himself asking, solicitously, "Is anything wrong?"

Then, realizing how ridiculous his words were, he burst into laughter. Judy began to heave with laughter, as she sat there, not even lifting her head. Then she rose, resignedly. "This is the story of my life," she said. "I'm about to shoot myself and I'm asked if there's anything wrong—" And she came out.

But what he remembered most vividly was a scene in which Vicki Lester had to turn on a young actor who, in the film, insisted upon her doing something she did not wish to do—while she, Judy, was deeply depressed.

She looked at Cukor, and he realized she would have to dig it out of herself, even in her depression. She said, "Do I really let myself go?" Cukor said yes.

She played the scene, pushing at it, and Cukor had never seen such controlled fury; it rose out of her with a power so real, so overwhelming, that he had goose-pimples. He thought, *Oh, wow, wow, wow* . . . He was afraid the other actor would crumple under it. Cukor had never witnessed an explosion of such terrifying power.

"Judy, that was just glorious!" he exclaimed. "My blood froze."

She looked at him, tears still in her eyes, and said, "You should come out to the house, George—I do that every afternoon."

That wit, that mordant wit, it seemed to Cukor, was her saving grace in such moments.

But there were genuinely terrible times, too. There was one period when it was impossible to get Judy even to the studio. Nothing Sid could say, or Warner, or Cukor, would get her to leave the house. She sat about, depressed, remote, unreachable. Finally Harold Arlen was prevailed upon to call on her at home, and see what he could do. Her respect for him was tremendous.

It was a time fairly early in the making of the film, before the Ojai experience. For days shooting had been at an impasse. Cukor had, as usual, shot around her. But this was no longer possible. Now they

380

were at their wits' end. Expenses were soaring, she was hurting only herself, so much rode on *Star*, her very future. . . .

Harold had not only written "Over the Rainbow" for Judy; he had dated her even before she had known David Rose. He accepted the mission reluctantly. A shy, reclusive man, everything in his nature shrank from exerting pressure on Judy when she was going through some dark private torture which he could only imagine but had never been able to understand.

He went to the Mapleton house. It was late afternoon. Sid was out, the children were out. The front door was open. He walked in. Judy was there. She welcomed him. By her manner he saw at once that she was medicated, yet she could manage a weak smile, and accept his kiss on her cheek and, as he held her, cling to him for a moment.

He made no mention of her absence from the set. Instead: "Judy, I have some new songs Ira and I wrote—I'd like you to hear them." He sat down at the piano, she snuggled next to him on the bench, and he sang and played his songs.

Then he began to talk. What he said, in essence, was this:

"Judy, you came just a little while ago from a triumph in San Francisco, and before that Los Angeles, and before that the Palace. They loved you. They greeted you there as no other person has ever been greeted. They adored you. Before that you came from a tremendous triumph at the Palladium. In England they love and adore you. You have two beautiful children, you have a man who loves you dearly, and works for you. You are in a film, your own film, which has tremendous possibilities."

Judy sat silently.

"You are loved and adored all over the world. You have had successes beyond number." He paused. "Don't you realize what you have, Judy? Few persons on earth have as much as you." He put his arm about her and held her close.

After a moment, she rose and sat down in a big armchair. She said, slowly, "With all that you have told me, Harold, and in spite of what you have told me, if I had a barrel of Dexamyl, I would take it right now." She looked out the window. Her face was pale and drawn. "I don't know where to turn or what to do," she said. Her voice was utterly without hope.

His heart went out to her. He left a few minutes later. He had not mentioned the set, nor her absence from it. He could not bring himself to do so. At the door she clung to him again for a moment. He thought, *This is really a lost soul.*

But he was wrong.

For, three days later, restored from whatever magical resources she had within her, she was back on the set, again enthusiastic, full of spirit, driving like a pile driver in her scenes; her voice, when she sang, inimitable—again the incomparable Judy.

There were no rules to deal with her.

FINALLY, *A Star Is Born* WAS FINISHED. It had begun late; on October 12, 1953, Luft gave Judy a bracelet appropriately engraved: "Columbus discovered America on October 12, 1492. Judy Garland began principal photography on A Star Is Born on October 12, 1953. With all my love—Sid."

Actually, there had been weeks of prerecordings and other work before that Monday morning. Records show that they had been ready to start shooting in June, but that Warner's indecision over what method of photography to use considerably delayed matters. The "Born in a Trunk" sequence, an afterthought, was not shot until July 1954; the first preview of the rough cut occurred in August. The picture had been a long time in the making, the budget had soared to nearly $5 million, but they had a picture running three and a half hours—compared to the usual hour and forty minutes.

One day Warner called Luft to his office. He showed him a wire from Sam Goldwyn: "Dear Jack: You have a fantastic picture. I just saw the rough cut. I love it. With proper handling, it should gross $25,000,000. Regards." If it grossed that figure, Judy and Sid's share would be four or five million dollars. Goldwyn was known as one of the shrewdest judges of a picture's potential. Said Warner, "Looks like we've got a hit."

As Luft remembered that meeting, Jack was so delighted that he offered Judy and him a bonus—a trip to the South of France. He had a villa at Cap d'Antibes, where he usually spent August. Sid returned to tell Judy: a month's vacation in the South of France. Jack, he said, had offered to "blow them" to the entire thing, but Sid told him, "If we're going to make that kind of money, we don't want you to blow us to a trip. Why not advance us the money from the profits?" Otherwise, it would be an in-house thing—as at Metro—and Judy's independence would be destroyed, the one thing she treasured.

Jack had said, "Better yet, I'll loan it to you."

So Sid had signed a note for $30,000—what with the expenses of maintaining the Mapleton house while they were away, taxes, staff, the children, he had estimated that they would need that much money, including their expenses abroad—against the expected four- or five-million profit from the film, and in return, Jack had given him a check for $25,000, the remaining $5,000 to be delivered to Sid and Judy in French francs, once they arrived in Paris en route to Cap d'Antibes. Sid wanted to take Vern along, and it was all set.

Judy said, "I don't want to go." Sid stared at her. "All I'll be doing will be a promotional tour for the picture. It won't be a vacation. Let's go somewhere else."

They argued. He said, "Look, darling, I sort of made the deal." She said, "How will we go?" He said, "We'll fly." She said, "I don't want to fly. I want to relax. Let's get on a sailboat and sail somewhere." "Oh, Baby," he said, "really—this is all part of the business." She said, "I know it is. When is it going to stop?" He said, "Not until this picture gets off the ground." She said, "What you should do is stay here with Cukor and help cut the picture." He said, "Judy, I've had it up to my fucking gourd. I'm beat. I'd like to go away someplace. Let's go, we'll have some laughs. If we don't, we'll take some side trips. Look," he said. "I got this $25,000." He snapped the check in his fingers.

She said, finally, "You've got your head set that way, so I might as well make up my mind I'm going to go."

One week later they were in Paris: Judy, Sid, Vern, Jack, his houseman, two other friends, having flown to France in a chartered plane owned by Howard Hughes. Sid and Judy dined at Maxim's; at five in the morning they had onion soup at Les Halles, after Judy, glowing, had walked through the market; and the next day Judy went on a wild shopping spree. Sid took her to Hermès, the internationally known leather shop. Watching her, he said, "You've gone bananas!"

She bought nearly $1,500 worth of gloves, scarves, belts and umbrellas, but particularly gloves: gloves with little dots on them, with roses, medium gloves, long gloves, black, white, faun, green, blue gloves. One night Judy, lovely in a brown suit and hat Jean Louis had designed for her, with Sid and Vern—Jack had continued on to his villa —went to Monseigneur, a nightclub celebrated for its troupe of serenading violinists. They remained there from 1 to 5 A.M., teaching the musicians to play "Rock-a-bye," "Swanee," "Danny Boy"—Judy's songs—they tangoed, ate, drank, and when they left, Sid paid a bill of $1,200.

Then they were on the Blue Train to Nice, and having drinks with Jack in his villa, Aujourd'hui—"Today"—not too far from the fashionable Hôtel du Cap, where Jack had reserved a suite for them.

And now—Judy had foreseen it from the beginning—began a series of Command Performances on her part. The day after they arrived, the three of them on a long walk to the Eden Roc came upon everyone they had just left in Hollywood—the very people Judy wanted to get away from. Here were Elsa Maxwell and her friends, Jane and Darryl Zanuck, Swifty Lazar, Sam Spiegel and his chartered yacht, which Judy promptly named the "U.S.S. Dramamine," and every night it was dinner at Jack Warner's with all the social obligations that entailed.

On the fourth day Judy had had her fill. "What did I come here for?" she demanded of Sid. "Let's go to London." Sid said, "That wouldn't be nice. We can't do that to Jack." Judy: "What do you mean? We're not his guests. We're paying our way—we're paying the hotel." Jack had taken care of their passage over, but that was it. She protested, but there was always another party, or nightly visits to the gambling casino in Nice, and, clearly, Jack wanted their company.

The second night Jack had an idea. Marlene Dietrich was to be guest of honor at a gala charity in Monte Carlo. "Fine, fine," cried Judy. "Anything to get out of this joint." She had spent most of every afternoon in her suite playing her own recordings, listening to them endlessly, while Sid swam, played tennis and kibitzed with Jack. Judy hated the pool, the rocks one sunned oneself upon; she invariably burned and blistered in the sun.

She was tired of the Hollywood crowd. They were always with each other, they had to be at the right place at the right time, and to be at Cap d'Antibes and Hôtel du Cap and the Eden Roc and

Monte Carlo in season was being at the right place at the right time.

It was Judy's misfortune that she and Sid were driven by Jack's chauffeur in his car, and that Jack chose the Grande Corniche to Monte Carlo, a high mountain road with breathtaking curves, and on which, nearly two years later, Warner was to suffer a near-fatal crash in the same car with the same driver. For Judy, to whom anything over twenty-five miles an hour was speeding, the trip was torture. She was screaming at the chauffeur, "You son of a bitch, slow down. You're a lousy, goddamn driver, you're a reckless driver, you're going to kill everybody, let me out of this car—" Jack, sitting next to the driver, thought she was giving an amusing performance.

At Monte Carlo, in a gathering of beautifully gowned, bejeweled and befurred women of arresting loveliness, wealth and social background, Judy entered quietly—and it was like what had happened when Vern Alves, traveling with her for the first time, after the Palace, from New York to California, stopped for a four-hour layover in Chicago. They had gone to the celebrated Pump Room of the Ambassador East Hotel for lunch, and when she entered, everyone at the tables looked up and seemed to stop breathing; then after a moment life resumed: her presence changed an AC current to DC. So it was now in Monte Carlo. Judy entered, and everyone knew a Presence had arrived. Buzz, buzz, buzz—then absolute silence, and heads up, like deer suddenly alerted, as everyone stared. Judy, with Vern at her side, had to make her way to the table reserved for them, and as she passed, a susurration flowed after her like the train of her rustling dress: "Judy Garland . . . Judy Garland . . . that's Judy Garland . . ." When she sat down, Judy looked about her, and there were the Zanucks, and Elsa Maxwell, and the same people they had seen nearly every night at Warner's villa. "Ah, well," she said, resignedly, "I hope the food is good."

She was asked to walk on stage and select the winning number for the door prize, a Cartier miniature top hat embossed with diamonds and rubies. She was given a standing ovation. She had not sung, she had not done anything. Dietrich sang, and later she and Dietrich greeted each other backstage.

Now, trouble. Aly Khan wanted Sid to come to Deauville to see his stud farm there. Sid wanted Judy to go along; she didn't. She wanted to go to London. The result: words again. The result of this: Judy sought escape in pills and liquor, and suddenly Vern got a hurried telephone call from Sid to come up to their suite. When Vern entered, Judy was screaming, pacing back and forth in her pajamas, in intense physical and mental anguish, like a caged, mistreated animal. Finally a doctor was called, and she was taken to a psychiatric clinic in a nearby town, assigned a gigantic psychiatric nurse, wrestled into bed and strapped down. It was mid-August 1954.

At six the next night, a telephone call to Vern. It was Judy. "Come and get me, they're trying to murder me!" She had called Vern, not Sid; after all, Sid had precipitated this by wanting to go to Deauville to see horses instead of taking her to London. The two men hired a cab to the clinic. Sid waited outside (there was no telling how Judy might react if he walked in on her) while Vern went in. He was led into a tiny bedroom with a cot, a table and a lamp, dominated by what appeared to be an at least three-hundred-pound nurse in uniform. The bed was empty. Then he saw Judy. She was cowering on the floor in a far corner of the room, arms hugging herself, her hair tousled as though she had been tearing at it, dressed in a long white coarse nightgown: a gibbering, wild-eyed creature. Vern said, "We're taking her back." The nurse said, "Fine." Apparently Judy had simply asked to use the telephone and they had allowed her to.

Now the nurse went to the corner and picked Judy up like a child —she permitted it, because it was a way to get out—and put her on the bed. Vern left the room. Judy was dressed, taken out to the cab. She got in the back with Vern; she and Sid exchanged not a word. At the hotel in Monte Carlo, she said to Vern, "I want to go to your room." Sid said nothing. He could not know how much of this was act, how much truth. Judy went to Vern's room, washed her face, combed her hair, came out of the bathroom and sat on Vern's bed.

"I don't know what happens now," she said.

"Don't you want to go to your suite?" No, she said. "Can't I stay here?" Vern said, "I don't think that's a very good idea." But, all right, she could stay in his room, because there was another small room adjoining with a cot which he could use. "So I won't be very far away if you need me."

He left long enough to report to Sid, who said, "Take her whatever she needs, and stay with her. If she wants you to. Or come back here. I'll wait here."

She told Vern that she had been treated with incredible cruelty, beaten by nurses, locked in her room, not given even a glass of water.

He listened, falling into her mood as he always could. Sometime during the night she finally fell asleep out of sheer exhaustion. Vern reported to Sid, who said, "She'll come out of it. When she wakes up, she'll be ravenously hungry."

They waited. She woke about noon—ravenously hungry.

When the food arrived, she was saying to Vern, "I just can't understand people like that in that place I was in. So inhuman." Yes, said Vern sympathetically. Meanwhile, she was devouring ham, eggs, potatoes, toast, marmalade—her usual truckman's breakfast.

Then the bad time was over for Judy, for Sid and for Vern. They left the South of France for Paris, and then to the Savoy Hotel in London, and a night at Les Ambassadeurs, the "in" club in London, where Judy and Sid danced, slowly and romantically—to anyone not privy to the astonishing adventures of Judy Garland, the couple dancing together might have been honeymooners.

Through all this both Sid and Vern knew a fact which seemed to make this unreal period only one more chapter in the unfolding story. As she and Sid danced at Les Ambassadeurs in late August of 1954, Judy was more than two months pregnant. She had discovered this, to her delight, just before leaving California; both Sid and Vern thought perhaps the entire melange of events—the change in her career, the discovery of her pregnancy, her sense of being trapped in Cap d'Antibes—were responsible for what had happened in Monte Carlo.

They returned to the States on Labor Day, in time to attend repeated previews of the film, in small suburban Los Angeles theatres. The first time Judy saw the completed, edited and scored film was at a sneak preview in Huntington, California, where she and Vern sat in the balcony loges. (Sid and Jack had gone to another preview in Encino.) It was like opening night at the Palace, for word had got out that the picture being sneak-previewed was *Star*. Judy's fans had lined up outside the theatre hours before, and when she drove up, she saw them.

She was very nervous. All the months of work, the publicity, were over. She had finally done it: she had *completed* it! "Do you think we're all too close to it and we really don't have a good picture?" she asked Vern. "But that can't be true." She went on, building everything up. "Of course it's a good picture. It's a great picture. Mason's great, the score is great, I'm great, the photography's great, it's a great picture. . . ." And then, a little weakly: "Isn't it?"

When they went into the theatre, by some telepathy everyone seemed to know Judy was sitting in the balcony; they applauded her, they stood yelling, cheering, *"We* love you, Judy!" So Judy and Vern sat there, Judy with vodka and grapefruit juice in a paper cup, and waited for *A Star Is Born* to begin. The moment the credits came on the screen, it was impossible to hear anything. It was bedlam. The audience went hysterical: they saw her name on the screen, and they knew she was there herself in the balcony. After every song, there was an ovation; after every dance, an ovation; there was no way to know whether the audience liked the picture, they were hysterical at everything. It was like a festival, a family wedding, a celebration of occult emotional rites.

When, later, the film had its spectacular official premieres in Hollywood, Chicago and New York, with Judy and Sid attending all three, Judy's reviews, and those of Mason, were superb. *Look* magazine said, "The year's most worrisome movie has turned out to be one of its best." *Time* called Judy's performance "just about the greatest one-woman show in modern movie history." Mason made a new name for himself, and if Judy's performance could bring Cukor to admit "my blood froze," she did the same to the audience. The scene in which she puts on a private show for her husband, dancing and singing to entertain him, a choreographed delight by Dick Barstow, the film's dance director, and the moments when, seconds after she receives her Oscar in the film, her drunken husband comes to the stage to humiliate himself and her, and in his clumsiness strikes her sharply in the face, and how she takes that, and goes on—these are particularly memorable. It was inevitable that Judy be nominated for an Oscar as the best actress of the year, with almost everyone agreeing she was sure to get it. Though she had received a juvenile award for her work in *Wizard of Oz*, this was the real thing, and if it were to come true, what a triumph after everything!

There were extraordinary scenes at the premieres. At the Pantages in Hollywood, twenty thousand people were estimated to line the streets, and it took two columns in the newspapers to list the celebrities who attended. There were utterly ridiculous but typical Judy incidents—particularly in New York, where the sidewalk crowds were the most unruly. Judy was then four months pregnant, and frightened. Jack Warner and Sid tried to protect her with a flying wedge of policemen as they walked from the limousine into the lobby of the Paramount. But the crowd, eager to reach and touch Judy, broke through the restraining barricades; they were so hysterical that Judy, Sid and Warner, despite their protective wedge of police, found themselves pushed not into the lobby but into the side street, Forty-fourth Street. Judy, surrounded by mounted police, unexpectedly found herself next to a horse which chose that moment to lift his tail and relieve himself. Judy, all dressed up in a full-length crimson gown, a long white coat with a luxurious mink collar, doubled up with laughter. "Everyone's a critic," she managed to say to Sid. Finally, however, they were inside, and the night was hers.

Judy and Sid gave an after-premiere party at the Waldorf. There was Tennessee Williams, looking like someone out of the 1800s, with his black velvet jacket, red brocaded vest, four-in-hand tie, black-and-white striped pants and high shoes, his mustache and long ivory cigarette holder; Pat Lawford and her brother, the promising young Senator Jack Kennedy, who was to become a lifelong friend of Judy's; and Tennessee's companion, the Italian actress Anna Magnani. To Judy's delight, Magnani not only knew most of Judy's repertoire, but sat down at the piano and played for her while Judy sang, and the future President of the United States and the country's greatest living playwright sat listening with complete and admiring attention.

No one seeing Judy enjoying herself at the round of parties given in her honor in New York, Chicago and Hollywood would know that just before she left for New York there had been meetings with her obstetrician, Dr. Morton, Dr. Marc and her current psychiatrist. It was a strenuous time for Judy, moving further into her pregnancy and revved up by everything happening to her. Dr. Morton wanted to ensure that she had the smallest possible amount of medication. When the Lufts returned after all the openings, Judy had a number of sessions with her psychiatrist. Sid, too, went to an analyst for several weeks, to help him cope with Judy as the time drew nearer not only to the birth of her third child but to the resolution of the mounting uncertainty as to whether she would win the Oscar.

They returned to the Mapleton house and their excited children with a great sense of relief, and a memento. One night while staying at the Plaza, Judy had been invited to dinner by the Duke and Duchess of Windsor. Not feeling well, she had had to beg off. An hour later a messenger arrived at her suite. He bore on a silver platter an envelope with the words "The Colony" engraved on it. Inside, on cream-colored Colony Restaurant stationery, was a little message in verse in the Duchess' handwriting:

> Somewhere up in the Plaza,
> Way up high,
> There's a gal that we miss,
> Oh me, oh my, oh my.
> Etc. . . . etc. . . . etc. . . .

Apparently, after four lines, the muse left her. It was signed, one name under another in round-robin fashion, by those at the dinner: Wallis Windsor; Edward; Babe Paley, wife of the president of CBS; Bob Young, president of the Penn Central Railroad; Bill Paley; and finally, Charlie Cushing, who added as a joke, "Your next husband."

Judy kept it in her small memory book.

She had two little books. One was her memory book, one her bitch book. In the latter, when she was outraged at anyone, she wrote the name down and ripped the page out, casting a black Irish spell upon the victim as she hurled the crumpled sheet away.

Now there was nothing to do but wait, hopefully, for the Oscar, scheduled to be announced at the Academy Awards Dinner at the Pantages March 30, 1955, which she would attend—and for the birth of her baby, which Dr. Morton was scheduled to take from her by Caesarean section some two weeks later.

29

SINCE LITTLE IN JUDY'S LIFE WENT PRECISELY ACCORDING TO PLAN, it is understandable that around 11 P.M. of the night of March 28, less than forty-eight hours before the Oscar ceremonies, Judy unexpectedly began showing preliminary signs of labor, and Dr. Morton hurried her to the Cedars of Lebanon Hospital.

While she was upstairs in the operating room, in the lobby below the festivities had already begun. Sid, as soon as he learned the baby was on its way, had arranged a party. A few minutes after she went up, Frank Sinatra and Betty Bacall arrived, both excited. "Has it happened yet?" Betty asked. Vern was sitting there on a sofa. He said no, and the two joined him. Luft came downstairs; his necktie was askew, his face was perspiring, but he was happy. They were preparing Judy in the delivery room, she was funnier than ever, keeping the nurses in stitches (pun), all was fine, nothing to do but wait. They sat on the sofa whispering while strangers in the lobby watched, fascinated, from a discreet distance.

After a little while Frank jumped up. "Be back in ten minutes," he said. Fifteen minutes later a delivery man arrived with a hot cart, such as hotels use to serve food for room service; Frank had ordered pizza, salads, sausages, red wine—a feast. They had their welcoming party there, on a coffee table in the stately lobby of the Cedars of Lebanon Hospital, with the busts of Jehovah and Moses and a photograph of Rabbi Nussbaum looking down on them as they gorged themselves on Italian delicacies.

Every little while Sid checked the desk. No news. By now Sinatra had brought out the wine. There was much talk. Judy had had two girls, she wanted a boy badly. And this would be her last child. She had privately told Dr. Morton to tie off her Fallopian tubes after the birth.

Now Sid had gone up again; moments later the elevator door opened and he emerged, a grin from ear to ear. His shirt, open almost down to his belt, was soaked with perspiration, his hair was mussed, but he was ecstatic. "It's a boy!" he exclaimed. "Judy's O.K.—everything's fine."

Now they celebrated in earnest. It was 2 A.M., March 29, 1955.

Actually, everything was not fine, as Luft learned after he had hurried home, showered, changed clothes and returned to the hospital. Dr. Morton greeted him; with him was the pediatrician Dr. Dietrich, and Dr. Marc, who had worked so hard to save five-year-old Judy so many years before. One of the baby's lungs had failed to open, a condition that could sometimes be fatal and occurred occasionally in a Caesarean because of the lack of struggle to be born. Dr. Morton was seriously concerned: this was a premature baby, weighing five pounds eight ounces; he had to tell Luft he gave the baby at most a fifty-fifty chance to live. Privately, he thought the infant would die.

The doctors walked up and down the corridor with Sid, explaining how powerful nature could prove itself, that the baby was in an incubator, that everything science could do was being done. Fortunately, because of Judy's choice of Cedars, her son was now being cared for in one of the largest, most modern and highly reputed hospitals in the country.

It was nearly 9 A.M. when Sid walked into Judy's room. She was up and bright, and her first words were: "Darling, I'm the mother of a son, and I'm so thrilled, and God bless us." Sid bent over and kissed her. He said, "I've just come from the doctor, I've seen him, he's beautiful—small but beautiful." It was a serious few moments. They had joked a week before about the name. If a boy, Judy wanted him named Joshua—this to Sid's violent protests. "Can you imagine me going into a schoolyard full of kids and calling, 'Hey, Joshua, come on home!' He'll get slammed around, and it'll be rough on him." So they compromised on Joey—Joseph Wiley (Jack Cathcart's middle name) Luft.

Both knew their son's condition, and neither wanted to let the other know, in the belief that it was not serious, that it was unthinkable, that it must go away. Judy had said to Vern, "I'm sorry, I just won't accept it. Don't even tell me about it. I don't accept it. He's going to be all right." She had rejected it even more strongly to Liza, whom she had telephoned to tell her that it was a boy. Liza exclaimed, with all her nine-year-old enthusiasm, "Oh, Mama! That's what you wanted." And Judy said, "They tell me he's going to die, but he's not going to—I promise you that. I won't let him." Liza didn't know what to say, but she never forgot her mother's voice. "I just wanted to call you and tell you that. It won't happen."

It was not until four the next afternoon, however, that word came that Joey's other lung had opened—it had been the left lung—and that there was no question that he would live. In those hours from early Tuesday, the twenty-ninth, to 4 P.M. Wednesday, the thirtieth, Judy and Sid went through hours of agony, she in her way, Sid in his, and only when the good word came did they reveal to each other that each had known. It had been almost as one seeks to avoid the evil eye: See nothing, mention nothing, and nothing will happen.

The first time Judy was permitted to hold Joey brought her to tears. She held him against her shoulder, patting his back gently, hoping to stimulate and strengthen the weak lung, and discovered to her astonishment that her baby's tiny right hand was seemingly patting the back of her shoulder, as if to comfort her, in turn, as if to say,

"Mama, I know what you've gone through, it's all right, I'm O.K. now. . . ." That special mutual caress would exist between Joey and his mother always.

Judy had expected to attend the Academy Awards. Now, knowing she would be photographed in bed if she won, she had ordered the prettiest bed jacket she could find—and then discovered herself the subject of more electronic attention in bed than she had ever imagined. Her competitors for best actress were formidable: Dorothy Dandridge, Audrey Hepburn, Grace Kelly and Jane Wyman. But Judy had been encouraged by an earlier award: *Look* magazine had chosen her and Bing Crosby as winners of their best-acting prizes, she for *A Star Is Born,* Bing for *The Country Girl*—the picture in which Grace Kelly appeared.

Maybe *Look*'s award was an augury. She seemed sure of it when her room was suddenly invaded by TV technicians. They were laying cables along the corridors into her second-floor room, and through it, to a television platform being built outside her window, through which a TV camera would shoot her. Gundy would be lying under the window, and the moment Judy's name was announced Gundy would release the blind and Judy would be on camera. "My God," she said, "they're wiring me up like a radar." There was a wire up her nightgown, to which a microphone was attached, and wires under her. It took considerable time: they worked all afternoon, and then went through a dress rehearsal.

That evening before seven o'clock they returned, and now when they completed their work, Judy was so trussed up she could hardly move. She could not leave the bed to go to the bathroom. She felt computerized, she complained, and lay almost rigid, afraid if she turned her head she might detach a wire.

It was like a scene from an old Buster Keaton film: men were climbing in and out the window, silent and purposeful, adjusting the camera; others were crawling under the bed checking cables, or adjusting the wires to Judy; and she was enjoying it all. She was the perfect hostess, despite her harness, full of regal solicitude: "Boys, wouldn't you like a drink, you're working so hard?" When they declined that, she insisted on ordering coffee and sandwiches for them. Her hair had been done, she was wearing a peignoir, she looked beautiful.

They were calling to her: "Judy, can you move a little to the left

—we can frame you better—get you better in the lens." They directed her with the aplomb of a George Cukor. "Now, you'll be watching the TV." A TV set had been put up in one corner, so she could watch the proceedings at the Pantages, where Bob Hope was master of ceremonies, and where, if she won, Betty Bacall would run up on stage to accept the Oscar for her, the circuits would open between the Pantages and the hospital, and Judy and Bob would banter with each other and she would make her little acceptance speech.

Luft, meanwhile, had prepared for a celebration. He had brought two buckets of champagne in ice, caviar, shrimps; he had a buffet set up against one wall. There would be very few in the room save the technicians: Judy, Sid, John Royal, an NBC executive and an old friend, and Gundy, lying uncomfortably under the window.

At the Pantages the program began. Everybody in Judy's room watched, Sid holding Judy's hand. The first presentations were, as usual, minor ones, one to a group of Japanese movie-makers for best foreign-language film. The awards went on. Finally came the moment. The envelope was opened, the name announced: "Grace Kelly, for *The Country Girl!*"

Gundy stood straight up. Sid put his arms around Judy. "Baby, fuck the Academy Awards, you've got yours in the incubator. Why, those sons of bitches, they'd give it to a fucking Jap who shot up Pearl Harbor, but they wouldn't give it to my baby!"

From the TV technicians came a disgusted "O.K. Wrap it up!" And without another glance at Judy, they began unceremoniously pulling out cables from under her bed, and detaching her from the microphone, pulling the wire from under her nightgown. One man pushed open the window. "Take it down," he said, and the cameraman scrambled to the ground level with his camera, while the carpenters began dismantling the scaffolding outside. That morning the technicians had entered Judy's room all solicitude and courtesy; now it was as though the girl in the bed were someone they'd never seen. Judy, half in tears, half in hysterical laughter, could not help saying as she turned one way, then the other, releasing the tangle of wires beneath her, "Boys, don't short me." Her hands were clenching and unclenching, but, as Luft continued to curse, she said, "Forget it, darling. Open the champagne. I have my own Academy Award."

Luft had always had some doubts about Judy's winning. He had

394

been told the odds were against her. All Paramount, where *Country Girl* had been made, and all Metro, to whom Grace Kelly was under contract, were rooting and voting for Grace; and Warner, who was having his differences with the Academy of Motion Picture Arts and Sciences, in the view of the trade had done little to lobby for Judy.

Corks popped. Luft drank steadily; he intended to get as drunk as possible as quickly as possible. He poured a drink for Judy. She sat up straight in her new bed jacket. "Well, I knew I wouldn't get it," she said. "They wouldn't give it to me, although I deserved it. They just wouldn't give it to me."

Vern Alves arrived a few minutes later, his face pale, a little embarrassed as he walked in. He was carrying another bucket of ice with champagne. He had been at the Pantages, expecting to hear Judy declared the winner. After his shock, he had debated: ought he go to the hospital? He had decided to go.

Sid had left for a moment. Judy was sitting up, staring straight ahead, the bed quilt drawn up almost to her chin, her fingers playing on the quilt. It was a habit of hers. Once, when Vern had been talking to her early in their association, she had begun to drum with her fingers on the arms of her chair. "Honey, am I boring you with this?" he had asked. She replied, "No, no, darling—I always do this. Haven't you noticed? It's a tune—there's always music in my head—that's what it is."

She had accepted what was much more of a disaster to her than anyone knew, and now she was already shielding herself behind the only therapy that had ever really worked for her—music. She had retired into her own world and was nursing her wounds there.

Alves did not know quite what to say to her, standing by her bed, feeling silly with the bucket and champagne, but at that moment Sid returned and said, "Give me that," and Vern gave him the champagne and Sid poured another round for everyone.

Judy spoke. "At least I have my son," she said. "My son."

Then Betty Bacall was there, Oscarless, and hugging Judy, helping answer the telephone calls, indignant, outraged, comforting, and reading the telegrams, among them one saying, "Dear Judy: This is the biggest robbery since Brink's—Groucho Marx."

Joey had to remain in the incubator until he was strong enough to come home, and then Judy doted on her son in a way that was beyond belief. She held him, she caressed him, she carried him about, he was the be-all and end-all of her life. She would be up at all hours to steal into his nursery—he had his nurse and a nurse to spell her on her day off—and gloat over him. *She had a son.* And he grew, and gained weight, and he was as healthy and lusty as any little boy. For the first months, at least, the other children in the house felt like second-class citizens; Judy seemed to have eyes only for her son, and that special wonder would remain with her as long as she lived. Of all objects in a world which often baffled her and, as she sometimes thought, seemed determined to destroy her, her greatest pride lay in her children, and of the three, Joey was the priceless one. He was the love of her life—always.

Liza accepted it. When her mother was with her, she could give Liza so much attention, she treated her so much like an adult, that nine-year-old Liza felt she had her own special relationship with her mother, and so could accept this obsession with Joey as a private matter between her mother and Joey. Lorna, so much younger, found it more difficult. Once, when Joey was not yet a year old, three-year-old Lorna managed to climb up into his crib and scratch his face; when Judy rushed in, hearing Joey's screams, there was Joey crying, his face bleeding, and Lorna cowering in the farthest corner of the crib. Judy immediately took her on her knee, turned her over and spanked her soundly. "Don't you ever do that again, never, never, never!" she cried. Fortunately Lorna was always to be strong and self-reliant—as frightened of Judy when Judy was in anger as any child (Judy in a fury made strong men tremble!), yet able to stand up to her and even sometimes to talk back. Now, having learned her lesson with respect to Joey, Lorna had to accept the fact that he was the apple of his mother's eye.

Judy's punishment of her children was always old-fashioned: spank them, spank them hard, then make up for it later with an unexpected treat. Ethel's methods had been far more Draconian. Once when Liza was almost three, Judy brought her over to Ethel's house. Liza wanted something that Judy didn't want her to have, whereupon Liza stuck her thumb in her mouth and blew hard. It was similar to holding one's breath. The child was beginning to turn purple. Judy panicked; she became almost hysterical. All right, all right, she was saying frantically, you can have it, but Ethel marched into the kitchen, came out with a pitcher of cold water and poured it over

396

Liza's head. Judy promptly threw up. But Liza never had another tantrum in Ethel's presence.

How busy that year of 1955 was! Sid was engendering all kinds of plans for Judy's career. Both were unhappy with their Warner relationship. To the disappointment of losing the Oscar was added their despair, as well as that of Cukor, Moss Hart and others, at what they considered the final inept cutting job done on *Star* by Harry Warner, Jack's older brother and head of the studio. From a running time of 182 minutes it was cut, finally, to 153 minutes. (Cukor's words were furious: "It was edited brutally, stupidly and arbitrarily, and many of Garland's finest moments were taken out.") The picture, however much Judy and Mason were praised, never achieved the box-office popularity expected. There were endless disputes between Transcona and Warner's over a dozen different aspects of *Star*—over the bills Judy ran up in New York, Chicago and Los Angeles while making personal appearances to publicize the film, charges of lack of cooperation and even an embarrassing cutting off of her credit at the Ambassador East in Chicago—all of which finally resulted in the ambitious nine-picture multimillion-dollar deal's beginning and ending really with *Star*. Jack had talked vaguely of Judy's doing a second film; but after the disastrous cutting of *Star*—the rave reviews had been based upon the full-length version, which Sid and Judy had hoped would be distributed by Warner's as a road-show production like *Gone With the Wind*—based on Harry Warner's decision to shorten it so that it could be seen by as many audiences a day as possible, a coolness developed, and ultimately Transcona and Warner's went their separate ways.

Nonetheless, Judy and Sid were going forward. No more films for a while, but other projects: new records, an album of earlier recordings to be released, a three-week concert tour through Southern California and the Northwest, to be followed by a nationwide tour in which Judy would take what was basically her Palace show from coast to coast . . .

But Judy was not to escape unscathed from a period of depression, whether post partum or post-Oscar. In May she was still heavy, and disgusted with herself. Dr. Pobirs came nightly to see that she got proper rest, in preparation for her tour. Pobirs was trying to maintain her medication at a minimum level, but she had reached a point of toxicity which could not have come from the medication he was giving her.

"She's getting something else," he warned Sid. But where? How? One night when Judy was knocked out completely for several hours, he and Sid methodically turned everything upside down in Judy's suite. There were four walls of heavy black drapes, for Judy slept much during the day, and when she drew these, her quarters were dark.

Sid rarely went there when she was not present. She spent much time there by herself; she had her own private telephone in her bathroom; he tried not to overhear her calls, or in any way invade her privacy. But now he and Pobirs were free to search. They found small envelopes of Seconal and Benzedrine hidden everywhere: Scotch-taped inside the drapes; Scotch-taped under the carpets; in the bedsprings; in the lining of Judy's terry-cloth bathrobe; tablets and capsules buried deep in her bath powder and secreted behind books. They got rid of it all.

Then they went downstairs. Pobirs left. Sid waited. It might be ten hours, twelve hours, before Judy would wake up and want her usual big breakfast.

When that happened, he joined her. She began cutting into the steak she had had the cook prepare as she liked it, charred on the outside, rare inside. She looked at Sid.

"You found them all, didn't you?"

"Yes, we cleaned you out," said Sid. "It's for your own protection, Baby."

She took another bite of steak. "You're a gumshoe, Sid," she said. "You missed your calling." But there were no recriminations.

Yet, no sooner was she back on the careful program of medication that Pobirs had established than Gumshoe Luft made another discovery. Judy's favorite drink was either Canadian Club and water or vodka and grapefruit juice. At the moment it was the latter, because of the vitamins in the juice. Judy usually took a few sips from a tall glass, then put the glass down. In the course of the evening there might be half a dozen partly full glasses about, with Vern usually called upon to "Darling, please freshen up my drink." He would pour a little more vodka in one of the glasses, add ice and give it to her. The idea was that there should always be a drink, in case Judy wished

The famous "Swanee" sequence from *A Star Is Born*. (Richard Barstow)

An informal moment between Judy and James Mason on the set of *A Star Is Born*. (Cinemabilia Inc.)

Off-camera, *A Star Is Born: (l. to r.)* Director-choreographer Richard Barstow, Judy and assistant producer Vern Alves. (Richard Barstow)

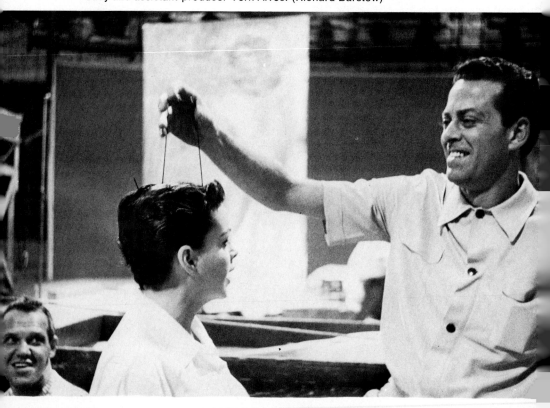

At Ciro's: *(l. to r.)* Dick Powell, June Allyson, Sid Luft, Judy and Humphrey Bogart.
(Pictorial Parade)

(Above) In Hollywood, 1954.
(Pictorial Parade)

(Right) Off to Cap d'Antibes:
(l. to r.) Jack Warner, Judy
and Sid Luft, 1954.
(Pictorial Parade)

With Joey and Lorna Luft in England, 1960. (London Daily Express)

At El Morocco: Judy, Sid Luft and Liza Minnelli, 1961. (Nancy Barr)

(Left) With Liza, Joey and Lorna, leaving England to live in New York, 1960. (Nancy Barr)

(Below) An almost unrecognizable Judy, with Sinatra and Liza, at the Cocoanut Grove, 1958. (Nancy Barr)

Debut at the Palace, 1951.

The famous clown, at the Palace, 1956.

At Arie Crown Theatre, Chicago, 1962. (John Fricke)

From *The Judy Garland Show,* with Dean Martin and Frank Sinatra, 1962.
(Springer/Bettmann Film Archive)

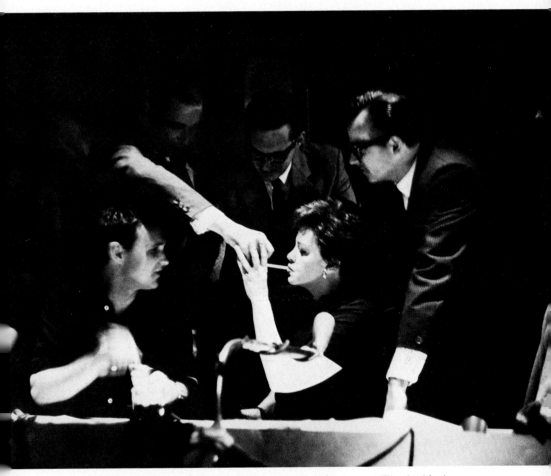

In rehearsal for her TV special, 1962. (Springer/Bettmann Film Archive)

The last Palace appearance:
(l. to r.) Joey and Lorna Luft,
Judy and John Bubbles, 1967.
(Richard Barstow)

Singing "That's Entertainment"
at the Westbury, L.I., Music
Fair, 1967. (Richard Barstow)

At midnight recording session in New York, April 1962. (Springer/Bettmann Film Archive)

Judy and Mark Herron, 1964. (Pictorial Parade)

From *I Could Go On Singing,*
1963. (Don Smith)

From *Judgment at
Nuremberg,* 1961.
(Pictorial Parade)

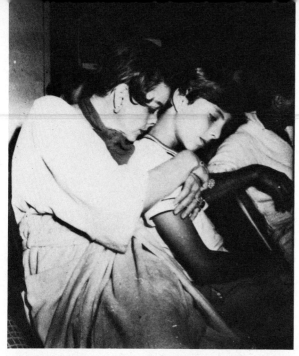

Backstage with Joey, at the Palace, 1967. (Nancy Barr)

With her fifth husband, Mickey Deans, March 1969. (London Daily Express)

In London Palladium TV show, January 1969.

Performance in Copenhagen, March 1969. (Pictorial Parade)

Portrait by Roberto Gari that now graces the lobby of the Palace Theatre.
(Richard Barstow)

it, no farther than arm's reach away—whether she was seated or moving about. This characteristic of Judy's drinking—that in hotel or home one always saw half a dozen hardly touched drinks standing about—gave rise to the belief that Judy actually drank little. This was not true. One of Sid's first discoveries was that Judy always needed liquids. The medication she took made her throat dry. But he had never thought of her as one who drank heavily. Pills had been his original concern.

Sid had built an elaborate mirrored bar before their bookcases in the den, with room for dozens of bottles. One day he poured himself a vodka and tonic. It tasted like pure tonic. He examined the bottle, three-quarters full, then took a swig of it. It was half-water. He tried another; it was watered, too. They had all been watered. Obviously Judy had quietly been helping herself, and replacing the vodka with water so that the levels remained the same.

Sid waited until Judy walked into the den that night.

Then, as she watched, he swept a dozen bottles of liquor—he had discovered water in the whiskey, in the Scotch, in the bourbon, in the gin—into a wicker basket, and, in front of Judy, proceeded furiously to smash the neck of each bottle on the edge of the sink and pour its contents down the drain. Then, carried away, he began on the bottles that had never been opened, smashing them, too.

Judy watched him, arms akimbo. She said, in a matter-of-fact voice, "That's your own liquor you're pouring down the drain, Sid." Sid halted, shocked. "My God!" he exclaimed. "You're right. What am I doing!"

There was nothing now but to burst into laughter and hug each other. "You drive me batty, darling," he said. "My old gumshoe Sid," she said. Next day Sid decided to make a formal apology. This was no way to treat Judy. There was a key to the bar. He replenished the bar with liquor, and left the key out. "Darling," he said, "I don't want to feel like I can't trust you. If you want a drink, that's up to you." "Oh, you're beautiful, Sid," she said.

But presently the liquor was being used, and entirely too swiftly for Sid's peace of mind. Judy surprised him at dinner one night. She had a new hairdresser, who had been coming in to do Judy's hair each time they went partying. Judy said, "Darling, do you know that she's an ex-alcoholic? She's found religion—she's a member of AA." She looked at Sid. "You know, you drink too much, too. Why don't we both go to her AA chapter in Pasadena?" "Great," said Sid. He meant it.

Two evenings later they drove there, Judy sitting next to him in the front seat with a silver flask of Canadian Club in her lap. Sid said, "You're not supposed to go to an AA meeting with liquor." Judy made a face at him.

At the meeting, held in someone's house, they had coffee and cake, listened to several men and women stand up and proclaim, "I am an alcoholic," and then drove back. Judy still had the flask but did not drink. "No more whiskey," she said. The spell held at least for the drive home.

Then Judy learned that a chapter of Drugs Anonymous met each week in the San Fernando Valley. She said, "I want to go there." Sid said, "Great." He never gave up hope.

They drove there one night. Inside the house it was like a Frankenstein movie: low-keyed green lighting, men and women standing up to announce, "I am a user of drugs." After twenty minutes Judy nudged Sid. They rose and left. "This place has really done me in," said Judy. "Let's go where it's a little gay." They ended at Romanoff's and had a drink. Judy summed up their experience: "I can't go for that—either AA or Drugs Anonymous. That will never do me any good."

They both looked on these two visits—their only ones—as a lark.

But, for all the fun and games, Sid worried. Pills. Liquor. And cigarettes. Even cigarettes posed problems. Though Sid was himself a chain smoker and Judy far less of one, she often smoked late at night and when she was alone. She would sit up in bed, with a large 18-by-24-inch drawing board, drawing endless landscapes in pencil, erasing them, then drawing them again. Sid had a talent for sketching and tried to teach her; she had taken it up as a kind of therapy, for she had to be constantly doing something. The radio would be on, the TV would be on; there were just so many books she could read, although she spent hours reading, and had a standing order at Hunter's Book Shop for the latest best sellers. Now the drawing board seemed part of her routine. But she smoked a great deal, and more than once Sid had come home to find a lit cigarette still glowing in an ashtray, and Judy asleep.

One night he returned late. Judy's quarters and his were both enormous, with a connecting bathroom and dressing room so that he had two means of access to her. The doors were sliding doors.

There were lights in her room; the TV was going full blast. He did not go in to see her, because if she had, perhaps, fallen asleep and he woke her, it would mean so much torture for her before she fell asleep again. He awoke suddenly, later, smelling smoke. It was just beginning to be light outside. It must have been around 6 A.M. He raced into Judy's quarters. The huge black drapes were columns of flame, a hole was burning in the ceiling, fire ran like hot yellow streaks along ceiling and walls, fed by the ancient paint, and was sweeping with lightning-like speed toward Judy's bed, where she lay asleep. The flames were no more than five feet from her when he grabbed her, pulled her out of bed and carried her downstairs. Awake, but still drowsy, she was crying, "The children!" "Don't worry," he managed to say, putting her on the lawn. The children's nursery was at the other end of the huge house. He rushed back, woke up nurse and children, and got everyone out. The firemen were there in a few minutes. Judy had left a lit cigarette among the cushions of an easy chair, slipped into bed and fallen into a drugged sleep.

What enabled the firemen to contain the flames and save the house was the result of an almost comic circumstance. When Sid and Judy first looked over the Mapleton house, Judy, as befitted a careful housewife, examined the closets. There was a huge one off the large entrance hall. When she opened the door, she found it completely filled with a professional-size fireman's hose, with a gigantic nozzle. Judy took one look and laughed. Hunt Stromberg, who'd built the house, she told Sid, was known as a pyromaniac at MGM. Once, according to the story that went around the lot, he had almost set Hedy Lamarr on fire. He had been interviewing her in his office. He smoked incessantly, lighting his cigarettes with large kitchen matches, which he invariably threw, still lit, into a wastepaper basket. Hedy's chair stood near it; the basket caught fire, the flames began licking Hedy's dress, there was a near-tragedy. Since he had this habit of tossing lit matches about, he had equipped his house with great lengths of hose, such as one found in a theatre, long enough to reach throughout the house. Judy, laughing then, could never have anticipated that it would be this hose that helped save their house. One entire wing, however, was a wreck and uninhabitable. The family moved into the Bel Air Hotel for several months until repairs were made. So far as the press was concerned, the fire was attributed to ancient electric wiring.

It was an arduous training course Luft was being given in the care and management of Judy, and yet it would have been difficult to find anyone better suited for it. Luft himself had almost burned to death when he was trapped in a Douglas plane he was testing during the war, flying so low over the Santa Monica airfield that even if he could have bailed out—that was impossible, his leg was caught—it would have meant instant death. He had ridden the flaming plane to the ground, followed by a screaming ambulance, was somehow extricated—he was hanging head down, burning—wrapped in a sheet and rushed to the hospital, severe burns on his left leg, the side of his face, his lower back. He remained there for three months. For a full minute, trapped in the plane, he knew he was going to be burned alive. It was an experience, he told Judy, against which no calamity in the future would compare; after that he could take on anything, the Devil himself. In the hospital he had lived on drugs, because the pain was unbearable, and then the grafts, the agony of withdrawal and six months of psychotherapy to make life livable again. If anyone was prepared for such a training course, he was.

What was interesting with respect to Judy was that after episodes in which she deliberately or accidentally harmed herself, she never engaged in a post-mortem. Either Judy had no memory of what she had done or, if she did, she could not explain. At the beginning he tried to discuss the episode, but the mere fact of his asking only made it worse. It was difficult, almost impossible, for her to apologize, to say, for example, that she was sorry after an attempt to cut her wrists, or nick—that was the usual word, "nick"—her throat. To have said, "I'm sorry," was tantamount to admitting that she hadn't meant it. She had to be taken seriously. When, that night, years before, married to Vincente, Judy had gone to the Gershwins' to lie on Lee Gershwin's grandmother's couch and scream, only to pause for a moment, open her eyes and ask, "Do you believe me?" and when Lee said, "Yes," to resume screaming—this came out of the same psychological pattern. She was saying, *Do you believe that I am in agony, that I am beside myself, that my screaming is genuine, that I am actually suffering?*

When Sid was not watching her, he assigned Vern, or Taylor, the butler, or Harry Rubin, the man of all work—always someone. Even those who had looked askance at this marriage had to admit that at this point, whatever Luft's bad press, his penchant for horses and gambling, Judy had chosen well. The number of times in the years to come he would save her life—many of them unknown and unpublicized—would add to a startling figure.

Rubin, a roly-poly man with unruly black hair and a belly sense of humor, was an electrician whom Sid transformed into a man of all work. He also had special backstage duties. One of his jobs when Judy was on tour was to carry two thermos containers, one of vodka already mixed with grapefruit juice, the other filled with ice cubes. Someone was always assigned this task when Judy was on tour. Another duty was to stand in the wings when she did her closing "Over the Rainbow" number, armed with three necessities: a shot of Canadian Club and water; a toothbrush; and an ammoniated capsule. Judy blacked out her two front teeth as part of the tramp makeup. The moment she finished "Rainbow," she'd come through the curtains, grab the toothbrush, brush her teeth clean, take a shot of liquor, Rubin would break open the capsule under her nose to revive her —and back she'd burst through the curtains again, to wild applause.

The tour in July under Transcona auspices—three weeks of one-night stands in such towns as San Diego, Long Beach, Portland, Spokane and Vancouver—was a mixed blessing. Once or twice she became ill, and had to cancel. On one occasion it was almost impossible to get her out of her dressing room. Who could understand what ordeal she was going through?

Sitting there, in the dressing room, she feels the old terror come upon her. She will not go out; she cannot. The tingling of the fingertips, the numbness of the lips, the dryness of the mouth, the sense of impending doom—the more frightening because you know it's not rational, there's no rational reason for it, but it's there, it's waiting there for you. . . .

Anxiety! How do you explain it? Your heart is pounding, and you talk to yourself frantically: I'm not going to die, I'm not going to have a heart attack—I'm just anxious. Everything . . . is . . . all . . . right. I'm fine. Goddamnit, I'm fine! But something is wrong, and I can't explain what it is. . . . I must hunt for it, put my finger on it, and it'll go away. But maybe it's something so dreadful, so horrible, so awful, that I don't want to find it. . . .

She leaps from her chair, and sees the drawn, terrified face of herself in the mirror. *Judy, get hold of yourself!*

She takes a tranquilizer, then a second. . . . They should work. She knows she really shouldn't take them. She knows that if you are truly anxious, too many tranquilizers distort rather than dispel anxiety. Now—has it been five minutes, ten minutes?—she is still anxious, but a little confused, a little less in control of the situation.

And her fear is growing. To have this fear, and not be in control, is even worse. Now it is: Oh, my God, I took this and it didn't work. It really didn't work, it made it worse. Maybe whatever I have can't be handled by anything, it will only get worse and worse. . . . Maybe there *is* something wrong with me! Maybe it really *isn't* rational. . . .

There's a sharp rapping on the door. "Miss Garland—Miss Garland —please, they've played the overture twice."

"Oh, please, two more minutes, five more minutes." There's panic in her voice, and she knows they hear it. "Give me five more minutes, please." It'll go away. It'll stop.

She talks to herself, beginning to babble: It's going to be fine. I've had this before, and I got out of it, didn't I? Judy always manages, doesn't she? I'll be all right once I get out there, I always am. . . . But what if they see it out there? What if I disappear?

The words begin to revolve in her mind like horses on a merry-go-round. What if I go out there and just disappear, disappear, disappear? I know it's wild, but it could happen.

The rapping on the door. The imploring voices: "Miss Garland . . . Judy . . ." It's not the people pounding on the dressing room door, she thinks, despairingly, dying little by little. It's the people waiting in their seats: sitting there, waiting, ready to punish you for what you've done. . . . And they're expecting you to turn them into raving maniacs, applauding, screaming, shouting, cheering, because you're so good—*you're the best in the whole world*—and you're trapped, because if you let them down, they'll tear you apart. They want what they came here to get from you. . . .

And you can't give it to them! Not now! Later, sometime later . . . please!

"Go away!" you scream. "Let me alone!"

And behind the locked door, in the bright dressing room, with all the world outside waiting for you to give them what they want

404

. . . you can't, you can't, you know you can't, not now, *not after everything you've taken to fight the fear . . . you can't.*

The tour, too, meant a different hotel bedroom each night, train bedrooms in between, entertaining onstage and at the parties that followed, Judy forced to be gay whether she felt like it or not, with people pulling at her from all directions, and she homesick for her children, to top everything else.

If anything enlivened the tour, it was what can only be called a Frank Sinatra spectacular. Frank had inaugurated the idea of renting buses to bring guests to Judy's concerts in and about the Los Angeles area. He hired a Greyhound bus, set up a bar, appointed Humphrey Bogart admiral and chief bartender, and brought scores of celebrities to Long Beach, where Judy appeared at a benefit for the Exceptional Children's Foundation. These were, of course, retarded children. Although her opening in San Diego was what *Variety* called "a dazzling performance," three days later, on July 8, the Long Beach benefit was the high point of the tour. She had never forgotten her experience in Boston, and how audiences of children responded to her. She told Sid, "I want to do it. We've got such beautiful, healthy children of our own, I'll do anything to help kids who don't have these advantages." This one night was like a circus: Judy performing, and then bringing onstage to entertain the youngsters a staggering assortment of stars; they included Sinatra, Bogart, Sammy Davis, Jr., Dean Martin, Van Johnson, Eddie Fisher and Debbie Reynolds, June Allyson and Dick Powell, Betty Bacall, every girl singer in Hollywood. Afterward, as a grand finale, Sid and Judy took Frank and his guests to Romanoff's for a midnight supper celebration.

Then, finally, a most important event—Judy's TV debut that autumn before the largest audience so far recorded in television history —from which Judy once more emerged, battle-scarred but herself, under circumstances that might well have destroyed anyone else.

30

JUDY WOULD NEVER HAVE MADE HER TV DEBUT, and opened a new chapter in her career, had it not been that Sid, overambitious for both of them, actually outsmarted himself. With the Transcona-Warner deal in chill abeyance, and no films in sight, Sid decided to take Judy's "International Variety Show"—that was how it had been billed ever since she brought it from the Palace—on a nationwide tour of some twenty cities in the autumn of 1955.

The idea had come out of a discussion between them that summer following Joey's birth. Judy had been telling Sid how much she enjoyed touring the country during the war with the Hollywood Bond Cavalcade of Stars, when she and a score of other name performers traveled from city to city, living aboard a train night after night, and making whistle stops from coast to coast. The gypsy in her liked the informality of this life. (One night, at 2 A.M., when she felt like playing poker and nobody had a deck of cards, she had simply gone through the length of the train, waking people in their bunks, saying, "I'm Judy Garland—would you possibly have a deck of cards?" And she'd gotten them.) Wouldn't it be fun to try such a tour on their own train, like a traveling troupe? Let's do it, Sid had said, and that had been the inception of the new tour. Judy suggested an improvement for this one. She had been reading about Lucius Beebe, the elegant social columnist, who traveled about the country in his private Pullman. If Sid could manage to rent Beebe's Pullman, she and her company could live in it during the tour. It would be like a circus. Dr. Marc had once said, "Judy should have been a circus entertainer —then she'd have been happy—with popcorn and hot dogs and ice cream and costumes and clowning about. . . ."

Judy painted a persuasive picture. They'd hook up the Pullman to whatever train was necessary to take them to the cities they'd chosen. Traveling like the Presidents of the United States, going back to Abraham Lincoln, appearing on the rear observation platform to wave at their constituents—their fans—she loved the idea.

Sid found Beebe ready to rent his Pullman. But it would be an enormously expensive tour. It meant taking an entire show, sets and all, across the country. Judy always appeared only in the second half of the show. Beginning with Frank Fontaine, the comic, they'd have to take along all their first-half acts—tumblers, jugglers and the like, as well as Judy's dancing boyfriends, plus a complete personal and technical staff. . . . It would be economic suicide to attempt this without a guarantee of, say, at least $10,000 a night from each theatre in case the usual 60 percent of the gross was less.

Sid told Judy that MCA, now her agents, believed it could be worked out. She had been doing well ever since the Palladium. The Palace had made her the biggest name in show business, and she now had behind her a major film as well. Sid began signing contracts with theatres that offered the requisite guarantees.

Then he discovered that only seven of the proposed twenty had come through. The remainder refused to post guarantees. Not long before, Jerry Lewis and Dean Martin had toured many of these cities. It had been a disaster. They'd be happy, enthusiastic, to take Judy—but no guarantees. Suppose she didn't show one night? There had been stories of her failing to appear for days while making Star. . . . This troubled theatre managers.

Sid faced a dilemma. Either he went through with the tour, taking his chances—which meant signing contracts with the orchestra, putting up bonds for the musicians, paying expenses on the road and everything else the tour entailed—or else he canceled the tour. But if he canceled the tour, the theatres he'd already signed would sue. He faced an agonizing decision: either option could bankrupt them. And this, just when Judy was doing so well in her comeback.

He turned to Jules Stein, head of MCA. "I think we can get you out of your misery," Stein said. The theatre contracts already signed contained a clause that if Judy was called upon by a bona fide sponsor to do either a film or television special, they could be canceled upon forty-five days' notice. "And," said Stein, "I think I can get you a sponsor for an hour-and-a-half TV special."

This apparently was a deal he had been working on, for not long afterward he notified Luft that the Ford Motor Company was prepared to sponsor Judy for its Ford Star Jubilee, over CBS, Saturday night, September 24. A major event—CBS's first color-TV spectacular. And Judy's debut. It was a natural.

Great, said Sid. They were saved. He spoke to Judy. TV? A live show? An hour-and-a-half show? She was full of fears. She wasn't ready for it, physically. She'd never been on television. She'd be before those goddamned cameras again. She'd have to lose weight. That would be torture. And *television:* that was even worse than making a film. No retakes. No mistakes permitted. Everything had to be perfect the first time, because that would be the only time, with millions watching and listening. . . . Oh, Sid, she said, I'm scared.

He reassured her. In any event, they had no choice. But she could do it. On the recent tour, despite bad moments, which were to be expected, she had delivered. As Sid put it, "All Ford is buying is the same show you've been doing night after night. And it would be one night, not twenty."

Judy asked, "Do you think I'm too heavy?"

It was now late July. They would have more than eight weeks to prepare for that single night, those ninety minutes. "What with rehearsals and diet, you'll be in good shape," Sid said. Everything she'd done since they knew each other pointed to this, and before an audience bigger than a thousand theatres, ten thousand theatres . . . how could she not? So Judy agreed. The business details were worked out. Judy would receive a flat $100,000, and Sid $10,000 as producer.

Judy and Sid threw themselves into this new world. A CBS executive, Harry Ackerman, assigned as coordinator, said he had the perfect man to direct the show—a young TV director named Ralph Levy. As for the format, it would be the Palace show, with eight dancing boys, integrated with various comedy acts, with David Wayne, the actor, playing foil to Judy, doing her Fred Astaire tramp number with her, and acting as master of ceremonies. But in the latter part of the program Judy would be doing virtually a one-woman show.

One morning Judy and Sid walked on the TV set. They were talking with Ackerman, blocking out the ninety minutes, when a man in his late twenties, wearing shell-rim glasses, appeared. Ackerman introduced him. This was Ralph Levy. "Ralph's had a lot of directing experience," Ackerman added. Ralph and Judy shook hands. "I'm delighted to know you," said Judy, and Ralph said, "I hope we'll get along." He said it smilingly, but Sid was suddenly alerted: some kind of message was coming to him, but not clearly. He looked at Levy closely; the other was still smiling, but was it possible that his eyes were a bit bloodshot? At this hour?

Judy and Ralph were talking together now, Sid not hearing all their words, but suddenly, clearly, he heard young Levy say, "Well, you know, Miss Garland, I am not impressed."

Judy said to him, "You're fired," turned on her heel and said to Ackerman, "Now let's get on with the business." Levy stood stunned, uncertain, and presently wasn't there. Ackerman, taken aback almost as much, said, "Well, I'll get somebody else."

Only later did it develop that young Levy *had* been impressed— so impressed, and so frightened at meeting Judy, that he had fortified himself with three martinis before coming on the set. He said, sadly, later, "I guess the wrong words just came out." What he did not know was how terrified Judy herself was, and why, therefore, she didn't want anybody around who was not impressed by her: she needed to draw courage from their belief in her.

Final rehearsals started a full two weeks before the twenty-fourth. Judy worked six to eight hours a day, every day, supported not only by Sid but by Jack Cathcart, who as her conductor would lead the thirty-eight-man orchestra. Everyone knew how important this show was, important for Judy, important for CBS: CBS was in a ratings fight with NBC, and it would be a difficult show, too, because Judy would appear in fourteen numbers during the hour and a half.

Two days before the twenty-fourth Liza and Lorna, now nearly three years old, visited Mama's set at CBS, and Lorna found herself the subject of a full-page spread in *Life* magazine, imitating her mother dancing, while Liza, slim and pert in a little tailored suit, watched her mother go through her act. Judy, though increasingly nervous, seemed fine.

The night of the twenty-third, Sid took counsel with her. He was exhausted; she was exhausted; perhaps she should have a friend or nurse stay with her that night, so she could at least have someone to talk to if she couldn't sleep. It was very important that she get a good night's rest. The show would go on early, at 6:30 P.M. California time, 9:30 P.M. New York time; there'd be rehearsals almost up to the last minute, with the final dress rehearsal at 3 P.M. A long, arduous, terrifying day awaited her.

No friend was available. Sid hired a nurse to stay with Judy, sleeping on a cot in Judy's room. "Watch Miss Garland all the time," he warned her. "She's going to be very nervous, and if she needs anything, or there's anything out of the ordinary, just knock on my door." He set his alarm for 6 A.M. of the twenty-fourth.

He awoke, for no apparent reason, at 5:45. He walked into Judy's room. The nurse was not there. Judy lay in bed, breathing heavily. He knew there was no point in saying, as he then said, almost prayerfully, "Judy, it's nearly six o'clock," because there was no response, as he knew there would be no response. He lifted one of her eyelids; the pupil was dilated. Judy was out. What had she taken, and how much? He shook her, but she did not respond.

He ran down the stairs, and there was the nurse, in the kitchen, heating a pot of water. "Where the hell have you been?" he cried. "How long you been here?" She said, "Just four or five minutes, Mr. Luft. I just came down to make a pot of tea."

"You know, I can't get Judy up?"

"Oh, my God!" the nurse said.

"Oh, my God!" Luft echoed, in complete despair, and took the steps three at a time back to Judy's room, the nurse on his heels. In those four or five minutes—or ten or fifteen or whatever they had been—Judy must have taken something, most likely Seconal, and most likely a great deal. He shook her vigorously. "Can you hear me, Judy?" Her voice came weakly, little more than a whisper, "Yeah, Baby, I can hear you."

He said, "It's six o'clock and this is show time today, dress rehearsal —everything."

She said, slowly, "Darling, I know it, but I want to sleep. I want to sleep . . . so . . . badly."

He said, "Baby, you gotta get up. Baby, darling, Baby, you just got to get up." He shook her again.

Like a sigh, the words came back, slowly, slurred, "O.K. . . . I'll . . . try. . . ."

He sat her up, put his arms under her armpits and lifted her out of bed. She couldn't walk. He carried her into the bathroom, with its huge sunken marble tub, and turned on the cold shower. He took off her pajamas and got into the shower with her, still in his pajamas, and the water was ice-cold, and she was yelling, "It's cold, it's freezing," and he said, "Yes, Baby, it's freezing." He held her under the water, and they stood together for about five minutes—she could hear him, she could answer him, but she was powerless to move—and then he

410

carried her out into the bathroom, sat her down on the toilet, dried her off, and at the same time removed his wet pajamas, dried himself, put on a robe, put her in a robe, got her into her dressing room, sat her on a chair, rushed back to his room to put his clothes on. It took him a minute and a half, and when he was back in her room, she was asleep again in the chair. He woke her. He began walking her; now, finally, she could remain erect, but swaying. "Do you want anything," he asked, "food, anything?" She shook her head.

Holding her with one arm, he telephoned Dr. Pobirs. Pobirs said, "I'd telephone the drugstore and get some Benzedrine or Dexedrine, but they don't open until eight o'clock."

Luft walked Judy back and forth in her room until eight o'clock, then, with the nurse standing guard, he drove to the drugstore, picked up the prescription and gave the pills to Judy.

Luft was, simply, terrified. He had had his experiences with Judy, but now he had no idea how much of what she had taken and how long it would affect her. She had to be at her best; she had to be able to make the first rehearsal, the dress rehearsal, the show itself. Ford had bought an hour and a half of prime time; there was no better hour than 9:30 P.M. on a Saturday night. They had taken full-page advertisements throughout the country: Judy Garland's television debut—CBS's first color spectacular. *My God,* Luft thought, *this could be the most publicized flop of all time.* All she had to do was louse herself up here. . . . It would wipe out everything, all her successes of the last four years, back to the Palladium; the image of Judy on that screen tonight, bombing, would be the picture of Judy millions would carry about with them from now on. . . . He could have shot the nurse and then shot himself.

It was now 10 A.M. A full day of rehearsals lay ahead of her. By this time Judy's throat doctor had arrived. He said, "Order up Chinese food, put a lot of soy sauce on it, and make her drink as much iced tea as you can." The Chinese food would absorb the medication, the soy sauce would make her thirsty, the tea would wash some of the medication out through her kidneys.

Eleven o'clock: her voice was slurred. Twelve o'clock: Luft was pouring iced tea into her. At 1 P.M. she was to go through some of her songs. But she still couldn't talk without slurring her words. Sid drove her to CBS. One of the executives walked into her dressing room. Judy was trying to eat a huge mound of chow mein, and her husband was pouring iced tea for her. Judy mouthed to him: "I'm going to save my voice." Luft explained, "Judy's not going to sing now, she's just going to go through the motions, walk through it, mouth everything, and then she'll do the dress rehearsal just as she'll do the show. But she wants to save her voice now." He ushered the man out as quickly as possible.

Two o'clock: one hour to dress rehearsal. Judy said, "How am I doing?"

"You're coming along fine," said Sid. "Drink your tea."

"Oh, God," groaned Judy. Then: "Do . . . you . . . think . . . I'll . . . be . . . all . . . right?"

"You'll be fine," said Sid, fearing he might show his own panic. Because even if she could manage to walk without swaying, suppose someone asked her a question and she couldn't answer? She might be so terrified she'd be unable to talk. Or if she talked, she'd slur her words.

It was nearly three o'clock. Everyone was getting into their costumes. Sid instructed her: "Judy, don't sing, don't talk at all, just go through all the motions. I'm going into the main viewing room with Robinson—" Hubbell Robinson, vice president of CBS—"and the other CBS brass, and I'll try to figure out what to say. Remember, don't try to sing."

No one at CBS knew anything of what had happened. No one had seen Judy yet, really, save the CBS executive, who had seen her for only a moment.

Judy's first appearance was to be in a long, lavender gown, and her opening song was "You Made Me Love You."

Sid left Judy then in Vern's hands—Vern had come on the scene as the result of a hurried telephone call—and went into the viewing room. Here were not only CBS executives, but Ford executives, Technicolor executives, executives of the advertising agency that handled the Ford account, all watching the television monitor for the dress rehearsal to begin.

Judy was on camera now. The in-house applause was deafening.

They saw Judy's lips move, but they heard nothing. She was mouthing the words silently: "I'm going to save my voice. I'm going to do this whole dress rehearsal without using my voice."

Everyone in the viewing room looked at Sid. Somebody asked, unbelievingly, "She isn't gonna sing?"

412

Luft felt perspiration actually rolling down his temples. But he replied as though it were routine for singers not to sing at a dress rehearsal.

"No," he said casually. "This is only a rehearsal—she's going to save her voice." But when the others continued to stare at him, he added, easily, "She's just careful. Don't worry. You know, it's the first time, she's being doubly careful. . . ." He thought, *It's three o'clock, and in three hours she hasn't made much progress. Christ, she should have snapped out of it by now* . . . He wondered, did they know he was trembling? *Who needed this?* he belabored himself. *I did it, I trapped myself.*

Judy simply walked through the dress rehearsal. Her dresser got her into her tramp costume. Sid had told her to wear low heels, not her usual high heels, because she wasn't steady enough. . . . The rehearsal went on. He looked, finally, at his watch. Five-thirty. It had taken two and a half hours for the dress rehearsal, what with halts and orchestral redos of this section or that, and at each break Judy used the time to go to her dressing room, drink more iced tea and go to the bathroom.

Thirty minutes to show time—could she do it?

Sid had comforted her, she was dressed, he stood in the wings. The curtain opened, and Sid wanted to cross himself. They were on the air. He listened to the show-time applause. He didn't watch the monitor, he watched her: she was standing in a little cubicle, in her lavender outfit, waiting, and then she began to sing "You Made Me Love You." *Thank God*, Sid thought, *that we decided originally to make it slow-paced*, because slow-paced it certainly was—her voice husky, the words slurry. Well, the audience would attribute it to nervousness.

Jack Cathcart and the orchestra were far to one side, unable to see the stage, Jack watching the show on a huge monitor. He knew nothing of what had happened, but the moment he got the cue— "O.K., Jack—boom!"—and the camera opened with a tight shot on her face, he gasped: the pupils of her eyes were enormous. He thought, *She's on downers. Oh, God, too many tranquilizers, poor kid.* She must have been terrified. He knew his sister-in-law. And the voice, wavering, retarded, like a record slowed down—a very slow, very wide vibrato.

Fortunately, the next number, "Swanee," had been prerecorded.

Judy lip-synced it, and that worked fine; then David Wayne appeared, which gave her a rest, and she reappeared to do a medley —she managed to get through that, growing stronger each time. Luft stood in the wings, willing her to get through. Again, a pause—then song after song, she getting better each time, until by the fifth song she seemed herself; and when she did her tramp number with David Wayne—who was superb in his part—and then sat down on the edge of the stage and sang "Over the Rainbow," she sang it magnificently. Neither Luft, from where he was watching, nor Vern, backstage, nor Cathcart, far to the side with his orchestra, could believe it.

Sid caught her as she came offstage, and she walked, smiling, erect beside him, to her dressing room. They closed the door and embraced. She clung to him, utterly exhausted. When he let go of her, after murmuring he knew not what, he saw bloodstains on his shirt where she had held him. The insides of her wrists were bleeding. "Baby, what happened?" he asked.

"Well . . . I had to dig for those last notes in 'Rainbow,' and I didn't realize it, I had my hands behind me, and I just dug my nails into my wrists. . . . Oh, I had to dig for those notes, but I didn't know it." She held him again and put her head on his shoulder. She said, "We did it, Baby."

31

IT MAY BE SAID THAT THE MIDDLE FIFTIES were good years for Judy and Sid Luft, her third husband—these two who had been counted out so many times before. These years marked the making of *A Star Is Born,* her nomination for an Oscar; Joey's birth, which completed her family of three children; the purchase and furnishing of their palatial home at 144 South Mapleton Drive in Holmby Hills; her TV debut, which led CBS to give her a three-year contract, a spectacular once a year; and her Las Vegas club debut at the New Frontier Hotel, where she was to receive the highest salary ever paid an entertainer, and which opened still another door to her. Luft was the *deus ex machina* in all this. While he provided her with a greater family stability than she had known for a long time, it was a roller-coaster period: highs almost unendurably triumphant, followed by descents so terrifying they would have shattered anyone save a woman who could entertain a hundred guests singing with stitches in her neck still sore from a throat-cutting attempt, and a man who had survived hanging head down in a burning plane.

It was, too, a time of entertainment, partying and gadding about, and if Mapleton Drive was not Sesame Street or Peyton Place, it was, nonetheless, a center of continuous excitement. The four Crosby boys would be racing their souped-up Corvettes up and down the street, Liza would be gossiping with her friend Cheryl Crane, Lana Turner's daughter, over the back fence, and there'd be open house everywhere. Frank Sinatra's Rat Pack had come into being, with Betty Bacall as den mother, and Bogey and Peter Lawford and Dean Martin and Judy and Sid and Swifty Lazar as charter members. They even designed gold pins, miniature rats with ruby eyes. At 2 and 3 A.M., Frank would drive up in his Thunderbird, the better for a few drinks, jaunty in his white trench coat and straw hat with its white band, and knock on the Lufts' door. Judy and Sid, as everyone knew, were up all hours of the night.

Judy loved her English Tudor castle. At the beginning, it took getting used to. Each afternoon a sightseeing bus came down Mapleton Drive, and Judy, sitting in the den reading, or playing with her children, seeming hardly older than they, would hear, through the open windows, the stentorian voice of the tour director: "And on our left, we have the Judy Garland home, you remember, she tried to commit suicide at MGM. . . ." The first time, Judy slammed the windows shut and, when Sid came home, demanded that he do something about it.

Maybe we could put special insulation around the windows, Sid suggested helpfully. If it wasn't the sightseeing bus, it was tourists on their own. An old lady sat on a bench at the corner of Sunset and Mapleton, selling maps giving the addresses of the stars—"X marks Judy Garland"—and every time Judy, in a robe and slippers, her hair on end, opened the door to pick up the newspaper, there were crowds staring at her. "Buy up all the maps, Sid," Judy pleaded. "I can't do that," Sid protested. "Not to a little old lady. Besides, she'd only get more maps to sell."

But there were many rewards. The furnishing of the house became an exciting project and, for Luft, a matter of high personal satisfaction. When they first moved in, there had been little furniture. In the huge, baronial 24-by-40 living room, there was only a Ping-Pong table (Judy was a demon Ping-Pong player); and in the magnificent, circular marble-floored dining room, there was a green onyx table, with which Judy had fallen in love in San Francisco (the decorator said the original was in the Louvre). Save for the bedrooms, bar and den, that was it. Preproduction costs on *Star* had been so heavy that Sid could not afford to put money in furniture. But he had his own plans. In the Transcona-Warner contract there was a salvage clause which allowed the producer, after *Star* was completed, first choice in the purchase of the set furnishings at 20 percent of the wholesale cost, to be charged against the expenses of the film. Warner's then had a similar option to buy what it wished of what remained. The principal set in *A Star Is Born* was the living room and den of the Norman Maines' Malibu Beach house, from which, on the morning of his greatest despair, Maine, having overheard his wife, Vicki, tell Oliver Niles, the studio head, that she will sacrifice her career to take care of her broken, alcoholic husband, kisses her and, smiling, goes out for his morning swim in the Pacific—and drowns himself.

The sets had been designed by Lemuel Ayres, who had done superb work in Vincente's films, had won many awards and had been brought to *Star* by Judy. Ayres spared no expense. Sid, as producer, happily O.K.ed everything—the exquisite sofa, the chairs, the paintings (one by Maurice de Vlaminck, the French Impressionist), the hand-painted Chinese screens and Chinese butterfly lamps, the magnificent T'ang Dynasty camel that had graced the Norman Maine house, the lovely ornaments and beautiful bric-a-brac. Thousands of dollars were spent on those furnishings. After *Star* was finished, Sid invoked the salvage clause, chose what he wished and had the satisfaction of seeing a huge Warner Brothers truck bring the furnishings to 144 South Mapleton Drive, where they fit perfectly. Warner's then chose what it wanted, and allowed Transcona to have whatever else Sid wished—he wrote a check for $4,200 and got the rest of it.

Now, as he and Judy looked about at all these expensive, beautifully tooled furnishings in their home, gotten so cheaply, Judy was as delighted as he.

On a good day at the Mapleton house Judy would get up around 11 A.M. She'd have breakfast in bed (as her mother had accustomed her to since she was five), turn on the TV and watch the soap operas, which she lived through as intensely as though they were real life. She also loved the radio, and listened to it passionately. She had one in her bathroom, and Sid, when he was home, could hear her laughing there, especially when the very popular *Bob and Ray* program was on. This was her private period, the few hours after she awoke and ate; she'd put on a caftan, or a blue-and-white-checkered house dress costing a dollar ninety-eight, instead of pajamas. She had her own little rituals, and did not want to be disturbed then. After breakfast, the soap opera, radio, she'd read. She had never read much in school: Jimmy and Suzy would brief her on the newest books, and Judy would grasp the essence of the story at once, and be as well informed at a party as anyone else. Now, however, she read for hours at a time. She'd lunch by herself (Sid would usually be at his office). Her appointments were usually between four and six: a friend dropping over, whatever. Then, about six o'clock, began preparations for the evening: her bath, her careful makeup—she would now begin to live. This might be entertaining at home; or being with the children; or going with Sid to Romanoff's or Chasen's; or dropping over to the Ira Gershwins' for poker, or at least once a week to Peter and Pat Lawfords', often running into Pat's brother Jack, the junior Senator from Massachusetts.

Nonetheless, the relationship between Judy and Sid during this period fluctuated from the most violent fights (it must be reported that once while he was driving back from a party Judy took off her shoe and banged Sid in the eye with the sharp spike heel, so that he had a black eye for a week, and that Sid once seized Judy by the hair and actually flung her across the room, to land, unhurt but shocked beyond belief, on the *Star Is Born* sofa) to the most ardent lovemaking.

One Saturday afternoon there had been a furious set-to between them. She was on pills again, and matters weren't helped when Sid, beside himself, stalked out of the house, got into his car and went to the races at Hollywood Park. Judy felt deserted—and doubly depressed. The result was a telephone call to Vern at his home. "Vern," she said, "I just want you to know that this is the end of it. I'm killing myself. I've taken some medication—" This was only too clear from her speech, but her next words chilled him: "I've got Joey here and I may take him with me. I want you to pass this word along. Sid is not to have the children. Liza and Lorna are to be given to Dirk Bogarde or Capucine." Judy had visited the British actor at his Bucks County farm in Pennsylvania, and liked him, and Capucine was a French model whom Charlie Feldman, the agent, was grooming to become an actress.

Vern took no chances. He had to get Sid, and Sid was in his box at the track, where no telephones were permitted. The only telephones were in the racing secretary's office. Vern had to plead to have a life-or-death message gotten to Sid: get home immediately. Then Vern called the police (scandal or no scandal didn't matter under such circumstances) and rushed to the Mapleton house. He went in the back way and ran up to the nursery. Lorna was there with her governess; Liza had been picked up that morning by Vincente and was spending the day with him. Vern cried, "Where's Joey?" The governess pointed upstairs. "She took him."

Vern raced up to Judy's suite; the door was locked. He went around to Sid's suite; that was locked. Judy had locked every door that would allow anyone to get to her. Outside, he heard the police sirens. At this moment Sid came bounding up the stairs. He had driven at break-neck speed, stopping for nothing. He was terrified, he did not know what to expect. Vern blurted out what Judy had said, and Sid, who had a way of getting into her bedroom by some means Vern hadn't known, a moment later was in there, Vern on his heels. The draperies were pulled tight, but all the lights were on, and there in bed, asleep, angelically curled in each other's arms, like a painting by Botticelli, were mother and child. Joey, unharmed, was given to the nurse. Sid shook Judy into a groggy wakefulness, Vern sent away the police, there was another wall-rattling fight between the Lufts, and Sid came down later, trembling with anger and frustration and relief.

The next night Vern was there, to pick up a package. He heard them in her suite. It was: "Oh, honey, baby doll," and: "Darling, dearest, what do you want for dinner?"

There was a brief fallow period; then Judy, becoming restless, went to work. She began cutting a new album for Capitol Records. Sid put out feelers and with her agents negotiated Judy's Las Vegas debut in July of 1956 at the New Frontier Hotel for four weeks at $55,000 a week.

The contract came a few days after another windfall. Sid had won,

418

at thirty-to-one odds, $52,000 on a horse, Ozbeg, which he had bought from Aly Khan two years before. He paid several debts on the spot, bought his trainer a Cadillac he'd promised him if the horse won, changed the rest of the money into hundred- and five-hundred-dollar bills and came home. Judy was lying in bed, reading. Without a word, Luft began pulling the bills out of the pockets of his trench coat (he also carried a revolver) and began throwing this cornucopia of magic paper endlessly on the blue and gold coverlet. "Ohhhhh!" Judy squealed. "Sid, you great big wonderful lovable son of a bitch, you! . . . But, my God, we'll be robbed!" Sid produced the revolver, and grinned. They went wild, the two of them, dancing about, tossing the money into the air, letting it shower down on them, hundred-dollar bills, five-hundred-dollar bills, caught in Judy's red peignoir, falling on the turquoise carpet—it was a scene he'd never forget.

It helped balance the times he spent seeking out Judy's caches of pills and capsules, emptying the latter, mixing Seconal and flour (they looked alike) and repacking them so they'd have half their potency (Seconal always had a depressing effect on Judy), and diluting her greens and whites with confectioners' sugar; or the times he conspired with Dr. Pobirs to instruct Judy's favorite druggist that any refills of Pobirs' prescriptions without his knowledge be made up of harmless placebos. Once Judy had broken open a capsule Sid had doctored and tasted it. She knew what he was doing. "What does he think I am, a cup of coffee?" she demanded of Vern. "This is pure sugar. I'll die of diabetes before I die of drug addiction." Sid tried to explain it to her later. "Half these medications are pure dextrose— that's sugar, that's why it's so sweet, that's what gives you the energy." Judy pretended to understand.

These were the games they played with each other, and if they made no sense to anyone else, they made sense to them, for whatever they did or said to each other in anger could vanish in an eyelid's wink. Sid courted her: flowers every few days; little, unexpected, charming gifts of books or jewelry. When she had terrible nights, nausea she could not control for whatever reason, he tended her, hour after hour, and would finally, exhausted, manage his way back to his own bed.

His heart could only melt when he found on waking late one day the note she'd pinned to his pillow while he slept:

Darling, I was really so sick all this Goddamn night. It's now 5:20 and I'm going to take a crack at trying to sleep. Anyway, don't wake me for "nuttin'." In spite of my pukeiness—I loved you all through the night. Not an attractive thing to tell you, darling, but when you adore your husband—what are you going to do? God bless you, my Sid, for having so much *CLASS*. See you sometime today. All my devoted love, forever—Judy.

The Las Vegas engagement meant hard work. Roger Edens wrote three new songs for her; they had to tailor a show for a new, tougher audience, with Judy again singing fourteen, fifteen songs, one entitled "Happiness Is a Thing Called Joe." There were no new superlatives for her show. *Variety* summed up her opening night: "In an air of expectancy as electric as the atmosphere attending the opening of a promising new Broadway musical, one of the greatest modern-day singers caught fire last night in the first nitery engagement of her career."

The Vegas engagement was done in style. Judy brought up Liza, Lorna and Joey, and the family lived in two large suites on the same floor, the children far enough away so they could not hear Judy and Sid's quarrels. But Vegas had its drawbacks. The temperature was 105, 110 degrees. To walk in this furnace-like heat did dreadful things to Judy's throat, drying it, making it feel raw. Judy had a characteristic gesture: three fingers touching the hollow of her throat lightly, patting it gently, as if petting it, caressing it: there were her vocal chords; this was the essence, the vulnerable physical essence, of her. The condition of her voice and throat was the key to how she felt about herself; her entire body, her personality, seemed to take its cue from her throat.

Now, in Vegas, the climate was an assault on her, out-of-doors was impossible. But inside, the air conditioning, too, had a drying effect. Sid had her room steamed constantly, and Judy lived with the dedication of a monk. After her show she would play blackjack at the tables downstairs to wind down, then get into bed, get her sleep, wake up late, breakfast and steam her throat through the day, and spend some time with the children. She tried to talk as little as possible during the day.

In the second week she came down with laryngitis: she could not sing for two successive nights. Her voice had vanished. Sid evolved the idea of Judy sitting on a little coffee table in the center of the stage, mouthing the words, while Jerry Lewis, just separated from

420

Dean Martin and starting a career on his own, stood next to her, singing her songs, cavorting about. It was moving and hilarious, since both were masters of pantomime.

The four-week engagement was so successful that it was extended for another week. Since Suzy's husband, Jack, was conducting, and Suzy was there every night, and the children as well, Judy decided to make it a complete family affair. She invited Jimmy, Johnny and eighteen-year-old Judalein to come up from Dallas as her guests, air fares and all expenses paid, and moved them into a third suite, and the three Gumm Sisters were together again. When the engagement was over, Judy took Judalein back to the Mapleton house as a house guest for a week to get to know her young cousins better, and to give her advice which Judalein always remembered: *Stay out of show business. There are so few sincere people in it, and God, they're hard to find!* Judalein listened, fascinated, for her Aunt Judy at the time was eating a whole chocolate pie, interspersing her advice with a kind of helpless "I'm not supposed to do this" even as she took another forkful.

Two months later, in the autumn of 1956, Judy opened at the Palace Theatre in New York. The return had been almost inevitable. Sol Schwartz had told her the Palace was hers whenever she wanted it; her opening night in Vegas was hardly over before he wanted to know if she'd return for an eight-week engagement. Just bring her New Frontier show to New York.

"Oh, I'm always happy at the Palace," said Judy. Sid wasn't so sure about this engagement. The farther Judy got from home and children, the more the work took its toll. To leave them—the solidity she had at last achieved—made going on the road a torturous experience for her. The very circumstances that tended to make her content as wife and mother now conspired to make her career more difficult. If she went to the Palace, she would do so only if she could take Lorna and Joey along. From now on, wherever possible, she would take them with her. Pulled as she was between love of the children and the need for applause, maintaining an equilibrium was to become an even greater ordeal for her, and make Luft's balancing act still more hazardous.

And the expense! When they'd been at the Palace nearly five years before, there had been just the two of them: no responsibilities, no overhead. Now there was a family, an expensive nineteen-room house that cost nearly $100,000 a year to run, and if they went to New York, they would still have to keep on most of the staff.

Was eight weeks at the Palace worth it? It meant going back to Roger Edens for new and changed lyrics—what was suitable for Vegas was not suitable for the Palace—as well as the expense of transporting eleven dancing boys, a conductor, hairdresser, nurse, the children. . . . In Vegas, they and the children had lived rent-free in the hotel where Judy worked, and the children were no trouble, out in the sun or pool all day, just under their noses. In New York they'd all have to move into a hotel; the children—Lorna was nearly four, Joey eighteen months, still in his crib—would have to be locked up in a hotel suite or taken to playgrounds, with a governess for Lorna, a nurse for Joey. Ethel Merman had suggested the Park Lane Hotel, because it had apartment-like facilities. Two apartments there meant another $4,000 a week.

But Judy wanted to go to the Palace, and go she would. Not only that, but she wanted their Park Lane apartment to have the flavor of home. That meant shipping certain Mapleton house furnishings to New York. It's too damn expensive, Sid said. They fought about it, but Judy had her way.

This time Walters, who had again been loaned by MGM, devised an extraordinarily effective introduction. It was all glamour.

The curtain went up unnoticed by the audience, because the house lights were on; the house lights faded; the orchestra lights came up for the expected overture; the audience still didn't know the house curtain was up. What they saw was an expanse of blackness: the stage was black, and though it was not deep at the Palace, to keep it totally dark, black velvet had been stretched across the rear wall.

The overture began, the moving, evocative notes of "Over the Rainbow": and on the third bar—bom! *bom!* bom!—a pinpoint of light hit Judy's face, small, far-off, like an apparition in the distance against the black velvet background, that marvelous face materializing out of the darkness—Judy singing . . . incredible! Judy had contributed to this idea, too. It stemmed from the long-ago days at the Old Mexico in Chicago, and before, when she sang, her face swathed in black—that child's face, singing, so pure, with such power—and then, unswathed, twelve-year-old Frances Gumm. It had been mesmeric then; now it was even more so. The reviewers were, if possible, even more ecstatic than five years earlier:

"In magnificent voice, Judy belted out each number as though she were singing it for the first time. This was not a wan and tired Judy for whom life had become no garland of roses. It was a Judy with sparkle, zip and plenty of punch, at the very peak of her career." And "Queen Judy Is Back Again At The Palace," and "Judy Garland Now Owns Broadway." The Palace, instead of ending her engagement as planned, stretched it into January of 1957.

The strain showed. For her first eight weeks, Judy was fine. One night Richard Rodgers, the composer, joined her in a duet, singing from his aisle seat. Another night, a group of one hundred fans gave a dinner party for her at Nino's, with the Duke and Duchess of Windsor as honorary guests. The Duchess and Judy got along well: Judy admired the older woman's forthright opinions; she was down to earth, feared no one and said what was on her mind.

But then came a period of overmedication, and with that, more quarrels with Sid. Judy was fat, the newspapers had remarked on it, and she was unhappy about it; and whatever cure she sought seemed worse than the disease. She had to cancel eight shows and spent most of this time at Doctors Hospital. In the wake of these difficulties, Judy got into a dispute with CBS over a TV special they wanted her to do a month after the Palace engagement closed—one of the three annual spectaculars that grew out of her *Ford Star Jubilee*. She was to have script approval, she claimed no scripts were submitted, they claimed she had walked out, and in the end CBS canceled the entire contract. Out of this grew a libel suit by Judy against Marie Torre, radio columnist of the New York *Herald Tribune*, who quoted an unidentified CBS executive as saying that Judy was difficult, she obviously had an inferiority complex, and thought she was too fat. . . . Miss Torre refused to identify her source; ultimately she went to jail for ten days for contempt of court. It was an episode from which Judy did not emerge well.

It was in a generally exacerbated mood that Judy went through a series of engagements the first half of 1957. There was a month in Vegas again, at the Flamingo, a week in Detroit, two weeks in Dallas (where Judy and Jimmy and the children had another reunion) and then the Greek Theatre in Los Angeles—her first appearance in Los Angeles in five years, and she was welcomed back by audiences that broke all records. During these engagements, when she was in good voice—and she was in good voice on opening night always—the audiences were her slaves; but now there would be a night or two when medication could not be disguised, and Luft would do his best to smooth matters over, or she would use an excuse, as in Dallas on closing night, when she walked onstage and simply said, "I've just learned that one of my dearest friends, Bob Alton, the choreographer, has died." It was true. "I simply cannot entertain you tonight. I do hope you will forgive me. Dear audience, just go to the box office and ask for your money back."

Backstage Sid would all but tear his hair. Often that one night's proceeds (especially if it was closing night, which meant a full house) on a 60/40 breakdown against gross receipts—Judy to receive 60 percent, from which agent's 10 percent commissions and business manager's 5 percent commission and various salaries had to come— represented the difference between profit and loss for the entire engagement.

In the Mapleton house, on a summer day in 1957, Judy said almost wistfully, "I've got to go to London. I'm bored. I'm unhappy here, I'm sick of Detroit and Dallas and all these cities—I've got to get to London, Sid. It'll be good for my tummy. Get me the Palladium again, Sid."

She had not appeared in England since 1951. London was always to be a relief, a refuge, for her; they loved her there; it would give her a new lease on herself. She repeated it: "Get me the Palladium." And she went into her wing of the house.

Within a day Sid knew he had problems. The Palladium was booked for months. Another theatre, the Dominion, would be happy to sign Judy Garland for a four-week engagement beginning October 16.

This offer, however flattering, made no sense financially. The prices of theatre tickets in England were far below those in the United States. Back in 1951 Judy had played to a $4.40 top at the Palace. Last year it had been $6.60. In London, the most that could be charged for a ticket was a pound—$2.80.

Luft faced the same dilemma as when Judy wanted to return to the Palace from Vegas. It meant taking an entourage from California to New York and then by boat to London—Judy, himself, the children, the dancing boys, staff—nearly twenty-five persons, plus luggage and costumes. He estimated the cost at $1,000 a person, or $25,000 there and back. And Judy would not do more than one show a night. If they got 60 percent of a house crowded to the rafters, they would still lose money.

This was confirmed by Judy's business manager, A. Morgan Maree. Impossible to go to London for a four-week engagement.

Judy said, "I don't give a damn whether we lose money or not. I want to go. Sid, you're ingenious—figure out a way for us to make money so we can do it."

The only solution, said Sid, would be to finance the expected London deficit by having Judy play two one-week engagements beforehand in the United States, at U.S. ticket prices. Then they might break even or better on the London deal.

Judy said, "I don't want to play in the United States. I told you I'm sick of these cities."

But because there was no help for it, Judy reluctantly agreed to be signed for a week in Washington, beginning September 16, and a week in Philadelphia, beginning September 26. She would close there October 2, and they would leave on the *United States* October 4. There'd be time for rest and rehearsal in London before opening the Dominion on October 16.

It was a deeply worried Luft who made the arrangements. He knew that when Judy did something against her will, sooner or later there would be trouble.

He and Morgan Maree had added up a number of recent unblinkable facts. No money had been made in the two-week Dallas engagement in June because Judy had canceled the closing night: this meant an $18,000 profit had vanished. What they made in their one-week engagement in Detroit just before that had been dissipated in traveling and layovers; and though they had a profit from Judy's really spectacular Greek Theatre engagement in Los Angeles, MCA had informed them they owed $37,000 in back commissions, which had been deducted then and there, leaving them very little indeed.

The Washington and Philadelphia engagements *had* to be done.

The day before Judy's opening in Washington at the Capitol Theatre on September 16, as Sid and Judy dined in their suite at the Sheraton Hotel (the children, as usual, had their suite far down the hall), Judy said, "I think I'm getting the flu."

Sid looked at her. The flu was going around, but Judy seemed fine.

"Better send for a doctor," she said. Sid read this to mean that Judy wanted medication, her kind of medication. There was nothing he could do.

The doctor arrived. Judy, as always, insisted on talking to him alone. Sid, as always, accompanied the physician down the corridor to the elevator. On the way he warned him: "Doctor, please be careful of what medication you send up." Judy had a show to do the following night.

"Don't worry," the physician said. "I've just ordered mild sedation so she can sleep and fight off anything that might come along." When the package came up from the hotel pharmacy, Sid took it. He felt three small bottles. *Oh, God*, he thought. *This is going to be a nightmarish week.*

Next day Judy woke with a hoarse voice. Sid knew at once that the "mild sedation" had been Seconal, for that dried the throat; the second bottle must have been Dexedrine to give her the lift she needed after Seconal; but he had no idea what the third was.

That night, opening night, though her hoarseness was evident, Judy was excellent. She responded to the challenge and excitement of opening night, however terrified she might be of new audiences. How could it be otherwise when critics wrote fondly, "No one gets a frog in her throat or misses a note with more grace and enthusiasm than Judy Garland"? Judy particularly sparkled because Perle Mesta, former Minister to Luxembourg and Washington's most celebrated hostess, was giving one of her famous parties in Judy's honor after the show.

But as the engagement continued, Judy rose each morning with her voice a little more hoarse; each day the same doctor came; each night, backstage, Sid gave her a little more honey and tea between numbers to soothe her throat; and each performance seemed geared subtly slower.

Sunday morning—that night would be her closing one—Judy had ordered breakfast to be brought up at 11 A.M. She was asleep when it arrived. Catherine, the maid, was ready to carry it in. Sid walked into Judy's room and wakened her. "Darling, your breakfast is ready." Judy rose groggily and went into the bathroom.

Two minutes, three minutes later, she flung the door open. She was standing in her pink embroidered knee-length nightie. She said to Sid, like a child, with no expression on her face, "Look what I did—" and extended both hands, palms up.

Sid saw a small fountain of blood spurting from the inside pulse of each wrist. She had cut across them with a razor.

"Oh, God!" he shouted in horror, ran to her, grabbed each wrist, clamping his hands over the cuts and yelling to a transfixed Catherine, "Get me a bunch of my ties, quick!" In the next few seconds he used two ties to bind two tight tourniquets about her arms, above the elbows—first aid he had learned in the Ferry Command—and then used his handkerchiefs to bandage her wrists as tightly as possible. Judy sat throughout this, placid, emotionless, like a doll.

Then, while Catherine rushed downstairs to bring up Harry Rubin, who had chauffeured them and the children on the long drive from the West Coast, Sid got on the telephone. The hotel doctor was off on Sunday, said the switchboard operator. But if it was an emergency, she'd ring the nearest hospital. Sid thought hard. That meant headlines—he dared not. He got the doctor's home telephone number, and when he reached him, he blurted out what had happened and what he'd done.

"You think you've stopped the bleeding?" the physician asked. Sid said, yes. "How badly is she cut?" Sid could only say, "Pretty badly."

"I live in Virginia," the doctor said. "If you don't want to take her to a hospital and if you think the bleeding has stopped, bring her out here. I've got a small operating room here—I can take care of her." Good, good, said Sid. A forty-five-minute drive? He'd do it.

He hung up. Judy, sitting there, said plaintively, "Darling, can you loosen these tourniquets? My arms hurt, my hands hurt."

"Darling, you'll bleed to death," said Sid.

"But you can see the bleeding's stopped," said Judy.

"It'll only be a little while longer. We're driving out to the doctor's," said Sid. Meanwhile, Catherine was doing her best to wash out the blood on the hotel carpet. Sid and Harry began dressing Judy. Judy did' not struggle as they put her in pajamas, and then in a colorful, long-sleeved, kimono-like Chinese jacket, and a gray scarf about her neck.

How to get her through the lobby of the Sheraton, one of the busiest hotels in Washington, and out to their car, with no one the wiser? Sid opened the door of their suite and peeked out: the corridor was empty; the children had been taken out for the day by their governess earlier. From the Lufts' suite to the elevator seemed a hundred yards.

"Let's go," said Luft, and he and Rubin, one on either side of Judy, half-walked, half-carried her by the elbows down the corridor to the elevator. It came up at Sid's signal, fortunately empty; they helped her inside and although the car stopped twice on the way down, Sid said brusquely, "Sorry—you can't get in this elevator," and they continued down to the lobby. The door opened.

Sid whispered in Judy's ear, "Come on, Baby, start laughing and kicking." And it was in this fashion that Sid and Harry, both chuckling, holding her inches off the floor by her elbows, she giggling and kicking, carried her through the lobby—the guests looked on, smiling: Judy and her hijinks—and out the door and into the car; and then they drove, as swiftly as they could, on a hot, hot day to the doctor's home in Virginia.

Now and then Judy spoke, but only to complain about the heat, or the Sunday traffic, which sometimes had them moving bumper to bumper. Not once did she say, "Why did I do this?" Or "Sid, I'm sorry." Nothing.

At the doctor's house, nearly an hour later, Sid carried her in. The physician gave her an injection of Sodium Pentothal to knock her out, and took almost ten stitches in each wrist. Then they placed her on a sofa and waited.

After ten minutes, the doctor slapped her face gently. Judy woke up; she sat bolt upright. "What happened?" she asked.

Sid said, "Well, Judy, you had an accident."

She looked down and saw the bandages. "Oh, gosh, what did I do?"

Sid said, "I guess you don't know what you did, but you scratched your wrists up pretty good."

As though she had not heard him, Judy said, all business, "What time is it?"

Sid told her. Three-thirty.

"Let's get to the theatre," said Judy. "I've got a show to do."

Sid said, "Darling, you can't go." He had left word with Catherine to telephone the Capitol Theatre, to inform them that Miss Garland had come down with the flu and deeply regretted that she must cancel her closing show. Ticket money would of course be refunded.

They took their time driving back to the city. Judy slept that night.

428

There was no further talk of what had happened. Sid waited until she had had her breakfast next morning. "Darling, do you think we ought to cancel Philadelphia?" They were to open at the Mastbaum Theatre there in three days.

Judy: "Of course not. Why cancel Philadelphia? I'll be all right. I could do a show tonight."

They drove to Philadelphia. The children knew nothing of what had happened. Judy wore long-sleeved dresses, flesh-colored bandages and wide bangles on her wrists. Sid never knew what medication the physician had given her day after day, that week, that made her take leave of her senses and do what she had done. She could not have known what she was doing, for when she did, she always nicked herself; this was too deep. And perhaps it wasn't that medication at all. Perhaps she had got something from somebody else, which reacted upon the medication she had already taken. It was impossible to keep complete tab on Judy.

All Sid knew was that cancellation of closing night meant they left Washington with less than $2,000 profit. And they had counted on Washington to finance at least half of the London deficit.

On September 26 Judy opened in Philadelphia. She felt weak, but did well. The reviews were excellent. The second night she was better: there was the audience, screaming and yelling, as Garland audiences should, "We love you, Judy!" On the morning of the day before closing, Judy twisted her ankle getting out of the car. It swelled up enormously. A doctor taped it. Her leg looked as though it were in a cast.

She said. "How do I perform, Sid? I certainly can't go through the dances."

Sid said. "Do your show in your robe and bandaged leg." Judy had a white terry-cloth robe she wore in her dressing room.

"Are you crazy?" she said.

"They'll love it," said Sid.

Judy's part of the show—the second half, which followed several acts of vaudeville, with Alan King starring as raconteur and MC—began excitingly with Judy's dancers, billed as "Judy's 11 Boy Friends," appearing suddenly in the rear of the theatre, racing down the aisles waving huge blue and white pennants, leaping onstage and singing a tribute to Judy, meanwhile unfurling their banners in an intricately choreographed number so that everyone saw that each had a letter emblazoned on it, which together spelled "J-U-D-Y G-A-R-L-A-N-D." At that moment Judy would walk onstage casually from the wings, as if she had wandered through the curtain by mistake—to a tremendous ovation. The very simplicity of her appearance after that elaborate introduction was always effective.

This time, at the proper moment, with the dancing boys holding aloft their pennants, Judy limped on, slowly, a little figure in a floor-length white robe and a huge, cast-covered leg. She looked as if she had just come off a hospital bed. There was a gasp, and then deafening applause. As a stage hand brought over a chair, she announced, "I'm going to do the show sitting down—I hope you don't mind my making myself comfortable." She explained how she had twisted her ankle—and the audience was already hers. She began to sing; by the fourth or fifth number, she forgot about her ankle, the cast, everything, and was hobbling-dancing about. It was one of her best shows.

At noon the next day, with both matinee and evening performances scheduled, Judy said to Sid, "I have no voice. I strained it last night. I can't go on."

So Sid canceled the closing day in Philadelphia, that Wednesday, October 2, as he had canceled closing night in Washington little more than a week before.

Now Luft was at his wit's end. The two engagements upon which he counted had ended with no money. He had to pay Gordon Jenkins, the conductor; Alan King; Judy's eleven dancing boys; other help; the hotel bill. In two days he and his family and his company would have to be on the *United States,* bound for England. He sat down that night in their suite at the Hotel Warwick and wrote $15,000 in checks on his Los Angeles bank, with no money there to cover them. He could only count on the fact that it would take several days for the checks to clear. Then he said to Judy, "I'm going to fly to New York tomorrow morning and see if I can raise some money to cover those checks." Judy would come with the children by train later in the day. They would sail Friday at noon.

In New York Thursday morning Sid checked into the Pierre and got on the phone. Not only had he to raise $15,000 to cover the checks; he had to find another $5,000 to pay for passage on the *United States* for himself, Judy, the children and the dancers, and money to pay for expenses aboard the ship, expenses in London, where they'd already reserved an enormous, elaborate suite at the

Savoy Hotel, which cost $2,000 a week for food and lodging.

Luft spent the day on the phone. First to one of Judy's agents. Could he borrow $15,000? No, he couldn't. He called Jock McLean, whom he had met in Palm Beach with the Windsors. "Jeez," said Jock, "I'd like to help you, kid, but I don't have it right now." He tried to reach Ted Law in Tulsa. He could not.

The hours passed. It was 4 P.M. He had still not raised any money. In New York offices closed at 5 P.M. He had an hour to raise the $15,000.

At this point, precisely at this moment, there was a knock on the door. If it was Judy, he had no idea what he would tell her. She had made it clear, repeatedly, that money was Sid's department, and she knew he'd always manage. Anyway, Washington had been his idea, and Philadelphia, too, she'd been talked into both against her will, and she'd gone through hell—that was the way it was, and Sid knew it.

He opened the door. There stood Freddie Finklehoffe, small, dapper, smiling. "Hi, ol' buddy," said Freddie. "How you doin'?"

"Come in," said Sid. He told him. He had written $15,000 in bad checks. Maybe he could write a check to Cunard and get on the goddamn boat and get to England and just pray that something would come up.

It was a hot summer-like day, that October 3. Freddie sighed. "I need a drink," he said. Sid said, "You better order me one up, too, Freddie. Maybe I'll function better."

They were martinis. Both drank. "I'm going to have another one," said Sid. Freddie sighed. "Ol' buddy," he said, "I hate to add to your troubles, but by the way, have you got a horse running over at Belmont?" Sid nodded. "Called Rover the Second?" Sid nodded again. It was a horse he owned, half and half, with Charles Whittingham, a friend who was also a leading trainer. How he had bought a half-interest in it was a long story, dating back to dealings with Aly Khan.

Freddie said, "Well, ol' pal, I don't think you have a horse. I was reading the racing form last night and read that Rover the Second broke his leg."

Sid sat up. "You're kidding!"

No, said Freddie. Rover the Second.

"You positive?" Sid demanded.

"I can read, can't I?" said Freddie.

Sid said, prayerfully, "I hope so, I hope you're right, man!" And started to laugh. Freddie looked at him as though he were insane. Sid was on the phone. He was talking to Charlie Whittingham. Anything new? Yes, said Whittingham. "A tough deal. Rover broke his leg and had to be destroyed."

Sid was laughing because Rover was insured for $30,000. There— as providential as fate—was his $15,000.

He said to Whittingham, "Charlie, would you do me a favor? Can you send an advance of $15,000 to my bank in California? We'll be getting the money from the insurance company, right?"

Right, said Charlie. Sid put down the phone, ordered another martini for himself and Freddie, and went on laughing. "I'm out of the woods!" he exclaimed.

There was another knock on the door. It was now nearly 5:30 P.M. Sid opened the door. There was Judy, in a big, white hat, a black coat with a white fur. She had just got off the train from Philadelphia.

"Did you have a good trip, darling?" Sid asked.

Oh, fine, she said. And what had he been doing?

Out of the woods? Not completely. He had to pay for the boat trip. He had to have a few thousand dollars for incidental expenses; he had to send back payments to California on the house, and other bills there; and he would have big expenses in London. He recalled that several months before, a nightclub in Brooklyn—Brooklyn, of all places—had queried whether it could book Judy there. This was Ben Maksik's Town and Country Club, an enormous place, the largest in the city, seating nearly two thousand persons. Maksik would consider it an honor to have Judy Garland there sometime in the spring of 1958.

Luft called MCA. Would they get a message to Maksik to call him? At once? Within fifteen minutes Maksik was on the phone. Luft said, "I've discussed your proposal. Miss Garland and I are leaving for an extended tour of Europe tomorrow. I'd like to talk to you about your idea, but the only time I'll have would be around midnight tonight. Could you make it?"

They met at midnight, at the Pierre. Judy had gone to sleep. The upshot of their discussion was: Yes, Judy would sing at the Town and Country Club, taking a three-and-a-half-week engagement at $25,000 a week, beginning March 21, 1958. Luft would seal the deal

432

if Maksik brought $15,000 in cash and a contract down to the *United States* tomorrow morning before sailing time.

At 10:30 the next morning, while a festive farewell party filled the Lufts' stateroom, Sid saw Maksik, a plump little man with a mustache, on the outer edge of the crowd, trying to attract his attention. Luft and Maksik promptly retired to the bathroom of the suite. There Maksik produced $15,000 in cash. Sid signed the deal. Maksik, triumphant, left. He had gotten Judy Garland for his place in Brooklyn. Who would go out to Brooklyn for a night on the town? They would if Judy Garland entertained.

It was quite a balancing act Luft had pulled off.

In this unorthodox fashion, the Lufts sailed aboard the *United States* for England and the further adventures of Judy Garland.

32

WHEN, IN A MOMENT OF BITTERNESS toward Sid Luft and in fear of him, Judy had telephoned Vern Alves and said she was going to kill herself and might take Joey with her, but did not want Sid to have Liza and Lorna, she was foreshadowing what in later years would become an obsession: that Sid might seek to take her children from her on the ground that she was an unfit mother, and succeed because of her highly publicized behavior.

The marriage was moving into difficult shoals. There had been a day back in early 1956 when Sid came home to find Judy and the children gone. The staff had no idea where they were; and it was a nightmarish twelve hours before he learned she had taken the children to a friend's house, spent the night there and actually begun a divorce action on the grounds of "extreme cruelty." But the next day she was home again, all was well, and, though the newspapers carried a small squib about it, the episode was forgotten. Yet this frightening telephone call to Vern, and the threat behind it, showed that somewhere in the back of Judy's mind, whether triggered by some evil chemical or stemming from who knew what desperation over herself and her husband and her life, there still lurked the idea of bringing an end to their marriage. Evidently Judy feared in Sid the very strength she admired, his championship of her; and as their financial difficulties grew, their relationship became more strained. It is only truthful to add that, as much as she hated and feared him one moment, she idolized and loved him passionately the next. He, for his part, tried to accept her: who was there like her? Better than anyone else, he knew what darknesses she went through. Once he had found, though he never told her, a prayer she had scribbled on lined notepaper in one of her dark hours, as she hid in her room. He came upon it, stuck in a book where she had forgotten it. Written in her left-handed slanting script—it seemed to him tear-marked, he was not sure—the words were clear:

Dear God. I am asking for help. I need help. I need strength and some kind of courage that has left me. My soul needs healing. My needs are many. Give me the strength to crush my fear and cowardice. Let me face life and the fun it must hold. Help me with my bad nerves and illness until the whiskey is out of my body. Let me see the loveliness awaiting me. Help me find You. Help me make the most of my splendid life. I have lost my way—Please God —let me find it. Let me find dignity and health.

There it ended.

Was she sincere? Or was this Judy acting? Had she written it after their visit to AA, when the actress in her might have made her see herself as a true alcoholic, so that she could write "until the whiskey is out of my body"? There had been periods when liquor played almost as important a part in her life as pills, but never had she been a whiskey-soaked alcoholic. Yet the prayer had all the accents of truth, it seemed a plea from her heart, and Sid had no reason to believe it was not the real Judy speaking—*at that moment.* Judy could make herself believe anything; that was the power of her songs: she sang with utter belief.

If this was the real Judy speaking, it strengthened him in those moments when he felt he could no longer endure living with and caring for her. He came to a point where he felt he had had his fill as her husband. Her other husbands had had their own careers, he had none: his career was Judy Garland. He dreamed of work of his own, and Judy knew he had made ingenious deals in his time—at least they sounded ingenious to her. He once explained how during the war, when he was earning money as a test pilot, he had bought several parcels of land in Coldwater Canyon for 10 percent down—

a few hundred dollars each—and then sold them later, during the postwar boom, for twenty and thirty times their cost, and bought horses and traded them, usually to his benefit because he knew horses. And though he had gambling losses, he also had winnings (Finklehoffe told her Sid was one of the top handicappers in the country), and he had put some of these winnings and his know-how together with Ted Law's money—and that of other wealthy sportsmen—into the co-ownership of a racing stable. She knew he had dealt not only with Aly Khan but with C. V. Whitney and other important names in the world of horse racing. None of this she quite understood, though Judy accepted it as part of his character.

But, with all this, his career was still Judy Garland. As far back as Edinburgh he had realized it would be like this, but never had he anticipated how all-consuming the job would be. He wore every hat she required of a man: husband, lover, protector, knight-at-arms, manager, father, comedian, psychiatrist, cheerleader, errand boy, whipping boy—whatever. Judy was a difficult woman, and under medication an elemental force, unpredictable, destroying and self-destroying; an armful of tigers would be an apt comparison. Yet when she was herself . . . he had never experienced a woman like her: the sweetest, tenderest, most sensitive to his feelings, most understanding, most feminine creature he had ever known. Yet more and more, now, there were quarrels. Sometimes, in sheer anguish of spirit, he would find himself lying in bed close to tears of frustration. On one occasion, fortified by drink, he had sworn he would pack up and leave. "You're driving me out of my fucking mind!" he had shouted.

And she surprised him. She came clean. He had said, full of self-pity in the midst of his anger, "One of your problems is that you're never to blame for anything. It's always 'poor me.' Everybody is always doing things to you; you never do anything to anybody. You're always sympathizing with yourself." She had retorted—it was a line she would use to others—"Sid, sympathy is my business." But then she had added, surprisingly, "What you expect of me will never happen. You might as well get used to the fact that this is what you bargained for. This is what you're married to. I am what I am. I cannot change."

He said, touched, "Judy, in the past I've tried to think of you like somebody who has chronic tuberculosis. I tell myself you've got a sickness, and treat you as a woman with a sickness. But there's a difference. The person who has chronic tuberculosis is usually calm and pleasant, but when you start getting heavily involved with pills, you're a fucking monster."

She said, startling him again, "I admit it. I know it. And that's when you have to keep in mind that I have tuberculosis, and treat me that way."

He had to admit that she had a point. And that argument ended as so many others did—with love-making.

Now, in London, she had nine days before her opening at the Dominion. They were days of rehearsals and sightseeing, shopping, nightclubbing, entertaining, interviews. Her fans welcomed her back as though she had been one of their own all their lives.

The afternoon of opening night, she and Sid and Aly Khan lunched together (she had dined with Dirk Bogarde, and seen many other friends), and then Judy went on to a night of wild acclaim. Her audience of three thousand roared with applause: she "pulled the place down"; she was in superb command, whether singing old favorites or joking in her inimitable manner or overwhelming the hall with her personality, her warmth, her singing of "Me and My Shadow" and "Swanee," and her incomparable tramp act.

She was excited and keyed up. She had gotten in the habit now, just before going onstage, of gripping the curtains in her hands, and literally pawing with her feet, like a horse about to break from the gate, dancing with excitement, waiting for the note that signaled her entrance; then she would burst onstage, propelled by Sid with a smart smack on her behind and a "Go, Baby, go!"

The night was another Garland success. "A revolution in show business hit London last night," said the *Daily Express* critic. But there was at the same time no hesitation about writing of her in a proprietary, even patronizing fashion, as though she were still their Dorothy of *The Wizard of Oz* (as she said once, "Everybody thinks they own me—for at least ten minutes"): She was "pudgy, unrelaxed, dumpy Judy," she was "square-faced, homely, bang-it-out Judy." They spoke of her placing her hands "on her ample hips." She had to accept it, but she was furious. Yet none of this showed in her nightly introduction, written as always by Roger Edens: "It's so good to be back in London. . . . I come all undone when I'm in London."

During the engagement she brought Lorna and Joey onstage to introduce them, and on closing night, which—as was true so often—

was comparable or even superior to opening night, a delirious audience demanded that she do her tramp number twice, and finally she brought Sid onstage and together they sang "Swanee."

On Monday, November 18, a Royal Command Performance, with Queen Elizabeth, Prince Philip and the Queen Mother present, was sponsored by Val Parnell. It began at midnight. A stage full of America's and England's finest entertainers appeared, but Judy was singled out: everyone else was limited to three minutes to do their best for royalty; Judy was allowed eight minutes so she could sing "Rock-a-bye," change into her tramp costume and then do "Over the Rainbow."

She was presented, with the others, to Queen Elizabeth and Prince Philip, and the Queen said to her, "I've enjoyed you in all your pictures, Miss Garland, and you have been one of my favorites. Do come back more often." Prince Philip spoke to her a little longer, but she was so excited she could never remember their conversation, save that he was fabulously charming.

When the Lufts returned to the States after six weeks in London, it was clear that Sid's and Morgan Maree's calculations had been all too accurate. They were broke and in debt. Sid had been sending money home for expenses there; he had $1,400 in his pocket after paying off everyone. They had not even tickets to get back to California, where they had more bills they were unable to pay. Sid calculated that in the last three months they had gone in debt over $50,000—not to mention the debts from previous years. They could not even afford Morgan Maree's commissions as business manager. He gave Sid a parting piece of advice: Go into bankruptcy.

And a few years before they had been riding so high!

The only bright spot was a three-week engagement, at $40,000 a week, at the Flamingo, in Las Vegas, to start the day after Christmas —less than two weeks after Judy's return to California.

"I can't do it, Sid," she said. "I'm just too weary, too knocked out." After her ordeals in Washington and Philadelphia, the exhaustion of London . . . Sid appealed to the Flamingo management, but they refused to let her out of her contract. On such brief notice they could never obtain a major star to play over the New Year's holidays.

Judy had to appear—Bobby Van worked with her this time—and what infuriated her was that the holiday diners were noisy, often inattentive and rude. It was never easy to sing to people who were busy eating, chatting with others at their table, out to enjoy themselves and accepting the entertainer, however celebrated, as part of the deal.

On the third night the audience clearly didn't even want a show. They were eating, drinking, talking, and Judy simply stopped singing. Because it was the Christmas holiday, eleven-year-old Liza had come along. She had been backstage each night, all eyes. This night she was watching from the wings, wearing a floral floor-length robe with a long zipper down the front, and slippers to match. Judy came through the curtains, grabbed her by the hand, brought her out onstage, introduced her—"Ladies and gentlemen, Liza Minnelli"—turned to her, said, "Take it," and walked off.

Liza, all but overcome—this was the first time her mother had introduced her as an entertainer, not as "my daughter, Liza Minnelli"—sang four or five of her mother's songs—"The Man That Got Away," "Swanee" and several others. Judy had never formally taught these to her; she had learned them from hearing her mother sing them. The audience couldn't have cared less. But Liza loved it. When she came off, Judy, standing in the wings in a characteristic pose—her left hand extended, palm up, the elbow cupped in her right hand held tight across her stomach—said, "You were terrific." Years later Liza thought, "I couldn't sing worth a damn then—but it was nice of Mama to say that to me." No matter what bizarre occurrences took place at home or backstage, Mama always built her up.

The next few nights were, however, even worse. In every Vegas contract there is a clause prohibiting the serving of food or drinks in the main room once the star has appeared onstage, though one usually saw the waiters and waitresses, bending low so as not to be seen, distributing the checks to the diners.

New Year's Eve Judy, after her first songs, came off into the wings. Sid was not there; he had gone to Los Angeles to see about bills, but was due back later that night. Judy said angrily to Vern, "They're serving out there. I can't hear the feedback." When Judy sang, she heard her voice come back to her from two large speakers facing her on either side of the stage; these were monitors which enabled her to hear how her voice was adjusting to the acoustics of the room. But tonight there was a clatter—waiters and waitresses hurrying up the aisles, hustling plates of food from huge circular metal trays. Vern spoke to the maître d'. "They're still serving out there. Judy can't work with all that noise."

The latter shrugged his shoulders. "What are you going to do? It's New Year's Eve."

When Judy came off again, she said, "I can't work. These people don't want to be entertained. I can't do a good show."

Vern said, "Look, honey, why don't you cut it short? Just cut it short."

She went onstage again. They started yelling at her from the front tables, "Come on down, join us in a drink. Come on down and let's celebrate. Let's have some fun. We don't want to hear singing."

The last straw came when a drunken woman staggered up on the stage and tried to dance with Judy. The woman was guided offstage. Judy emerged with Bobby Van, both holding microphones; they joined in a duet, "Auld Lang Syne," and walked off. It was the end of the show. Judy was fuming, livid. "That's it," she said. "I'm not working here any more."

Sid, back by now, tried to mollify her. She had a contract to fulfill, they'd been unable to get out of it, she had worked only six days, and she hadn't even been paid for that week. The more Sid tried to placate her, the more furious she became. "Get your ass out of here!" she cried. "Whose side are you on? Are you going to protect me or are you going to be on their side? You know they've broken their contract! The hell with them! I will not. I'm sorry, I will not."

She went back to the cottage in which they were living, and Sid and Vern went to the casino. Sid said, "We've got to get some money." Vern said, "What'll we do, hold up the joint?"

Sid had been thinking. As always, he had a plan. He went to the cashier and got $5,000 in chips as an advance to play craps. He signed for the money, to be put on their bill.

As Sid played, every few minutes he would give Vern, standing beside him, a hundred-dollar chip, which Vern dropped into his pocket. Finally, when Sid stopped playing, he told Vern, "Go up to your room, I'll be up in a few minutes." When he arrived, Vern gave him the chips. Sid took them down to the cashier and cashed them in, then returned and gave Vern the money—something like $4,700, which Vern put in his shoes. Sid had actually wagered very little. It was all a maneuver to salvage as many chips as possible, which could be turned into cash. Now Vern had the $4,700 in hundred-dollar bills in his shoes.

Had the hotel management known they were leaving, it would

have immediately canceled Sid's credit, charging that Judy by walking out was breaking her contract: We can't pay you, this has to go to arbitration. (Later Judy was awarded $22,000 in the arbitration procedings, most of which went to lawyers.) Vern quietly took Judy's costumes and luggage from the cottage, locked them in his station wagon and, in his money-filled shoes, drove back alone to Los Angeles to the house on Mapleton Drive. Judy and Sid, with Liza, arrived shortly afterward.

At this moment the Lufts were anything but a loving couple. Her life with Luft was more and more moving into a stage where it was, as someone said, like a roller coaster in hell. Their business manager had left them. The only money that had come in during these terrible months had been the $15,000 insurance for Rover the Second and the $15,000 in cash Ben Maksik had advanced. Sid borrowed $25,000 from a bank to keep the household going.

Judy stayed for hours in her bedroom—reading, talking on the telephone to friends all over the world at all hours of the day and night, her drapes drawn, the lights on, the radio on, the TV on but its sound turned off, refusing to see or talk to Sid. Finally, husband and wife did talk to each other, and it was a calamitous no-holds-barred fight. "I've had it," Sid announced. He was white. "I can't get to you." He was moving out of the house into the Cavalier Motel, not far away on Wilshire Boulevard, and "cool it for a few days."

Judy promptly hired two detectives to guard her and the children from him. Some mornings later, Sid had a visitor at his motel: it was a man serving papers; Judy was suing him for divorce. The papers had come from the office of Jerry Giesler, the famous divorce lawyer. Next morning the newspapers had it: "SID CHOKED JUDY." Sid had beaten her, Judy declared in her complaint, he had tried to strangle her, they were separated, she wanted a divorce, she was compelled to live with guards, she feared harm for her and her children.

Sid telephoned Giesler. "Jerry, what the hell!" he exclaimed. "What are you doing to me? You know Judy."

Moments later he and Giesler were discussing the matter at the latter's house. Judy, Sid explained, was going through a bad period. "She's ill, she really needs hospitalization, she's medicated, and the medication is making her irresponsible. You know if I wanted to strangle her, there would be no such thing as 'tried.' " Giesler said if it was as Luft reported, he could forget it. "It'll blow over," he predicted.

Sid went back to his motel. A few days later there was a telephone call from Albert Gray, Judy's chauffeur.

"Mr. Luft, you better come over here. Mrs. Luft fell asleep with a cigarette, the mattress caught fire, she's burned her hip, not too badly—we got her out O.K."

Sid telephoned one of her detectives to say he was coming over, "because I know what's happening to Judy, and I've got children in that house." The detective said, "You can't come here. Mrs. Luft doesn't want you."

Luft said, "That's my home, and if you want me to, I'll get a court order. But I'm coming over now. I've got kids there and you're not responsible for them—I am."

He went to the house. The two hired guards and Sid confronted each other. Each man had a revolver. Judy remained upstairs. Luft said, "Now look, one of you men stay upstairs all the time. Watch her. She can kill you and the children and everyone in this house—you watch her! If you're going to guard, guard. And let me know what's going on! You don't know what a responsibility you have here!"

The episode of the burning mattress shocked Judy into activity. She had her engagement to do beginning March 21, 1958, at Ben Maksik's Town and Country Club in Brooklyn. She hated doing it; she was in no condition to work, not to mention going all the way across the country, but she consoled herself: Brooklyn was next to Manhattan, and anything was better than staying like a prisoner where she was. She packed and went to the train with Liza, Lorna, Joey and their nurse, and when they arrived in New York three days later, Maksik and Norman Weiss, the MCA agent who had signed the deal, were waiting for them.

At the beginning Maksik and Judy hit it off well. She made demands, but he accepted them. She wanted a house to live in with her children and their nurse, a car and chauffeur, and a twenty-four-hour guard to protect her and the children from Luft, who, she knew, would sooner or later be on the scene. . . . Maksik, with the club already selling theatre parties for Judy's three and a half weeks, and with Bobby Van once more signed up to appear with her, spell her, do her tramp number with her and generally act as MC, could do nothing but agree. He moved her and the children into a large beach house he rented in Neponsit, Long Island, and provided her with around-the-clock Pinkerton guards.

A few days later Sid flew to New York. He telephoned Maksik. "I don't want to harass Judy," Sid told him. "But she's not too well. I'm at the Warwick, in case you need me." Maksik told him that wasn't necessary. But, as it turned out, there was a problem. Judy owed over $8,000 in back New York State taxes stemming from her Palace appearance in 1951, and the state had put a lien on her salary.

Now Judy and Sid met together for the first time since Sid had moved out—with Maksik, in the New York State Collector's office. Judy was distant; Sid was formal. It was agreed that $3,000 would be deducted each week from Judy's $25,000-a-week salary until the taxes had been paid.

Opening night at Town and Country was fine, as always; the second night good, but by the third night it started going downhill again. She was living out on Long Island, and though the club was first-class, it *was* Far Rockaway, and Judy Garland was singing in Brooklyn. She was bored, she needed companionship, she needed doctors—whatever she needed was not there. In Vegas there had been maids, help of every kind; now there seemed to be only her and twelve-year-old Liza. Now Liza rubbed her back, sewed torn hems, got rid of a spot on her costume with cleaning fluid. In the midst of the engagement, Judy got colitis. She was too embarrassed to tell anyone—Liza herself didn't know about it until she caught her mother crying—again it had to do with Judy's privacy in the bathroom—and Liza thereafter was always running off to the drugstore for medicine. Judy felt wretched, performing became more and more difficult, she took medication to make herself feel better, which made her only more suspicious—not only that Sid would pounce on Lorna and Joey but that even Maksik might kidnap them, because, after all, hadn't he and Luft made the deal? Some nights she refused to go to the club unless Weiss baby-sat with Lorna and Joey.

The crisis came Sunday night, March 30, the night of her eleventh performance. Judy was really sick, but she still wouldn't tell them it was colitis. Maksik, according to Weiss, aware that she was not herself, was trying to keep Judy from going on; he wanted out of the whole business. When Weiss and Judy and Liza arrived at the club that night, Maksik was furious: "She's not going on! She can't sing any more! I can't do this to my customers!"

Weiss, as Judy's agent, said, "Judy is in her dressing room, getting dressed. She's going on. There is no breach of contract."

The band played Judy's overture. She went onstage. She sang her opening number, then her second, "Life Is Just a Bowl of Cherries," the irony of which at this point struck her so forcibly that she had to stop. She said, "Ladies and gentlemen, you'll have to excuse me. I have a terrible case of laryngitis. I wish I could go on with the show, but I can't. It really doesn't matter." Her voice quavered. "I've just been fired."

She tried to say more, but someone had switched off the mike. She hurried to the front of the stage, in tears, her arms outstretched appealingly to the audience. "It's wrong," she cried, "it's all wrong. You've been a wonderful audience. I love you all."

Later she said Maksik had fired her when she arrived that night. She had appeared "only to hold up my end of the bargain."

At this point Luft suddenly showed up. Judy had telephoned him at the Warwick earlier. "Sid—come and get your family. I'm in this goddamn Maksik's joint and he won't let me out of here, he's got me captured, he's got my jewelry locked up in his safe."

Luft found the principals in the lobby: Maksik and Weiss in hot dispute (they had been friends for years); Judy, dressed in a blue turtleneck shirt, a pair of slacks and boots, standing by. Maksik was shouting, "Get her out of here! She's crazy. Get her out!"

Sid said, "She'll go, but Judy told me you have her jewelry." Yes, said Maksik, he had it in his safe, and he was keeping it. What this Garland woman had already cost him! The money he had advanced, the expenses he had paid, the ticket money he had had to refund . . . Luft said, "You give her her jewelry and we'll leave." Maksik was doubly furious. March 29—the night before—had been Joey's third birthday, and Maksik had thrown a party for him, to boot. Finally he opened the safe and gave Judy her belongings.

The Lufts that night checked into the Drake Hotel. Later Sid and Judy dined with Aly Khan at Harwin's, a fashionable nightclub, and Judy and Sid danced cheek to cheek. Since Maksik had not paid Judy, the state had not received its first $3,000 payment on back taxes. There were to be suits and countersuits, but the state came first. Judy was put under technical arrest, and warned she could not leave the state until the debt had been paid. Aly sent over his lawyer to represent her, and Sid got on the telephone to raise money. There was hardly anything in his own account; before going to New York, Judy had gone to the bank where he had deposited the $25,000 loan to pay household expenses, withdrawn $9,000 of it—which represented most of what remained—given Jerry Giesler $5,000 and kept the rest. Sid was able to borrow $1,500 from Peter Lawford, several thousand dollars from Frank Day, a Detroit businessman who backed him in several ventures, paid the taxes, and then the Lufts returned to Los Angeles, reconciled—and very broke. The divorce suit was dropped. "I told you," said Giesler.

In July, Judy—fat, heavy—opened at the Cocoanut Grove in Los Angeles. What took place that night—Judy's success, her gaiety and happiness, Sid's delight, the ecstatic time enjoyed by the children when they were introduced by Mama—was impossible to square with everything that had happened to date. It simply could not have happened; or if it had happened, it had been to another Judy—not to the shining, adorable, full-of-fun creature who dominated the stage and captured the heart of everyone in the great room. The critics and columnists were at a loss for words. "How can Judy Garland's opening at the Cocoanut Grove ever be topped, or for that matter, how can it ever be equaled?" wrote one. It was "sensational," wrote another; Judy "sang her heart out and was never in better voice." Hedda Hopper, with whom Judy had carried on a feud because of Hedda's frequent lectures in print to Judy to mend her ways, wrote: "From the moment she appeared, that audience wrapped their arms around her with such love and affection as I've never seen before." Again, the biggest thing in Hollywood, that land of superlatives, since the last Oscar presentation.

How could anyone know what financial maneuvers had gone on behind the scenes to make that appearance possible? Luft had had to take out still another loan to get Judy's costumes out of hock so she could wear them that night; the bank refused, and not until Irving Schachtel, one of Sid's friends from New York, came to the house that afternoon and guaranteed the loan was Sid able to get the money—and Judy's costumes.

Then—to pay back some of the debts—appearances by Judy at the

Sands Hotel in Vegas, Orchestra Hall in Chicago, the Fontainebleau in Miami Beach and half a dozen other places during the remainder of 1958—a prelude to something entirely novel in her career, the consequence of one of Luft's more inspired ideas.

He and Judy had been drinking in the bar of the Mapleton house. He looked at Judy. She was fat, very fat, and uncomfortable, and low in spirits. All the excitement seemed in the past. It was early 1959. She sat about the house, watching her soap operas, marking time, miserable. Sid had a deeper understanding of her now. Calling on his own special knowledge, he likened her to a horse, a finely bred race horse. She was made to run; and when she was not running, she was restless. He called it "breezing" in horseman's parlance. Breezing was training for the main event. Brief two-minute gallops, then longer, then longer again, then the day of the race when you must run at top speed—that was opening night. That was the hysteria Judy loved: the screaming in the theatre, the lights, the music, the applause, the adulation. What living person had ever got such adulation? Sinatra had, but Sinatra was a man, he could duck it, or walk away from it by himself. Judy could not. There were things a woman could not do by herself. She was trapped. There was no escape. ... And the answer to the hysteria, the answer to the inability to slow down, the answer to the frustration, the boredom, the fears, the inflated terrors ... was pills. She would feed her brain with Benzedrine and Dexedrine and Thorazine and Seconal and Tuinal ... there was no end to them.

Sid had to come up with something. He had to prevent her turning again to too many pills. She was saying, "Look at me. I'm heavy. The telephone doesn't ring."

Sid looked at her. It was not only that she was heavy; her face had started to puff up. This was more than fat; this was a kind of bloat. And her mental condition matched her physical condition. It was apathy. She didn't wish to entertain, she didn't wish to see anyone, she didn't want to go out. Even if the telephone had rung, she would have made excuses.

Sid downed his drink. Sitting there on the couch, in her checkered blue-and-white gingham house dress, like a caftan, her feet tucked under her, Judy looked so fat, so plump, he thought: *She looks like a prima donna, an opera prima donna, at home for the evening.* He heard himself say aloud, "She ought to be in the Metropolitan Opera. Why not?" He spoke to her directly: "You ought to be in the Metropolitan Opera, Judy."

She said, "You better stop drinking, Sid. You've had enough." But Sid was moving now. "I'm going to put you in the Metropolitan Opera House in New York." She said, "Come around from behind that bar and sit down and stop it."

He came around the bar. He had seen a spark in her face. She was intrigued despite herself. "Darling, you're gonna play the Metropolitan Opera House." He himself had never been inside the Met. As far as he knew, no popular singer, certainly no vaudeville entertainer, had sung at the Met. A wild, wild dream.

On May 11, 1959, Judy Garland opened at the New York Metropolitan Opera House; she could appear there only under charitable auspices, because of the Met's franchise, as Rudolf Bing had explained to Sid at lunch with Harry Zelzer, an impresario; her elaborate show was for the benefit of the Children's Asthma Research Institute and Hospital of Denver; it was black-tie, $50 seats, as gala as any opening of the Met. True, some of the critics spoke more about her magnetism than about her voice, except when she went into old favorites, but suffice it to say that there were fourteen curtain calls. Roger Edens as usual had written special music and lyrics; Alan King, making an ever bigger name as a monologist, again appeared with her, doing the "A Couple of Swells" tramp number, along with John Bubbles, the dancer, choruses of dancing boys and girls—an elaborate, full-scale presentation with "a company of 100."

The Met appearance made history; nearly half a century before, Harry Lauder had appeared there, but not since then had a popular entertainer taken over the great stage. And since it was Judy, there were exceptional circumstances. A sheriff waited backstage to serve a court order attaching her salary obtained by Ben Maksik, who had filed a $150,000 breach-of-contract suit against her. It took all of Sid's persuasiveness to prevent the man from serving Judy onstage.

Then, in June, the Chicago Opera house, in July the San Francisco Memorial Opera house, later the Los Angeles Shrine Auditorium. In San Francisco those in the front row took off their shoes and pounded on the stage to add to the applause. She was a success in each opera house, but with each appearance, with certain proceeds going to charity, and the tremendous overhead (sometimes the unions demanded enough stage hands to handle the Bolshoi Ballet), the Lufts lost more and more money. They went thousands of dollars into debt. Their total expenses at the Plaza in New York alone were $9,000; their share of the net proceeds from the Met benefit was $8,000. It had cost Judy and Sid over $150,000 to put the show together. He had borrowed money everywhere: $15,000 from Charles Wacker, an old friend of his and Aly Khan's; $40,000 from Mark Boyer of Los Angeles, which meant taking out a mortgage for that amount on the Mapleton Drive house (followed, a little later, by a second mortgage of $50,000, which meant $90,000 in mortgages on the house, then valued at $200,000). The sets had cost $12,000, costumes $20,000, orchestrations $16,000, Gordon Jenkins $1,125 a week as conductor of fifty men (not the usual thirty or so), plus the salaries of Dick Barstow the choreographer, Vern Alves, Harry Rubin, press agents and lawyers. Then there were many additional costs—the rental of rehearsal halls for weeks before the openings, the parties given by Sid and Judy for two hundred, three hundred guests, agents' and business managers' commissions—the entire financial burden of supporting a star's elaborate entourage and way of life, not to speak of Judy's enormous medical expenses: it was not unusual for her to have three or four doctors in each town, one not knowing she was dealing with the other . . . and always the financial drain: taxes, mortgage payments, maintenance, month after month, on the great stone castle back in Beverly Hills.

But when she appeared onstage, heavy as she was, what did all that matter once she felt the audience reaction? Then she became, once more, an irresistible force. Fat as she was, and sick as she was—she would be in a hospital, near death, as the year ended—onstage she was giving more than a performance. She was in a championship battle, a battle to win every person in every seat. She would burst backstage, perspiring, winded, fists clenched, early in the show. "Who put that goon in the first row? He's not applauding! I'd like to belt him one!" Then a dash of cold water over her face, a hurried rubbing with a towel, a gulp of whiskey and water (straight hard liquor was too much for her throat), a quick warning—"I'll nail him! I swear I'll nail him!"—and back to the fray, to the arena, to shattering applause. Until, under the bombardment of her songs, her projection, the daggers of energy she directed at every last single soul, the man she aimed at broke and, like the others, was standing, applauding, not knowing why.

Was it, as someone said, "She had to have one more guy out there to love her"? She had been programmed to be loved from the age of three, and never was it enough. It had to be everyone, all of them, *everything*.

Back from the months of the tour, she barely moved out of the house. She grew more bloated, all but waddled. She could not sing, she could not dance, she could not make love. A former MGM publicity woman had opened a new and very expensive reducing resort in the San Fernando Valley, Comanche Ranch, which Judy dubbed "Come and See Me" Ranch. Judy, Sid and the children went there. Liza lost fifteen pounds on the carrots-and-cheese diet, Sid lost ten, but Judy lost nothing. Back to the house again, Judy was still bloated, and getting no better. "Judy, you need a doctor," said Sid. She did not want to see a doctor. Was it fear? (Years later she revealed to a friend that she had a phobia about cancer. Was it this?) What could be wrong with her? She hardly ate. Disgusted with herself, she began to drink. She swelled up until she could hardly catch her breath. Sid invited two friends over. Both were young, handsome; both were physicians, but introduced as musicians, because each was skilled in music.

One sat at the piano, playing and singing. Judy, in another part of the house, despite her desire to see no one, found herself entering the room. She liked what she saw. She sat down next to the pianist. The other visitor leaned over to examine the music; as he did so, he placed his hands gently on her shoulders.

Later, he took Sid aside. "She's waterlogged. All the way up. Her kidneys, her liver—something is very wrong. She should be in a hospital right now."

The one hospital Judy might be content in would be Doctors Hospital in New York, where she had gone during her second Palace engagement; she had liked its luxury, its hotel atmosphere. How to get her there, without letting her know the reason—first to New York, and then to the hospital? Sid, by a carefully worked-out scheme, in which Charles Wacker helped—telling Judy that Elsa Maxwell was giving a party at the Drake Hotel in New York for Aly

Khan, with Judy as guest of honor—managed it. Sid flew to New York. Freddie Finklehoffe was there, too. Sid counted on Judy's loneliness, and Wacker's persuasiveness, and Judy's liking for Aly and Freddie, to make her respond to the idea of a spur-of-the-moment trip to New York with Wacker. Anything to get out of her boredom. It worked. Judy went on the plane with Wacker. Her feet were so swollen she wore slippers; she was so fat that when she bent over to sit down, she split her slacks; someone gave her a large safety pin; she had to go to the ladies' room, and she made a hilarious production of that, to the laughter of everyone on the plane.

In New York Wacker took her to a room in the Beverly Hotel. Sid joined her. Freddie was on a lower floor at the same hotel. Sid had told him, "Hang around—I may need your help." Sid had another ace up his sleeve: his uncle, Dr. Israel Rappaport, whom Judy liked; and though he still didn't know how he would manage it, he hoped in some way to have Dr. Rappaport examine her.

At the Elsa Maxwell party Judy was not herself. She wasn't enjoying the party. She and Sid got back to the hotel late. Judy watched television; Sid fell asleep. When he awoke, the sun was coming up over the East River, and Judy was still sitting there, watching TV. She had not been to bed at all. She said, suddenly, "I'm very sick. I've got to go to the hospital."

Sid could hardly believe his ears. He said, quickly, sympathetically, "How about my calling my uncle?" Judy nodded.

It was now around 6 A.M. Dr. Rappaport would not be at his office until eight o'clock, and by that hour Sid had Judy dressed, a gray turtleneck sweater over her pajamas, a huge red coat wrapped around her swollen body, and took her to his uncle's office, not far away. Two other internists, alerted by Sid's earlier call, were there as well.

While they examined Judy, Sid waited outside. Then his uncle came out. Judy was critically ill. How she was alive, he did not know. Her liver was enormous; so was her spleen; she was blocked up, her whole body poisoned with fluid. She had to be rushed to a hospital at once. She could go into a hepatomic coma at any moment. She had a diseased liver (Judy was later always to say it was hepatitis, which is uncertain—Dr. Pobirs, who had attended her longer than any other physician, declared that she had been clinically treated for cirrhosis); the years of medication, the excesses of medication, the liquor, the abuse of herself—all had taken their toll. She could never touch liquor again, she was warned.

Judy came out and Sid told her, "We've got to get right to the hospital." They all helped her down to a cab. Sid got in and Judy said, "I've got to go back to the hotel and get some things first." Sid, almost frantic, cried, "Things? What do you mean, things! You got to get to the hospital!" Judy said, "We go to the hotel first or I don't go to the hospital." There was nothing for it but to let the driver take them to the Beverly. Once in their room, Judy packed a bag Sid could easily have brought to her, then picked up the phone and ordered up a triple vodka and water.

Sid all but screamed, but there was nothing he could do. The vodka arrived. Judy sat there with it, sipping.

"Put that damn glass down," Sid cried, finally. "You've got liver problems. That's the last thing you should do!"

Judy faced him. "Either I have my drink or I don't go and I die right here. With the vodka."

Five minutes passed. Ten minutes. Judy was killing time—and perhaps herself. Sid said, "For God's sake, Judy, let's get out of here." Judy said, "I want to finish this, do you mind?"

No, Sid said, meekly. After a moment she went to the bathroom, and Sid used the interval to telephone Finklehoffe. "Judy is very sick, Freddie, I've got to get her to a hospital," he said, and at the other end he heard, "Oh, my God!" a cry, then silence. "Freddie, Freddie!" Sid shouted into the phone.

Judy came out of the bathroom. "What are you screaming about?"

Sid said, "Freddie. Something's happened to Freddie."

Judy said, "Well, go down and see him," and returned to her chair and her drink.

Sid hurried down to Finklehoffe's room. Finklehoffe had in some manner tripped, struck his head against a table and knocked himself out. Sid put cold towels on Freddie's forehead, began chafing his wrists, thinking of Judy upstairs, with cirrhosis of the liver, drinking a triple vodka. This was no time for Freddie to pass out on him. But now Finklehoffe was groaning, coming to, a maid was at hand, the house doctor was on his way up, and Sid dashed upstairs again. Judy had still not finished her drink. He told her Freddie would be all right. "Now, let's go, please!"

Judy rose, the drink in her hand. "I'm taking it with me," she said, and when Sid stared at her, she said, annoyed, "Sid, if you want one, order your own."

Then, and only then, did he get her downstairs into the cab and to the hospital, and, while she was given a two-hour examination in her room, Sid moved in on the third floor, the family floor, where relatives of patients were permitted to live. Then his uncle appeared and, placing his arm around Sid, walked the corridor with him. It was as they thought. Her liver was at least four times its normal size. She hovered between life and death.

"I will tell you one thing," his uncle said, somberly. "The liver does not repair itself. We know you can live with only part of it function-ing, but we can only guess how much damage there is. If she does get out of this, you, Sid, must see that she never touches liquor again, or goes off heavily on pills—nothing a damaged liver can't handle."

She lay, desperately ill, in her room. Freddie Finklehoffe, to keep Sid's spirits up, moved in on the third floor of the hospital, too. The day after Judy entered, he was walking down the corridor outside her room and overheard three doctors talking quietly about her. One turned to him. "I have to tell you the truth," he said. "I don't think she'll make it."

Finklehoffe said, and he was surprised at his own passion: "Doctor, you're talking about flyweights. She'll make it. She will die on her own time, not on yours or anybody else's in this hospital." He thought, as he walked on, *She's got something else to do, I don't know what it is, but not until it's done, that's when she'll die.* He was sure of it. She hadn't played her string out yet.

Seven weeks later, on January 5, 1960, Judy emerged from Doctors Hospital, to return to California for months of recuperation. From 150 pounds she was down to 120—still plump. Her normal weight was 100. The doctors had withdrawn twenty quarts of fluid from her in twenty days. She emerged in a wheelchair, a semi-invalid, having been told she must accustom herself to the life of a semi-invalid as long as she lived, that she would never entertain professionally again, certainly never work a day again in her life.

Actually, it was only the beginning of a third comeback.

BOOK THREE

ENDINGS

*"When I think of all my goddamned,
marvelous, failing, successful but
hopelessly tragic and sorrowful years . . ."*

33

ON A DAY IN MID-JULY 1960, writing from her suite at the Savoy Hotel, in London, Judy sent off a chatty letter to Sid, in Los Angeles:

Darling, how much I miss you. London is not the same without you. Had a good trip over, after a lovely party at Roddy's in New York, and arrived in time to find beautiful weather. Had a hectic press conference, with the usual newspaper bastards—the result the usual—"fat, matronly, but happy." Fuck them! How are my babies? Tell them I'm thinking of them every minute and how I love them.

Judy had gone to England on July 11. It had taken her five months to recuperate from her long illness at Doctors Hospital, and when she came off the train that brought her home from New York, she was still in a wheelchair. She had sent fourteen-year-old Liza with a group of girls to spend most of the summer perfecting their French in a French summer school, while living with a local family in Annecy. Judy's trip had been her own suggestion. She had said to Sid, in June, after Liza had gone off, "Darling, we've been joined at the hip so long —I just have to get away. I've got to get out of here. I still have some recuperating to do and I want to do it in London. I need the change; it will do my tummy good; it's important to my health, my mental outlook." She had added calmly, deliberately, "I want to get off by myself and think about the future."

He had said, "Darling, we can't afford it, but I'll get you the money." She would need about $25,000 for wardrobe and expenses for the two or three months' stay she contemplated. There was the Vlaminck painting hanging on the wall. Originally it had been borrowed from an art gallery by Lemuel Ayres for the Norman Maine beach house in *Star;* then it had been bought from the gallery for $2,500, and ultimately became part of the furnishings moved from Warner's to the Mapleton Drive house. Sid sold it now for $11,000. He had nearly half the money. He turned to Vern. Vern had property in the Malibu Hills. Could Vern loan him $15,000 or so? Faithful Vern borrowed the money, putting up his property as collateral, and Judy had left, with a hug and a kiss for everyone. There had been farewell parties: Roger Edens gave one, in honor of her, Kay Thompson and Ethel Merman—the three would leave together—at which Judy and Ethel sang together until three in the morning. Then Judy had been guest of honor at a hundred-dollar-a-plate Democratic dinner seated with Jack Kennedy (it was three days before his nomination), Eleanor Roosevelt and Adlai Stevenson. So she had left on a high note.

Her letter continued:

I talked to Liza in Annecy and she'll either come to London for a few days or I shall see her in France. . . . I'm going to Dick's [Dirk Bogarde] in the country today at 5:30. There's a party Sunday and I'll be back here on Monday.

She gave him the gossip. She was making records at Capitol, which had just renewed a three-year contract with her, working with a man she called Noilly Prat, because she couldn't pronounce his name. They had just "passed a law here taking all the whores off the streets. It's a little like taking the trolleys out of San Francisco," and went on: "Some of the color has gone, but the girls still advertise on bulletin boards outside the pubs. It's either French lessons or massage, both interesting, but underground."

On their previous trips to London, Judy had always been intrigued talking with the girls who frequented Piccadilly Circus; the subject fascinated her. She went on to say how thrilled she was about Jack Kennedy's nomination, and she would campaign for him wherever she could. And she concluded: "Well, that's all for now. Write to me and tell me everything but mostly that you love me and miss me as I do you.—Judy."

The London trip had its clear, sane reasons. Sid had become interested in a project with Eddie Alperson, his partner in Transcona

Enterprises: the development of a stereophonic sound system to entertain passengers on commercial planes. TWA had its Inflight movie system, but musical entertainment was something else again. Here, Sid thought, might be the career he had been seeking, so he could be more than Judy Garland's husband/manager.

And Hollywood—Los Angeles—had changed. Friends had uprooted themselves and gone to New York. Bogart had died, Betty Bacall had gone east. Television had taken over; the great movie studios were falling apart. You could walk up Sunset Strip and see nobody you knew. The place was becoming deserted.

Yet her weeks in the hospital had been good for Judy. She had been taken off her drug syndrome and save for a new pill—Ritalin, a psychic energizer which doctors had begun to prescribe mainly for elderly ladies two or three times a day to build up their mood—she was virtually medication-free. During the first months she had been too weak to work; she couldn't perform in Vegas, or do films or TV. She really felt unwanted. To live in Hollywood and not be involved in it was itself a pressure. She had to escape that.

Everything close to Judy seemed pulling away from her at the same time: friends, work, husband, the children now at school. . . . Judy was always one for a complete change of scene, and she took it.

Her life in London was made gayer because of Kay and Ethel. And, important later, the presence of Liza, who, if she had been a precocious youngster at four—once she had walked into the living room just as a doctor gave her mother a shot in the rear end, exclaimed, "Oh, not again!" turned on her heel, and left—was now a sophisticated teen-ager, years ahead of her age, alert, vigorously alive, with her mother's sensitivity and sharp, intuitive perception. When Liza visited Judy briefly in London, the two were dining in Judy's suite, watching Marlene Dietrich and Noël Coward doing a mannered scene on TV. It got worse and worse. Judy and Liza reached into a little bread basket to get a piece of bread, and their hands touched. Without a word, they both picked up a piece of bread and threw it at the television; and then, still without a word, picked up the rest of the bread and threw it at the TV. Then they threw everything at the TV screen—salad, meat, potatoes, everything. As once years before a glance between Judy and Mickey Rooney had established instant communication, so it was now. At a party, a glance by Judy, and Liza knew her mother felt as she did—bored—and it was time to leave. Or Liza would be telling a funny story to someone, and catch her mother's signaling eye: "You're wasting it on him—he won't get the point," and she would stop, and go on to something else.

Liza began to realize how important humor was to her mother. Humor could get you through anything. Any crisis, if met with humor, could be turned into glorious laughter. Only later could Liza put it into words—her mother's uncanny ability to be her own person at one moment, and then step outside herself to see herself as a character in a situation—and how funny it was. To be on the brink of disaster, yet see yourself in your ridiculous, it's-just-too-much predicament, and describe it so that your listeners doubled up with laughter, and you with them—that was Mama's gift.

Now in London Liza began to understand that in a way she was becoming her mother's confidante—her "pal" as Judy called her. For the first time her mother talked to her about her "medication." That there was medication was, of course, no secret to Liza, but she had never quite understood about Mama's endless prescriptions, her terrible pains, the many doctors. She and Lorna had become accustomed to the fact that Mama had good and bad times. When they came home from school, particularly if they brought friends, their first question asked of the help would be "What's Mama's mood?" Mama would have awakened around one o'clock, and one never knew. If the signal was all-clear, everything was fine; Mama was the most wonderful, tender, understanding mama in the world. Otherwise, one remained downstairs, careful, circumspect, until everything was all right again.

Liza learned early that she would get different stories from her mother and from Sid, with respect to events; after a while she became skilled at determining what appeared to be the genuine emotions involved, and from them figure out where the truth lay. One never knew when her mother was on—and her stepfather had to be devious, one step ahead, for things to move as they should. In this bewildering, explosive household, Liza, then Lorna, then Joey, learned how to keep an even keel. Very early Liza realized that if her mother one night said of Sid, "He's the worst man in the history of the world!" or "Oh, God, he's lost all the money at the races!" the next night she'd be saying, "Oh, thank God, he's back. What would we do without him?"

So when her mother went through bad times, Liza didn't try to analyze, or seek explanation; what Mama needed then was support, Mama wanted to get rid of whatever awful feeling was weighing down on her, and Liza would agree with her, and comfort her. She knew a reason existed; it might have nothing to do with what happened that day, it 'might relate to an episode months before that suddenly had popped out of the past, enormously inflated, to torture her mother. If Luft's training had enabled him to cope as well as he had with Judy, so Liza had trained herself to cope with both Mama and Papa Sid. He was not the only virtuoso at balancing on a tightrope. Sometimes Judy would call her into her room, tell her something and say, "Don't tell Pop. Promise me." Liza would take three paces outside the door and Sid would grab her. "What did she say?" Liza would fumble with words, saying and not saying. If sympathy was Judy's business, subterfuge had to be Liza's. Liza was able to take it all in remarkable stride. Once, some years before, when Sid had left briefly after a quarrel, Judy said to her, "Liza, you are now head of the house." A couple had come, in answer to an advertisement for housekeepers. They waited in the kitchen. Out came an eleven-year-old girl who said, in a matter-of-fact voice, "May I see your references, please?" And actually got on the telephone and checked them.

In so many ways, despite her repeatedly hard-to-understand behavior, Judy was unparalleled as a mother. When the children were sick, she stayed with them. Lorna and Joey both suffered from sties: Lorna often had to stay home from school, two sties in each eye, painful, patches over them, with Judy sitting, crying, by the side of her bed. Even if Lorna fell asleep, when she awoke, hours later, there was Judy, still watching over her. Liza had frequent excruciating earaches (so had Baby Gumm), and often Judy would forgo a party to tend her, using an eyedropper with hot camphorated oil to relieve her pain. When it came to explanations difficult for most mothers, Judy was again surprisingly competent. She herself had learned about where babies came from from Jimmy, but on this delicate subject Judy was admirable. She had sat Liza down when the appropriate time came—as she would Lorna, later—and seriously, and with great delicacy and beauty, described the miracle of conception and birth. Judy told her she would become a woman when she had her first period, and she made that seem a magical achievement. "Oh, that'll be a wonderful day," she told her daughter. And when it happened, she would bring out the sherry and they'd drink a toast together to Liza's womanhood. "I will let you have your first sip of sherry then." It was all handled so beautifully, but when the time came and Judy went to get the sherry, she found Sid had locked the liquor cabinet and she and Liza had to toast each other in cooking wine.

Now, in London, talking to Liza of her medication, Judy explained, "When I was very young, I had to work so late and so hard. After I'd work, I'd be wide awake and I couldn't go to sleep, and I had to get up in four hours and start all over again. So I was given—" Judy hesitated over the words, and Liza didn't know whether her mother would say tablets, pills, medicine—"I was given . . . a pill—" she indicated with thumb and forefinger something very small—"to help me go to sleep and help me get up. And after years of doing this, my system functions well on these. I find they make me feel better. So I kind of need them—like vitamins."

What Liza did not realize then, but would later, was that Judy was revealing that there would always have to be a floor of "medication" for her. This was true by the time Judy had reached thirty. She had this need; this was her burden, and she accepted it.

Late in July, after a delightful trip to Capri, Judy telephoned Sid in Los Angeles. She was a house guest at Dirk Bogarde's country place. "Sid," she said, "let's move to Europe. Let's try it for six months—here in England."

In August, then, Judy and Sid, who flew over, rented two houses that had been knocked into one, belonging to Carol Reed, the British film director. Ellen Terry, the actress, had once lived there. It was surrounded by ivy-colored walls, and so was quite private; it was on King's Road, in the heart of Chelsea, with a double-storied living room with a small balcony, huge French windows looking out on a rose-bordered garden, fireplaces on each of three floors, the top floor having a guest room and bathroom, and four other bedrooms with huge beds covered with eiderdown quilts, under which Judy loved to sleep. They moved in, only to discover that Eddie Fisher and Elizabeth Taylor, house-hunting too, had almost taken it but turned it down because it had no central heating. Judy discovered there were electric heaters in every room, so that really didn't matter; and among their first visitors were the Fishers, blaming themselves for not grabbing it first.

One night Judy, in the shower, was singing at the top of her voice. She emerged in a cloud of steam. "Sid, I swear my voice is so much stronger," she said, as though she did not believe it herself. Sid agreed. "I've never heard you with such power," he said. "Well, I feel just marvelous," said Judy. She'd been taking long walks, she'd been out in the air all day, she felt like a new person. "I'd like to do something."

The result: Sid arranged two concerts, a week apart, at the Palladium, where Judy sent the critics into hosannas, Judy singing thirty-four songs in a two-and-a-quarter-hour appearance, with John Gielgud, Dirk Bogarde and scores of other entertainers cheering themselves hoarse; and two performances in Paris at the Palais de Chaillot, with the French critics writing front-page reviews in *Le Monde* and *Figaro*, and all kinds of high social events: lunch at Maurice Chevalier's home, a dinner given by the Duke and Duchess at their estate outside Paris, a dinner given by the Loel Guinnesses, of the famous Guinness stout family.

At the theatre, the first night, Liza, who had finished her Annecy stay, found herself seated next to the Duke. Now Liza was astonished to discover (as Judy already knew) that the Duke hummed the music under his breath when the orchestra played, and when Judy sang, he sang with her and knew every word of all her songs. At the Guinness party that night, Liza watched her mother with sheer admiration. She was surrounded wherever she stood or walked, she held an entire room with her conversation. Judy, the raconteur, whom George Cukor once called the peer of any storyteller in Hollywood, had everyone hanging on her words.

Judy that night, Liza saw, produced the princess in herself. She looked like a princess. She wore a black sable stole, her hair was jet-black, her face pale, the huge eyes dark and lustrous. She looked elegant, elegant. . . . As Liza watched, her mother *became* the princess. Judy did not change. She simply adapted. She segued from Judy Garland the performer into Miss Garland the ineluctable legend. Her personality did not change, but in ways noticeable only to someone who knew her well she altered herself: she sat a little differently, her head was tilted at a slightly different angle. As Liza put it later, "It was Mama being elegant . . . and she could do it."

A week or so later Lorna and Joey were flown over with their governess, and the Luft family were together, as happy as they had ever been, Lorna and Joey in Eden School, Liza enrolled in Miss Dickson's and Miss Wolf's School for Young Ladies. The Lufts had an Italian butler, Antonio, as well as a cook, who came with the Reed house; they had tea at the proper hour (with Lady Eden, the school headmistress, as a special guest one afternoon), with Judy, like any London mother and housewife, walking her children to school, or shopping for food and making out lists of necessities and attending the theatre and parties of an evening, and buying boxes of Bavarian mints she loved to keep by her bed.

There was one bad week, when Lorna had an emergency appendectomy. She remembered her mother, standing, watching her as she was about to be wheeled down the corridor to the operating room, Judy, tears streaming down her face, hugging to her Lorna's favorite doll. Lorna cried out, "Stop!" because she discovered she still had the doll's shoes in her hand. She said to her mother, "Hold these until I come back," and at that, her mother broke down and sobbed, and that picture of Judy crying, holding Lorna's doll in one hand, the doll's tiny white shoes in the other, would never leave her. Then Lorna was well again, with a scar she could show about, and all went swimmingly.

But Judy, even in her contentment as mother and housewife, after her successes in London and Paris began thinking of her career. The idea was spurred, too, by a telephone call from Pat Lawford in the States. There was a large U.S. Army installation in Germany, at Wiesbaden. Jack wanted to know if Judy would fly there to a Kennedy rally, to entertain the boys and stump for him. Yes, yes, yes! said Judy. Her reception can be imagined. This was a new audience, these young soldiers, and how they welcomed her! She took particular pride in attending an election-day party at the Dorchester, given by U.S. Ambassador John Hay Whitney, as Republican as could be. He appointed her an usher; she promptly pinned a huge Kennedy button on her dress and greeted everybody with a cheerful "I hope you voted for Jack Kennedy." She told Sid, "I wanted the Ambassador to know where I stand." And what a celebration at the Luft house on King's Road, everyone crowding about the TV on their small living-room balcony to watch Jack win! Her friend—the President of the United States!

It was at this point, with the Lufts living in London and Sid increasingly involved in his projects (he had met Douglas Fairbanks, Jr., who allowed Sid to use one of his offices), that a luncheon took place in New York that was diametrically to change the direction of Judy's and Sid's lives.

The participants at the lunch were two men: one, Arthur Jacobs, a highly successful actors' press agent, later to become a film producer remembered for his *Planet of the Apes;* the other, Freddie Fields, husband of actress Polly Bergen, vice president of the Music Corporation of America, and one of the brighter, more ingenious young men at that agency. At the moment, Jacobs was Judy's press agent.

Not long before, Jacobs had received a call from Sid in London. Judy was beginning to champ at the bit. She'd sung again one night at the Olympia in Paris, she'd done a midnight show in Amsterdam —"We've got to get her an agent," said Sid. "What's your advice? Look around and let me know." Sid was getting deeply involved in his own project. He had in mind a tape deck that would play four hours of stereophonic music; the sophisticated electronic equipment was being made for him (he and Alperson had put considerable money in it) by engineers in Florida. Sid knew he would have to spend much time during the next months not only in Florida but traveling about the country exhibiting the apparatus to airline executives.

At the lunch Fields revealed in confidence that he was going to quit MCA to form his own agency with no more than twelve clients. Polly, of course, would be his first. Phil Silvers had promised to come over. That made two. Now, he asked Jacobs who among those he represented were unhappy with their agent and might want the personal services a firm with only twelve clients could provide?

Jacobs pulled out his list. It was impressive. Henry Fonda, Rock Hudson, Gregory Peck, Marilyn Monroe, Richard Burton . . . Fields went down it, name by name. His finger stopped opposite one name. "There's one we want—Judy Garland."

Jacobs sighed. "Freddie, you realize that nobody can get her a job in the States at this moment."

"That's why I want her," said Freddie. He continued down the list. "I want him, too." He pointed to the name of Peter Sellers. Sellers had as yet had no great triumphs in American pictures.

All right, said Jacobs. And added, "Judy's thinking about an agent anyway."

Fields, excited, said, "Pal, I gotta see her!" Jacobs called Sid in London, and Sid worked on Judy, who was not happy about the idea. She considered most agents flesh peddlers and disliked them. "I really think this guy's going to be terrific," Jacobs had said. "He's sharp and savvy, and if he does what he says—handles only twelve clients—I think you should see him." Sid suggested that Fields fly over to London to meet them.

Judy finally agreed. Fields turned out to be full of personality and ebullience, young, ambitious, eloquent with plans, a first-rate salesman. She and Sid both liked him. Later Fields took into partnership a onetime MCA associate, David Begelman, like him personable, quick-witted, persuasive, able. Judy, when she met him later, liked him, too. Sid felt relieved. He hadn't let Judy down. He was putting her in good hands.

When Judy first met Fields, he looked as though he could have been a twin of Douglas Fairbanks, Jr.: the same mustache, the same build, about five foot nine, slender, his dark hair slicked back and cut long. But he soon divested himself of his mustache and looked even younger. He was electric with energy. Begelman was taller, heavier-set, more elegant in bearing, immaculately tailored; he wore blue shirts in the daytime, a blue so pale as to be almost white, and white shirts in the evening—it was almost impossible to tell the difference, but the difference was important to him. It was a nuance Judy would note—and appreciate.

Both men thought and worked in ways which intrigued Judy. They were witty—with a kind of Marx Brothers wild humor. Like her, they saw everything from slightly off-center; every problem, every crisis, was turned into something wry, hilarious; they were men of laughter. Begelman particularly endeared himself to her, after the Lufts and the children came back to the States before New Year's 1961, Judy already signed by Fields and eager to resume her career under their management.

Once, on the tour that followed, she and Begelman were sitting at a bar when a woman with huge sunglasses came up to her. "Oh, Judy, my God, you're so wonderful!" Meanwhile she was doing to Judy what so many other fans did: patting her face, tweaking her cheek as though she were a child, running her hand through Judy's hair— the Judy everybody owned—and Judy was helpless. Begelman walked over to the woman. "We think you're fantastic, too," he said, with great sincerity. "You're just marvelous." As he spoke, he removed her glasses; then he pulled off her hat; then he started unbuttoning her blouse; and she stood there paralyzed, while Judy clung to her chair to prevent herself from falling off it with laughter. Begelman continued undressing the woman—now he was pulling out her blouse, saying earnestly, "God, you're such a wonderful woman, Judy needs an audience like you. It's people like you that really make her day—"

Finally the woman was able to gasp, "How—how dare you!"

Begelman looked at her coldly. "How dare you do that to her?"

The woman staggered away.

This was humor Judy could understand. "Look how fat I am!" she had said at first. It didn't matter, they said. They made her feel beautiful, feel wanted. When they laid out their grand plan for her, she was completely theirs. They stressed they were not "handling" her, as big agencies did. She was not one of hundreds of clients. For the first time she felt as she had while making *Star:* she was in a partnership. These two were saying, Whatever we do, we do together. If it turns out well for you, it will turn out well for us. You're that important to us.

They outlined their plan: (1) Prove to the entertainment community that Judy Garland was anxious to work, willing to work and could be relied upon. That meant, establish her credibility by seeing that she made every personal appearance scheduled, first in cities like Buffalo or Albany, where, if she did fail to show, it would not be so great a calamity; then, later, in major cities. (2) Make her again the most important attraction in the nightclub field, in Florida, Vegas, Tahoe. (3) Then re-establish her importance as a motion picture actress.

When the Lufts first arrived in New York from London, they took a suite at the Carlyle, and as the two men unfolded their game plan, Luft was more than agreeable to it. He had his own money problems. He had lost nearly $150,000 in the tours that began with Judy's Metropolitan Opera appearance. London had been infernally expensive: $1,000 a month for the King's Road house, private school for three children, two nurses, a staff of two, travel, doctors, etc. . . . Judy had received $10,000 for her two Palladium concerts, and less for the others; the astronomical costs of her illness in New York, the months of recuperation with no money coming in; he had been selling off horses he owned in partnership with Ted Law; he was getting calls from the bank in California threatening to foreclose on the Mapleton house—it was a mess. He spent more and more time trying to raise money. The airplane executives he spoke with were difficult. . . . He devised, and devised, and seemed to get nowhere.

That February Fields laid out roughly a twelve-city tour for Judy, to begin late in the month in Dallas; but before that, a quick trip to Hollywood to talk to Stanley Kramer about a cameo part in *Judgment at Nuremberg*. At this point Vern Alves, who had been out of the scene for some months—he had been working in the Kennedy campaign—found himself invited to lunch by Fields at the Beverly Hills Hotel. There, around the swimming pool, where important deals were so often made, Fields explained that Judy needed someone to accompany her to the Coast, and then on tour, acting as a general production manager. Vern, Fields knew, always got on well with her. Would he accept the job?

Vern said, "Of course." He knew Judy could be a handful, but they *did* get along.

Then Fields, Vern said, went on: "Look, if I have a year with Judy, I can score big with her. But how do I keep Sid out of it?"

Vern's first reaction was surprise. Sid had introduced Fields to Judy. Fields, as if reading Vern's mind, said, "Judy told me: 'Let Sid down gently, but I don't want him involved in my business.' "

This seemed confirmed not long after when Judy gave a cocktail party in New York under Fields and Begelman auspices, and told Sid, "I don't want you to attend." She would see him later that night in their suite at the Carlyle.

When she came home about midnight, Sid blew up. He had been drowning his frustration and humiliation in liquor. "I don't like this," he shouted. "We're husband and wife and I should know what's going on." There was no resolution of their argument. Sid was not happy, either, with at least one of Judy's bookings. Fields had booked her into the Concord Hotel on the Borscht Circuit. This outraged Luft. Fields said he found strong resistance in trying to book Judy. He got her into the Concord because he had friends there. Sid thought, *Jesus Christ, after the Palace, the Palladium, the Palais de Chaillot, the Windsors, the Guinnesses . . . the Borscht Circuit?* But it was quick good money, said Fields.

Sid finally found himself talking to Fields about his problems with the Mapleton Drive house. He needed $10,000 immediately to stop a sheriff's sale—foreclosure. That was the amount he was delinquent in the first mortgage. Fields told him, Sid said, that he could make the money available from Judy's income, but if he did, Judy wanted the house put in her name. It was their joint property.

Sid indignantly refused. He borrowed the money from Ted Law in Tulsa. The possibility had come up of selling the house, by now encumbered by a third mortgage he had been forced to take out to pay debts. Fields had said Judy told him she didn't wish to live in California any more. This was a contingency—the selling of their house—that Sid fought. That house symbolized their family's unity; it was Judy's base; it was her home; and to be cut loose from that meant a breaking apart of everything.

As Luft saw it, Fields and Begelman were beginning deliberately to euchre him out of the scene, not only as director of Judy's career —here he had only himself to blame, he realized—but as her husband, so they could have complete control of her. If Judy appeared to approve this procedure, Sid maintained, it was because they were influencing her to get rid of him.

Stevie Dumler, Fields's secretary-assistant, insisted this was not the case: that Fields and Begelman specifically decided—first privately and then in Stevie's presence—that whatever Judy wanted was fine with them. If Sid was the man she wanted, then Sid would be terrific; if Judy wanted someone else, then someone else would be terrific; they would go along with whoever she wished to be the man of the moment. All they wanted was a happy, functioning Judy.

But there were more words between Judy and Sid, and Judy moved out of the Carlyle with the children. She had left no word where she had gone. When Sid called Fields, Fields would not tell him on the grounds that these were Judy's wishes. Sid learned that she was in an uptown hotel with the children, and he thought, bitterly, *There goes everything, our close ties, our family, Judy is going out on her own, not confiding in me.* . . .

For the next year Sid was separated from Judy, reconciled with her, separated, reconciled, living with her, not living with her. She told Sid she had formed her own corporation, Kingsrow Enterprises. She owned all the stock, she explained, and in turn had given Freddie and David power of attorney to write checks for her. Sid saw this as one more encroachment on his relationship with Judy.

Whether Fields or Kramer thought of her first for the part of the frowzy German *Hausfrau* in *Judgment at Nuremberg* seems difficult to answer. Kramer's memory is that Judy immediately came to his mind when he thought of the actress who could perfectly portray Irene Hoffman. He remembered Judy as Baby Gumm, but he had not forgotten her ability as an actress in later years. He had tremendous respect for her. She was one of a handful who could weep on take 9 precisely as they had done on take 1, though it had been done eight times in a row, the same emphasis, emotion, tears. He found out who was representing her and sent a copy of the script to her with a note to the effect: If you like this, please call me.

Judy had been told that her part would be shot in about eleven days. Every role of any consequence was being played by a star: Spencer Tracy, Burt Lancaster, Marlene Dietrich, Richard Widmark, Montgomery Clift, Maximilian Schell. Kramer needed an actress to play the German woman who had been very close—the German state charged "intimate," thus breaking a Nazi law—with an older Jewish man who had been her friend and neighbor.

When Judy walked into his office early in 1961, he was taken aback. He saw a heavy, unattractive woman in black slacks, but the tremulous smile was Judy's. She had yet to go on tour; she had yet to know how she would be received. He saw that she had the script with her. She sat on a chair opposite Kramer, he behind his desk, the script on her knees. "Do you like it?" he asked. She was obviously ill at ease, but yes, she liked it.

"I can't pretend that your role is anything more than a cameo part, but it's a very important one in the picture," he said. "This is a big thing for me," he went on earnestly. "I want you to do it and I'll tell you right off, if you won't do it, you'll break my heart."

There was a moment of silence, and Judy said softly, her eyes searching his, but the ghost of a wry smile trembling on her lips, "Mr. Kramer, haven't you heard about me?"

He was stopped for a minute, but then he came back: "Haven't you heard about *me*, Miss Garland?"

She looked surprised. What did he mean?

He was Stanley Kramer, he explained, he was the bleeding heart of the fifties, the discarded liberal of Hollywood with his Boy Scout approach and message pictures which had changed nothing. . . .

But none of this mattered; he told her he had great hopes for this picture. "You're not going to come off as the most attractive lady in this picture," he warned her. "This is a woman who's had it. She's been through it. . . . But I feel that you'll be able to reach everything in the character." He had his own insecurities about the character, but he knew that in Judy one saw not only the Judy of today but the girl she had been twenty years before, and that she possessed the emotional power. "You'll do it for me?" he asked.

"Goddamn it, you *believe* in me, don't you?" she said.

"Goddamn it, yes, I do. How much money would you want to play it?"

She looked at him, and her next words almost brought tears to his eyes. She said, as only she could say, carefully, "How much do you want me to pay you to play it, Mr. Kramer?"

He could only brush that aside by getting up and saying, almost brusquely, "Then it's agreed."

She nodded, as if she still could not believe it. "I want to play it, and if you think I can do it, that'll be enough for me." And then: "Besides, I'll be right for this. You don't want anybody too pretty."

Kramer, a man slow to anger, exploded despite himself. It was no longer Miss Garland. "Judy, for Christ's sake, if you want to go to some spa and drop a few pounds, if you want to look pretty, O.K., but it's not right for this." He said, hardly trusting himself to speak, "I'll pay you fifty thousand dollars for the part, and I'll settle it with Freddie Fields."

And so the deal was made, although Fields wanted more—the first picture since *A Star Is Born,* her first under the auspices of her new agents, who had named their firm Freddie Fields Associates. Later it would become Creative Management Associates, Ltd., one of the giants in the agency industry.

Kramer *had* chosen well. When it came time to make the picture and Judy played her role, the magic was there. Kramer had always thought that, when Judy performed, what she was saying was: "Here is my heart, break it. Hit me, be mean, because people are mean to me. I overreach myself all the time!" Kramer realized he had two difficult persons in his cast; not only Judy, but Montgomery Clift, who was physically and emotionally very ill at the time. Clift could not remember his lines, until finally Spencer Tracy, who played the chief judge in the Nuremberg trials, said, "Monty, just look at me. Stanley doesn't care about the lines, you know what it's about. Look at me and play it: you don't have to say anything, just react." And that was what Clift did, in the role of a victim of the Nazis who had been sterilized in his youth. Most of the time Clift did not know what he was saying in the picture. When Judy had her great moment on the witness stand, denying that she had had an affair with her elderly benefactor, while Maximilian Schell, the state prosecutor, bore down on her mercilessly, Clift, watching in a corner, was like a strange little ape, so pathetic, huddled up, holding his knees, the tears rolling down his face.

Judy had prepared hard for her role. While still in New York, she had gone to Uta Hagen, the German-born actress, to learn the proper accent. She discussed the part with Liza, and let her read her lines. "It's a great role," Judy said. Liza didn't see it; it wasn't on the paper.

Judy explained to her: "Acting is hearing something for the first time, and saying it for the first time. Do you understand me, Liza?" Liza said, yes. Her mother went on: in acting, you rarely say what you think; you must have a whole story going on back here—her mother tapped the back of her head—and the words that come out are connected to this, not to what you seem to be saying. Later, after the picture was made, Judy told Liza that when she geared herself up to react to the ugly accusation made against her—that she had been intimate with this older man, who had been so kind to her as a child, bringing her candy when there was no candy to be had, a man whom she loved and respected—she thought of her own father, Liza's grandfather, Frank Gumm; and that charge so horrified her that it gave her the emotional power to play the role. Cameo part though it was, when the time came, it won her a nomination for an Oscar as best supporting actress, but she did not win.

Judy's tour in early 1961, under the auspices of her new agents, was as triumphant as any she had ever made. She was plump, but no one cared. In city after city—in view of everything she had gone through—she was incredible. That was the only word. On February 21, her first engagement, in Dallas (it meant a reunion with Jimmy), singing thirty songs for two hours, "Her pipes were never better"—this from Variety. Two days later, in Houston: "Unquestionably the greatest show ever given in Houston." So the reviews went, time and again. Then Sid was back in her life (Joey's sixth birthday, March 29, brought them together), and the Luft family squeezed in an Easter holiday in early April in Florida—Sid, Judy, Lorna, Joey. One might have thought it was the Judge Hardy family. Judy and Sid went together to Washington, D.C., where Judy sang at Constitution Hall; they lived together at the Mayflower Hotel, with Vern Alves in an adjoining suite.

President Kennedy had just flown back from Key West, where he had conferred with the British Prime Minister. The day after the Constitution Hall concert on April 8, Bobby and Ethel Kennedy invited Judy and Sid for a buffet dinner at the Kennedy home in McLean, Virginia. They had a marvelous time, and did not return until 4 A.M.

About 9 A.M., a telephone call for Judy: it was from Ethel Kennedy. Judy picked up the phone and squealed, like a little girl: "Of course, absolutely!" She turned to Sid. "The President wants to see us at the White House—we've only got an hour because he's got to go to the baseball game and throw out the first ball of the season." Kennedy wanted to thank her personally for campaigning for him in Germany.

It was a wild twenty minutes while she prepared: deciding what to wear, she and Sid wolfing their breakfast, then Judy sitting at her makeup table, carefully fixing her face, her bare legs outstretched under it so Vern could shave them—it was like a stage farce, Vern at work under the table, Judy precisely applying her lipstick brush.

In the Oval Office at the White House, the President greeted her with a hug and a kiss. He took her behind his desk, pushed away his chair and said, "You see all those tiny pinlike holes in the floor?" Judy looked. "What are they, termites? In the White House?" No, said Kennedy. They were made by the spiked golf shoes of President Eisenhower. There had been a putting green where the rose garden now was. Ike would go in and out in his golf shoes.

Now Kennedy had to leave for the baseball park. He turned to Sid. "Do you like baseball?" "Not particularly," said Sid, the horseman.

Kennedy grinned, and said with his hand to the side of his mouth, "You Commie bastard!"

Then Sid was off on his business, and Judy and Vern on hers: Birmingham, Atlanta, Charlotte, Greensboro—an appearance every other night.

The triumph that spring was her historic success at Carnegie Hall on April 23, but that spectacular appearance was sandwiched between two nightmarish episodes which for depth of anguish matched any previous ones—episodes caused perhaps by separation from her children, who were in New York, or by medication prompted by a sudden relapse into hysterical fear.

The first occurred in Charlotte, North Carolina, a week to the day before the Carnegie Hall triumph.

Judy and Vern were in her suite at the hotel in Charlotte, when Judy said suddenly—she had done a good show—"I don't know why I'm so depressed." Vern suggested, "Would you like to take in a midnight movie or something?" No, she replied. He remained silent. He had learned that Judy could not always focus on what troubled her at the moment. It took time, and finally, almost without realizing what she was saying, it would come out. It happened now. She said, "I want to talk to my children." And: "I'd like to have them brought to me."

Vern said, "But, honey, you know we have only one more engagement on this leg of the trip—in Greensboro, two nights from now—and then you'll be back in New York, for Carnegie Hall."

Judy: "Why can't the children come here?"

Vern: "Well, you know, honey, we'll be home in a couple of days." To bring the children meant taking them out of school, making arrangements. "You'll be home in seventy-two hours or so, and then you'll have ten days with them."

Judy wandered silently to a chair. Like a child, she spoke under her breath, plaintively. "Can't even have my own children. . . . Goddamnit, I work my ass off, making money for everybody, can't even have my own children with me!"

After a few drinks, and watching television in the sitting room of the two-bedroom suite, they went to their rooms. Sometime during the night—he was not sure whether it was only a few minutes later or an hour or two after he fell asleep—he awoke suddenly: he could hear a low moaning, a sobbing and catching of breath, and with it a steady, dull pounding.

Vern, when he traveled with Judy, always kept his bedroom door partly open. He leaped out of bed and ran across the sitting room to her room. Her door was open. Judy was not in bed, and he realized that the sound of pounding came from behind her open bedroom door, and that someone was there, between the door and the wall.

He looked. It was Judy, in her nightgown. She was hitting the door with her fists, and from her came a crying, a moaning and sobbing, with words intelligible between—a totally lost soul, *Perdu, I want out*

472

of limbo—the sound of someone suffering the deepest anguish.

He pulled her out from behind the door. She came unresisting, inert, like a sack of potatoes. He helped her to the bed. He knew that Judy could always be soothed by the gentlest running of one's fingers over her skin, the skin of her face, her forehead, the back of her neck. So Lee Gershwin had done many years before; so Sid would do; so Liza, and Lorna, and Joey; and Vern had of course learned it from them. Judy could actually be put to sleep in this fashion, if one's fingers barely touched, and now Vern soothed her, comforted her, saying softly, "It will be all right, honey, don't worry. . . . I'm going to stay right here."

Finally she calmed down. She slept that night taking only one pill, an antibiotic a doctor had given her for an ear infection. Her ear had hurt her, slightly—could this, invoking the memory of her childhood, and her father's death, have brought on the depression?

Next morning it was as though nothing had happened. Judy was in top form. She had along as a companion a brilliant, highly attractive writer, Shana Alexander, who was doing research for a piece on Judy in *Life* magazine. Judy took to her at once when she learned that Shana's father had written "Hard-Hearted Hannah" ("the vamp of Savannah"). They all drove together to Greensboro: Judy was happy, full of energy, and put on a great show, now that she was bound for New York and the children.

Shana would watch her with wonder, preparing herself backstage, literally puffing herself up just before she went on. Where she used to grab the curtains, waiting to go on, literally pawing the ground, now she had a variation: when the big, pounding introduction came, all percussion, and just before she came out, she would grab the curtains and, in tempo to the music, say, "Fuck 'em! Fuck 'em! Fuck 'em!" to the audience, and seem to grow bigger and bigger, like a balloon being inflated by a bicycle pump: then, full of air, she'd sail out on that stage.

It was 11 P.M. The show was over. In the lounge of the country club where Judy had appeared, several musicians were playing poker. Judy walked over. "Can anybody sit in this game?" They put a chair at the table. She sat down, took off her coat, said to Vern, "Darling, would you make me a drink? Just one drink? I'll play a few hands and I'll be up."

Vern went upstairs and made her a drink, but after waiting fifteen minutes, and Judy had not appeared, he went down again. Judy and five men were playing poker, sleeves rolled up, the room filled with smoke, cigarettes drooping from their mouths.

Vern went to bed.

He woke about 7:30 A.M. He was having his toast and coffee, when Judy walked in. She looked about twelve years old—like Tess of the d'Urbervilles—refreshed, happy, positively glowing with health.

"Oh, what a marvelous—" she began. "You won't believe the experience I've just had. It was right out of a dream."

She had not slept. She had played poker until 5 A.M.

"I didn't get even until then, so I thought, I'll take a walk and get some air. I walked out through the woods and down the greensward and out on the golf course. Everybody else was tired and pooped, but I was feeling refreshed. I took off my shoes and walked barefoot, and it was marvelous. In some parts of the course it was wet, and the gardener was sprinkling, and I could feel the freshness of the spray and then I met a wonderful dog—he was a mutt—and he took me for a walk, and we walked all over, everywhere. And the only reason I came back in was because people were coming out to play golf and I realized what time it was."

She drank the rest of the coffee in Vern's pot, and went to bed.

He thought, marveling, *This girl hasn't had two minutes' sleep, she hasn't had a bit of food since before her show twelve hours ago, she's had nothing but exercise, peace, quiet, fresh air and a companion she couldn't argue with!* What he did not know was that she had had another companion on her walk: Shana Alexander. But Judy, as always, had improved the story.

The Carnegie Hall appearance a week later, Fields and Begelman's big attempt, was an incomparable success. Judy's voice was at its zenith for a two-and-a-quarter-hour performance reminiscent of her Palladium and Palace openings; twenty-eight songs sung, ovation upon ovation, Mort Lindsey leading the orchestra, the entire show taped for an album which became *Judy at Carnegie Hall,* her most successful recording to date; an audience (many of them Arthur Jacobs' clients, whom he encouraged to attend) which included Richard Burton, Henry Fonda, Julie Andrews, Carol Channing, Spencer Tracy, Betty Bacall, Roger Edens and Chuck Walters (reveling in Judy's triumph), Mike Nichols, Myrna Loy, Harold Arlen—name upon name, applause upon applause, a thousand people waiting at the stage door. Later there was an ecstatic reception at Lüchow's.

And exactly one week later it was followed by a night of pure hell.

It is difficult for the mind to embrace the hades and the heaven built into Judy. One can only wonder what volcanoes lay buried there which fueled this overwhelming contradiction, yet beggared description: one leading to such explosions of joy, talent and showmanship, the other to eruptions of unendurable anguish and terror, the terror of one possessed.

It began with, of all things, a compliment.

Vern and Judy were in her suite at the Warwick Hotel, Philadelphia. It was midnight. She had concluded two tremendous shows there.

Judy was sitting on the sofa in the large living room, lost in her own thoughts. Vern knew of her difficulties with Sid, the charges and recriminations, Sid's guilt at having brought new managers into her career, her feelings of rejection by Sid. Vern knew how she was torn, and that this must be affected by increased medication: she was taking not three, but ten and more Ritalin a day, and who knew what else, and who knew what hallucinatory affects these combined drugs had upon her? He knew the irony of her triumphs: *What did it all matter?*

Into this tortured silence, David Begelman walked. It was 1 A.M. He had just arrived from New York with a batch of newspaper clippings his office had received. Begelman was literally in charge of Judy, Fields having opened an office on the West Coast, leaving Begelman to run the New York office and concentrate on Judy, particularly since her contract contained a clause that a representative of the office must always be with her. The clippings covered the entire Southern tour she had just completed, and he counted on their making her happy. He wanted to read them to her himself.

Because Judy had been so quiet, Vern had paced himself with her mood: he had not attempted to start a conversation; he had been sitting quietly opposite her in an easy chair. Begelman swept in, vital, ebullient, full of good cheer. "Judy, you won't believe these reviews," he began. "You could have written them yourself—they're absolutely fantastic!" He almost bounced down beside her on the sofa, and showed her a clipping. "Look at this!"

Judy was gently touching the hollow of her throat with three fingers—her characteristic gesture. "I have a sore throat," she was saying. "My throat is very sore." And then, in a plaintive voice: "I'm getting laryngitis."

Begelman, carried away by the reviews, went on excitedly, "Oh, honey, you're all right. What do you care about your throat? You're finished with the tour. You did a great show tonight. You don't have to work tomorrow, or the next day, or the day after that." He waved a clipping. "Listen to this—just listen to what they said in Greensboro." He began reading aloud.

It was the wrong thing to do, Vern knew, but David did not know her well enough; when Judy was serious, joshing her, pushing aside her complaint when she wanted sympathy, would roil her. He should have said. "Oh, honey, I'm sorry! What can I do to help? Would you like me to get you some tea and honey?"

So when Begelman began reading, she exploded. "Oh, fuck you!" she cried and, leaping up, ran into her bedroom, slamming the door.

Begelman sat, stunned. Then he sighed several times, and shook his head. "Well, I sure blew that." Vern said, "Yes, David, you did." Begelman said, resignedly, "There's nothing left for me but to get out of here." There were no more trains to New York that night; he called the hotel desk, arranged for a car, returned to his room, packed and left.

Vern waited a few minutes. No sound came from Judy's bedroom. He crossed to the door and gently tapped on it. Still no sound. He pushed the door open slowly and walked in. In the darkened room he could make her out, lying fully dressed on her bed, her hands clenched at her sides, and she was sobbing like a little girl who had been spanked by her mother for something her brother had done.

Vern sat on the edge of her bed and reached out to touch her hand, to see what her reaction would be. There was no reaction. That was good. He began to soothe her, running his fingers over her arm, barely touching it, back and forth, back and forth. She said, not looking at him but at the dark ceiling, "I don't know how people can treat people that way. It's inhuman!" It echoed her lament after the clinic in France, it echoed so many of her hurts, going back, back into her life. Vern reached to her bedside table and handed her a Kleenex, and she dabbed at her nose. "I could be *very sick*"—she gave the two words a full reading—"and what sympathy would I get?"

Vern continued to murmur encouraging words to her until she stopped sniffling. She blew her nose and he helped her off the bed, and she went slowly into her bathroom, changed into a nightgown and came back. By this time he had turned down her bed. He helped her slip under the covers. Was there anything she wanted? No, she said. But would he stay with her until she fell asleep?

There were twin beds in the room. Vern lay down on the other bed, pushing himself back until he rested, half-sitting, against the backboard. He would remain there, watchful, a companion and protector and sympathetic listener, as long as she wished.

She seemed very, very tired. Lying there in the semidarkness, she said, "I don't want the children to know about this." She had taken Lorna and Joey with her on this leg of the tour, and they had their own room down the hall. "I don't want them to know I was upset." Silence for a moment. "I'll be all right tomorrow." Silence again. Then, in sudden anger and hurt: "It's just those goddamn insensitive people!"

After a little while, she was asleep.

He tiptoed out, across the living room and into his bedroom. It was quite late; he fell asleep almost the moment he was in his pajamas.

Suddenly he was wakened, as if by a cyclone. Something had shot into his room as though fired out of a cannon, and seemed to strike and carom off everything in the room. It was Judy, stark-naked and, it seemed to him, stark, raving mad. He had no idea what time it was; it must have been four or five hours later; daylight had come. As always, he had kept the door of his room ajar. What had happened was that she had hit his door, slammed it back against the wall, continued into his room like a fury, grabbing whatever she could get her hands on and throwing it, yelling and screaming.

For a moment Vern was paralyzed, in such shock at this apparition in the dawn—without robe, without nightgown, without slippers. She had obviously taken pills, stimulants of some kind—who knew how much, and how long they had been building up in her?—and they had revved her up to a maniacal pitch: she had relived everything painful, her marriage, her frustration, the indifference of those she saw as cruelly, callously, cynically using her, she always being caught in the same intolerable pressures, and finally she had simply in that moment gone out of her mind.

He leaped out of bed and tried to grab her, but it was like grabbing a ghost. She slipped through his hands, whirled away and rushed into the living room. She tried to push her foot through the television screen. Then she saw the window, and made for it, screaming hysterically, grabbing the top pane and trying to pull it down. They were on a high floor. Even in his frenzied attempts to seize and hold her, Vern thought, the *top* of the window! If she wanted to go out that window, she had only to raise it from the bottom and plunge through. To go out the top meant clambering up and trying to climb over it —almost impossible. He grabbed her; he could make out her screaming words, "Let me go, I'm going to jump—just let me go, goddamn it, let me go!" fighting him, struggling as he held her. If she wanted to go out that window, why rush into his room and wake him? Why not simply dive out the window, glass or no glass?

He was wrestling her now, trying to protect himself as she punched and kicked at him, aiming for his groin. Finally he threw her on the couch and himself atop her, holding her down with his weight. She struggled less and less as he pleaded with her, "Honey, what is it, Judy? Judy, is it something I've done? Let's start with that, honey. Something I've done . . . ?"

She was sobbing softly now, trying to catch her breath, but no longer fighting him. Her entire body quivered under him, and it took some minutes before she stopped trembling, and was finally calmed down. He ventured to release her slightly; she lay quiescent; so he dared lift himself off her, find her robe and cover her. She lay there, her face shockingly white, drained of all color and of all emotion. Then she said weakly, "Let me go and clean up."

As he rose, he saw that she was herself again. The rapidity of change in her moods, the lightning-like transformation of personality, never ceased to astonish him. It was as though the wild-eyed cursing madwoman at whom he had thrown himself a few minutes before had been pure imagining on his part, a momentary hallucination; in her stead was Judy, tear-stained but recognizable Judy. Tying the belt of her robe about her as she walked away, she said in a calm, matter-of-fact yet resigned voice, "Oh, shit, Vern . . . I guess—what the hell, it's no different now than it's been all my life. Why should I expect something different now? Why should I expect people to be considerate and understanding? They never were. So what the hell! Why am I killing myself over this?"

It was Judy, playing out her scene.

She went into her room, bathed, dressed and came out to ask for

Lorna and Joe. When they were up, would they come in and have breakfast with her? She ordered the inevitable trencherman's breakfast: orange juice, two eggs, ham, potatoes, toast and tea—everything. Her throat still hurt, she said.

Vern packed. Later, with the children and the governess, all unaware that anything had happened, they took the train back to New York.

It was May 1, 1961.

Five days later Judy opened in Chicago, at the Chicago Opera House. The critics raved. "The best singer since Caruso," they said.

34

EARLY IN 1961 FIELDS'S ASSISTANT, Stevie Dumler, at Judy's request, found an apartment in New York for her. Judy wanted to remain east, where the action was. Joey and Lorna had been put in Public School 6, and Liza happily enrolled in the School of Performing Arts, spending almost every night going to a Broadway show. The apartment—huge, eight-roomed, high-ceilinged, gloomy—was in the Dakota, an almost legendary residence on Central Park West. It was a sublet from John Frankenheimer, the director, a Fields-Begelman client. Here Judy, Vern and the children returned from Philadelphia before she went on to the Chicago Opera House a week later. Her throat hurt her, she said; she telephoned a physician, who prescribed a medication to be poured into a basin of hot water and inhaled. Vern set up the apparatus. After about three minutes, Judy had had enough. "Well, that ought to do it," she said. She hadn't even gotten her nose wet.

Vern helped her into her bed. She said, "Won't you stay with me?"

He said, "Honey, I'm *so* dirty, I have no clothes with me." (He'd taken only one change to Philadelphia.) "I'll stay with you until you go to sleep, but I'd like to go back to my hotel, have a bath and get some sleep." He had, after all, been up hours tending her through that *Walpurgisnacht* at the Warwick.

She said, "Well, all right, if that's what you want to do . . ." She was obviously displeased. He thought to himself, *Oh, fuck it, I'm going to do it,* and so he did. He left.

The next day Sid, who had spent most of early 1961 on the road demonstrating his equipment, showed up. He got into an argument with Judy. He telephoned Vern to come over. The apartment was very quiet, the children subdued. When Sid, breakfasting in the kitchen, saw Vern, he raised his eyes to the heavens in his characteristic way—"Here we go again." Judy rang her bell from her room; it sounded in the kitchen. The housekeeper answered it, came back and said to Vern, "Miss Garland would like to see you."

He found her propped up in bed in the gloom. He said, "Hello, dear, how are you?"

She said, "Well, you really did it, this time."

He thought, *Oh, Christ, what could it be?* Aloud: "What do you mean, Judy?"

She said, "Just because of your selfishness last night, you wouldn't stay here with me, now I'm really sick."

Vern, nonplused, sat on a little stool at the foot of the bed. "But I stayed with you until you went to sleep, which was our agreement, then I went back to the hotel."

Judy said, "If you had stayed here, I would be well today, because we would have continued the medication for my throat. Now I've got laryngitis." Her throat was as clear as a bell; she could have sung *Tannhäuser.*

She looked at Vern, sitting on his little stool. "Get Luft!" Vern said, O.K. He walked into the kitchen and said to Sid, "You're on."

Sid went into her room, and there was a loud, abrasive quarrel. She accused him of being insensitive, of being a disruptive influence, of turning the children against her; that she had to work and couldn't work under such conditions; and "You can get your ass out of here and take that little boyfriend of yours with you!"

Vern heard that and left. He walked out, signed out of his hotel and returned to the West Coast. It would be years before he and Judy would see each other again.

Sid, too, left, and went back on the road. When he returned to New York, it was late May. Judy had interrupted her tour for a brief visit with the children; when Sid saw her, she seemed under heavy medication, he thought, and nervous.

They got into one of their inevitable arguments, shouting at each other, in the middle of the night, in Judy's bedroom. Sid, fearful that Joey, whose bedroom was nearby, would awaken and be upset, took the sleeping child out of his bed and put him on the living room sofa. The sight of Sid picking up Joey triggered that fear always in Judy's mind: that he would take the children from her.

At 8 A.M. that morning, the doorbell rang. A huge policeman in civilian clothes entered the apartment. Sid was to leave at once, on orders from Judy.

"If you want me to leave," Sid retorted, "you get a uniformed cop in here and see if he can get me out. My wife isn't well, I know goddamned well she isn't. You can't get me out of here." Sid quoted the officer as saying, "This is Miss Garland's apartment, she is paying the rent, she doesn't want you here." Sid said, "You try to put me out and you're going to see violence." The other said, "There won't be any violence," and showed Sid a .38 in a holster on his belt. Sid thought, *This is ridiculous.* He took Joey back to his bedroom (Judy, in her own bedroom, had not appeared), and left. Sid checked into the Sherry-Netherland, where his partner, Eddie Alperson, was staying.

A little while later, Judy, who as usual had tracked him down, telephoned him. "Are you out?" she asked. "Out where?" demanded Luft. Judy said, "Out of jail." Sid did not know whether to laugh or curse. "I'm really concerned," Judy was saying. "I was told you were arrested."

No, said Sid, he had not been arrested. But, he asked bitterly, why should she order him out of her apartment? Why should a city policeman come into their private life? The upshot was that Judy and Sid went to dinner that night.

There had been an experience earlier that Judy could not overlook. Sid's role in her success at Carnegie Hall the month before had, ironically enough, only led to new difficulties. The night before the concert she said to him, "I want to get away from everything and get a good night's sleep for tomorrow. I've had a rough tour and I need the rest." Sid was all for it. "Let's check into the Sherry-Netherland," he said. "We'll have an easy dinner, just the two of us, play some cards, and when you're tired enough, you'll go to sleep." One thing they both agreed upon: she'd take no pills. Tomorrow night she must be at her best. Carnegie Hall was sold out; the show would be taped for an album, she had to be at her best.

They dined, played cards, talked. Judy did not fall asleep until 5 A.M. Sid, with the memory of what had happened the night before the *Ford Star Jubilee*, took no chances. He remained awake, keeping an eye on her, for the next ten hours, until she awoke, fresh and in fine spirits, at 3 P.M. Two hours later he took her to Carnegie Hall; half an hour before she went on stage, Freddie and David showed up in her dressing room, surprised to see Sid there, and, he thought, apprehensive. Perhaps Judy and Sid would take off on each other, and ruin everything. But nothing like that happened. Judy did the concert of her life, and they all went together to the after-theatre reception given by Jan Mitchell, owner of Lüchow's, and Judy and Sid did not get to sleep until 8 A.M.

That day Sid had to make another hurried trip out of town, and returned exhausted to the Dakota. He had been up nearly forty-eight hours. After a few hours' sleep, he was told by Judy, "I've got good news." She, David and Freddie had held a meeting while he slept. "I told them what help you'd given me, everything, the pressures on you, that I want to help you, so we've decided to put you on the payroll of Kingsrow as associate producer at four hundred dollars a week." With that, she said, "Let's go out and celebrate."

Sid, surly, but not showing it, took Judy to P. J. Clarke's. There, into the small hours of the morning, he talked about horses with another sportsman and the manager of the restaurant, who was a horse enthusiast, too. Judy and Sid closed the place at 4 A.M., got into Judy's limousine to return to the Dakota, and as they rode through Central Park, Judy said, "That was some goddamn celebration."

Sid said, placatingly, "Well, the guy kept the place open for us, he loves to talk about bloodlines."

Judy said coldly, "I'm not interested in bloodlines. I'm interested in what I thought was something I did for you."

"You mean that four hundred a week?" demanded Sid. "Why, that's a two-bit tip for a groom, compared to what I've given and done for you. You don't know a fucking thing about finances. If you think that four hundred dollars a week is anything when you're making a hundred thousand a week, and four hundred is what I need, you're misinformed."

482

Judy slapped him in the face. He held himself back. With the house on his mind, and all the money he had invested in his sound system with discouraging results, and the debts piling up, he said, "Shove it! I don't need that four hundred from you."

They had returned to the apartment in silence.

Judy was moving as though nothing could stop her, appearing in a steady succession of alternate nights in different cities, a rigorous routine she had been rarely able to maintain. She was as unpredictable and as pixilated as ever. An enormous outdoor audience awaited her on a summer day at the Newport Jazz Festival. At her first rehearsal, she complained to Stevie that the microphone looked awful. "It's too—it's too phallic," she said, giggling. "I can't sing into that." How to disguise it? Judy herself came up with a solution: she had a workman cover it with a rubber contraceptive. Nobody was aware of what had been done, but it remained a private joke between the two for a long time.

Sid, traveling about the country, now and then spoke to Judy on the phone. Once there was a telephone call to him from a lawyer: Judy wanted a divorce. Cool it, said Sid. Nothing would happen. But Judy did write a will, on June 30, 1961. The income from her estate would be paid to each child when the child reached twenty-one; at twenty-five, each would receive $250,000; at thirty, another $250,000; and at thirty-five, the remainder of the principal. Sid was not mentioned. She named Freddie Fields and David Begelman as her literary and residual trustees; her lawyer, Aaron Frosch, as executor. She wanted to be cremated, "and my remains disposed of as my Executor, in his sole discretion, shall decide."

A few days later she wrote Sid a letter: he was in New York, and about to go to California to sell the house, like it or not, if he could get a good price—one that would pay off all the debts. He had turned down an offer of $170,000. Judy was taking a summer place in Hyannis Port—Stevie had found it for her across the street from the Kennedy compound—Liza would work backstage at the Hyannis Port Playhouse, painting scenery, for which she would be paid $15 a week, Joey and Lorna would have a fine summer, and it would be a wonderful rest for Judy. She wrote:

Dear Sid:

I'm sorry that I was so short on the phone last night. I'm afraid the heat got me. . . . I have lots of things I must do today, but in case I don't see you before you leave, good luck and God bless. I'll be talking to you in California concerning the children and Hyannis Port. We have a very good house and the children will have plenty of other children to play with. Have peace of mind—we'll all be fine—I wouldn't do anything to hurt them—and I know you feel the same. Goodbye for a while.—Judy.

P.S. Will make a list of things in the house today and send it to you in California.

Sid stared at the letter. It wasn't cold, it was warm, but it was distant. They were wider and wider apart. Neither knew how to cope with their situation.

In California he succeeded in selling the house for $225,000. That would pay off the three mortgages, pay Lynn $14,000 he owed her in back child support and alimony, the $15,000 Vern had loaned him to enable Judy to go to England, the $10,000 Law had loaned him. There were eighteen attachments, and Lord knew how many liens. When it was all over, Sid had $10,000.

A day or so later he read that Judy had been hospitalized in Hyannis Port with a kidney attack. Kidney attack? It had to be an overdose. Sid telephoned Judy at the hospital; she was asleep, he was told. He learned the name of her doctor—a Kennedy physician—and telephoned him.

"I've just learned that my wife had a kidney attack," Sid said. "I don't believe it, Doctor. I'm the husband, and I'd like to know her condition. I'm sure you've heard about Judy and medication. Apparently she's taken some kind of overdose."

The doctor said, "I'd rather not discuss it on the telephone." Sid got no satisfaction, but, the next day, an angry call from Judy. She was in her hospital room. She was in good hands, and she was furious. "How dare you start probing into my personal life? Calling my doctor behind my back!"

"I was concerned about you," Sid said.

"Well, don't be concerned. I just had a little kidney attack."

Sid said, "I want to see the children."

Judy said, "If you want to see the children, talk to my lawyer." There was nothing to do but get in touch with Judy's attorney, who, as Sid recalled, said: "Judy doesn't feel well now. I have talked with

484

her. You may go up and see the children if you wish, but she'd rather not have you stay at her house."

Sid drove to Hyannis Port on a hot July day, and registered at a motel. He telephoned Judy; her voice was like ice. He made no attempt to see her that day. Next morning he found the children on the beach, and romped with them. Eight-year-old Lorna had a marvelous story to tell Daddy. On July Fourth six-year-old Joey and one of Bobby Kennedy's boys were watching the fireworks. The Kennedy youngster turned to Joey. "Do you know the Gettysburg Address?" No, said Joey. "Can you recite the beginning of the Declaration of Independence?" Joey shook his head. "The first words of the Constitution?" No, said Joey, and then he came back, so brilliantly: "Can you whistle *West Side Story?*" And so a Luft had shown up a Kennedy!

The following day Sid played a round of golf with Pat Lawford and Eunice Shriver. They invited him to the Kennedys' that evening. Then, and only then, he wandered over to Judy's house, and found her in the living room. "I've been invited to the Kennedys' tonight," he said. It turned out that Judy had, too. She said, "Under the circumstances, Sid, I'd rather you not go." She was quite firm. He accepted her dictum.

Next afternoon he called on her again. She looked adorable in a gray turtleneck sweater, gray slacks and golf shoes. He sought to approach her, but she backed away from him.

She poured them both a drink and then said casually, "You know, Sid, I'm going to divorce you." Had it been said in heat, in anger, in anything but a cool, matter-of-fact tone, he would have dismissed it as he had so many times before. Now, for the first time, he believed her. He fumbled for words. "Well, if that's the way you want it—but think it over carefully." He left.

Back at his motel he began to drink, and as he drank, for one of the few times in his life he began to fall apart. He called her on the phone; he was shaking. He could not control himself—he was weeping. He thought, *Either I'm more in love than I think I am or I'm so afraid of what a divorce will do to this family . . . the children need me . . . I've a wife who demands so much watching . . . God knows what she can do to herself, to the children . . . no one but me can handle her. . . .*

He sounded so upset that within five minutes Judy was at his motel. She said, "Sid, what's gotten into you?"

He managed to say, "I don't know." He was sobbing, he was almost hysterical, and she tended him until he was calm, and then, as aloof as before, she left.

It was some time before he saw her again.

In September Stevie found Judy and the children a house in Scarsdale, a wealthy New York suburb. Judy chose it because it had excellent schools. Lorna and Joey were enrolled in the Scarsdale Elementary School, and for Liza it was a new opportunity: she joined the Scarsdale High School Little Theatre Group, was given the lead in the play *The Diary of Anne Frank,* and did so well that it was agreed the entire cast would go to Israel and Greece the following summer and put the play on there. When Judy saw Liza at the opening in the high school auditorium, she wept all through it into her powder puff, because she had no Kleenex, and later hugged Liza backstage with a half-tearful, half-laughing "My God, I've got an annuity."

Judy herself was busy. She had resumed her concert tour—Atlantic City, San Francisco, Hollywood—as well as arranging to dub the voice of Mewsette in *Gay Purr-ee,* a cartoon film about a seductive French cat and her lover, Jaune Tom, a Place Pigalle tomcat whose voice was to be dubbed by Robert Goulet (Fields got her $50,000 and 10 percent of the gross, an excellent fee), and doing retakes on *Judgment at Nuremberg,* which Kramer was then editing. At the same time she was preparing for an open-air concert at the Hollywood Bowl.

Out of all this: near-disaster.

At 4 A.M. of the morning of the night she was to sing at the Bowl, September 16, Kramer was awakened by a frantic call from Fields. Judy was in a tantrum, he had to come to her place immediately. She was hysterical, pounding the floor, screaming, "I won't, I won't, I won't!" How could she sing at the Bowl while she was working on a film! It was too much. Kramer hurried over; there was Judy, on the floor, kicking her feet, screaming—Fields, Walters, a wardrobe lady, others, trying to help her and getting nowhere. Kramer got through to her finally: "All right, all right, forget the retakes. I'll change your schedule. Just sing at the Bowl tonight—that's the important thing. I'll use you the day after."

At 8 A.M. Kramer, Walters and the others staggered home. They had managed to get Judy calmed down. But they got no sleep, and neither did she. That night Judy sang at the Hollywood Bowl before more than twenty thousand people who jammed even the exits.

There was a strong wind. It rained intermittently. But not a single person left his seat. Some had raincoats, some umbrellas, some newspapers, some nothing, but no one left. It was Carnegie Hall all over again. When she sang "Chicago," the place rocked; she ripped apart the audience, she galvanized them into one mass of hysterical people paying homage to her. She was supercharged; and in their seats those who had been up all night with her—Kramer, Fields, Walters, the others—could barely keep their eyes open: they were sick with loss of sleep. But Judy? Kramer thought, *I know about actors and performers, but this is unholy: she is vitality, spirit, energy, rejuvenation, everything.*

This was what she loved, as only those close to her knew: the more it rained, the better; the harder the wind blew, the better; she loved fighting, throwing herself into a contest with the elements—this was living! She leaned against the music, drawing her own special mescaline from the combined tumult of music, audience and weather. . . . She had herself a ball. She sang, she joked, she did every little trick. Mightn't the rain short the microphone cord and electrocute her? Mightn't she slip off the glistening wet runway and land in the lagoons over which it extended? A moth, attracted by the lights, buzzed about her and suddenly flew into her mouth; without losing a beat, she tucked it between gums and cheek with her tongue, and continued to sing. And the songs went on, and the encores went on, and still they begged for more. The Los Angeles *Examiner* critic wasted no words: "Perhaps the most memorable night in show business history."

On Halloween 1961 she was back in Scarsdale, after finishing a forty-two-city tour—in her first eighteen months with Creative Management, she was to sing in sixty-one cities and make three films—tricking and treating with Liza, Joey, Lorna and her cook, Judy dressing like a little clown, squeezing tubes of shaving cream on the windows of the good burghers of Scarsdale.

One November night Sid attended a dinner party at the home of Eleanor and Seymour Berkson in New York, where they watched the first TV showing of *A Star Is Born.*

Halfway through Sid rose, made his apologies and left. He returned to his hotel and watched the conclusion of the film in his room. He was counting on something, and he was not wrong.

At midnight, an hour after the picture ended, there was a telephone call from the lobby. "This is Miss Garland's chauffeur," came a man's voice. "Miss Garland is here, in her car, and she would like to see you."

He had known it must happen. How could Judy watch *their* picture—as he knew she must have, in her house in Scarsdale—and not be so moved that she had to see him again? When he went downstairs and walked outside, there was Judy, dressed to perfection, sitting in the rear seat of a limousine, a fur blanket over her knees, beside her an ice bucket with a bottle of champagne.

"Hi, darling," she said, as though they'd seen each other a few hours ago. "How are you?" He said, "Just fine." She said, "You watched the picture?" He nodded, not trusting himself to speak. "Wasn't it great?" she asked. And then: "You produced a great picture, Sid." He said, "Judy, it was your picture and you were great in it and it's great to see you again."

She said, and her voice broke, "Let's celebrate."

They did—at El Morocco.

That night Sid went home with her to Scarsdale. On the drive back he noticed she was wearing neither her wedding ring nor the engagement ring he had bought her later. "Where are they, darling?" he asked. She snuggled up to him. "Somewhere between here and Scarsdale," she said, her voice muffled in his shoulder. "I got sore at you one night and threw them out of the car."

Sid spent the next several nights in the Scarsdale house. Judy had to go off on several concerts, always returning to him and the children, and then to West Berlin in mid-December, for the world premiere of *Judgment at Nuremberg*. She made personal appearances with Spencer Tracy, Montgomery Clift, Richard Widmark and Abby Mann, who had written the script. One night in her Berlin hotel, overcome by the Germany she saw and the Germany she had lived through in the film, she talked into a tape recorder just before she fell asleep. She was in a strange mood. "Don't call it witchcraft," she said. "I am hearing, feeling, sensing, all the lunacy of the human race that was put upon the German people. . . ." Then, in a moment of self-pity: "I am at the height of my career, and the depth of despair, because of being alone, in a miserable, Godforsaken country where a race of people happened to want to follow a madman." It was as though she were back in the days of Hitler. And again:

"I feel so bad and despondent and depressed and despairing"

(there had been the gayest of parties only a few hours before) "because I am in Berlin and I'm alone . . . and I'm in a Hilton hotel. The combination is not good, with the gray carpets which look like they came from Omaha; the gray rugs that have no particular character; the gray walls and the gray outdoors, heavy with guilt, that somehow I take upon myself." She paused, and said suddenly, emotionally, "The Germans were part of *my* generation. The Nazis were part of *my* life. . . . My God! My God! How can we stand on this bloodied ground and think, even dream, of another war or of cruelty toward one another? . . . My God, my God, keep us from it!"

With her on the trip was Al Paul, her hairdresser, a quiet, resourceful man in his thirties, who had been recommended to her by Pat Lawford when she went to Hollywood to shoot *Judgment* in early 1961. Paul became devoted to her; so much so that when Fields asked if he would become her permanent hairdresser, and accompany her on her concert tours, he gave up his own flourishing beauty shop in Beverly Hills to do so. Judy always had to have someone in her entourage whom she liked, trusted, could confide in and whom she found unabrasive. At one point in her tour, she told him, "This is the first time in my life I feel I've accomplished something on my own, that producers haven't pushed me into. I've paid off the government something like one hundred thousand dollars." When she was working on *Judgment,* Paul would do her hair in her Beverly Hills Hotel bungalow, then accompany her in her limousine to Kramer's set at United Artists. She would study the script of her day's shooting as she sat in the back of the car, a pair of glasses on the end of her nose; by the time they reached the studio, she would have tossed the script on the floor. She knew her lines for the day.

Now, in Germany, Judy suddenly decided to go to Rome. Abby Mann and Al Paul accompanied her. Rome was full of her friends; Elizabeth Taylor was filming *Cleopatra* with Richard Burton, there were Eddie Fisher, of course, Roddy McDowall and Kay Thompson, whom she tried to find and apparently couldn't. After the second day Judy came down with a virus; Elizabeth Taylor's physician treated her, but she got no better, and decided she would fly back to the States, via Paris. She was dressed in leotards, blouse and heavy topcoat as she walked through the snow up the ramp to the plane. Paul, who had managed to thread his way carefully through a few Garland-Luft crises, feared she might be coming down with pneumonia, and put through a transatlantic call to Sid, whom he found in Florida. Sid immediately flew to Paris—Creative Management provided the fare —on December 19, landing at Le Bourget, only to learn that Judy was waiting for him at Orly Field, the other side of Paris. He drove there at top speed: at the edge of the field, a plane waited, about to take off for the States. Sid went aboard. Judy sat, all bundled up, shivering, in an aisle seat, her eyes closed. He gently tapped her on the shoulder. "Judy," he said. She opened one eye. "Where were you?" she demanded and closed her eye again.

What was one to do with her?

A few days later, with Judy back in Scarsdale, well again save for a hoarseness in her voice, Sid moved in once more with his wife and family. Sid and Al Paul went shopping for Christmas gifts in New York at F. A. O. Schwarz, and two days before Christmas the entire Luft family put on its own little holiday pageant.

First, Judy, as mistress of ceremonies, very portentous: "Good evening, ladies and gentlemen. I wish to introduce you to an important member of the Luft family, a Miss Lorna Luft. This little lady is about two, three feet high, she has blondish hair, beautiful blue eyes that are slightly crossed," (giggles from everybody) "a turned-up nose with freckles all across it marching down her—and no chin and very peculiar knees. Here she is, Lorna Luft! Take it, Miss Luft!"

Lorna, who has just marked her ninth birthday: "Good evening, ladies and gentlemen. Welcome to our family. This is Station L U F T. We're selling—what are we selling? Fab-fabulous. We are going to trim our little Christmas tree tomorrow. And now I give you back to Miss Judy Garland."

Judy: "And now, ladies and gentlemen, I am going to introduce Mr. Joseph Wiley Luft. He is a very handsome, strapping boy who happens to be my son. Here he is now, Joey Luft."

Joey (whispering): "What should I say?"

(Whisper by Judy.)

Joey: "Ladies and gen'emen, we're going to decorate the Christmas tree tomorrow. We're going to go to school . . ."

Judy (whispering): "Are you going to stay all day at school?"

Joey: "No."

Judy (whispering): "You're going to come home."

Joey: "Then I'm going to come home and decorate the Christmas tree all day with Mommy and Daddy."

Judy (whispering): "And who else?"

Joey: "And Liza and Lorna and Joey."

Judy (whispering): "Say good night, everybody."

Joey: "Good night, ev'ybody, ladies and gen'emen."

Judy: "That's very nice, Mr. Luft. Thank you very much. We now give you a most peculiar girl, a girl named Liza, who's sitting right here now, looking like something I should say in the zombie family." (Burst of laughter from Liza.) "Along with her mother, she has a ripping case of the flu. Ladies and gentlemen, I give you—and you won't take her—Liza Minnelli."

Fifteen-year-old Liza: "Good *even . . . ing*, everyone! This is Typhoid Mary coming to you" (interrupts herself with laughter) "from the Luft house, which is at this point pretty *icha!* My brother is doing the twist, or what is commonly known as the twist, and I have absolutely nothing to say, because I feel rotten! I give you my mother again!"

Judy: "Daddy?" (Sid has walked in.) "Come here. We're trying to get the head of the household, ladies and gentlemen. It's a very difficult thing. He's coming through the crowd now—Mr. Luft, will you give us a few words?" (Much hand-clapping from the children.)

Sid: "Ladies and gentlemen, unaccustomed as I am to public speaking," (Liza's laughter interrupts) "you know that old jazz—but it's nice to be with my beautiful family, Liza, Lorna, last but not least, José—who is now going to bed and we're going to start to decorate the Christmas tree tomorrow, bright and early, and we'll have a ball. Good-bye, all."

Chorus from the children: "Good night, good night, good night everybody."

Judy: "Good night from Mommy and Daddy. Good night, Lorna."

"Good night." (from Lorna.)

Judy: "Good night, Liza."

"Good night." (from Liza.)

Judy: "Good night, Joey."

"Good night." (from Joey.)

And Joey's piping voice again: "Good night, ev'ybody, good night, ladies and gen'emen!"

That Christmas of 1961, in Scarsdale, though it may be difficult to believe, was one of the happiest in the bewildering, baffling, perverse story of the Lufts. The record is there: a taping of idyllic nights, of loving games by Judy and Sid and Liza and Lorna and Joey, of little songs and gleeful skits, and through it all laughter and affection and the miracle of being together again.

35

ON A SPRING DAY IN 1962, Judy Garland and her husband Sid Luft had one of their most serious confrontations. Before it was over, Judy had fled with the three children to England, leaving an impotent, cursing Luft struggling in the iron grip of two private detectives, to the accompaniment of tabloid newspaper headlines, charges and countercharges of kidnaping and assault and battery, the whole manifesting all the earmarks of a Chaplinesque tragicomedy.

For both husband and wife, the situation had reached a stage of complete distrust. As for Sid, he felt he was being coopted by Judy's alliance with Fields and Begelman. Stevie Dumler, Fields's cool, competent and resourceful right hand, had found the Dakota apartment for Judy, the Hyannis Port house for Judy, the Scarsdale house for Judy—his family was being moved about, taken out of his domain. . . . Vern had reported what Judy told Fields: "Keep Sid out of it." All right, he thought, he'd keep out of it. He did not deprecate what they had done for her. More power to them. But however it would end, he saw it as a tug of war between himself and Fields and Begelman.

In 1962 Judy went to California, work awaiting her. The Scarsdale house was closed by Sid, who then joined her on the West Coast, where she took a house with the children in Bel Air. Those poor kids, he thought: dragged from one coast to another. (Before Liza was finished, there would be sixteen schools.)

In these early months of the year, Sid was putting together his four-hour tape-deck program of comedy, music and songs, to which Judy, Bing Crosby, Nat "King" Cole and other stars lent their talents, each acting as his own disk jockey, in a Luft Production which Sid hoped to sell to the airlines. Judy had taped a CBS special with Frank Sinatra and Dean Martin, which was shown in February 1962. (Fields had straightened out her legal difficulties with CBS.) Jack Gould in the *New York Times* put it succinctly: "Judy Garland held television in the palm of her hand last night. In her first video appearance in six years, the singer carried on the music hall tradition of Al Jolson and the other greats." Frank Sinatra and Dean Martin got their mention in the second paragraph; it was Judy's show. She was still the champ.

This behind her, she threw herself into Kramer's second film, *A Child Is Waiting*. In this she starred again with Burt Lancaster, with a new young director, John Cassavetes. The making of this picture, in which she played Jean Hansen, a too sympathetic teacher in a home for Mongoloid and other retarded children, became a traumatic experience. Once, years before, when Sid had taken Judy to watch the running of the Kentucky Derby, they had gone through a hospital in Lexington filled with hundreds of birth-damaged children, some of whom, Judy had been told, had been given lobotomy operations; it had upset her. In *A Child Is Waiting* she had difficulties with Cassavetes, with Lancaster, who, interested in the subject himself, had definite ideas as to how the role should be played. He and Kramer, he and Cassavetes, had their disputes. Each day Kramer brought the children from two actual homes for retarded children. And each day Judy had to drive to the set to be confronted not by make-believe but by grim reality. Some of the pressure was relieved by Liza, who would often go over Judy's scenes with her in her dressing room. The heavy scenes overwhelmed her; sometimes she was medicated, and under the care of a new doctor who had been brought in to help keep her on an even keel.

Meanwhile, hanging over her head was the realization that within three weeks or so after finishing *Child*, she would be going into another picture, *The Lonely Stage* (later changed to *I Could Go On Singing*), to be made in England.

Judy needed breathing time between performances, whether concerts or films. Deadlines terrified her. To perform when she was not ready to perform, when she was not at her best, was a torment. When she finished *A Child Is Waiting*, she had less than a month in which to pack up everything in the Bel Air house, get off her medication and restore herself to a condition in which she could fly to New York, then to London and take on a new film. There were several reassuring factors. She would be working with friends. Her co-star would be

Dirk Bogarde (although it was because of his busy schedule that she would have no rest), the title song would be by Arlen and Harburg, the musical director would be Saul Chaplin. And again it was a musical, with all the work that meant.

Judy told Sid, "I want to go to New York alone, ahead of you. You close up the house and bring the children to New York." The plan, as Sid had envisaged it, was for them to go to London as a family. While Judy worked on her picture, he would exhibit his tape deck to European airline executives. He and Nicholas du Pont, whom he had known since their school days, had become interested in another project—a Norwegian spruce which might be used to revolutionize house construction—and he would commute from London to other capitals, always returning to his family. But Judy going on ahead by herself? Sid was highly suspicious.

Unexpectedly, Judy moved out of the Bel Air house into the Beverly Hills Hotel with Lorna and Joe, days before she was to leave for New York, separating herself from him. (Liza was staying with Vincente.) And, confirming Luft's worst suspicions, he received a telephone call from Grant Cooper, a well-known divorce lawyer. Judy wanted a legal separation. Luft told Cooper he would refuse to sign a letter of separation. "It'll blow over," he said. "Judy always acts this way. That's the way she takes out her frustrations and fears—on me. She's done it before."

Nonetheless, Judy considered herself separated from him.

Then, in quick order, a succession of events:

On Thursday, April 12, Judy flew to New York, Al Paul accompanying her.

On Friday Dr. Lester Coleman, a New York throat specialist, who had treated Judy's laryngitis when she made her Vegas debut years before, and had become so intimate a friend of the Lufts that they had named him Lorna's godfather, telephoned Sid. He had spoken, he said, with Dr. Kermit Osserman, who was treating Judy in New York, and Dr. Osserman had said he was concerned about Judy's condition.

The next morning at 9 A.M. Sid received a telephone call from Judy. "I'm very ill, Sid," she said. "I'm going into the hospital. Please take care of the children." Luft checked and found Judy was in the Columbia Presbyterian Hospital. She had entered for two weeks.

This was Sunday, the fifteenth.

494

Four days later, having closed the Bel Air house, Sid flew to New York with the three children and a nurse. That Thursday evening they all checked into the Hotel Stanhope, on upper Fifth Avenue. He telephoned Judy at the hospital. She was testy with him. "You better get out of town," she said. "You're way behind in our taxes, and if it wasn't for David, the IRS people would have broken down my door, because you failed to file 1958, 1959 and 1960 tax returns." Luft said Begelman, who had to be in almost constant attendance on Judy (later, when Begelman and his wife, Lee, had separated, Mrs. Begelman would not conceal the fact that the attention Begelman had to pay to his star client had played a role in the breakup of their marriage), had already warned him by telephone not to stay in New York because the IRS was looking for him.

On Easter Sunday, April 22, Judy suddenly left the hospital. Two days later Luft had to fly to Germany to exhibit his equipment; when he returned on April 27, he found Judy planning to leave for England the next day, taking the children.

Now Judy, Sid and the children were all in the Stanhope Hotel, Judy on the eleventh floor, Sid on the sixth. According to Sid, at 9 A.M. Saturday, Judy knocked on his door. "As soon as I'm finished with this picture, I want a divorce," he quoted her as saying, and himself as replying, "Judy, let's not discuss that now. You go off to England and get well. I'll come along shortly with the children because you're not well enough to take the kids. I'm whacked out and you're tired."

"No," said Judy. "I'm taking them with me today."

Sid said, "I don't think you will, Judy. That's my decision."

She left.

According to Stevie, what happened then was this: That Saturday morning Judy sent Lorna and Joe out to play in Central Park, across the street from the hotel, with Stevie and the children's nurse in charge. Liza was staying at the home of Dr. Coleman and his wife, Felicia, three blocks away. She had a crush on a young actor whom she was seeing, and had no wish to go to England.

When Stevie saw that everything appeared fine—the children playing happily under the nurse's eye, Sid nowhere about—Stevie left the park long enough to telephone Judy, "Everything's O.K." Judy said, "Oh, I'm so relieved."

When Stevie returned to the park, she could find neither children nor nurse. She searched the play area hurriedly, then dashed back to the hotel to report to Judy. "Oh, God," Judy cried. "Sid must have them." Had the nurse been in Sid's employ?

Stevie hurried down to the sixth floor and listened. She heard the children's voices, and promptly knocked. "Who's there?" Sid asked. "Stevie," she said. Sid opened it. With her usual self-possession, Stevie spoke up: "I've got to take the children upstairs, Sid. They're in my charge."

With that Sid pushed her out and slammed the door.

Stevie went back upstairs. Maybe Judy should call Liza at the Colemans' and get her over. Liza was ingenious. She might come up with a way to get the children back.

Judy did so, telling her daughter, "Sid's got Lorna and Joe—get here quickly. Hurry, hurry, hurry—you're the only one who can talk to both of us."

Liza threw on a pair of blue slacks, a T-shirt, and made her way to the Stanhope. The lobby seemed full of police. When she got to the eleventh floor, she found two policemen guarding the door. Judy let her into her suite. Judy's lawyer, Irving Erdheim, was there, as well as several of Judy's friends.

"Hello, darling," Judy said, and Liza knew at once that her mother was playing a role for the benefit of the others. Judy added, in a voice of doom, "He's got the kids." She made it sound, Liza thought, as though they had been bound and gagged.

Liza spoke up brightly, "Well, let me go down and see them."

Judy said resignedly, "Oh, you can't get in."

"Of course I can," said Liza. She went down to the sixth floor and rapped on the door of Sid's suite. "Who is it?" came her stepfather's voice, from behind the door. "It's me," said Liza. The door opened and she walked in. Joey and Lorna were on the floor, watching TV. "What's going on?" Liza asked innocently. "Nothing," Luft said. "I just don't want the kids to go to Europe." Lorna and Joey chimed in, "We don't want to go to Europe either."

Liza knew that in the end she and Lorna and Joe would go with their mother. Judy would not be defeated; also, wherever Mama was, was home for them. But playing, as always, the sagacious moderator, she said, "Well, Pop, look. I don't really want to go either. But isn't there a way we can do it without the whole New York police force in the lobby?"

Luft looked hurt. "I didn't call them, you know."

"Yes, but you didn't get rid of them," said Liza. Sid replied, "I can't."

After a few more minutes of inconclusive conversation, Liza left and went upstairs to report. "Well?" demanded Judy. Everyone in the room looked at Liza. She had no heart to say, "Mama, they're fine, they're watching TV." She had to rise to the occasion, with her mother looking so pale and drawn, in her best Duse role, and other people there. She said, "They're O.K." She said it as if to suggest that she'd managed despite enormous risk to catch a glimpse of them through the peephole of their dungeon and, though trussed up and helpless, they were still alive.

Judy: "What did Sid say?"

"He didn't say anything, Mama, except that he wanted them with him. He doesn't want you to take them to Europe."

Judy's mouth compressed. "Liza, he's not going to take them from me."

Time passed. Word came up to the eleventh floor that Lorna and Joey and their nurse were walking in Central Park, with Luft nowhere in sight.

Judy summoned Liza to her side. Standing as a backdrop behind her mother, now, were four huge men—bodyguards, obviously. Judy's voice became conspiratorial. "Here's what you do, Liza. You go into the park and get them, then bring them to the side entrance of the hotel and I'll have these men waiting for you."

"O.K.," said Liza. This was a game, and she could enjoy it. She hurried downstairs, trotted into the park, made out Lorna and Joey and their nurse on one of the walks, and started running after them. Presently she heard someone behind her, puffing hard. She looked over her shoulder; it was her stepfather. She thought, *My God, what are we doing? This is getting to be like a Mack Sennett comedy.* She veered suddenly to take a path to the left, her stepfather on her heels. She stopped suddenly, and turned. "Wait a minute, Pop! Just what are we doing?"

Luft, trying to catch his breath, countered, "What are *you* doing?"

Liza said, "I'm going to get the kids."

Luft demanded, suspiciously, "And take them where?"

"Nowhere," said Liza. "I just wanted to talk to them."

"Oh," said Luft, and they fell in step. When they came upon the two children and their nurse, they all strolled together and, after a few minutes, all returned to Luft's suite.

Liza was no sooner there than a call came from Judy. Apparently she had observers who were reporting to her. "Come upstairs!" Liza went. "What happened?" Judy demanded. "Nothing, Mama," and then: "Look, Mama, I'll go to Europe with you." She knew her mother didn't want to go alone.

"Then go get your clothes," Judy ordered, and Liza dutifully hurried over to the Coleman residence. She literally grabbed an armful of clothes and ran back to the hotel. She had not even time to put on shoes; she was wearing sandals. A limousine waited at the side entrance. One of the guards was there to direct her. "Get in," he said. As she slid into a corner of the limousine, she saw her mother, Lorna and Joey, all three, bursting pell-mell from the side entrance and hurrying toward the car. Joey had on two unmatching socks, Lorna wore a sun dress, Judy a huge straw hat. They all scrambled into the limousine, and it drew away almost before the door shut. Now everyone was caught up in the spirit of the thing—here they were with Mama off on a new adventure—they had completely forgotten they didn't want to go.

"How'd you do it, Mama? Tell me! Tell me!" Liza all but squealed, and Judy, with interruptions and emendations from Lorna and Joey, triumphantly explained. She had gone to Sid's apartment with her bodyguards and rapped sharply on the door. "Sid?"

"Who is it?" Sid's voice was cautious.

"It's me."

"Are you alone?"

"Yes, Sid."

"I don't believe you," Luft said. "No, no, please," Judy said. "I just want to talk to you. Maybe you are right, Sid. Maybe they should stay."

Again he asked, "Are you alone?" And again Judy swore she was.

He opened the door. Judy went in, the door was all but closed— here Lorna spoke up: "Mama screamed, 'He's hitting me, he's hitting me!' "—when the four bodyguards burst in. Two grabbed Luft, pinning his arms behind him; Judy with the other two grabbed Lorna and Joey, shepherded them out and, as she left, turned and thumbed her nose at Luft, struggling and cursing like a man bereft. Then they were on the elevator and down to the lobby and out the side door and into the waiting car just a moment after Liza had slid in.

Three days later, Judy was at the Savoy Hotel in London, poised, pert, chic and remarkably self-possessed, being introduced to the press by David Begelman. No, the children were not with her at the moment. "They are being guarded day and night in a hideout in Surrey," she said. Her "estranged husband," she had told reporters at Idlewild Airport, was attempting to take Lorna and Joe from her on the grounds that she was "an unfit mother." That was completely ridiculous.

Yes, she expected Luft to follow them to England, to try to take the children. He would never succeed. There was no chance of a reconciliation. "My marriage is finished," she said. She would start shooting her film in a few days. Begelman added, "The studio will see that no unauthorized person—even Mr. Luft—will be able to see the children at this stage."

The same day Judy had her children made wards of the High Chancery Court of Britain. It meant they could not be taken out of the country without the court's approval, by either parent. That would fix Sid.

Not altogether. A week later, Judy turned to Lorna. "Dad's here," she said. Sid had arrived, and had quietly registered at the Carlton Towers Hotel. He had telephoned Judy a day or so after his arrival. It had been: "Hi, darling, can I see the children?" As though nothing had happened. Judy had agreed. Sid lunched with them and their governess at his hotel that Sunday and spent the rest of the day with them.

Joey and Lorna had arrived with a proper British nanny, who introduced herself as Miss Elizabeth Ann Colledge, a state nurse and former school matron, to whom Sid took an instant dislike because of what he considered her proprietary attitude toward his children. But that Sunday went well. Three days later Judy started shooting her film.

Now began three months of a cat-and-mouse game, with Gumshoe Luft employing a private detective, Judy employing private guards, and lawyers busy on both sides, arguing over Sid's visitation rights. All Lorna and Joe knew was that something called a "custody battle" was going on, and that Mama, working on her film, was repeatedly ill—either stumbling down the stairs and hurting herself, or taken by a sudden stomach upset that sent her briefly into a hospital.

Judy rented a house for those months at 33 Hyde Park Gate, one of London's loveliest, most peaceful residential areas, but that summer saw occasional violent scenes there. Sid learned that Begelman flew in from New York frequently to see Judy, and he was upset by this close managerial relationship. He felt helpless and began to drink heavily. There was at least one wall-shaking encounter when he came to visit the children. Miss Colledge laid down Mrs. Luft's precise instructions, and Sid, who thought the children were not properly taken care of, told off Miss Colledge in language she and Judy later described in sworn depositions as full of such adjectives as "fucking" and worse. Miss Colledge summoned the police to oust Mr. Luft. The police arrived, said courteously that this was a "domestic affair" and as courteously left, leaving Luft triumphantly there.

Liza, fortunately, missed some of this turmoil because on July 3 she flew to Israel to join her Scarsdale Little Theatre Group in their presentation of *The Diary of Anne Frank* at the Hebrew University in Jerusalem. Al Paul, who had been given a small part in Judy's film so he could receive a work permit as her hairdresser, trying his best to keep impartial, accompanied Liza to the Tel-Aviv airport, saw her safely met by her colleagues and returned on the next plane to London. But it was impossible for him to avoid becoming involved. He accompanied Judy to a hospital (she had taken suddenly ill, the papers said), but he stated in a deposition he was required to make that she had had her stomach pumped. In the end, she dismissed him.

The legal actions and depositions continued. Sid charged that Judy had at least ten doctors during these months; that on July 4 Judy called him, told him she was in Regent's Park Nursing Home (she had fallen and cracked her head on a bathtub, she explained) and asked him to take the children for a week. On June 10, her fortieth birthday, Sid had sent her a huge bouquet of red roses. Now, nearly four weeks later, she thanked him for them. After his week with the children Judy, coming out of the nursing home, asked him to accompany her to a recording session. Then they returned to her home and for the next three days lived there as husband and wife. That reconciliation was brief: a second was attempted, even more brief.

Among the depositions were statements by three psychiatrists called by Judy, one of whom said Luft tried to prevent him from giving Mrs. Luft necessary sedation one night; a deposition by Judy that she had been the breadwinner during their marriage, that she had paid off numerous of Sid's debts, that he had sold her services without her knowledge, that he did not contribute "a penny piece" to the children's upkeep; countercharges by Sid as to her unfitness as a mother; and a counter-countercharge by Judy that Sid telephoned her on July 26 and told her, "You still love me," whereupon she replied, "You are mad," and at once moved with her children to the Savoy for protection.

All this came to an end, in England, on August 12, when Judy and the children, accompanied by Begelman and Miss Colledge, flew to the States. Judy had finished shooting *I Could Go On Singing.* Ironically enough, the film was in some ways almost autobiographical: it dealt with a famous American singer with emotional problems, one of them growing out of her having had an illegitimate son fourteen years before by Dirk Bogarde, her lover, and how she came to play the Palladium in London and attempted to find, and get back, her son. Ultimately she loses him because as an entertainer she is considered an unfit mother. In view of the pressures on Judy, not only in her personal life but in making a film that must have touched so many raw nerves, the fact that so acute a critic as Penelope Gilliatt in the London *Observer* could speak of her as "a harrowingly good actress" and praise her "thrilling technique" is only one more measure of Judy.

She left the country with the children after attending a court hearing with Sid, where she explained she had to go to Nevada to carry out engagements and to take up residence in order to file a divorce suit against Luft.

That autumn of 1962 was a witch's brew for Judy as personal and emotional problems of every kind assailed her. Immediately upon arriving from London, she had taken a suite at the Beverly Hills Hotel in California before a brief stay in Tahoe and then Vegas. Suddenly, there was an emergency call to Jimmy in Dallas in the middle of the night from Vegas: her sister Suzy had attempted suicide with an overdose of pills. There were no planes flying then, no way she could get to Vegas immediately. Judy, reached through Harry Rabwin, at once chartered a plane and flew up, sat all night at Suzy's bedside and literally talked her back to life. That extraordinary healing power over men, women and children worked its magic. By the time Jimmy arrived next day, Suzy had come out of it and seemed fine.

The three Gumm sisters had met infrequently in recent years. Judy had seen more of Suzy than of Jimmy, because Suzy's husband Jack conducted for her for several years after the first Palace engagement in 1951. Then Gordon Jenkins became her conductor, and Jack went on to become musical director of the Riviera Hotel in Vegas. Not only that: Jack had fallen in love with a girl, and had left Suzy to marry her. Suzy, who loved children, had always envied her sisters theirs, but had never had children of her own. She had even wanted to adopt a child. Now Jack had not only married a younger woman, but she was giving him a child. Suzy had always been in her sisters' shadow; older, more proper, suffering from chronic colitis, she had taken to drinking heavily. The breakup of her marriage, which had lasted for nearly twenty-five years, had left her in an unbearably depressed state. (Later it was learned that she had been living for years with a skull fracture suffered during a fall, so there was an additional physical reason for her malaise.)

In any event, the three sisters were together again. Judy was to open a month's engagement at the Sahara Hotel September 18, and file her divorce suit on September 28. Since she would be there at least six weeks, she brought the three children with her. It was then she learned that Sid was filing a countersuit in California to restrain her from divorcing him in Nevada on the grounds that neither was a bona fide resident of the state.

It is difficult to sort out exactly how the next series of events played upon one another, because so much emotion was engendered by all the parties, but Judy took too many pain-killing pills because of an excruciating kidney attack which hospitalized her while vacationing in Tahoe before going to Vegas ("HARD-LUCK JUDY O.K. AFTER OVER-DOSE," read the Hollywood *Citizen-News*), fought bitterly over the telephone with Sid, made arrangements to hide Joe and Lorna on a secret, fenced-in ranch protected by armed guards and police dogs against any attempt by Sid to kidnap them, and got into a furious fight with her sisters.

This quarrel took place while the three children were still in Judy's suite in Vegas. Judy had just been on the phone to Sid; they began trading obscenities, which were overheard by everyone—Liza,

Lorna, Joey, the children's governess, Jimmy, Suzy and her escort, and the hotel hairdresser, who had been waiting patiently in an adjoining room to do Judy's hair. Everyone pretended not to hear. Liza was telling Jimmy about her exciting trip to Israel that summer, talking loudly to drown out her mother's voice. Judy, growing more and more enraged on the telephone, hung up and, beside herself, strode into the living room, slamming the bedroom door behind her. She had been going repeatedly to her bathroom, and nobody knew how much medication she had been taking either to calm herself or to stoke her courage.

Her eyes fell on the two children. "Go to your room!" she ordered. "Nanny, take Lorna and Joe to their room." Lorna spoke up—of them all, she alone dared talk back to Judy—"I don't wanna go." Judy: "Go to your room!" Lorna, muttering to herself, obeyed, Joey trailing along with the nurse.

Judy, even more agitated, hurried back to the bedroom, slammed the door, called Sid back, and the battle picked up where it had left off.

Then, after some moments, she emerged and strode into the room where the hairdresser waited. She sat down before the mirror and he began his work. In the living room everyone relaxed. They then heard Judy's voice, obviously incensed because everyone had pretended nothing had happened: "None of you care anything about me!"

Jimmy, from her chair where she had been sitting quietly smoking, answered her: "What are you talking about?"

"You don't care anything about me!" came Judy's voice, even louder. "When I was sick in the hospital in New York with hepatitis, did either of you come to see me?" Her anger and self-pity built up as she went on. "Look, I do all this for you, I pay for all this stuff—and have you, either of you, ever done anything for me? Did either of you so much as send me a flower or even a note? I almost died!"

Jimmy's voice rose. She was outraged because the children had heard Judy's end of her vituperative telephone conversation with Sid. "Look, Judy," she said. "I didn't even know you were sick."

Judy: "Well, you should have known."

Jimmy, dryly: "Honey, for twenty years I didn't know where you were unless I read it in the paper, and then I couldn't be sure about it."

"No," Judy retorted. "You just didn't give a damn."

Jimmy: "I didn't think you gave a damn if I gave a damn."

Judy: "If you loved me, you'd know what was happening to me. You'd have found out. You would have—"

At this point Liza spoke up: "I think I'll go make a Spanish pudding," and left the room. Under any other circumstance Judy would have roared. It was one of her own favorite stories. When George Gershwin died, the entire Gershwin family had returned from the funeral and sat about the house, quiet, grieving, their minds on George, how tragic his death had been, when one of his sisters unexpectedly rose, saying, "I think I'll go make a Spanish pudding," and disappeared into the kitchen. Judy had always told Liza it was "the non sequitur of your dreams." But she was too upset now to appreciate it; otherwise she might have noticed, too, that sixteen-year-old Liza had deliberately absented herself so she could listen, unseen, in the next room, so that if the storm threatened to become too intense, she could gallop back among them, pretending to be deathly sick, crying, "I'm going to throw up!"—and so draw their attention away from each other.

But no one seemed to notice her leaving.

Suzy said angrily: "How about me? I've been in the hospital a lot. When did you ever come to visit me?"

"How did I know?" Judy demanded, coming into the living room. She grew even angrier. "How about the last time I was in the hospital up here?"

Suzy said, "What did you have?"

There was a long pause. Judy seemed to be swallowing her bile. Then out it came, her sense of humor getting the better of her even now: "Clap! That's what I had! What difference does it make what I had?"

There was a giggle Liza couldn't suppress in the next room, followed by a moment's shocked silence, and then the quarrel went on again. In the midst of it, Judy remembered an incident the night of their mother's funeral. The three sisters had gone back to Judy's house, a number of friends had come over for a kind of Irish wake, and Judy had asked, "Does anyone want an after-dinner drink?" Jimmy said, "I'd love a brandy." Her husband, John, said he would like one, too.

Judy went behind the bar, took two large brandy snifters, poured each half full and brought them to her sister and brother-in-law. Jimmy, for all her grief, could not help bursting into laughter. "My God, honey, I don't drink that much. Don't you know, Judy—you just put a shot in the bottom, then you warm it up in your hand."

Now it came back to Judy like a blow. "Remember how, in front of everybody, you put me down at Mama's funeral? You wanted it to look like I didn't know anything."

"I don't know why you're so all-fired sensitive about that," said Jimmy, "when you're not sensitive about the sort of language you use in front of your own children. You shouldn't talk like that on the phone in front of them—all those four-letter words—"

Now Judy was in a fury. She had been drinking her liebfraumilch, and she shouted, "Who are you to tell me what to do?" She confronted Jimmy, even as Liza dashed in to soothe her mother, too upset herself to play her little trick. But Judy was beyond soothing. "Get out!" she was saying to Jimmy. "Get out!"

Jimmy said, "Honey, don't do that, don't say that, it's wrong, it's dumb!"

But Judy was beyond hearing. "Get out!" Jimmy walked to her room, packed her suitcase and left. She never saw Judy again.

Whether this explosion was triggered by medication, liquor, the subterranean pressures brought to the fore on the relatively rare occasions the three sisters were together, or by the sudden memory of her mother's funeral—no one can know. But it would appear that in the back of Judy's mind there always remained a subtle tormenting guilt about her mother. Only a few months before, talking to her good friend and confidante Ellie Schachtel, the wife of Sid's friend Irving, Judy first revealed that for years after her mother's death she had the recurring nightmare of searching for her mother. She had confessed, suddenly, "You know, my mother didn't have to work in that defense plant. I had the money then—I could have taken care of her, I really could. But don't you think I was right? After all the things she did to me?"

The day after Judy was suddenly taken to the hospital in Tahoe after her overdose/kidney attack, Luft telephoned her from Los Angeles, and when she got on the phone in her Carson Tahoe Hospital room, there followed a bitter exchange:

Sid: "What happened?"

Judy: "What do you mean, what happened? Did you hear what happened?"

Sid: "I heard garbled—"

Judy, contemptuously: "Garbled? Or are you listening garbled?"

Sid: "I didn't call to argue. I wanted to find out how you were."

Judy: "I'm doing awfully well. For two years I've been working and supporting the children, and all these kind of things. You try to do as well. And in the meantime, don't bother my friends—or me."

Sid: "I would like to see the children, by the way."

Judy: "You can see them when the court says you can see them." And after a further exchange: "I just won't take any more of this nonsense from you any more, ever. You've got two weeks to go—and then you're out of my life forever!"

She was talking about the divorce suit she would file.

After another exchange, Sid: "Ummmmm. Well, you'll get on your knees one day."

Judy: "Oh, you won't find me on my knees unless I'm singing 'Mammy.' "

More words and then the conversation ended when Judy said, "Oh, get off the phone and stop bothering people here. Get lost. Just get lost. You can't win." Sid said, "I'm not trying to win anything. I'm trying to do the decent thing as I always have," and Judy snapped, "Decent thing! You don't know the meaning of the word. Get lost."

And she hung up.

It is understandable why she came down with laryngitis while singing at the Sahara. Fortunately, she found a new cure. Stan Irwin, vice president and executive producer at the hotel, had an excellent rapport with Judy. He knew how to handle talent. She had been appearing in shapeless sack dresses; he found new, more attractive costumes for her. And since Judy obviously did better the later the hour, he introduced for the first time in Vegas the 2:30 A.M. show, to help her—and even at this hour there was standing room only.

Also, Irwin had a remarkable facility as a hypnotist, something he had been practicing for more than twenty years. When Judy's voice troubled her, he explained how he had helped other singers. "Hypnosis fights infection," he told her. She could check this with her doctor. She should continue taking whatever medicine her doctor prescribed for her throat, but was she game to let Irwin hypnotize her? There was no mystery to it, it was simply the deepest form of relaxation. You didn't go to sleep, you relaxed, utterly, and once you had experienced this, in later life if you were told what to do, the same state of pure relaxation would return.

"I'd love it," she cried. "Yes, yes." A new toy, a new adventure.

The first time he hypnotized her was at 10 P.M. in her suite. She curled up in a big easy chair, her feet under her, and looked expectantly at him. "Any time you want to ask a question, you go ahead," he said. "Ready?"

Judy nodded.

"First, close your eyes," he said. "Now take three deep breaths, hold each one for a count of five, then release the breath, as slowly as possible." She followed his directions. "You're a balloon allowing the air to come out, and as the balloon folds up, so do you. You hear nothing but my voice, you will enjoy my voice, and you will relax completely. . . ."

Judy's eyes were closed. She had ballooned, and folded. "Your throat is fine," he said, in a gentle voice. And he gave her then what he called his induction. She was to count backward from ten to one. Each time she counted a figure—at ten, nine, eight, and down to zero —he would say, and she would repeat after him, "At the count of three, each and every muscle of my body will unwind and unpinch itself, align and adjust itself perfectly for physical and mental health and complete relaxation." She carried out his instructions, and by the time she said "zero," and went through the magic sentence, she felt utterly at peace.

She sang that night perfectly.

"Stan, it's wonderful," she cried. But what if he was not around? She could do it herself, he said. He would establish a posthypnotic word that would instantly put her in a state of relaxation. He had to travel about, signing up acts. He had a special phone installed in a room adjoining her dressing room, and it was agreed that each night at nine he would telephone her and put her back into a hypnotic state. But what should be the cue word? It must be something pleasant. "I've got it," said Judy, excitedly. "Irish Mail." When she was a little girl, an Irish Mail was very popular; it looked like a little tricycle, and you pumped a handle back and forth to propel yourself, like a handcar on a railroad. She had wanted one so badly, but had never had one. "O.K.," said Irwin. "That'll be the word."

At nine o'clock every night she appeared, then, Judy's special phone rang. She dashed over, sat down with the phone, and the following dialogue took place:

"Hello, Judy?" "Hi, darling." "Are you ready, Judy?" "Yes, darling." "All right. Hold the phone close to your ear now, and the phone will remain at your ear no matter what I say, at all times the phone will remain at your ear. Are you ready? Take a deep breath . . . *Irish Mail* . . ." Silence. Then Irwin: "How do you feel?" Judy's voice when he first spoke to her had been a nervous or tense, even high-pitched "Hi, darling." Now he heard her say, slowly, "All . . . right."

When she went on, she did beautifully. One night she had come back after the usual wild applause to her bungalow, with a few friends, who were now sitting about her feet, all idolizing her: "Oh, Judy, you were so fabulous. You're so fabulous!" She suddenly said, "I can't say 'Thank you' any more! I just can't!" Clenching her fists, she got up and ran into her bedroom. That ended the party.

Yet how did one hypnotize Luft? Shortly after Judy closed at the Sahara, Sid obtained the California court order temporarily restraining Judy from going through with the divorce. A few days later, November 21, was Lorna's tenth birthday. Sid asked through an intermediary if he could visit Lorna and Joe on the ranch. A furious Judy sent back a message by the same means: "The weather isn't right for you to come up here." An equally enraged Luft decided he would drive up to the ranch—a little gumshoe work led him to discover its whereabouts—and take the children back to California. He would bring along a friend, a former weightlifting champion of the world, and a good man to have in his corner, because he was so little yet so strong—he weighed only 134 pounds and he could press 327!

Sid waited a week, then quietly drove up with his friend. He had it planned carefully. The gates of the ranch were open; he saw Joey and Lorna swimming in a pool, which was not far from the entrance. It was three in the afternoon. For the first twenty minutes or so Sid played with the children, then he told them, "Let's take a little walk," and, holding each by the hand, began casually walking toward the gate, where his friend was sitting behind the wheel of the car, with the motor running.

Suddenly Sid picked up the two children and made a run for the

508

car. A guard materialized from nowhere with a drawn .45 revolver, which he stuck in Luft's face: "Put the children down." Lorna and Joey began to cry. Sid released them. He cursed himself—and his weightlifting pal. He was always to say, "My timing was a little off. I was still twenty feet away, the motor was running—" The friend had failed him, for he was to have helped seize the children.

Yet Sid realized that had he succeeded, or were he to try again, Judy would hold all the cards in the deck. Whatever happened would have to happen in due and legal course.

One January day in 1963, at 4 A.M., a call came to Sid Luft in the Beverly Rodeo Hotel in Los Angeles, a place where nobody should have known he was, and the voice at the other end was only too familiar.

"Hi, darling," said Judy. "Do you think we'll ever have a chance?"

"Judy," Luft said, as if three months had not passed since they'd talked, "we'll always have a chance. Where are you?"

"I'm in Miami," she said. "Do you think we can sit down and talk —that there's any chance after what we've gone through?"

"We always will," he said. "You know as well as I do, we love each other."

She made no reply to this, but went on, sounding cold-sober: "I'll meet you halfway so we won't waste any time. Let's meet in Chicago, at the Ambassador East." No, he said, it was cold and dreary in Chicago. "Let's make it closer, you don't like to fly anyway. I'll meet you in New Orleans." They arranged where. When he hung up, he threw cold water on his face.

"What in hell is going on?" he asked himself.

It was a good question.

36

IT TURNED OUT, ON THE FACE OF IT, to be one more attempt at reconciliation, and an important one: Judy had before her a TV special for CBS with Phil Silvers and Robert Goulet, but, far more significant, in the works now was the biggest project of her career:

Creative Management was beginning to negotiate a multimillion-dollar deal with CBS for Judy's own TV series, a weekly one-hour musical variety show to be called *The Judy Garland Show*. Thirteen shows it would turn out, at $150,000 each, on prime time—9 P.M., Eastern Standard Time, Sunday night—opposite *Bonanza*, NBC's most popular show, with an option for an additional thirteen if CBS and Judy agreed. If successful, Judy would be a rich woman for the rest of her life and she and her children would never have to worry again.

Aside from the problem whether Judy was up to doing such a series, with endless rehearsals and unalterable deadlines, there was the problem now of her domestic life. Hard enough to keep Judy on an even keel when all went well; if the fight with Luft continued, and the custody battle, too, only catastrophe could result.

How much of this, and of other troubles which not even Sid knew, was behind Judy's telephone call to him can only be conjectured. Sid flew down to meet her, somewhat suspicious, the next day; he became even more so when he found her waiting at the New Orleans airport with a bucket of iced champagne, and two bags of confetti to throw on him as they hugged each other; confused again when he discovered she had registered them in rooms on separate floors at the Prince Conti Hotel; reassured when, as they danced closely together at a nightclub, she whispered in his ear, "This is it, Baby! This is it!"; then completely bewildered when she said, "Darling, you go to your room and I'll see you in the morning. Good night." He said, "Good night, Mrs. This-is-it," and went to his room. Yet they did travel about New Orleans for two days, see the sights, try to come to some sort of an understanding, until both agreed that there was "something missing." "Perhaps we're both too scarred up," said Sid. Judy said, "I'm tired, Sid, I'm going to bed." The next morning when Sid woke very early, there was an envelope under his door. The note inside read:

Dearest Sid:
    No matter what way or manner you handle what's ahead for us in our divorce—your children need, love and want you. You're their father and always will be! Our marriage failed—but I'll be your friend forever.
    With deep sincerity,
                                                                    —From J.

It was only 6 A.M. A call to her room disclosed she had checked out. Two weeks later they met in New York again, with lawyers prepared to take their divorce depositions. Unexpectedly Judy refused to give hers. Instead, she suggested that Lorna and Joe be flown in from Nevada, where they were going to school, join her and Sid, and the family take a two-week vacation in the Cat Cays, in the Bahamas, and try another reconciliation. This one succeeded. Everyone ultimately flew to Los Angeles; by late spring the Lufts had signed an official document of reconciliation, dismissed all pending suits, and Judy, as president of her corporation, Kingsrow Enterprises, which would produce the TV series, had bought a house in Rockingham Drive in Brentwood.

And the deal, the long-awaited, all-important CBS deal for the Judy Garland weekly TV show, went through.

The events leading up to it would almost make one think the fates were conspiring against Judy. As CMA was about to sign with CBS on Judy's behalf, Begelman had come to her with appalling news. Unknown persons, he told her, had obtained a dreadful photograph taken of her while she lay unconscious, nude from the waist up, on a hospital table in England, having her stomach pumped out after an overdose. These persons wanted £20,000—$56,000—or they would sell the photograph to a London newspaper. Judy *had* been in hospitals more than once in England; she *had* had her stomach pumped out; such a photograph *could* have been taken. She told Begelman in panic to get the picture and negative and pay whatever was asked. Begelman told her later he had met the blackmailers, who had flown over from England, in his apartment in New York, while Judy waited in his office at 410 Park Avenue, paid them with a check for $50,000 on money transferred from her account in England, and returned to her with negative and prints. She looked at them in horror and burned them. There was nothing else to be done. The $50,000 was as nothing compared to what she stood to lose once such a scandal broke, for CBS would have immediately dropped their entire deal with her. This awful secret of the picture and the payment she kept to herself for a long time, but it was one more emotional burden placed upon her.

That spring had been arduous. Judy had flown to London for the world premiere of *I Could Go On Singing*, she had flown home especially for Liza's seventeenth birthday party on March 12—a complete surprise—then to the Bahamas, then again to New York for Liza's opening, April 2, in *Best Foot Forward,* an off-Broadway show. Liza had reserved a seat for her mother, who she knew was in New York, but all through the play that empty seat stared at her. Her mother hadn't come to her opening! At the intermission, backstage, others heard Liza on the telephone to Judy at the Plaza, saying tearfully, "But, Mama, how could you make such a mistake? I told you it was tonight, not tomorrow night." Only later did Liza realize that Judy had deliberately absented herself from the opening, lest her presence detract from her daughter's night. But the following evening she was there.

Now, in June 1963, Judy began production on her TV series, the first show to be taped June 24, with Mickey Rooney as guest star, for network showing in September. The series was tantamount to producing a one-hour motion picture in color every seven days. The CBS staff was first-rate; George Schlatter was producer; there were skilled writers and costumers; Mort Lindsey was her conductor; Mel Tormé, the singer, was writing special musical material; and CBS had even built a replica of the little yellow brick road in *The Wizard of Oz,* which led to her dressing room trailer, decorated in the style of her new Brentwood home. Judy, fortified by liebfraumilch, showed up every day. Sid, meanwhile, was living in the Rockingham house, going to his own office, where he was involved in the Nick du Pont spruce wood deal and various other projects.

Judy was at both her best and her worst during the months of the TV series. Once she held it up for a week: she "just didn't feel like doing it." This was not willfulness. There had been an angry dispute with Sid. In July after two months in the Rockingham house he simply walked out and went to Newport for a ten-day period to cool off. Judy promptly had all his clothes and possessions put in storage and sent him a wire to that effect. Now they were separated again.

Judy, without Sid, was lonesome for Liza, who was happily beginning her fourth month in *Best Foot Forward* in New York, and going steady with Tracy Everitt, a young dancer. Judy telephoned her. "I miss you," she said. "Come back here, darling." "Oh, no, Mama," said Liza. "I really can't."

Judy managed things her own way. She telephoned Tracy Everitt. She needed another male dancer on her TV show. Would he take the

512

job and come out at once? It was an opportunity he could not turn down. He went to California; and Liza, who, like her mother, when in love was all in love, quit *Best Foot Forward* and returned to California to live in the Rockingham house.

It was now, in July 1963, that Liza grew to know her mother. If Judy had made her her "pal" in London when she was fourteen, now at seventeen she found herself becoming her mother's best friend and confidante. They talked and talked. Had Mama really had a romance with Tyrone Power? And what about Mickey Rooney, in those early musicals? Oh, said Judy, she and Mickey were only the best of friends, like brother and sister, but they loved and helped each other. And what about Fred Astaire in *Easter Parade?* Oh, said Judy, he was a wonderful, wonderful gentleman. Liza sat at her mother's feet and listened, entranced. How festive, how enchanting, she made everything seem. She could describe a scene, a city, an emotion, so you could almost taste it. More and more Liza began to understand this bewildering, prismlike personality, and, with growing respect, to learn that however bizarre her behavior might appear, there was always a reason; to understand that under the extremes of "Oh, God, everything's falling apart!" and "Isn't it just marvelous!"—under the laughter, the tears, the spontaneity, the mischievous irony, the inflating of fears and delights, the acting, the need to make life high, exciting, dangerous but always thrilling adventure—"God, Mama was so *alive!*" Liza was to say later—there was a hard core of logic: *Let's get this show on the road.* Time and again, talking to her three children, keeping in mind her own convoluted life and the endless public psychoanalyses printed about her, Judy would say, "You are all happy, healthy kids in spite of me," or, "You are all happy, healthy kids because of me." It depended upon how Judy was feeling about herself.

In those endless talks with her daughter (when she was not at CBS), Judy taught Liza something of her own craft. She gave her insights which became invaluable in Liza's own career.

She told her that in singing, "Just because you're holding a note, don't think that the emotion of the word is over." She illustrated, there, in the den of the Rockingham house. She began to sing, quietly, beautifully, "A very quiet thing . . ." She said, "You keep the thought going, as if the sound is in slow motion, and you're trying to get it over to that chair, and it'll only get there if you hang on to it and keep it going." You watched the note, almost as though it were a physical, seeable object, you watched it moving to its destination and continued the emotion even after it struck; you might have finished the word, but the emotion was still in you, and the audience would feel it, too. "You never lose the thought behind the word: *you are not just singing a note.*" In a song, she said, you must play different people as you sang it. *Singing was acting, too. A song was a scene in a play.*

Once Liza brought home a script she was to try out, and Judy gave her an unforgettable acting lesson. It was a hospital script, and Liza's part was simple. She had to read a scene dealing with a girl who had had an abortion. The dialogue was:

DOCTOR: How do you feel about this?
GIRL: Fine.
DOCTOR: Are you sorry?
GIRL: No.
DOCTOR: It had to be done, but you can have other children.
GIRL: I know. Thank you, doctor.

Liza said to Judy, "It does seem simple, doesn't it, Mama, but I want to make it unsimple, because it really *isn't* that simple. Will you help me?" Judy said, "Sure."

They were sitting on the floor of Judy's enormous bathroom, which was always her refuge, and Judy said, "O.K., I'll read the doctor's part, but I'll also read what's going on in your head and then you insert the lines." She shut the door, sat with one leg bent in front of her—to sit cross-legged put a strain on her back—stuck her glasses on the end of her nose and studied the script, biting the inside of her cheek as she thought. She spoke the doctor's line: "How do you feel about this?" Then she looked at Liza and told her what should actually be going on in her mind: *How do you think I feel about it? I feel empty. I feel drained. I feel terrible. I wish I were dead.* Then again, the actual line of the script: "How do you feel about this?" And Liza replied, "Fine," as the script read, thinking the thoughts Judy had given her.

In this fashion her mother went through the script and made it full of meaning. When the doctor asked, "Are you sorry?" and Liza had to reply, simply, "No," actually in her mind she should be thinking: *How would you know? . . . How would you know how much I wanted this, how much I would have liked to, how embarrassed I feel, how degraded I feel!* Then Liza said, "No," but behind the "No" was all the yearning, the embarrassment, the degradation.

Judy added, "I think the emotional break should come when he says the words 'but you can have other children.' I think your thought pattern at this point should be: *I don't want other children, I wanted this child.*"

Judy, the professional, was thorough. She studied the part again. "Do they know who the father is?" "No," said Liza. "They don't make it too clear." Then you must have it absolutely clear in your mind, said Judy. What does he look like? How old is he? What is he doing at this point in his life? What sort of flowers did he send you? Question after question, until Liza had a clear image of this man whom she loved, but who obviously didn't love her . . . a marvelous lesson from this mother of hers, so much of whose world seemed illogical yet who could seize an hour to be the very paragon of logic.

It had not been easy for Liza to get her mother's permission to go on the stage. Hyannis Port and Scarsdale were all very well, but a professional career? It had all begun in the late summer of 1962 when Judy would call Liza, whom she had sent to the Sorbonne after her return from Israel. Judy was constantly calling her to come home, and one day Liza said, all right, and she walked out of the Sorbonne and flew to New York, en route to the Coast. In New York she confronted her father, there for a meeting. He was staying at the St. Regis, in a beautiful, all-gray suite, having breakfast, as always with style: silver tray, silver coffee pot, a discreet servitor—it might have been a scene from one of his own lovely films. Liza sat down opposite him. "Daddy, I want to come back here to New York and go on the stage."

Minnelli said, "Yes, I think it's about time. You have so much energy you might as well start using it."

Liza said, "But I've got to tell Mama."

Her father said, "Well, I'm all for it, if that helps. Just tell her as you told me."

When Liza reached the Coast, she chose to tell her mother as Judy was sitting in front of her makeup table. Liza had prepared an eloquent sales pitch: "I think it's really time, Daddy is all for it, I really want to study, I want to be very good"—and Judy interrupted with a simple "I think it's wonderful." Liza nearly fainted from shock. Judy added, "But if you do it, you're going to do it on your own. Not one penny from me."

Liza said, "That's what I want to do."

Fine, said Judy. Did Liza know who she wanted to study with? As Judy talked, she picked up a pack of cigarettes from her dressing table and extended it to Liza. "Do you want one?" She had never before offered her daughter a cigarette.

Liza, backing away, said, "Oh, no—"

Her mother said, "It's O.K. You can smoke."

Liza took a cigarette and her mother lit it for her. They sat, two women, smoking.

Judy's TV show was in trouble. CBS had made a survey after the first few shows were taped: some executives thought Judy wasn't herself, that she was nervous, that she was touching everyone too much, that an obviously unhappy woman was trying to entertain them. Most of the top production staff were fired, and a new production team hired. Judy came home, obviously worried. She sat down in the kitchen, where Liza was making herself a snack, elbows on the table, chin in her hands, pondering, while her daughter, knowing when to keep silent, continued spreading strawberry jam on a piece of toast. Judy mused aloud. "It just doesn't make sense. . . ." And then, suddenly: "Jesus! It's just like the government." She jumped up, excited. "That's it, I'll just call the President."

And while Liza watched incredulously, her mother telephoned the White House. She said, "This is Judy Garland." Those words could open any door. "May I speak with the President, please?" Then, after a short wait, she was chattering away. Liza caught only snatches from her mother's end. "How are you, Mr. President," and then, after a few words, "But I'm really going nuts," then a peal of laughter; apparently Kennedy had said something like "Me, too," and asked, "What's wrong, Judy?" Her mother: "The studio politics are just driving me crazy. I don't know how to handle them. People are being fired right and left, new faces appear on the set, I don't know who they are—"

More conversation, and suddenly her mother's voice changing, and Judy saying, in a tone of disbelief: "Oh, no, you don't really. . . . You do? Really?" A pause, then: "All right," and then, with Liza watching and listening and not believing her ears, her mother sang into the telephone the last eight bars of "Over the Rainbow."

When Judy hung up, she began to cry, and Liza with her. The President of the United States!

For some time afterward this became an almost weekly ceremony for Judy and Liza. Judy managed regularly to telephone the White House, sooner or later reaching Kennedy, and despite the pressures of her TV series, her altercations with Luft on the telephone, her own personal problems, when she spoke to Kennedy, there would be the quick, delightful, lighthearted, bantering exchanges, laughter and warmth and affection, the conversation always ending with Kennedy asking her to sing the last eight bars of "Over the Rainbow" and Judy, perched on a white kitchen stool, singing into the phone for her audience of two, the President and her teen-age daughter, after which she would slowly hang up, look unbelievingly at Liza, and then mother and daughter would dissolve in tears.

It was an emotional time for Judy. After Sid had left in July, husband and wife had long, before-dawn calls. In one long conversation the night of August 29, 1963, one sees their individual torment: married eleven years and their marriage over in all but name, forever joined by their two children, yet finding it impossible either to live together as husband and wife or to live apart. It was a sad conversation, so much in contrast to the bitter, punishing dialogue when he telephoned her in her hospital room in Carson City the autumn before, Judy's voice regretful, full of heartbreaking nuances, fearful, too, that this man might in some way explode, even as he fought against it, and yet revealing—though Sid would not accept it —an unmistakable, melancholy finality.

The conversation came a few days after she had been reported in the Cedars of Lebanon Hospital, as the press put it, for her "annual checkup," though Sid suspected it was pills again. Sid was in financial straits, there had been further staff changes in her show, and their talk ranged over many subjects. He said, if one of his deals went through, "I might be getting some money in a couple of weeks—"

Judy: "Oh, I hope so, honey."

Sid: "I've had such damn bad luck. . . ."

Judy: "Don't blame it on yourself. I have had damn bad luck and I've blamed it on myself. . . . You'll be all right, Sid. You really will. You're a good man. You are."

Sid: "Thank you. I think I am, too. Oddly enough."

Judy: "I don't wish anything bad for you, and I don't think you want anything bad for me."

Sid: "Of course I couldn't. How could I?"

Judy: "You couldn't. . . . This is a nice conversation."

Then they talked about how lucky they were in their children, and Sid, when she said, "Oh, I get mad and I get scared," said emphatically: "Remember what I'm saying now, darling. I said it to you time and again, and I'm going to say it to you now: *Don't be afraid.*"

Judy: "Of you?"

Sid: "Yes. Please don't! *Don't be afraid of me!*"

Judy: "All right, darling. I guess you're right."

Sid: "Call me. I'm with *you.* Remember that."

Judy: "Do you mean that? . . . Even if I can't be in love with you any more? Even if I can't be with you?"

Sid: "I know why you're not."

Judy: "You know what it is? You want to hear it?"

Sid: "Yes."

Judy: "I—I—am . . . Ruth Reject. . . . And I did love you, so much. That's about all there is. It's as simple as that."

Sid: "What do you mean, you're Ruth Reject? I don't understand."

Judy: "You know," (she gave a small laugh) "I'm so ready to be rejected, always have been. I wanted your love, but I felt that you rejected me, and I don't know whether you did or not. Maybe I was wrong. Maybe you didn't."

Sid: "Darling, I never did want to reject you. I was replaced, unfortunately, in such a manner—" She looked in the wrong places for love, he went on, "and you get a hand to hold yours, and maybe some dialogue, but that's not love. There's no substitute for what we had, and there never will be; you're confused about so many things, darling, you're lonely, and so am I.

"That's one contributing reason why you don't sleep," he said. "I understand it. You think you want a divorce—maybe you do. I don't know how positive anyone can make up their minds about that. That also adds to somebody's confusion."

Judy's voice had been soft, caressing, agreeable. Now it changed. "No," she said. "I still want a divorce, Sid. I still need a divorce. I need your respect."

Sid: "I understand that."

Judy: "I need it so badly, so deeply, because I need it, because . . . I must breathe. . . . But I still think you're a hell of a wonderful son of a bitch."

Sid: "Thank you. Well—"

Judy: "And any time I can help, Baby, any time . . . call me up. To hell with the lawyers."

Sid: "I appreciate it."

Judy: "Oh, darling! You don't have to say that. We have two children we love and respect. We have a wonderful, wonderful relationship, I think. Don't turn on me. There's no reason to—"

Sid: "I'm not turning on you."

Judy: "I'll never turn on you. Unless we turn on each other. And then we'll go over that, too. But always call me—for money, for moral support if you're lonely, because I'm going through the same thing you are."

Thus they spoke to each other, that late August, and finally the subject came up: the picture taken of Judy. Sid said that no one had taken a photograph of her in that condition, the whole thing was a hoax; if any photograph existed, it was a fake.

Judy: "Darling, I saw the picture and I got the negative and the whole thing."

Sid: "No newspaper in the world would dare to print it."

Judy: "Yes they would." Didn't the British always love her, she asked, and yet they loved to say how fat she was, too. Of course they'd use the picture.

Sid talked to her about it. When did she see the picture? About four days before she was going to sign the contract with CBS.

Judy: "I saw the picture, and it wasn't very pretty."

Sid: "What was the picture, darling?"

Judy: "I didn't have any clothes on. My bosom was out, and there was a stomach pump down my throat—I was having my stomach pumped out . . . on a table. I was nude and unconscious."

She did not know when it had happened, but something had come up at her house in London which made her mad, "and I took maybe three, maybe four extra pills, and then I got very Bernhardt about it, and there wasn't anyone there from the agency to protect me, and Al Paul called the police. They took me in an ambulance. I was sound asleep, but" (embarrassed laugh) "I wasn't that . . . drugged. They took me in an emergency ward, took my clothes and . . . do what they do. And there was a nurse there and she went into the other room and couldn't resist getting a picture. Then she sold that picture to gangsters, blackmailers, whatever. She was a bitch . . . and that was it. It was so ugly. I looked so ugly—and it was worth it to me."

Sid: "Blackmail, Baby."

Judy: "I know it. It put me through agony to have to pay, but it would have been worse agony for it to be shown."

Then the conversation veered to Sid's charge that he had been "substituted out"—something he could not take. "You don't know what I went through."

Judy: "You don't know what *I* went through."

Sid: "If you want to leave me and divorce me, I'm going to give you a divorce and a decent one, but if you don't appreciate my love for my children and for you, you've got to get yourself somebody else."

Then each asked the other to search their souls, that they would talk again, but no more now, Judy said, because she was too tired, she was going to bed and turn off her phone, she would talk to him tomorrow. It ended with:

Sid: "All right, darling."

Judy: "All right, honey."

Sid: "Good night."

Judy: "God bless—"

Sid: "You, too."

Judy: "Good-bye."

Sid: "Good-bye."

The next night Judy charged that Sid had climbed the fence surrounding her house, terrorized the help and children, taken several possessions; she asked for a court restraining order denying him the right to visit the house. She placed it under a twenty-four-hour guard. They were furiously embattled again.

There was still one more dramatic confrontation—and it was the last between Sid Luft and Judy Garland as husband and wife. It came a week later. On September 6, the court gave Judy custody of the children and gave Sid visitation rights.

In accordance with these, the following night he went to the Rockingham house, dined with Lorna and Joey, and was about to leave around eight o'clock when Judy suddenly appeared in the living room. Would he like a drink? Sid, surprised, said yes. "A Scotch, please." She made him one, and made herself a vodka martini—an unusual drink for her, because she was a sipper and liked long drinks. Obviously, she had something on her mind.

It was a curious discussion. First she complimented him. He was a good producer. She'd like him back on her team. At one point she said, "I know you're in financial bad shape while I'm making a lot of money."

"I'm busted," said Sid, "but I'll get by."

"I owe you a great deal, I really do," she said, "and I want to help you. You helped me when I needed help." She sat down and wrote him a check for $10,000. "That ought to help for a while and get some debts off your back."

"I can certainly use it and I appreciate it," he said, and stuck it in his pocket.

She went around the bar and got another drink—not a long one, but a quick martini tossed down almost in one gulp. She turned to him suddenly: "I'm so fucking mad at you—to think that we could be so good, so right together, but you're insisting on digging up all our past financial troubles. I want to forget it, darling."

Sid felt alarms going off somewhere within him. "Judy, I don't think I can get to you. I'm confused about us. We get along momentarily, and then we don't. You never want to hear about your tax problems. You have them, Judy, and I'm going to level with you. Things that happened in the past will catch up with both you and me when the government does an audit."

Judy: "Sid, I don't want to hear what's going to catch up with me."

Sid: "What I'm trying to tell you is—and you won't accept this— but in the very near future I have either to join you or disown you as a husband, as far as our taxes are concerned."

Judy: "But, Sid, why didn't you take care of those things then?"

He tried to explain the complexity of the returns. Judy snapped, "You just do the goddamn income tax. Do it, and I don't want to hear about it. I'll do my shows, and don't interfere. Don't bother me or else I'll be so upset I'll blow the whole thing."

They began shouting at each other, they both drank more, he could not remember what precisely she said that set him off, but he demanded, "Is this the way you really feel now?"

She retorted, "Yes, that's it!"

He cried, "Oh, fuck, Judy," reached into his pocket and said, "Here, take your check. I cannot accept it this way. I could if we were on a friendly basis, but there's too much hostility between you and me and I don't need your money. You just aren't going to make it, these programs aren't right for you." He tore up the check and strode out the door.

He got into his car, but when he reached the electric gate which he had opened by pressing a button on a post halfway there, he found it closed. He returned to the house. "Judy, let me go home. I'm tired." She had obviously pressed another button in the house; she could see his car and the gate from the kitchen window. He said, "This is too goddamn serious now. I can't live this way, in this house or out of it. . . . This is a walkout, Judy, as far as I'm concerned. I'm going to walk out of this house and I'm going to walk out of your life."

He went back to his car, drove to the gate, on the way pressing the button to open it—and again it shut before he reached it. He went back again. "Judy," he said, "I'm exhausted. Open the gate." She was smiling, a kind of naughty child's smile, as though she were thinking, *Come back, you son of a bitch, don't leave me now.*

Sid: "Judy, I've got to get out of here. Now, for Christ's sake, let me out!"

This time the gate was open when he reached it. He went to the hotel in which he was staying. At 4 A.M. his phone rang. It was Judy, sounding hysterical. "There's prowlers about, come back here, you son of a bitch, and guard your family!"

"Call the police, Judy," he told her, "there are no prowlers, just keep those gates closed," and hung up. The phone rang again, and each time it was Judy, "You son of a bitch, you're no husband, you don't love me, you don't love your children—"

Finally he told the switchboard to cut off his calls.

When he awoke the next morning, he was deeply depressed.

He had a revolver on his dresser. Still in his pajamas, he picked it up, flipped open the barrel, saw that it was loaded, aimed it at the mattress of his bed and pulled the trigger. It was a small room and it sounded like a cannon had gone off. He expected any moment someone to pound on his door. Nothing happened. He thought, *You could murder someone in this hotel and they wouldn't even know it.* Firing the revolver made him feel a little better, but it solved nothing.

522

It was true. He had walked out of her life—as a husband. He knew it. And Judy, he knew, knew it too.

The next day he flew to New York, to throw himself into his sound work. He was not to see Judy for many months—and no longer in a husband-and-wife relationship.

There was a vacuum now, and it was filled quickly enough. Judy and Glenn Ford rediscovered each other. In the autumn she began going out with him. Glenn had been in and out of her life since she was twelve, and a Gumm Sister. He, eighteen at the time, was assistant stage manager at the Wilshire Theatre in Santa Monica, where the girls appeared. He had helped her backstage, and had been her slave from then on.

Now, having found each other again, night after night they spent evenings at his home, around the corner from the Beverly Hills Hotel, holding hands like two teen-age lovers. And sometimes she was a teen-ager. She came upon a lettering machine that stamped letters on tape, and went mad over it. Like a little girl she constantly stamped out tapes reading "JUDY AND GLENN," "GLENN AND JUDY," and pasted them on her fireplace, his fireplace, on gifts she sent him, on the hood of his car, her car. For hours they would sit in front of his stereo, listening to records; they felt they were having the most marvelous conversations without words. She was a romantic, he was a romantic, he was convinced they spiritually touched each other. She made him buy a grand piano for his huge living room. "What do I need a grand piano for?" he asked. Judy said, "You need it, you just need it—the *room* needs it—" and Glenn bought a grand piano.

Often she called him up at ungodly hours. Everyone knew this about Judy, of course—telephoning friends at 3 and 4 A.M. to talk or ask them over to keep her company because she could not be alone. But Judy knew when she called Glenn that he was busy on a film. She said, "I know how late it is, I know you have a 6 A.M. call, darling, but please—please just talk to me." He talked to her, gently and lovingly and reassuringly, for nearly half an hour, until she fell asleep.

Next morning, on his set, there was a bouquet of two dozen red roses, with a note in her handwriting: "Thank you, Glenn. You are a gentle man." Above his fireplace he hung, to remain always, a photograph she had sent him of herself, with her inscription, "Glenn, dear one, Now I can look upward and see the beauty of the sun and moon, and the love you give to me. You have my heart and I adore you."

Now Glenn's physician became Judy's physician. This was Dr. Lee Siegel, who had many film stars as patients. Glenn telephoned him one night: "Lee, Judy's here, she wants to talk to you." A happy Judy got on the phone. She had met Dr. Siegel often at parties and several times he had attended her. She said, "Lee, I like you and want you to become my doctor." That night Dr. Siegel drove over to Glenn's house and the three had a drink together. Judy obviously "was firing" her current doctor, presumably because he balked at 2 A.M. house calls. Dr. Siegel accepted Judy as a patient because he thought he had a different approach to her need for medication. A new drug—Valium—was just being introduced. He found it useful in converting patients addicted to barbiturates. It was an antispasmodic and tranquilizer; it was used on wild animals, even lions, the medicine being shot into them from a distance.

But in Judy he faced a particular problem. She had faith only in the red bullets—Seconal. Dr. Siegel went so far as to ask a druggist to grind up the Valium pills and fill the red Seconal capsules with them. Soon he had Judy off all barbiturates, which had always had a depressing effect on her, and on Valium. Judy, thinking they were Seconal, took them, and they worked. Dr. Siegel was overjoyed. It was a tremendous achievement.

Then he was defeated by an exasperating technicality. Seconal was made by Eli Lilly & Company. The druggist notified him that he was no longer willing to take Valium—a product of Hoffmann La Roche, Inc., a competitor—and place it in Lilly capsules.

"Look," said Dr. Siegel, "I'll assume any medical responsibility—"

The druggist said, "You won't assume anything, nor will we. The drug companies won't permit it. You can't play that game."

Dr. Siegel said, "I'm playing with saving somebody's life, that's what I'm playing with." But the druggist refused.

Defeated, Dr. Siegel had to return to Judy's earlier regime, minimal doses of barbiturates, plus uppers—and no one knew how many of these she was taking to fend off the barbiturate depression. It was a shame, because Valium was so much less harmful. Dr. Siegel also realized that Judy, little by little, had returned to her favorite drink, vodka (this time with orange juice), and that the combination of liquor and barbiturates was dangerous. Both were depressants; both were synergistic—that is, each reinforced the other's effect, making each more than twice as strong. The patient drinks, forgets he took pills, takes more pills—the result is an overdose, if large enough, fatal. He was sure that Marilyn Monroe's death the year before had been the result of this synergistic effect of barbiturates and wine, which was Marilyn's favorite drink.

Now, frequently, as the shows were taped, Glenn and Dr. Siegel and his wife, Noreen, sat together in the studio audience. Sometimes a throat specialist would treat Judy with a cortisone derivative for her vocal chords. Now, instead of Judy's pounding on some other doctor's door at 3 A.M.—"I'm in pain, help me!"—forcing him to come out in his pajamas and robe to give her medication, and even sometimes put her to bed in a guest bedroom, Dr. Siegel became the recipient of this attention.

One solace he had. He doubted strongly that Judy would ever deliberately kill herself with a fatal overdose. For one thing, her tolerance had reached unbelievable limits. For another, she once confessed to Noreen that one of her greatest fears was of dying. It was quite possible that some of her insomnia was based on a fear that death might sneak up on her in her sleep, when she would be helpless to fight back. One of the first, important and comforting facts Liza learned about her mother was that Judy's overdoses were never really suicide attempts; they were desperate calls for help, for attention, for someone to take care of Baby Gumm. They were not really attempts to die: she never took poison; she never used a gun on herself; she never threw herself in front of an automobile. Her apparently self-destructive acts always had something awry about them, calculated to frustrate their success: dashing for the *top* of the window, as in Philadelphia, taking too many pills only when someone was around to find her, or a telephone call to a hotel desk clerk announcing she was going out the window—giving him time to send someone up to grab her at the dramatic moment.

At one point Liza actually told this, in substance, to her mother. People were no longer rushing to the Rockingham house when she threatened to put an end to it all, when she took an overdose. Judy knew exactly how much she could take. "Mama, you'll simply have to think of something else," Liza, the pragmatist, said. "It's just getting boring. Nobody comes. I call up and they ask, 'What's the matter?' and then, 'Oh, not that again.'"

Judy said, "You're kidding."

"No—you've got to think of something better." So the two tried to cook up something nutty yet effective. One night, when Judy had tried to get both Fields and Begelman to the house, and each had promised but had not shown up, Judy was both angry and guilty. Why hadn't they come? Was it the fact, which she didn't want to face, that she might be giving them trouble? But she was under tremendous stress because of her TV show, and her troubles with Sid over the children. They *should* have come over.

The scheme Liza and Judy cooked up was simple. First Liza drove Judy's car several blocks away, where it was not likely to be found. Then she telephoned Freddie: "Mama's disappeared!" "Oh, that's great!" said Fields. "Are you sure?" He was difficult to convince, but Liza was an excellent actress. The same word went to Begelman, and within the hour both men, after cruising about looking for Judy, were at the house, really upset.

Judy had gone to the car, where she waited for Liza's signal—a light turned on. Meanwhile, Liza was putting on an act: What might have happened to Mama? She was worried, she had so many pressures! . . . When a sufficient time had elapsed, she went into a back room and switched on the light, and returned to the others. Fields and Begelman had been on the telephone to everyone, and were worried. Presently the front door opened and in walked Judy.

"Where were you? What happened? Why didn't you call?" they started in on her. "What are you all getting so upset about?" she demanded. "Ludicrous! No privacy at all!" and walked into her bedroom and slammed the door.

The two men left. But Judy had satisfied herself. She had proved that they still cared for her.

Then came the awful Friday in November—November 22, 1963 —and the unbelievable news from Dallas. Judy had heard the bulletin on the radio, just before ten o'clock. That evening was to be Lorna's eleventh birthday party. Though the birthday actually fell the day before, on the twenty-first, Judy chose Friday night because there was no school next day and she wanted to invite many of Lorna's friends. On this terrible morning Lorna and Joey were at school. Only Liza was in the house, in her room. She heard the door swing open.

A white-faced, shocked Judy stood there. She could hardly get the words out. "They—they've assassinated . . ." Liza stared at her. Kennedy had been shot in Dallas, he was seriously wounded. . . . Judy's voice moved from uncertainty to a fierce anger. It seemed to Liza her mother was suddenly determined that she could, she *would*, do something about it. "I'm going over to Pat's," she said, got hurriedly into a pair of slacks and left. Pat Lawford was at the Lawford beach house in Malibu.

An hour later Judy was back. She and Liza sat in Liza's room watching the TV screen, staring helplessly at it when Chet Huntley appeared, looking as though he were about to break into tears, to announce that the President was dead.

At his words Judy rose and disappeared into her room. A moment later Liza, trying to control her own tears, tiptoed to her mother's door. She listened. A chill came over her. Her mother was praying.

Liza, shaking, returned and stared at the unfolding tragic story on TV. She became aware that her mother, in her robe, had come into the room, sunk into a chair and was silently watching, too.

Liza stole a nervous glance at her. Judy was staring at her now, not at the screen. "What are we going to do?" she asked, in a trembling voice. Then, a pitch higher: "What are we going to do? What are all of us going to do now?" She repeated the words, now biting them off in desperation. "What-are-we-going-to-do, what-are-all-of-us-going-to-do?" Her face was growing more pale, then more flushed, her eyes were becoming feverish, and Liza braced herself for whatever would happen.

Then Judy broke. She fell to the floor and began to scream piercingly, "Oh, God! God!" and, like a child in a tantrum, lay there kicking her feet and screaming, a child suffering punishment unjust beyond endurance. Liza ran to her, threw herself to the floor, grabbing her by the shoulders and shaking her. "Stop it, Mama, please stop it!" But Judy would not, and Liza wrestled with her as she flung herself about, tried to throw herself against the wall, Liza pleading, "Mama, don't, don't, please don't, you'll hurt yourself, he wouldn't want you to hurt yourself!"

She had never seen her like this before, and she had witnessed her mother suffer such agony from migraine that she had ripped a bed sheet apart as though it were paper. Finally Judy lay there crying, Liza hugging her close as though Judy were her child, not her mother, and trying to comfort her. In a voice drained of emotion, Judy managed to say, "It's like—it's like hopelessness without hope." Liza said, not knowing what to say, "I know, Mama, I know . . ."

Then even the tears stopped, and Liza helped her mother up and to her room, where she tucked her into bed and sat by her until Judy fell into a heavy sleep.

Lorna had heard about the shooting in school. The maid came and they ran home together, Lorna terrified not only at the news but at what it might do to her mother. When they had lived in the Carol Reed house in London in 1960, and they all sat about the TV watching the election returns from the States that November (she having just returned from her appendix operation) and Kennedy had won, she couldn't dance about with the others because her incision hurt. It must have been eleven o'clock when the telephone rang—an overseas call for her mother. Mama had answered it, suddenly turned bright red, and began jumping up and down. "Please don't do that, Mama," Lorna had said. "It makes me laugh and it hurts." But Judy was saying, "The President called me—the President's called me." He had telephoned her immediately after his election—why, she must have been one of the first persons he called!

It was Glenn Ford who helped comfort her in the days that followed—she had Thanksgiving dinner with him—but their relationship was over by Christmas. A new man had appeared.

37

WHEN PRESIDENT KENNEDY WAS ASSASSINATED, the shock was shattering to a young American actor named Mark Herron, then living in Rome after spending several years abroad following his graduation from the City College of Los Angeles. Herron had played a small part in Fellini's masterful film *8½;* he was thirty-one, tall, slim, blue-eyed, with a deep love of the drama and a quick sense of humor. Kennedy's death appalled him; he seemed to have nothing to cling to away from the United States, and within a week he was back home in California.

Early in December 1963, Ray Aghayan, the designer, who was costuming Judy's TV show, and had been a classmate of Herron's, invited him to a party. "There'll be someone there you ought to know," said Ray.

It was Judy Garland. When they were introduced, Herron said, "We've met before." He had been a fan as far back as he could recall. Once he had seen her at Pacific Ocean Park in Santa Monica. Judy had bought every bizarre disguise at the booths. She wore huge buckteeth over her own, an arrow seemed to have pierced her head from ear to ear, and she had in tow Lorna and Joey. She thought she had disguised herself, but everyone knew it was Judy Garland, and she had been followed by a whispering, admiring group of fans. Later he'd been dining with Margaret Whiting, the singer, with whom he'd appeared in *Bell, Book and Candle* on the West Coast. Judy walked in. Everyone oohed, Margaret introduced him to Judy, Mark rose, bowed, and, when he sat down again, he missed his chair, and slipped right under the table. Judy asked, with a straight face: "What happened to him? He was here a minute ago."

Ray had obviously told Judy about Mark, because when she came to Ray's party and they shook hands, she said to Ray, "You told me he was going to fall down, that he'd faint. Why, he doesn't even have two heads!"

They all went out later for a midnight supper, she and Mark separated from the others, they had so much to talk about, and they ended that night in Judy's house, talking until the rising sun showed through the windows. She was fascinated by his kicking around the world, his sensitivity—that Kennedy's death, which had so affected her, could have made him come home—he was handsome; he spoke gently and poetically, he had a kind of fawnlike face with enormous soft blue eyes, a face which reminded her of the young Keats. . . .

She confided in him. She had wanted so badly to sing "The Battle Hymn of the Republic" on her show after Kennedy's death, because she felt the country wanted a return to old-style Americanism and religious fervor, but Jim Aubrey, that ——— (Herron was amused and impressed that, for all her delicacy, she could curse like a man), had refused. "We want to forget it," they told her. "The country's mourned Kennedy, it wants to go on to other things." She said,

"Forget it? Are you crazy?" And she added passionately, "Fuck it! I'm going to do the show I wanted to in the first place, and I'm going to do it in concert version."

She did; it was sensationally successful—one of the occasions when the producers, directors, staff, everyone who'd been having their difficulties with Judy, and the problems of the show's format, actually had tears in their eyes.

Judy invited Mark to the remainder of the tapings through the early months of 1964. Now where once Glenn Ford had sat, Mark Herron sat, beside Dr. Lee and Noreen. They, too, were taken with him. Mark had been with Judy, too, when she taped her Christmas show, with Liza, Lorna and Joe all taking part, while Judy, the proud mother, watched.

Those first months of 1964 were difficult and bewildering for Judy. She fought to keep her show going, but it was obviously doomed. She and Sid were in endless contention over custody. Ultimately, Sid won the right to pick up the children outside the gate of the house each Saturday at 10 A.M., and return them no later than 8:30 P.M., and to visit them inside the house for three hours on alternate Wednesdays, but he had to telephone an hour in advance. Lorna and Joe were seeing a psychiatrist recommended by Dr. Marc three times a week to help them cope with their parents' problems. They were to say later that Judy told them unbelievable things about their father, accusing him of poisoning their pet dog, for instance, in an attempt to have them testify against him when the ultimate custody hearing came.

Trying to trace Judy's movements now is comparable to following the zigzags of quicksilver on a hot stove. She made a sudden flight to New York to visit Liza, who was hospitalized with a kidney infection. Later she was to get into a tug of wills with her daughter: Liza wanted to appear in *Carnival* in winter stock in Mineola; Judy didn't want her to—"You're not well enough"—and when Liza insisted, Judy said, "Over my dead body," and when she still insisted, Judy telephoned the newspapers to announce that Liza had dropped out of the cast; Liza promptly telephoned them to say nothing of the sort had happened. She appeared in the play. (Months later, in the Rockingham house, standing behind the bar, Judy turned to her and said, "You know, that was the first time you defied me, and it infuriated me—but God, how I admired you for doing it!") While in New York

Judy, with Peter Lawford, had visited Jilly's, Sinatra's favorite New York bar. She had been so impressed by Bobby Cole, the pianist, that she hired him in a not too clearly defined musical capacity for $1,000 a week for her show. There were more staff changes, litigation against Judy by Mel Tormé and various other principals. Sometimes the show was fine, sometimes less than fine; there were arguments and jealousies behind the scene, yet at the same time high moments of pure entertainment; and as its ratings dropped, Judy, after pleading with Arthur Freed himself to produce it for her (he refused), announced that she was giving up the series with the taping of March 13 to "give more attention to my children."

But she could not disguise from herself or anyone else that the show had not been the success everyone had hoped for. Newspapers put it bluntly: "What caused Judy to fail?" Her best Nielsen rating was on her first show, September 29, with Donald O'Connor, though it was not the first one she had taped. The O'Connor show rated 18.7. Then the series dropped, to hover around 13! Meanwhile, Judy's competition, *Bonanza*, was reaching 40.

However much Judy's magic was on tap, she was often fidgety and nervous. The problem of format troubled everyone; for Judy to do each show concert style—which meant to sing one song after another —no matter how enormous her repertoire, week after week, was too much to expect; on the other hand, to play a professional host, like Jack Paar or Garry Moore, was also too much to expect. And above everything there were Judy's own troubles, which led her to be sick, to be late, to be a perfectionist, to be too high or too low, to find herself unendurable when she was not at her best, and often impossible to please. For a time everyone had to come to her house to rehearse; she refused to go to the studio. Yet there were happy periods, too: Lorna remembered parties on the set, laughter, gaiety —that happy Judy who seemed to pop out of the desperate Judy time and again.

Her final show was nearly a shambles. But it had good reviews. The trouble was Judy herself, singing (and heartbroken at it all), unable even to finish. It was a sad affair. Scheduled to begin at 6:30 P.M., with a faithful group of her fan club on hand, it began taping late, halted in the middle when Judy simply would not or could not appear— even her fans were ordered to leave—and the taping did not resume until after 2 A.M.

By now Herron had moved into the Rockingham house, and he and Judy were reading play scripts. They'd find one—preferably a two-character play—to do after Judy finished a concert tour in Australia in May, which Fields and Begelman had booked. The idea of Mark and Judy's acting together had come up unexpectedly.

One evening he came home to find Judy in bed, where she'd been for the last two days, brooding. She said, "I'm never going to get out of this bed." "O.K.," said Mark. That night she was still there. "Really, aren't you ever going to get up?" "Never" said Judy. "Why?" "There's no reason for it," she said. "Oh, c'mon," he said. "You mean to tell me there's nothing in your life that you haven't done and you'd like to do?"

There was a faint tinge of interest in her voice. "What do you mean by that?"

"Exactly what I said. You've really fulfilled your life? There's not one thing left you'd like to do?"

Judy sat up. "Yes. I would like to do a play with you." With that she got out of bed, sat down at her dressing table and began to put on makeup.

Was she serious? Mark wondered. Or was she saying this only to please him. He decided she meant it. "What would you like to do? he asked. She retorted, "Well, what do you do best?" He said, with a grin, "Good parts."

"All right," said Judy, "we'll find good parts." She asked Begelman to find a play for the two of them, and sent Lionel, the butler, to the bookshop to return with an armful of plays, and she and Mark sat on the love seat that came from the set of *Star* and began reading.

Mark suddenly held up *Sweet Bird of Youth,* by Tennessee Williams, which had been a Broadway hit a few years before with Geraldine Page and Paul Newman—a play in which an older, love-starved actress picks up a handsome young adventurer named Chance Wayne.

"This is really hysterical," Mark said. "Because that's what people are saying about us—the actress and the guy nobody knows whom she picked up. We couldn't do that!"

Judy grabbed it. "Oh, this would blow everybody's mind!" she said. If that was the picture the world had of her and Mark, it wasn't the picture they had of themselves. They read *The Glass Menagerie*— "You know," Judy said, "I always wanted to play Laurette Taylor's part, and she once told me I was the one to do it. Liza could play Laura, the daughter, and you Tom, the son." Mark bristled a little at that. "Oh, no, I couldn't play that part. But I'd like to direct it."

Judy kept reading. Then she got up and paced back and forth. Suddenly she said, "If I didn't have this fucking voice—" she clawed at her throat, making as if to tear out her voice box—"I could have been the world's greatest actress! I could have been a brilliant actress! Nobody gave me the chance!"

As for the Australian tour she was going on, she said, "I've paid my dues, damnit. I've done God knows how many concerts and ended up with no money. Now I've done my goddamn TV show, I've got a little money, I might as well go away." She turned to Mark.

"Will you come with me to Australia?"

He was stunned. Everything between them had happened so suddenly, and so perfectly, on every level—intellectually, spiritually, sexually, their very personalities seemed to merge—they were very much in love. Herron had never married. He had always been something of a loner, dedicated to drama and books, and Judy had always been surrounded by a formidable entourage—secretaries, hairdressers, assistants, managers, advisers. Finally he said, "Honey, if there's a chance of our going on from here, just you and me, why don't we try it, just us two, without any of these people?" He suggested they stop in Honolulu, on the way to Australia, and spend a week at Waikiki Beach—steal a week away from the world; no doctors, no nurses, no secretaries—a test for her and for himself.

On May 2 they flew to Waikiki, with about thirty pieces of luggage—Judy always carried unbelievable amounts of luggage, each piece numbered, with contents listed in a little book, so she knew what to take into her suite, and she demanded, even if it was only a one-night stand, that everything she took into the suite be unpacked and neatly placed in drawers, even if it all had to be removed the next day—and always with her photographs of her three children and one of Kennedy, inscribed, "Love to Judy." They also took the "typewriter"—this was a carrying case for Judy's vodka and Mark's Scotch, as well as a tape recorder and tapes of her TV shows she most enjoyed, especially the Christmas show with her children. She played and replayed Lorna's first solo, "Santa Claus Is Comin' to Town," and the Christmas carols she, Liza, Lorna and Joey had sung together.

Mark thought the trip excellent therapy for her. He had discussed it with Dr. Siegel. It would help Judy get over the traumatic TV series. She actually didn't look forward to appearing in Australia—two nights in Sydney, May 13 and 16, one in Melbourne, May 20—but she and Mark agreed that, rather than think of it as a working trip for Judy, they'd consider it a pleasure journey around the world.

It didn't quite turn out that way. At every stop everyone knew Judy and nobody knew him. The press didn't quite know how to describe him, beyond explaining that he was her "traveling companion." He found himself painted as a nurse, a homosexual, a dancer, a gigolo, an adventurer. Judy would laugh with him over it, sometimes bitterly. He said, "Judy, I really don't care. I know what we are, I know what I am."

As the concert dates drew near, the pressures began building. Judy became glum. "I don't want to make the tour," she said. "I wish we could just forget the whole thing and stay right here."

The advance crew—Mort Lindsey and several others—met them in Honolulu, en route to Sydney. There Judy suffered a humiliation which none of her audiences would know about. In Australia, customs officials were adamant that no drugs be brought into the country. Judy now habitually carried in her personal luggage a small case which contained barbiturates and amphetamines—each in its own bottle or box, all packed in neat rows in cotton batting, as in a druggist's sample case. According to one witness, the authorities confiscated everything she had. No one was immune from a rigid search. Judy was panic-stricken; only through the offices of a Chinese abortionist who had black-market connections was she able to replenish her stock, but they were European drugs with dosages unfamiliar to her, and they were to play a role in some of her catastrophic moments in Australia.

She had arrived in Sydney utterly exhausted; it had been a fifteen-hour flight from Honolulu, and she had hated every minute of it. There had been a bad moment after customs, too. A reporter asked, "Is it true, Miss Garland, what Sid Luft said? That you tried to commit suicide twenty-two times?"

Judy: "What did you say?"

The reporter repeated his question. Judy, distressingly thin and frighteningly pale, said, "Why don't you ask Mr. Herron that question?" The man did so. Mark, not knowing what to reply, quipped, "Who counts?" Judy broke up laughing over that. Mark thought,

What else can the girl do? You've got to be able to laugh—or it will kill you. That, he realized, was her defense through life. Her sense of humor. It was Oscar Levant's refuge, too. Once, playing poker with a group of friends, he heard a radio report that Judy had taken another overdose. He had said dryly, dealing the cards with no change of expression, "She's two up on me on suicide attempts—but I'm three up on her on nervous breakdowns. Or is it the other way around?"

There was no theatre in Sydney large enough to hold the crowds who demanded to hear Judy, and she had been booked into the Sydney Stadium, usually reserved for boxing matches. She had to thread her way past toilets and cubicle dressing rooms. The place was packed—more than ten thousand persons, real Judy fans. They waited nearly an hour for her to appear, and when they saw her, they screamed, they stood on their chairs, they applauded, they cheered.

"The greatest reception any entertainer ever received in Sydney," said the newspapers. Though the rehearsal hadn't gone too well (most of the orchestra had to be recruited in Sydney, and they did not know her ways nor she theirs), and there were other difficulties, she was stunning one moment, not so memorable the next. But she was onstage for nearly two hours.

After the second show, three nights later, real trouble, however. The dressing room was under the stage. Judy had gone back up for two encores; she was completely drained. One of the theatre executives asked, "Judy will you take another call? Listen to them!" The chant almost shook the building. "We . . . want . . . Judy! More . . . more . . . more!"

"No," Judy said. "I'm tired."

The executive said to her, "Listen, they're going crazy. Only a jerk singer like you could produce such a response."

Judy asked, unbelievingly, "Will you say that again?"

Again Mark heard the words: "Only a jerk singer like you could do that to that many thousands of people—"

Judy stood up and slapped the man hard across the face. Mark was stunned. He could only think, *He didn't mean to put it that way, but that's how the words came out.*

The executive looked at her, his face red where she had slapped him. "Do you feel better doing that?" he said.

"Get the hell out of here!" she cried. She appeared shattered.

If Sydney was a success, Melbourne was a disaster. Judy was to sing in Festival Hall, which is comparable to New York's Carnegie Hall. A huge crowd had waited for hours for her arrival at Melbourne's Essendon Airport on Sunday; but at the last minute Mark had changed the published travel plans, deciding they should go by train, thinking it might be more restful for Judy. It turned out the opposite. The trip was long and boring, the train was little more than a milk train, forever stopping, she was wretched throughout the ride, and the fans waiting in vain at the airport were irate. When Judy arrived at the train terminal, she and Mark went directly to their hotel with the announcement that no interviews would be permitted.

The press, to their anger, could not get to her for the next three days. One reporter disguised himself as a waiter, carrying a tray of food; when he got into their suite, Mark threw him out. Everything was beginning badly.

Nonetheless, her fans jammed Festival Hall. Judy was to have appeared at 8:30; she did not show up until after 9:30, before an impatient audience that had begun a steady slow handclapping. Not only was the press incensed at her; the producer was almost apoplectic. It had taken him nearly two hours to get Judy from her hotel to the theatre. He had invested a tremendous sum of money in her tour, and here she was saying she couldn't remember anything, she couldn't possibly do a performance, and he had to face the possibility of returning thousands of dollars to ticket holders. Finally, with the help of Mark and others in her entourage, Judy was gotten into a car and brought to the theatre.

Mark escorted her onstage, Judy began an apology, stumbled over her mike cord—there were immediate, shocked cries from the audience, then applause and cheers: they *were* pulling for her, late or not —and she went into her first number. She was singing off-key, she was forgetting lines, but she finished it. Then she took the baton from Mort Lindsey, tapped him playfully with it and conducted the orchestra, moved about the stage, joking with the audience, working to make them like her. She began her second number and, halfway through, suddenly dried up. She couldn't remember a word. The silence was horrible. The audience couldn't believe it. They were shocked. Was she drunk? Drugged? (Had it been the unfamiliar pills?) She tried all her tricks to win the audience, but when someone shouted, "Have another brandy!" it unnerved her the more. She

536

moved unsteadily on her high heels, she knocked over a chair, she got tangled in her mike cord. Someone shouted, "You're drunk!" and several in the front row were abusive. They hooted her. Lindsey kept striking up music cues to jog her memory—she was able to get through a few songs. At one point she sat down on a stool facing the orchestra and the audience heard her say, "Why don't we just play cards?" She turned around: some of the audience were already leaving.

"Where are you going?" she cried out. "Home," someone replied, "and that's where you should go." Finally she began "I'll go my way by myself," and when the audience continued to heckle her, she placed her microphone on her stool and walked off.

Mark thought, *That's it, she's never going back on that stage,* and grabbed her in the wings to get her downstairs and out the rear of the theatre. The audience howled in anger; they wanted their money back. They had been promised a show of some two hours and Judy had sung perhaps ten songs, the rest had been talk and clowning and disaster.

The departure from Melbourne was torture. Thousands had come to the airport to see her off—and boo. The headlines had been cruel: "JUDY STONED—DRUNK—DRUGGED."

She did not realize at first that she was being booed. It was simply inconceivable to her. As they were about to go through the turnstiles at the airport, a woman stood nearby holding a baby. Judy had to stop; she had to touch that child. She hugged the baby for a moment. "Hello, you sweet little thing—" Then, in a momentary silence, she heard the noise outside. She said, startled, "What is that? That can't be—" Then she realized that they were indeed booing her. She collapsed; her head dropped, her body caved in, and if Mark had not caught her, she would have crumpled to the floor. "Hang on, sweetheart, hang on," he begged her. It was a scene out of purgatory: the booing, a powerful wind blowing across the field as he half-carried, half-helped her to the plane, her hat suddenly blown off, the boos growing louder. . . . Then they were on the plane that would return them to Sydney.

When they arrived, she said, "I don't want to go back to the States." She didn't want to sing again. She wanted to go, go—anywhere. Go around the world. That had been their plan, anyway, hadn't it? "O.K.," said Mark. "We'll start with Hong Kong." Everybody else returned to the States, after Judy had signed all the required checks, and Judy and Mark went on to Hong Kong.

As for Melbourne, Judy simply dismissed it. They were barbarians. Everybody knew Sydney was civilized, and Melbourne boorish. She would never appear there again.

Mark understood something of her problem as a singer. Once she had complained, "How can I bring new life to these same old songs, over and over and over again?" Few of her arrangements had been changed since they'd first been written. She had sung "For Me and My Gal" more than twenty years. Now her voice had grown deeper. Mort Lindsey had to lower some of the notes to make them easier for her to sing. Those same old songs, she said.

"I know," Mark said. "It's like acting forever in the same play."

He was in favor of a world tour. He knew Judy was not ready to face the press at home. He had tried his best to keep the local press from her, as well as the fan mail. Some of the latter were pure poison-pen letters. One read: "Judy, get rid of Herron. God in heaven will punish you. Go back to Sid Luft. You're a rotten mother. Go back to your children."

Then they were in Hong Kong, staying at the Mandarin Hotel, in a suite on the twenty-second floor of the twenty-five-floor building. As usual, the moment Judy entered a hotel room, she turned on the TV and radio. Everything was in Chinese, so Judy and Mark sat before the TV and tried to invent a plot, a hilarious dialogue in English to go with the action. They were each other's best audiences.

It *was* a love affair. She called him "Marko," and he called her "Dearest," "Darling," "Sweetheart." Once when he called her "Judy," she turned to him: "Have I done something wrong. Have I hurt you?"

They had talked repeatedly of marriage. To interviewers, she had always insisted that Mark be included in any photographs taken of her, and had said that they would be married "in a few days." This, though the divorce from Luft would not come through for nearly another year. They considered themselves married. Mark bought Judy a ring, a jade stone surrounded by diamonds. "Marko, let's both get wedding rings," she said. They settled on two simple gold bands, each putting the ring on the other's finger.

In the four days they were in Hong Kong, they visited every exotic corner, exploring the shantytowns, the fifth-rate bars, the docks. In a bar at 3 A.M. one morning a sailor walked over to Judy. "I've bet twenty dollars with my buddy—" Judy smiled sweetly. "No, I just look like her. Isn't that amazing? I get that wherever I go." At that moment the pianist broke into "Over the Rainbow," and Judy had to burst out laughing—nobody had her laugh, she had fooled no one.

The sailor said, "Wouldn't you like to see our submarine?" He and his companion put them in his convertible and drove to the submarine. "You really want to go down there?" Mark asked. "Of course I do," said Judy, game for anything. They went aboard and walked through. It was just dawn and the day crew was getting up. One said, "Jesus Christ, I just had the weirdest dream. I could have sworn Judy Garland just walked past here." His buddy in the next bunk said, "She just did." Then excitement, like wildfire, everywhere. "I don't believe it, I don't believe it, good God, Judy Garland down here, in this sub, in Hong Kong!"

She adored it. Who in Hollywood could have thought up a better party?

But on the night of Thursday, May 28, 1964, the worst typhoon in Hong Kong history struck the city. Radio warnings had sounded through the day: Typhoon Viola was on its way.

It was brought home to Mark when at dusk he went to one of the large picture windows, below which the Bay of Hong Kong was spread out in all its glory. This morning ships with white sails and gleaming prows had filled the glittering, spanking-sunny, blue, blue waters of the bay, a Chinese print seen through the morning haze. At night, breathtakingly lit up, the scene was even more spectacular.

Now, at dusk, the bay was empty.

"My God," said Mark. "Everything's pulled out. They must mean it. Maybe we should get out of here."

They hurried down to the lobby. No, they were warned, stay inside. The weather bureau had estimated winds at ninety miles an hour. They'd be blown off their feet if they tried the streets. The ferries had stopped operating. In the lobby all the shops were closed. Only the newsstand remained open.

Judy said, trying to be calm, "We need some magazines." Mark grabbed a handful, and the two returned to their suite. Mark switched on the TV and radio. Yes, the typhoon was on its way. Even as they watched, the wind roared, the building actually trembled.

Judy sat down on the sofa and started to thumb through a magazine, but she was obviously terrified. Mark tried to reassure her. Everything would be fine. Typhoons were routine here, buildings were constructed for such eventualities. But he did not believe his own words.

Among the magazines was the new, May 29, 1964, issue of *Time.* Judy, her hands trembling, was looking through it. Mark heard her wail, "Oh, my God, it all comes back!" It was a scathing review of her Melbourne disaster, cruel and unsparing, which began: "At 41, Judy Garland may have gone over the rainbow for the last time." The audience, it said, waited over an hour for her "and this was one time Judy was not worth waiting for." It quoted the remark, "Have another brandy," with the reviewer's comment, "She didn't need one," and described her antics onstage, down to the audience beginning to leave "long before she did." As if to distress her even more, the story's last paragraphs dealt rhapsodically with Marlene Dietrich's triumph in Moscow, where she had opened a one-woman show the same week. "Oh, God!" Judy repeated, as she read again every painful word. In the days they had explored Hong Kong and its fascinating corners, she had appeared to have forgotten Melbourne, but now, as she read, the torment returned.

The storm increased. The wind howled about the windows. The building did more than tremble; at that height it swayed from side to side. The huge windows, which had seemed so attractive, now terrified them. The furies were at work outside; the rain came, suddenly, like solid sheets of water hurled again and again against the glass.

Judy could bear it no longer. She jumped up. "Oh, my God," she cried, "I'm not going to go this way. Jesus Christ, it'll really be Dorothy going over the fucking rainbow! We can't go this way. Gimme those pills and we'll die together!"

Mark, who with Judy's agreement was in charge of her medication and the doling out of pills, had a cache of Tuinal hidden away. He grabbed her and tried to comfort her.

Mark had no idea how deep-seated was Judy's terror of any natural convulsion. Ethel Gumm's one fear had been of violent storms; the times she had herded Suzy and Jimmy into the basement when there were lightning and thunder had terrified Judy. Judy herself had had a bad experience when, at the age of twelve, she was taking dancing lessons from Maurice Kusell in Los Angeles, and the floor trembled, pictures rattled on the walls: an earthquake had struck California. Judy began screaming, running hysterically in circles, and Kusell grabbed her, took her struggling in his arms into his office and held her close until it was over.

Mark thought they would be safest in bed. While the building swayed and trembled, they lay side by side, very still. Mark closed his eyes and prayed. He assumed Judy was praying, too. For if there was a hell, it was here, on the twenty-second floor of this perilous tower in this ancient city of the East: the shaking of the building, the roar of the elements, the look of the mad water below, the sensation that an ocean was exploding just outside their windows and might at any moment inundate them.

At some point during the night, Mark reached over to find Judy's hand—and she was not there.

He sprang up and ran into the bathroom. Judy lay unconscious on the floor. At some time she had slipped out of bed, had somehow found the bottle of pills and had taken—how many?

Mark frantically rang the manager. It was dawn. She must have taken the pills hours ago. His words tumbled out: "Miss Garland is sick, get a doctor, an ambulance—she's got to be taken to the hospital at once."

Impossible, said the manager. The wind was so powerful there was no traffic in the streets. An ambulance would be blown away.

Mark knew there was a Catholic hospital three blocks away, on a small hill. The manager brought a wheelchair up; Mark threw a robe around the unconscious Judy; the manager and a nurse helped them get her into it, took her down the elevator, were lucky enough to commandeer a taxi, and in a scene directly out of *The Wizard of Oz*, with trees bending over in the gale, they managed to reach the hospital.

Now, once she was in a room, began a terrifying wait. When Judy arrived in Sydney, she could not have weighed more than ninety pounds, and her pallor had been observed by everyone. Now she weighed even less. They pumped out her stomach. The doctor muttered, "It's too late, she's got it in her blood stream by now. Nothing's coming out." Judy lay in a coma, under an oxygen tent.

To Mark the doctor said, "You'd better get out." Mark refused. "I'm not leaving here until you tell me that she's all right." The doctor said he could stay if he allowed the physician to give him a shot to knock him out; otherwise he'd have two sick patients on his hands. Mark submitted, saying, "Get Dr. Lee Siegel in Los Angeles —he's her doctor, he'll know what to do." If not, Dr. Kermit Osserman, who had treated Judy in New York.

Neither man could be reached. Not until hours later did Mark get Lee on the phone, and have him advise a local physician.

The next thing he knew the doctor was passing by. "What, you still awake?" Mark: "I told you I won't leave until you tell me she's all right and is going to live."

The doctor said somberly, "If she regains consciousness, there's every possibility that she'll catch pneumonia, and that will kill her."

Mark sat on a chair in the corridor outside her room and waited, chain-smoking. Now and then he spoke with Dr. Osserman in New York, and again with Lee, in Los Angeles. Judy, meanwhile, lay in a coma. It was to last more than fifteen hours.

At one point a nurse came out, agitated. "Mr. Herron, you better come," and he walked in. There was no movement under the oxygen tent. Mark found himself shaking like an epileptic, his head jerking back; he grabbed a napkin and stuffed it into his mouth to keep from making noises; he found himself striking his head against the wall and sobbing. He heard the nurse say distinctly, "She's dead." The words galvanized him into action. He cried out, "No, no, no, she's not, get another oxygen tent—"

"But she's dead—"

He shouted again, "Get another oxygen tent." They were fumbling as they worked to tighten something on the oxygen supply line. He screamed, "Goddamnit, tighten it properly! Fix it!" Somehow they fixed the valve, and after what seemed an eternity, he discerned the slightest motion under the tent. The mask over Judy's face moved, ever so little—there was life there!

Mark remembered that at one point one nurse did leave the room and announce, "She's dead." That word spread swiftly through Hong Kong, and then was on the radio in Los Angeles, and Lorna, riding with her governess, Mrs. Chapman, heard it over the car radio and always remembered it, and how her governess immediately turned off the set when Lorna asked, "What did that man say about Mama? Did he say she died?"

Lee Siegel, in Los Angeles, had left for Hong Kong. He and Noreen, with Karl Brent, Judy's secretary, had their passports expedited through Attorney General Robert Kennedy's intervention, and all flew to Judy's bedside.

When Judy came out of her coma, her first words were: "Spyros Skouras choreographs the Rockettes." Mark, not quite believing what he heard, said, "Honey, Lee Siegel is on his way." Judy gave the slightest of nods. When Mark saw Brent later, Brent told him he had come to take the body back.

Just before they arrived, Mark thought he would go out of his mind if he did not get away from the hospital for a while. Judy was out of the coma, at least. The storm was over, but it was still raining furiously. He walked back to the Mandarin Hotel to check for messages. There was a cable from David Begelman in New York. It read: "Tell Judy—this at your own discretion—that her sister Suzy just died." Suzy had succeeded, this time, in taking an overdose, two days before in Vegas. The cause of death had been announced as cancer. Mark thought, *How can I tell Judy about her sister? She's just come back from the grave herself.* He told her, much later, when she was up and about, and Judy wept: "Poor Suzy," and kept to herself for a little while. Mark never knew more about it than that.

As he stood reading the wire, the clerk said, "Mr. Herron, if you should want a drink, you'd better not go to the bar. It's crawling with the press looking for you. Order it in your room." Mark sneaked out of the hotel by the back way, and facing him, across the street, was a sign: "THE STARLIGHT ROOM." Under it, the words: "NOW APPEARING: THE ALLEN BROTHERS & ADRIANA." Herron thought: *I've got to hear some music, maybe it's the only way I'll hold on to my sanity.* He went in and stood at the bar. The entertainment was good. Someone recognized him, and a message was brought to him: the Allen Brothers would like to meet him, so he went back and met them.

When he returned to the hospital, he hardly recognized Judy. Her throat was black and blue. The oxygen tent lay discarded to one side. She looked at Mark and said in a voice that sounded like that of a male midget, deep and bass and very slow, "Where . . . have . . . you . . . been?"

He said, "I went out to hear some music."

Judy: "Did . . . you . . . meet . . . any . . . pretty . . . girls?"

He said, "Yes, I met one."

Judy: "Did . . . you . . . fuck . . . her?"

He said, "No, I was too weak—"

Judy said, a little more spirit in her voice, "Son of a bitch, here I am dying, and you're going out to nightclubs. I'm getting out of this goddamn bed."

"For God's sake, Judy, you can't move," he cried.

With that she threw herself out of the bed, onto the floor. "I'm getting out of this fucking hospital!"

The nurses were there, fighting to get her back in, when Lee arrived. She had pleurisy in both lungs. Lee took over for several days until she was able to be moved back to the hotel to recuperate, with a Chinese nurse, called Snowda Wu, who spoke English and was remarkably competent, to watch over her.

Judy had been told that she would never sing again. Her throat had been injured—the stomach pumping, the other procedures—her heart was damaged. She had one reaction: anger. Mark felt almost relieved. If she couldn't sing again, it might be a blessing; she could turn to drama and prove herself as an actress.

Several nights later she said, "I want to see those people you heard in the Starlight Room." There was no stopping her. Her recovery had been astonishing. In days she had gone from seventy to nearly ninety pounds. She put on a little hat, makeup, a scarf about her neck—no one would have dreamed she had been given up for dead less than a week before. They went to hear the Allen Brothers—Lee and Noreen, Judy and Mark. After the show, the Allen Brothers and Adriana joined them for dinner. Judy looked radiant. She was herself once more. Never sing again? She stood up on that floor and *sang*, the Allen Brothers applauding the loudest. She got along splendidly with them; they were bright, quick, talented. She could not know—or she might have known even then, in the back of that cunning mind of hers—that one of the brothers, Peter, would, sooner or later, become her son-in-law, Liza's husband.

Then the calls from New York. Even in the hospital, as soon as Judy felt well enough, she had ordered merchants to send up jade and pearl ornaments to examine, was surrounded by her court of admirers and telephoning friends all over the world. She called Dr. Marc and Marcella, and told Marcella, "Well, now I have my Mark, too."

The New York newspapers were on the line. "Was she married?" "Oh, yes, yes." Mark was appalled. Judy said, "To hell with them. If we want to lie, we'll lie." She was angry at the entire world, she'd suffered as no one else had, why couldn't she play any game she wanted to play?

That began a new story. Judy announced that she and Mark had been married on June 6 on a Norwegian freighter, the *Boda*, in Hong Kong waters by a Captain Thorvald Norvik, because her lawyers had informed her that "my former marriage to Luft" had been dissolved in the Mexican courts and "I've got custody of Lorna and Joe though they're still with Luft." There had been, of course, no Mexican divorce, or marriage dissolution, no Norwegian ship named *Boda* and no Norwegian captain named Norvik—Judy had invented it all.

In Los Angeles there were astonished denials. *Newsweek* called Luft. "We understand you're still married to Miss Garland." Luft said, "If you ask me, they got married on the Good Ship Lollypop. It's a fairy tale. I'm sure Judy and Mark are aware of their legal status. She and I are still married."

Then Judy changed the story. A Chinese Buddhist monk had blessed her in an elaborate ceremony, full of burning joss sticks and incense because of her miraculous recovery. In some way that had led to the "rumor" that they'd been married. But she was going to marry Mark as soon as her divorce was final.

The Allen Brothers, Peter and Chris, turned out not to be brothers, but close friends, talented singers, pianists and songwriters, and made to order as company for Judy.

Mark and Judy continued their trip: Tokyo, for three weeks, aboard the *President Roosevelt* with streamers, a wedding cake and photographers—so far as anyone was concerned, they were married and their twin wedding rings seemed only to confirm it—then Alaska, and finally London, where they took a house in Chelsea, and Judy was soon entertaining such friends as Vivien Leigh, Roddy McDowall, Peter Lawford, Rex Harrison and others.

One day one of Liza's albums came in the mail. Judy listened. "Where did she get that voice?" She went into absolute ecstasy. "Oh, my God, she must have worked her little old ass off!" There was nothing for it but for her to come to London. She telephoned Liza. "How would you like to sing with me at the Palladium? Judy and Liza at the Palladium?" Liza said, "Oh, no, Mama, why? It's too much, Judy and her kid. Why don't you do it yourself?"

"All right," said Judy, hung up and immediately notified the British press that she and Liza were going to do a concert together. It was sold out in an afternoon. She called Liza back the next day. "We're sold out, isn't it great!" There was nothing Liza could do but say, "Right," call up her friend the composer, Marvin Hamlisch, who years later was to win three Oscars in a single evening, and ask him to prepare several arrangements for her. What Liza did not know was that Mama also had Peter Allen in mind. She had decided the Allen Brothers were so good she wanted to manage them, she was making bookings for them in London, and once Peter was in London, Judy was sure he'd serve as an excellent reason to keep Liza there with her. They'd make a wonderful pair. In a way Liza's insistence on being on her own, on doing *Carnival* despite her mother's wishes, had started the whole thing. But Liza had to admit that her mother's *fait accompli*—going ahead with their concert no matter what Liza had said—was a neat trick. She thought, *If Mama wants it that badly —why, then, yes, wonderful. And I love her for it.*

On September 10, 1964, Liza arrived in London. Mark and Judy met her at the plane. Mark had seen Liza only briefly in the Rockingham house; he felt in her the same shyness and tenderness that he felt in Judy. He knew Liza was sizing him up, as they sat in the car returning from the airport. He would have been astonished to know what was going through her mind. She was thinking, as she saw them then, and later at parties, so much in love, Mama slender and beautiful and happy, Mark lean, handsome, poetic, *They're like Scott and Zelda, you'd look at them and it was like a small conspiracy was going on between them.* She could almost visualize them jumping fully clothed into the Plaza Hotel fountain. . . . Aloud she said, suddenly, "Well, Marko, I've checked up on you."

Mark thought, *Oh, Jesus Christ, oh, boy! So? So?* Liza had certainly read the headlines about them, the phony marriage on the phony boat, and who, anyway, was this Mark Herron? Liza explained almost apologetically, "I just had to have you checked out. I found out two things: one, that you're a hell of an actor, and, two, that you're a hell of a nice guy. So I said, 'Mama's O.K. I don't have to worry about her.'"

So that was settled.

Now, Judy said, would Mark direct their concert? It had been scheduled for November 8. Mark was dumfounded. Direct Judy? Yes, if Judy would sing new songs—not the old ones she'd been singing all her life.

"But, Marko, that's what they want to hear," said Judy.

"Yes, but what about you?" he asked. "You treat yourself sometimes like an old Sophie Tucker. You don't have to go down that memory lane, that nostalgia-trunk stuff you had on your TV shows. You're a young woman. You can do new things."

He sold her on the idea, but it was difficult, and a typical Garland scene. Mark wrote down a list of songs he thought Judy should sing, and left spaces between for Liza's. He and Judy were sitting in the living room of their house. Mark said, "Well, sweetheart, here it is. My idea." He handed the paper to Judy.

She put on her glasses and looked at it, then looked back at him. "You are out of your mind!" She stood up and started to walk away, crumpling the sheet of paper and throwing it on the floor. "I'm leaving," she said. "You-are-out-of-your-fucking-mind. Nobody—nobody could do that. Completely impossible." She was walking away, taking a step back to him, then stalking off and vanishing into her room.

Mark sat and waited.

She reappeared at the other end of the room. She said, "You know, this is humanly impossible. Nobody could do these. You've put down five ball-breaking songs in a row. Nobody could do that."

Mark said, "*You* can."

Judy: "You really think so?" She bent down, picked up the crumpled paper, smoothed it out and looked at the list again.

"Of course," said Mark, "or I wouldn't have put them down." There were four songs she had never done. He wanted her to open with "Once in a Lifetime," because it was so apropos: *This is my moment, my own special moment, Liza and me, the first time together.*

He added, "If you don't want to do it my way, then get somebody else. But if my name is going to appear, I don't want it to be Carnegie Hall, which you've done and done and done."

Judy yielded. She learned "What Now My Love?"; she learned a song from *Funny Girl*—even though she disliked learning new songs —and threw herself into work again. She had had an enormously encouraging experience—one she needed after the fiasco in Melbourne—a sensational last-moment appearance during the summer at an annual British benefit, *Night of 100 Stars*, which began at midnight at the Palladium. The Beatles were masters of ceremonies. The mere mention of her name—a few hours after she left a nursing home, where, as announced, she'd been resting several days after accidentally cutting her wrists while trying to open a brassbound trunk with a pair of scissors—stopped the show, and her coming on second to last, singing "Over the Rainbow" and "Swanee," created such a tumult that the Beatles found it necessary to cancel the grand finale. That was simply part of the Garland legend. Nobody could follow Judy.

Now she was rehearsing industriously. "All right," she said to Mark, "so I'm going to do it." She'd sing four of the new songs he'd listed for her. Then she'd introduce Liza by singing "Liza, Liza . . ."

No, said Mark. Don't do it that way. Give her the dignity she deserves. Say simply, "Ladies and gentlemen, Liza Minnelli." Judy had forgotten that was precisely how she had introduced her daughter years before in front of an unruly audience in Vegas. Judy said, "I'd love that. Yes, I'll do it that way."

Herron set up the opening scene, using Sean Kenny, who had done the sets for the highly successful musical, *Oliver!* A ramp was built on each side of the stage; when Judy said, "Liza Minnelli," he wanted Judy to be stage center, Liza to come down one ramp, they would meet, bow to each other, then Judy would walk off the other ramp. It was theatrical, and effective. Liza sang four songs. At the end of the fourth song, the lights lowered, and as it grew dark, one heard Liza's voice, "Mama?"—tentative, and then again, "Mama—?"; and as the entire theatre went dark, Judy's voice, gentle at first: "Hel-lo, Liza"; then the lights came up slowly, showing Judy with her mike, Liza with hers, walking toward each other; then all the theatre lights came up and they were singing together, Liza: "You're looking swell, Ma-ma. . . . It's nice to have you back where you belong—"

That each stumbled over their lines once or twice made little difference. It was indeed a memorable evening, a black-tie Sunday night event, so successful that it was repeated a week later, and the Capitol Record album made from it, *Judy Garland and Liza Minnelli "Live" at the London Palladium*, became an immediate best seller.

This success, gratifying as it was, had the edge taken off it by a bitter custody hearing Luft had obtained only a couple of weeks before, in late October, in Santa Monica. Reading about Judy's and Mark's antics abroad, Sid had been growing angrier and angrier. Once he strode into the Rockingham house, fighting drunk, took off his coat, threw it on the floor, as if ready to take on all comers, and demanded to have the children. Gradually he was placated by the help, and, remembering his experience when he had tried to kidnap Joe and Lorna in Nevada, he grew less combative and finally left. Before this hearing, Judy had had full custody; he wanted it changed on the ground that she was an unfit mother. His lawyers asserted she had used barbiturates and intoxicants for years, recently to even greater excess; Luft produced a house worker who testified she had found bottles of whiskey or wine hidden everywhere, in the bathrooms, behind books, wrapped in towels in the linen closets. Luft's lawyers stated that Judy's "course of conduct . . . has been habitual and continuous and the court can draw inferences as to what her conduct is and to what we can expect in the future." Though Judy's counsel presented witnesses to deny these charges, the result was a court ruling giving Luft joint custody with Judy. Her lawyer, explaining that Judy and Liza were to appear together in London on November 8, said: "I would like to make a motion for the children to go to London for one week and see their mother and sister opening at the Palladium." His wife, he said, would take them over, and a tutor would go along as well.

No, said the judge. "These children have been uprooted too often. They are remarkably well adjusted in spite of that, but I'm not going to approve a two-or-three-day junket of that sort with a long flight, even though they would be in custody of someone who is entirely responsible."

When Judy read the report of this hearing, her reaction can be imagined. She had had full custody; now she had joint custody. That was a body blow. She missed her children; how wonderful it would have been for Lorna and Joey to have seen Mama and Liza do their show together, see how happy Mama was with Mark, see that Mama seemed to have gotten it all together at last. . . . Through those closing months of 1964, Judy, Mark and Liza were attending party after party, Judy receiving ovations at theatre and film premieres that often eclipsed those of the stars themselves. They spent evenings with such companions as Noël Coward, Rosalind Russell, Peter Sellers, Rex Harrison and Lionel Bart, whose *Oliver!* had been such a success, and who privately confessed that he wrote every song with Judy in mind; they dined with Fonteyn and Nureyev; Judy brought Peter Allen and Liza together (expecting to hate each other at first sight after Judy's matchmaking efforts, they discovered the opposite to be true). Though all this was going on, the court decision of late October back in the States threw its pall over everything.

Finally Judy could stand it no longer. One night, sitting with a long drink, she took out the tape recorder and, in what was at once a plea, an accusation, a defense and a declaration of independence, spoke her heart out. Perhaps this would be part of the book she would write someday. But it was Judy, almost artless in her wish to make everything clear, speaking to the world, saying, *This is me, Judy, this is how I feel, this is what I want. . . .*

"The time has come for me to talk, to put the pattern straight. I am outraged, outraged about many things I have read about myself . . . written about in a shocking manner, smeared, scandalized, and I'm sick of it. . . . I've come to a time in my life when I don't want it any more, and I can't rise above it.

"First of all I don't understand, I don't honestly understand, why I've been made the victim of so many untruths. Perhaps you don't understand what it's like to pick up the paper and read things about yourself that aren't truth, read loathsome things that have nothing to do with your life, or you or your heart or your beliefs or your kindnesses or your willingness. . . . I've spent years trying to please through singing or acting. There's nothing wrong with that.

"And yet I've constantly been written or talked about, by certain individuals that I'll get to later, as an unfit person. . . . Well, what kind of people are they, what kind of business are they in? They're dead people. But they've tried to kill me along the way, but by God, they won't! Because I'm mad!"

Then, more calmly: "In some ways I'm a very lucky woman to have come to this time of my life and to have found happiness with a fine man—a man who is able to love me. Not just that I'm able to love, but the fact that he loves me, *just me,* whether I sing or dance or whether I don't.

"It's made me prettier than ever. That's what my oldest daughter, Liza, tells me. I'm prettier than ever. Liza has grown up to be a strong, beautiful, talented, fine, sensitive, courageous young woman.

550

I'm proud of that. I did that alone. I raised that little girl alone. Because nobody cared about us. Oh, they cared about the money I brought in, because it made them rich. Lots of people got rich off me. My children didn't get rich. I didn't get rich, and Mark Herron didn't get rich. But we have a love, my little boy Joey, my little girl Lorna, my young-lady grown-up daughter Liza, Mark, myself—we have a love that makes everything else look just stupid."

She inveighed furiously against Luft, against the judges who ruled "that I can't even get to see my children now that I'm living in England." She grew increasingly bitter. "Because I can't live with the stench of the Santa Monica courts, and the stench of lawyers who rob me, and just keep it going, keep the case going, Judy's crazy, Judy doesn't know what she's doing—I know well enough how to raise three kids, and damn well!

"I know how to be loved by a man who understands the pressures I've had to go through, and it's worth it. It's worth it and the hell with all the crazy so-called fan mail. The letters say, 'You've sinned, Judy, turn to Christ'—I've got God in my heart. That's more than most of you have. My children have it. Mark Herron has it. And we represent an army, we represent strength and goodness, and by God, justice had better prevail!"

She brooded for a little while, and then, speaking with growing hurt:

"Being Judy Garland—sure I've been loved by the public. I can't take the public home with me. And I've been ripped to pieces— *ripped to pieces!*—by the public and the critics and the newspapers and people who don't know what they're talking about. And I demand, I *demand*, to be heard, and I *will* be heard, and I'll keep talking for the rest of my life because now I can talk, now I'm happy, now I *know* there's no *Gaslight* in my life; and the people who try to present it are the criminals. And it all comes down to the unholy dollar."

Now she spoke confidentially: "Nobody has ever encouraged me to talk before. . . . It's a little difficult to sit and talk about yourself. I'm a very modest woman. I've always believed in that terrible cliché: whatever is printed in today's newspaper is yesterday's news. That's a lot of nonsense!" She grew angry. "I get mail—and fie, fie on the rotten poison-pen letters—the people who write those are demented! I'm going to live a life as splendid as my surroundings are, my man and my children. *I'll get my children.* I support my children, I brought them up and I love them and they love me. I respect them. I worship them. They give me the same respect, the same love, in return. They're brave children. . . .

"It's not that I'm wailing like an old-fashioned mother. I need them. I need them as much as they need me. I need their laughter. I need their arms around me, until they grow up and it's time for them to go about their own lives. I want them with me, I want them with me, I gave birth to them, I supported them, I loved them, I still do; but for goodness' sake, for God's sake, what about the lawyers? What about the judges? They're being handed over to a man . . ." She could not vent enough of her anger at Sid.

"I've been working my head off. Somebody had to feed my children, and that was me; and it was my pleasure, but it was damned hard to keep from climbing up the wall with frustration. So I'm not going to be frustrated any more. I'm going to talk, and somebody's going to print this, even if I have to put up the money myself. I'll print it in a little book. Maybe somebody will read it and maybe somebody will learn a little of the truth about this so-called legend. That's what I'm supposed to be—a legend—Judy Garland. All right, then read about it, but read the truth, though!

"I want to love. I want to be friendly. I want to work. Don't get in my way! And don't let other people get in my way! Get off my back! Let my loved ones stay around me. Let me stay around them. Let me live, for God's sake, let me live!

"If anyone's going to print anything about me, or write anything about me, it will be me. I'll print about me. I'll write about me because I'm the only one who knows, and I just refuse to stay silent any more while everyone else makes news about me—so-called news. And I'll never again be made the target for some demented sick mind that just wants to print bad things and to hell with the good things. And there've been a lot of good things!"

Again silence. And again that voice, giving each word its meaning, now rueful, now impassioned, now pleading:

"I'll never be that kind of target any more. There's no more over the rainbow for me. I've grown up. Those days are over. There's nothing about me to threaten by exposure. I've been exposed since I was a little girl, wrongly exposed. *News* was made—bad news. I know exactly who did it, how it was done, why it was done. I'm not a stupid woman. Now those people are going to be exposed and it's going to be fun. I've waited a long time for this; and revenge can be very sweet . . . when it is proper and right.

"I'm a very revengeful person now. I don't want any more lies printed about me. My children read the newspapers; they have to put up with their schoolmates and what they're made to say about me—they do the best they can, they don't pay any attention to it, they've learned better, and they're smarter. But I don't want somebody who is retarded writing columns or saying things, like Miss Hedda Hopper or Miss Louella Parsons—they seem to be terribly important. I don't want them to say, 'Poor, poor Judy,' right after I've triumphed at the Palladium in London. Write something good about me. I've been nice to them, I've been polite. You ought to see the condition they're in. Oh, boy! I know their makeup men. I know the tricks they've got to do to pull those women's faces up so they can look human. No more. No, sir. I'm going to talk. . . .

"Yes, this is a rough story, and I sound like a rough woman. I am, about Sid Luft. I am, about a lot of people. Except my son and my two daughters, and the man I'm in love with. And I have a right to be in love and I have a right to be loved and I have a right to get a divorce from a man like Sid Luft and to be married properly." A pause. And then, in a voice of infinite tenderness: "I want my son Joey to give me away at my wedding to Mark Herron. Mark Herron wants Joey to be his best man.

"I want my Lorna, my daughter, to be bridesmaid.

"I want Liza to be—to stand up with me. I'm going to wear white. White. White satin. And white lace. And white pearls. I am pure! And I'm marrying pure. And my children are pure. So you see, it's not all crazy and insane, the way people like to write it.

"Mark has given me courage. Mark has given me love. Mark has given the children love. Mark is so wonderful that it's hard for the rest of mankind to understand him. I understand him. I understand what he's given to me. I understand what he's given to Liza and to Lorna and to Joe. They understand it, too. . . . He's gentle, but by God, he's strong. And I love Mark Herron and Mark Herron loves me.

"What's so silly about that? What's so crazy? We will be married. We are correct, nice people. I will have more babies with my husband, Mark." She did not pause. She must have completely forgotten that she had directed her doctor, after Joe's birth, to make it impossible for her to bear more children. "We will have a wedding ceremony. There'll *be* over the rainbow for me."

Her voice rose to an impassioned plea:

"I've just about got it made! All I have to do is talk, and all you have to do is read, or listen, and *believe me,* the way you-believed-me-when-I-sang-all-the-songs! Well, now, I'm talking—and *listen* to me, for goodness' sake. . . ." Her voice reached a crescendo: "For goodness' sake, don't make a joke of me any more!"

Then, in a sudden change of mood—one can only imagine that she was up most of the night, thinking, talking, thinking, talking:

"People say and print and believe—the stupid ones, and that's the minority—that I'm either a drunk or a drug addict. It's a goddamn wonder I'm not! But I'm not, because there's Joe and Lorna and Liza and Mark and me, and whoever wants to love us is welcome; whoever is against us, get out!"

She came to a final, long peroration, and again this was tied up with her children:

"My three children—they're great successes unto themselves. Without an awful lot of help. I gave them so-called instant love, because I had to work to support them. That meant I had to leave them many times. And that meant I had to make them believe in my love when I left them; and that meant that they had to know that I would come back. It also had to mean that I had a life, that I would be well, and that when they grew up, they could leave me, and that I would be all right then.

"It's not easy to take. . . . If you're all alone and raising children, you do the best you can. Well, I've done a hell of a good job.

"You take a look at those three children. They're people, not children. They're children, not people. Whichever way you want to put it. I respect them. I disciplined them, because that was the only way I could give them security. I objected many times. I will not have spoiled children: spoiled children won't get along well with the rest of the world. They're not spoiled, but they're smart, loving, talented, and I'm a terribly, terribly lucky woman. I've been able to be honest with them and I have enabled them to be honest with me. If for nothing else, for that I'm proud.

"In whatever part of the world we're in, whether it be in England, America, Rome, wherever—Mark, Liza, Lorna and Joe . . . we're here, we're now, we are—is—of—and now . . ." and in a curious rhythm, her voice rising to what was at once a challenge and a promise . . . "and will conquer the world!"

What one must know is that at this time Judy had received a letter, dated October 29, 1964, from Herbert Schwab, her attorney in Los Angeles, indicating that she had the following matters on her mind:

1. Depositions, *Luft* vs. *Luft*
2. Depositions, *Mel Tormé* vs. *Judy Garland*
3. Delinquent Federal income taxes
4. Furniture appraisal re Kingsrow
5. Preparation of a new will
6. Possibility of her forming a Lichtenstein corporation to avoid certain tax liabilities

Legal cases then pending included:

Luft vs. *Creative Management Associates, Inc.*
Bradford vs. *Kingsrow & Judy Garland*
Tormé vs. *Kingsrow & Judy Garland*
Gary Smith vs. *Kingsrow*
Dan Dailey vs. *Kingsrow & Judy Garland*
Sultan & Worth vs. *Kingsrow & Judy Garland*
Garber vs. *Kingsrow & Judy Garland*
Alan Sussman law firm, $70,000 indebtedness, settled ultimately for $15,000
Oscar Steinberg vs. *Judy Garland*
Harry Zeever vs. *Judy Garland and Sid Luft*
Closed Credit Corporation vs. *Judy Garland and Milton Holland*
A legal bill for $55,815 for 1,273 hours of service

Judy and Mark returned to the United States several days before Christmas 1964, with happy plans to reunite with Lorna and Joey in New York on Christmas Day. Christmas Day came—and no children. They were somewhere on the West Coast with Sid, and no one could find Sid. Judy had obtained a court order a few days earlier for Sid to return the children to the Rockingham house so that Mrs. Chapman could fly them to New York in time. Instead, Luft had taken Joey and Lorna to celebrate Christmas at the home of twenty-three-year-old Bridget Somers, a girl he said he had hired to look after the children. A warrant for his arrest was issued and he successfully petitioned to have it dropped. "I had a wonderful time with my children on Christmas," he said later. "I would rather have gone to jail than miss it—my first Christmas with them in three years, and it was a happy and delightful holiday."

But several days later the children and their governess did fly to New York, and on the late afternoon of December 29, Lorna and Joey were gathered ecstatically into Judy's arms in the TWA waiting room at the airport.

Present, too, were Liza and Peter—engaged.

Indomitable was the word for Judy Garland.

38

AT 1:30 A.M., NOVEMBER 14, 1965, JUDY, carrying a white Bible and a single white rose, became Mrs. Mark Herron in the small wedding chapel of the Little Church of the West in Las Vegas. Her divorce, long awaited from Sid Luft, had become final some weeks before.

She had walked out of court that afternoon in Los Angeles, and to reporters who asked, "Will you marry Mr. Herron?" she had replied primly, "If he'll have me." Then she hurried home. "I'm free, I'm free," she cried, grabbing Mark and dancing about the room. "Now what are we going to do?"

"Let's celebrate," Mark said. They went to the Daisy, a popular discotheque. They talked marriage. "Why is that so important?" Herron asked. "We are living as man and wife, aren't we, sweetheart? Why that certificate?"

Judy, proper as only a Gumm from Grand Rapids could be, said, "That's the only way I'll know you love me." She added, "My children need a father." They set the date.

Herron kissed her, they went to a telephone and called Liza in New York. "Darling, Marko and I are getting married. May we have your permission?" And when Liza said, of course, Judy said, "Please come." She'd called Lorna and Joe, to ask their permission, too, and to invite them, but Sid said, "No, they're in school, they can't come."

Liza really couldn't come, and said, "Mama, I can't, but I promise I'll come to the next." Then she realized what she had said, and added quickly, "Oh, Jesus, I'm sorry, I didn't mean it that way, Mama, I'm sorry, I didn't mean it to sound that way." At the other end there was silence—then a shriek of laughter—Liza could see her at the other end roaring with laughter, and heard the phone fall. Judy had to call her back twenty minutes later, still choking with laughter, and Liza could see her wiping her eyes from laughing.

Sid had met Herron on the telephone just before the divorce became final. He was at the Rockingham house, about to take the children out for the afternoon, when the telephone rang. Judy answered it. "Hello, darling. Yes, darling." Then she put her hand over the mouthpiece. "It's Mark," she said to Sid. Luft thought, *She says it as though he were royalty.* "Would you like to say hello?" Luft agreed.

He picked up the telephone, to hear a young man's voice. "Hello, Mr. Luft." "Mark, how are you?" Sid said. "I'm so glad to have an opportunity to talk on the phone," said Mark. "Well, I am, too," said Sid. Mark: "I just want to tell you that I'm very much in love with your wife, we plan to marry soon, and I'm going to try to make the best father to your children." Sid could scarcely control his voice when he hung up. *Father* to *his* children!

At the wedding there had been three witnesses: Snowda Wu, who had tended Judy with such infinite tenderness and skill in Hong Kong that they brought her back to the United States; Guy McElwaine, Judy's publicity man, who was Mark's best man; and Guy's wife, as matron of honor.

Weeks before, Judy and Mark had had a tug of wills. As always when in love, Judy's passion over a man—for him or against him— had to be volcanic. She had been booked into the Circle Star Theatre in San Carlos, just outside San Francisco. It meant appearing on a turntable stage, she discovered. "Never," she told Mark. "I can't do that." But he'd done it, said Mark, he'd appeared in theatre in the round. "Oh, no," said Judy. "I'm not a record. I'd fall down. I'd get dizzy."

They were staying at the Mark Hopkins Hotel in San Francisco. Judy added, "Anyway, I've caught a cold." In brief, she wanted to cancel the appearance. A turntable and a cold to boot—oh, no. Mark said, "Darling, you're not that sick." Judy, annoyed, left to get something in the lobby, then came up to find Mark lying on his stomach on the bed, watching baseball on TV.

"What the hell are you doing," she demanded, "watching a god-damn ball game again?" Mark said, "Yeah—Dodgers and Oakland." Judy said angrily, "I don't give a damn if it's Susanna Foster and Deanna Durbin! Pay attention to me. Don't you understand, I'm sick! Now, you call up and say I'm not going on."

Mark said, "I'm not going to do any such thing." They began screaming at each other. Sid, Mark—what did it matter who?—they were always telling her what to do. Finally Mark telephoned Fields. She wasn't going to go on? O.K., said Fields. He'd get somebody to replace her.

When Mark relayed this to her, it led to a violent extension of their first argument, and they found themselves screaming at each other, Judy crying, "I'm going out the window!"—they were on the twentieth floor—and Herron clinging to her with the aid of Snowda Wu, who had already called the hotel doctor. "I'm going to jump!" she screamed. Mark, clutching her—it was not too hard to hold her back —said, just as the doctor entered, "If you jump, darling, that would make such an idiot picture of you in the papers—you don't want that." And Judy listened. "O.K.," she said. "But I'm still not going on. Call them and say I canceled." She lay down to rest.

Mark thought, *What am I going to do?* Then an idea came. He left her for a moment in the care of the doctor and Snowda, then returned excitedly. "Darling, guess what?" "What?" Judy asked, angrily. "You won't believe this, but I just phoned Barbra Streisand in New York and you know of course she just had a triumph at Forest Hills. Barbra's coming out, she's bringing all her musicians, and she's going on for you tonight."

Judy leaped up. "All right, all right, I'll do it! I'll do it! Damn you, I'll do it, I'll do it!"

Mark said, "No, no, no, sweetheart. I won't allow you. You're much too ill. Your throat, I won't want you to hurt your—"

"Fuck you!" said Judy. "I'm going on."

Mark immediately notified Fields no replacement was necessary.

In the car driving to San Carlos that night, Judy suddenly turned to him. "You bastard! I feel like opening this door and shoving you out." She had suddenly realized it had all been too pat, that Mark had tricked her. Of course he'd made no phone call to Streisand.

She went on that night, and she was fine. Mark was already for-given. When, as usual, he escorted her onstage, the applause was so warm that Judy spontaneously announced: "Ladies and gentlemen, I want you to meet the man I'm going to marry, my beautiful Marko." Mark, red with embarrassment, escaped to his seat.

Several nights later, as they were walking through the hotel lobby to go to a party—they had no limousine that night and would pick up a cab in front—a heavy-set masculine-appearing woman joined them. "I want to talk to you," she said to Judy. Mark said, "Excuse us, please," and they hurried their steps. The woman kept pace. "I want to talk to you," she said insistently to Judy, gesturing Mark away. Judy groaned under her breath, "Oh, Jesus!" This woman was very drunk, and dangerous. Mark said, as politely as he could, "I'm terribly sorry—" but still she was at their side.

Now they stood under the hotel awning, in a pouring rain, while a doorman ran for a cab. The woman suddenly said to Judy in a loud voice, "You goddamn bitch! You're just like whatever I've read about you. You're a dope fiend, you're a drunk, you're a filthy—"

Mark said, "Please, lady, please stop saying those things."

But she only continued her tirade. "And here you are, marrying someone so much younger than you, a goddamn pimp—"

"I warn you," Mark said. "You say one more thing and I'm going to beat the shit out of you."

The woman paid no attention. Suddenly he slapped her, hard, and then again, and then a third time, until she fell. No one tried to stop him. The other doorman did nothing, the spectators who had formed a little circle did nothing. They heard it all, they were shocked, and Judy was putting her hands up before her face, like a blind person, saying, "Oh, my God, oh, my God," and then the cab was there, and Mark helped her in. He found himself shaking. He had no idea he had that much violence in him.

Judy turned to him. "Nobody ever did anything like that for me. Thank you."

But one afternoon, for whatever reason, Judy turned on Snowda, whom both Dr. Siegel and Mark considered one of the most tender and competent nurses they had ever known, and Snowda, accused beyond endurance, walked out. She was returning to Hong Kong.

That night Judy asked Mark, "Where's Snowda?" Mark said, "She's gone, Judy. She's gone—poor thing." Judy stood up in bed and held him in her arms and said, "I always bury the wrong people, don't I?"

He said, "That's right, sweetheart."

She clutched his arm. "Don't let me bury you. Promise me that. You're too nice a man." Mark held her close. "I won't, dearest, I won't."

There had been, a few months back, a difficult period in Los Angeles. Judy had signed to appear June 15 at the Thunderbird in Vegas, but she was gaining weight. Months before, in London, she had once asked him, "Marko, would you leave me if I ever got fat again?" He had said, "You bet I would. I'd go in a minute." "Well," she said, "I promise you, I won't get fat."

Now she said to him, "Marko, I feel I'm going to lose you if I don't shape up." Mark read between the lines. It wasn't weight she was talking about. He replied, "That's right, sweetheart." She checked herself into a hospital. Mark visited her doctor every day. She did not want to see him, or speak to him on the phone. Her doctor assured him, "She's doing beautifully." He added, "She's on withdrawal." But when it came time for her engagement, the doctor told Mark, "Please don't let her go from here. We've got her fairly clean. I won't be responsible for the consequences if she leaves now."

Judy said, "I have no money, I'm deeply in debt, I've got to take the Vegas engagement." Mark said, to Judy's agents, to Dr. Lee, to Judy herself, "I don't care. Sell the house, do anything." But the final decision was hers.

She insisted on leaving the twelfth, but was almost immediately rushed back because of an "emotional rash"; after two days she again left for the Thunderbird. Once they were in their room, Mark said, "Don't you want to go down and see the band?" "I don't know if I'm up to it," Judy said. But they got on the elevator; as it descended, she began to giggle at a joke, started to have convulsions, and when the elevator door opened, she fell out unconscious on the lobby floor. They gave her first aid and got her back to her room.

That night, once more—how often could this continue?—Judy came up off the floor. She played to two weeks of full houses, as if her collapse had been only a dream. But she had been too ill to rehearse; and when the opening night show was over, and she was taking her encores, she could not help it, she broke into tears.

Who was there to know how badly she needed the money?

The fact was that Judy's finances were now crashing down upon her. All that year whatever she earned was eaten up by past debts, liens, taxes—unpaid bills ranging from $901.25 for four days in May at the Ambassador Hotel in Chicago, to $2,400 for limousine service, $8 to a baker, $1,200 to a Las Vegas haberdashery, $13,065 to her lawyers, Bautzer, Irwin & Schwab. The list was endless.

A. Morgan Maree, once her business manager, was hired again, at $10,000 a year, in the hope that he could help keep her head above water. As early as February, she had to borrow $25,000 from Capitol Records against her earnings; that month, a Federal tax lien of $32,405 was slapped on her Decca Records account, and she received a letter stating that a check for all moneys due her was being sent to the government, as well as any future royalties until the debt was paid. But she kept going: she had to earn money, and she concertized; she appeared on *The Sammy Davis Show*, Perry Como's *Kraft Music Hall*, an *Ed Sullivan Show*; she sang in Toronto, in Hollywood, Florida, in Miami, in Charlotte, in city after city.

Something new had been added to her show: now the first part featured the Allen Brothers and, though Sid Luft was always on the periphery—and sometimes called in to see if he could help maneuver her out of her worst difficulties—most of 1965 and 1966 saw the same succession of concerts, triumphs and disasters, illnesses and hospitalizations, that had marked the years before.

And yet there was a subtle difference. She took happiness where she could find it. In the midst of everything, in April 1965 she, Mark and the two children had flown for a two-week vacation at Waikiki Beach, where she and Mark had been so happy that week they stole from the world. (This time they fought, were in each other's arms, fought, and once Judy cut up Mark's suits with scissors so skillfully that he didn't know it until he tried to put them on.) When they returned, there was a desperate Cincinnati appearance where she canceled the second half of her show, claiming a virus, and enraged patrons actually jammed her dressing room shouting for their money back. Melbourne, it appeared, had marked the beginning of a period of a kind of audience treatment she had never known before, and a blow from which it would take a long time to recover.

Bills flowed in to Judy, to the offices of Karl Brent, her secretary, to the offices of Schwab, her attorney.

She had hired Maree as her financial adviser and business manager (or magician) on July 8, 1965. From that date an endless series of letters with bills came to her from him, some dating back years. He had worked out her fixed monthly charges: $600 for automobiles; house payment, $700; monthly staff salaries, $3,000; monthly legal retainer for Bautzer, Irwin & Schwab, $3,718; $833.33 to Morgan Maree, Jr.; $1,283.88 to Guy McElwaine & Associates, public relations; and $3,000 a month to Sid Luft.

This last had been an ingenious arrangement. In their property settlement—California had community-property laws—Judy wanted to keep the Rockingham house and its furnishings. The house was appraised at $300,000, the furnishings, artwork, books, etc., at $100,000. Sid said, "Let Judy keep the house and everything else, but I want half of $300,000, paid out over a five-year period." Judy didn't have the money. Sid said, "All right, pay me $3,000 a month, and she keeps everything." But Judy could not afford to pay him $3,000 a month, so he was employed as her producer, so she could write off as much of the amount as she could for a tax benefit. She had had virtually no income in 1964—that had been her year abroad with Mark—but considerable expenses for their extensive travel, for the house they rented in Chelsea, for her critical illness, for hotels, parties, entertainment.

Since most of these monthly charges were not paid because she was always living on advances, or finding her moneys seized by creditors or liened by the government, the debts (and the interest) mounted, month by month.

But she kept busy. Her engagements, in number and effort, were staggering. From Forest Hills, New York, to the Greek Theatre in Los Angeles—where a six-night engagement was cut to two when she broke her left elbow tripping over her dog at home, and had to sing the second night in great pain, her arm in a cast, spelled, fortunately, by Mickey Rooney—to her triumphant two weeks in Vegas, to a tremendous appearance at the Houston Astrodome.

As 1965 moved into 1966, the dunning letters to Schwab increased. On March 9, 1966, there was a sheriff's attachment on the Rockingham house; unless something happened quickly, it would be sold for moneys due. There was a Tiffany bill of $1,600, due over a year. On May 6 Schwab himself wrote a letter to the lawyer for the Mark Hopkins Hotel, where Judy's bill had remained unpaid for months. There was no money to pay the bill, he wrote, and since the IRS had levied on "all moneys due my client," the filing of a suit by the hotel, and even the winning of a judgment, would be little more than an academic exercise at this time because there were no assets which could be subject to execution.

A month later S. A. MacSween, of Maree's firm, wrote Judy directly. If there was one thing she wanted not to be harassed about, it was the complexity of money and those enormous debts. How could she owe so much when she had worked so hard? And hadn't her salary and fees been good? Why, for that single night at the Houston Astrodome on December 17, 1965, she had received the highest fee ever paid a performer there—$37,500. But look how that tremendous sum alone had vanished into thin air: reduced by $4,000 held in escrow, $1,300 for fares and excess baggage, $3,750 commission to Creative Management Associates, and an additional $28,735 due them for past commissions they hadn't been able to collect even off the top of her fees because of government liens, which took everything—hers and theirs. That came to more than the $37,500, and she'd still be responsible for taxes on that sum, not to mention salaries of staff and accompanying acts, and expenses involved in the production. "Take from my purse what you need, Baby," Ethel Gumm used to tell her. That purse was not only empty, but not even there. . . . So MacSween decided he must put it down, tersely and unmistakably:

DEAR JUDY:
As you know, we have been running into some serious problems and we have been unable to pay your bills. We had hoped that we would receive a little money from your Hollywood Palace engagement on April 1, to keep things moving. However, the IRS stepped in and filed a levy and have taken the entire check against your income tax liability.

I wanted to advise you that this is getting to be a serious problem and we have unpaid bills with no funds to make payments of over $60,000. In addition to the foregoing bills from hotels, travel bureaus, stores, there will be a large income tax payment due with the 1965 return, which you will of course be unable to meet. I know that Herb Schwab has gone over these things with you, but I thought that if it was submitted to you in writing, it would be more understandable.

He then listed individually more than 120 creditors.

And by June 1966 Maree could write to Schwab: Judy's assets, $12,163.29; her liabilities, $122,001.08.

By then, the Garland-Herron marriage had already fallen apart. Within six months after the ceremony they separated, and ultimately divorced. There were many reasons. From the first Herron had been restive at not acting. He had asked Judy's agents to get him something; he'd read for a part in a new play in New York. Everyone was enthusiastic; he had won the role. He was so excited he ran first to tell Liza, whose apartment was nearby, and then to Judy, at the Regency, where they were living. "I got it, I got it!" Judy looked at him strangely. "What's the matter?" he said. She said, "No, sweetheart, you haven't." He said, "I know when I've got something." She said, "They called, they said you were brilliant, but after you left, someone came in and just read you off the stage."

Was it possible that she had intervened to make sure that his evenings would be spent with her, and not on stage in his own play? One thing led to another. There was that bizarre episode when she telephoned Peter Lawford before dawn one morning back in California.

She was sobbing: something terrible had happened, he must come quick. He dressed hurriedly and rushed over. Judy met him at the door; blood was streaming down her face. Peter put his arms around her and led her to a lamp so he could examine her face. There appeared to be many fine, small cuts. "My God, what happened?" Peter asked. Judy managed to catch her breath long enough to say, "Mark went after me with a razor." Where was Mark? He had vanished. Was anyone else in the house? Only her maid, Judy said, in her room.

Peter helped Judy to the den and laid her out on the bar, under a bright light, while he tended to her. Peter could find no antiseptic anywhere, so he used vodka, dabbing her wounds as gently as he could. He knew Judy had nothing less than 100 proof in her bar, which meant 40 percent alcohol. Then he got hold of some BFI surgical powder, and tried to get the powder to coagulate the tiny nicks. He told her, "Stay there, don't move," and went down the hall to the bathroom. As he passed the maid's room, the door opened and she beckoned him over. She whispered, "I think I ought to tell you, Mr. Lawford. It wasn't Mr. Herron who did that—she did it herself."

Who was to know, in Judy's despair—no money coming in, debts piling up, her house threatened with foreclosure, her husband going off on his own career—what she had taken? They separated, and Herron moved out, with indignant statements from both sides.

Judy's statement was given to the press by Tom Green, a Dartmouth graduate in his late twenties, employed by Guy McElwaine with Judy as his specific assignment.

Green was handsome, dark-eyed and efficient, and the transition seemed surprisingly smooth. Now Green, not Herron, escorted Judy about, willingly and admiringly. He had met her just before she married Mark, when McElwaine himself took Green over to the Rockingham house the preceding October. Green was trembling, because of what he'd heard about her, and how she turned strong men into gibbering idiots if she was in a bad temper.

He had expected to find a miserable, mean old bitch—and he found, instead, the funniest-looking, screwed-up, unmade-up, untamed little frightened rabbit awaiting him in her front hall. It astonished him: he kept looking up for a star, and here was this girl standing in front of him, her right arm still in a sling, one sleeve ripped off her dress so the sling would fit through, she wore slippers, her hair wasn't done, and she looked terrified.

When Guy introduced them, Green thought, astonished, *This kid is scared stiff!* Then it was his job to be on hand when she did a late-fall *Ed Sullivan Show* in 1965 at CBS. He was amazed at the attitude of some on the set. If she asked for a bobby pin, someone would groan, "Oh, for Christ's sake, what does she want now?" A little later she said, "I'd like a hot dog." "Oh, Christ," came the comment, *sotto voce*, "now she wants a hot dog! There aren't any hot dogs around here."

Green spoke up. "Judy, if you want a hot dog, I'll get you one—all I have to do is go next door." He did so, and she thanked him. She had to wait for the cameras to be adjusted. She said, "I'd like a little music." So Green hurried through the building, found a portable radio and brought it to her, so she could listen to music while she waited. Someone said to him, "O.K., O.K., but you'll get tired of this shit, you'll see."

But he didn't. By early August 1966 Green had quit McElwaine to work full time for Judy as her personal publicist at a reported $500 a week, was managing her house and accepted everywhere as her escort.

Autumn 1966.

In the den of her Rockingham house, the house which was about to be sold from under her at a sheriff's sale to pay back mortgages, she sat alone, hunched before a tape recorder. Of all her terrible times, this was one of the worst.

Everything seemed to be falling apart. She was more than $100,000 in debt; in addition, she owed more than $400,000 to the Federal and state governments.

It was before dawn. She sat and tried—as she had so many times before—to put something down for her autobiography. She spoke bitterly; she was trying to sum up "all my forty-four goddamned, marvelous, failing, successful but hopelessly tragic and sorrowful years." Swifty Lazar, seeking to find some money for her, had told her: "Just begin anywhere, just put it down as it comes to you." She had begun pouring out her rage and frustration and sense of betrayal from childhood on:

". . . I laughed at myself when I should have cried! and I've cried because I had every reason to. I'm so goddamn mad! I'm an angry lady. I've been insulted, slandered, humiliated . . .

"I'm a woman. I'm not something you can wind up and put on the stage that sings a Carnegie Hall album—and then is put back into the closet. . . . I wanted to believe, and I tried my *damnedest* to believe, in the rainbow I tried to get over, and I couldn't!" Her voice rose in anger and challenge. "So what? Lots of people can't!" It was not easy for her to talk about herself, she said (as she had said so often before). "I went through five years of psychoanalysis going back over a life that was no good to begin with, no fun." She had gone into this "true Judy Garland or Frances Gumm project" purely for money, she went on. "I deserve it. I've sung, I've entertained, I've pleased your children, I've pleased your wives. I've pleased you, you sons of bitches!" Her voice rose to a shout: "And you can't deny that!" Out had come the ever-present hate-love relationship between performer and audience, the performer knowing that the audience expects and demands to see, hear and feel what it has come to see, hear and feel, and, if deprived of that, is ready to tear apart the performer, to hoot and ridicule and shame her off the stage—hadn't it happened in Australia, hadn't it happened in Cincinnati? *We-love-you*, the audience cries, but it could turn on you like ravening wolves if disappointed, and if the audience becomes not wolf but sheep, if the audience becomes pitying and embarrassed, how much more the performer tears herself apart.

566

The tape is silent for a while; then her voice begins again. There is no indication whether this is hours or days later; her voice is slurred, it is a medicated Judy, whose bitter attacks on virtually everyone—agents, Sid, others: CMA, CBS, MGM—poignant as they are, must be taken with that realization. Sometimes the words are hardly intelligible; but, however medicated, it is a heartbreaking lament, and doubly so in view of the gaiety and joy she could produce in herself, and in the thousands she had held in the palm of her hand, and would again in the future.

"I want my money. . . ." Her voice was hoarse, like a man's, painful, as though every word were ground out from her. "All . . . I . . . want . . . is . . . my . . . mon-ey. I worked hard. . . . They used me and used me. . . . It was a month of blackmail. I want my money . . . the money belonging to me and to my children . . . That's all. *Just my money.* I worked hard. I was never protected in any way, emotionally, financially. . . . Promises that I was given that I would be financially independent never came true. . . . I have been used physically, mentally, emotionally." And again, a plea almost unendurable to hear: "*I . . . want . . . my . . . money.* I want my children to have money. . . . I was told I would never have to work after I did my television series. I was . . . not protected. . . . I hate people who have stolen from me. I won't have it any more." As she continued to speak, she sounded a little less medicated, it was wearing off, there was a growing sharpness to her words, an emotion breaking through: "I was a patsy. But they'll all pay. I want my mon-ey. I want it all *now.* Nobody will be protected by me, because of emotions. I want things straightened out. And I'll ruin—*ruin*—through newspapers, through courts—I've been blackmailed, I've allowed it because I was lonely and scared. . . . I wanted friendship and protection and I didn't get it. I'm not only ashamed of myself for being so—a terrible thing!— dependent! But I'm not that way any more."

She paused. She cursed MGM. She warned—and these were her last words before only silence: "Metro and every son of a bitch who's ever stolen from me better get it up—or they'll be hauled into court just by *me* and exposed!"

She had nowhere to turn, so, despite her inclusion of him among the people she inveighed against, she turned to Luft.

She had come back in late August from Mexico, where she had gone with Tom Green to appear at El Patio, one of Mexico City's top

nightclubs, for $15,000 a week—twelve days, fourteen perform-
ances, with a stipulation that she must be paid in cash at the end of
each night's performance—an engagement from which she expected
to emerge with a net of $20,750.

She was able to do only two shows. Though the Mexican critics
used such words as "glorious" and "electrifying" for her opening
night, she canceled after the second performance. The altitude—
Mexico City is nearly eight thousand feet above sea level—and the
pills she took worked together to give her laryngitis, and she had to
be replaced suddenly—and ironically—by Betty Hutton, who had
replaced her years before in *Annie Get Your Gun*.

So the $20,750 dwindled to a fraction and, after costs and other
expenses, to less than zero.

She had not seen Sid, nor talked to him, for months. On his visits
to the children in the Rockingham house, she had absented herself.
She telephoned him now. "I want to see you, Sid," she said, and he
came over in the afternoon. She started pacing back and forth. "I
don't know where to begin." He kissed her on the cheek. "I don't
know what to do." And then: "I'm broke. I have no money. I have
no resources." She showed him the sheriff's attachment on the
house.

She needed his help. The children needed his help. "I'm too sick
to work. We're going to be on the street, Sid." He had been shocked
when he first saw her. She could not have weighed ninety pounds,
her face was drawn, but she was sober. He suggested that she come
that evening to the apartment he'd taken on Manning Avenue, near
Westwood, where she would be away from the children, from everything, and he and she would talk it over and "I'll try to map things
out." Sometimes Joey and Lorna spent the night at his apartment,
but Judy had never been there.

When Judy came there, they had a nearly night-long discussion.
Sid said he would help. She had made certain deals in her capacity
as president of Kingsrow. Sid suggested she hire a lawyer who would
give him power of attorney to represent Judy to renegotiate certain
contracts she had made. This was done, with the result that $25,000
was realized, and Sid obtained an extension on the sale of the house.
With the money Judy and Tom Green were able to go to Lowell,
Massachusetts, where Tom introduced Judy to his parents; then they

568

visited Dartmouth, and Judy returned to spend Christmas with the Greens, climaxing the holiday season with the announcement that Tom had given her an engagement ring.

39

MONTHS BEFORE, at a fashionable house party in Connecticut crowded with show-business people, entertaining themselves happily in a huge rumpus room, Judy found herself talking to a tall, vital, dark-eyed woman who'd just been introduced to her as Mrs. Irving Mansfield, wife of a well-known TV producer. It was "Judy, meet Jackie," and the two hit it off at once. "Do you play poker?" Judy asked. Mrs. Mansfield smiled yes, and Judy said, "You're my girl. Let's play."

They joined a table of others. As they played, Judy asked, "What do you do?"

"Well, I'm a writer," said Jackie, "and I wrote a book about my dog."

Judy squealed. "Oh, *Josephine!* Right?" She loved dogs, she had read the book, she was delighted with it. Mark Herron was still with her then, and she called him over excitedly. "She wrote the book about the dog." Then they all bent to their cards, and Judy said, "You know, poker's my big game." Jackie said, "Yours and mine. When I was in Broadway shows, I used to make more money playing with stage hands than I did with my salary."

Judy burst out laughing. "Hey," she said. "I like you. Let's be friends."

Jackie felt constrained. She had just finished writing a book called *Valley of the Dolls*—for a long time after, Judy would call Jackie Susann "You know—Irving's wife"—and the book was not to be published for some time. If Judy read it when it did appear, she might think Jackie had based Neely, the pill-taking young singer, on Judy.

So Jackie came out with it. "I'm a writer now, Judy—no more acting—and I've written another book. It's a *roman à clef*—"

Judy, curious, asked, "What's a *roman à clef?*"

"It's a novel supposedly based on real people. This is not a cute little book like *Josephine,* and there's a character in it that a lot of people are going to think is you, but it's not."

Judy stared at her. "Why? Is she a child star?"

No, Jackie said. "She makes it when she's seventeen. But she's a third of a dance team—"

Judy pursued it. "Does she have a Mickey Rooney in her life? You know, I was in love with Mickey when I was young, but he never took me seriously. He treated me like a boyfriend, like we were pals."

"No," said Jackie. "This is nothing like that." And ventured: "This girl is on pills. Everybody in the book is on pills."

"Everyone?" Judy asked, and laughed.

Then, after a moment: "Was she a child star at Metro? Or at any studio?" No, said Jackie. "And there wasn't a Mickey Rooney in her life?" No, said Jackie. "And she wasn't a big star as a child?" Jackie shook her head. "She was a vaudevillian."

"Well, I *was* a vaudevillian," said Judy.

"But she was third-rate," Jackie said.

"So was I," said Judy.

"But then at seventeen she makes it in a Broadway show. And she doesn't get into show business until her second marriage. She becomes a hell of a good singer, and she's married several times and she has twin sons."

Judy dismissed the whole thing. "Oh, that's not me."

The meeting and the story are of interest because after *Valley of the Dolls* was published and became one of the best sellers of all time and Fox bought it, Jackie Susann was telephoned by David Weisbart, the producer. He had a problem: he had a cast so far of three lesser stars—Barbara Parkins, who had done soap opera, Sharon Tate, whom few had heard of, and Patty Duke, who was great on Broadway but was just building a name in films; and while Jackie had no control of casting, Fox wanted her to be happy, because they respected her ability to publicize the property. What would Jackie think of signing a really big star, Judy Garland, who hadn't done films for a long time and could use the chance, to play Helen Lawson, who many thought (though Jackie denied it) was based on Ethel Merman: a tough, hard-talking, hard-drinking but great singer? Jackie's first choice had been Bette Davis. No, said Weisbart, they were making everyone younger in the film, and, with Barbara, Sharon and Patty,

Bette would be too old. They needed someone in her forties, and Judy would fit the bill.

"Physically she's all wrong," said Jackie. "Why, you could blow Judy over with a strong wind. I don't care how iron Judy is underneath, on the screen she appears vulnerable."

After further discussion Fox decided they still wanted Judy as Helen Lawson. Patty Duke would play Neely. Sid was consulted, hired John F. Dugan, an agent, to negotiate, and in February 1967 Judy received a letter from Dugan: he'd made the deal, $75,000 for eight weeks, then $25,000 a week if she was needed longer, Judy required to sing only one song.

Judy excitedly telephoned Liza about it in New York, where Liza was preparing for her marriage to Peter Allen the following month. "I'm going to do a new picture," Judy said excitedly, "the latest book by Irving's wife."

Liza said, "You don't mean *Valley of the Dolls?*"

Judy said enthusiastically, "Yes, it's a best seller now. It's No. 1." Had she read it? asked Liza, who had read the book. "No, not yet," said Judy, "but I hear it's great and a marvelous part." Liza herself had tried to buy several properties for her mother and herself but they had all fallen through.

"I don't think it's a good part for you, Mama," said Liza. Because there had been talk that Neely was based on her mother, Liza was under the impression that this was the part Judy had been asked to play. Liza talked about a horrendous hair-pulling scene in which Neely pulls off Helen Lawson's wig and tries to flush it down the toilet. It made Liza shudder. She didn't want, she didn't think the public wanted, to see her mother do a thing like that.

"I'm an actress," Judy retorted.

"Yes, but we're talking about a commercial movie. If it was an Ingmar Bergman film, it would be different."

Judy said, "I think I can do it."

"Yes," said Liza, "there's no doubt that you can do it brilliantly, but do you want to do it? Do you think the public would like to see you in that role?"

Well, said Judy, Mayer refused to let her play the Esther Blodgett part in *A Star Is Born* when she was at Metro, saying, "People don't want to see you as the wife of an alcoholic." And Judy had done it, in her own picture, and it had become a classic, even if she didn't win an Oscar for it. So she responded to her daughter, "That's not the point. If I'm good in the part, the public will buy it."

"But, Mama, do you *want* them to buy you in that role? Because you can make them do it, you're a good enough actress to make them buy you in anything—"

But Judy would not be budged. She'd play the part.

Now she had to fly to New York for two purposes: on March 3, Liza's wedding to Peter, and the day before, a joint press conference with Jackie Susann to announce Judy's acceptance of a role in *Valley of the Dolls.*

As a wedding present Liza wanted an old Irish linen tablecloth. Judy simply didn't have the money. One of her close friends and long-time romances was John Carlyle, an actor, who lived with a group of fellow actors and artists on Norma Place, a short street of old-fashioned, white-painted frame houses with picket fences built about Norma Talmadge's original mansion in the silent-film days. It was a beautiful area, fragrant with bougainvillaea, and one reason Judy wanted to play in *Valley* was that she hoped to use the money to buy a duplex apartment for herself, Lorna and Joey on Norma Place, after selling her Rockingham house. It represented old, lovely Hollywood to her. Carlyle was tall, slender, handsome, witty, as were the others who formed a clique of Judy admirers who adored her, often flew en masse to her openings at Vegas and later put her up on visits to the West Coast after the house was sold the following summer. Sid knew some of them; more like an uncle than an ex-husband, his instructions to John and his friends were always "Take good care of her." John's favorite name for Judy was Madam Gumm, and he was sometimes an even more constant companion than Green.

Judy borrowed money from Lionel and Alma, the butler and maid, checked out tiny caches about her house where she hid money—as she did Ritalin—and she and John went to the Maison Blanche, a fine Beverly Hills shop, to buy Liza her gift. They were about to settle on a cheaper tablecloth because it cost $88—all Judy and John could scrape up between them—when the salesgirl said, "But, Miss Garland, you have a charge account with us." Judy said, "I do? Oh, how marvelous! All right, let's have the one you showed us first. And charge it." Her face lit up, and they walked out of the store giggling, Judy saying, "My God, when will they get their money? How will they get it?" Then she went home to get dressed, and John took Joey to buy a gift for Liza—a bottle of bath salts—and Judy and Joey flew to New York, followed by Sid and Lorna.

Now everyone was in New York, Fox putting Judy up at the St. Regis with the children, Sid meanwhile negotiating a series of summer concerts in the East to follow *Valley*. He was now booking Judy again, Vern Alves at his side—the old team was back.

At the press conference Judy was absolutely brilliant. Jackie Susann felt like the amateur, and it was *her* book that was being filmed, and she was the lady author who was supposed to be sharp, tart and knowledgeable, and Judy the vulnerable, helpless one. It turned out to be nothing of the sort.

When Jackie met her now, at her suite at the St. Regis, moments before they were to go down to the conference, Judy treated her first as though she were Hemingway. "Miss Susann!" she said, holding out her hand. Jackie thought, *Maybe she's forgotten how we met in that rumpus room and played poker and told stories.* But she followed suit. "Hello, Miss Garland." Then Judy said, "Well, I guess we're ready," and the two went into the elevator taking them down to the floor where the press awaited them in a room set aside for the purpose.

As they got off the elevator, Jackie stayed behind a step, to let Judy go ahead. "You're the star," said Jackie. "No," said Judy, "the author is the star," making a graceful gesture indicating that Jackie should walk into the press room first.

Jackie did. It was packed. Only then did she realize that she was the opening act, she was a minor introduction; Judy would make the entrance. Which was precisely what happened. Judy entered, and the place erupted.

Now they were both at the microphone. A reporter asked Judy, "Do you think there are a lot of pills being taken by people in show business?"—a scare question, they thought, for Judy, but one she couldn't get angry at, since pills were a legitimate issue in the book. Judy said, "Why don't you talk to the Lilly Company? They sell a hell of a lot of pills all over the world." Someone else asked, "Do you think actors tend to drink more than other people?" "No," said Judy, "I've met more drunken newspapermen." When it came to questions about the story, the plot, the book, Judy, who really still hadn't read it, fielded them skillfully by saying, "Why don't you ask the author?

She's right here." Question after question, whether intended to be embarrassing or not, Judy answered to perfection, and Jackie was revising her opinion of Judy.

As they walked out, Judy looked at Jackie. It wasn't "Miss Susann" any more. "How'd we do, Jackie?" And then: "Little did I know that day when I met you in that basement rumpus room that this is the book you were talking about. Now," said Judy, completely in command of the situation, "let's go out and have a few drinks."

Jackie got hold of herself. "Judy, I just can't go now. I've got to rush off." When their photographs appeared in the press, there was Judy, poised, her hair perfectly coiffured, her long, perfectly shaped fingernails, the essence of delicate femininity, while Jackie, with the blunt, short-nailed fingers of a writer, looked like the Dragon Lady. *Helpless little Judy?* Jackie thought. *My God, she always manages to appear as poor Little Butterfly, but she knows exactly what she's doing.*

Liza's wedding went off beautifully. The girl who had grown up riding on Van Johnson's back, dancing at Gene Kelly's garden parties, entertaining at Lee Gershwin's gatherings, was now a married woman. Now mother and daughter's lives alternately merged and separated, Liza now on Broadway and Judy in Hollywood, or joined together in New York or the West Coast. Liza was on her way, and Judy, the mother, was eminently proud—and jealous—Judy being Judy.

Judy was due in California a few days after the wedding. At 4 A.M., March 6, Charles Cochran, a handsome young New York pianist and singer, one of John Carlyle's close friends, had a telephone call. He had been a fan of Judy's from childhood. When he was fifteen, he had met her and Sid at a party in Palm Beach given by Tony Pulitzer, after Judy's sensational 1951 Palace appearance, and had seen her last when Carlyle threw a party for her at his Norma Place house. The guest list consisted of Tom Green and five of Carlyle's friends, and Hedy Lamarr, Cheryl Crane (Lana had been invited, couldn't make it and sent her daughter instead) and Judy. An incredible party, with wit, gaiety, delicious food, unbelievably beautiful surroundings, and Judy singing with a voice pure as a bird's. Cochran now was playing a Second Avenue club in New York, and had just come home.

The call came from a young girl. She introduced herself: "I'm Lorna Luft." It was Judy's daughter, whom he had never met. She had gotten his number from John Carlyle, whom she'd just called on the West Coast, because Mama had been up all night, sick, without sleep; she had to leave in a few hours to fly to the West Coast to start shooting *Valley of the Dolls,* and she needed stimulants, Ritalins, wake-up pills. Judy asked Lorna to call Carlyle because John might know someone in New York who had pills, for Judy simply had to be alert, at her best and not groggy, or everything would be ruined. Carlyle had said, "Try Charlie Cochran," because Charlie, as a nightclub entertainer who worked until dawn, might have wake-up pills. Cochran said, regretfully, no, but he knew a lot of entertainers who kept late hours; he might be able to get some. He'd check and let her know. He contacted several people, including Mickey Deans, a pianist-singer who lived down the street, who was one of his closest friends and with whom he used to take turns as pianist at Jilly's bar after Bobby Cole's departure to the Coast for Judy's TV show.

At 5:30 that morning Deans, also in his early thirties, met Cochran in the lobby of Judy's hotel and they went up to her suite. Joey and Lorna opened the door. Both men thought, *Such incredible kids: how they manage, how capable they are.* Cochran introduced himself: "I'm Charlie." Judy had told the children he was a good friend of Carlyle, whom everyone liked. Because of the hour and the situation, Cochran introduced Deans as "Dr. Deans" to the children. Dr. Deans would help Mama.

Deans went into Judy's bedroom, gave her what he had brought, remained very briefly and left. It was his first meeting with Judy.

Cochran stayed for a while, to make sure Judy'd be all right; little by little she began to wake up, to put herself together: the makeup went on, the hair was done, the spirits perked up, the records started playing (it had been silent when they came in). Judy had been sitting up in bed in her nightgown, seemingly half-alive, utterly exhausted, when they arrived. Apparently she hadn't slept for a long time. Now alert, alive, she was listening to her own record—*Judy at Carnegie Hall*—to bolster her morale. Then she was on the phone, there were lawsuits she was involved in, she was calling her agents, she had problems with her house. . . . Cochran thought admiringly, *If this had happened to me, I wouldn't be able to fly out there, to laugh, to crack jokes.* . . .

Then Cochran went back home and slept all day. He assumed Joey and Lorna slept all the way back to the Coast.

At the beginning of *Valley* on the Fox lot, everything seemed fine. Preproduction sessions, wardrobe fittings, all went perfectly. David Weisbart telephoned Jackie, who had come out with Irving because she was to play a Hitchcock-like bit role in her own picture. Weisbart was ecstatic. "Oh, God, Jackie, Judy recorded the song, it's fantastic. It's not the final take, of course, but it's going to be wonderful. Her voice is just great."

Several evenings later, when Weisbart and his wife and Jackie and Irving were dining at the Bistro, David said, almost too casually, "Look, if anything went wrong with Judy . . . do you have anyone else in mind?"

Jackie thought, *Oh, oh!* Well . . . perhaps Anne Baxter, perhaps Rita Hayworth . . .

Weisbart did not bring up the subject again, but Jackie talked to Barbara Parkins, who described what was going on at the set, once shooting began. Judy came in at 7:30 or 8:30 A.M., with a cheery "Hi! Hi!," had her hair done, was very funny, made you double up with laughter at her stories, but at eleven o'clock everyone was still waiting for her to come out of her dressing room. She wouldn't come out. Mark Robson, the director said, "All right, we'll try it after lunch." But after lunch when Judy appeared, she wasn't drunk, she was glazed. Obviously, she was on something.

The second day Tom Green telephoned Sid, who had been keeping away from the set, trying to line up future projects. "You better get over here, Sid." When Luft walked into Judy's dressing room, one glance and he knew what had happened. He could imagine how terrified she was, and how she had been stoking herself with pills to give her confidence. "I'm a little rusty, Sid," she said. "But I'll make it all right. Tell them out there not to worry—I'll get it." She was wearing a beautiful sequined pant-suit costume created for her by Travilla, a distinguished designer. But there were no takes that morning. Nor could they get Judy out of her dressing room that afternoon. "I'll be right out—I've got to fix a snag in my blouse." But she didn't come out.

The third morning she mislaid her portable caps for her front teeth, and there was a wild dash about town with John Carlyle, to have them made, and by the time she got back to the set, and was made up to her satisfaction, it was 3 P.M.

576

Her first appearance was an occasion: workers came down from the catwalks to see her, Barbara and Sharon and Patty were like awed schoolgirls, Joey and Lorna had hurried over after school, Tom and John stayed in the background—but all this delayed the shooting.

Judy's opening scene, in her role as an over-the-hill, ill-tempered singer, was with Barbara Parkins. She had to say something like "Who the hell are you? Get out of here!" Whether it was the pills, the fear, the pressure of expectation, whatever, the words emerged with surprising mildness—her "Who the hell are you?" was kind of halting, poignant. Robson, had he been Cukor, would have said, "You're marvelous, Judy, but be a bitch! Freeze my blood again!" Instead, Robson said, "Darling, that's wonderful, but just try to make it a little rougher, a little tougher." Somehow Judy couldn't get it: take after take, and nothing that could be used that day.

At home, at the Rockingham house, the situation was desperate in another way. There was no food in the refrigerator. Lorna telephoned Dr. Marc at 11 P.M. one night. "Come over, please, please, we have nothing to eat, Mama needs something to put her to sleep, she has no medication." Dr. Marc knew that Judy was taking some 200 milligrams of Ritalin a day—twenty tablets, instead of the usual three. Now Lorna pleaded with Dr. Marc: "Mama's screaming, she's in agony, she needs something, there's nothing in the house, you have to come over!"

Dr. Marc, with his medical kit and a bag of hamburgers he'd hurriedly bought, drove swiftly to the Rockingham house. Judy needed something now to calm her down. He could not give her a hypo; it had to be a specific sedative that wouldn't harm her, what with everything else she'd been taking. "I'll be right back," he told Lorna, and began driving through Brentwood, looking for a pharmacy still open. None was. He drove into adjoining Santa Monica. None open there either. He turned around and drove all the way back into Beverly Hills, found the Beverly Wilshire Hotel pharmacy just about to close, got the sedative, paying for it—Judy's credit had been cut off at all the pharmacies, and they actually would have feared to issue any medicine if they had known it was for her—and speeded back to Rockingham Drive. By now it was nearly 12:30 A.M. He had spent more than an hour traveling about to find the dose—six capsules—he would give her.

He hurried into the house—and Judy was locked in the bathroom, where she had knocked herself out with a sedative she'd had all the time! He could not even get in to treat her.

"Where'd she get it?" he demanded. Lorna could only say, "She must have had it hidden away."

Dr. Marc thought, *She made all this trouble for an extra dose,* and when he hadn't returned quickly enough, she had dug out what she had hidden. She was anticipating the panic that would come later after whatever he might bring would have worn off!

As he drove home that night, he recalled another episode in which she had locked herself in her bathroom. It had happened not long before. That time he had been able to get her out and put her to bed, and treat her. She had been able to rouse herself enough to talk for a few minutes, and she had spoken lovingly of her father, his gentleness and tenderness toward her. Then she had asked suddenly, "Dr. Marc, is it true that my father was a homosexual?" In all these years, she had never said anything like this to him, and he had been taken aback; he had heard rumors, but had no evidence that would confirm them. His reply was: "I have no reason to believe so." She had put out her hand and held his for a moment, and then she was asleep. But obviously this was something she had been turning about in her mind —and for how long? Who was to know what she might have heard far back in those before-dawn quarrels between her parents? He could only wonder how much of this, if true or believed, had had to do with Judy's attitude toward Ethel, and Judy's own understanding of and attraction to the homosexual and bisexual men who were so much a part of the show-business world and so often in her audiences.

But that episode was not Dr. Marc's principal concern at this moment. The first thing next morning he called the studio. "Judy has got to have somebody with her—she has no money, you should provide it." Fox hired a nurse to stay with her, they gave Judy a check for $5,000, they did everything they could to enable her to go on with her work in *Valley of the Dolls.* It did not help.

David Weisbart finally telephoned Jackie Susann. "We'll have to fire her. We've been shooting almost a week, Jackie, and we haven't one foot of film we can use. You know, she's used to the star system where, when she comes in, everyone asks, 'Are you all right, Judy? O.K.? O.K., do it, kid, do it.' And maybe it means eighteen takes, but so what—they do eighteen takes, and the eighteenth is fine, and they've got it." But here Judy was up against twenty-three-year-old

Barbara Parkins, who'd learned how to do two full soap operas a week in *Peyton Place;* against Sharon Tate, who'd done a couple of nondescript films but had Roman Polanski to help her; against Patty Duke, who'd had a Tony, an Oscar, and was all of twenty years old —and suddenly Judy couldn't keep the pace. "Those kids are so adroit, so quick," said Weisbart.

Jackie sighed and hung up the phone. Then she went into Judy's dressing room. There it was: the huge pool table she had demanded and pictures of Liza, Lorna, Joey and Jack Kennedy. Jackie, taking her own clothes out of the closet—she had finished her bit in the film, and they had allowed her to share the room—saw a little white pill on the floor in a corner of the closet. She picked it up and put it to her tongue. She recognized that bitter, telltale taste. Demerol. Jackie had undergone a mastectomy and had been given Demerol. The maid saw her with the pill. "Oh, that must be one of Judy's nerve pills," she said. "If she knew she'd dropped it—when she drops one, she tells me, 'My God, they're diamonds, find them.'"

Poor Judy, thought Jackie. So she had been taking Demerol, at the least, to ease her tension, and all it had done was make her float, impervious to everything.

On Thursday Judy was fired, but it would not be official until it was announced the next day. That day, Jackie and Irving were to leave for New York. Late Thursday night John Dugan, Judy's agent, telephoned Irving. Judy's fired, he said, and it's so terrible, because no one called her, no one talked to her. "She feels dreadful."

Jackie said, "Give me her number. I'll call her right now."

When she tried to reach her at her home, a maid said Miss Garland was taking no calls. Jackie said, "Just tell her that Jackie Susann called, and is very sorry."

Judy called back five minutes later. Jackie heard a medicated Judy: "Lissen, I wanna ask you something. Am I a star?"

"Of course you're a star," said Jackie.

"Well, then, where did everyone go?"

"What do you mean, Judy?"

"Well, I put in a call for David Weisbart, he won't talk to me, I put in a call to Mark Robson, he won't talk to me, I even called Darryl Zanuck in New York. Where'd everyone go? I'm fired. . . . I'm calling a press conference and I'm going to say I quit."

Jackie asked, "Judy, how much money do you have?"

"None," said Judy.

"Well, you realize that if you say you quit, you're not going to get any money. But if they fire you, they've got to pay you off. So, is it your pride or your money you want?"

Judy: "Oh, lady, you're very bright. You're really wonderful, you're the only one who called me." She sobbed. "Jackie, I want the part back . . . I had a virus."

Jackie: "Judy, you were loaded with sleeping pills and Demerol. Right now you've got pills in you."

"No, I haven't!"

"Judy," said Jackie, "I've known too many friends on pills. I know the sound of pills as against the sound of booze. You're loaded with pills; I don't know what you're on, but you're on either Seconal, Nembutal, Ritalin or you're on Demerol."

"Well," said Judy plaintively, "I have a virus, that's all. I don't know what the doctor gives me."

"Judy, you're a chemist. You know what pills you're taking."

"Well, let me call a press conference. I'll tell everyone I was fired."

Jackie tried to explain again to her, patiently. "One, you don't call a press conference on Friday, you won't get anything on Saturday. The weekend's no good. Why don't you call a big columnist and tell him—" Suddenly she had an idea. "Look, Judy, I'm flying to New York tomorrow. I will call Darryl Zanuck. They want my next book. I'll demand one more shot for you because they haven't got anyone to replace you yet. But you've got to promise this weekend that you will dry out, and if I'm going to go on the line for you, you've got to do this for me."

Judy, sobbing: "Oh, I love you. I'll never forget you, you're a great lady. You're a star. Can't you come over now, can I come to your place?"

"No, Judy, I'm packing. I've got to make the plane."

Next afternoon the Mansfields were already on the plane when a TWA agent came aboard. There was a telephone call for Miss Susann from Judy Garland. Both left the plane and Jackie went to the nearest TWA phone. "This is Judy," came Judy's voice. "I just told them I was Judy Garland and to get you off that fucking plane."

Jackie: "What is it, Judy?"

Judy: "Are you going to tell Darryl what you said? Is that a promise?" Yes, said Jackie. "Well, fuck em!" cried Judy. "I don't want it.

I want it in the paper that I've been fired, and I'll have all the public on my side, then they'll have to come back to me because I'll dry out like you said, but I want it. Who do I call?"

Jackie suggested Earl Wilson in New York. Judy: "What's his number?" Jackie gave it to her: JU 6-6969.

Judy giggled. "That's a funny combination of numbers." Then she suddenly began to cry again. Jackie asked, "Judy, are you alone?"

"No, I've got very dear friends here with me, I'm all right, I want the part." She was sobbing.

"All right," said Jackie. "Promise me you won't take anything, and I'll go to Darryl tomorrow. I'll give him first and last refusal if they'll give you a shot for another week. Now, I'm really going on the line for you."

Judy: "O.K., and I'll tell you how much I will be able to do it. I've got my doctor here, and he'll talk to you." A man's voice came on the phone. "Hello, Miss Susann." Jackie asked, "Is she all right?" He said, "Yes." Jackie went on: "Judy says she'll be all right to go to work Monday. Doctor, will she be able to report for work on Monday?"

"She says she will."

"Look, Doctor," Jackie said, explaining how she was sticking her neck out for Judy. "I'll do this if you give me your word as a doctor, can she do this? Can she hold out for ten days to make the picture without taking pills?"

"She says she can."

"Then you're not saying *you* think she can."

"I'm telling you, Miss Susann, she says she can."

"What is your opinion?"

"No."

At this point Jackie heard Judy's voice: "What are you saying?"

Doctor: "I'm telling Miss Susann you say you can be there Monday and do the job." Jackie heard Judy say, "That's right."

The call ended. Once in New York, Jackie went to Zanuck. He told her how much money they had already lost because of Judy. They could not take her back.

Meanwhile, Judy had called Sid. "They fired me!" She was in tears. "They fired me! I don't know why they wouldn't give me a chance." And then she really began to cry. "Sid, get it back for me!" as though he could work miracles.

Sid tried, but of course it was impossible.

He went back to Judy. "Fuck 'em!" he said. "The hell with the goddamn thing. That part wasn't for you anyway. And you didn't come out so badly." Judy stared at him. Fox had been decent about it; they'd agreed to pay Judy half of the promised fee—$37,500—for her time. Sid said, "That's not too bad." The agent took $3,750, the government took $23,500, Judy was left with $10,000—and the knowledge that at least $23,500 in government taxes had been paid.

At that, things were beginning to pick up a little. Sid had worked out a concert tour; Vern, always his capable self, moved into the Rockingham house to close it, after Sid negotiated its sale in May so that thousands of dollars of back taxes were paid, and another $15,000 made available to Judy. Just the month before Judy had had an experience with the Rabwins that represented both a low and a high in her life. When the City of Beverly Hills gave a dinner at the Beverly Hilton Hotel honoring Marcella Rabwin for her civic activities, the Rabwins invited Judy, Lorna and Joe as their guests, to sit at their table. It would help bring Judy out of her financial doldrums, for a while at least. Jimmy Stewart would be master of ceremonies, Rudy Vallee would be among the entertainers, and, as a special attraction, Judy promised to sing. She would do it for Marcella.

Then in June she'd start off the concert tour at Lee Guber's Westbury Music Fair, celebrating her forty-fifth birthday with Tom Green en route, in the Pump Room at Chicago's Ambassador East.

Not only had Marc and Marcella Rabwin been through much of what had happened to Judy in these recent years, but more than once Dr. Marc had filled the pantry at the Rockingham house; more than once he had been there to comfort and reassure Judy, busy as he was; he was now chief surgeon and one of the trustees of the Cedars of Lebanon Hospital. He was immensely proud of the honor now being bestowed upon Marcella, and delighted that his Judy and her two children would be their guests on this great day.

But, as with all things relating to Judy, events took their own turn.

Rudy Vallee was the last entertainer before Judy, who would close the evening. And Rudy, it developed, insisted on using all the time allotted to him—and more. He sang and sang, he told jokes, he would not give up the stage. It grew late. He had begun a long, long routine, and he was going through with it. Meanwhile, Judy, all prepared, excited, sitting at the table of her oldest friends with her children, began showing more and more signs of nervousness.

Finally she excused herself. Marcella thought, *Oh, my God, I hope she's only going to the bathroom.* But Judy, not only nervous but angry at Rudy, and terrified as she had to wait longer and longer to go on, lest she make a spectacle of herself before her best friends and her children, had gone to the bar to fortify herself.

She came back: Marcella could make her out at the back of the hall, standing there, watching Rudy, waiting for him to finish, and when he launched into another song, she suddenly turned and vanished again.

When Rudy finally got off, Judy was drunk. While she tensely waited for his routine to end, her terror had become overwhelming, and Marcella knew she really now didn't want to do it—but her children were there, she was doing something for a woman she loved, and she had to do it.

She was introduced to cheers, and weaved her way to the stage. What happened then was a calamity. Marc and Marcella cringed. Judy was impossible. She wandered about the stage with the microphone, not reaching anybody, mumbling her songs, asking the audience, "What do you want next? No, that's too big," or turning to the orchestra: "No, we'll do—" then, to the musicians a moment later: "What's the matter with you!"—an exhibition beyond belief.

Marcella could only think, *It's too awful. Poor Judy. She wanted to do so well,* and thinking, *My party, my big night, and Judy, of all people, who wanted to do this for me, who would do anything for me, is ruining it for me.*

If Rudy had refused to get off the stage, Judy was even worse. She had been terrified of going on; now it was almost impossible to get her off. Finally she was helped down, and rejoined the Rabwin table. A place was made for her and she sat down, heavily. The man who led her to the table had followed her with the microphone. At this moment someone in the audience cried out, as always, "Judy, sing 'Over the Rainbow.'"

Judy put out a trembling hand and took the microphone. And sitting there, holding the microphone before her and looking at Marcella, she sang her song. It was incredible. Her voice was perfect, it was exquisite, it was in perfect pitch, every emotion she had ever expressed in that song she expressed then. It was the most sudden, the most dramatic change. She turned an embarrassed, hostile audience into an adoring one. Marc and Marcella were in tears—tears of relief, of gratitude, of wonder, of the knowledge of Judy's awareness of how disgraceful she had been, how agonizing to those she loved so dearly, and how she had risen to this moment as only she could.

40

To LAUNCH JUDY ON THIS, the latest resurrection of her career, a new corporation had been formed—Group V—the third in which both Judy and Sid were involved, each with its own checkered history. The first had been Transcona, under whose auspices *A Star Is Born* was made; the second was the Gamma Corporation—"GA" for Garland, "M" for Michael, Sid's first name, and "MA" for Judy's proud career as a mother—the aegis under which Judy had given many of her concerts.

Group V was different. Sid had met in Los Angeles a former New York stockbroker named Ray Filiberti, about thirty-eight, who drove a Rolls-Royce, admired Judy and suggested the corporation. Under it Sid and Judy would have employment contracts, Sid as president and producer to receive $1,000 a week and Judy guaranteed $1,500 for every night she performed. Filiberti would advance the necessary funds, and hold all the stock. It was, indeed, an unusual ironclad document, for by its terms Judy possessed nothing: not her voice track, her music, even her own services, and deliberately so, so that there would be nothing for the government to attach during her tour. Filiberti, owning all the stock, owned Group V; Judy and Sid were his employees. But in return, Group V would pay all her expenses—household, hotel, medical, entertainment, clothes, aides— the complete retinue of a star. In addition, they ultimately made an arrangement with the IRS. The IRS would take $300 each night from Judy's $1,500 and $100 each week from Sid's $1,000. It seemed an ingenious resolution of their problems.

Judy and Filiberti, who was clever, amusing and exuded confidence, took to each other at once, especially after Judy, having read through the clauses of the contract, discovered that one of them demanded that she give him twenty-four hours' notice before she died. The same rapport did not exist between Judy and Filiberti's wife, Sherwin, who was twenty-eight, a tall, beautiful blonde of considerable independence.

Filiberti tried to explain to Sherwin that a comeback for Judy was most difficult. She was approaching fifty—actually, she was forty-five —she had been to the top, bottom, top, bottom, a dozen times; and he concluded that she was really strong only when Sid was at her side to support her.

At the moment, Sid was in a motel with Judy in Westbury, where she was to open that night—June 13—at Lee Guber's Westbury Music Fair—and Filiberti was in New York. Sid telephoned him. Did Ray know a good throat man in New York? Sid had been unable to reach Dr. Coleman. Otherwise, Judy couldn't go on tonight. Filiberti thought, *There goes my $100,000 or more,* so far invested in Group V.

He called a distinguished throat specialist who was visiting his family in Great Neck. Filiberti had his chauffeur drive him in his Rolls to Great Neck, pick up the physician and drive him to see Judy. Sid had said she couldn't speak, she was mentally distraught—"We'll never get her on the stage."

The physician, a man of great dignity, with a stiff white banker's collar, examined Judy's throat. Judy said, "For a throat specialist, you have bad breath."

The doctor reddened. (He did not know this was one of Judy's favorite gambits: she liked to say that Toto, the dog in *The Wizard of Oz,* had such bad breath she could never get near him. Such was her bizarre sense of humor.) In this instance, Judy clearly did not want to appear; she didn't want a doctor to make her well.

The physician said later, to both men, "I don't see how she can go on. Her throat is completely raw." He went back, treated her, came out again. "I might be able to fix it, though. It means spraying her throat between songs each time she comes off the stage. She's on Ritalin, gentlemen—it dries the throat—enough Ritalin, so far as I can determine, to kill three people."

Show time arrived. Judy's first songs were bad: the voice broke. Filiberti realized that, though people came to see Judy perform, they also came for a diabolic reason: to witness a catastrophe. But Judy threw herself into every performance, for a star of such caliber, with incredible intensity. He thought, *Her guts are on the stage.*

Garland had to be Garland.

At a certain point in her Westbury performance she hit a couple of notes that were unbelievable, considering the condition of her throat that night. The audience went crazy. Sid and Ray looked at each other. That's what they needed to kick this concert off. Now the bookings would follow because she'd made it the first night. *She could do it; she had done it.*

The doctor was proud of himself. When Judy walked backstage, the beaming physician said, "Let me spray your throat." She demanded, "Hear that applause? Who needs you?" And she walked away.

But there was a reason for her apparently inexcusable hostility. Sid had warned the doctor: "Don't give her any pills. She will manipulate you into a position in which she will get what she wants from you" —and the physician had remained firm. This explained her reaction to him. He, however, had had enough. "I stop here," he said. "I no longer treat you." And he left.

Judy arrived two hours late at a party Filiberti gave—the new Judy Garland with Tom Green. Ray's wife, Sherwin, had already taken a stand on Judy. "I don't want you to get involved with this woman. I just don't like her." Judy had said to Ray, "I am relying on you." He was someone new and important on the scene. They danced, cut up, laughed together. Later Judy left with Green. But Filiberti knew that from now on he'd be on call. She must win him over for Sid, because a financial backer was good to have.

Westbury *had* started out beautifully. One could not say that Judy and Sid had been reconciled—he was now her manager, held at arm's length. He had hired to support her in the show John Bubbles, the singer and dancer Judy liked, and Rip Taylor, a wild comic. The Westbury reviews were ecstatic; Liza and Peter were there, Earl Wilson came out to cover it for his widely syndicated column, and John Wilson of the otherwise staid *New York Times* wrote: "Her voice was tight and husky at first. . . . Then she reached back for one of her old, familiar belting climaxes—and she found it, all of it. It came through in an electrifying burst of power that brought that eager audience to its feet once more." He caught the adoration: " 'We saw her,' a girl cried ecstatically to a group of friends. 'We really saw her. And I touched her!' 'You touched her!' exclaimed a young man. 'Are you kidding? I kissed her hand!' "

This was the old Judy, *Valley of the Dolls* debacle or not. She brought Lorna and Joey onstage, Lorna singing, Joey playing the drums (Buddy Rich, one of Judy's oldest friends, had given him a drum and a few lessons), and when Sid saw the success of this family combination, which had come about in impromptu fashion—most of the summer engagements were in tent theatres, all quite informal— he incorporated the children into the shows following, in Springfield, Massachusetts, and in Camden, New Jersey, where they found themselves in July.

Somewhere along the line Judy quarreled with Tom Green, and for a while had been escorted about by Paul Millard, one of John Carlyle's friends, and his landlord, on Norma Place. And Sid had a major surprise for Judy. Without telling her (lest it fall through suddenly), he signed her for four weeks in the Palace. "Oh, Sid!" Judy almost forgot their arm's-length relationship when she learned about it.

This had come through unexpectedly. Gwen Verdon had been playing the theatre in *Sweet Charity*, which was to continue until September 1. In late June Miss Verdon became ill; ticket sales began to drop. Sid said to the Palace management, "Why don't you close the show next month and give Judy the month of August?"

Once more Judy was back at the place of places, this time with her children in the show: Lorna, long-legged, singing like a tornado, unstoppable, unflappable, Joey beating his drums like mad, and Jackie Vernon now the comic. Judy was in complete command. She had kept the beautiful, sequined pant suit designed for her for *Valley;* she was slim, beautiful, and her entrance was, again, pure surprise.

The house lights went down; a spotlight roved over the curtain, finally centering on one spot; slowly the curtain rose, everyone expecting to see Judy standing there, bowing to a wild reception. But the stage was empty. At that moment, there were sudden screams and cheers from the rear of the theatre; everyone turned to look: there was Judy, making her entrance, not from the wings onstage, but from the back of the theatre, like a late-comer, waving, smiling, shaking hands as she came forward, letting the people reach out and touch the living magical Judy herself as she made her way down the center aisle to the stage.

Once onstage, it was not only that she sang, that she used all her inimitable graceful little tricks, but that she engaged in the deftest of dialogue with the audience; no matter what came from them, Judy caught it, played with it, replied to it; it was repartee, delightful, captivating, spontaneous, done with wit, charm and enormous personal magnetism. This was no studied casting off of shoes, or practiced spontaneity of tears at precisely the same moment night after night; this was pure Judy.

She missed not a single performance, although she was sometimes on too many uppers (she *had* to take Seconal to sleep, and so she *had* to take uppers to give her even the smallest lift), and was not always at her best. Often she couldn't hit a high note, but the audience never knew it. Sid handled the sound; when she couldn't hit the note, she threw back her head, flung up her hands characteristically and screamed—and at that moment Sid turned up the amplified sound of the orchestra full blast, the audience erupted in applause, and nobody knew the difference.

On closing night the audience did what only a Garland audience would do: they rose and sang "Auld Lang Syne" to her. Paul Millard, sitting with friends in the front row, had them all put their feet against the orchestra pit railing to prevent those who had rushed down the aisles toward the stage from engulfing her. They brought posters of her old movies, and they were waving them to get her attention. They threw flowers onto the stage. One girl actually carried a small trunk to the stage, filled with memorabilia of some kind. And Judy, whose "Born in a Trunk" had made musical-film history in *A Star Is Born*, and in so many of her shows, accepted it with tears.

Outside, the streets were roped off; the police had to knock on Judy's dressing room and say, "We won't be responsible if you don't leave very soon. The crush is getting too much." Somehow she and Paul managed to be escorted to her limousine, the crowds cheering on either side, and as they pulled away, Judy said, "Paul, you look marvelous, I look marvelous," and to the chauffeur: "Driver, please turn on the lights inside the car so everyone can see us." The chauffeur turned the switch on his dashboard—but nothing happened. The interior of the limousine remained dark. "I've been driving twenty-seven years and this never happened to me before," he said, crestfallen. The lights must simply have burned out.

They went on to a party Millard gave for her in a huge apartment on the twentieth floor of 784 Park Avenue, at the corner of East Seventy-fourth Street, loaned to him by friends, and he had decorated it with twelve dozen red roses in her honor. The guests included Robert Fryer, who had produced *Sweet Charity* and *Mame* on Broadway, and Jerry Herman, who'd written the songs for *Mame* and so many more hits, and Sid, and Liza and Peter and the children and dozens of friends. There had been the Palace, 1951, and the Palace, 1956, and now the Palace, 1967—Judy would go on forever!

Paul and another friend stayed overnight. Late next morning they went into Judy's bedroom—she was sitting up in her red velvet robe in the very middle of a king-sized bed, looking like a fourteen-year-old, waiting for them. The moment they entered she invited them onto the bed to sit on either side of her. The sun shone golden through the east windows, the room had red roses everywhere, a huge terrace ran the length of the apartment, and in the distance the bridges over the East River were silhouetted against the bright blue sky. She was in excellent spirits.

"Oh, Paul," she said. "You know that tribute last night, that ovation I had—it was fantastic. And your party was so great. And all these beautiful roses—and to be here with somebody I love so much . . ." She reached over and kissed him. She said, *"I'm so happy!"* And then those snapping brown eyes of hers looked at him, and she said in a gruff, lower, satiric voice, "Who needs a happy Judy Garland!"

She knew, thought Paul. Somehow he felt that one sentence was the clue to her life.

Days before, just preceding the Palace, Judy, Sid and the children had been staying at the Stanhope Hotel, in their separate suites. The Stanhope had been the scene of Judy's melodramatic flight with her children to England, while Sid had been held cursing in the grip of two bodyguards—was that five full years ago?—and Judy now called Sid to her suite.

It was late afternoon, she was dressed beautifully, as though to go to a tea party. "What is it, darling?" Sid asked. More than once, when Judy, Sid and Tom Green had been together at parties, Judy, introducing them, had found herself saying, "You know my husband, Sid—" though they had been divorced for two years, and Tom, her fiancé, was standing beside them.

Judy said now, "Sid, I've done Westbury, Springfield, Camden, all for you, and now I'm going to do the Palace. What about us?"

Sid walked to the bar and poured himself a drink. "I don't quite understand, Judy." Judy said, "You know you understand." Sid said, "I guess you're talking about some kind of reconciliation." She said, "That's exactly what I mean, you and me. You know how I feel about you and I always will feel."

He said, "Well, I feel the same way, but I'm not ready for that, Judy."

She looked at him. "Sid, has something happened to you?"

Sid said, yes, something had happened to him. He meant that emotionally he was a confused and a wounded man.

Judy said, "Don't tell me you've switched and become a fag!" and walked out to an appointment,

The Palace success definitely made New York Judy's home, and while she was still at the Palace Group V had rented for her a brownstone on East Sixty-third Street, a few doors off Fifth Avenue, around the corner from Central Park. She had always dreamed of a New York brownstone; now she had one. It belonged to a popular lecturer on psychology and sexual mores. He had had it decorated in a fashion which convulsed Judy: everything seemed imported from Venice—Venetian-glass decorations, a winding staircase with wood banisters and hand-blown twisted Venetian-glass rods, and eight-foot-high blackamoors guarding each level, and a priceless Buddha, as well as French and Chinese statuary. Judy claimed the Buddha stared at her when she tried to sleep, so she had it perched precariously on the slanting outside ledge of a window; and that the blackamoors followed her around the room, so she moved them out to the small lawn in front. She had her trademark—an enormous pool table—placed in the center of the magnificent dining room, sending a massive imported dining room table seating eighteen into storage. A large Chinese mural with dancing girls covered one wall of the music room; Judy amused herself throwing darts at the girls. The place depressed her, even though there were lovely bedrooms for Joey and Lorna and quarters for two maids. She complained to Filiberti. "It's like living in a mausoleum." "Well," said Ray, "I'll cheer it up." He hired Enzio, a guitar player at the Sherry-Netherland, for $300 a week to come each night as a wandering troubadour to keep Judy company. Every time Sid or Ray dropped over, they heard Enzio singing "Come Back to Sorrento," accompanying himself on his guitar, as he wandered about the house, upstairs and down. At the same time Bobby Cole, whom she'd originally hired away from Jilly's during her TV series, and was now her conductor at the Palace, would drop over to entertain her on a huge antique gold piano. Delores, his wife, would sometimes come along.

Then, one morning, Ray got a 2 A.M. call from Judy. "Ray . . ." Her voice was like a stage whisper. "I feel sick . . . I'm dying. . . ." He was to come over, quick. While Sherwin watched, controlling her anger, Ray dressed, kissed her apologetically and rushed over. All the lights were on, all the television sets were on, their sound muted, all the radios were on full blast, everything was going simultaneously. A terrified Judy clung to him. "I want to get out of this house! This man who owns it—he's a sex maniac. I found dirty books, I found a whip—"

Filiberti tried to explain that these were books on sex and props used by the lecturer, and calmed her down. It was the first of what would become a series of predawn summonses.

Yet she could play little-girl let's-pretend games—if that was what they were. If she decided to go out quite late, Alberto, her hairdresser, would come to the house at night. Once he knocked on the door, and there was no answer. He walked in. The place was dark. He waited in the hall. He had never liked the place; the statues, huge and menacing, frightened him. Suddenly he saw something moving ghostlike down the stairs. He began to tremble. Then as the figure neared, he saw it was Judy, dressed in a clown costume. "Hello," he said, but she didn't answer, continuing silently down the stairs. When she neared him and saw that he was frightened out of his wits, she exclaimed, "My God!" and began to laugh, turned around and hurried up the stairs. "Come up and fix my hair," she called.

During the day fourteen-year-old Lorna came into her own. She ran the house for her mother, and took the responsibility magnificently; rarely had she had that much attention before. Now she was looking after Judy, picking out what she should wear, loaning her her clothes—Judy could wear Lorna's dresses, and often did—and frequently Lorna would drop over to Liza and Peter's and borrow $10 for groceries. But nights could be difficult.

The fact was that at this period in her life Judy generally slept all day and was up all night. Since she could not bear to be alone, Lorna often had to keep her company. Lorna would say, "Mama, I'm so tired," and she'd say, "Wait—wait." When Lorna and Joey slept with

Judy, all three in Mama's bed, neither child really slept. Lorna was nervous that her mother wasn't sleeping. Judy could carry on conversations, reminiscing about her childhood, lying there, staring at the ceiling, and talking, talking. "You know why it's painted like that?" she'd ask, and Lorna would think, *Oh, God, Mama, go to sleep*, and then Judy would continue. "What did you do today?" It was now 5 A.M. "I can't remember." "You can't remember what you did today?" "Mama, please, I—" If Lorna or Joe answered the question, Judy would go on to something else.

Lorna had never seen anyone like her mother: she would come into a room, put the radio on, put a record on, put the TV on, keep the lights on and go to sleep. If they traveled, and came to a town where there were no late TV programs, Judy would turn on the test pattern. Sometimes, when Lorna would think she was asleep, and whisper this to Joey, there would be a sigh from Judy. "Lorna, are you awake?" "Yes"—reluctantly. "I'm hungry," Judy would say. "Mama, it's five in the morning." Judy would make herself mashed potatoes and lima beans, mix them together and eat a bowl happily.

Or, if all three were lying together in bed, Judy would sometimes tell her favorite stories. One was about a French train wreck. Scores of people were hurt, they were all laid down on the adjoining track, bleeding, bruised, bones broken, groaning, waiting for the Red Cross relief train—which came along and ran them all over again. Or about the two hippopotami that had stood for centuries face to face in the La Brea Tar Pits in Los Angeles without saying a word to each other until one day one said, "I keep thinking it's Wednesday." That was Mama's humor—wild.

Once when Lorna told Judy she wanted to go into show business, her mother just looked at her and said, "Why? Why are you going to do this to me?" Lorna said, "To you? I'm not doing anything to you." Judy said, "Don't hurt me so much." Lorna couldn't figure out why it would hurt her. Sometimes her mother was very difficult to understand.

Like Liza, Lorna and Joe had to become teen-age psychiatrists and first-aid specialists. Each began to know their mother well at a different period in Judy's life. But all had the same concern. Lorna would have to think: When was the best time to tell Mama this—or that? It was more than the average child's fear: *I'll get in trouble*. It was: *I'll get her in trouble. Suppose she gets really upset, then she won't*

be able to work and Daddy will get upset, and then I'll get in more
trouble myself. . . . I'll have to pick the right time.

Yet there were times when Judy loved to play the hostess. She decided one night to make a shepherd's-pie dinner. This was the one dish she felt was her masterpiece. She herself would cook dinner for Liza and Peter, Joey and Lorna, and Vern and Sid—a dinner for seven. She went about it efficiently. First she dictated a shopping list to Lorna, and since one did everything in style, she called up Carey Cadillac and had a chauffeured limousine take Vern, Lorna and Joey out to do the buying.

First, however, she needed money. She said to Vern, "Find Sid." No one knew where Sid was, save that he was in New York. Judy made it sound simple. Vern and the children drove through half the town—they began at two o'clock—until they found Sid at his tailor's. "I need money," Vern explained. Judy was making a simple dinner; he had to buy a dozen chicken breasts, a leg of lamb, various vegetables and the like. Sid gave him $200. It seemed a considerable amount of money, but they both knew Judy—particularly since one of the first orders on Lorna's shopping list was to go to Hammacher Schlemmer, one of New York's most expensive stores, and buy an electric meat grinder, twelve crystal goblets and twelve liqueur glasses.

After Hammacher Schlemmer came the meat and vegetables. Vern's favorite shopping place was a huge supermarket on the West Side, at Broadway and West Ninety-second Street. The imposing Cadillac drove up, parked, and while the chauffeur waited, Vern, Joey and Lorna began pushing shopping carts through the store. Lorna's handwriting was all but illegible; as much time was spent deciphering as buying. But in the end, they had bought the chicken breasts, the leg of lamb, potatoes, peas, lettuce, salad dressings, condiments and other sundries Judy wanted.

They had spent nearly the entire $200 at Hammacher Schlemmer, so Vern had to dig into his own pocket to meet the grocery bill.

By the time they got back to the house, it was six o'clock. They deposited the groceries in the kitchen.

Judy walked in, in high spirits. "Well," she said, "you know, it's too late now. I simply don't have time to do a leg of lamb, grind it, then do the chicken breasts. Call Sid."

Vern: "What time is dinner, Judy?" Judy: "Nine o'clock. On the dot." And she added the cabalistic words, "Find Sid" (again, no indication where he might be) "and tell him to go to P. J. Clarke's and get a dozen chicken breasts, have them ground, and do the same with the roast leg of lamb."

All she would have to do, then, was open a can of gravy.

Vern found Sid, ultimately. He was hysterical. "I knew this would happen." But they drove to Clarke's, got what she wanted, brought it to the house, and around 11 P.M., with their dollars' and dollars' worth of food in the refrigerator untouched, the electric grinder as pristine as the moment it had been bought, they sat down to dinner.

Meanwhile, there was work to do. Judy had done splendidly at the Palace: the largest gross in the theatre's history. Then came a tremendous one-night outdoor stand on the Boston Common—a free concert sponsored by the Knickerbocker Beer Company for its hundredth anniversary, which brought out 110,000 cheering people— and there were to be, after that, half a dozen other engagements. With everything else, Judy was to be, in the next few weeks, as busy as she had ever been, working heroically. By October, she was ready for a vacation.

The idea came from Sid. Sherwin and Ray were going to London for two weeks on October 11, Ray to book some halls and look into other deals. Why not take Judy along? Sid, living at the Plaza, a few minutes from Judy, had been on call twenty-four hours a day—he needed a rest badly, too. He was beginning to suffer neuralgia headaches of his own, so painful that Ray had to hold Sid's head under a tap of nearly searing water to relieve the agony. London would be a wonderful change of pace for Judy, Sid said. "She has Dirk Bogarde there, and a lot of friends. . . ." And so it was agreed. Sid had another reason. He wanted not only two weeks' rest from Judy, but two weeks to relax with Marianna Hill, a young actress who had been quietly his girlfriend for many months.

Judy was delighted to go. Sid rode with her and the Filibertis in the limousine to the airport; they kissed good-bye—as though they were still married—then Sid returned to town—and to Marianna.

Once aboard their plane, at 5 P.M., Sherwin and Ray would have liked to sleep—everyone had been up all night and busy through the day—but Judy was alert, full of vigor and eager to play gin rummy. So Sherwin, who literally dragged herself onto the plane, sat alone, nursing a martini, while Ray and Judy, also with martinis, began

594

playing cards. The three of them had the first-class lounge to themselves, and Judy had made herself comfortable, changing to a robe and slippers.

As they began to play, Judy's eyes became tearful. "What's the matter?" Ray asked. "I miss Sid," said Judy. "You've got to make one promise. I want him to come to Europe. We were so happy in Europe together." Ray didn't quite know how to take this; he knew that he was dealing with half a dozen personalities when he spoke with Judy. But whether or not she was playing a game now, she was confessing a love for Sid—at this late date and after everything.

Ray said, kiddingly, "I'll put my property in Spain up against your $200,000." She certainly had no $200,000, but you couldn't gamble with Judy Garland for stakes of $200. O.K., said Judy. They ordered more drinks. Judy began to lose, and grew angry. Ray thought, *I better start losing.*

At this moment the captain of the plane came back from the cockpit. Judy was trying to win back what she lost, Ray was saying, "My hotel against your $100,000," and the captain was talking to Sherwin, a few seats behind, when Judy turned and said, "Captain, will you do something for me? Shut your flapping yap?" The captain reddened, and Sherwin said, "Judy, that's no way to talk to this gentleman."

Judy turned to her: "And I'm tired of hearing your flapping yap back there, too."

Sherwin, no mean belligerent herself, especially with several drinks in her, said, "Judy, you better apologize right away."

Judy: "I'm not apologizing to you—even if you have all the money in the world. There's no way I'd apologize to you."

Now Sherwin exploded. "You broken-down singer," she cried. "Ray and Sid may have to put up with your bullshit, but I don't— I don't have to earn my living from an old worn-out bag like you. . . ." And within a few seconds the two women were hurling their drinks at each other, and a battle royal was going on 35,000 feet in the air, until both women quit of their own accord, Judy sitting by herself and Sherwin pummeling and kicking Ray, who was defending himself as best he could.

Finally, when she paused, he said, "My God, what have you done? You know she's had a few drinks, and pills, and Sid is depending on me."

Ray ventured to go up to Judy and sit down with her. "Judy—"

"Ray, I'll do business with you any time, but I don't want any part of your wife."

"Fine, Judy, just relax yourself and be calm."

Now the plane was coming down. Ray was in a dilemma. He couldn't leave Judy alone, he had to escort her off the plane—but that meant letting his wife get off by herself, in which case he might have a very angry wife on his hands. He thought, miserably, *I should have brought Vern along.*

While all this took place in the lounge, in the rear the entire planeload of passengers had been watching with great interest.

By the time they got off the plane, the news had spread and they were surrounded by reporters. Judy said to Ray, loudly: "I'm returning to New York on the next plane."

A reporter asked, "Why is that, Mr. Filiberti?" Ray thought fast. "While we were in flight, we got a wire that Joey Luft, Judy's young son, is running a high fever, we've got to return at once—"

Judy interrupted. "That's a lot of shit!"

Sherwin had gotten her luggage and flounced off. "To hell with you and your friends. I never want to see you again." She took a cab into London, to the Dorchester, where they had all made reservations.

Judy, meanwhile, was holding a press conference. Filiberti thought, *I can imagine what she's telling them,* and then he realized that he had left his attaché case with Judy. He had tried to get away as quickly as possible, so as to have no more questions to answer; he had had a few brushes with the law in the past and wanted as little to do with the press as possible. But that attaché case—in it were all Judy's pills. That had been his responsibility. If she got hold of all those pills . . . He thought her problem so serious—he was not yet aware of her survival power—that whenever he and Sid took a hotel room on tour, if at all possible they took one across the building setback from hers, so they could look into her window and watch her all night.

He had to get that attaché case. Judy was nowhere to be seen. He began running through the airport, trying to avoid reporters, hiding at intervals in one shop or another, looking for Judy. Then he saw her, waiting for the next plane, his attaché case next to her. He grabbed it. It was empty. "Judy," he said, "now cut the crap. Where is the medication?"

Judy said, "I'm not giving it to you."

Ray: "Look, I want those pills." He fought with her and got them back simply by wrestling her purse from her and removing the pills from it.

Judy boarded the next plane back to New York. Ray took the following one, an hour later. He used the time to telephone Sid, waking him at 4 A.M. in New York. Sid knew all about it: Judy had already telephoned him. She was humiliated by Sherwin and she was coming right back. Would he meet her at the airport? "To hell with it," said Sid to Ray. He wasn't going to pick her up. "What she's put us through and what she's going to put us through." Please, Ray begged. Sid finally agreed to send Vern to pick her up.

Then the reporters in New York at the airport. Someone asked Judy, "Miss Garland, were you—er—high when this fight took place?" Judy retorted, "I sure was—thirty-five thousand feet in the air."

What smoothed things over for a while was another coup by Sid. He had swung a deal at Caesar's Palace, the newest, glossiest, most luxurious hotel in Vegas, beginning November 30: an unprecedented one show a night for $30,000 a week and other inducements, which no entertainer had yet achieved.

Judy really didn't want to do Vegas. She had walked off a show that New Year's Eve because of an inattentive audience. Vegas really wasn't for her; the audiences weren't sensitive, sophisticated or, like so many audiences for such women singers as Judy, Dietrich, Sutherland and Streisand, crowded with homosexuals, who loved her. Vegas audiences were interested in gambling, eating, drinking and talking during the entertainment.

But she went anyway. Sid had made it easier for her by taking along Paula Wayne, a well-known singer and friend of Judy's, whose manager, Alan Sher, also acted as Judy's manager. At each performance when Judy wanted a rest, she'd say, "There's a dear friend of mine in the audience—Paula Wayne. Paula, won't you come up and sing a few songs?" This gave Judy a respite for at least ten minutes each evening. Also, Judy had secretly telephoned Tom Green to come to Vegas for the last two weeks—he was now to be in her good graces again.

She was angry at Sid. There had been a party earlier at El Morocco, in New York, at which Sid had shown up, finally, with Marianna on his arm. Sid and Judy were divorced, Judy had remarried and divorced since, she had a fiancé—certainly Luft was entitled to take out another girl. But he knew it was a risk. Because Green was then still on her blacklist, she had telephoned John Carlyle to fly in from the coast and escort her to the party. But she was still jealous; she wanted Sid, she wanted Ray, she wanted John. Each time Sid danced with either Marianna or Sherwin, Judy cut in. "I want to dance with this man," she announced, and there she was, dancing with Sid. Several times when Sid was dancing with Marianna, she hurried up to the ladies' room to have him paged over the telephone, without giving her name, just to disrupt him. But Sid refused to answer the page. He knew his Judy.

All this helped explain Tom Green's sudden reappearance on the scene in Vegas after a four-month separation.

On December 4 word came of Bert Lahr's death; Judy, saying backstage she was overcome—her Cowardly Lion was dead— refused to go on. Finally one of the hotel owners announced that she would not appear, adding angrily, "She may never appear here again." All tabs would be picked up and the audience was invited into the lounge to see Eartha Kitt as the hotel's guests.

The next afternoon Ray visited Judy. "You're going on tonight?" Yes, said Judy. "But you must fire Sid Luft."

Why? asked Ray.

"I don't want Sid on the premises," said Judy.

Ray used all his charm. "Well, Judy, you know, Sid's a friend of ours, he's a great help."

Judy: "I insist on it; otherwise I'm leaving, right now."

Ray went downstairs and found Sid. "Sid, the only way I can get her on tonight is to fire you." Sid retorted, "Fuck her. I'm not getting fired. Tell her any goddamn thing as long as she gets on."

Ray dutifully went up to Judy's dressing room later. "Judy, Sid is fired."

Judy: "I want him off the premises."

Ray: "I can't do that. The man has no money, I'll have to give him a lot of money to leave the premises—"

Judy: "I don't care what it costs." Finally, however, she agreed that Sid could leave later, but as soon as possible. And Vern, who had come along, had to leave, too. O.K., said Ray.

He thought, *How long ago was she crying how much she missed him, that he was the only man in the world for her?*

While Judy was onstage, Sid was backstage in the dark on one side, Vern on the other, both hiding behind pillars. Sherwin, not to cause further trouble, hid behind a third.

Judy went through the first portion of her show. When she returned for the second, she caught a glimpse of Sid, hiding behind his pillar.

She said to the audience, "Ladies and gentlemen, I need help. I am working for two people who are worse than Goebbels and Göring."

From the audience, not quite knowing what Judy was talking about, applause and shouts. "We're with you, Judy!"

Ray, backstage, to Sid: "What do we do if she gets the whole audience to storm back here and lynch us?"

What enlivened the days at Caesar's Palace was the presence of John Carlyle and two of his friends—Tucker Fleming, whose father was a distinguished neurosurgeon, which impressed Judy, and Charles Williamson, who shared with Tucker one of the most beautiful houses on Norma Place, with a lovely swimming pool bordered with cypress trees forty feet high. The three men flew up—each handsome, witty and urbane—and all were Judy's special guests at a front table. "Now, darlings," she had told them, "I want you to be at this table"—not only for the security of their presence and adoration, but so that, when she wished, she could lean down from the stage and pick up one of their drinks to wet her throat.

She was enchanted, too, by her new conductor, Gene Palumbo, whom Alan Sher introduced to her for her Vegas appearance. Palumbo was something of a musical prodigy: he was only twenty-two. When Judy first met him in her brownstone, her reaction was: "Why, he's a baby!" But she found him skilled, worshipful and a marvelous audience for her stories, and helpful when she forgot lines. She stood onstage, appearing to sing her song to him—actually, he would be whispering the lyrics to her. To Palumbo, she was "the kindest, dearest, sweetest person to work for," and he got her to do new songs and songs she hadn't done in years. He was so youthful that he always carried a briefcase hoping it made him look older. Judy loved that. He remained her conductor from then on. (Later, when Lorna achieved her own career as a singer, Gene became her conductor and musical director.)

But the year ended with a disaster—for which Sid blamed himself.

Originally it promised to be a coup. Judy would be the first performer in the Felt Forum of the new Madison Square Garden in New York, beginning Christmas Day. She would sing "The Battle Hymn of the Republic," with a huge chorus; Lorna and Joey would participate, Lorna with her own chorus of youngsters, all dressed in white sweaters, white pants and white shoes—a seven-day holiday show for parents and children, to run through New Year's Eve. Sid arranged this while Judy was still at Vegas. Now, after he had signed contracts, hired a choreographer, the youngsters, a male chorus, orchestra, costumes, everything, Judy said, "I won't be able to do it, Sid. I'll be too tired from this." Sid, whose headaches had now become excruciating neuralgia attacks, for which he took codeine which whacked him out for hours at a time, said, "My God, we can't cancel now!" Finally Judy said, "Oh, I'll do it, but I don't like it, you're making me do it, and don't forget: If anything goes wrong, it's your fault." Sid had heard these ominous words before, and felt even sicker.

Everything went wrong. The Garden had a public-address system suitable for announcing prizefights to audiences of thousands, not the sophisticated sound system required by a singer. Judy's first visit was appalling; she stepped into a bucket of wet cement. The place wasn't finished. She found herself in a huge structure of steel seats and concrete, and her dressing room turned out to be the men's locker room. (She said, "Those urinals are rude; the least they can do is put some plants in them.") Despite everything, Judy did enormous business, but she sounded flat opening night, because of the PA system, and as the curtain fell, she summoned Filiberti: "Cancel the rest of this date. I'm not going on."

"Judy, you've got to go on. We have more than $150,000 in this show, and we're having a tough time paying for the stuff—I'm still having new costumes coming in without paying for them."

Judy: "I hope they beat the two of you up." And then: "Would Frank Sinatra sing under these conditions?"

Filiberti had to say, "No, he wouldn't. But you're not Frank Sinatra. We're in debt to Uncle Sam for $400,000, and if you miss a performance, everybody reads something else into it. You're perfectly legitimate in your right not to go on with this concert, a star of your caliber, but—"

They argued until three in the morning. He saw to it that the sound system was improved, but she complained that Sid and Ray had been to blame, and the fifth night she refused to appear. She had a sore throat from adjusting to the PA system, she was doubled up with pain, and finally she spent New Year's Eve dining with Tom Green in her hospital room at the Medical Arts Center. At the Garden there had been havoc: shouted demands for return of money, Ray dashing about to find cash to pay off, management refusing certain payments to Group V because Judy had canceled. Sid, taking double whiskeys for his neuralgia and, when that didn't help, taking Seconal, managed to buy Christmas gifts for the children, set up a Christmas tree next to the pool table, and then vanished to Acapulco to forget everything.

A wild, catastrophic ending to a year that had begun so promisingly.

41

JUDY WAS RUNNING OUT OF TIME. Yet, tracing her days and nights, the people she met, the shimmering cobweb of fantasy she wrapped about them and herself—she had spoken in recent months of marriage to five different men—to watch Judy these days and nights, to hear her, to know her thoughts as revealed by her, requires words, silences, music . . . a wandering of one's imagination amid the mysteries of a personality so complex as to defy any attempt to measure or capture it.

What man was sufficient for her? What stage large enough? What mosaic of words, however intricate, detailed enough? What humor varied enough: baggy-pants, Noël Coward–like, ironic, self-deprecating, delicious, roguish, mischievous? And always the Judy with her arms about somebody, always touching, always in embrace against the lonely everywhere about her. She fought against what she once described as "a space that keeps me apart from the world." She loved, she hated, she yielded, she conquered, she took, and the moment her grasp was sure, it no longer existed, she no longer wanted it; she was a child who had never grown beyond the age of five, but had reached a hundred.

One may apply many labels to Judy: that she was infantile, narcissistic, that in a very early period of her life she was emotionally damaged, imprinted with a fear of desertion and emptiness (perhaps through her near-fatal illness when at the age of one she was separated for almost a month from her mother in the hospital in Duluth, an experience repeated when she was five, suffering that irreparable damage Freud speaks about when an infant is taken from the mother at a crucial period of development). Or that Ethel's all-consuming attention was partly an unconscious attempt to fulfill her own needs, so that Judy was deprived of an ego, an identity, never knew who she was, and thus always played roles, overwhelmingly effective because they were her only reality. All this, in turn, added to the impact she had upon people—that is, they wanted to protect, to comfort her. There was a hysteria there, intensified by all her fears and inadequacies. When that hysteria showed itself in her work, she tore apart her audiences; when it appeared in her private life, it tore her apart and all those close to her. Howard Dietz, for years Loew's chief publicist, put it in words: There's a heartbreak in her, even in the midst of her greatest gaiety. Do we not all of us know that heartbreak, in greater or lesser measure, and is not our recognition of it what makes us kin with Judy—and so deeply touched by her?

Nineteen sixty-eight—an antic year! So full of action—and increasing disaster, halted now and then by nights of such superb performances that even the critics forgot whether the voice was what it had been before—indeed, whether it was voice or phenomenon they had come to see. She was like a whirlwind: a call might come from her from anywhere, at any time; she was like a dragonfly lighting now here, now there; but whatever was pursuing her was alternately catching up with her or halting in its tracks while she paused to thumb her nose at it . . . and moved on, a *force majeure.*

While still at the East Sixty-third Street house, she made a valiant attempt to get Angela Lansbury's role as Mame in the Broadway musical, which Angela was to leave early in the spring. The producers and director were invited by Filiberti one evening to meet Judy at the house and discuss it. The men were downstairs, talking to Filiberti, with Gene Palumbo playing softly on the great antique gold piano, when suddenly Palumbo began the opening strains of "Mame," and down the magnificent Venetian spiral staircase came Judy, swaggering—and she *was* Mame! Dressed in a long, slinky gown, holding cigarette holder and cigarette, she was insouciance, flashing eyes, independence, chutzpa—the works! When the men left later, no one had given Judy a definite refusal, but her antennae were sensitive: the moment the door closed on them, she ordered Filiberti, "Quick! Open the window!" and as their guests were only a few feet toward Fifth Avenue and the cab they sought, Judy was singing "Mame" at the top of her voice, Palumbo accompanying her on the piano. Fifth Avenue and Central Park rang with the sound. She was either telling them, "See, you bastards, what you're getting!" or, more likely, "See, you bastards, what you're turning down!"

Later Filiberti told her it had been no. One man had said, Look, why should I punish myself? Suppose the audience asks for an encore: "Sing 'Over the Rainbow' "! It's not impossible. What happens to Mame? Mame vanishes and becomes Judy Garland. She's just too strong a personality. And will she like her wardrobe, and will she come out of her dressing room, and will she be able to go through with it night after night—who needs all that? So she was turned down. She could have played Mame in masterful fashion; she wanted the part desperately; she had never been in a Broadway musical; she would have had first chance at the movie role; it could have meant so much to Judy.

Then came a dreadful period for her in the East Sixty-third Street house, whether because of the loss of *Mame* or her general fear and despair, her financial problems. The medication she took to cope with the furies pursuing her, the "enemies" all about her, made things even worse. She did incredible things. She raged at Lorna: "You go in there and make your bed." Lorna did so. Half an hour later she heard her mother's voice: "Lorna, come here." Judy was in Lorna's bedroom. "I told you to make your bed! Why didn't you?" Lorna stared, uncomprehending. The bed was unmade. Her mother had pulled it apart and left it as it had been before. "Mama!" Lorna cried, then bit her tongue and silently made the bed again. "That's better," her mother said and left the room.

There was no peace for Judy in the late hours. As one night went on, she raged at herself, at the house, at the children. She broke things. Mirrors crashed, the ornate twisted-glass staircase rods shattered. And finally, battling the pain, the guilt, the hallucinations, Judy exploded at Lorna and Joey, "Leave me alone, get out!"

Lorna and Joey fled. They got into a cab and went to Liza's apartment. It was very late. Lorna rang and rang, and finally the door opened and there stood a sleepy Liza. She put her arms about them and took them in. "I expected this," she said. "It's happened to me." Peter was helpful, sustaining. The three of Judy's children talked. Mama was upset. Mama was unhappy. Mama was sick. Joe summed it up. "Maybe she's just lonely," he said. It made Liza think, *This little woman, rambling about that huge, stupid house, unmaking beds, ranting, alone . . .*

At 3 A.M. the telephone rang. It was Judy. "Hi," said Liza. "How are you?" Fine, Judy said, adding, "What are you doing?" Liza replied, "Oh, nothing." She knew that Judy knew the children were with her, that if they had been told to leave, they'd simply taken a cab to the apartment of their married sister.

"Let me talk to Lorna," Judy said. And presently Lorna was in tears; her mother was shouting at her, "Lorna, don't come home," and hung up. Liza thought for a minute, and called Judy back. "What's the matter, Mama, what's happening?" Judy bore down on Liza. She was a traitor, stealing the affection of her children. . . . Liza thought, *Suddenly I'm an enemy, too.* "I'm sorry, Mama, how can you say something like that?" And Judy: "That's right, stay together, all three of you. Leave me all by myself here, I don't care," and hung up.

A moment later the telephone rang again. Joey answered it. His two sisters had tried, it was his turn. But Judy was still furious; now her words, however, were "If you two don't get your rear ends home, I'll spank hell out of you!" And hung up.

Lorna and Joe didn't know what to do. What kind of situation would they walk into if they returned? And Liza knew she could not help. "I'm scared," she said. "And I know you have to go back, and I know you're scared, too."

Peter took over. "I'll take them," he said. He got a cab and went with them back to the East Sixty-third Street house. Presently, he returned. He shook his head and sighed. "I am now the stinking son-in-law," he said. Judy had sent him out the door—"Get out of my sight!"—and hugged the two children, as if to say, "Oh, that terrible man is gone. Thank God you're home and safe."

So everything ended well . . . all things considered.

She moved out of the East Sixty-third Street house. "I'm bored," she said to Filiberti. "Get me out of here." She and the children went to the Hotel Stanhope, which they had to leave, and then to the St. Moritz, where they had two suites, as always.

Judy was still seeing much of Tom Green, her off-and-on fiancé. Nearly a year before, she had written in a women's magazine that she would marry Tom "in the chapel of his college, Dartmouth," and: "This is the first time I've known what real happiness is." She was to marry him in May of 1968. She began dictating into a recorder another attempt to tell the story of her life. By now, her version of it was an even stranger mixture of fact and fiction: Now she saw herself as the mute little girl in the Children's Hospital in Boston, and when she sang "Jingle Bells" on the stage of her father's theatre in Grand Rapids, those were the first words she had ever uttered.

"Here I was," she said, "this orphan, Frances, who hadn't spoken a word. I'd suffered awful ear infections from the day I was born. I didn't hear very well. Nobody said anything to me . . . I was treated like a misfit. . . . My mother saw to it that somehow I got some kind of food." Had she, Jimmy and Suzy once collected bees in canning jars? Now the story changed: Her sisters took her into a room, opened the jars so the bees could escape, and ran out, closing the door, so the bees could sting her at will. Had Ethel given them all hot chocolate malted milk after they made angel figures in the snow? Now her sisters gave it to her to make her sleep, so she wouldn't bother them. Her father dared pick her up in his arms "only when my mother's back was turned," and if she caught Frank at it, "she bawled hell out of him and he had to put me down again." Then came the day her grandmother, to spite her mother, whom she hated, got her a dress with a bow and put her unexpectedly on the stage in Grand Rapids. "I felt the spotlight hit me and I was terrified and I made the first sounds I ever made by singing 'Jingle Bells'—I hadn't talked, no one had listened, no one had done anything but torment me; I opened my mouth and a sound came out—I was so glad to be allowed to make any sound that I sang seventeen choruses. Maybe those seventeen choruses made up for the silence I had maintained."

But at other times, in rare moments of candor, she would say, "Nobody's to blame; I did it all myself, nobody did it to me." It is not impossible that she set up failures and cataclysmic denouements because deep in her was the need to prove that she could rise from the floor, that she could make the comeback—that curious, incredible arrogance made up of two absolute opposites: a conviction that she was a fraud, without talent, and could only fail miserably and humiliatingly, and an equal conviction that she was the champion of them all, the omnipotent superstar. These two opposing obsessions tormented her, fought within her simultaneously, and when they were distorted or intensified by excesses of Dexamyl or Ritalin or alcohol or Demerol or Seconal or Tuinal or any other chemical compound, Judy found herself ravaged and all but destroyed. It is incredible that she survived such torments so long—not only survived them in life but surmounted them in performances that were of such quality that they are today, years after her death, still the stuff of legend.

She and Tom were not married in May. On March 18, she slipped in her tub at the St. Moritz, injured her shoulder and was hospitalized. There was no money to pay the hospital bill. Sid was in California, beleaguered by troubles ranging from neuralgia to IRS investigations. Judy told Tom, he said, to take her two rings from her dresser at the hotel and pawn them, so they could pay her bill and get her out of there. The next day Tom pawned the diamond-and-jade ring she and Mark had bought in Hong Kong, and a diamond-and-cultured-pearl ring she also owned, for $1,000 at the Provident Loan Society, at Park Avenue and Twenty-fifth Street. Three weeks later Judy had Tom arrested, charging that he had stolen the rings, which were worth, she said, $110,000. She appeared in night court to press the charges on April 11. Tom was released on bail. His lawyer said that Green had been "emotionally, physically and financially sustaining" Judy for the last three years. Tom later drew up an accounting which asserted that he was owed over $48,000, which he had loaned on her behalf, or was due him for salary, or which he had borrowed from his parents—even to the pawning of his mother's ring —in order to carry out these duties. Later the charges against Green were dropped, and she was to resume her friendship with him.

All this had come upon the heels of what can only be described as a heartbreaking fiasco at the Baltimore Civic Center, where Judy and Tony Bennett gave a joint performance in February. Judy admired Tony, as a person and as an artist. It seemed a wonderful idea.

Tony sang the first part of the program; then, after an intermission, he led her on. They were, at one point, to sing together.

But Judy was in bad shape. Apparently she had gotten to her pharmaceutical case. No one knew what she had taken, or how much, except that she had been known to take as many as forty tablets of Ritalin a day. Tony escorted her on stage, holding her about the waist. She could scarcely walk; she balanced herself as on a tightrope, faltering with each step, until she reached the microphone; then she clung to that with both hands. When she tried to sing, the sound was more croak than voice. Sid, watching the performance, though Judy had sent a message she did not want him about, was appalled. She wore one of her beautiful white sequined costumes, but she simply could not hit any notes. He wanted to race to the stage, grab her and run with her somewhere—anywhere—in shame and humiliation. People were already leaving the hall. Judy pleaded with them: "Please don't go, I'll be all right. Don't go! Come back—oh, come back!" A small group of fans ran down to the stage, which was raised five feet above the pit; they formed a ten-tier semicircle at her feet, cheering her on: "Go, Baby, go! Go, Judy!" and she saying, "Don't worry, we'll do something here. We'll get through this, stick with me . . ." her words slurred, but fighting her way back. *And she did the show,* young Gene Palumbo helping support her, keeping her on a stool lest she fall off, she clinging to his arm, as many times before, as he whispered the lyrics that had gone out of her mind.

Later there was an explanatory item in the columns. She had been suffering from food poisoning.

She was everywhere, she was doing everything. She began spending time with Mickey Deans, now night manager of Arthur, a popular discotheque in New York, where she often helped Mickey close up the place at 4 A.M. It is quite possible that she never knew Mickey was the "Dr. Deans" who had been brought over by Charlie Cochran that morning, a year earlier, she so desperately needed to be alert to fly back to the Coast to begin shooting *Valley of the Dolls*—or that Cochran was the man who had brought him over.

One night in mid-May, this year of 1968, about 4 A.M., Charlie, just home from his nightclub engagement, was watching the *Late Late Show* when the telephone rang. It was Mickey.

"Listen," said Mickey. "I'm with Judy Garland. We're finished here at Arthur. I was wondering if I could bring her up for a drink." Sure, said Cochran. "But I don't have any vodka—better bring up a bottle."

Within half an hour they were there. They played records, they talked; Mickey had been about, not only as a pianist at Jilly's but as an entertainer at various nightclubs here and abroad, and was full of stories. After a little while Judy said, "I'm kind of tired, I'm going in and lie down." There were two bedrooms in Cochran's suite. Judy went into his bedroom, turned out the light and fell asleep. He and Mickey talked and drank, and around dawn Cochran went to bed in his guest room.

When he rose, early in the afternoon, there was no sign of Mickey. As he moved about the living room, he saw the door of his bedroom open slightly, a little hand came out with a Bloody Mary in it, and set it down on the carpet for him. He realized Judy was there. "Hi," he said, and "Hi" came her voice. They spent the day together. At one point he went back with her to the St. Moritz, to find a double lock on the door of her suite.

Yes, said the man at the front desk, Miss Garland owed something like $1,800, and she could not get into her suite until something was done about the bill. Something was done—how, Cochran was not clear—but some of Judy's possessions remained confiscated, and Judy simply moved into Cochran's apartment for the next week or so.

Yet she worked. Sid made a deal for her to sing Friday and Saturday, May 24 and 25, at the Back Bay Theatre in Boston, putting her up in a suite at the Sheraton Plaza, while he took another suite with the children at another hotel.

Nobody having seen Judy that painful night in Baltimore with Tony Bennett would have recognized the Judy who swept into Boston, and conquered it. Thursday afternoon, the day before her first night's performance, with Joey and Lorna along, she paid a visit to the crippled and paraplegic at the Chelsea Naval Hospital. She was tireless, going from ward to ward, even insisting that a piano be wheeled behind her so she could stop in each ward and sing "Over the Rainbow" to the men.

A retinue of officers accompanied her. At one point the officer in charge said, "Wouldn't you like to stop a minute and rest—have a cup of coffee perhaps?" Judy said, "What do you mean, stop? Rest? You're a strong healthy man—now get up and let's go. Look at me. I'm a little fragile lady, and I can do it." They continued on. She went to every bed, she spoke to every patient; if a man was asleep, she asked his nurse if it was all right to wake him, so she could hold his hand and talk to him. She had something different and cheering to say to each patient—their faces lit up. She introduced herself, she introduced her children, and after a while Lorna and Joey didn't need to be prompted; they engaged the patients in conversation themselves. Judy, with her soft, soothing voice, with her tenderness, was a healing presence moving through the hospital, and the naval officers with her were beside themselves with gratitude and something akin to worship.

The next night, at the theatre, she was beyond belief. She sang and sang and sang—there was no stopping her. She finished her concert, the audience screaming and carrying on. If her voice was uneven, the spirit and power were there. "Come closer!" she cried, and everyone rushed down to stand en masse about the orchestra pit, and Judy gave them a second show. She sang, she strutted, she joked, she exchanged witticisms, she answered song requests. It was now 11:00 P.M. If the musicians continued, they must be paid overtime. The theatre manager, a short, heavy-set man whom Judy dubbed Mr. Five-by-Five, hurried into the pit to order the orchestra to call it a night. Now there was a confrontation: the orchestra leader, the manager and Judy, onstage.

Judy: "Mr. Five-by-Five, get out of the pit, please, and let me sing. This is a great audience, I can't let them down." The audience itself was ready to seize the manager and throw him out of the pit. Judy egged them on; this she loved, a knock-down-drag-out fight. "Get out of the pit!" she cried again. "Let me sing!" The manager left, shaking with rage and frustration. Double time not only for the musicians, but for the electricians, the lighting men, the stage hands, everyone on the job. And from Judy, onstage, standing in her parade-rest position, defiantly: "I'm going to stay here all night!" Not until nearly midnight was it over. Judy had been onstage for almost two and a half continuous hours. Then she went out to dinner and celebrated in earnest.

There had to be a perverse sequel. It began at 7 P.M. that Saturday, her second and closing night. The reviews had been typical Garland. Word of Judy's bravura performance was all over town. The Back Bay Theatre would be packed.

Judy decided she would not appear.

At 7 P.M. Sid Luft telephoned her from the theatre office, and Judy took the call in her hotel suite. "Judy, it's nearly seven—you know the show starts at eight-thirty."

Judy: "I'm not coming, Sid. I'm not singing any songs tonight."

Sid, after a choked silence: "Is there any reason?"

Judy: "No reason at all. I'm just not going to sing tonight. It's as simple as that, Sid."

Her voice was not slurred. This was Judy cold-sober.

Sid tried another tack. Perhaps there were problems she and he should discuss, something he might not know about.

"No," said Judy. "No problems. I'm just not singing tonight. I sang all the songs I wanted to sing last night. I gave them enough—how much more do they want?"

Lorna and Joe, meanwhile, had come into the small office. Daddy was talking to Mama, and there was obviously trouble. Sid said, "Well, what can I say, Judy? For God's sake."

"There's nothing to say." A flat statement. "All right, Judy," said Sid. "It puts me in a hell of a bind and it's going to affect both of us, you know that."

"I know all about it, Sid," she said, and hung up.

The theatre manager entered. Luft said, "I hate to tell you this, but I just talked to Judy and she says she's not going on tonight."

The other's mouth dropped open. "She's not going on?" His voice rose shrilly. "Is she crazy? Half of Boston's here tonight. We've got the Mayor and—" He began listing the admirals, the captains, the commanders. And: "I've made arrangements for all the paraplegics, the boys in wheelchairs, from the hospital she went through Thursday—they're all coming, they'll be in early."

The two men stared at each other. Luft said helplessly, "I don't know what to tell you. You're welcome to call her yourself."

The manager sat at the desk and telephoned Judy. He repeated to her what he had told Luft: the audience filing into the theatre this very minute, the special guests, the very paraplegics she'd visited like an angel of mercy two days before—they were all there, and she would not come?

He listened, perspiring despite the air conditioning, and put down the phone. "She isn't coming. What'll we do?" He jumped up and paced back and forth. "Oh, my God, this is terrible." He whirled on Lorna. "Lorna, please call your mother. Maybe she'll listen to you." Fifteen-year-old Lorna dialed the number. They heard her: "Mommy, please come. All the soldiers and sailors—please, Mommy—" As she listened, she began to cry. "But, Mommy, all the crippled soldiers are being wheeled in—" and through her sobs: "Just a minute, Mommy, here's Joey," and Joey got on the phone as Lorna said, half-hysterically, "She said that if they can wheel them in, they can wheel them out."

Thirteen-year-old Joey was saying, "Please come down, Mom." Pause. "Joey, you have to understand. I'm not coming down."

He, too, began to cry. "Just a minute, Mom," and Lorna was back on the phone, listening through her tears. Finally she put down the phone. "She hung up. Daddy, she's not coming. She really isn't."

Again the two men stared at each other. Luft said, "All we can do is wait. There's a possibility that she might change her mind after these calls."

Eight-thirty. Nine o'clock. Since the show was to have started half an hour ago, the audience began to clap impatiently. Sid had hired a comedian for a forty-minute warm-up. "Go on," he said. "Give them everything you've got. Stay on as long as you can." Then would come the intermission, and perhaps by then Judy would have relented.

The comedian worked for an hour and a quarter. Then intermission. No Judy.

By now there were shouts of "We want Judy," and a rhythmic, metronomic handclapping. At 10:30 a loudspeaker announcement: Miss Garland is on her way from her hotel. Cheers, applause. Another twenty minutes, a second announcement: "Miss Garland has been held up by traffic—please be patient, folks." Again cheers and applause, but also grumblings, half the audience already out of their seats, waiting at the box office for their money.

At 11:15 a final announcement over the loudspeaker: "Miss Garland is ill tonight and will not appear. We're awfully sorry. All your money will be refunded at the box office."

The people milled about the lobby. The children cried in the manager's office. Sid kept his face impassive when the manager said, "Sid, I'm sorry, you've lost your money, the advertising, whatever we got for program sales—we can't pay you a quarter."

At 2:30 A.M., finished with whatever accounting remained, Sid took Lorna and Joey to an all-night cafeteria for ham and eggs. Then they returned to their hotel suite.

About 3 A.M. the phone rang. "Hello, Sid?" It was Judy. As though nothing had happened: "Sid, I'm going to remain up here for a few days. The children O.K.?" Sid: "They're right here, darling." Judy:

"Will you take them back to New York? I'll be coming down there later. I might even check into the hospital for some tests. I'm not well." Then: "May I speak to the children?" Sid put Lorna on the phone. Judy whispered, "Lorna, watch Daddy—remember Kim Novak," told her she loved her and asked to speak to Joey. "I love you, Joey, I love you both, take care, I'll be seeing you soon."

For a long time Lorna could not puzzle out her mother's cryptic "Watch Daddy—remember Kim Novak." Then she remembered that she and Judy had once watched a film on TV, starring Kim Novak, in which she was menaced by a man with a gun. That was it. For whatever reason, Mama worried because she knew Daddy had a gun, and should be watched. Always that fear that Sid might take the children. Or harm them.

Then, because it was very late, and because Lorna and Joey Luft could have found themselves in the Kingdom of Oz without batting an eye, the two children went to bed, as did an exhausted Luft.

There is no point in dwelling on Judy's appearance at the new ten-million-dollar Garden State Arts Center in Holmdel, New Jersey, which she officially opened for a scheduled five-night engagement on June 25. The month had begun badly with Bobby Kennedy's assassination; this seemed to be working its own subtle torture in the back of her mind far more than anyone knew. While in Boston, she met Wesley M. Fuller, Professor of Music at Clark University. She had driven down to Asbury Park a few days before her appearance with Lorna and Joe, who would be onstage with her, and with Fuller, who had been signed by Sid, under Group V auspices, as her sole artistic adviser at $350 a month. Fuller, a quiet, divorced man in his thirties, with a small daughter, had met Judy after her failure to show up the second night at the Back Bay Theatre. He had sent her flowers and a beautifully turned note saying he could understand how an artist might find it impossible to appear.

Her Arts Center engagement, however, came to a poignant end when, closing night, Judy, on the apron of the stage, slowly slumped over on her side and fell asleep while singing "What Now My Love?" the mike still in her hand. Sid, unable to wake her, immediately summoned an ambulance from the nearby Monmouth Medical Center. She had seemed perfectly fine until then, taking walks with Fuller on the boardwalk every morning; now her fans watched in silence and awe as she was carried out on a stretcher from backstage.

612

They knew this was her birth month and, as the vehicle drew away, they burst into spontaneous applause: "Happy birthday, Judy! We love you, Judy!"

Next morning she telephoned Sid: "Darling, please take care of the children, I'm going back to Boston with Wes."

Judy had several things in mind, the most important of which was becoming an outpatient at the Peter Bent Brigham Hospital so she could fight her way back from excessive medication. Mickey Rooney had telephoned her, to build up her spirits. She had said to him, "Do you think I can make it, honey?" He had said, "I know you can make it, Baby. I made it, and I know you can make it. You can make it with God. That's the only way you can make it." She said, "Will you be there with me?" He said, "I'll be with you always, honey."

Rooney was convinced that if three or four of Judy's friends got together, in some way arranged matters to take the pressure of her debts off her, allowed her to have at least two years of rest from work —to hell with that crap that work was therapy—and from the worries that were drowning her: fears for herself, for her children, for their future, for her future—she could go on, strong as ever. He began lining up physicians to take care of her; he had plans to do whatever would help.

But Judy went on with her own plans. She wanted to sign again with Creative Management Associates. On March 15, 1967, in New York, she had filed a complaint against Fields, Begelman and CMA alleging that they had improperly withheld moneys due her, had mishandled her funds and, so doing, had caused her to be delinquent in payment of income taxes. She was now staying as a house guest of Fuller and his parents; through the Boston Bar Association she obtained the name of an expert contract lawyer, Benjamin S. Freeman. Freeman prepared for her signature documents in which she ultimately released CMA from all claims she had made against them, and Judy was once more a client of CMA. (Luft, because he had signed joint returns and was therefore jointly responsible for any tax deficits, was granted the right to pursue the case on his own behalf. He later filed a complaint, to which Fields and Begelman filed a general denial, and there the matter stood.)

Judy hit it off beautifully with Freeman, and particularly with his wife, Pearl, who was Judy's age and, like her, a Gemini, born in June; they became bosom companions. Presently Judy moved from the

Fullers', to become the guest of the Freemans, in Brighton. .

Her social life was busier than ever. Sid had placed Lorna with friends on Long Island and taken Joey back to California, where Sid now began taking shots to relieve his neuralgia. Judy, meanwhile, was seeing Fuller, dining with Tom Green, who was back in her good graces, seeing much of the Freemans, and confiding some of her problems to Ken Mayer, a former newspaperman who was confidential secretary to Edmund McNamara, Boston's Chief of Police, and a sympathetic, resourceful friend in high places. Mayer was fascinated by her. Dining with her one evening, he learned she had pawned a ring that morning because she had so little cash, yet she had a hired limousine and chauffeur waiting outside the restaurant to take her to a nightclub after dinner. What kind of sense did that make? he asked her. She said, "Ken, once you're a star, you live like a star."

On July 20 she was in Philadelphia, where she gave what the public later believed was her last singing appearance in the United States —at the John F. Kennedy Stadium, with Count Basie's orchestra. More than twenty thousand screaming fans were on hand, there were seven curtain calls, the stadium was so enormous that a screen projection showed Judy's face two stories high. Gene Palumbo conducted and had to tell himself, *It's incredible, her voice is back from God knows where, it's back, she's great!*

That night, just after midnight, Palumbo had a call from her in his hotel room. They were staying at the Warwick. Would he come to her room? Her words were a little slurred; she had obviously taken her sleeping pills—usually she kept them in a little egg cup by the side of her bed. She was in her nightgown, in bed. She said, "Do you have anybody in your room? I mean, is anybody waiting for you?" No, he said. She had always treated him as a son, and he adored her in a filial fashion. She said, "Would you mind lying here for a while and just let me rub your back a bit?" He lay down beside her, fully dressed.

She talked, almost as if thinking out loud, while slowly rubbing his back, as she might have rubbed Joey's back. "It's so strange what singers like myself have to go through. I stand on that stage, in front of all those thousands of people, and all I can hear is 'We love you, Judy; we love you, Judy; we love you, Judy.' And then I come home, and if it weren't for a few friends like Wes and you, I'd be all by

614

myself." She paused for a moment. "I like it when they say, 'I love you'—they're nice people, all of them, my audience. . . . What would I do without them, where would I be without that? But I just want someday to hear one voice say it to me in bed, when the lights are off, and I want to wake up in the morning and have somebody's back next to me, and just rub it, and wake them up."

Palumbo was moved. He thought, *Lady, you just said everything that you are in this world.* . . . And then she let him go, and he returned to his room and went to bed.

On the last day of July, Judy telephoned John Carlyle on the Coast. Would he pick her up at the Los Angeles airport? She was coming in for a brief visit to see Joey and to collect some music she needed.

Carlyle met her at the airport. She arrived with one small suitcase, a Bloomingdale's shopping bag containing an extra dress, and her purse. Later they picked up Joe at Sid's apartment, and Judy, Joey and Carlyle went out to dinner together.

When she had still been at the Rockingham house, and the marriage with Mark was tottering, John had been one of her closest, most intimate friends. One night she was playing Monopoly with the two men. Liza had just won the Tony Award for *Flora, the Red Menace*, a Broadway musical. John said, "Well, I think Liza is marvelous, but she didn't deserve the Tony Award." Judy got up and, without a word, poured her drink over his head and rushed into her bedroom, got on the intercom with Mark and said, "Tell John to leave the house! Tell him to get out at once! He had no right to say that!"

Next day Judy apologized. "I'm always too brusque with people I love." Then, presently, Mark was out of her life, and Judy would drop over and stay a week at a time with John on beautiful Norma Place. He would keep up with her until, exhausted after a week, he would telephone Lionel, the butler, and ask him to call for Judy on the pretext that he, John, had to go out of town. A few weeks would pass, and Judy would again join him.

During one hot night, when she was staying with him, he and Paul Millard were her total audience as Judy, engulfed in John's bathrobe, went on a singing spree from 3 A.M. to dawn. The two men sat on the floor, laughing, crying, applauding, until the first rays of the sun began coming through the open windows.

There was a knock on the door. "Madam Gumm, be quiet," John said. "It must be the police." Her voice obviously had been sailing out the open window. Lord knew how far it carried.

There, standing on his porch, was a middle-aged woman in pajamas, bathrobe and slippers. She said, "I apologize for knocking at this hour. I live about two blocks away. I opened the door to let out my dog, and I thought I heard someone playing Judy Garland records. Then I realized it was not a recording, but a live voice, and I just followed it here." She paused, and added embarrassedly, "I have worshiped her all my life. Please, if she's here, would she let me come in for a minute or so?"

John hurried inside. "There's a lady here—could she please come in—she loves you—and sit quietly and listen to you for a while?"

Judy said, "Of course, darling."

The woman's name was Kate, and she was a schoolteacher; they gave her a vodka and tonic, she sat on the sofa, Judy sang, and the woman completely fell apart. She began repeating again and again, "Nobody will believe me." After some minutes of this, Judy grew nervous. She whispered to John, "Darling, please take her home."

John explained that Judy was tired and going to bed. He walked Kate to the corner. She kept saying, "Nobody will believe me."

Days later he found a note under his door: "Dear Judy and John —nobody did believe me.—Kate."

One day, in that period, John had taken her over to visit Tucker Fleming and Charles Williamson in their own house on Norma Place. Tuck and Chuck were then preparing to remodel it, and the four went over the plans with the architect. "You're going to have a guest room, aren't you?" asked Judy. They said, of course. And Chuck added, "And it can be yours whenever you want it."

Judy was enchanted. She began calling it "my room." She dropped over to see how the remodeling was progressing on February 27, 1967, a few days before she was to fly to New York for Liza's wedding to Peter Allen, and brought two azalea plants as belated St. Valentine gifts for Tuck and Chuck. Then she went upstairs to see how her room was coming along, humming and singing as she watched the workmen. When she came down, she said, "I think one of those men knows who I am." Tuck said, "He doesn't know who you are at all. He thinks you're the afternoon hooker." She loved that bawdiness.

Now, on this summer visit in 1968, she and John went over to see how her room had finally turned out. It was a lovely little suite, with its own dressing alcove and bathroom. "May I stay here?" she asked.

She turned to John. Would he mind? "Of course not," he said. So Judy immediately moved from John's apartment to the Fleming-Williamson house. Once she was installed, she was all efficiency. She sent her dresses out to be cleaned—John had brought over a favorite red velvet robe she delighted in wearing—and she insisted Chuck keep a record of her bills. "I want to keep the list," she said. "You're being very generous having me here, and you know, I have to pay you back."

In the past, someone else had always handled her medication, doled out her pills; hereafter she had to be in charge of herself. Her doctor had given her a prescription for a four-week period. She began looking through her purse for it. She took everything out and put it on the table—notes, a bit of cash, Kleenex—"I have nothing for this week. What happened to it?" Chuck said, "Well, Judy, obviously if you had it, either it's already been filled or you've lost it."

Judy looked at him icily, scraped up everything from the table, put it back into her bag and went up to her room. She stayed there for half an hour before relenting and coming down. Then she said, "You know, it's humiliating to be dependent on any sort of medication."

During the day she swam in the beautiful oval pool. "This is my Shangri-la," she said, and read for hours in their library. Once, rummaging among the books, she found the new Random House Dictionary. She came running excitedly into the living room. "Look, I'm in the dictionary!" And there she was. "Judy Garland," immediately following "Hamlin Garland," the writer.

She spoke to the men of Wes Fuller in Boston, and how decent he had been. She might become Mrs. Wes Fuller. "Then we'd have a house in Boston, and there'd be snow in the wintertime. . . ." It seemed that now, as her life became ever more directionless, she yearned deeply for the idyllic scenes she remembered—winters in Grand Rapids as a child, the lovely Christmas scenes in *Meet Me in St. Louis*. . . . Several times she telephoned Fuller, as well as Ben and Pearl Freeman, and her physician at Peter Bent Brigham.

No one knew how long she would stay on the Coast, but she cut her visit short, and suddenly. On Wednesday, August 6, Tuck and Chuck had been invited to a dinner party. It was eight o'clock when they left; they planned to be back at ten.

About half an hour later, while they were at their host's table, the butler came to Williamson. There was a telephone call from Judy.

"Chuck, I'm going back to Boston," she said. "There's no need to leave your lovely dinner party. I'll just take a taxi to the airport."

Williamson was shocked. "Judy, what do you mean? We'll be right there." They had made reservations to go the next night to hear Tony Bennett open at the Cocoanut Grove, she'd told Joey they'd take him.

The two men immediately made their apologies and hurried home, to find Judy all dressed for travel, her tiny bag at her side, her hat on her head, sitting in the hallway. She was leaving on a 10:30 plane. No, she really had to go. Would Chuck wire Tony saying they'd not come to his opening, but not hold her responsible, adding love and all the rest? And telephone Joey tomorrow and explain that she had to return to Boston, it was very urgent?

They sat a few minutes over drinks, then drove her to the airport. She kissed them, thanked them and went aboard.

When they returned home, Williamson found on his desk a note she had scribbled on the pad he kept there, the only written communication he had ever received from her. It read: "John, Chuck, Tuck, I love you, always—Judy."

Back in Boston, Judy telephoned Lorna, on Long Island. Sid learned about it when Lorna called him in California.

"Daddy, I just talked to Mommy, and Mommy wanted me to come to Boston, and I just couldn't."

"What did she say?"

Lorna: "We had a terrible row on the phone. Mommy insisted that I come there. I said, 'Judy, I cannot come.' She said, 'Miss Garland to you,' and hung up. Then I called her back and she said, 'All right, if that's the way you want it, don't come.'"

Sid said, "Lorna, there'll be a ticket for you at the airport in New York. Come home." She flew back to California.

In the following months John and Tucker and Chuck read about Judy. After Boston, at Lincoln Center in New York for a tribute to her friend Harold Arlen, then appearances on TV talk shows—Dick Cavett, Johnny Carson, Merv Griffin—and one day, in Earl Wilson's column, the announcement that she would marry Mickey Deans.

Charlie Cochran telephoned Mickey. Charlie could not believe it. He knew that she had been at Arthur night after night, that Mickey and Judy were close . . . but marriage? Yes, it was true. And a little later, when Charlie was invited to a Christmas party given by Stan

618

Freeman, a pianist and arranger, he asked if he could bring Mickey and Judy. The two were going to London, where Judy had been booked into a five-week engagement at London's popular Talk of the Town restaurant, beginning December 30, 1968, and she needed a new opening number. Stan might come up with something.

At the party Stan said yes, he had an old song that might be perfect, entitled "I Belong to London." He played a recording of it. Judy said, "It's wonderful." Stan wrote a new arrangement, and in a few hours Judy mastered it, and turned it into a Garland number with a skill that seemed as remarkable now as it had ever been.

Mickey turned to Charlie. "Will you come to London with us?" he asked. "Help me set up Judy for Talk of the Town? We're going to be married there—will you be my best man?"

Charlie said yes.

On December 28, Judy, Mickey and Charlie flew to London, playing poker all the way over, not for castles in Spain or for sums such as $200,000, but for the fun of it—with Judy humming her song, "I Belong to London."

42

IT WAS LIZA WHO NOTICED IT FIRST.

It was May 1969, and Judy had flown quietly into New York with Mickey Deans. She had married him first on January 9, at a secret Catholic Church ceremony in London (Mickey was Catholic, she was not) because of a complication in the Herron divorce papers, but she wanted to be married in the eyes of God; then she had married him in a public civil ceremony at the Chelsea Registry Office on March 15.

The second, official marriage would have occurred earlier had not Judy and Mickey gotten into a violent dispute, he had flown off to the States, and Judy, staying with Johnnie Ray, the singer, an old friend, and his manager, Bill Franklin, had said to Johnnie, "I don't know if he's ever coming back, and I don't care."

They were living in a house in Cadogan Place Johnnie had found after Judy's triumphant opening at the Talk of the Town. She almost did not appear; months before Filiberti, who had lost thousands because of engagements Judy did not or could not finish, had, without informing either her or Luft, turned over his Group V stock, and Judy's contract, as collateral for a loan. Now, as she was about to open, the new holder of the contract claimed her services and tried to use the very clauses which had been devised to protect her in the United States to prevent her from performing in London. Fortunately, a British court ruled in Judy's favor. But Mickey did come back, there was the usual ecstatic reconciliation, and Mickey had immediately announced to Johnnie, "We're getting married this Saturday at noon—" only five days off—"and you're going to be my best man."

Johnnie had sat down and sent off the invitations for a postwedding reception at Quaglino's, one of London's most famous restaurants. The guest list included some of the most prominent names—John Gielgud, Bette Davis, Ginger Rogers, Margaret Leighton, Peter Finch and many others—but none of them showed up. It was incredible. Johnnie, trying to soften the blow, said, "Maybe they didn't get the invitations in time." However she felt, Judy, frighteningly thin, danced gaily with Mickey, and two hours later they were on a plane bound for a brief Paris honeymoon.

Then, in April, Mickey called Cochran from London. Judy had completed a ten-day Scandinavian concert tour with Johnnie Ray, and he, Mickey, had an idea: the promotion of a chain of Judy Garland Theatres in the United States. He and Judy planned to fly to New York. "Can we stay at your place?" he asked Charlie.

"Sure," said Charlie. He had a house guest at the time—Anita O'Day, to whom Judy, by coincidence, had back in 1944 presented the Best Jazz Singer of the Year Award. But he'd arrange it.

The Deanses arrived in New York in late May. Cochran, the perfect host, moved out to stay in the apartment of a friend, and his three house guests shared his Lexington Avenue apartment, with Cochran stopping in every day to see that everything was all right.

Hardly anyone knew that Judy was in New York. Liza was one of the few, and she dropped in on her mother one evening. She had met Mickey Deans many times, of course; there was a kind of John Garfield toughness about him. He was a sturdy, muscular man, who could wheel and deal as well as sing, play the piano, entertain, manage a discotheque—all of which, she realized, must have attracted her mother. It was a toughness, an I-can-handle-it assurance reminiscent of Sid. Of Judy's four other husbands, Mickey was the only one who had that same quality.

When Liza entered the apartment, there was her mother, sitting down, reading, her granny glasses on, quite peaceful, but it was not the calm of tranquilizers or of liquor. Suddenly it occurred to Liza: *She looks just like a middle-aged lady. Mama? And she talks about subjects which aren't Mama's subjects. . . .*

First, Liza asked, "Hey, where's Mickey?"

Judy said, "Well, he went to see . . ." She was vague. This surprised Liza. She knew her mother. Whoever her man was, he had to be on the spot; if not, Judy had to know exactly where he was. His eyes could not even wander around the room without her noticing it; his eyes had to be on her, or looking for her. If not, she would do something outrageous, or say something arresting, to bring his attention back to her. Liza knew that her mother possessed this uncanny sense (Sid had felt it often enough) of keeping the man under constant surveillance, apparently with the back of her head, knowing what he was saying, knowing what he was thinking, knowing what was happening to his body, his emotions, what he wanted, what he felt like doing. . . . And here was Judy saying, vaguely, "Well, he went to see . . ."

Liza, prepared for a typical night with Mama until dawn, said, "Well, are we going to meet him later, Mama?"

Again her mother surprised her. "No," said Judy. "He's doing this theatre thing, it'll be such a comfort, because we'll finally have some money we can depend upon. . . ."

Then Judy went on to talk about their house in London, in Cadogan Place. "I wish you could see it," she said. And suddenly: "Liza, did you ever try Teflon ware?"

Liza looked at her. This wasn't Mama. This wasn't Judy Garland. This was a peaceful housewife who might be living in Queens. Not knowing where her man was. Talking about Teflon ware. This was what was called normal, and Liza couldn't stand it. She was accustomed to Mama—or to Judy Garland. There was a real distinction there. They were different, one would change into the other—but neither was this middle-aged lady talking about Teflon ware and not even sure where her man was.

Judy's forty-seventh birthday was June 10. She spent it mostly in bed, in Cochran's guest room. Somehow Harold Arlen learned she was in town, and sent her flowers. That day she telephoned John Carlyle on the Coast. He had no idea that she was in New York. And she said, "Oh, darling, let me come to California."

John said, "Look, Madam Gumm, you're a married lady now. I can't ask you. I would, you know I would."

Judy said sadly, "I've lost my audience."

John: "You never will, Judy. You must try to get stronger. Behave yourself and take care of yourself." She was obviously unhappy that day. They began talking about other matters, and she said, suddenly, "Darling, how's Judy?" John had two cats, one named for her, and he took care of them almost as though they were children. He replied now, "Love, she's very sick."

"What do you mean?"

"I've been taking her to have shots, and I don't think she's going to live much longer."

"Oh, darling, put her by the phone," said Judy. John got the cat from under the bed and placed it by the receiver—and this was the last time he really heard Judy Garland's voice in song. She sang softly, tenderly, over the telephone: "Ju-dy . . . Ju-dy darling, get well, darling, for John and me, please get well. . . ."

They spoke a little longer, she seemed tired, and she said, "Good night, love."

John thought, *Judy's birthday, and she's in bed all day, in Charlie Cochran's apartment. . . .*

When Judy had first arrived, Charlie had not been too surprised at her appearance. She had been thin when they flew over, but he had been a little shocked by the photographs he had seen of her March 15 wedding to Mickey. She had been even thinner, a wraith. When she had opened at Talk of the Town, she had not been herself, even if the reviewers spoke of her as "a riveting performer." The critics went even so far as to call her "gaunt" and "haggard." Now she appeared so fragile that, after he arranged for them to stay at his place, he took Mickey aside. "Don't you think Judy ought to go to a hospital for a few days of rest and treatment?" Mickey said, no, but he called his physician, who examined Judy, suggested rest and took her off her usual sleeping pill, Seconal, and put her on Thorazine instead.

Judy had been ill off and on in England. One night at Talk of the

622

Town, after she had arrived late and obviously in a bad way, one table of four drunks began throwing bread rolls, crushed cigarette packs, whatever other debris was on their table, at her, and began shouting obscenities; she ultimately walked off the stage and did not return to Talk of the Town for three nights.

She and Johnnie Ray had decided on the Scandinavian tour during Judy's brief separation from Deans. They had found a wall safe in the house with 150 pounds in it, and delightedly used it on their trip. Judy had always gotten on well with Johnnie; as long ago as her appearance at Caesar's Palace in Vegas, he would watch admiringly from backstage, and now and then she would bring him on to sing with her. That was really the genesis of their decision to work together on their tour—Stockholm, Göteborg (which she had to cancel because of an overdose), Malmö and, on March 20, Copenhagen. There, standing backstage, after he had finished his turn, Johnnie watched Judy singing, and suddenly found himself sobbing. Bill, his manager, grabbed his arm. "What is it?" Johnnie said, "I just have the feeling I'll never see Judy alive again." He and Bill left late that night for another tour. He had been right.

Now, in New York, Judy followed the doctor's instructions and got as much rest as she could. One night, when she felt better, she and Mickey drove to New Jersey to meet his parents. Another night they spent at The Apartment, on Second Avenue, where Charlie was entertaining. And Sunday night, June 15, they all went to hear Anita at the Half Note, a club in Greenwich Village where she sang. Judy looked sparkling that night, in a black dress with a huge picture hat.

Anita invited Cochran to join her in a jazz duet they often did together. Then Anita, in the applause, said, "That was my roommate, Charlie. How about my other roommate coming up and doing a song?"

Judy laughed, rose and came on stage. She sang "Day In—Day Out"—she was in good voice, as always when she was rested. Then she sang "Over the Rainbow." Anita joined her, and they sang "April Showers" together, Judy singing the melody, Anita the fill.

It was the last time Judy sang in public in the United States.

Two days later the limousine came to take her and Mickey to the airport for their flight back to London. It was Tuesday, June 17. The Judy Garland Theatre project had fallen through. Cochran kissed her. He said, "Love, you've been a perfect house guest."

Four days later, Saturday, June 21, Cochran, not quite knowing what to do with himself, flew to the Coast and dined with John Carlyle. They went to a late entertainment at a nightclub, and then returned to Cochran's motel in the San Fernando Valley for more drinks and talk.

They were watching the *Late Late Show*, but Judy had been the subject of their conversation, as always.

Now, around 2 A.M., John said, suddenly, "God, I miss Madam Gumm, I want to talk to her. Let's call her." Both had had enough liquor to feel deeply sentimental and indifferent to the cost of a call to London. Charlie said, "Terrific! John, go ahead, you place it."

If it was 2 A.M. Sunday morning in Los Angeles, it was 10 A.M. Sunday morning in London. Judy and Mickey would be asleep. But John gave the overseas operator Mickey's number. A moment or so later, at the other end, in London, Mickey's sleepy voice answered. No, no, he didn't mind—not really. After a few more words, John said, "Can I talk to Judy?" Mickey said . . . a beat of time elapsed . . . "John—" there was a little pause again—"I don't know where she is. I guess she's in the bathroom." "Well, go get her," John commanded, alcohol giving him more than usual assurance. "All right," Mickey said. "Hold on." After what seemed a long two or three minutes, he was back on the phone. "Look, she can't talk to you right this second. Give me your number and she'll call you back in half an hour."

The two men waited in the motel. Charlie poured another drink. The telephone rang. John picked it up with "Madam Gumm, we miss you—" But it was not Judy. It was Mickey. "John, Judy's dead."

John held the telephone, paralyzed. The sheer brutality of it stunned him. "You're kidding, Mickey," he managed to say. "You're kidding." No matter what Judy did to herself, he knew she was indestructible. How many grim witticisms had those who loved her exchanged among themselves! You could fill Judy full of pills, bop her over the head with a floor plank, lash her ankles together, tie her to a manhole cover and drop her off a Malibu pier into the Pacific—and she'd reappear, blithe and gay and ready to tear the house down, that very night. He said again, "You're kidding," and Mickey's voice came back hysterically, "John, if you say that to me one more time, I'll kill you. She's dead. She's in the bathroom. Please go over to Westwood and tell Lorna and Joey so they won't read it in the newspapers—"

624

His voice broke and splintered into something shrill and choking, and he hung up.

Like two automatons Charlie and John drove to the Luft apartment, climbed to the third floor and rang the bell repeatedly, and when there was no response, they began pounding on the door. Still no sound from within. Only later did they learn that, not only was Luft's bedroom far in the rear of the apartment, but that he had taken the phone out of his bedroom so he could sleep undisturbed —he had been up very late the night before; that Lorna was at a girlfriend's house, and Joey spending the night with a classmate. Finally they stopped. It was nearly 4 A.M., and they feared neighbors would call the police. They went to John's house. They still did not believe it. John switched on the radio, and they were shocked: it was Judy singing. A moment later, a man's words, superimposed over Judy's, said in sepulchral tones, "This voice was stilled . . ."

Then they believed it, and John kicked the screen of his front door out, in helpless anger at her for dying, in fury at the world that had allowed her to die. . . . He called Vern Alves, who later that morning reached Luft and broke the news to him.

That Saturday night Joey had slept over at the home of his friend Jack Kimball. Early Sunday morning he woke suddenly; Jack's mother was standing at the foot of his bed, Jack like a shadow behind her. She said, "Joey, is there some way I can get in touch with your father? There's no answer at the apartment."

"Why, what's wrong?" he asked.

She did not reply, but mother and son both turned and walked out of the room. Joey was left alone, sitting up in bed, his fists clenched. He felt some kind of horror, he didn't know what. A moment later Jack came back into the room, and the expression on his face—he simply stared at Joey as though he had never seen him before—gave Joey the feeling instantly that his mother had died. He said to himself, hearing the words somewhere between his eyes, "Could she have died?" He answered his own question: "No . . ." Yet there was that flat feeling in his mind that yes, she had died.

Then Mrs. Kimball returned and took him into another room. There she said to him, "Your mother died." She had her arms around him, comforting him. He could only think, in the grip of a kind of numbness, of the last time he had seen his mother. She knew something then; but how could she have? His mind turned dizzily. It had been months before, on that quick visit when she'd stayed with Chuck and Tuck for a week or so before returning to New York and ultimately going to London and her marriage to Mickey Deans.

Mom and he had seen a great deal of each other on that visit in August 1968. One evening—as it turned out, it was the night before she left Los Angeles—they had had a wonderful time. Together with Chuck and Tuck they had gone to The Factory, the most exciting discotheque around. At the table Judy had turned to him. "Joey, aren't you going to ask me to dance?" He had said yes, blushing—he had turned thirteen only a few months before—and he had been very proud to dance with her. It was the first time mother and son had danced in public. Judy had marveled at how tall he had grown, and was beside herself all evening because of what he had whispered in her ear as they danced. "Mom, when I grow up, I'm going to be a banker so I can support you." "Oh, Joey," she had said, thinking, as she told John Carlyle later, *Thank God, there's one sensible member of the family who doesn't want show business.* And adding, much impressed, "He's a young man! He's just growing up, but Joey's a young man!" And with almost a note of awe: "I'm the mother of a young man!"

When they returned to the house, it was after 1 A.M. Judy said, "I'm going to slip into something"—it was her favorite red velvet robe— and she had vanished into the guest room they'd set aside for her. Minutes passed, but she did not come out.

Joey went up to say good night to her. He had a dentist's appointment early the next morning. Sid had cautioned them all to make sure that he did not come home too late.

To Joey's surprise, his mother was in bed. He had expected to see her in her red robe, seated before the dressing table in the little alcove, putting a deft touch to her makeup before returning to join the others. He knew that for his mother the evening had hardly begun.

He bent over and kissed her. Nestling down in bed, the covers almost enveloping her, her little girl's face so small against the pillows, she appeared hardly older than himself. "Good night, Mom, I got to go," he said. He started to leave. At the door he looked back and saw there were tears in her eyes. He went back to her. "What's wrong, Mom?" She said, "Oh, Joey, don't leave, don't leave." Her hand clutched his arm. "Stay here with me tonight." He said, "Mom,

I'll see you again. Why are you crying?" He knew they'd made reservations at the Cocoanut Grove two nights later for Tony Bennett's opening. She had never acted like this before. "I'll see you again." He bent down and kissed her on the cheek once more.

But he actually had to pull away from her grasp, and her eyes followed him as he left, and when he was outside her room, he hurried downstairs and said to Chuck, "Please go upstairs and talk to my mom and make her feel better. I don't want to hurt her, but I promised Pop I'd be home early. I can't stay."

Chuck and Tuck went up to talk to her, and then Tuck came down and drove him home.

Now, Joey thought, as he sat shivering beside Mrs. Kimball taking him home, she must have known, somehow, all those months earlier, that she would never see him again.

That Saturday night Lorna and Joady Henderson, her best friend, had gone to see the Young Rascals, a rock-'n'-roll group that was simply the greatest. They had come home late and, after a midnight snack, gone to bed. For no reason, sometime during the night Lorna awoke with a start. She was wide awake, and frightened, but she could not focus on what was frightening her. Then she realized her whereabouts—she was sleeping in a twin bed in Joady's bedroom, and Joady, across the room in her own bed, was sound asleep. Her fear subsided, and she fell asleep again. When she awoke, it was around nine o'clock. Joady's bed was empty. Lorna, in pajamas, walked into the kitchen. Joady and her mother were both up and dressed—it seemed very early for a Sunday—and talking in hushed tones. They stopped when they saw her.

Mrs. Henderson looked at her strangely. "Lorna, I've got to tell you something," she said. Joady hurried out of the kitchen, and Lorna began to freeze. A panic was coming upon her, a panic somehow connected with the terrible fear that had wakened her so suddenly hours ago. Mrs. Henderson said, "Your mom died."

Lorna backed away. "I don't believe you!" she said, accusingly. "I don't believe you." She fought a mounting hysteria. Why, she'd talked to her mother only three days ago, and she was fine. Mama had called them from London, she was in a good mood, everything was wonderful, she wanted Lorna and Joey to fly over later in the month and spend part of the summer with her and Mickey, she had talked to Daddy and he had agreed. But . . . Lorna rushed to the telephone and called home, but, though it rang and rang, her father did not answer. *It couldn't be true,* ran through her head. Once before they'd told her that, and it hadn't been true then. She and Mrs. Chapman, her governess, were being driven somewhere, she was eleven, Mama and Mark Herron were off on that trip around the world, and the car's radio suddenly said what sounded like "Judy Garland is reported dead in a Hong Kong hospital." It hadn't been true then, and it couldn't be true now.

Unable to reach her father, Lorna called Liza in New York, but only the answering service replied. Then Lorna found herself being taken home, where Joey and her father, his face gray, awaited her. What Sid had always feared—that he might wake some morning to read the headline "JUDY GARLAND DEAD"—had happened.

Liza, that weekend, with her husband, Peter, his sister Lynn and a friend, were house guests in the Hamptons, two hours from New York.

Their host came into the bedroom Sunday morning; there was a phone call for Liza. Peter said he would take it. He came back into the room and she heard him say, "Darling, you better wake up. I've got something to tell you."

Liza jumped up, her heart racing. Something terrible had happened. She knew it. It was one of her parents—but which one? Not her mother—Mama was indestructible. She said, tentatively, "My father's dead." Peter said no. "Is Mama sick?" Peter said no. It came to her in a rush then, and she started to shake. "Is Mama dead?" Peter said yes.

As he told her what he knew, she was to remember how light the room was, how brightly the morning sun poured through the window, how green, how Technicolor-green the grass outside, everything so vivid, every color so sharp—almost as though she were part of an extraordinary photographic exhibit—and yet everything trembled about her as though she were in an earthquake, because she was shaking so. She thought, *I've got to control myself, I've got to pull everything together.*

She was taking deep breaths, fighting to get enough oxygen into her lungs, as though she had just come offstage after a wild, impossibly strenuous dance number. *Lorna! Joey!* she thought. She must reach them at once before they read or heard it. She ran to the telephone and called her stepfather's number in Los Angeles, but

628

there was no answer. Where *were* they all! She thought, *I've got to have an autopsy done right away so Lorna and Joe will know it's not suicide.* She knew, as well as she knew that she was alive in this terrible moment, that it was not suicide. It could not be. Mama would never dream of suicide, no matter how often she played at it. She would never deliberately leave them. Not only that: Judy Garland was a master of entrances and exits, and she would never depart in this fashion.

They had to get back to New York. Liza dressed, throwing some kind of clothes on, and walked downstairs, through the kitchen and out the back door into the bright daylight, and onto the lawn, and sat on the grass for a little while, waiting for the others to get ready for the long drive back to the city. For the space of a heartbeat she almost broke down, because the day was so pretty, so golden, everything suffused with a kind of saffron glow—just the kind of a day *she* would have loved. It had shadows, it had definition, it wasn't flat, it was three-dimensional, filling your eyes. *I'm not going to let you down now, Mama,* she thought, *I'm not going to panic and run away from this. I'm not going to let anybody else handle it. I'll do it the way you wanted. . . .* They had talked about this many times and in many places. They had a favorite phrase: "If you go before I go, or I go before you go . . ." Judy had a bracelet given her by Kay Thompson when Liza was born, and Judy had given it to Liza and they'd given it back and forth. It was good luck. "If I go before you go, I want to be wearing this," Judy said of the bracelet. "I don't care what dress you put me in, but I'd like to be wearing this." And she wanted to be cremated. She had claustrophobia, she shuddered at the thought of being encased in a tomb, or put into a coffin under the earth. Her mother, for all her fears, Liza knew, could joke about death, and how she would go. Wouldn't it be wonderful, she had said once, if you had those tiny suicide pins spies carry, and when the doctor said, "I hate to tell you this, but you have terminal cancer," you'd say, "Never mind," and prick!—you'd have nothing to worry about any more. Thank you very much, sir!

And thinking about her mother, her indomitable, indestructible mother, she was seized by a strange elation. That energy, that power that could turn audiences of thousands into manic worshipers, that mischievous wit and antic humor that could so entrance and delight, that aliveness that could burst from her to electrify all about her, that extraordinary perceptiveness that could catch the faintest nuance of a glance, a word, a thought behind one's eyes, that utter tenderness that could envelop you and make your knees weak—all that energy, that vitality, that *essence*, would no longer be contained in that small, frail body, it would be dispersed into the air about her: it would always be part of the world surrounding her, Liza realized. *Mama would never be gone.* Always she would be with her, to talk to, to confide in. . . . Sitting there on the grass, she spoke aloud to her mother: "O.K., Mama. Now, we'll get this done. It will be terrific, we'll do it with dignity, you'll be so pleased. . . ." And then Liza broke. She began sobbing, chokingly, convulsively, feeling her body straining as if to burst out of itself. She cried very hard for two or three minutes, and as quickly as the storm came, it subsided. She thought, *This isn't in the schedule, this crying. Save this for later.*

She rose, walked around to the front of the house just as the others emerged from the front door, and they got into the car and began the endless, endless drive back to New York.

Now the funeral. She must handle that, whatever it involved. She threw herself into activity. Stevie Dumler talked to her: "Do you know that Kay Thompson just got in from Rome?" The last time Liza had seen Kay, her godmother, had been at least eight years before. She had been a vaporous figure that floated in and out of her life, although she knew she had had a great influence on her mother's style.

She telephoned Kay. "Hel-lo!" came from Kay. "Kay—" Liza began. It was clear from the "Hel-lo" that Kay had not heard. So Liza said, "Mama passed away." There was a long pause. Then: "How are you?" "I'm fine," said Liza. Kay said, "What has to be done?" Liza felt a surge of relief. "Look," said Kay, "I'm going to throw on a pair of slacks. I'll be right over. Let me tell you something before I hang up: she had one of the most wonderful lives that anybody ever could ask for. She had everything she ever wanted. There was nothing that, if she wanted it, she wouldn't go after. . . . No matter what her complaints and tragedies and all that—" "Yes," said Liza.

Kay arrived. Liza said, "I know two things she wanted for sure. I know I want to do it. Can I?" Kay said, "Let's find out. Why don't you just get started? Actually her husband, whoever she's married to now, has final say in everything."

Liza had just talked to Mickey in London. He was a wreck. There would be an inquest in three or four days. Liza said, "Mickey, don't worry about anything. I'll handle everything." He said, O.K. Liza thought, *Well, I guess I will handle everything now.*

She reached Lorna, Joe and Sid in California. It was one of those terrible, awkward conversations. What did one say? Are you O.K.? Yes, I'm O.K. But they felt together, strong, united. Liza said, "I'm going to try to start arranging things. I'll call you back."

Where would Mama want the services held? In London? No, because that was not the central place of her life. Either New York or Los Angeles. People could more easily get to those cities, and, after all, the services were for people. New York, then, because it was most central.

Now, where? Kay said, What about Frank Campbell's, at Madison Avenue and Eighty-first Street? It was dignified, small and pretty.

Each time Liza was about to break down, Kay was there to ask a question, make a suggestion. "What color flowers? Your mother wanted to be cremated, right? We'll do that." Liza began to fantasize. If she could carry Judy's ashes about with her, and throw them to the wind—throw them to the air, to be carried all over the world . . .

Nobody to wear black. No funeral colors. They'd have yellow flowers. Judy's favorite color. How does one obtain thousands of yellow flowers? Liza had already decided.

A phone call from Sid. The services would be in New York, said Liza. Sid wasn't sure. He'd call back. "I don't think she should be buried in New York. California is the place that made her—"

Liza: "She hated California."

Sid: "But all her friends are here."

Liza: "What friends? Anybody who cares enough will come to New York. And from London, too, and it's harder to get to California from London. . . ." Then she said, "Pop, I've arranged the whole thing. It'll be beautiful. Trust me."

Sid: "All right. Where is she going to be buried?"

This led to a dispute, a tearing one, particularly when Liza told Sid that Judy wanted to be cremated.

"God!" he screamed, horrified. "No, you mustn't, no, you can't." She could hear Lorna and Joey crying. Judy was still too alive for them—too alive for them all. So Liza said, O.K., O.K., all right. That's what she wanted, but let's talk about it.

No, no, no, they said. And when Liza heard Judy's son and daughter crying for this not to happen, she knew Judy wouldn't want it. It was as though her mother were still with her saying, *Oh, look—let's not upset them any more.* So Liza said, O.K., we'll do what you want.

Liza remembered that in one of the discussions they used to have Judy had said she wanted Gene Hibbs, a well-known makeup man, to make her up for her funeral. "I want to look so—well, just glamorous and perfect." Liza had promised her that.

But then it was discovered that Gene Hibbs was making up Eva Gabor for her TV series, *Green Acres,* and would not be permitted to take the time to come to New York. Then Liza thought of Charles Schram, who had made up Mama for *The Wizard of Oz,* years ago. Would he do it? He would know how she would want to look and he agreed. Liza burst into tears of relief.

The inquest was held. The coroner announced that Judy Garland had died accidentally from an "incautious self-overdosage" of sleeping pills. The medical examiner had found no evidence of a deliberate overdose, which officially ruled out suicide. She had undoubtedly taken her usual Seconals, then awoke at some point and, in the words of Westminister Coroner Gavin Thurston, "Miss Garland had taken —perhaps in a state of confusion from previous doses—more barbiturates than her body could tolerate."

When John's telephone call woke him, and Mickey found Judy not on her side of the bed, he had hurried to the bathroom, knocked on the door—locked as usual—gotten no reply, come back, told John that Judy would call him soon herself, then dashed back to the bathroom. "Judy!" he called. There was no answer. Perhaps she had fallen asleep in there. He was able to reach the bathroom window by climbing out the window of their dressing room and walking across the roof. Judy was there, sitting, her arms, as he remembered it, on her lap, her head resting on her arms. Asleep, he thought, with tremendous relief. He worked open the window and climbed in— and then he saw that she was sitting there dead.

Now Judy's body was on its way, and almost before Liza and the others knew it, it had arrived, with Mickey on the same plane. Schram had already been to Campbell's. Lorna, Joey and Sid had come in from the Coast.

Lorna said, "I want to go and see her."

Liza said, "Oh, Lorna, you really don't want to do that, do you, honey?" Lorna was strong, but she was also sensitive. She was sixteen —at that point in her life, to look upon her mother's dead face?

Lorna said, "No, I want to do it." Liza thought, *Well, I must go with her. Because suppose something happens. I won't let her go alone.*

Sid said, "I'll go, too."

Joey said, "I don't think I can go."

As they were about to leave, Joey pulled Liza over and said, out of Lorna's hearing, "Liza, don't let her get too close." To the coffin. "She might . . ." Liza understood. Joey—he had such sharp perceptions in his quiet way—was saying, *Don't let her get too close so that she can see that she really is dead.*

They went to Campbell's. Liza was beginning to shake. Lorna walked in, marched her staunch little body over to the coffin, looked down at her mother and stood there, staring. Then she started to tremble, came away and sat down by herself. Now it was Liza's turn. It was strange what she had to do to reach the coffin. First she sat down on the chair farthest from it. Then she rose, took a few steps and sat down in a nearer chair. And so, by stages, until she found herself, knees trembling, seated in a chair directly in front of the coffin. She stood up and looked down on her dead mother.

It was the most incredible experience she had ever had, because Mama's hands looked beautiful; her feet were pointed as they should be; she was wearing a lovely, lovely gown; and on her wrist, the bracelet she and Liza used to trade back and forth, the good-luck bracelet.

It was not a waxen image of Judy. It was Judy. Her lipstick was on as it should be, she was smiling slightly, her eyes were closed peacefully. And Liza found herself saying, "Goddamn it, you do, you do, you do!" In Liza's head she was hearing Judy's voice: "Don't I look swell, terrific, just beautiful?" And Liza was answering her, "Yes, Mama, you do."

And then the services.

Those who had been invited—only Judy's closest friends—entered to find on each seat a mimeographed sheet with the words of "The Battle Hymn of the Republic" on it, and they sat down, holding the sheets in their hands. Kay and Liza had agreed there should be singing. Why not? A great part of Judy's life had been singing. Liza remembered, too, how her mother had insisted, after President Kennedy's death, upon singing, on her TV show, "The Battle Hymn of the Republic," with its magnificent chorus, "Glory, glory, hallelujah!" That's what Judy would want sung at her funeral.

Liza had pondered hard: Who would deliver the eulogy? Mickey Rooney, who knew her from her earliest MGM days, those two who had gone through so much together? But poor Mickey—he might fall apart up there, talking about his Judy. Then she thought: James Mason. Perfect. They had worked together, Mama admired him, and she loved his voice. She would always tell Liza, "Listen, the way he talks, doesn't he talk terrific? Why, his voice is enough to ride home on!" And Mason had agreed, although he had not known Judy that well. Which was all right, because then he would not be so emotionally involved that he might depress, rather than exalt, those who were there.

She had talked repeatedly to her father. Whatever Liza wanted, he would agree with. And so they had had the services, and everyone there looked right: they were dressed in floral prints, in pastels, in white, pink, yellow—it looked like Easter Sunday.

The Reverend Peter Delaney, who had blessed the marriage of Judy and Mickey, read with the right power to his voice. James Mason said just the right words: " . . . The little girl whom I knew . . . when she was good, she was not only very, very good, she was the most sympathetic, the funniest, the sharpest and the most stimulating woman I ever knew."

Now they all stood up to sing "Glory, glory, hallelujah!"

Liza and Lorna and Joey and Sid, standing in a row, holding hands, started to sing. Liza sensed they would all collapse unless she said something. She whispered fiercely, "Lock your knees! Sing! Sing!" But their voices were squeaking, Joey's little voice, tears streaming down his face, and tears streaming down Lorna's face, and Liza, holding Lorna's hand, felt her begin to crumple—and at that moment, there was a swish of satin behind them, and it was Kay. She whisked in, put her arms around the three children and said, "Sing, goddamnit!" She was stomping her feet in time, and Jack French, musician and old friend of Liza, played the organ, and everybody was singing now, "Glory, glory, hallelujah!"—crying and laughing and smiling, and smiling and crying and laughing, and the hall rang with the voices and the music.

For a day and a night, more than twenty thousand persons had filed by the coffin in which Judy lay, under a glass covering—Camp-

634

bell's had never had so large a crowd, greater even than at Valentino's funeral, so that they had been forced to remain open all night, so enormous and continuous were the crowds filing by to look for a moment at Judy, lying in state in the gray chiffon gown in which she had been married to Mickey little more than six months before, in the casket lined with pale-blue velvet, wearing, after the French fashion, a triple gold wedding band on the small finger of her right hand, which clasped a black prayer book. For the service itself, the casket had been closed, completely covered with yellow flowers.

They had come out for Judy's funeral. She always drew well.

Seated by himself was one man in whose life this event was an extraordinary chapter. It was Dr. Marc Rabwin, now a man nearing seventy. Judy existed because of him; he had persuaded her parents to allow her to come into the world. Now he was here, witnessing her departure. How much he knew of this girl; how much compassion and admiration he felt for her; how proud he was that, however troubled, however frightened, however alert to the slightest whisper of a falling leaf or a breaking heart, this girl had made the world stop, and listen, and feel, and go outside itself. Magician, illusionist, sorceress, weak as the weakest, fearful as the most fearful, strong as the strongest, funny as the funniest, indomitable as the most indomitable —was there ever anyone like her, who could wrap her arms around the entire world, and about whom the entire world could wrap its arms? She spoke to them all, and all understood her, and felt her: man, woman, man-woman, child, parent, grandparent.

Seeking love, she had had many men, yet she had never found it; for finding it, she could not believe it; or if she believed it, suspected it; or suspecting it, denied it. One wonders. Frances. Frances Gumm. Judy Garland. Was there ever a Judy Garland? Was it not all Frances Gumm, endlessly playing the part, endlessly in search of herself?

Yet there she was, in a coffin, Judy Garland. There were the thousands outside, blocking the streets. There were the millions all over the world, mourning and missing her: she had taken from life, despite everything, what she had wanted; despite unimaginable ordeals, she was gaiety, magic, wonder, all caught up in this incredible child. . . .

Then the services were over, and as they rose and sang "Glory, glory, hallelujah!" Marc with them, he saw a scene he had never witnessed before. Eight huge men came down the aisle, they lifted the coffin, they raised it high above their heads, and they bore it out —so a queen, high above the heads of her courtiers, resting on her funeral bier on their uplifted hands, might be borne from the great mourning hall. Marc, standing there, thought, *They are carrying her into Eternity.*

There was a song Judy loved. It was called "Great Day," and its lines went:

> *When you're down and out,*
> *Lift up your head and shout:*
> *There's gonna be a great day!*

Now back in Liza's apartment after the funeral cortege had taken Judy to a crypt in Ferncliff Cemetery in Hartsdale, New York, which Mickey had chosen, the family were together. Kay had prepared food, but it was not food Liza, Lorna and Joey wanted; it was music and song. And with Kay at the piano, getting them to sing each time it seemed they were about to collapse, they sang this song again and again.

This must not be funereal, this day, Liza had insisted. That was why she wanted nothing black, everything bright, springlike, happy flowers. She had let herself go when the elevator man at her apartment building broke into tears: "Oh, that poor, poor thing!" Liza found herself almost shouting at him: "For God's sake, don't feel sorry now: smile! That's all she tried to make you do. She entertained, she tried to make people happy. If there's any favor in the world you want to do for her right now, it would be to smile!"

And so the three children sang until they could sing no more. Liza would make tea, they'd grab a bite, they'd sing again. As evening came, Lorna said to Liza, "Mickey wants to take you and me to a friend's house to go swimming tonight. It's out in the country." Lorna added that Mickey was trying to control himself, and "I think we should go with him."

All right, said Liza. Joey was so tired he had gone to bed. Sid and the others had gone elsewhere. She and Lorna and Mickey and one of Mickey's friends got into the car and they began to drive. It was a beautiful June night. Liza thought, *When you die, you go to heaven and become a star.* She looked out the open window of the car, looking for the brightest star, because that would be Mama. There was one there! She said, "Look, Lorna, I betcha anything it's her."

Lorna looked. "Yes," she said, "the brightest one is Mama."

Mickey, driving, turned on the radio. It was a shock: they were listening to the overture of the record, *Judy at Carnegie Hall*! Mickey, almost in horror, moved to switch it off, but Liza cried, "No, no, leave it on."

Judy sang—and her two daughters sang with her, filling the car with the sound.

Then they reached their destination, a small house, with a trailer parked nearby. Mickey introduced them to their hosts, two brothers whom they did not know. The men went to another part of the house for a moment, and Liza and Lorna sat down on the sofa in the living room. It was very silent. Then they began to hear a strange sound: "Hunhh! Hunhh!" They looked at each other, startled. It sounded like heavy breathing—but where was it coming from? The two girls rose and went in the direction of the sound, and clearly it was coming from behind a door. As they came nearer, they became aware of an incredibly bad odor. "It's coming from there," Liza said. She opened the door. It led downstairs, apparently to the basement. The odor was very strong. 'C'mon," Liza said to her sister. "Are you game?"

Lorna nodded. The two girls stole down the stairs, into the increasingly stronger odor, turned the corner—and there were five large wire cages filled with baboons.

The animals took one look at them began to grunt furiously, "Hunhh! Hunhh!" and began hurling the lettuce, bread, bananas they'd been eating.

The girls rushed upstairs, slammed the door, looked at each other and burst into laughter. They had ended this day in a house with baboons. They sought out Mickey. Yes, he said. The people who owned this place were animal trainers. They trained monkeys, chimps and baboons for circuses.

"Oh," said Liza. "How Mama would have loved this!"

ACKNOWLEDGMENTS

Among those whom I have not thanked earlier, I am deeply grateful to the following:

Stella Adler; Shana Alexander; Harry J. Anslinger; Harold Arlen; Fred Astaire; Mary Astor; Richard Barstow; Fred Bartholomew; Phil Berg; Joan Blondell; Ray Bolger; Margaret Booth; Lucille Bremer; John Carlyle; Whit Carter; Saul Chaplin; Cyd Charisse; Jack Chertok; Charles Cochran; Jewel Cohen; Joseph Cohn; Bobby Cole; Delores Cole; Jackie Cooper; Bosley Crowther; George Cukor; John Darrow; Frank Day; William Dozier; Mrs. Stevie Dumler (now Mrs. Stevie Phillips); George Feldsher; Dorothy Fields; Ray Filiberti; Sherwin Filiberti; Fred Finklehoffe; Tucker Fleming; Glenn Ford; Hugh Fordin; Myron Fox; Benjamin S. Freeman; Lucy Freeman; Pearl Freeman; John Fricke; Leonard Gershe; Lee Gershwin; Robert Gilbert; Ruth Gilmore; David Gilruth; Kathryn Grayson; Tom Green; Lee Guber; Margaret Gundy; Jack Haley, Sr.; Billy Halop; Margaret Hamilton; E. Y. "Yip" Harburg; Maria Haver; June Havoc; Charles Higham; John Hoagland; Stan Irwin; the late Arthur Jacobs; George Jessel; Van Johnson; Danny Kaye; Doug Kelly; Gene Kelly; Patsy Kelly; Stanley Kramer; Maurice Kusell; Eleanor Lambert (Berkson); Abe Lastfogel; Peter Lawford; Jerome Lawrence; Cloris Leachman; Mervyn LeRoy; Sammy Lewis; Patty Luft; Joseph L. Manckiewicz; Toni Mannix; Irving Mansfield; Jesse Martin; Lorraine Martin; Tony Martin; Ken Mayer; Tex McCrary; Patricia McMath; Mrs. Karl Men-

638

ninger; Johnny Mercer; James Michener; Paul Millard; Ann Miller; Albert dei Monticichi; Mrs. Virginia Mortenson; the late Charles C. Moskowitz; Carmel Myers; Donald O'Connor; Gene Palumbo; Al Paul; Otto Preminger; Barron Polan; Harry Rabwin; Johnnie Ray; Mickey Rooney; Leon Rothschild; Harry Rubin; Ann Rutherford; Mrs. Ellie Schachtel (now Mrs. Ellie Krach); Roger Schachtel; Vernon Scott; Artie Shaw; Lloyd Shearer; Sidney Sheldon; Lillian Burns Sidney; Noreen Siegel; the late Bill Spier; Helen Strauss; the late Jacqueline Susann; Howard Teichman; Emily Torchia; Mel Tormé; Myrtle Tully; Lana Turner; Charles Wacker; Irving Wallace; Sylvia Wallace; Charles Walters; Rose Warwick; Lella Waxman; Norman Weiss; Arthur Willi; Charles Williamson.

INDEX

651

Tate, Sharon, 570, 577, 579
Taurog, Norman, 194
Taylor, Elizabeth, 73, 324, 460, 489
Taylor, Laurette, 532
Taylor, Rip, 586
Taylor, Robert, 58, 67, 81, 98, 117, 154
Tell Me That You Love Me, Junie Moon, 372
Temple, Shirley, 32, 54, 56–57, 114, 121
Terry, Ellen, 460
Thalberg, Irving, 62
"That Old Black Magic," 154
Thau, Benny, 61, 83, 102, 107, 117, 162, 163, 251, 266, 267, 277
Thin Man films, 154, 175
"This Time the Dream's on Me," 154
Thompson, John, Jr., 244, 364–367, 421, 504
Thompson, Mr. and Mrs. John, Sr., 366
Thompson, Kay, 105, 173, 184, 207–208, 212, 315, 456, 457, 489, 629–631, 633, 634, 636
Thompson, Dr. William G., 220
Thorn, Dr. George W., 253, 254
Thoroughbreds Don't Cry, 103–106, 117
Three Smart Girls, 83, 93
Thurston, Gavin, 632
Till the Clouds Roll By, 219, 221
Time, 221, 388, 540
Tokyo, 545
Tormé, Mel, 243, 512, 531
Torre, Marie, 423
Tracy, Spencer, 67, 175, 283, 468–470, 474, 488
Transcona Enterprises, 353, 357, 358, 362–363, 369, 397, 403, 406, 416, 456–457, 584
Travilla, couturier, 576
Treasure Island, 65
"The Trolley Song," 211, 215, 314, 331, 375
The Trouble with Cinderella, 346
Tucker, Sophie, 35, 36, 45, 94–96, 98, 101, 103, 335, 547
Tully, Myrtle, 281, 282, 289, 297, 298, 304, 305, 307, 308, 312, 315, 325, 351, 352, 356, 365
Turner, Lana, 67, 73, 117, 118, 122, 127, 128, 135, 141, 145–149, 150, 153–156, 161, 168, 202, 415
20th Century–Fox, 54, 67, 83, 85, 93, 114, 121, 190, 375, 570, 571, 576, 578
Two Girls on Broadway, 146

Universal Pictures, 33, 67, 83, 141
Ustinov, Peter, 324

Vallee, Rudy, 582–583
Vallee, Rudy, Show, 74, 95
Valley of the Dolls, 569–572, 575–582, 587
Van, Bobby, 437, 439, 441
Variety, 53–54, 56, 111, 211, 215, 325, 405, 420, 470
Velez, Lupe, 283
Verdon, Gwen, 587
Vernon, Jackie, 587

Wacker, Charles, 447–449
Waikiki Beach, 533, 561
Walker, Nancy, 194
Walker, Robert, 208, 210, 219, 279, 304
Wallace, Irving, 159
Walsh, Fred, 78
Walters, Charles (Chuck), 173, 175, 190, 208, 234, 237, 249–251, 267–270, 272–276, 278, 312, 330, 331, 333, 334, 335, 338, 354, 474, 486, 487
Warner, Ann, 363
Warner, Barbara, 363, 364
Warner, Henry, 114, 397
Warner, Jack, 58, 363, 370, 374, 375, 380, 382–384, 387–389, 395, 397
Warner Brothers, 67, 114, 347, 363, 369, 374, 375, 397, 406, 416
Warren, Harry, 215
Washington, D.C., 425, 428, 429, 471
Waxman, Lella, 173, 221, 227, 249, 250
Wayne, David, 408, 414
Wayne, Paula, 597
"Wedding of the Painted Doll," 105
Weisbart, David, 570, 576, 578, 579
Weiss, Norman, 441–443
Welles, Orson, 323
Westbury Music Fair, 582, 585, 586
"What Do I Care?" 36–37
"What Now My Love," 547, 612
Whiting, Margaret, 529
Whitney, C. V., 435
Whitney, John Hay, 462
Whittingham, Charles, 431, 432
"Who?" 219
Whorf, Richard, 128
Widmark, Richard, 468, 488
Wilder, Thornton, 155
Wilkerson, Billy, 53
Williams, Andy, 208
Williams, Esther, 117, 167, 208

653